C0-AKK-007

WHAT THE SPECIAL FEATURES OF THIS HANDBOOK DO . . .

- Lists of **Terms you need to know** define the key terms in a section or chapter. Look here when you aren't certain what a particular word means.
- **Troubleshooting** sections at the opening of many sections explain problems writers may have with mechanics, usage, punctuation, style, or an aspect of the writing process.
- **Fine Tuning** sections examine issues of mechanics and usage you may not encounter routinely, but which you may find pertinent or intriguing.
- **Diagnosis/solution** headings direct attention to problems in sample passages and offer recommendations for correcting the difficulties. These heads appear only in the chapters on punctuation.
- **Tip** boxes furnish practical information or provide a bit of advise.

WHERE TO FIND USEFUL CHARTS, TABLES, AND BOXES . . .

THE SCOTT, FORESMAN HANDBOOK WITH WRITING GUIDE

MAXINE HAIRSTON
University of Texas at Austin
JOHN J. RUSZKIEWICZ
University of Texas at Austin

THE SCOTT, FORESMAN HANDBOOK WITH WRITING GUIDE

HarperCollins*Publishers*

Executive Editor: Constance Rajala
Development Editor: Marisa L'Heureux
Project Coordination: Proof Positive/Farrowlyne Associates, Inc.
Text Design: Lucy Lesiak Design
Cover Design and Illustration: Lucy Lesiak Design
Production: Michael Weinstein
Compositor: Weimer Typesetting Co., Inc.
Printer and Binder: R. R. Donnelley & Sons Company
Cover Printer: New England Book Components

Acknowledgments for the literary selections appear on the page
on which the copyrighted material appears or in the Credits section at the back of the book, which is to be considered an extension of the copyright page.

The Scott, Foresman Handbook with Writing Guide
Copyright © 1991 by HarperCollins Publishers Inc.

All rights reserved. Printed in the United States of America. No
part of this book may be used or reproduced in any manner
whatsoever without written permission, except in the case of
brief quotations embodied in critical articles and reviews. For
information address HarperCollins Publishers Inc., 10 East 53rd
Street, New York, NY 10022.

Library of Congress Cataloging-in-Publication Data

Hairston, Maxine.
  The Scott, Foresman handbook with writing guide/
  Maxine C. Hairston, John J. Ruszkiewicz.
    p.   cm.
  An expanded edition of the Scott, Foresman
  handbook for writers.

  Includes index.
  ISBN 0-673-46304-4
  1. English language—Rhetoric—Handbooks,
    manuals, etc.

  2. English language—Grammar—1950—
    Handbooks, manuals, etc.
  I. Ruszkiewicz, John J., 1950-   II. Title.
  PE1408.H2969   1990
  808' .042—dc20   90–45206
                                              CIP

90 91 92 93   9 8 7 6 5 4 3 2 1

Contents

PART 4 GRAMMAR AND USAGE 313

Preface

The idea behind *The Scott, Foresman Handbook with Writing Guide* seemed irresistible: why couldn't a complete guide to mechanics and usage also cover the genres of writing most typically assigned in college classrooms? Existing writing textbooks typically emphasize one aspect of composing at the expense of another. As a result, the handbook sections in rhetorics often look like token efforts. Similarly, the treatment of "patterns of exposition" or "aims of writing" in handbooks can seem perfunctory. Our intention in *The Scott, Foresman Handbook with Writing Guide* is, within a single volume, to give students a rhetoric and a handbook composed with equal care and energy. We cover in detail the composing process, all important genres of college writing, and the activities of research; we offer a thorough guide to style, mechanics, usage, and punctuation—complete with illustrations, exercises, and an exhaustive glossary. And all this information is set within a consistent framework that enables writers to move confidently from one type of discussion to another.

Creating this new textbook involved more than just stuffing chapters with writing assignments into *The Scott, Foresman Handbook for Writers*. The *Writing Guide* is an expanded edition in almost every one of its sections—fuller in its coverage, its explanations, and its exercises. Because it is more deliberately designed to serve as the only classroom text in a writing course, *The Scott, Foresman Handbook with Writing Guide* has its own, more expansive format, an augmented glossary, and a modified table of contents—one that places each potential writing assignment (whether an essay of evaluation, a position paper, or a memo) in its own chapter. It also has many new features and sections that instructors and students will welcome.

The new version, however, retains the distinctive character of *The Scott, Foresman Handbook for Writers:* its friendly tone, its problem-solving structure, its down-to-earth tips and guidelines. So the student using *The Scott, Foresman Handbook with Writing Guide* has access to all the advice on the writing process, mechanics, usage, and punctuation he or she would find in a complete English handbook—and a great deal more.

The Writing Guide

The most distinctive part of *The Scott, Foresman Handbook with Writing Guide* is, of course, Part II, "College Writing." The seven chapters here provide a detailed introduction to academic writing. They do not, however, stand isolated, but follow five carefully revised chapters on the writing process. This comprehensive introduction to inventing, organizing, drafting, revising, and editing gives students a framework for understanding each of the assignments in Part II.

Part II opens with a friendly, but challenging discussion of college composition, one that explains what makes writing in college different from similar work students may have done in high school or on the job. There's advice in this chapter on finding and evaluating sources, understanding academic audiences, and framing effective arguments. Chapters 7–12 then guide students through six general kinds of writing: narration, cause and effect, exploration, evaluation, proving a thesis, and persuasion. Each chapter includes both a basic assignment and a number of variations to encourage students and instructors to approach genres from several directions. Like the discussions of mechanics and usage in *The Scott, Foresman Handbook for Writers,* the explanations of rhetorical strategies in these chapters are concise and lively.

Drawing from earlier material on the writing process, the chapters in Part II reprise the major stages in producing a text: finding an idea, discovering or locating materials, drafting, revising, and editing. Writers will appreciate the wealth of detail; the advice given is down-to-earth and practical, not abstract and generic. That's at least in part because we wrote these chapters out of our own classroom experiences and materials. Each was actually composed while one of our freshman English classes was working its way through a similar assignment; each was revised with a fresh stack of student papers in hand. The comments and suggestions we make in these pages reflect how we work with our own students.

Not surprisingly, then, the sample student papers (with one exception) came from a single freshman class and represent honest examples of the kind of writing many instructors see daily. We considered that users of the book might be interested in watching individual writers respond to varying assignments, so we included papers in three different genres from a single writer, Luis Garcia, and two papers by yet another student, Michael Contreras. The sample essays are tough, wry, and thought-provoking; we think they'll prompt discussion and analysis.

The Scott, Foresman Handbook with Writing Guide supports many writing assignments in addition to those in Part II itself; Part VI, "Special Assignments," covers literary analyses, position papers, and abstracts. The basic business forms—letters, memos, and résumés—each have their own chapters too. There is even a short chapter with sensible advice (and some encouragement) about preparing an oral report—an increasingly familiar assignment in college courses.

Expanded Coverage

The larger format and new focus of *The Scott, Foresman Handbook with Writing Guide* gave us the opportunity to expand our treatment of selected topics. For example, the chapter on writing with a computer (Chapter 51) now includes individual discussions of planning and organizing a paper (51C), drafting an essay (51D), and revising with a word processor (51E). These pages augment two more general sections that introduce writers to computers and word-processing.

We believe the additional material will be especially valuable to students who use writing labs or computer networks.

Similarly we've been able to expand our coverage of language. We've incorporated a full range of grammatical terms into the glossary—almost doubling its size. Both the discussions and the exercises in chapters on mechanics and usage are fuller in this version, for instructors who prefer more illustrations and longer exercise sets. But because some teachers like to treat grammar and usage as a secondary matter in writing courses, we've provided a chapter (21) that we call the *Mini Grammar*—a quick review of the parts of speech and of twelve matters of usage that trouble even skilled writers. Finally, there's a new section on vocabulary development that offers a brief history of the English language, placing the subsequent presentation of word roots, prefixes, and suffixes into a sensible context.

Like any good handbook, *The Scott, Foresman Handbook with Writing Guide* supplies the materials and advice students need to prepare a college-level research paper. In these chapters, writers will find discussions of important research techniques, including explanations of new tools such as CD-ROM indexes and Boolean searches. The lists of indexes and research volumes are especially extensive in this volume, as is the coverage of MLA and APA documentation. A special feature of *The Scott, Foresman Handbook* new in this edition is a checklist for setting up papers in either documentation format: simple guides help writers be sure they've gotten everything right, from the width of margins to the placement of page numbers.

Acknowledgments

We think students and teachers alike will find *The Scott, Foresman Handbook with Writing Guide* a practical and friendly introduction to college writing. We're particularly grateful to our editors, Anne Smith, Constance Rajala, and Marisa L'Heureux, who recognized the potential of this project and supported it enthusiastically. They were the same people who helped us shape the original edition of *The Scott, Foresman Handbook for Writers;* this time around, they made it possible for us to develop two new versions of that original edition simultaneously. Together, we learned a great deal about audience, purpose, revision, and scheduling.

We appreciate the kind remarks and helpful suggestions of our reviewers on this project: John Dick, University of Texas at El Paso; Carol Adams, Delaware Technical and Community College, Terry Campus; Craig Smith, University of Northern Colorado; Kirsten Figg, Kent State; Wendy Bishop, Florida State University; Christine Briggs, Henry Ford Community College; Bob Schwegler, University of Rhode Island; Lisa McClure, Southern Illinois University; Karen D'Agostino, Brookdale Community College; David Mair, University of Oklahoma.

We read our colleagues' comments thoroughly and learned a great deal from them. As we hope our reviewers will see, we took what they had to say to heart, especially suggestions that pushed the manuscript toward greater concision and clarity. Bob Schwegler deserves a special nod of thanks for helping us realize the dimensions of this project initially and then commenting so perceptively on our draft as it moved toward completion. We appreciate, too, the work of Joseph Kelly, a graduate student at the University of Texas, who prepared the answer key for the exercises and carefully proofread the sections on MLA and APA documentation.

We owe a special debt of thanks to the writers whose essays we used in this textbook, all of them students at the University of Texas at Austin: James Balarbar, Ruth Blumenthal, Michael Contreras, Luis Garcia, Lori McWilliams, and Michael Minor. We enjoy being among the first to publish their work. We hope this book inspires other students like them to write and publish.

Finally we'd like to thank Andy Hess and Proof Positive/Farrowlyne Associates, Inc. for a truly remarkable job in readying this book. We have never worked with a more conscientious, careful, or accurate editor, nor with a more diligent production group.

Maxine C. Hairston

John J. Ruszkiewicz

**THE SCOTT, FORESMAN
HANDBOOK WITH
WRITING GUIDE**

THE WRITING PROCESS

We write in order to produce writing. That makes writing both a process and a product. In this first section of the handbook, we examine the processes that produce various kinds of writing, and we suggest ways to make composing more productive and, we hope, more enjoyable.

1 What Is Writing?

A Myths about composing
B Writing as process

Troubleshooting

Writing is not a mysterious activity at which only a few people can succeed; rather it is a craft, like weaving or playing an instrument, that can be learned by almost anyone willing to invest the necessary time and energy. Contrary to what many people seem to believe, the main qualities you need to succeed as a writer are not inspiration and talent, but confidence and determination—confidence that you are an intelligent person with something to say and determination to work at your writing until you become competent. If you feel insecure about your writing skills, remember this. In our information-dependent world, millions of people have to write on their jobs every day, and they do so successfully. If they can, so can you.

1 A   WHAT ARE COMMON MYTHS ABOUT WRITING?

Myth 1.   Good writers are born, not made.
Fact: People become good writers through wanting to write well and working at it.

Myth 2.   Good writers work alone.
Fact: Good writers frequently rely on others for suggestions and help, and writers often collaborate to share ideas and work out their writing problems.

Myth 3.   Good writers know what they are going to say before they start writing.
Fact: Good writers often begin with only a general idea of what they intend to say. Frequently, they discover what they want to say as they write because they know that writing is a way of generating ideas and finding out what they know.

Myth 4.   All good writers make complete plans and outlines before they write.
Fact: Many good writers make only preliminary plans and outlines. They continue to plan as they compose, reorganizing, changing, and adding material as they write and revise.

3

Myth 5.   Good writers get it right the first time.
Fact: Although experienced writers can sometimes produce good prose on the spot, for important jobs professional writers usually write several drafts.

Myth 6.   Good writing comes from knowing all the rules of grammar.
Fact: Success as a writer does not depend on knowing grammatical rules, and learning rules won't make anyone a good writer. Mastering the conventions of grammar, however, makes most people more relaxed and confident writers.

Myth 7.   All writers use the same process.
Fact: Writers work differently, and the same people write differently in different situations. The craft of writing cannot be reduced to a single method.

EXERCISE 1.1

Review the myths above. Pick out one or two you have thought to be true and write a short response telling where you first encountered the myth or myths. How do you think those myths affected you at some time when you needed to write?

EXERCISE 1.2

In the course of this book, you'll be meeting many students, faculty members, and citizens associated with Clear Lake College's two campuses: one in Ruralia, Illinois, where it's scenic but sometimes a little dull, and the other upstate in Chicago, where there's more action but also more snow. Students who get together in the student union on the Ruralia campus often compare notes about their writing. Connie Lim, editor of the campus newspaper, insists writers shouldn't start writing until they know what they're going to say and can make an outline. "How else can you tell if you're getting it right?" she asks. Her friend Travis Beckwith twits her for being an unimaginative hack. "Why don't you just start writing and count on inspiration? That's what I do."

How do you think Connie and Travis are being influenced by myths about writing? What do you think they might learn from each other?

1 B   HOW DOES THE WRITING PROCESS WORK?

To understand writing . . .

➤ **View writing as a process.** It's tantalizing to think there is a formula for writing papers and that if you could just discover it, you'd have a secret that would make your life much easier. We assure you that no such formula exists, and you're not a dolt because you haven't discovered one. Nevertheless, researchers who have studied how writers work do agree that there are discernible patterns among writers, and that, generally speaking, they seem to work through the following stages, which parallel the stages of other creative processes.

PROCESS MENU
PREPARING
PLANNING
INCUBATING
DRAFTING
REVISING
EDITING AND PROOFREADING

PREPARING
In this stage, writers consider what they want to write about and use a variety of techniques to select their topics and generate ideas for composing.

PLANNING
In this stage, writers think about ways they might organize their materials, and many writers make tentative plans—lists, outlines, summaries, or charts.

INCUBATING
In this stage, writers give themselves time off to let their ideas "simmer" or take shape in their subconscious mind.

DRAFTING
In this stage, writers start composing and produce a first draft. They may spend additional time reorganizing and planning as they write.

REVISING
In this stage, writers look back over what they have composed, reconsider their ideas and language and, if necessary, rewrite.

EDITING AND PROOFREADING
In this stage, writers edit, polish, and proofread to get their work ready for public reading.

Though broadly accurate, this skeletal view of the process is sketchy and oversimplified—the process of writing is never as neat and uncomplicated as such a summary makes it seem. Different writers work differently. No one pattern works for all writers or for all writing tasks, and each person has to adapt the process according to his or her temperament and habits. Nevertheless, this general outline of a process that goes from preparation to finished product provides a useful plan for starting your writing projects.

▶ **Think of writing as cycling through stages.** Many successful writers find that they cycle through the stages of writing several times in the course of a writing task. As they develop their ideas, they move back and forth, sometimes planning, sometimes writing, sometimes stopping to revise.

Most writers begin with some preparation—brainstorming or making a list or roughing out an outline—but they don't try to map out their whole paper ahead of time. Instead, they may plan just enough to get started, write for a while, then stop to reread and plan the next section. Some wait to do major revision until they have a first draft, but others also revise as they work. Many experienced writers have learned to allow time for incubation between planning and starting to write, or they may prefer to keep working but take frequent breaks for reflection.

Individual writers also vary their writing processes according to the kind of writing they are doing. One writing task, such as a term paper, may require a great deal of preparing and revising; another, such as the summary of a report, may take very little.

So writing is not a one-two-three process by which one marches straight through from outlining to editing. Rather it's a dynamic, **recursive** activity in which writers begin by planning and end by editing, but loop in and out of the different stages as they work. For complex assignments, they may repeat parts of the operation several times before they produce a finished paper.

1 B

Process

EXERCISE 1.3

If you have done some writing you were proud of—perhaps an article in the student newspaper, a letter to the editor that was published, a song or story, or a personal statement that won you a scholarship—write a paragraph telling how much preparation you put into it, how many times you revised it, and why you think it was successful.

EXERCISE 1.4

Working in a group, each person pick out some piece of writing he or she likes: perhaps a regular column in a newspaper or magazine, a favorite novel, the commentary on a record album, or a film or television program (remember, someone has to write those scripts). Write a brief description of how you think that writer works. What kind of temperament and habits do you think he or she has? After writing for ten or fifteen minutes, compare descriptions and see what common features you find among them.

EXERCISE 1.5

Write a paragraph or two candidly describing how you typically write papers for your college courses or how you wrote them in your high school courses. How late do you wait to write them? What do you do first? Do you spend more time planning or writing? Do you revise? Which stage causes the most problems? How do you think you might improve on your writing process?

2 How Do You Prepare to Write?

A Analyzing kinds of writing

B Analyzing the writing situation

PROCESS MENU
PREPARING
PLANNING
INCUBATING
DRAFTING
REVISING
EDITING AND PROOFREADING

Troubleshooting

Almost everything in your life contributes to your preparation for writing: things that have happened in your family or on your job, your hobbies, your experiences in sports or with your car, your social life and your relationships with friends or lovers, your experiences in college. In other words, your memory bank is stocked with a wealth of material that you can draw on for the content of your papers. You also have ideas or opinions you can develop and beliefs that are worth explaining. All this adds up to such a rich stock of resources that you shouldn't run yourself down by saying, "I have nothing to write about." Of course, you do! You have an abundance of human experience that will be interesting to other people. And the more you train yourself to be alert to what's going on around you and to keep notes or a journal, the more ideas you will generate for writing and the more material you will have to work with.

So approach your writing with confidence. Even if you haven't written much before, you have the inborn ability to communicate with others. With practice, there's no reason you can't communicate as well in writing as you do in speaking.

EXERCISE 2.1

In a first draft to share with your classmates and instructor, write a paragraph or two about an experience you have had with writing that you think shaped your attitude, either positively or negatively, about composing. Then meet with a small group of other students and compare your experiences.

2 A   WHAT KINDS OF WRITING DO YOU DO?

Terms you need to know

EXPLANATORY WRITING. Writing that explains or presents ideas, theories, or data. Explanatory writing usually focuses on facts or events, and the writer has a specific goal in mind.

EXPLORATORY WRITING. Writing that explores, reflects on, or speculates about concepts, ideas, or experiences. The writer often discovers content while writing and may not have a specific goal when he or she starts.

COMBINATION EXPLANATORY/EXPLORATORY WRITING. Writing that mixes explanation and exploration, using facts and explanations to support reflections and speculations or using exploration and reflection to comment on facts and information.

Troubleshooting

People do many different kinds of writing, but we believe that most of the writing students do in college, aside from taking notes and completing lab reports, falls into two general categories: explanatory writing and exploratory writing. We think you will write more effectively if you learn to distinguish between the two.

For instance, if you are planning for a writing assignment that asks you to gather information, classify it, and draw conclusions from it—for example, a paper reporting on an experiment you saw done in a psychology class—you're going to be doing mainly explanatory writing. You probably wouldn't gain much by starting to write without having thought your paper through ahead of time, although as you worked you might polish your style.

On the other hand, if you have a writing assignment that asks you to identify a crisis in your childhood and write about how that crisis affected you—for example, a paper for your early child development class—you're going to be doing mainly exploratory writing. Although you need to do some planning, you probably shouldn't try to plan out the whole paper ahead of time since you really don't know what you're going to say. You need to start with notes and impressions, but develop your content and organization as you write.

To approach explanatory writing projects successfully . . .

➤ **Recognize when your writing will be explanatory.** If you know what the content of your paper is going to be and what you want to accomplish in it, you're likely to be doing explanatory writing. For example, suppose you were asked to write a paper for a nutrition course in which you report on current medical theory about the relationship between diet and cancer. The content for such a paper already exists. You just have to look it up and synthesize it. Your goal in writing—in addition to learning about the topic—is to inform the readers and hold their interest.

Other assignments that would call for explanatory writing could be an essay for a classics course about the development of rhetoric in ancient Greece or an engineering report about the environmental impact of a proposed chemical plant. The content for those papers exists; the writer's goal is to present it effectively.

Many of the papers you write in college are going to be explanatory pieces, and certainly most of the writing people do in business and the professions—writing that keeps information flowing and gets the job done—is explanatory. It's an important kind of writing that all of us need to master, and it doesn't have to be dull to compose or to read. Explanatory prose at its best is clear, accurate, lively, and wonderfully informative. You can learn from and enjoy it both as a writer and a reader.

2 A

Prep

➤ **Understand the process for explanatory writing.** If you like to plan ahead and organize your ideas before you write, you're probably comfortable doing explanatory writing. It is the kind of writing task for which it helps to identify and analyze your audience and take a systematic, problem-solving approach. If that is not your style, however, you can still do a good job with explanatory writing. In the next section and other parts of the book, we give you strategies for gathering, organizing, supporting, and presenting your material for explanatory papers and suggestions on how to write them clearly. The techniques are not difficult to learn.

EXERCISE 2.2

Make a list of fifteen possible topics, general and specific, that you think you might enjoy writing about—topics on which you have some information and which you find interesting. Consider, for instance, organizations you belong to, magazines you read, music you like, sports you play or watch, jobs you've had, special people you know, and so on.

EXERCISE 2.3

Make a list of the kinds of writing you have done in the past week, such as leaving a note for someone, writing a letter, a lab report or exam, or writing in a journal. Which composing do you think would be classified as explanatory writing?

EXERCISE 2.4

Working with other students in a group, look over two or three issues of the student newspaper published on your campus and pick out three or four items: editorials, reports, news stories, feature stories, and so on. Discuss which pieces seem to be mainly explanatory writing. On what do you base your judgment?

To approach exploratory writing projects successfully . . .

➤ **Recognize when your writing will be exploratory.** If you have a general idea what you want to accomplish in a paper, but haven't figured out the specific content or plan for organization, you're likely to be doing exploratory writing. You might have your idea—for example, writing a sociology paper about your experiences as a recent immigrant to the United States or a paper for a women's studies course about returning to college as a single parent—but you count on getting fresh ideas and insights as you write. Typically, in exploratory papers writers reflect on experiences they have had or speculate on the implications of cultural phenomena. An example of the latter would be an article about the effects of car owning on American high school students.

2 A

Prep

Writing about values and problems is likely to be exploratory—for instance, essays about teenage pregnancy, the aftermath of divorce, sex or race discrimination, personal loss, and so on. Many of the essays you find in an anthology for a college composition course are examples of exploratory writing.

➤ **Learn to work with exploratory writing.** If you are working on an exploratory assignment, don't be intimidated or reluctant to express your views. Your instructor may have made the assignment to encourage such expression. And remember that although you certainly want to do some planning, you probably can't plan everything ahead of time. You need to start writing in order to generate ideas and think of examples, and you need to make abundant notes as you write.

The first draft of an exploratory paper is often a discovery draft. That is, the writer composes it to find out what he or she knows and the direction to follow. The process will be messier and less predictable than drafting an explanatory paper from an outline, but ultimately readers expect exploratory writing to be as organized and clear as explanatory writing. Thus, exploratory writing nearly always requires much revision and rethinking. What follows is a chart that lists some examples of different kinds of writing.

Explanatory	*Explanatory/Exploratory*	*Exploratory*
Report on laboratory experiment	Comparison of child-care programs in Sweden and the United States	Article about coming to the United States as an immigrant
Environmental impact study	Account of the decline of communism in Eastern Europe	Paper in a literature course interpreting a short story
Case study of pregnancy-induced diabetes	Commentary on the economics of professional basketball	Speculative article on the psychological attractions of dangerous sports
Term paper on superconductivity and its applications	Argument paper on how to combat homelessness in one city	Article about Americans' fascination with celebrities

To approach a combined writing project successfully . . .

➤ **Recognize when you need to use a combined writing strategy.** We have divided writing into these two classes to help you realize that there is no best way to write a paper. Sometimes you will do well to make extensive plans and a full outline; at other times, you'll do better if you make a few notes, then just start writing to get your ideas flowing.

We suggest that each time you write, you take a few minutes to assess your job. Think about the material you are going to be working with and about what you want to accomplish. For instance, if you are writing a paper in history or science, working from data and facts, and your main purpose is to explain an event or document a theory, you're clearly going to be doing explanatory writing. You should invest considerable time in planning and getting your material in good order before you start. But if you want to write a paper for your sociology course on what can happen to young people who grow up poor in an American city and intend to use your own experience, you're likely to be doing exploratory writing. You'll need some planning, but you'll probably produce a better paper if you begin to write early and see what emerges.

2 A

Prep

Often you may want to combine the two kinds of writing. You can use explanatory writing to organize and present information, then switch to exploratory writing to speculate about the meaning of that information. For instance, you might start by documenting the concrete differences between American and Japanese schools—number of school days, length of days, required subjects, kinds of examinations, and so on—and then reflect about the implications of these differences. What do they say about American priorities and about Americans' temperament and their attitudes toward their children?

You will often find that combining explanatory and exploratory writing also works well when you're writing a persuasive or argumentative paper because, typically, such papers mix information and emotion. For example, you might begin a paper in which you argue for enlisting the help of television networks to combat drug addiction by giving facts about such addiction and about television watching; then you might speculate how television could get through to drug addicts and influence them.

➤ **A Caution about Classifying**

Both explanatory and exploratory writing are useful, and it's important that you feel comfortable doing either kind of composing or with mixing them. Don't jump to classify everything that you write and don't worry if you can't determine which kind of writing you should be doing. Explanatory and exploratory writing are simply terms to help you understand the differences between writing processes. Neither the terms nor the processes are absolute or completely separate from each other. Writing is too complex for any such simplistic formulations.

When you understand the distinctions between these kinds of writing, you may better understand why you feel differently about the various kinds of writing jobs you do. Some seem congenial, even easy; others are formidable and challenging. You'll probably like best those assignments suited to your temperament and that you do well, but that doesn't mean you can't also learn to manage other kinds of writing just as skillfully.

2 B

Prep

EXERCISE 2.5

Think about writing you have done in the past several months—perhaps an editorial for the student newspaper, a paper written for a course, a personal essay for your college application, a report on a trip you made, or some writing you did on your job. Which pieces of writing would you call exploratory writing? Why? Which ones were mixed?

EXERCISE 2.6

Working in a group, each person write a paragraph telling which kind of writing he or she prefers, explanatory or exploratory. Why do you think you prefer one kind over the other? If you can, tie your preferences to other kinds of activities that you like or dislike. For instance, if you like mechanical gadgets and your room is always neat and your office well organized, you probably feel more comfortable with explanatory writing. If you love to cook and frequently improvise on recipes and if your closet always needs reorganizing, you're probably more comfortable with exploratory writing. Compare notes with others in your group—it could be interesting.

EXERCISE 2.7

Write the first draft for a medium-length paper (around 300–400 words) in which you compare a typical day's routine for you at your college or university to the typical day of someone you know who goes to a very different kind of college or university—for instance, a community college versus a four-year institution; a small college versus a large university; a small-town residential college versus an urban commuter college.

Begin with a factual account (that doesn't mean it has to be dull) that illustrates what you see as your typical day at school and compare it with the typical routine of your friend at a different school. Then comment on the effect you think these differences have on the kind of education you and your friend are getting. A suitable audience would be students at either or both institutions or, perhaps, parents who are trying to decide what college their son or daughter should go to.

2 B   HOW DO YOU ANALYZE YOUR WRITING SITUATION?

Troubleshooting

Every time you face a new writing task, you should ask the same question—what am I supposed to be doing and why? A good way to answer that chronic question is to learn to think each time about your *writing situation,* the social context in which you are writing. Except for personal journals, writing is social, a way of interacting with other people; thus, every time you write you are trying to

say **something**

to **somebody**

for **some purpose.**

Unless a piece of writing does these three things, it doesn't really exist *as* writing. It's just an exercise, rather than a communication going on between people in order to accomplish something.

2 B

Prep

Since we think everyone becomes a better writer when he or she learns to think in these terms—*what* do I want to say to *whom* and *why*—we want to condition you to think *meaning, audience,* and *purpose* every time you write. Probably no single habit will do more to help you become an effective writer.

To evaluate a writing situation . . .

➤ **Ask yourself whether your topic is something worth writing about.** Do you have an idea worth spending your time to write on and worth someone else's time to read? Will your paper tell your readers something they want or need to know? We don't mean that every time you write you should come up with a fresh idea or that you always have to write about serious and complex topics. But you should try to tell your readers something informative, interesting, or surprising.

Perhaps you can give your readers useful information, perhaps entertain or amuse them, or perhaps just give them fresh insights on a familiar topic. If you were writing an exam for a professor, "informative" might mean writing an essay that demonstrates your understanding of a basic concept—for instance, pulsar stars in astronomy. In an essay written for an English class, "interesting" could mean a paper that vividly narrates a personal experience.

Don't underestimate your ability to write something other people will enjoy reading. Anyone who has held a job, pursued a hobby, traveled, or who simply talks often with other people has gathered experiences and information that can be developed into intriguing papers. Chances are good that if you write about something you know well or are curious about—even something as simple as observations about students you see on the bus every day—other people will find your paper worth reading.

Chances are also good that if you select a topic that seems easy but bores you, your content will prove trivial, and your readers will yawn. A paper that relies on conventional wisdom and clichés to tell readers what they already know will surely be insignificant writing.

EXERCISE 2.8

Walter's Do-It-Yourself garage in Clear Lake is a favorite Saturday afternoon hangout for the mechanically inclined who like to watch other people work. On any given Saturday afternoon, you're likely to find Big Stevie tinkering with her motorcycle, Jasper Rhodes, Clear Lake College's football coach, dreaming of next season and tightening something or other on his drooping Vega, Colonel Ringling giving orders, and Christy Rasmussen predicting what the next bestselling records will be. Deciding to do a feature story on the garage, Connie Lim made this list of topics discussed at Walter's in the course of a single Saturday afternoon.

> What happens when aluminum auto engines overheat?
> The merits of Japanese versus German cars
> The metric system versus good old American measures
> Lite Beer commercials
> Lite Beer
> Passing teams versus running teams in college football
> How rock and roll has corrupted American youth
> How a single-parent college student juggles his or her schedule
> Million dollar salaries in professional basketball
> The demise of the television program "Miami Vice"
> Do women make good mechanics?
> Who can lift more, Big Stevie or Walter?
> Do bulging muscles make either sex more attractive?
> Will Clear Lake College win a football game this century?

Which topics do you think might furnish material for intriguing articles? Discuss how a writer might develop one of the more promising subjects.

EXERCISE 2.9

Write a paragraph about some aspect of one of your hobbies that would be interesting to other students in your class. You might choose, for instance, new developments in ski boots, the latest gimmick in electronics, or the most recent album of your favorite singer.

EXERCISE 2.10

Make a list of some of the people and things you see every day when you are going to and from your classes. Which are potentially good topics for a paper? Why?

➤ **Ask for whom you are writing.** Direct your writing to somebody. "Somebody" can be an **audience** of one, a group of people (perhaps your classmates), or a much larger group, such as the readers of a newspaper or magazine. As far as possible, you need to know

> what your audience expects from you;
>
> how much they already know about your topic;
>
> what questions they are likely to have about it;
>
> what values and attitudes they have that will affect the way they read your paper.

You also need to consider what reasons the potential members of your audience could have for reading your paper and to decide how you are going to appeal to those readers. You can help yourself do that by creating a mental picture of your audience or by choosing one individual you think would typify that audience. Keep that picture or that individual in mind as you write. The Audience Analyzer in this section shows how to create such a picture for yourself. (See also the section on audience adaptation in revising, Section 5A.)

Sometimes you may want to postpone audience analysis until you get to a second draft. For instance, if you are furious about a recent proposal to raise the tuition in your school and want to write an editorial about it, you can just blow off steam in the first draft. Such explosions are often an effective way to start, but they don't do much to impress the people you need to persuade. When you start the second draft, however, think about who has the power to prevent the tuition raise and consider how to appeal to those readers. Then you can revise your essay to reach them.

Learning to analyze your audience skillfully takes time and practice, but we strongly believe that no step in learning to write well is more important than developing a sense of audience. The best way to develop this all-important audience awareness is to do what student lawyers do in moot court and student pilots do in flight simulation trainers: practice in a mock situation. For this reason, in this book we suggest many writing activities that ask you to write as if you're writing for a real audience in a specific situation.

EXERCISE 2.11

Very briefly analyze who your readers would be and what they would expect if you were writing in these situations.

1. Writing an autobiography for a college admissions board.
2. Writing a description for the Division of Motor Vehicles of an accident you had.
3. Writing a letter disputing a charge on your Visa account.
4. Writing out an application for financial aid.
5. Writing a description of an experiment you carried out in psychology class.

EXERCISE 2.12

Write a paragraph describing a time when you had to be particularly sensitive or cautious in writing for a particular audience. Why was it so important to you to understand that audience?

EXERCISE 2.13

Working with another student in your class, select a magazine—some possibilities are *Sports Illustrated, Rolling Stone, Omni, Car and Driver, Women's*

Day, Esquire, Ms., to name just a few—and study the ads and the kind of articles it carries. Then draft a description of the kind of people you think the editor and publisher of the magazine assume their readers to be.

➤ **Analyze your readers by using this audience analyzer.**

Audience Analyzer

1. **Who is going to read this essay?**
   Is the audience already specified?
   Can I specify the audience?
   If so, who would be the best audience?
2. **Are the readers likely to be interested in the topic and willing to read?**
   Are they likely to be receptive to my ideas? Why?
   Do they have the power and ability to act on my suggestions?
   Are they going to be willing to learn or be persuaded?
3. **What do my readers already know about my topic?**
   How much information on this issue can I expect them to have?
   Can I use specialized language? Should I?
   How much of what I am writing is news to them?
   How can I give them new information or ideas?
4. **What attitudes about this issue do my readers have?**
   What values do we share that I can appeal to?
   What biases do they have?
   What kind of approach might alienate them?
   How will their age, sex, social, economic, or educational level affect the way
      they react?
5. **What do my readers expect to get from reading this essay?**
   What specific questions will they have that I should try to answer?

➤ **The Audience Analyzer Applied to an Essay**

In Chapter 4, "How Do You Write a Draft?" you will find the first draft of an essay by a student named Ruth Blumenthal. In it, Ruth, the youngest in a family of twelve stepbrothers and sisters, writes about the adventures and disasters that happened on a family ski trip her father and stepmother dreamed up in the hope the children from the two families would learn to get along better. The title is "We're Taking a Trip—All of Us?"

Here is an analysis of some of Ruth's preparation for writing the paper.

1. Ruth knew she wanted to write something about the turmoil of living
   in her family of twelve children and knew her first audience would be
   her professor and other students in her writing class. She also thought
   her essay might be interesting to many young readers outside her class
   since so many young people she knew had stepbrothers and sisters because of their parents' divorces and remarriages. She decided to aim for
   young readers of a general magazine such as *Mademoiselle.*
2. Ruth thought most readers would probably be interested in her narrative about her father and stepmother taking eight children on a ski trip
   if she could make it lively and funny.

3. Ruth assumed most of her readers would know something about the problems that two sets of children can have getting along when families are joined, because many of her readers have direct experience.
4. Most readers are interested in stories about family adventures—witness the success of television programs such as the "Cosby" show—and they like young people, so Ruth can assume they'll be sympathetic readers. By choosing to write for *Mademoiselle,* she knows she's writing mostly for young women, many of whom are familiar with the kind of family she writes about.
5. Ruth assumes her readers want to be entertained by her essay, but they might also want to get insights into how stepbrothers and sisters can learn to get along. Her readers might have these questions: Did the children learn to get along better as Ruth's father had hoped? What's the family like now?

2 B

Prep

EXERCISE 2.14

Think of three different audiences for whom you might write something connected with your job. For instance, if you have a new job at college, you might want to describe it for your parents, for a former employer, and for other students who might be interested in taking such a job. In each case, write down two questions that readers might expect you to answer.

EXERCISE 2.15

Here are the titles of several magazine articles. Who do you think are the likely readers for each one?

"How to Save Our Schools"
"The Airborne Auto: Flight of Fancy?"
"Tracking the Mighty Gulf Stream"
"What's New with Zoos?"
"Is Breathing Hazardous to Your Health?"

EXERCISE 2.16

Make a list of the different pieces of writing you have done in the past week. Who was the audience for each one?

➤ **Consider your purpose for writing.** Except in a very few instances, writing is not an isolated activity that you do just for yourself. Usually it's a social act between human beings; you write to someone to accomplish something. In college courses, you write both to learn and to demonstrate learning. Out of school, you may write on your job or you may write to report a stolen credit card, to protest a proposal you don't like, or to ask for information. In every case, you have a purpose, and usually you'll write more effectively if you think about that purpose ahead of time.

Sometimes, particularly in exploratory work, you may begin writing about your topic in order to explore it and may not know exactly what your direct purpose will be. You could ramble a bit in the first draft to find out what you know, then pin down your purpose in the second draft. With most writing, however—especially informative or persuasive writing—you should try to figure out your purpose before you begin to compose so that you don't waste time writing around your topic rather than on it. The purpose analyzer given below can help you discover what you want to accomplish with your paper.

2 B

Prep

➤ **Analyze your reason for writing by using this purpose analyzer.**

Purpose Analyzer

1. Why are you writing?
What need or situation are you responding to?
Is your purpose specified for you? What is it?
Can you specify your own purpose? What is it?

2. What do you hope to accomplish with your writing?
To entertain?
To inform?
To share experience?
To provoke emotional response?
To bring about change?
To persuade?
To make readers feel good?
To challenge readers' thinking?
To reinforce existing ideas or attitudes?
Several of the above?

3. What action do you want your readers to take as a result of reading?
Join you in a cause?
Reflect on experience?
Consider a new point of view?
Take up a new activity?
Other?
None?

4. What change do you hope to bring about?
Readers will alter their behavior?
Readers will adopt your proposal?
Readers will change attitudes or opinions?
None?

➤ **The Purpose Analyzer Applied to an Essay**
Now see how the purpose analyzer can be applied to Ruth Blumenthal's "We're Taking a Trip—All of Us?" (See Chapter 4.)

1. Ruth chose her own purpose. She's responding both to her instructor's assignment to write a paper using specific personal experience and to her feeling that many young people have problems learning to get along when they join new stepfamilies and that she might give them some insights.

2. Primarily, Ruth wanted to entertain her readers, but she also wanted to inform and persuade them by suggesting that it's possible for children in stepfamilies to learn to get along with each other.
3. She does not want her readers to take any particular action.
4. She's not seeking to bring about any change in her readers.

EXERCISE 2.17

What purpose might you have in the following writing situations? Think about the impression you would want to make as well as the immediate goal for the writing.

1. Writing an autobiographical sketch to accompany an application for admission to college.
2. Writing an ad to sell your used car.
3. Writing to your college president to protest poor security on campus at night.
4. Writing a report for the supervisor at your job.
5. Writing a former teacher to ask for a letter of recommendation.

EXERCISE 2.18

Working with two or three other classmates, collect and analyze a dozen brochures you find around campus or in grocery stores, banks, health agencies, and so on. Study them to determine the purpose of each. How does the way the brochure is written seem to promote that purpose?

EXERCISE 2.19

Here are the titles of several brochures. Where do you think such brochures would be displayed? What purposes do you think the people who wrote them might have had in mind?

"How to Establish Credit and Protect It"

"Ten Ways to Feed Your Family Better"

"Alcohol Is a Drug, Too"

"Get an MBA on Nights and Weekends"

"Adopt an Animal"

➤ **Consider how audience and purpose work together.** Although we have discussed the concepts of audience and purpose separately in order to define and explain them, experienced writers know that one can never really separate the concepts in actual writing. Inevitably, the audience you choose to write for will, to some extent, be determined by the purpose you have in writing.

For example, if you are angry about a proposal to double student parking fees and want to stop it, you have a choice of audiences. If you want direct action, you need to write to the person in charge of such matters, perhaps the university vice-president for business affairs. For such a reader, your purpose in writing would be to make a calm but convincing cause-and-effect argument demonstrating the harmful results of the increased fee: hardships for commuting students, reduced enrollment, and so on. If, however, you want to get other students to join you in a protest and try to get the fee reduced that way, you could write an angry editorial to show the fee is unfair.

EXERCISE 2.20

Write a sentence or two about each of these writing situations summarizing how you would adapt your writing to your audience in order to accomplish your purpose.

1. You write a fundraising letter to local businesspeople asking them to give money to a charitable project you're interested in—for example, Recordings for the Blind, adult literacy, Big Brothers and Sisters, or a center for battered women.
2. You write a letter to one of your college instructors asking for an interview to discuss the D you received from that person in summer school.
3. You write to an agency that grants funds for overseas study to students asking that it finance a year abroad for you.

3 What Goes into Planning?

A Finding a topic
B Narrowing a topic
C Exploring a topic
D Planning and outlining a paper
E Devising a thesis statement
F Organizing for emphasis
G Finding a title

3 A HOW DO YOU FIND A TOPIC?

Terms you need to know

BRAINSTORMING. Randomly jotting down all ideas about a topic as they come to you without worrying whether they're logical or "right."

FREEWRITING. Writing continuously about a topic for ten or fifteen minutes to generate ideas.

CLUSTERING. Grouping similar ideas about a topic together.

PROCESS MENU
PREPARING
PLANNING
INCUBATING
DRAFTING
REVISING
EDITING AND PROOFREADING

Troubleshooting

Sometimes an instructor may give you a specific topic, define its limits, and explain clearly what you need to do. In such instances, you don't have to find your topic, so you can begin immediately to generate material, plan your paper, and start writing.

Often, however, instructors prefer to give students only broad suggestions for their papers and let them find their own topics, believing that many students work better and enjoy writing more if they can write about something they're interested in and know about. "That's fine to be able to choose," you may say, "but how do I find a good topic, one that I'd like to write about and on which I can find something to say?" We have several suggestions.

To find a workable topic . . .

➤ **Choose something you're interested in.** When you have to invest as much energy in a task as you do in writing a paper, be good to yourself by choosing a topic you'll enjoy, one that won't bore you. Find a broad subject that appeals to you and one on which you already have some ideas. Start by writing down possibilities that sound interesting. One such list might look like this:

exercise	architecture
children of divorce	folklore
women's changing roles	Indian art
college basketball	sexism in advertising
credit cards	modern ballet
musical comedy	science fiction
yoga	drinking in college

After generating such a list, run through it quickly and reject those topics that seem too broad or complex—you could quickly bog down in topics like architecture, children of divorce, or modern ballet, for instance—and focus on two or three that seem workable and appealing. You may find it helpful to talk with other students in making a preliminary choice; they might see possibilities that don't occur to you or may point out problems you don't anticipate. After you make your preliminary choice, explore it by using one or more of the following strategies.

➤ **Talk your topic through with a friend.** You'll be surprised at how productive conversation about your topic can be. Be sure to keep notes. If you can't find someone to confer with, talk about your topic into a tape recorder, explaining it as you would to a friend. You'll find that the very act of talking out loud, even to yourself, will generate new ideas.

➤ **Brainstorm your topic either in a group or by yourself.** Write out your topic on paper or on the board, then jot down any words, phrases, or ideas that come to mind. Don't stop to evaluate them—just get points down in no particular order or priority. Accept all suggestions. Remember that in brainstorming, one idea piggy-backs on another and there are no wrong answers.

➤ **Freewrite about your topic.** Write down sentences about your topic as they come to you without worrying about correct spelling or usage. Compose continuously for ten or fifteen minutes without stopping, then pause to read what you've put down. Continue to work as long as ideas come and don't cross out or reject anything you write.

➤ **Create clusters of words.** In the middle of a blank sheet of paper, write down a word or phrase that summarizes your topic. Circle that word and then, for about ten minutes, write other associated words in a circular pattern around the original. Circle the additional words as you write them and draw lines connecting them to the word that triggered them. Look at the second group of words, think of words you associate with them, and make additional clusters, drawing lines linking them to the word that triggered them (see diagram). Review the clusters to see which groups seem to have the most potential for development.

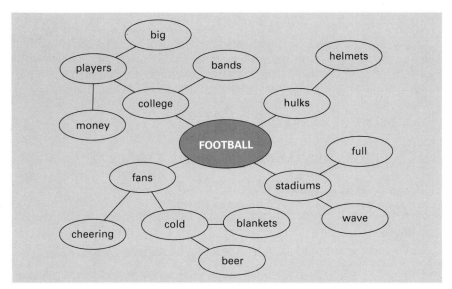

➤ **Look for computer programs that help you generate material.** Many campus writing centers or writing labs have software programs that will help you generate ideas about your topic. Spending an hour with such a program can get you off to a good start on defining your topic. Some programs even help you organize and outline material.

> **TIP: Don't feel you have to work through all these explo-ration strategies before you decide on your angle. As you work, you may find you're drawn to some particular as-pect of a topic. If you think that's the one you want to pursue, go ahead and start generating material.**

EXERCISE 3.1

Working with a group of two or three classmates, have each person brain-storm one of his or her topics on the board. Help each other to select the material that looks most promising.

EXERCISE 3.2

Freewrite on your topic for fifteen minutes. Then go back and underline those sentences that seem most interesting or have the most potential for devel-opment. Working with two or three classmates, talk about those sentences and make notes about how you might develop them.

EXERCISE 3.3

If your school has a writing center with computers and several invention programs, pick one and work through its questions to explore your topic. Write a paragraph explaining how you think the program either helped you or failed to help you.

3 B HOW DO YOU NARROW AND FOCUS A TOPIC?

Terms you need to know

INVENTION. In writing, the process of discovering what can or should be said about a subject.

NARROWING. Reducing a broad and general topic to a smaller, more specific one.

FOCUSING. Concentrating your attention on one limited area or section of a larger, more complex idea.

TREEING. Dividing and subdividing a large topic into smaller subtopics.

PROCESS MENU
PREPARING
PLANNING
INCUBATING
DRAFTING
REVISING
EDITING AND PROOFREADING

Troubleshooting

Writers often try to do too much in one paper. They start out with a topic so broad they couldn't possibly do justice to it in a short essay, and if they don't stop to narrow the topic down, they wind up writing a superficial paper, long on generalizations and short on details. You may fall into this trap if you try to use all or even most of the material you have generated on a topic through brainstorming, freewriting, or using a computerized invention program. We offer two suggestions to help you narrow your topic and avoid this problem.

First, when deciding what to write about, keep these guidelines in mind.

• Don't try to tell everything you know.

• Write more about less—pick a small topic but include abundant details.

Second, use some of the invention strategies discussed in this chapter to narrow a broad topic on which you have a great deal of information down to a smaller, more manageable subtopic.

To narrow a subject . . .

➤ **Focus on your topic.** Think about narrowing your topic in the same way that you focus a flashlight. If you adjust the beam to its broadest range, you will throw diffused light over a large territory and not be able to see details. But if you want to see the details, you will have to narrow the focus of your light and concentrate its power to throw an intense light on a small area. You can reduce a writing topic in the same way. For example:

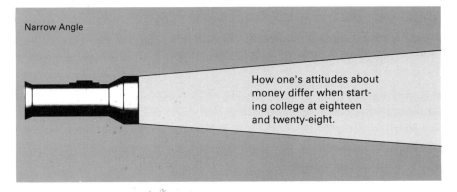

➤ **Tree down your topic.** Another way to narrow your topic to manageable size is to draw diagrams that "tree it down." To do this, make a chart on which you divide and subdivide the topic into smaller and smaller parts, each of which branches out like an inverted tree. The upside-down tree helps you see how many ideas you can generate under each division and which branch offers the most promising material. For example:

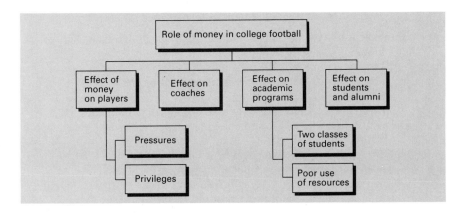

Sometimes you can pick out the most promising part of your first diagram and tree it down a second time. For example:

3 B

Focus

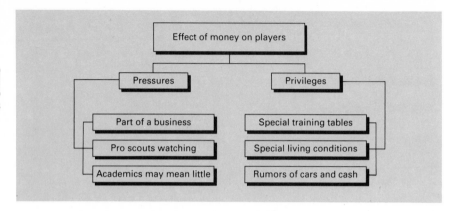

▶ **Select and develop one segment of your material.** Think of your general topic as an accumulation of possibilities from which you can select the most promising one to develop. Skim over what you've produced in freewriting or brainstorming or even in your initial discovery draft and focus on that part that appeals to you most or seems to have the most potential for expansion. Set the rest aside and concentrate on generating more material on your chosen subtopic. Here is an example of how you can focus on a subtopic.

Assignment: Write an article for your student newspaper about some personal experience in college.

Writer: Marty Green, returning twenty-eight-year-old student at Clear Lake-Chicago.

General topic chosen: Contrasting the experience of being a freshman at twenty-eight and at eighteen.
 Possible subtopics to include:
  difference in motivation at different periods
  contrast of attitudes toward studying and homework
  contrast of preferences in social life and recreation
  contrast of finances and financial management at each time

Subtopic chosen and developed: contrast of finances and management.
Ideas for specific development:
 At 18: parents paying bills, personal allowance
  no experience managing checking account or credit cards
  naive about the cost of living
  expensive tastes in entertainment—costly stereo, ski trips, etc.
  result: financial disaster in one semester, parents suspended support,
   dropped out of school
 At 28: self and wife holding part-time jobs
  borrowing money from student loan program
  experience living on Navy enlisted man's salary, realistic budgeting
  modest tastes—country dancing and movies on VCR
  result: living frugally, pushing to get degree

EXERCISE 3.4

Working in a group, everyone write down several subtopics that you might write about under the broad subject of credit cards. Then compare your lists of subtopics and decide which ones are still too broad and which are narrow enough to be worked into lively, informative papers.

3 C

Explore

EXERCISE 3.5

Working with two or three other classmates, draw tree diagrams for two broad topics, perhaps women's changing roles and college basketball. Look back at the examples in this section to help you get started. In discussion, decide which branches of each topic look like good possibilities for writing.

> **TIP: After you write your first draft, you may find that your topic is still broader than you thought it would be and that you need to narrow and focus it even more. That is particularly likely to happen with an exploratory paper.**

3 C   HOW DO YOU EXPLORE AND DEVELOP A SUBJECT?

PROCESS MENU
PREPARING
PLANNING
INCUBATING
DRAFTING
REVISING
EDITING AND PROOFREADING

Troubleshooting

When you finally have your topic, what's the next step? It's finding supporting ideas and details. By using one or more of the invention strategies discussed in this section, you can begin to generate specific examples and details.

To explore and develop a subject . . .

➤ **Write a zero draft.** You may find that your best device for generating material is simply to start writing. The very act of writing, of seeing your words on paper—or the computer screen—will often set the creative juices flowing and help you come up with ideas and make connections that you hadn't thought of before. Think of this first try as a "zero draft," a trial run that doesn't really count. Zero drafts are cheap to write, but they can help break through writer's block and produce a rough draft you can work on.

➤ **Use the journalist's questions.** Beginning reporters for newspapers are taught to keep six questions in mind when they write a new story. They are

Who?	When?
What?	Why?
Where?	How?

Not every question is useful in developing every topic, but they can help you generate information. For instance, you could use the journalist's questions if you had decided to write a paper on stepfamilies similar to the paper by Ruth Blumenthal we have reprinted in the chapters on drafting and revising. Stepfamilies are those new family units created when people with children from previous marriages remarry. Questions you might consider follow:

3 C

Explore

Who are the individuals involved in stepfamilies?
Who do you know who is part of a stepfamily?
What are some of the issues that arise in stepfamilies?
What are some advantages of stepfamilies?
Where are stepfamilies most often found?
When are stepfamilies likely to have problems?
Why do stepfamilies pose special problems?
How can stepfamilies solve some of their problems?

EXERCISE 3.6

The journalist's questions—especially *Who? Where? What? When?* and *How?*—work particularly well with factual or explanatory writing assignments. If you are working on such a paper, apply these questions. To what extent do they help you get your material together?

EXERCISE 3.7

The journalist's questions *Why?* and *How?* can also work well with exploratory assignments that are reflective and loosely structured. Think of some serious problem in your college or in your community—perhaps drug pushing or an unusually high high school dropout rate—and write an introductory draft paragraph on *why* the problem exists and a concluding paragraph on *how* it might be handled.

▶ **Use patterns of thought to generate ideas.** People seem to think by processes that fall into certain patterns, and writers sometimes use these patterns to explore their subjects. The most familiar patterns are

Description	Cause and effect
Narration	Comparison and contrast
Process	Circumstances
Classification	Testimony
Definition	

Here are ways a writer might use these patterns to find material for a paper on the modern American family.

Description: Describe three generations of the same family and show how their living patterns have changed through those generations.

Narration: Tell stories to illustrate certain points about modern American families. (A dramatic anecdote can be a good attention-getting opening for a paper.)

Process: Show some process that seems to typify a modern American family—for instance, the pandemonium of everyone leaving for work and school in the morning.

Classification: Set up a system for classifying some typical kinds of modern American families—stepfamilies, two-working-parent families, single parent families, traditional one-working-parent families, and so on.

Definition: Make a list of important traits of the modern American family—more educated than in past years, more members of the family working, more dependent on day care for children, and so on.

Cause and effect: Speculate about some of the forces that have created the modern American family and changed it from the typical family of fifty years ago.

Comparison/contrast: Compare two categories of modern American families—rural vs. urban, single parent vs. two parents, working mothers vs. nonworking mothers, poor vs. affluent. You could also compare American families with families from another culture—Japanese or Arab, for example.

Circumstances: Analyze the circumstances that have brought about the modern American family. How are they different from previous circumstances?

Testimony: Use case studies of modern American families you are familiar with to illustrate your points.

3 C

Explore

EXERCISE 3.8

Choose three of the thought patterns described above and write three short paragraphs in which you apply them to one of your hobbies or sports interests; for example, skiing, sports cars, soap operas, hockey, dancing, stamp collecting, photography, or something similar.

➤ **Collaborate with others to talk about your assignment.** In many writing classes, the instructor arranges for groups of students to meet before they start work on a writing assignment so they can help each other to generate ideas. Take advantage of the opportunity to talk through your topic. You'll find that as you start to explain your topic to others, more and more ideas will come to you and you'll begin to think of examples and arguments to use. You'll also see problems you may face as others ask you questions and give you suggestions.

➤ **Go back to the computer.** When you have narrowed your topic to one that you think looks manageable and interesting, you can work up additional material by going back to the computer and running through one of the available invention programs, using your more specific topic this time. Now your responses to the computer prompts and questions will be focused more directly on your topic and should produce ideas and examples you can use immediately.

3D HOW DO YOU PLAN AND OUTLINE A PAPER?

PROCESS MENU
PREPARING
PLANNING
INCUBATING
DRAFTING
REVISING
EDITING AND PROOFREADING

Troubleshooting

No matter how good your ideas are, your readers will not understand what you write, or even stick around long enough to read your paper, unless it comes in some organized form. At a minimum, your readers expect that most papers will have a beginning, a middle, and an end. You cannot safely ignore these expectations.

If you don't make the effort to organize a paper, your readers will try to impose a design on it anyway, and if your writing doesn't meet their expectations, they'll blame you for the confusion they feel. So don't think that good organization is optional, something you can add to an essay if you have time; it's the foundation.

When you write, you usually need a plan to keep you on track. True, you may have one worked out in your head, but don't trust your memory—you need something written down. Your plan doesn't have to be a formal outline, however; you can choose from among a number of simple but effective planning strategies. Here are some possibilities:

> sentence outline,
> scratch outline, or
> working list.

Once you have a plan, keep referring to it, but stay flexible. Don't lock out good ideas. To control your material and arrange it effectively for readers, you usually need a specific plan when doing explanatory writing. But you also need at least a tentative plan when you start doing exploratory writing. With reflective or personal pieces, a plan gives you a sense of direction and a tentative goal.

Compare the difference between planning for explanatory and exploratory writing to the approaches two different people might use driving from Chicago to Albuquerque. Driver One's objective might be to make the trip as quickly and cheaply as possible with no delays, avoiding cities when possible, and spending only two nights on the road. To do that, he would have to plan ahead carefully, lay out his route on a map, check a travel guide to find moderately-priced motels, and estimate how far he could drive in a day.

Driver Two's objective might be to have a leisurely trip and explore the country along the way, getting off the interstate highways as much as possible and finding interesting hotels. She wouldn't have to do much specific planning, but she'd have to know in which direction she was heading and where she wanted to wind up. She would also have to expect to do more planning as she went along. A comparable amount of planning is about the minimum a writer can get by with.

To plan a paper, you can . . .

➤ **Make an outline.** For some writers and for some situations, outlining works well. For example, both John McPhee, who writes for *The New Yorker,* and B.F.

Skinner, a noted psychologist, swear by outlines. They claim that, because they put so much time into their outlines, they can write much more easily and quickly. But Jacques Barzun, a writer and philosopher, finds outlines "useless and fettering." He favors lists. One author of this book almost always outlines; the other rarely does. Neither is necessarily "right."

Sample Informal Sentence Outline for a Paper

Family Meals—A Lost Institution?

I. In olden days—thirty or forty years ago—families usually ate their meals together.
   A. Family gathered for breakfast at beginning of each day. Mother cooked and kids ate the food whether they liked it or not.
   B. At dinner time, everyone sat down to eat. Family meals were sentimentalized by Norman Rockwell paintings and Betty Crocker-type advertising.
      1. Mother spent hours in the kitchen preparing food and felt guilty if she didn't.
      2. Family often had good times at the table but lots of fights, too—place for sibling rivalry to surface.
      3. Lots of arguments came from trying to make children eat stuff they didn't like.

II. One of major changes in modern family is that all members seldom eat together.
   A. Everyone works or goes to school—often both. In the morning, people leave at different times, usually in a rush. They grab breakfast on the run as they leave or they pick it up at fast food places.
   B. Teenage children have many commitments and different schedules . . . often can't be home at same time.
      1. Teenagers have jobs.
      2. "Career" teenagers have demanding schedules.
         a. Competitive athletes or cheerleaders.
         b. Dancers, skaters, musicians, and so on.
         c. Club activities.
      3. Schools schedule practice for athletics and other events during traditional meal times.
   C. Two working parents often have heavy schedules, and there are many single-parent families.
      1. They work overtime at jobs and sometimes have to travel.
      2. Because women work too and have less time to cook, most people eat out more.

III. New pattern has disadvantages, but also advantages.
   A. Disadvantages are these:
      1. Parents and children may have less time together and less conversation.
      2. Sometimes children may not eat as well and eat too much fast food.
   B. Advantages are these:
      1. Often teenagers learn to shop and cook for themselves—fosters independence.
      2. Wives and mothers are less tied to kitchen, not expected to wait on everybody.
      3. Fewer family fights occur at the table.
      4. Kids don't have to eat food they don't like.

3 D

Outline

Notice that although the writer uses a sentence outline, she arranges her points informally as if she is still sketching out her essay, not yet sure where she is going to take it. As she writes the essay, she may develop additional material that will help her to make up her mind.

If you have the temperament for outlining, and particularly if you are doing explanatory writing, you may find outlining a useful tool. A sentence outline often helps you articulate your main ideas and put them in order. And don't let worries about putting an outline in proper form keep you from making one if you think it will help. Probably no one is going to see it except you.

Powerful outlining programs are available on personal computers. They allow you to write, revise, expand, contract, and rearrange your ideas in outline form quickly and easily. Some programs even work directly within word processing programs, enabling you to plan, write, and revise all on the same screen. Computerized outlining programs combine the organizational power of the traditional outline with the flexibility of less rigid planning strategies. Investigate such programs if your writing center or library has them. (See Chapter 51 on using computers.)

TIP: Outlines are only tools to aid organization; they are *not* blueprints that must be followed faithfully once they are written.

➤ **Make an informal or scratch outline.** Many writers like working from outlines but dislike the formality and restrictions of formal sentence outlines. For them, informal or scratch outlines that give main points in categories and subcategories work just as well as sentence outlines. Not only are they less trouble to make, but they seem more flexible to work with. A writer doesn't invest as much in an informal outline, so it becomes easier to adapt and change as he or she writes.

Sample Scratch Outline for a Paper

Topic: What's happened to family meals in today's average American family?

The traditional practice of families having meals together seems to be changing.

> Most families used to eat breakfast and dinner together; now both children and parents may be working shifts and hardly see each other.

> Everyone got caught up on family news at the dinner table and had a chance to tell about their triumphs and exasperations of the day.

> But often the worst family fights also took place at mealtimes when family members got together.

Why have things changed?

> In many modern families, everyone works, sometimes on shifts or at odd hours. Makes more hectic schedules.

> Today's teenagers apt to be involved in lots of activities—sports, clubs, computer labs, etc. Schools' extracurricular stuff cuts into family meal times.

(margin) **3 D** Outline

With so many women working, harder for them to cook and get regular meals on the table. More eating out and more fast food.

Consequences

Bad: Less family time together and there's not as much communication. Probably don't eat as well or as regularly. School activities sometimes overwhelm kids. Can miss some good times at the table. Harder to pass on family traditions.

Good: Fewer fights between children—not as much opportunity. Sometimes parents have the chance to have peaceful meals by themselves. Individuals have more choice about what they eat. Children learn to fend for themselves.

With this kind of outline, you have a good working plan that you could start developing with additional information and concrete details. It's also possible that in working out the outline, you might be struck by some part of it and decide to build your paper around that, thus narrowing it from your original idea. At this stage of your writing, that possibility is still open.

EXERCISE 3.9

Choose one of the topics you wrote down in Exercise 2.1 as something you might be interested in writing about. Sketch out an informal sentence outline you might use for developing some aspect of your topic.

➤ **Make a working list.** The working list is the most open-ended and flexible of all outlines. Start by putting down the key points you want to make, leaving plenty of room under each one. Then working from your brainstorming or freewriting notes, choose subpoints that fit under the various points and write them down. You might want to jot down some cue notes in the margin to remind you of anecdotes or examples you could use to illustrate certain points. A typical cue note to yourself might say, "Check article in Jan. *Rolling Stone*" or "Use story about Uncle Henry."

When you think you have enough material, look over your list to decide which point you want to put first and how you might arrange the others. Then start writing and, as you work, refer to your list occasionally to see that you are staying on track and not forgetting important items. You will probably cross off some items as you write and add others.

Lists can work well with both explanatory and exploratory writing. For explanatory writing, the list helps you to gather facts and information and start arranging them by some plan. For exploratory writing, making a list will help you to jot down ideas and reactions you want to incorporate into the paper even when you don't yet know how you will use them.

Sample Working List

In today's family, eating patterns are different.

Fewer meals together	Eat out more
More people work	People favor different foods
Different schedules	School activities clash
Fast food—eat on the run	with mealtimes

New patterns have altered the dynamic in some American families.

Effects

On parents
harder to spend time with children
feel contrast with own childhood
may feel frustrated, guilty
spend less time shopping and cooking
don't have to listen to children fight at table

On children
some miss contact with parents
may fight less among themselves
spend more time with others their age
might not eat as well but don't have to eat stuff
they don't like

EXERCISE 3.10

If you have a job or have recently had one, make a working list for an explanatory paper you might write about your job, a mainly factual paper that would let someone who was interested in applying for a similar job know what qualifications he or she needs, what kind of work is required, hours and salary, and what benefits and drawbacks you find in the job.

EXERCISE 3.11

Working in a group, each person make a working list for an exploratory paper as a response to an invitation by your school newspaper to describe the single most important improvement you would like to see on your campus or in your college. Get together to compare your lists and make suggestions.

> **TIP: Whatever plans you make to develop a paper, keep them flexible. Actual writing may spark ideas that incinerate your original plans. If you can—that is, if you have the time—consider these new ideas and adjust your outlines or lists to accommodate them. Don't moan over the ashes. Don't close down too quickly if you can avoid it. Just because you have a finished plan for a paper doesn't mean you have found the best way to treat a topic.**

3 E   HOW DO YOU DEVISE A THESIS SENTENCE?

Terms you need to know

THESIS SENTENCE. A carefully constructed sentence that expresses the point of a paper or summarizes its main ideas. Note that a *thesis sentence* differs from a *topic sentence*, which states the main idea of a paragraph.

3 E

Thesis

PROCESS MENU
PREPARING
PLANNING
INCUBATING
DRAFTING
REVISING
EDITING AND PROOFREADING

Troubleshooting

Many writers like to work out a **thesis sentence** for a paper early in the composing process and use that as one of their major organizational tools. By keeping that sentence in mind as the paper develops, they can be sure they will cover their main points. If you are writing a primarily factual explanatory paper for a college course, you can strengthen the paper by writing a clear and full thesis sentence and including a version of it early in your paper. Such a sentence sets the direction of the paper and lets your professor know what to expect.

A full thesis sentence can also be useful when you're planning an exploratory paper because it sets down the main ideas that will underlie your writing even if you don't yet know exactly how you're going to develop them. You don't need to use the sentence in your paper but it can serve as a good anchor.

In either case, you'll need a carefully thought out thesis sentence if it is to serve as a working guide for a paper. It should be comprehensive—that is, mention the major points you want to make—yet succinct—that is, brief and to the point. Here is a thesis sentence with both these qualities.

> In the last fifteen years, the number of high school students holding down part-time jobs has more than quadrupled, changing the traditional role of a seventeen-year-old as a carefree youngster to that of a harried young adult.

The sentence could use some polishing, but a writer who organized a paper according to this sentence and developed its points through examples should have a tight, easy-to-follow paper.

Don't assume that your thesis sentence must be the first sentence of your paper, although it can be. Often you can find a more interesting or dramatic sentence with which to open your paper. You can put the thesis sentence aside and use it only as a planning tool, or you might place it at the end of your first paragraph, especially if you have spent some time developing it.

To write an effective thesis sentence . . .

➤ **Make a comprehensive statement.** A thesis sentence won't help you much unless it enumerates the points you intend to develop and sets a direction your readers can follow. Begin by making a statement about your subject. That means, write a complete sentence (not a phrase, not a fragment) that explains what you expect to write about.

{**Not**}   Many high school students have jobs.

{**But**}   Today so many high school students have jobs that they have become an important block of consumers, specially targeted by advertisers.

➤ **Make a strong point.** Does your thesis sentence provoke reactions? Can someone legitimately disagree with it? If not, change it to say something that sparks interest or raises expectations. Take a stand.

{**Not**}   For several reasons, Michael Dukakis was defeated in the 1988 elections. (True, but that's news?)

{**But**}   Some political analysts believe that Lyndon Johnson's civil rights policies of the sixties helped defeat Michael Dukakis for president in 1988.

➤ **Be sure your thesis sentence gives direction to your paper.** Does it tell readers what they can expect or what you intend to cover in the paper? If not, check where in your thesis sentence you need to include the central points you intend to make.

{**Not**}   Perfume ads show us an unreal world.

{**But**}   Television advertisements for cologne and perfume portray a false world, where everyone is beautiful, rich, happy, and in love.

➤ **Be sure your statement is worth making.** Read your thesis sentence aloud, and then ask yourself whether an intelligent member of your audience would respond to it with "So, what's your point?" or "Big deal!" If they might, look for a more significant idea, or give pertinent specifics of your general point.

{**Not**}   Returning to college at thirty-three, I faced many big adjustments. (That's hardly surprising.)

{**But**}   Returning to school at thirty-three, I had to learn to listen actively, think critically, and balance the new demands in my life with those of my children.

> **TIP:** Write your thesis sentence early in the writing process if you want it to serve as an anchor and guidepost for your paper. Then from time to time as your paper develops, test the thesis sentence against the paper you are writing. Sometimes you may find that as you write the second and third drafts, you will continue to focus and narrow your topic so that some of the earlier points in the thesis should be dropped or revised.

EXERCISE 3.12

Write a preliminary thesis sentence you might use for a paper on why you had a job while you were in high school or why you didn't have one. Then get together with two or three other students in the class and decide who has written the most informative thesis sentence.

A representative from each group could present the winner to the rest of the class.

EXERCISE 3.13

Working in a group, review the guidelines for an effective thesis sentence; then collaborate to rank the following thesis statements as "pretty good," "not too bad," and "won't do the job." Why? Which survive the "So what?" test?

1. Although Clear Lake College is not a large university, it offers excellent programs in play writing, interior decoration, forestry, and business administration and has graduated many well-known figures in those fields.
2. The story of Clear Lake College is an interesting one.
3. Clear Lake College's early commitment to education for women has helped it produce some of the state's outstanding women scientists and enhanced its reputation nationally.
4. Students from Mexico, Vietnam, Germany, Hong Kong, and Muleshoe, Texas, give Clear Lake College an international atmosphere and a unique cultural flavor.
5. Returning older students often change the atmosphere in a college's classrooms.

3 F   HOW DO YOU ARRANGE A PAPER FOR EMPHASIS?

PROCESS MENU
PREPARING
PLANNING
INCUBATING
DRAFTING
REVISING
EDITING AND PROOFREADING

Troubleshooting

As one part of organizing your paper, you need to decide what points you want to emphasize and how you are going to do it. In an effective paper, you can't just present ideas at random or you'll have your readers wondering which points are more important. You need to establish a sequence that gives readers signals about priority.

To provide the right emphasis in a paper . . .

➤ **Put your main ideas up front in most informative essays.** In the first paragraph, give readers a clear idea of what to expect. Then you can follow with subordinate or supporting ideas and build toward a strong concluding paragraph that will leave your readers with a clear impression of the main point. For example, from a paper that Marcia Daly wrote for a course in women's studies, here is an opening paragraph that makes a direct statement about the subject of the paper.

3 F

Emphasis

At the end of the 1980s, one-third of the doctors graduating from medical schools were women. Women doctors will soon be in the majority in specialities such as obstetrics/gynecology, pediatrics, and psychiatry, and they are rapidly making inroads into traditionally male territories like surgery and orthopedics. This shifting balance in what up to now has been a male-dominated profession is changing American medicine in a number of ways. One can already see changes in medical education as the number of women professors in medical schools increases.

For more indirect and speculative essays, consider catching your readers' attention with an intriguing first paragraph that indirectly signals what's coming. For example, Marcia could have used this kind of opening paragraph if she had been writing a speculative rather than an informative essay about the increasing number of women in the medical profession.

A slight woman with long, blond hair tied back in a ponytail, Melissa Gaines is used to having her patients in the Veterans Hospital refuse at first to take her seriously in spite of her stethoscope, white coat, and a name badge that says M. Gaines, Ph.D., M.D. One gruff veteran complains, "I don't want any teenage doctors." Another insists on asking her to fix his pillows or rub his back. But veterans who have been at the VA several months see in Dr. Gaines a new kind of doctor and they like the change.

In an argumentative paper, you could start out emphatically by raising the key question you plan to answer and finish memorably by giving your solution. You particularly need to put the most important idea last in argumentative papers since most people remember best the last point that they read. (You'll find more on opening and closing paragraphs in Chapter 14.)

➤ **Announce key ideas with phrases that underscore their significance.** Such phrases might include remarks like "the major points we must consider are"; "the chief issue, however, is"; "now we come to the crucial question." You can also mark your important points by labeling them "first," "second," "third," or using phrases such as "I want to stress," or "it is essential to. . . ." All such phrases signal readers to "Take this seriously."

➤ **Keep the amount you write on each point roughly proportionate to the importance of that idea.** Be careful not to write a lopsided paper that misleads readers. If an introduction takes up half the paper, it's no longer an introduction. If you write a long argument but conclude it with only a one-sentence summary, your readers are going to feel your paper fizzles out at the end.

➤ **Allow enough time to write a strong conclusion.** Because conclusions are so important, be sure to leave time to write a good one. If you have only limited time you can invest in a paper, don't put a disproportionate amount of energy into the introduction and body of your paper and then skimp on the conclusion.

EXERCISE 3.14

Working in a group, discuss the main point a writer might choose to empha-size in papers on these topics.

1. In an African-American history course, the role of African-American musi-cians in early jazz.
2. In a newspaper editorial, a claim that the city's schools are not giving enough attention to Southeast Asian refugees.
3. For a freshman English paper, a report on AIDS education on your campus.

3 G

Title

3 G HOW DO YOU CHOOSE A TITLE?

PROCESS MENU
PREPARING
PLANNING
INCUBATING
DRAFTING
REVISING
EDITING AND PROOFREADING

Troubleshooting

Your readers want and expect a title; in fact, they depend on you to give them one. They'll be particularly annoyed if they don't find one that helps them anticipate what they're going to read. So don't let them down. You may not have considered, however, that finding a title is an important step in organiz-ing a paper.

To find a good title . . .

➤ **Use a working title as a tool of organization.** Choose a preliminary title early in your drafting process to help you keep your writing focused. For instance, if you are writing an article about a computer business that a college friend of yours has started, you might begin with the title "The Student Computer King of Central University." The title contains several cues to keep your writing on target: *student* reminds you that you're limiting the paper to this one student, *king* reminds you that you'll need to show why he's so impressive, and *Central University* reminds you to show his connection with the university.

> **TIP:** When you're doing informative, explanatory writ-ing—and college papers often fit this description—be sure your title accurately reflects the content of your paper. No cute titles, please. People doing computer searches work by looking for what are called "descrip-tors" in titles—that is, key words that help identify the content of a book or article and direct the researcher to the place where he or she can find it. Thus it's essential for your title to give accurate signals to someone looking for information.

➤ **Revise the working title to reflect your finished product.** When you have finished an essay, you need to look at the title again to be sure that the title and essay are tightly connected and that the title acts as a predictor for your readers. For instance, as you worked on your paper, you might have been struck by parallels between your friend's efforts and the early work of Steven Jobs at Apple Computers. You refocus your essay in this direction and, after some tinkering, come up with this: "Computer Genius at Work: Another Steve Jobs at Central University?" It is a clearer, more specific title containing all the major cue words your readers need.

3 G

Title

EXERCISE 3.15

Working in a group, have each person write a title that might work well for papers on these topics. Compare titles and see if you can agree on the best ones.

1. A complaint about the way your campus book store is run.
2. An exposé of a drug-selling operation on campus.
3. A satire on the kind of shoes fashionable on your campus.
4. A review of a rock or folk group at a favorite music spot.
5. A feature story about student fathers at your college.

EXERCISE 3.16

Which of these titles seem to you as if they would be good predictors of content in a paper. Why?

1. "Cruising Around Black Holes with Physicist Stephen Hawking"
2. "Beautiful Daydreams"
3. "Choosing the Best Car Stereo for You"
4. "Tricking Your Body into Losing Weight"
5. "What's in a Name?"
6. "Drugs"
7. "My Father, My Mentor"
8. "An American Problem"
9. "Keeping the Faith: Fundamentalism in the 1980s"
10. "Insurance Costs Keep Rising"

4   How Do You Write a Draft?

4 A   HOW DO YOU GET STARTED ON A PAPER?

Troubleshooting

Most writers agree that actually getting those first words down on paper can be the hardest part of writing. Even professional authors have described the paralyzing anxiety they sometimes feel as they sit before a typewriter and stare at a blank sheet of paper. Columnist Russell Baker tells of pulling one blank sheet of paper out of the typewriter and rolling in another one that might be "friendlier." Today, instead of staring at the typewriter or gnawing on a pencil, many of us listen to our computers hum, and we look in frustration at the blinking cursor. The problem is the same though; how do you get started?

Well, first, recognize that beginnings *are* hard. If you have trouble getting those first few sentences down, don't assume it's because you're a bad writer or that you don't have anything to say. It's just that, in the short run, it's always easier not to write than it is to write, so we put it off. Before long we have built up a barrier of inertia, and then we have to work at breaking through it. In this chapter, we offer several suggestions for managing that first difficult stage.

To get started on a paper . . .

➤ **Find a place to write and gather your equipment.** If you can, get away from other people and find a place to write where you won't have distractions. If you're using a computer, turn it on and let it hum. That's a working noise you hear. Gather up all the materials you need—computer disks or a typewriter, your notes, paper, pencils—and lay them out where you can see them. Be sure you have a copy of the assignment. Preparations like these aren't just fussing or procrastinating. You're creating a writing environment, giving your brain signals that you're going to write and committing yourself to the job.

➤ **Set your own pace.** If you are not sure what pace suits you best, start by making yourself write quickly. Concentrate on composing and try not to worry too much about details at this stage. If you hit a snag and can't think of the precise words you want or the specific example you need, "island hop" around the troublesome parts and go on. Writing a first draft quickly will give you a sense of accomplishment because early on you will have an actual copy you can see and begin to work with.

If, however, you're the kind of writer who just isn't comfortable composing quickly, don't feel bad. Many competent writers work slowly. They may take several hours to turn out a page or two, but their first drafts often are quite polished. In the long run, slow writers may not spend any more time composing a paper than writers who seem to be working faster.

Whatever your pace, remember that writing itself is a creative process that stirs up the unconscious and generates new material. Thus even when you know most of your content before you start writing, you should expect fresh ideas or useful examples to turn up as you work, and you should have a plan to capture them.

➤ **Collaborate with other writers.** You can often come up with good ideas and improve your work by collaborating with other writers at several stages during the writing process. You can brainstorm together, give each other examples and anecdotes, suggest possible audiences, and remind each other of the constraints those audiences impose. As members of a group, you can also act as the first audience for each other's drafts and give immediate feedback. You will also get insights into your own work by viewing it through the eyes of others.

This kind of collaborative work helps to create a community of writers who are interested in each other's work and can strengthen each other as writers. It also reinforces the social element of writing. Because most of us necessarily do much of our writing alone, it's easy to forget that writing is a social activity that we engage in to communicate with each other. Working in groups reminds us of that.

> **TIP: At the end of this chapter, you will find a set of questions and guidelines that will help you work with others in a group to respond to their writing and make suggestions for improving it.**

➤ **Don't take beginnings too seriously.** Think of your first paragraph as a device to get you started—a runway, a starting block, a launching pad. It's something to push off from to get you moving; it isn't necessarily a permanent part of the paper. Some writers agonize over that first paragraph, tinkering endlessly until they get it exactly right. Unfortunately, often they're also the writers who don't get their papers written at all or turn out a poorly developed paper because they spent so much time on the beginning. The important thing is to get going. Write two or three sentences to get started, no matter how bad you think they are. Just lay down some tracks so your thoughts can start moving and you can build momentum.

➤ **Don't criticize yourself as you write.** When you are working on a first draft, give yourself a break. Don't say, "Oh, this is awful" or "I hate my writing." You wouldn't say that to a friend who was struggling to write a first draft, so don't say it to yourself. Remember that writing anything complex is a slow and challenging business—you should congratulate yourself when you're getting it done at all. Most pieces of good writing develop over a period of time; you can't expect something to be polished and satisfactory when you first write it.

➤ **Don't edit your writing prematurely.** When you're working on early drafts, try not to worry about mechanical problems, such as punctuation and spelling, or style problems, such as parallelism or sentence fragments. You can go back and fix those later after you have captured your ideas in writing. If you fuss over details this early in the writing process, two bad things can happen. First, you may lose your momentum for writing. Second, you may limit yourself to writing easy sentences and thus write a much less interesting paper than you are capable of.

➤ **Make a contract with yourself and anticipate rewards.** Promise yourself that you will write for two hours or write two pages, whichever comes first, before you get up from the typewriter or computer. When you do take the break, have a reward waiting for you—a bag of popcorn or a cold drink. Then go back for another two-hour session and reward yourself again. Plan a bigger reward when you finish the first draft—perhaps a computer game or a movie.

EXERCISE 4.1

Working in a group with two or three other students, have each of you write a paragraph about your strategies for getting started on a paper. Encourage each person to read his or her paragraph aloud, and then compare notes. What useful suggestions can you give each other?

EXERCISE 4.2

Working with a group of two or three other students, each of you write down two or three sentences that might work as one way to start a first draft for the following writing assignment. Then read the beginnings out loud and discuss their potential as "launching pads."

> **Assignment:** Write a paper about a violent incident that happened to you or to someone you know well.

| EXERCISE 4.3 |

Analyze the kind of writer you are by answering the following questions.

—Do you write quickly or slowly? Do you make a lot of changes as you work? How long can you work at one stretch?

—How often do you stop to reread as you are writing? Do such stops seem to be necessary?

—How often do you get up to do other things when you are writing? Do such breaks usually help you think?

—Where do you prefer to write? Is there something about that place that helps you write?

—What time of day do you prefer to write? Can you work at any time?

—What kind of atmosphere do you like? Must you have quiet? Do you like music while you write?

—What tools do you use? Pencil and paper? Typewriter? Word processor? Can you switch from one to another without getting disrupted?

—Do you write regularly? Do you keep a journal or diary?

—How do you feel about writing? What words describe your attitude?

| EXERCISE 4.4 |

Get together with two or three other students in your writing class and compare your answers to the questions in the previous exercise. What strong similarities do you find? What major differences are there among your methods? Write out one idea you got from others that will help your writing.

4 B   WHEN SHOULD YOU GIVE YOURSELF A BREAK?

Terms you need to know

INCUBATION. In writing, an interval during which the writer stops composing for a time to let ideas "cook" or germinate in the subconscious.

PROCESS MENU
PREPARING
PLANNING
INCUBATING
DRAFTING
REVISING
EDITING AND PROOFREADING

Troubleshooting

Sometimes you start writing and then suddenly find yourself stumped. You look at the computer screen or listen to your typewriter hum, but nothing comes. Some people call the problem "writer's block," but it may signal nothing more serious than a creative lull. At such times, you need to stop to let your thoughts *incubate*. Put the writing task aside on the conscious level and do something else.

We don't really know what happens during these incubation periods. The creative or problem-solving part of the mind seems to go on a fishing expedition into the subconscious. It sorts through what it finds there, discovers fresh ideas and makes new connections. You can't force or rush incubation. The only thing you can do is be ready to grab the idea or solution when it surfaces.

To help ideas develop . . .

➤ **Expect both major and minor incubation periods.** Like the other elements in the writing process, incubation is an ongoing activity that may occur several times during one project. For most authors who write consistently, these periods of rest are absolutely necessary. When they've written themselves out for the day, it's fruitless to stare at the computer or typewriter any longer. Time to quit and let the creative juices replenish themselves.

4 C

Develop

The periods that lapse between writing the first, second, and even third draft of a paper can be tremendously productive, but minor incubation periods can also help greatly. When you are stuck for a word or can't think of the example you need to illustrate a point, getting away from the desk long enough to do an errand or go in the other room to chat with your spouse can trigger a flash of insight that breaks up those blocks temporarily obstructing your writing. So you don't have to keep yourself glued to the chair all the time in order to write—minor interruptions can be productive, too.

➤ **Don't use incubation as an excuse for procrastination.** You can and should relax occasionally and take time out while you're writing, but you can't wait indefinitely for inspiration to strike. If you're still having problems after a few hours (or a weekend), you need to get back to work and hope that the act of writing will help you break through the blocks. Review your notes or outline; reread what you've already written or talk to a friend about the assignment. Most important, just write! Chances are good that your conscious and subconscious will mesh and you will write yourself out of a hole.

EXERCISE 4.5

Recall a time when you solved what seemed like an insoluble problem after taking a break from worrying about it. (The problem does not have to be connected with writing a paper.) Describe that experience in a short narrative. Was the solution you arrived at obvious? If so, why do you think you didn't discover it earlier?

4 C   HOW DO YOU FIND A PATTERN OF DEVELOPMENT?

Troubleshooting

When you start your draft, you shouldn't torment yourself by thinking that there's one right way to organize a piece of writing and that you have to find that way. For most writing, you have a choice of several workable patterns; if you learn the basic features of several common patterns of organization, you can choose among them when you need one. Here are some useful patterns.

Select as a pattern of development . . .

➤ **Introduction/body/conclusion.** This is the basic formula, simple but also powerful if used well. Begin by introducing your subject to give your readers a clear signal about what they can expect and in what direction they'll be going. Follow with examples and explanations that expand on your topic and support your claim. Conclude with a section that ties your points together and leaves your readers with a sense of closure.

Although this elementary pattern can produce mechanical, dull writing, it doesn't have to; it can also produce interesting writing that's easy to follow. It works well for essay exams, placement exams, or any impromptu writing in which you have to organize your ideas and get them down quickly. This pattern is easy to outline and readily expandable as you think of ideas.

A variation of the introduction/body/conclusion pattern is:

1. Introduction
2. The problem defined
3. Its causes
4. Its effects
5. Recommendations

This can be a good pattern for writing college papers, particularly in the social and physical sciences.

➤ **Problem and solution/question and answer.** You can use this pattern effectively for papers in which you argue for change or propose a solution to a problem. You start by explaining the problem or posing the question. This first part could run only a paragraph or it could take up half or more of the paper. The second part of the paper lays out the solution or answer.

For example, when Connie Lim was writing an editorial for the campus newspaper complaining about a group of students monopolizing the lounge of the Student Union to watch daytime soap operas, she began by defining the problem, explaining how thirty to forty obstreperous students took over the lounge every day to watch "Search for Tomorrow" and "All My Children." She then suggested the solution of putting several television sets in the Union's third floor conference rooms, which are seldom used.

➤ **Comparison/contrast.** In writing comparison/contrast papers, you'll usually find yourself using one of two basic plans, either describing the things you are comparing one at a time or describing them feature-by-feature in alternating sequence. Alternative scratch outlines for a paper on wild game viewing by Luke Scandino, who works for a Chicago travel agency, illustrate the difference.

Entire Subject at One Time

1. **Introduction:** Seeing wild animals in Africa and in India
2. **Subject 1** Viewing game in Africa
   Feature A (Quantity) Abundant game in Africa, easy to see

Feature B (Variety) Distinct African species: zebra, lions, etc.
Feature C (Mode of viewing) Landrovers, expert drivers
Feature D (Accommodations, transportation) Tented camps, access by small plane

3. **Subject 2** Viewing game in India
   Feature A (Quantity) Far less game in India, sometimes hard to see
   Feature B (Variety) Distinct Indian species: tigers, black rhino
   Feature C (Mode of viewing) Elephant back, jeeps, blinds
   Feature D (Accommodations, transportation) Tented camps, lodges, hotels; access by bus and small plane

4. **Conclusion**

4 C

Develop

Feature-by-Feature

1. **Introduction:** Seeing wild game in Africa and in India
2. **Feature A** (Quantity)
   Subject 1 (Africa) Game abundant in preserves
   Subject 2 (India) Game rather scarce, smaller preserves
3. **Feature B** (Variety)
   Subject 1 (Africa) Distinct species: lions, zebras, hippos
   Subject 2 (India) Distinct species: tiger, black rhino, cobras
4. **Feature C** (Mode of Viewing)
   Subject 1 (Africa) Landrover, expert guides as drivers
   Subject 2 (India) Elephant back, jeeps, blinds
5. **Feature D** (Accommodations, mode of transportation)
   Subject 1 (Africa) Tented camps, lodges; access by small plane
   Subject 2 (India) Tented camps, lodges, hotels; access by small plane and bus
6. **Conclusion**

If you are using comparison/contrast in a short paper and making only one or two comparisons, you can use the one-subject-at-a-time plan successfully because your readers won't have to keep a large quantity of information in mind as they make comparisons. If you're doing a longer paper, however, you'll do better to use the alternating feature-by-feature pattern; otherwise, your readers have to hold too much information in mind, and they'll lose track of the features being compared. For the paper on viewing game in Africa and India, for example, Luke has so much information that he should use the feature-by-feature pattern; otherwise, his readers will forget his first points about game viewing in Africa by the time they get to the comparable points about India.

▶ **Cause and effect.** When you're writing an argument or an explanation, you can often use a cause and effect pattern to organize your material. You can create such a pattern in two ways. You can start your essay by identifying and describing an effect and then go on to explain or hypothesize about the causes, or you can start by listing a number of events or facts and show how they cause a certain effect. Cause and effect patterns are particularly popular with lawyers when they argue cases, and they work well for many kinds of college papers.

Here is a possible scratch outline for a cause and effect paper that Marty Green, who attends the Chicago branch of Clear Lake College, plans to write for a philosophy paper about why the study of rhetoric flourished in ancient Greece.

Effect/Causes

Part I—Effect. In fifth and fourth centuries B.C., the art of rhetoric originated in Greece and became established as major study.

1. Famous rhetoricians—Plato, Gorgias, Isocrates, Aristotle.
2. Schools—Plato's Academy, Sophists' schools. Itinerant teachers. Aristotle teacher for Alexander the Great.

4 C

Develop

Part II—Causes. Rise of democracy in Greece in fifth century B.C. made public speaking and persuasion important.

1. Government by public debate and vote. Political power came from being good speaker.
2. Legal disputes settled in public forum—citizens had to be their own defenders.
3. Citizens eager to master rhetoric—demand for teachers and schools.

Marty could write an equally effective paper by simply flip-flopping the pattern and moving the causes to the first section.

▶ **Assertion and support/claim and evidence.** Lawyers, scientists, environmental analysts, and writers in many academic fields especially favor this pattern of organization because it underlies much logical argument. The method is simple enough. The writer makes an assertion or a claim in the introduction, then gives supporting reasons or evidence. This pattern of organization is another one that works well for much of the writing you do in college because when you make a claim or assertion in a paper, professors expect you to support it with evidence.

Here is an outline for an assertion/support paper that Mavis Solomon, a returning older student, wrote for her English class after she made a trip to India with a group from the Museum of Science and Industry in Chicago. Notice that her assertion can also act as her thesis sentence.

Introduction

Assertion: Although I had misgivings when we were planning our trip to India, I found the culture rich and diverse, the architecture stunning, and the people beautiful and dignified.

Support:

1. Preconceptions about poverty and crowded cities in India made me apprehensive about going there.
   a. Expected to see people living in misery.
   b. Expected Indian cities to be overcrowded and squalid.

2. New Delhi and Jaipur are beautiful cities with poverty and homelessness no more striking than in some American cities.
   a. Crowded, but that's partly Indian way of life.
   b. Rich panorama of diverse street life makes cities more lively and interesting than most American cities.
   c. Hindu and Moslem religious practices help the poor.

3. India is full of exquisite architecture, especially from Moghul period.
   a. Taj Mahal.
   b. Red Forts at Agra and Delhi.
   c. Fetaphur Sikri.

4. People, especially the women, are beautiful and dignified.
   a. Handsome people, slender and smooth skinned.
   b. Women in colorful saris walking everywhere.
   c. Affectionate families.
5. Conclusion: Although some things about India are unsettling, its rich cultural diversity and vitality make it very worth visiting.

➤ **Commitment and response.** Writers using this important strategy consciously make a *commitment* or promise to their readers early in a paper, then use that commitment as a foundation upon which to develop the rest of the essay. The commitment can be direct or indirect. In a *direct commitment,* the writer addresses the issue in the opening paragraph. For example, here is Derek Mott's opening paragraph for an editorial in the campus newspaper.

4 C

Develop

> Because once more a stingy Board of Directors has failed to appropriate money, students at the Clear Lake-Chicago campus again face a semester of cancelled courses and overflowing classes.

Such an opening statement presents an issue and commits the writer to developing a response to it. Another kind of direct commitment can take the form of a provocative question. For example,

> Why must students at the Clear Lake College campus face another semester of cancelled courses and overflowing classes?

Derek could also have begun the editorial with an anecdote or example making an *indirect commitment.* For example,

> Did you leave fall registration today with a rearranged schedule because two of the courses you planned to take had been cancelled? When you got to your first class, did you find standing room only? If so, welcome to the club.

With this opening, Derek has committed himself to making a response to the issue he has raised.

➤ **Classification, narration, and process.** Three other possible patterns for your essay can be these three, described and discussed briefly in an earlier chapter (Chapter 3, pages 28–29) and in the next chapter on paragraphs (Chapter 13, pages 215–219). You can consult those sections if your instructor suggests that you might try one of these patterns. Briefly, here is how they work.

If you want to use **classification** as a pattern, do it like this.

1. Describe your system of classification; for example, cars could be classified by price range, origin (Japan or U.S.), model, and so on.
2. Explain why you chose this system.
3. Give characteristics of the classes.

For instance, when Rita Ruiz wrote an honors paper about Picasso's changing painting styles for her art history class, she began by saying she would classify his paintings by chronological periods and discuss the important features that characterized each of the periods; she justified her system by pointing out that it was the one adopted by the new Picasso Museum in Paris, and then she analyzed how the style and subjects of Picasso's painting changed over his more than sixty years as an artist.

If you choose to organize your paper by a pattern of **narration,** you probably will use a chronological structure and recount a story or event as it occurred, or you could begin with a dramatic anecdote, then flash back to the events that led up to the event.

4 C

Develop

For instance, when Travis Beckwith needed to write a paper about pulsar stars for his "History of Astronomy" course, he chose to use a narrative structure. He began with an anecdote about the scientists at Bell Labs who first interpreted the signals coming from pulsar stars as possible radio signals communicated by intelligent beings in outer space. Then he went back to tell the story of their discovery.

If you organize a paper by a **process** pattern, start at the beginning and work your way carefully through the steps of the process, explaining each one. Be especially careful to include all the steps in the proper order. Process is an important kind of organizational pattern for giving instructions and for some engineering and scientific writing, particularly technical reports. When Darwin Ferguson wrote a paper in his "Computers and Writing" course about a new program for peer response created in the writing center at Clear Lake College, he wrote a process paper stating the rationale for the program and detailing how it worked, step by step.

> **TIP: Although we have classified and described several useful patterns of organization here, you shouldn't assume that each pattern is separate and distinct. Several of them overlap or resemble one another. If you're not sure how to describe the pattern you're using, don't worry about it. What counts is that your paper have a design your readers can follow.**

EXERCISE 4.6

Working with two or three other students, consider what patterns you might use for writing about two of the topics given below. Give reasons why you think those patterns would work well.

1. The popularity of horror movies.
2. A trip to Mexico during spring break.
3. Choosing a stereo system for your car.
4. Why fewer students are applying to medical school.
5. The prospects that face a pregnant teenager.

EXERCISE 4.7

How could you set up a comparison/contrast pattern for two of these topics?

1. Choosing your major in college.
2. How to find good music in your college's town.
3. On-campus jobs.
4. Life as a single-parent student.
5. Choosing between downhill and cross-country skiing.

4 D

Draft

4 D   HOW DO YOU PRODUCE A FIRST DRAFT?

PROCESS MENU
PREPARING
PLANNING
INCUBATING
DRAFTING
REVISING
EDITING AND PROOFREADING

Troubleshooting

Sometimes, particularly with exploratory papers in which you're developing ideas as you write, you can get off to a promising start by just writing to generate material. Often you will wind up with a first draft that you like well, although you know it needs work.

Take, for example, the first draft of a paper Sheila Moore wrote for her freshman English course about her first visit to New York City. She wanted to stress how confused she felt by New York's mixture of affluence and poverty, beauty and squalor, people brimming with energy and those sunk in dejection. She started her draft by describing her Sunday morning walk through Central Park, past the Metropolitan Museum of Art, and down Fifth Avenue past elegant hotels and apartment houses to the dazzling Trump Tower. As she wrote, she remembered and added more details—polar bears in the newly opened Central Park Zoo, oriental men doing tai chi exercises in the park, open-air book stalls on the sidewalks along Fifth Avenue.

As she continued to write, she also recalled how she cringed when she saw people sleeping under the bridges in the park and the disgust she felt going by walls that smelled of urine and were defaced with obscene graffiti. She was most upset, however, by seeing old women huddled against buildings, clinging to grocery carts that held everything they owned. Then she felt herself get caught up again in the charm of Greenwich Village and the excitement of the city at night. She also remembered how shocked she was by some New York prices.

Her first draft was rich with details, but they were jumbled together in no particular pattern, and her readers told her they got lost. They had thought at first that she loved New York, but then they got confused because she went off in a new direction and talked about how depressing and expensive it was. Sheila agreed that she hadn't realized how much she was going to write. She knew her material wasn't well organized.

So she went over her draft, condensed each point into a sentence, and numbered the sentences; in effect, she made an outline *after* she wrote her first draft. She drafted a new opening paragraph that began, "New York is the best of cities; New York is the worst of cities," establishing her comparison/contrast pattern and signalling her readers what to expect. Then she arranged her summary sentences in pairs and used description to contrast the elegance and security of the expensive apartment houses with the insecurity of the old women on the street, the glamor of the Trump Tower with the squalor of filthy underpasses, and so on. She deleted any mention of prices, realizing it wouldn't fit her paper.

4 E

Draft

When she finished reading over and evaluating her draft (with a little help from her friends), she was ready to revise. She knew that with her word processor she could move her points around easily and tinker with her phrasing without losing the freshness of her first impressions. She also felt more confident because she knew now she had a plan for her paper.

4 E WHEN DO YOU HAVE A DRAFT?

PROCESS MENU
PREPARING
PLANNING
INCUBATING
DRAFTING
REVISING
EDITING AND PROOFREADING

Troubleshooting

As the deadline approaches to turn in that first draft, relax and assure yourself that although a paper you are laboring over may not be as good as you'd like, it *is* a draft that you will have the chance to work on again. Take comfort, too, in knowing that most other people's first drafts probably aren't in great shape either. If you are in a class where writers exchange papers and comment on drafts, you'll see evidence of that quickly. But how do you know when you have a rough draft that's worthy of the name, one that your teacher is going to accept as a legitimate effort?

When you can say "Yes" to the three questions below, you probably have a draft that will satisfy you, your instructor, and your classmates reasonably well.

To determine if you have a draft, ask yourself . . .

➤ **Does the draft represent a good-faith effort?** Have you made an honest effort to write something worth reading and discussing? A decent first draft, such as the one Sheila had ready for her group (see Section 4D), shows that you have invested some time and thought in your writing. If, however, you write a sloppy, superficial first draft because you're not going to be graded on it, you're not writing in good faith, and you shouldn't expect anyone else, including your instructor, to spend time responding to what you've written. You're also passing up an opportunity you may not get again—the chance to get substantial and useful criticism on your paper *before* it is graded.

➤ **Is the draft reasonably complete?** Have you stated a thesis or main idea, developed it with some supporting arguments or examples, and finished with some kind of conclusion? If so, you can legitimately claim that you have a working draft that is a starting point. An outline or a few paragraphs don't qualify as working drafts. If you want useful feedback from others, you can't give them only part of a paper. In Sheila's draft, her conclusion was fuzzy, but she had a main idea and plenty of examples, and she got good feedback from her group and the instructor.

➤ **Is the draft legible?** Can someone else read the draft without having to struggle to decipher it? Give your readers a break by typing or printing out your paper, double-spaced. Be sure your typewriter or printer has a ribbon that's dark enough to make a good copy. If you can't type or have the paper printed, write in ink on every other line. Legibility is particularly important when you're going to have the paper copied and distributed. Again, you can't expect others to try to decipher a paper that's almost unreadable, much less respond to it helpfully.

4 F

Draft

EXERCISE 4.8

Evaluate a draft you have written against the three criteria discussed above. Does your paper meet the standards? Or is it back to the drafting table?

---

4 F   WHAT DOES A DRAFT LOOK LIKE? (AN ESSAY IN PROGRESS)

Here is the first draft of a student paper for which the author, Ruth Blumenthal, could say "Yes" to all the questions in Section 4E. It's a good draft in many ways. The paper is lively and the tone is light, but it also deals with an underlying theme likely to touch many young readers: the conflicts that so often rise in what are usually called "stepfamilies," the new family units formed when divorced or widowed parents remarry. Ruth has brought in many vivid, specific details and included some comic incidents. The paper is certainly readable, with no pretentious language or tangled sentences. The conclusion is fairly good.

The draft does have weaknesses. The opening doesn't get to the main issue quickly enough, and the organization is jumbled at times. The biggest problem, however, is that Ruth hasn't focused well enough on the theme of her parents trying to bring all the children closer together through the ski trip. Neither has she developed the paper's narrative potential as well as she might nor given enough details.

Her instructor read the draft and gave Ruth the following summary comments:

"The paper needs lots of polishing, but the material you have to work with is promising. Without turning the piece into a novel, you've got to flesh out the details in many places, often with no more than a word or phrase to make your brothers, sisters, and parents more real to us. You've missed opportunities to show us the war zone and the need for some communal identification.

You could also give more serious attention to your theme: how the trip forged you into a more generous and loving family, despite the fights. Give emphasis to those incidents that show some bonding—perhaps the hitchhiking; de-emphasize those that don't—your sunburn."

Here is Ruth's first draft. As you read, see if you agree with the instructor's evaluation.

4 F

Draft

We're Taking a Trip--All of Us?

¶1   "If we're going to get along as one big family, we need to get used to doing things together. And what better way than to all go skiing in Colorado? You'll see, it'll be great and we'll all have fun."

¶2   I can still hear the excitement and anxiety in my father's voice as he informed me and my family that we were all going skiing for Spring break.

¶3   Before I go any further, let me fill you in on my not-so-average family. I have four brothers and sisters, nine stepbrothers and sisters, and I'm the youngest of all fourteen. When my father married my stepmother and we all moved in together, our friends used to compare us to the "Brady Bunch," only we fought more. Everyone had a difficult time adapting to our newly formed family and, for a while, our house resembled a war zone. Even though only ten kids lived at home, we had more than our fair share of arguments, to say the least.

¶4   So my parents got this great idea that to help everyone get along better, we should take a family trip. According to them, we would drive to Colorado, have an exciting and memorable ski vacation, and return home as the best of friends, or at least civil to one another. Well, they were right about the memorable and exciting part, but the rest I'm not so sure about.

¶5   While my stepmother Joyce raided Sears of every pair of long underwear from children's 6X to men's large, ski pants, hats, gloves, and everything else nine kids could possibly need for a week of skiing, my father went out, with the help of my oldest brother Paul (he was eighteen) to find a vehicle big enough for all of us to travel in.

¶6   After carefully checking out every auto dealer in town, Daddy and Paul pulled into the driveway honking the horn of a brand new 1979 Volkswagen bus. But this wasn't just any bus. Daddy decorated it to make it more "hip," as he put it. He carpeted not only the entire floorboard but the walls of our candy-apple red bus, too. And if the bus didn't stand out enough already, he painted flame-like designs on the sides, tinted the windows, applied a gold eagle on the front, and mounted two chrome sidepipes along the bottom.

¶7   At first we thought he was joking, but when reality set in, so did panic. We pleaded with my father to show us some mercy and not force us to be seen in such a monstrosity. We knew he tried to make the bus into what he thought a bunch of teenagers would be proud to ride in, but his attempt failed. Can he help it if he thought a 1960s decorated bus was cool?

¶8   Three days later, the bus was all packed up and we departed Pasadena, Texas, ready to handle what was supposed to be a twenty-six hour, nonstop trip to Breckenridge, Colorado. Things were running pretty smoothly, with a fight here and there, until we got to Amarillo. It was there that Margaret, one of my stepsisters, came down with the flu. From there on, things only got worse.

4 F

Draft

¶9   By the time we reached New Mexico, not only was Margaret deathly ill and my brother Kenny coming down with the flu, but the bus wasn't doing too well either and it finally broke down in what seemed to be a deserted town. So there we were, nine kids, two of whom were curled up in blankets, throwing up on the gas station floor, while we impatiently waited for the town's only mechanic to repair our bus.

¶10   He fixed the bus long enough for it to barely make it to Denver, where it broke down again. This time the problem was more serious and the bus had to stay overnight in Denver, with Daddy and Paul staying with it since they were the ones who had picked out the newly named Circus Lemon. The rest of us boarded a Greyhound bus. When we finally arrived in Breckenridge, Margaret and Kenny were getting better, while Joyce and Linda, another stepsister, were coming down with the flu.

¶11   We settled into our condominium and were ready to go rent our ski equipment. Joyce, my stepmom, was so sick she could barely move, but she refused to let us go alone. The ski shop, she said, needed fair warning that we were coming. There were so many of us that they thought we were a church group or something and gave us the group rate on our skis and lift tickets. Once they found out we were all one family, the salesclerks kept telling Joyce that they understood why she looked so sick. With our skis, boots, and poles, we were ready to hit the slopes bright and early the next morning. But were the slopes ready for us?

¶12   We were the first ones to arrive at the mountain and after Joyce set us all up in ski lessons, she went home to bed. We took a group lesson and by lunch, our ski instructor was ready to be committed. Nine kids, between the ages of seven and eighteen, would be enough to drive anyone crazy. After lunch, we were assigned three different ski instructors, a wise choice. We caught on to skiing pretty well except for Shari, another stepsister. She just couldn't seem to get the hang of it and after crashing into her third tree, the ski instructor carried her down the mountain with a broken toe. Luckily she was our only fatality. Barry and Amy, my real brother and sister, were a different story. They thought they were such hot-shots that they didn't need to ski with the rest of us. Taking off on a quest for speed and adventure, they set off a minor avalanche, which was enough for our instructors to call it a day.

¶13   When the ski slope closed and we drank all the hot chocolate we could stand, we were ready to go home. Joyce promised us she would pick us up at 4 P.M. but when 5 P.M. rolled around and she still hadn't shown up, we decided to take the matter into our own hands. Because we had missed the shuttle bus and couldn't get through to Joyce because we didn't have a phone in the condominium, our only choice was to hitchhike. We lined up in single file along the roadside and stuck our thumbs out. When that didn't work, they made me stand in front, pretend to cry, and wave money. Finally a hippy-like guy in a beat-up old Volkswagen bus, of all things, picked us up. My parents almost died when they saw us file out of the bus. They claimed that with all the excitement, they just forgot to pick us up, but how any parents could forget to pick up nine kids is beyond me. I still think that they subconsciously forgot us on purpose.

¶14   We skied for three solid days, wearing no sun or wind protection. On the fourth day, our faces were so red and blistered, everyone looked like raccoons, except for me. My windburn was the worst, and instead of a raccoon, everyone called me Bozo the Clown. My dad found the nearest emergency center and started me on special cream and medicine. Needless to say, I didn't get to ski anymore.

¶15   Well, when it was time to head home, we were all tired, sick of each other, and dreading the ride in the circus bus. On the way home, the flu managed to strike everyone else, except my dad. But at least the bus didn't break down until we reached Houston. Although it was a tough trip, my parents were right. It was memorable, exciting, and we did understand one another better than before we left. We still fought as much, but at least we understood why.

¶16   After all the trouble we went through, you'd think my parents would refuse to ever take us anywhere again, especially skiing. But in the following four years, we never missed a Spring break ski trip, traveling in our circus bus, which continued to break down every time. My parents must be insane, but wouldn't you be if you had to put up with fourteen kids?

4G   HOW DO YOU WORK ON A DRAFT COLLABORATIVELY?

PROCESS MENU
PREPARING
PLANNING
INCUBATING
DRAFTING
REVISING
EDITING AND PROOFREADING

4 G

Peer Rev

Troubleshooting

In many writing classrooms, students help each other to write by working in groups to read each other's drafts and respond to them. Often the instructor also responds to and comments on drafts and makes suggestions to students. We see at least two advantages to this method of responding to drafts. First, it gives writers the benefit of a real audience, people who actually read their writing and can ask questions and give useful feedback. Second, it allows writers to profit from other people's reactions to their writing *before* that writing is completed and submitted for a grade.

If you are working in this kind of learning situation for the first time, however, you may have trouble figuring out how to respond usefully to your fellow students' writing. To help you, we have some suggestions to offer. We've also prepared a response sheet to guide you in commenting on a colleague's paper.

We suggest that you first read your fellow students' drafts straight through for information, just as you would any other piece of writing. Then go back and reread them, using the guideline questions to formulate useful responses. It's important that you say more than "I really like your paper" or "Well, you could maybe add some examples." Specify *what* you like about it, such as a colorful turn of phrase or a memorable anecdote. Specify where you think it needs examples. It's also important to comment about large-scale concerns; don't focus on misspellings or omissions that are really proofreading problems.

When you use the response sheet, write out your answers so you can give them to the writer for his or her study. You can also use the questions as a guide for evaluating your own drafts. Both as a reader and as a writer, you will find that employing the guidelines will help you participate actively in revision conferences.

> **TIP: When you read and respond to other writers' drafts, enjoy them for what they are—someone's attempt to tell you something interesting. Don't start out by being overly critical or by assuming that you are supposed to take the place of those students' writing instructor and "grade" their drafts for them. You can help colleagues most by showing an interest in what they are writing, asking questions, giving them reinforcement, and making constructive suggestions for future drafts.**

Response Sheet for Drafts

Author of the draft _____

Title of the paper _____

Person responding _____

1. What do you like most about the paper? What particularly impressed you when you read it?

2. Do you think the writer has a good sense of his or her audience? What suggestion might you make about audience adaptation?

3. What does the writer's purpose seem to be? Where does the purpose come through clearly?

4. What suggestions can you make about focusing the topic? Should it be made narrower?

5. What questions do you have for the writer? What additional information, discussion, or examples would you like to have?

6. What two or three specific suggestions can you make that might help the writer improve the next draft?

7. What general comments do you have for the writer?

5 How Do You Revise, Edit, and Proofread?

5

A Large-scale revision
B Small-scale revision
C Editing/proofreading
D Finished essay (an essay in progress, part 2)

Terms you need to know

REVISING. Rethinking and rewriting the draft of a paper; making substantial changes to improve it.

EDITING. Correcting and polishing a late draft of a paper; cleaning it up to submit for evaluation.

PROOFREADING. Checking a finished paper closely to correct omissions, typographical errors, or any mistakes in mechanics and usage.

Troubleshooting

When your instructor asks you to revise a draft, you may be baffled about where to start and what to do first. You may also be confused about the difference between the terms *revising, editing,* and *proofreading.* What's the difference and how do you go about doing each one? The terms are not interchangeable; they describe different processes and different stages in the whole task of getting a paper from an early draft into final shape. When you understand those differences and how to manage each process, you'll find the job of improving your drafts becomes much easier.

Remember that revising and editing are different processes. When you start **revising** a draft, try not to think in terms of *fixing* or *correcting* your writing—that's really not what you are doing. Rather, you are working on a paper in progress, reviewing and rethinking what you have written and looking for ways to improve it. You may get new ideas and shift the focus of your paper, and you may decide to cut, expand, and reorganize. You're thinking about several things at once: large concerns, such as accuracy, support, and focus, as well as lesser ones, such as tone, style, and word choice. If you write slowly, you may do substantial revising as you go along; if you write quickly, you may not revise until you finish your first draft.

When you **edit** a paper, you may rewrite sentences you find awkward or wordy, delete or change words, and correct usage problems, such as sentence fragments, dangling modifiers, misleading pronoun reference, or faulty subject/verb agreement. Editing also includes correcting spelling and punctuation.

When you **proofread** a paper, you go back over it line by line, reading carefully to correct typographical errors, checking for words that may have been omitted, verifying details, and looking for inconsistencies, to eliminate pesky, embarrassing mistakes. You're getting the paper ready to appear in public.

Editing and proofreading are important steps for all writers because the appearance of a paper matters. A sloppy paper full of careless mistakes gives readers a bad impression. However, for most writers, it's a good idea to postpone editing and proofreading until the last stages. If you start correcting errors while you are composing or revising you're liable to bog down in details.

<table>
<tr><td>**5 A**</td></tr>
<tr><td>**Glob Rev**</td></tr>
</table>

5 A   WHAT DOES LARGE-SCALE REVISION INVOLVE?

PROCESS MENU
PREPARING
PLANNING
INCUBATING
DRAFTING
REVISING
EDITING AND PROOFREADING

Troubleshooting

After completing a draft, you may feel good about what you have written but know that much work remains. Or you may be in despair about the draft—that happens to everyone at times. In either case, when you start revising, don't try to work through your draft paragraph by paragraph, making changes as you go. The problems of a first draft are likely to be **large-scale** problems of focus, organization, balance, and audience and purpose—problems that you need to think about before you start fixing individual sentences. You'll waste time if you stop now to revise sentences or paragraphs that you may discard entirely in the second draft. At this point, **think big.**

Turn your attention later to **small-scale,** mainly stylistic changes. Large-scale changes include revising for focus, purpose, proportion, commitment and response, audience adaptation, organization, and sufficient information. Working with a paper copy if possible, read over your first draft from start to finish, thinking about the following suggestions.

> **TIP: Don't turn to the grammar and usage section of your handbook yet. Wait until you finish your first revision to start checking specific problems.**

To make large-scale changes that affect content . . .

➤ **Read your draft through thoughtfully,** keeping in mind the comments your instructor and fellow writers may have made about it. Ask yourself how *you* feel about the draft. What's good that you definitely want to keep? Where does it seem weak? Then consider these suggestions for large-scale changes.

➤ **Refine the focus of the paper.** A well-focused paper concentrates on one limited point or concept and develops that point; the author avoids overgeneralizing or including too much broad information.

To check for focus, ask yourself these questions.

- Do you suspect you have taken on too much and may have gotten in over your head?
- Have you generated more material than you can possibly deal with?
- Are you generalizing about your topic instead of giving details?

5 A

Glob Rev

One of the most common problems with first drafts is that writers over-extend themselves by picking a topic too broad to deal with in a short paper. They end up with a superficial paper full of generalities. If your instructor or class-mates suggest that you're doing that in your first draft, read back over it to see if you can focus in on one part of your topic and develop it. (See Chapter 3, pages 24–27, on narrowing your focus.)

➤ **Consider your purpose.** Ask yourself whether someone reading your draft would quickly understand what you're trying to accomplish. To check whether your purpose is clear to both you and your readers, ask these questions.

- If you're writing an explanatory paper, in the first paragraph or two did you state clearly what you intend to do? In an exploratory paper, were you able to express the ideas important to you?
- After reading the draft, were other readers able to summarize your main idea?
- Does the draft develop all the main points you intended to make?

Although you may not have had a strong sense of purpose when you started your first draft, now you need to decide what you want to accomplish with your paper and to be sure that your intentions are clear to readers.

➤ **Examine the proportions of your paper.** "Proportion" means the distribution and balance in the content of a paper. You should develop your ideas in proportion to their importance. Ask yourself these questions:

- Are the parts of the paper out of proportion? That is, have you gone into too much detail at the beginning and then skimped on the rest of the paper in the later parts?
- Can your readers tell what points are most important by the amount of space you've given to them?

➤ **Check that you have made good on promises made to readers.** The first part of your paper creates certain expectations in your readers. When you revise, it's important to see that you meet those expectations, so ask these questions.

- What did you promise or imply to your readers at the beginning of the paper?
- Did you finish what you started? Have you raised questions you haven't answered?

On second drafts, it's time to start tying up loose ends.

➤ **Check for audience adaptation.** Have you adjusted a paper to the needs and interests of your readers? Ask yourself,

- Have you identified your readers? What do you think they want from your paper?
- Have you considered what they already know about the topic?
- What questions would they have that you need to answer?
- What changes do you need to make in order to adapt to your audience?

Sometimes a first draft is what we call *writer-centered;* that is, the writer has concentrated mostly on getting his or her ideas down without thinking much about the audience. Such an approach can be productive, but a major goal of revising should be to change writer-centered writing to *reader-centered* writing. You do that by trying to put yourself in the place of your readers. How will *they* respond to what you have written? Working with the audience analyzer on pages 16–17 can help you make this shift.

➤ **Check the organization.** A well-organized paper has a plan and a clear direction. Readers can move from the beginning to the end of a paper without getting lost. To check for organization, ask:

- Do you move from an opening statement to development of that statement?
- Does your writing have a clear plan or pattern that will make it easy for readers to follow your thought?
- Would the paper work better if you moved some paragraphs around and changed your emphasis?

You usually need a typed or printed copy of a draft to work on organization because it's difficult to see problems in organization on a handwritten paper or on a computer screen. A typed or printed paper can be marked up and cut-and-pasted to test various schemes of organization.

➤ **Check that information in the paper is sufficient.** When you revise, you may find that you need to add information to give your paper more substance, especially if you have decided to narrow your topic and focus on only one of your points. Ask yourself these questions.

- Do you need more details to satisfy your readers' curiosity?
- Can you add specific examples and concrete information that will make your case stronger?
- Have you answered the questions *who, what, where, when, how,* and *why?*

At this point, you may need to stop and think of examples or do more research to give your paper the "weight of facts."

> **When doing large-scale revision, you should**
> - focus your thesis more sharply
> - test your thesis
> - check the distribution and balance of your ideas
> - analyze the effectiveness of your organization
> - judge whether you have fulfilled your readers' expectations
> - decide how well your essay suits its intended readers
> - fill in any gaps in information.

5 B

Local Rev

EXERCISE 5.1

Apply the criteria for large-scale revision summarized in the box above to a draft you have written.

5 B WHAT DOES SMALL-SCALE REVISION INVOLVE?

PROCESS MENU
PREPARING
PLANNING
INCUBATING
DRAFTING
REVISING
EDITING AND PROOFREADING

Troubleshooting

The large-scale changes you have made should give you a better-focused, clearer, and more interesting draft. You are ready now to make small-scale changes, revising for concrete and specific language, word choice, transitions, wordiness, and better introductions and conclusions.

TIP: Now is the time to use the handbook to check on details of style, mechanics, or usage.

To improve specific features of a draft . . .

▶ **Go over the paper after you've made the large-scale changes.** It's probably quite different, closer to what the final version will be. If you're reasonably well satisfied, now is the time to start making small-scale changes with words and sentences and to look for minor problems with usage and style. Check the draft to see if you need to make the following improvements.

▶ **Make the language more concrete and specific.** Language is *concrete* when it describes things so that they can be perceived through the senses: colors, textures, sizes, sounds, smells, actions. Language is *specific* when it names particular people, places, or things.

Early drafts of a paper often turn out to be too abstract or general because a writer developing ideas may not be thinking about the anecdotes, interesting examples, or vivid language that would enliven a paper. When you start revising, however, look for ways to add people, reinforce generalizations with specific details, and give your readers more images. For more suggestions, see Chapter 9, "What Kinds of Language Can You Use?"

➤ **Consider your choice of words.** Now is the time to tinker with your words to see if they can be improved. For instance, you might consider whether to change "world-famous" to "legendary" to make your writing less hackneyed or whether to write "poor" instead of "economically deprived" to make your language more direct. Check to see if your style is "noun-heavy." If it is, look for ways to fix it (see Chapter 17, Section D).

This is also the time to be sure you are using language accurately. Check any words you're not sure of. Other people who have read your drafts may also have questions about words that you need to resolve now.

➤ **Test your transitions.** Transitions are words and phrases that connect sentences, paragraphs, or whole passages of writing. To determine if your paper is choppy and disconnected, read it aloud. If you pause, stumble, and sense gaps, you have a problem. Let others read what you've written to see if they lose the thread anywhere. If they do, you may need to add transitions or to create a pattern that links the parts of your essay. See Chapter 8 for more suggestions on improving transitions.

➤ **Cut excess words.** Many writers produce wordy first drafts, especially when they are generating ideas. When you're writing second and third drafts, however, it's time to start looking for places you can cut. Perhaps you explain too much or you have used more examples than you need. For specific suggestions about how to trim the fat, see Chapter 10, Section D on wordiness.

➤ **Polish the introduction and conclusion.** Most of us know intuitively that the introduction of a paper is important enough to merit special attention. Nevertheless, it makes sense to postpone revising that first paragraph until after you have dealt with other major problems in a paper. After you've made your changes and know where your paper is going, it's time to rework your opening paragraph so it draws them into the paper by predicting what's to come.

Conclusions also warrant special care, but they may be even harder to write than introductions. So don't fuss too much with them until you have the main part of the paper under control. Then try to work out a strong ending that pulls the paper together and leaves your readers satisfied.

> **When doing small-scale revision, you should**
> - sharpen your language
> - check your word choice
> - test your transitions
> - cut excess words
> - polish your opening and closing.

For more specific suggestions, see Chapter 14, "How Should You Manage Opening and Closing Paragraphs?"

EXERCISE 5.2

Apply the criteria for small-scale revision in the box above to a draft you are working on. Give your essay all the attention to detail it deserves. Don't back away from more complicated revisions if they are necessary.

5 C

Edit

5 C   WHAT DO EDITING AND PROOFREADING INVOLVE?

PROCESS MENU
PREPARING
PLANNING
INCUBATING
DRAFTING
REVISING
EDITING AND PROOFREADING

Troubleshooting

When you are reasonably satisfied with the content, organization, and style of your paper, you're ready to put it in final form to make a public appearance. Just as people form their first opinion of you from your appearance, your readers are going to be strongly influenced by the surface appearance of your paper. So it's worth your while to invest time in editing and proofreading. Like checking your clothes and grooming in the mirror before an important date or appointment, editing and proofreading provide the final degree of **quality control.** The more you care about the impression a paper makes, the more important it is *not* to neglect this last step.

> **TIP: Now use your handbook again to check on punctuation, correct usage, or the conventions of edited American English.**

To edit and proofread thoroughly . . .

➤ **Check your weakest areas.**

• If you are a poor speller, pick out words that you suspect might be misspelled and look them up in a dictionary or get help in some way. If you can, get a good speller to read your paper. If you are using a word processing program that includes a spelling checker, run your text through it. However, a spelling checker won't catch many serious misspellings, such as writing "their" for "there" or "know" for "no." (See Chapter 35, "How Good Is Your Spelling?")

• If you know you're likely to write sentence fragments, review all your sentences to be sure they have both subjects and verbs.

• If you are likely to put commas where they're not needed, check all the commas to be sure they're not interrupting the flow of ideas where they shouldn't.

➤ **Check for inconsistencies.**

- If you promised you were going to discuss three points, did you do it?

- Did you mention issues in the first part of the paper that you never followed through on? (Remember a director's suggestion to playwrights: Never hang a gun on the wall of the set unless someone is going to fire it before the end of the play.)

- Is the tone of the paper consistent throughout, not light and informal in some places and stiff and formal in others?

5 C

Edit

➤ **Check capitalization and punctuation.**

- See that proper names (*E*nglish, *A*merican, and so on) and "I" are capitalized.

- Check for periods after abbreviations and titles.

- Check for both opening *and* closing quotation marks and parentheses.

- Check for comma splices—that is, joining a balanced pair of independent clauses with a comma instead of a semicolon.

- See the various chapters on punctuation in Part IV of this handbook.

➤ **Check paragraphs to see if they seem too long.** If they are, try to find a place to split them. See Chapter 13, "Making Paragraphs Work."

➤ **Check sentence structure.** See if some sentences could be joined together or rearranged to get a smoother, tighter style. See Chapters 12–18.

➤ **Check the format of your paper.** Be sure to number your pages, keep accurate and consistent margins, underline titles that need to be underlined, put other titles between quotation marks (See Chapter 34) and clip your pages together.

➤ **Proofread for typographical errors.** They count even if they aren't your fault (writers tend to blame typists, typewriters, and printers). Look especially for transposed letters, dropped endings, faulty word division, and misplaced or forgotten apostrophes.

> **When editing and proofreading, you should**
> - **double-check spelling**
> - **eliminate inconsistencies**
> - **get the punctuation right**
> - **check grammar and usage**
> - **eliminate all typographical errors**
> - **evaluate the readability of your paragraphs**
> - **make last-minute improvements in sentence structure**
> - **check the format of your paper.**

➤ **Get some help from your friends.** Exchange papers with another student or get your roommate to read your paper for mistakes and lapses. After a point, we no longer see mistakes in our own papers—a fresh eye helps.

Edit this excerpt from a draft of Colonel Ringling's history of Clear Lake College. Make changes, as needed, in spelling, punctuation, paragraphing, sentence structure, and so on.

5 C

Edit

(¶1) An annual event at Clear Lake College has been the annual snowball fight. Following the first major storm of the winter season.

(¶2) This melee regularly pits an outnumbered freshman class against the remainder of the student body. The event seems to have originated around the turn of the century. When snow sports were the main recreation of the college

(¶3) Year after year for more than a generation, timid freshman were trounced in the snow battle usually centered in the college quadrangle between the living quarters; and sent fleeing into full retreat by barrages of snowballs hurled by triumphant sophomores, juniors, and seniors who then raced into Peabody Hall, pillaging like Vandles and Huns. Freshmen and their possessions' would reign from the lower floor windows. Until the school administrators, finally stirred from an unexplainable lethargy, declared the war over.

(¶4) The tide turned, however, in 1940 when jolted upperclassmen awoke one night early in december to discover freshman in full dress, armed with snowballs, iceballs, and a few mud-balls, racing through their corridors. Snow had started falling just after midnight, and the freshmen, led by a bold commander, had taken the initiative. While ice missiles volleyed and thundered, upperclassmen struggled to some semblence of deceny, feeling, no doubt, a little like the Trojans must have fealt the night their long-triumphant city was assaulted by the Greeks.

(¶5) Sheer numbers enabled the upperclassmen to drive the freshmen into the quadrangle at last and then the tide shifted, or so it seemed—the frosh raced back to Peabody Hall, chased by a furious bands of upperclassmens. But as these elders reached the doors of the building where they had plundered unchallenged for almost forty years, they were blasted by two fire hoses careful positioned at the portals, assaulted on thier flanks by a fresh band of frosh gorillas, and charging from behind a band of frosh women with water ballons! (Women had never before taken arms in these struggles.) As the Angle-Saxons are wont to say in their poetry, the frosh soon possessed the slaughterfeild. For the first time in the history of Clear Lake College, the upperclassmen surrendered at the gates of Peabody Hall and were compelled to run a jeering gaunlet across the icy quadrangle, barefeeted.

(¶6) The commander of the freshmen assault in 1940 soon left school to serve his country in World War II and Korea. He made a career in the army, retiring only recently. He has since returned to Clear Lake College to complete his interupted education and; at age seventy, once again has plans for leading the freshman to gloious victroy.

EXERCISE 5.4

Edit and proofread a paper you are working on, using the criteria summarized in the box on page 66. If you need to cycle back to small- or even large-scale revision, do it.

5 D THE FINISHED ESSAY (AN ESSAY IN PROGRESS, PART 2)

Troubleshooting

Here is a revised version of Ruth Blumenthal's paper. She has made several large-scale changes, partly in response to her instructor's comments and partly in response to questions from students in her revision group. All of her readers suggested she reorganize her paper to get off to a livelier start. They also wanted more specific information about her family and about the skiing trip.

First, she revised to show immediately the conflict in her family and her father's hope to resolve it with a ski trip. She starts out with her father's declaration, "I'm sick and tired of living in a war zone all the time with everyone fighting." She highlights that drama by including several lines of dialogue, then satisfies her readers' curiosity by saying, "Let me fill you in on my not-so-average family." She now focuses much more on the ski trip itself.

She has strengthened the picture of the family by adding interesting specific details, such as her family installing commercial plumbing and the tension caused by siblings going to rival high schools. She dramatizes the children's disgust with the decorated van and adds details that make the individual brothers and sisters come to life. She cut some details about getting sunburned and getting the car fixed, and she has strengthened the ending.

She has also cut the last sentence from paragraph eleven—"But were the slopes ready for us?"—realizing that it was an unnecessary cliché, and deleted the exaggerated statement about buying ski clothes in paragraph five. She has combined sentences in a few places, shortened them in others, and divided up several paragraphs to make them more readable. The result is a tighter, more vivid, and more interesting paper than her original draft.

We're Taking a Trip--All of Us?

¶1 "I'm tired of living in a war zone all of the time with everyone always fighting. If we're ever going to get along as one family, we need to get used to doing things together. If after going skiing together you still can't get along, at least we'll give the appearance of a family that can go out together without killing one another."

¶2   As my father told our family of his plans for a family ski trip, he didn't get the reaction that he expected.

¶3   "We have to be in a car for how long?" complained Shari.

¶4   "There's no way I can be around Paul that long, especially if I have to sit next to him," cried Amy.

¶5   "Don't you think I'm a little old to be going on a family trip?" asked Jimi.

¶6   Before I go any further, let me fill you in on my not-so-average family. I have two brothers, Paul and Barry, two sisters, Julie and Amy, six stepsisters, Patty, Kathy, Suzie, Margaret, Shari, and Linda, and three stepbrothers, Chris, Jimi, and Kenny, and they all think that I (being the youngest of all fourteen) am around just so they can have someone to torture when they are bored. When my father married my stepmother, Joyce, and we all moved in together, our friends used to compare us to the Brady Bunch, but we fought more.

¶7   Everyone had a difficult time adapting to our newly formed family and, for a while, our house resembled a war zone, as my father called it. Getting ready for school in the morning was impossible because everyone would fight over who got to take showers first. Eventually, my parents had commercial plumbing installed, along with an additional bathroom. With ten kids living at home, six of whom were teenagers and went to rival high schools, we had more arguments in one week than most families experience in a year.

¶8   So my parents decided that to help everyone get along better, we should take a family trip. According to them, we would buy a new car and drive from Pasadena, Texas, to Breckenridge, Colorado. We would have an exciting and memorable ski vacation, get to know each other as more than just brothers and sisters, and return home as the best of friends, or at least civil to one another. Well, they proved right about the memorable and exciting part, but about the rest I'm not so sure.

¶9   My stepmother, Joyce, raided Sears, buying long underwear, ski pants, hats, gloves, and everything else eight kids could possibly need for a week of skiing. Meanwhile, Daddy went out, with the help of Paul, my eighteen-year-old brother, to find a vehicle big enough for us to travel in. After carefully checking out every auto dealer in town, Daddy and Paul made the great purchase and pulled into the

5 D

Sample

driveway honking the horn of a brand new 1975 Volkswagen bus. That's right, a candy-apple red Volkswagen bus. Daddy had carpeted not only the entire floorboard but the walls of our new vehicle. And if the bus didn't stand out enough already, he had painted flame-like designs on the sides, tinted the windows, applied a gold eagle on the front, and mounted two chrome sidepipes along the bottom. Everyone was disgusted at the sight of our Circus Lemon, as we named it, and no one could imagine the thought of having to ride in it.

5 D

Sample

¶10   At first we thought Daddy was joking, but when we realized how serious he was, everyone began to panic.

¶11   "Bern, you can't be serious," was all Margaret kept repeating.

¶12   "Daddy, there's no way I'll ever be seen in that thing, even if it's by total strangers," cried Amy. "What will my friends think?"

¶13   "It's definitely goofy looking, but at least people will know when we're coming," laughed Barry.

¶14   We pleaded with my father to show us some mercy and not force us to be seen in such a monstrosity. He put up with the complaints for a while, and then informed us that, whether we liked it or not, this was our new car, and all the complaints in the world would not make him take it back. We sadly accepted our defeat.

¶15   Three days later, we departed Pasadena eager to complete what was supposed to be a twenty-six hour, non-stop trip to Breckenridge, Colorado.

¶16   Despite a fight here and there, usually between Paul and everyone else because, being eighteen, he thought he was so old and sophisticated, the trip ran pretty smoothly until we got to Amarillo. It was there that Margaret, one of my stepsisters who's always sick, came down with the stomach flu. From there on, matters only got worse.

¶17   By the time we reached New Mexico, not only was Margaret deathly ill, but Kenny, my fourteen-year-old stepbrother, was also coming down with the flu. Meanwhile, the bus wasn't doing too well either, as it broke down in what seemed to be a deserted town. So there we were, eight kids, two of whom were curled up in blankets and throwing up on the gas station floor, while we waited for the town's only mechanic as he attempted to repair the bus.

¶18   The mechanic's repair job on the bus didn't last long. We barely made it to Denver, where it broke down again. This time the problem was more serious and the bus had to stay overnight in Denver with Daddy and Paul since they were responsible for selecting the Circus Lemon. The rest of us boarded a Greyhound for Breckenridge.

¶19   We settled into our condominium, rented a car, and went to rent our ski equipment. Joyce, my stepmother, was so sick, she could barely move, but she refused to let us go alone. The ski shop, she said, needed fair warning that we were coming. There were so many of us that they thought we were a church group and gave us the group rate on our skis and lift tickets. Once they found out we were all one family, the sales clerks told Joyce that they understood why she looked so ill. With our skis, boots, and poles, we were ready to hit the slopes bright and early the next morning.

5 D

Sample

¶20   We were the first ones to arrive at the mountain and after Joyce set us all up in ski lessons, she went home to bed. The eight of us took a group lesson, and by lunch we had already worn out our instructor. Eight kids between the ages of eight and eighteen would be enough to drive anyone crazy, so after lunch, three instructors were assigned to us.

¶21   We caught onto skiing pretty well, all except Shari, my clumsy stepsister. She couldn't get the hang of it, and after she had crashed into her third tree, the ski patrol carried her down the mountain with a broken leg. Joyce, crawling out of her death bed, picked Shari up and took her to the hospital. Luckily, she was our only casualty.

¶22   Barry and Amy, ages ten and fourteen, were convinced that they were too good to ski with the rest of us, so they decided to ski ahead. In their quest for speed and adventure, they set off a minor avalanche, which caused an entire trail to be closed. This was enough for our instructors to call it a day.

¶23   When the ski slopes had closed and we had drunk all the hot chocolate we could tolerate, we too were ready to call it a day, with only two dollars left between the eight of us. Joyce promised us she would pick us up at 4 P.M., but when 5 P.M. rolled around and she still hadn't shown up, we decided to take the matter into our own hands. Because we had missed the last shuttle bus to our condominium and couldn't call Joyce because our condominium didn't have a telephone, our only choice was to hitchhike. We lined up in single file along the roadside and stuck our thumbs out. When that didn't work, my bothers and sister made me, the youngest of the bunch, stand in front and pretend to cry while Kenny waved our only two dollars.

¶24   Finally, a hippy-like guy in a beat-up Volkswagen bus rescued us. My parents almost fell over when they saw us file out of the bus. My parents claimed that with all the excitement of Shari's broken leg and Paul and Daddy arriving, they just forgot to pick us up.

¶25   We skied for four days and by the fourth day, we were ready to head back home to Pasadena. On the way home, the flu managed to strike everyone else, except for Daddy. But at least the bus didn't break down until we reached Houston. Although the trip had been tough, my parents were right. It had been memorable, exciting, and after all of the illnesses, injuries, and crazy experiences we went through together, we felt closer and understood one another better than before we had left.

¶26   In the following four years, we never missed a Spring break ski trip, traveling in our Circus Lemon, which continued to break down every time. Nevertheless, it became a fixture in our family—we almost learned to love it. Everyone said my parents must have been insane, but wouldn't you be if you had to put up with fourteen kids?

COLLEGE WRITING

Like Part I, The Writing Guide is also about processes of composing. But in these chapters we suggest how you might respond to actual academic assignments, using various processes and strategies to produce effective, perhaps even memorable, papers. Because you need to understand what college instructors require, we open with a chapter on college writing. Then we outline six types of writing—narration, cause and effect, exploration, evaluation, proving a thesis, and persuasion—and explain how to manage each stage of the writing process effectively, from the discovery of an idea to the editing of a final draft.

6 How Do You Write College Papers?

A Special requirements for college writing
B Thinking critically
C Explanatory and exploratory writing

6A WHAT IS DIFFERENT ABOUT WRITING PAPERS IN COLLEGE?

Troubleshooting

As a college student you may not believe that the only things one can count on are death and taxes. When you're in college, you can also count on having to write papers, a prospect that may seem more daunting than either death or taxes. If you had to write only a few papers in high school or if you have been out of school for several years, it's hardly surprising if you get a little panicky when you think about writing papers—not only in freshman English, but in history or philosophy, and even in your science courses. What do you do? How do you start? What do professors expect?

Marty Green, a returning student and Navy veteran, came close to withdrawing and asking for a tuition refund during the first week of classes at the Chicago campus of Clear Lake College when he looked over the syllabi for his courses in government and in American Studies. In American studies the professor specified that 60 percent of the course grade would come from three short papers and a fifteen-page term paper; the government professor required a one-page response paper to the reading assignment every week, plus a ten-page paper at midterm and another at the end of the semester. Returning to college at the age of twenty seven after one long-forgotten year in community college and two four-year hitches in the Navy, Marty found the thought of writing those papers more frightening than the times he had stood on the dark deck of an aircraft carrier waving lighted wands and watching a fighter plane come straight toward him as he guided it in to a night landing.

After the initial panic, however, Marty decided he could figure out how professors thought and what they wanted, just as in the Navy he had figured out how petty officers thought and what they wanted. He would read directions and ask a lot of questions. He reasoned that writing papers couldn't be as hard as a lot of things he'd learned to do in the Navy. It would just be different.

And that's the key—understanding that writing in college is different from other kinds of writing because professors are readers with special requirements. Those requirements are not mysterious, however, or unduly hard to meet. Once you understand them, you should do well.

75

For writing in college you need to . . .

➤ **Remember that when you make a claim you are obligated to support it with reasons and evidence.** In our daily conversations, most of us are inclined to talk with people who think as we do, so we seldom have to make a strong case for our opinions or back up our claims with solid evidence. In those circumstances, it's easy to get by with sloppy thinking. When you're writing for professors, however, you face a different situation.

If one word could be used to describe professors and college instructors, it would be *skeptical,* especially when they read an argument. For them it's not enough that a writer asserts, on the basis of opinion or feelings, that something is true or recommends that an action be taken. Their immediate response to any claim is likely to be "Why? Show me." In the margins of papers they put comments and questions like "What's your source?"; "Who says so?"; "I'd like to see more evidence"; "Do you *know* this is true?" and "You're claiming too much here." College instructors act like this not because they're cantankerous, but because they want students to examine their ideas, think about where those ideas came from, and decide whether they're justified. They also want students to realize that, in academic writing, claims must be supported. (See Chapter 11, on proving a thesis.)

In the first draft of his first paper for Professor Collins's government course Marty proposed that the U.S. government should consider dropping criminal penalties for using or selling drugs, and then put the money and energy saved from law enforcement into rehabilitation and education programs. He was in a hurry when he wrote the draft and just put down the first reasons he could think of. He gave two reasons: he argued that first, by putting addicts in jail we expose them to a worse drug culture, and second, he suggested that if drugs were legal, they would seem less attractive and glamorous to young people. The teaching assistant who looked over his draft pointed out that his arguments were flimsy, that they were based on no more than feelings and an untested hypothesis. He warned, "I think Professor Collins is going to expect something more substantial. What evidence can you find for either of your claims?"

When pushed, Marty found he could do better. He remembered walking along streets in Amsterdam where drug addicts congregated. There, addicts can buy drugs legally from licensed distributors, although the addicts are also invited to go into rehabilitation programs. Marty decided to find out more about why the city had legalized drugs, whether the number of addicts had dropped, how well the program worked, and so on. After doing some research, he had enough evidence to write a documented and informative paper in which he concluded that his proposal was a possible solution to the drug problem but one complicated by serious drawbacks.

➤ **Remember not to take on too much in your paper.** When you're writing an academic paper, make it your golden rule not to take on too much. When you make a claim in a paper, think of yourself as having staked out a piece of territory; you've asserted what you believe, drawn lines around it, and now you have to defend it. You don't want to find out before you're through that you've taken on more than you can handle, that your boundaries are so overextended that you don't have the resources to back up the commitments you've made. You'll do better to stake out a smaller territory you know you can defend, one you can explore thoroughly. Then you'll have a chance to explore and write about your topic in detail.

In his American Studies course Marty quickly found himself in deep trouble with the first draft of a paper on the history of rock music. He was so enthusiastic about his topic that he started his paper with the exuberant statement, "Rock and roll is the crowning achievement of American popular music." Within two paragraphs he had bogged down trying to survey popular music in America for an uninformed audience. When he went to the college writing center for assistance, the tutor helped Marty see that he needed to pick a smaller topic on which he had more information. As a result, Marty backed off from his sweeping statements and wrote an informative paper about both Bon Jovi and Springsteen getting their start in the music business by performing at The Stone Pony, a New Jersey nightclub.

6 A

College

➤ **Understand what constitute evidence and good reasons in academic writing.** Since we live in a society where people are encouraged to express themselves, most of us are used to voicing our opinions freely even when we haven't thought about them carefully. Thus it's not unusual to hear a student saying, "Well, that's *my* opinion. Isn't it just as good as the next person's?" Most professors would reply, "Outside the classroom, yes. But not here, not unless you can give me good reasons." In ordinary conversations or arguments you can advance any opinion you like, but when you're writing academic papers, the professor or teaching assistant isn't going to take you seriously unless you can show you've given your opinions some thought and can back them up with evidence and good reasons.

In academic writing that evidence should be rational and factual: historical material, eyewitness accounts, expert testimony, research data, case studies, statements from authorities, and other kinds of arguments designed to appeal to readers' intelligence. A single personal incident or an example drawn from an unreliable source doesn't count. For instance, one student in Marty's writing group in freshman English argued vigorously for his claim that since there were so many planets in the solar system and life existed on one planet, Earth, then life certainly exists on other planets. Others in the group finally convinced him that, however attractive that chain of reasoning seemed, it wasn't based on any verifiable evidence and didn't count as proof.

Remember also to document your sources. If you write "It is generally believed that . . . ," your professor is likely to ask "By whom? Where?" If you cite statistics or research, a professor wants to know where you got your data. If you quote a television program or a magazine article, college instructors want the title and date. Documenting sources takes time, but it's not that difficult once you know where to find the guidelines (See Chapters 37–40), and careful documentation pays off by enhancing your credibility as a writer.

When writing papers for most academic courses, what will count as good arguments are the kind of arguments lawyers present in court: precedents, analogies, predicted consequences, speculation about cause and effect, and so on. Sometimes you can include personal experience in your reasons, but be sure it's relevant to your argument and illustrates a point. (See Chapters 10 and 11 on proving a thesis and persuasion.)

When you're writing an academic paper, remember that you can seldom prove something absolutely, irrefutably true. So don't overstate your case. Settle for a forceful, well-supported case with high probability. And remember that reasoning means just that—appealing to your readers' intellect and rational faculties. Most professors find emotional appeals out of place in college papers although they'll grant they have a place in other kinds of writing.

▶ **Understand the constraints on your writing.** When professors ask students to write papers, they often specify a certain length: four to six pages, ten pages, fifteen pages, and so on. In one sense that's helpful—you do want to know whether you're being asked to write a short paper or a long one. But in another sense, such limits are not helpful at all. You wonder how much you can do in five or six pages. How big a topic can you manage in ten pages? In twenty pages? Hard questions to answer out of context, but there is one useful rule of thumb. It's this: Make the scope of your paper proportionate to the length of your paper. Sounds simple enough, but it's not always easy to follow. As a result, some of the worst papers instructors receive are those in which the writer takes on too large a topic, tries to cover it in a short paper, and bogs down in vague generalities. On the other hand, if you're asked to write a twenty-page paper for a history course and choose a very narrow topic, you may not find enough to say on it without padding your writing.

Early in the semester Marty Green fell into the trap of trying to do too much in a short paper when, fascinated and appalled by what he read about the decline of urban schools, he decided to write an argument paper for freshman English entitled "What's Wrong with Our City Schools?" When he finished the first draft of the paper, however, he found that he had three pages of generalizations about the problems of finances, discipline, inner-city poverty, teacher flight, tax-payer indifference, and local corruption. Each of the issues was so complex he couldn't begin to develop any one of them in such a short essay. In despair he went to see his instructor who suggested he shelve his title for the time being and go read some articles about the problem. After he did, he decided to focus on some of the surprising successes in urban schools and wound up writing about one school and one person: the controversial principal Joe Clark, who used unorthodox methods to clean up a drug-ridden, inner-city school in Newark.

After that experience, Marty thought about the twenty-page term paper due in American studies at the end of the semester. He decided to talk to the professor ahead of time to sketch out a topic that would be substantial enough to warrant twenty pages but limited enough to be manageable. Knowing Marty was planning to get his degree in Radio/Film/Television, Professor Gibson suggested that he combine his interest in rock music with something about current trends in television. After talking the topic over with his friends, Marty decided to explain how rock stars like Madonna and Michael Jackson have used MTV, music video, to bring their music to a much wider audience than they would ever reach through concerts, and to explore some of the effects of that development.

A paper of that scope would require research, which Professor Gibson expected, would lend itself to an in-depth analysis of current trends on MTV, and would allow Marty to recount the short history of MTV. Twenty pages proved to be about the right length to include everything he needed. Researching the paper

6 A

College

turned out to be fun; Marty discovered some astonishing things. Professor Gibson also learned from Marty and complimented him on turning in a paper that wasn't just a rehash of material from the textbook or classroom lectures.

Remember, too, that you have constraints other than length when you're writing college papers: consider how much time you're going to have, whether the computer or typewriter you need will be available when you need it, and where you will have to go for the materials you need. Before you get too far into a topic, consider how much research you may have to do to come up with supporting data and examples and whether you can get good material. How long is the research going to take? Some books you want may not be available, particularly if you wait until the last minute. If you have to write your paper at home during spring break, what's going to happen if all your sources are on campus? Are you planning interviews for your paper? When can you do them? If you need files of recent newspapers, does your hometown library have them? Do you have to check important facts?

In other words, think ahead about possible snags in your writing process and adjust your plans to avoid a last minute crisis. College instructors take the attitude that they're teaching responsible adults, and they're not interested in or very sympathetic to excuses.

They also expect you to have your facts straight. It won't do to say that Joe Clark was a principal in the Chicago schools or that the great push for democracy in Eastern Europe started in 1991 instead of 1989. And saying you didn't have time to check your facts will just make matters worse.

➤ **Remember that college instructors expect the papers you turn in to look good, to be carefully edited and proofread, and, if possible, to be typed.** Such a caution seems obvious, but Marty was amazed at some of the grubby, barely legible papers he saw being stacked on his teachers' desks on days that papers were due. He was surprised, too, by the number he saw returned with spelling and grammar errors circled by the dozen. If nothing else, his Navy experience had convinced him that appearances always count, and he thought, "I work too hard writing my papers not to clean up the grammar, spelling, and type them neatly. Why antagonize a professor before she gets beyond the first page?"

Even if your instructors have been lenient about usage or punctuation errors when they were reading your drafts or haven't given special warnings about using standard English when they assigned papers, they do care about those details on the final product. And it's not that hard to turn in a presentable paper. If you have access to a computer, run the spelling checker. (Remember, though, that it doesn't catch words that sound alike but have different meanings; for example, "there" for "their" or "no" for "know.") If you can't use a spelling checker, get help from a friend who can spell. Proofread for faulty punctuation, agreement errors, and so on. Again, get help if you need it. If you possibly can, get the paper typed, double-spaced, and with a dark ribbon; if you have to write in longhand, make sure it's readable. Professors quickly get annoyed when they can barely read a paper. And use decent quality paper, not stuff so thin you can see through it; *never* use pages torn out of a spiral notebook with the ragged edges still attached. That makes professors apoplectic!

6 A

College

➤ **Remember that one of the major reasons you write in college is to develop your capacities for critical thinking.** More and more in colleges, professors and instructors are less interested in having you feed facts and information back to them than they are in having you acquire the habit of asking questions, checking sources, questioning authorities, looking for connections, and learning how to support your ideas. They believe that the best way for you to acquire that habit is by writing because writing stimulates thinking and helps you make connections and see things in a new light. So when you can, use college writing assignments to explore new intellectual territory and try out new ways of thinking. Like Balboa or Columbus, you could find the joy of discovering something you didn't know about before.

6 B   **HOW CAN YOU BECOME A CRITICAL THINKER?**

Terms you need to know

ASSUMPTION. A statement or belief that is taken for granted and considered so obvious that it does not need to be stated or explained; something that is self-evident. An *unwarranted* assumption is a statement that has been assumed to be true but proves not to be.

ANOMALY. An irregularity or abnormality; an event or observation that doesn't fit into an expected pattern.

Troubleshooting

Few of us go out of our way to read books and articles we don't agree with or to talk to people whose views differ sharply from our own. That's human nature—most of the time it's easier and more pleasant not to argue. The problem is, however, that people who stay in their own comfortable and isolated worlds too long lose the power to think effectively. Their minds are like boxes in which they've arranged all their ideas neatly, then closed the lids so that nothing will upset the order. When they do encounter new ideas, they can't fit them in or revise an outdated concept. They are limited and inefficient thinkers.

One of the main reasons for going to college is to break through those limits and develop the inquiring, reflective mind that marks the critical thinker. In college, your chief instrument for developing that ability is writing; it is mostly through writing that you will do the inquiring, exploring, testing, speculating, and reflecting that is the essence of a college education. And it is through critical thinking that outdated concepts and theories are discarded and new ones emerge. Much of the information you absorb in college today will be obsolete ten or twenty years from now, but if you develop the habit of thinking critically you will acquire analytical and problem-solving abilities that will serve you the rest of your life.

To develop your abilities for critical thinking . . .

➤ **Remember that learning to think critically means cultivating an attitude of inquiry rather than learning any special skills.** Critical thinking is not a difficult process practiced only by brainy and highly educated people, nor is it a set of skills or a process you can run through. Rather it is an intensified version of ordinary thinking, one directed toward asking questions and solving problems. All of us engage regularly in critical thinking so we can function successfully in our world every day. That is, we try to look at the elements in a situation and think about them carefully in order to make a decision. A person shopping for groceries is thinking critically when he or she simultaneously checks on advertised specials, thinks about what the children will and won't eat, considers the nutritional value of products, and takes into account the family budget and the time available to prepare meals. So is the person who reads *Consumer Reports,* compares prices, tests the equipment, and talks to owners before he or she buys a stereo or compact disk player.

6 B

Crit Think

For instance, Marty Green is an expert critical thinker about the process of getting from his home near Lincoln Park in Chicago to O'Hare airport to catch a plane. An experienced traveler, he does more than figure the distance from home to the airport and calculate how long it would ordinarily take for him to drive that many miles. He looks beyond the obvious to take into account weather conditions, especially in winter, alternate routes, especially if one is under construction, how long it will take him to leave his car in reduced rate parking and take a shuttle to the terminal, and whether he has to check luggage or get a boarding pass. If he's traveling on Friday afternoon when traffic is notoriously heavy, he figures on extra time. And if his father is traveling with him, for the sake of family harmony he adds an extra thirty minutes knowing that his dad will be a nervous wreck if he isn't at the departure gate at least half an hour ahead of time.

This is critical thinking, the kind all of us have to do when we have to juggle our finances, organize a household around two jobs and a child in day care, or decide whether to change jobs. It is what doctors do when they make a diagnosis and what detectives do when they solve crimes. Each situation that calls for critical thinking is a little different, but the good critical thinker asks questions, draws on experience, gathers the best evidence he or she can, considers alternatives, makes educated guesses about outcomes, and reaches conclusions. The more alert and informed any thinker is and the more he or she concentrates on solving a problem, the more solid the conclusions are likely to be. We're never absolutely sure of those conclusions—for all his figuring, Marty could still encounter some obstacle that would make him miss his plane—but we know they're the best we can do under the circumstances.

The critical thinking you have to do in college differs from this kind of daily thinking primarily because you deal with different, more abstract issues and then often have to write about your conclusions. Now, instead of analyzing all the elements you need to consider before you decide on what kind of car you want to buy, you may be writing a paper analyzing the data on which a Harvard psychologist's study of ethical development is based. Nevertheless, your thought processes are the same. To each task you bring the same kind of skeptical, "show me" attitude that prompts you to ask questions. A car manufacturer advertises the anti-lock braking system that you want, but is it available on all models? A Harvard psychologist generalizes about stages of ethical development in young people, but did he include young women among those he surveyed? In each case the answer is "No"; thus you have good reason to challenge the claims being made.

➤ **Learn to look closely at claims being made to decide if they seem reasonable on the basis of the evidence or if they seem excessive, more than the evidence warrants.** Often when you think critically you're just using your common sense to see if what someone is claiming seems sensible and agrees with your perceptions and experience. If it doesn't, you have good reason to contest the assertion although, of course, after you investigate you may concede that it's valid. But it's still a good idea to use the test of common sense.

For instance, in her speech communications course Kate Green was asked to read and evaluate an article in which the author claimed that there are definite patterns in the way young men and women talk to each other when they are courting. He quoted several such conversations to support his assertions. On her first reading, Kate was skeptical. The examples didn't sound like the way she and Marty talked in the months when they were dating before getting engaged. When she reread the article she found that the author was using as his evidence sample conversations he had taken from twelve fairly recent novels about young people in love affairs. "That's ridiculous!" she said. "What makes him so sure that those authors know how young people talk when they're falling in love? Sounds like a bunch of romantic cliches to me." She based a critical paper on that common sense reaction, pointing out that dialogues in novels *might* accurately reflect real conversations, but it might also reflect only how writers thought lovers were supposed to talk. All the author could legitimately claim was that the courtship conversations of young characters in some novels seemed to follow a pattern.

➤ **Get in the habit of asking questions about evidence and examples.** How big is the sample on which claims are being based? Who gathered the evidence? How sound is it? What possible biases should you take into account? If a writer cites authority, what are that authority's credentials? Since people who are explaining something or arguing a position usually depend heavily on evidence and examples, it's important that you train yourself to ask questions about the evidence they present. Such questions don't have to be hostile; you're just checking.

For instance, you need to know how much evidence or how many examples a writer is drawing on when he or she makes a claim. Suppose a newspaper features a story about a special city high school that provides child care and vocational counseling for teenage mothers and uses the example to demonstrate that city's commitment to deal constructively with the problem of teenage pregnancies. Kate Green would say, "That's wonderful but let's also ask some questions. How many young mothers is the program serving? Six? That won't make much of a dent. Where did the money come from? A private contribution? How long is the program funded for? Just this year? That's not much of a commitment." What Kate is doing is probing beneath the glossy surface of the newspaper story to put her finger on some realities and counteract the implication that the city is actually doing something substantial about a serious problem. That's critical thinking.

We also need to watch out for bias in our own thinking as well as that of others and to guard against the tendency all of us have to select evidence that confirms what we already believe. Kate was delighted when her economics professor Samantha Grealy suggested that one of the topics for the midterm paper could be to argue for or against the merits of the comparable worth doctrine, that is a pay scale that establishes comparable salaries for men's and women's jobs requiring about the same level of skill and responsibility. While Marty was in the Navy, Kate worked as a ward clerk at a Chicago hospital, and when she had been there only a few months found out that she was paid $300 less a month than a male orderly who had less education than she did. Thus, for Kate, the topic was a provocative one.

Kate found an abundance of articles about comparable worth, more than she could read carefully or use in her paper. So she began to skim judiciously, setting aside the ones she thought she would like to use. She ended up using ten articles and two interviews and felt good about the first draft of her paper, which started off, "Nearly everyone agrees that the doctrine of comparable worth is an idea whose time has come." When she showed the draft to Marty, he thought it was fine until he looked at her bibliography. "I really like the paper, dear," he said. "You make some good arguments. But look at your bibliography. Out of twelve references, eleven are women. Aren't there men writing on this idea too? I think Professor Grealy is going to take exception to your one-sided sample even though she may agree with your conclusion."

➤ **Learn to look for what's *not* there; develop the habit of looking for the unstated assumptions that underlie an argument.** A writer or speaker's assumptions lie at the heart of any argument because they represent what writers or speakers consider common ground or agreement between them and their audience. Thus it's important to know what that presumed common ground is and to check to see if it *is* shared. If it isn't, the argument rests on shaky premises and can be challenged.

Marty's government professor asked each student to write a paper explaining what he or she considered the two major problems for government in this country and suggesting some solutions. Marty argued that his first priority for the federal government would be to strengthen education by rebuilding inner-city schools and increasing incentives for good people to go into teaching. His second would be to combat the drug problem by increasing the number of judges, building more jails, and doubling the number of rehabilitation programs. Such noble goals require a great deal of money, of course, and Marty believed he knew where it could come from. "Our defense budget is bloated and out of control, particularly with weapons such as tanks and airplanes that cost several million dollars apiece. Because of recent international developments, most Congressional representatives would agree that we can start to cut defense spending, perhaps by a third. Then we can channel the savings to the education and drug problems," he wrote. It didn't occur to him that anyone could challenge such reasoning.

Professor Collins, however, did challenge it. She wrote, "First you assume that most legislators would agree we can cut defense spending . . . are you sure, given how many of them have big defense contractors in their districts? Then you assume that if indeed we do cut defense spending radically, Congress would automatically vote to spend it on education and drug control. You'll find a lot of people who don't share that assumption. They'll say, 'What about reducing the federal deficit, increasing the coverage of Medicare, rebuilding our crumbling bridge and highway system, and so on?' I think you need to convince your audience about your priorities rather than assume they share them."

The reverse side of trying to avoid faulty assumptions in your own writing is watching for them in other people's arguments. Notice places where you're not quite comfortable with a writer's reasoning. For example, if you read an article about what the best jobs are going to be in 1995, does the author seem to assume that the sole criterion for a good job is how much money a person makes? Many people won't agree. Does another writer laud a program like Outward Bound, which takes people on wilderness survival trips or gets them involved in activities like mountain climbing, because it teaches people to push themselves to the limits? Does that writer assume everyone will agree such a goal is a worthy one? Not all people are competitive or interested in proving themselves so the underlying assumptions wouldn't hold for them.

People's assumptions can also cause them to fall into stereotyped thinking. For example, the assumption that women are not good at math kept women from going into fields like engineering and finance for many decades. The truth, of course, is that many women are excellent math students and thousands are now doing well in engineering programs. Moreover, almost as many women as men get master's degrees in business administration. Nevertheless, Kate Green found one of her advisors still reluctant to believe she was serious about getting a degree in economics.

6 B

Crit Think

▶ **Learn to look for anomalies, those spots in an argument or explanation where inconsistencies pop up.** One of the marks of critical thinkers is that they are continually alert for those places where things don't quite fit, where a contradiction sticks out. When they find such inconsistencies, they begin to ask questions that reveal the weak spot in an argument or line of reasoning.

In a rhetoric course, Kate read an article in which an eminent rhetoric scholar asserted that the most ethical appeal a speaker can make is to establish a definition and argue from that definition; for example, Lincoln's argument that slaves are men and thus, in the United States, entitled to freedom. The scholar of rhetoric claimed that such arguments appeal to the basic nature of things. The more Kate thought about that claim, the more skeptical she became. Finally she said to her professor, "This man claims arguments from definition are morally superior to other kinds of arguments. But it seems to me that some of the most immoral arguments I can think of are arguments from definition. What about Hitler defining the Jews as inferior, evil people? That led to six million Jews dying in the Holocaust. And what about all those 'authorities' who have defined women as intellectually and morally inferior to men? Arguments from definition underlie all kinds of discrimination."

On the other hand, spotting anomalies can be creative and open pathways to new ideas. As the philosopher of science Thomas Kuhn points out in his book *The Structure of Scientific Revolutions,* major new theories in science come from scientists who notice anomalies that don't fit accepted patterns. In recent years a new way of thinking in physics and mathematics called chaos theory arose because the meteorologist Edward Lorenz noticed that the results of a mathematical equation didn't fit predictions. So it pays to look for anomalies and, when you find them, to ask "What's happening?" Often that's the beginning of critical thinking that leads to discoveries.

▶ **Learn to look critically at the language a writer or speaker is using and consider the context in which it is being employed.** Being a critical thinker doesn't mean you should always doubt what people say or write or that you can't take any statement at face value—that would be carrying skepticism to the point of paralysis. It does mean, however, that at a partially conscious level you keep running a kind of "bias check" as you read or listen. Marty Green does that almost automatically when he encounters advertising; he smiles at claims that reading a "how-to" book can make him rich and laughs at the idea that switching to a different coffee would improve his disposition at breakfast. It has taken him a while, however, to get in the habit of thinking about possible bias or misleading language in serious factual writing, news stories, and even textbooks.

Marty's professor in a history of science course drew his attention to an example that set him thinking. In the textbook for the course, the authors wrote "Professor *X* devotes 25 pages in his book to a brilliant refutation of Professor *Y*'s widely accepted theory." By using the words "brilliant refutation" the authors revealed their bias; the rest of the chapter confirmed that their own thinking parallels that of *X* so they have a vested interest in discrediting *Y*'s theories. Marty's bias detector begins to buzz when he encounters phrases such as "Mr. *A* correctly argues . . . " or "The obvious conclusion is. . . . "

Both Kate and Marty are becoming adept at checking out a source before they accept something they read at face value. Using a phrase they've picked up from murder mysteries—*cui bono,* which roughly translated means, "Who benefits?"—they regularly exchange examples of hidden bias in the language they encounter everyday. For instance, Kate showed Marty a book that bore two glowing endorsements on its back cover, one saying the book was "groundbreaking and exciting," the other calling it the "finest example I've seen of this genre." Then she turned to the acknowledgments at the front of the book and said, "I just happened to notice that the people making these endorsements are listed as major consultants for the book. Makes you wonder, doesn't it? *Cui bono?*"

Marty showed Kate a guest editorial from their hometown paper in which a local business leader was recommending moving the present overcrowded airport to a location fifteen miles north of the city in order, as he said, "to bring the city into the twenty-first century and ensure its prosperity for years to come." "Remember him?", asked Marty. "He's the head of that 21st Century Group that five years ago bought up about 2000 acres of land in the area where the airport would go. Is it the city's prosperity he's thinking about? *Cui bono?*"

➤ **Pay attention to a writer's metaphors and analogies and be aware of their underlying implications.** From a linguistics class Kate is learning to pay attention to the metaphors and analogies she encounters in her reading. Although she knows that such "figurative expressions" are an integral and important part of our language, she also now realizes the extra meanings they often carry. For instance when she read an article that says "A battle is brewing over the politics of the new educational bill," she realized that the author was using a war metaphor to dramatize and draw attention to his point. When she read *Notes of a Native Son* by the black author James Baldwin, she noticed he used the metaphor of disease to describe the anger he feels at racial prejudice, saying he suffers from "a rage in the blood," and "a blind fever." She realized the metaphor evoked both her sympathy and understanding. Her linguistics instructor also pointed out that people promoting our space program often use an analogy which compares space travel to breaking new frontiers because Americans draw good associations between advancing frontiers and our own history.

▶ **Be suspicious of simple solutions to complex problems and polarized thinking.** In his government class, Marty listened in amazement to a heated class discussion between a fervent gun control advocate who argued that we could virtually eliminate violent crime in the United States by banning all sales of guns and an ardent member of the National Rifle Association who claimed that if more citizens owned guns, there would be less violent crime. After ten minutes, Professor Collins intervened to say, "Well, as some sage once said, 'For every problem there's a simple solution, and it's almost always wrong.'" That kind of comment is typical of professors, instructors, and other critical thinkers who reject either/or, black/white thinking as simplistic and uninformed. They know that serious problems have no easy solutions. Most problems our society wrestles with are so complex that anyone who hopes to address them intelligently needs to recognize that there aren't just two points of view to consider, but several.

6 B

Crit Think

"Let's take a look at some of the complicated questions involved in this issue about violent crime and gun control," said Professor Collins. Within fifteen minutes members of the class had come up with these. 1. Although the Constitution does guarantee the right to bear arms, what does that right mean? Does that include handguns? Rapid-fire machine guns? Does it mean carrying a gun in your car? 2. How many violent crimes involve guns? How did the criminal obtain the gun? Legally or illegally? 3. Is owning a gun a right or privilege? Who decides? 4. In most European countries, it's difficult to buy any kind of gun. Do such restrictions seem to affect the violent crime rate there? 5. In the United States, is there less violent crime against people who own and keep guns? 6. What legitimate reasons are there for someone to own an automatic machine gun such as the Uzi? 7. Does a United States citizen have an inherent right to hunt? If so, with what kind of weapon? 8. Who should control guns? The federal or state governments?

When Professor Collins asked class members to name some other issues which they suspected would prove just as complex, a partial list included the regulation of traffic in Chicago, the cost of medical malpractice insurance, the effects of raising the minimum wage, and the quality of education at Clear Lake College. Any of these issues, when examined through the lens of critical thinking, raises so many complex questions that a thoughtful observer would quickly reject looking at it in black/white, either/or terms. Critical thinkers also know that any solution, however good it may seem, always has consequences, and they are willing to look at long term implications. If you raise the minimum wage, some employers will hire fewer people. If you close the center of a city to reduce traffic congestion, some businesses will suffer. If the board of regents decides to strengthen the faculty at a college, student tuition may have to rise.

In summary, to become a critical thinker is to learn to observe, reflect, ask questions, test answers, and to refuse to settle for easy explanations. It's a complex process that can, at times, lead to disconcerting conclusions. But it can also be extremely gratifying and productive. If you become adept at it, and learn to incorporate it into the writing you do for your college courses, you'll get more out of those courses. You may also improve your grades.

6C EXPLANATORY AND EXPLORATORY WRITING

In the next six chapters of the book you will read about some of the different kinds of writing that you will do in college; the chapters move from narrative to persuasive. Each of these types of writing has broad applications, with purposes that range from strictly explanatory to predominantly exploratory. (See Section 2A.) For example, a narrative could be a report of a technical process, or a personal account of a painful discovery. A cause and effect paper could analyze statistics or speculate on the effects of AIDS on show business in the next decade. What we want to suggest is that the many different types of academic writing are often closely related: a cause and effect paper could explore as well as explain; an evaluative paper could explain as well as explore. In short, you can use one or more of the methods described in the next six chapters in a wide range of writing situations. The chart below plots some of these kinds of writing along the scale of explanatory and exploratory writing discussed in Chapter 2.

6 C

Expl

Explanatory   Exploratory

Explanatory		Exploratory
Narrative		
Exploration of a process		Personal narrative
Cause and Effect		
Analytic report	Case study	Politcal analysis
Evaluation		
Product evaluation	Personnel evaluation	Movie/book reviews
Exploration		
	Diagnosis of a problem	Speculation about the future
Proving a Thesis		
Reports, historical account	Explanation of population changes	
Persuasion		
Brochure	Literary interpretation	Political protest

Explanatory   Exploratory

7 WRITING A PERSONAL NARRATIVE

Terms you need to know

NARRATIVE. A paper that tells a story or explains a sequence of events: what happened, how it happened, why it happened. Narratives typically arrange events in chronological order, but other organizations are possible.

7 A UNDERSTANDING NARRATION AND PERSONAL EXPERIENCE

It's hard to resist a good story because people are interested in people: what they do, how they react, what they think in particular situations. Any time you put a story on paper, you are writing a narrative. But the process of writing a narrative may range from a mainly explanatory exercise to a purely exploratory one. In a broad sense, a narrative can be any organized retelling of events.

> **Some narratives**
>
> | | |
> |---|---|
> | Diaries | Minutes of a meeting |
> | Personal journals | Travelogues |
> | Personal letters | Accident reports |
> | Autobiographies | Obituaries |
> | Confessions | Court testimonies |
> | Biographies | Research journals |
> | Case histories | Ethnographies |
> | News reports | Novels/short stories |

Yet even the simplest narratives require some art. Take, for example, the report you file with an insurance company after an automobile accident. Writing such a report might seem easy at first. But the need to be concise and clear, and to present events in a sensible order, can make even a nuts-and-bolts "explanation" anything but simple.

When you want to tell a more complex story—something that moves readers to laughter, tears, or deep thought—you'll likely follow an exploratory process. Such an open-ended process of writing is particularly important when you compose a personal narrative—that is, an account of something that has happened in your life.

> **Places to Find Personal Narratives**
>
> **In lifestyle sections of newspapers**
> **In biographies and autobiographies**
> **In anthologies of personal writing**
> **On religious programs: testimonials**
> **On talk shows**
> **In some political campaign speeches**
> *Cosmopolitan*
> *Esquire*
> *Paris Review*
> *Rolling Stone*
> *The Saturday Evening Post*
> *The Sewanee Review*
> *Sports Illustrated*

7 A

Pers Narr

Finding a subject for a personal narrative shouldn't be too difficult. Everyone has a story to tell, even a person who has never had the fifteen minutes of fame Andy Warhol predicted we'd all enjoy in the future. A personal narrative, however, need not be about the sensational demolition of your father's Buick or the day you set the chemistry instructor on fire; it will probably be better if it isn't. Out-of-the-ordinary events that disclose little about a writer's day-to-day life often aren't good subjects for personal narratives.

Potentially more satisfying are stories that explore relationships between people, or narratives that examine routine moments that make life both difficult and interesting: an incident that illustrates what it's like to be poor in an affluent nation, a woman in a man's profession, a solitary Asian in a suburban classroom, a high school cheerleader stereotyped as an airhead, an ambitious executive trainee given real power for the first time, a tired father desperately needing a promotion, a working mother with two kids considering an abortion, a student editor resisting pressures for censorship, a confused teenager trying to make sense out of her parents' recent divorce, a young hunter confronting his first kill.

Here are just a few of the many potential reasons for writing an exploratory personal narrative:

- to tell a story about yourself so that other people know you better;
- to learn more about yourself;
- to explain how something happened;
- to understand some past experience better;
- to tell the truth about something—what really happened;
- to tell about the people, places, and things around you—your neighborhood, friends, and family;

- to get something off your chest—something has been bothering you;
- to tell about something extraordinary that has happened to you;
- to tell a good story—something suspenseful, inspirational, or exciting.

7 B   EXAMINING A NARRATIVE PAPER

Here is an example of a personal experience paper written by a college student.

AUTHOR: Michael Jarrett Minor, Student at the University of Texas
AUDIENCE: His classmates in an English course
ASSIGNMENT: Write a narrative about an event in your life that changed you
REQUIREMENTS: Length: not specified

The Voices

(1)   Hurrying up the mountain, I fell only twice as the West Texas sky turned a light morning purple. I jogged across the floor of Downey Draw, wanting to reach the riverbed before the sun cleared the peaks of the Sierra Orientals. I moved quickly to keep warm, pushing through the brush and cactus. Everywhere the sotol and Spanish dagger assaulted my thighs, their points just missing me. I reached the river unscathed and just a little winded as the sky turned a lonely bluish yellow.

(2)   I was cautious, lurking slowly along canyon walls lined by hundreds of caves. My feet were unsteady on rocks which, ten thousand years ago, rolled along the bottom of a deep and furious river. Today they resembled big marbles, discarded and sunbleached white. While negotiating the canyon edge, I scanned the floodplain on the other side. I'd seen many a deer come trotting out of those trees and I wasn't about to miss anything. But today--nothing for two hours except an occasional rabbit. Preoccupied by my searching, I did not sense the change in weather. It was going to snow.

(3)   I looked up and noticed the clouds, heavy with ice. "Dang it," I said, as I watched my shadow disappear completely. Perfect for a blizzard. The first thing a deer does in inclement weather is bed down, and the only way to find one then is to step on him--and that is a dangerous proposition. I decided to hole up in one of the caves as the first flurry melted on my cheek.

(4)   I chose a low cave since it was easier to get to, and hauled myself and then my rifle inside. The cave was just big enough for me to sit up straight and it went

back about fifteen feet. I sat in it with my legs crossed Indian style, my rifle resting across my middle.

(5)   The walls and the ceiling were black with soot, the residue of ancient fires, but as I looked to the very back wall I saw that it looked uncharacteristically clean. I slid backwards to have a look. There was something on the wall, on the exterior, a painting. God knows how long it had been there. The elements had taken their toll, but enough remained to make out a man tossing a spear at the sun. Beneath the sun was an animal, a bison perhaps, and it had reddish markings on its side which I took for blood.

(6)   This was a portent, I considered. This was my sign. In my mind I reenacted the scene of the hunt and thought of the men who brought down beasts with flint-tipped spears.

7 B

Pers Narr

(7)   From the riverbed below I suddenly heard the sound of rock on rock. I turned to see one of the biggest bucks in Texas moving near the entrance of my cave. I silently moved to raise my rifle. The snow was falling hard now, the wind picking up , but I didn't care--I had the fever. My hands shook so bad I could barely get the animal in my sights. He was about a hundred yards away, a cake of a shot.

(8)   I kept losing him. I cursed myself under my breath. One moment in, the next out. "Hold him," I whispered to no one. "Steady son, steady."

(9)   I thought of the painting, I thought of the kill, the spear and the sun, the bloody bison. Those long-dead hunters would laugh if they could see me, I knew. And I believed they could. I could almost hear their scoffs at my quivering. No, I would not embarrass them today, three days into my seventeenth year. I would enter their clan with my kill, my initiation.

(10)   The buck remained in my sights. I pulled the trigger. The rifle cracked with thunder, and I was almost deaf as the murderous echoes bounced off the walls of the cave. For a solid minute I was disoriented. When I could finally see, my heart sank like a sack of boulders. Nothing. There was no deer anywhere. Could I have missed. How? It had been perfect. I had never been so sure of a shot in my life.

(11)   Immediately the voices returned. "Some hunter you are," they mocked. "You are not a man, you are still a boy. Go play beside your mother."

(12)   I ran over the unsteady rocks to where the deer should have been. Hope was alive. There on the ground ahead of me I saw the blood and hair lying together, new, and still visible from the snow that piled up fast over it.

(13) Now I praised the storm; it is easy to track over the white of snow. I began to follow the drops, hurriedly, before the blizzard covered all traces.

(14) Quickly, quickly--I pushed myself hard over the rocks. I fell, crushing my knees but saving my rifle. The snow came faster and harder with every step; the wind bit into my face like blue steel. I imagined the voices urging me on, "Find him and you are one of us." I was sweating. I removed my coat and laid it on a tree branch. I would come back for it later, or freeze to death. Just penalty if I failed in my quest. I knew the voices would agree.

(15) I crossed the riverbed in a blind fury--blind to everything but the drops of blood, which diminished with each treacherous step. I slipped again, and I could feel the broken skin and my own blood run warm and quick beneath my trousers. I arose, continued the search. I could no longer feel my nose, or was it my fingers that were numb?

(16) Still the voices urged me on. "A hunter who could not track is no hunter," they said. "He but wastes what God gives him."

(17) My whole body was exhausted, and I stumbled once more. This time I couldn't get up.

(18) "I must not waste!" I mumbled, "I will not waste." I sat there exhausted on the ground with the snow blowing straight at me. I stopped sweating and imme-diately felt a freezing chill. The voices were gone now. They had deserted me. I was still only a boy. I wanted my mother.

(19) I looked around through tear-filled eyes. I looked at nothing. Then sud-denly, unbelievably, I saw a dark shape lying on the ground thirty yards ahead. It moved slightly. I jumped to my feet and ran as fast as I could toward it.

(20) My soul filled with triumph when I finally stood over my buck, yet my glee was short-lived. For as the gallant beast looked up at me, I noticed his split abdo-men and the entrails spilling out their testimony to my marksmanship. A deep shame filled my breast.

(21) I stared into his eyes of green nickel and he blinked twice. They begged me to finish the job. I saw that his face was very old, very grey, and the ice of his breath hung to his whiskers like beads. I wished him peace.

(22) "Forgive me," I said, and pulled the trigger.

➤ Analysis of Michael Minor's "The Voices"

Purpose: Would you characterize "The Voices" as mainly explanatory or mainly exploratory? Which parts of the story lead away from straightforward explanation? Where have you read similar pieces? Where might a narrative of this kind be published?

Audience. Does the story seem better suited to some specific audiences than to others—to men more than women, Westerners more than North Easterners? What assumptions does the writer make about his audience's knowledge? Does Minor convince you that he has the knowledge and ability to write this story? How, or why not?

Characters. How much does Mike Minor reveal about himself in the narrative? What details about him can you locate? What does he leave out? How do you interpret the voices in the narrative? Where do they come from and what do they do? Is it significant that we don't hear them at the end of the story?

Setting. How does setting play a role in this narrative? What details of the descriptions in the story strike you as most memorable?

Language. In general, how would you describe the language of the story— is it formal, informal, elaborate, bare? Do any of the lines strike you as particularly unusual, memorable, or appropriate? Would you recommend changing any particular lines? How does Minor make use of dialogue?

Reader's Response. Did you enjoy reading "The Voices"? As precisely as you can, explain why or why not. Does the narrative connect with anything in your own experience? Does "The Voices" remind you of other stories? What assumptions does the writer make about hunting and the rites of initiation or manhood? Does Minor make other assumptions you might not share? What does the story reveal about the writer's world and culture?

7 C CHOOSING A TOPIC FOR A NARRATIVE PAPER

> **The Basic Assignment**
>
> Write a personal narrative about an event in your life that reveals something about who you are—a story that someone who knows you well would read and say, "Yes, if you want to understand my friend _____, just read this." The narrative can be serious, comic, bittersweet, but it should give us a glimpse into your world. Plan on following an open-ended, exploratory process of writing.

▶ **Variations**

a. Write about an event that has changed the way you think or behave. Maybe you got cut from a sports team or had to move away from a city you liked. Let the process of telling the story illuminate what you learned from the event and how the circumstances changed you.

b. Write about an event or moment that you look at much differently now than you did when it actually occurred. Let your retelling of the incident explain why your perspective on it has shifted. The incident may have been as simple as not making the dean's list or as painful as a forced separation from a parent.

c. Write about something happening to someone else that also affected you. (The person could be a friend or member of your family.) Be sure you know enough about the story to do a good job revealing and illuminating what happened.

d. Write about a change in someone's life that you caused. Narrate the impact of some decision or action for which you were responsible.

e. Write a travel narrative. Describe what happened to you on a trip recent enough to evoke strong memories of people, places, cultural differences, and particular incidents. Don't explain what happened every single day; both you and your readers would be bored. Instead, focus on one or two major events: what is really worth remembering about the local culture and people, or about your encounters with them. One thing—you don't have to travel to an exotic location to tell a good travel story. A day trip to a local farm co-op, factory, or artist's studio can be as good a topic as an excursion to Paris on the *Concorde*. Read some travel narratives as a warm-up.

f. If you have a job, write about something odd that has happened while you were working there. Or focus on routine events, giving readers insights into characters who work with you and how they interact.

g. Form a writing group with three-to-five students to produce a collection of personal narratives on some common theme. If possible, try to form groups united by some shared trait: age, ethnic background, shared sports experiences, single-parent families. Or deliberately seek diversity—in racial and ethnic background—to provide a variety of perspectives. Then write personal narratives on a common theme everyone agrees upon: rites of passage, religious training, death in the family, economic worries, encounters with prejudice, the big game, dealing with older/younger siblings, adventures in baby-sitting, choir practice, the first date. Edit the collection as a group, adding a paragraph or two of introduction.

7 D

Pers Narr

7 D   PREPARING AND PLANNING A NARRATIVE PAPER

Given a choice of a writing course assignment, most college students, we believe, would compose a personal narrative. The paper seems easy to organize and the content is a given—no research required. Begin at the beginning, explain what happened, and let the story speak for itself. That's really all there is to effective narration, right?

In some cases, yes. Writers who struggle with explanatory reports and arguments can sometimes weave gripping narratives without blotting a line. We all have so much experience with narratives—from our run-ins with novels, short stories, TV programs, and films—that we acquire an expert's sense for how a story can be told. Whether we know it or not, we're competent critics of the narrative form.

But while some stories seem to write themselves, most require a passel of midwives. Narratives get into trouble when a subject isn't made compelling for a reader, when incidents and characters aren't developed, when the plot plods for lack of shape or focus, or when there's a shortage of details or a plague of generalities. Fortunately, these problems are easy to diagnose and even have a tendency to correct each other. Clarify the motives of a character, and dialogue becomes easier to write; give surer structure to an endless, wandering story line, and important details also seem to snap into focus.

To write an effective personal narrative . . .

7 D

Pers Narr

➤ **List possible subjects.** You want to choose an intriguing subject. So begin with a list of all possible candidates, and don't be too demanding at this point. Allow yourself room to explore. A trivial incident, a remembered word or gesture, a cherished tune or aroma can provide starting points. Don't dismiss an incident that seems to lack a story complete with beginning, middle, and end. Just put down whatever comes to mind, as in the following list.

Winning the lottery—almost.
Losing my six-year-old sister in the subway.
Seeing crack pushers in our block.
Watching Aunt Agnes die of cancer.
Finding a bullet on the sidewalk.
Meeting our Korean neighbors for the first time.
Being falsely accused of shoplifting.
Remembering incense and church bells.
Getting arrested at a protest rally.
Losing the class election.
Feeling like an outsider for the first time.

It might be easier to come up with a list if you think about rituals, holidays, or occasions: graduations, spring breaks, family reunions, Monday mornings on the job.

Two other useful ways to find and explore a subject are freewriting (see page 22) and looping. Put "What of importance has happened to me?" at the top of a blank sheet of paper. Then write on that subject nonstop for five or ten minutes. Don't let your pen stop for the entire time. If this initial freewriting has produced a topic idea, you are set. If not, read over your first selection and look for an intriguing sentence or phrase in it—one that might be a spark for another freewriting attempt. Put that sentence or phrase at the top of another blank sheet and freewrite a second time. This is the looping phase, a combination of focusing and freewriting. You may want to loop a topic idea several times until you find one that interests you enough to proceed.

When choosing a subject, follow your better instincts. Many writers will abandon a subject they suspect contains a strong idea for another story that seems technically easier to execute—writing a complex exploration of race relations, for example, would be more work than a step-by-step account of your latest skiing accident. But which narrative will give you more worthwhile material to develop? An accident is an accident. When it is over, it's done. Look for subjects that reverberate, that have significance for readers who don't know you personally.

Also look for subjects which leave you a bit uneasy in the telling. If you are narrating a tale that has no loose ends for you—all the personal conflicts are resolved, none of the implications are troubling—then you aren't likely to discover much in telling the story. The paper might show technical competence, but readers may find it trivial or predictable. This is often the problem with personal narratives about subjects such as car wrecks, practical jokes, or even serious matters like deaths in the family. The writer has either no conflicts to resolve ("Gosh, was Joe surprised when his bed exploded!") or has dealt with them in understandable, but conventional ways ("I will always miss my grandfather and treasure the love he gave me.") You are more likely to create a powerful narrative if you tell a story that explores deep and unexpected rifts in family or personal relationships or in the workings of society. We don't mean to suggest that good narrative topics must be dour or painful, but that a mature writer might use a personal narrative to explore issues of substance. It often helps to discuss subject possibilities with your friends or classmates; hearing their ideas may foster some of your own.

When you have decided on a possible story, try listing or brainstorming again, this time homing in on key moments or incidents. If your original idea already had the shape of a story, you might list the major incidents—what you expect to cover.

> Riding in a pickup with my father, heading for West Texas.
> Drifting off to sleep.
> Remembering an earlier trip.
> Hunting in the cold of the morning, alone.
> Starts to snow.
> Enter a cave; see drawing of ancient hunters.
> Spot a buck; take a shot.
> Track the injured buck through freezing snow.
> Give up, then see the injured animal.
> Shoot the buck.
> Awaken in the truck traveling west.

At this stage, everything about a narrative remains tentative. Notice that this outline sketch of what would become "The Voices" does not even mention the thematic center of the story: the imagined words of the ancient hunters. But it does include a framing story (traveling with his father in the truck) that eventually will be dropped.

If the original idea is just a flickering memory—incense and church bells, for example—you might freewrite on the subject to locate a narrative center, an incident triggered by the memory.

> The sweet, exotic smell of incense. I remember it from the days when I
> was an altar boy. Used only on solemn occasions, especially funerals. At
> the end of a funeral, the priest would use a tiny golden spoon to sprinkle

beads of incense onto a glowing charcoal. The rich odor would fill the air as he swung the vessel containing the incense and, at the same time, the church bells would start to toll. We knew to expect tears from the congregation then. I remember especially one occasion when we buried an elderly woman to whom I had just spoken days before. . . .

➤ **Decide what you want to emphasize.** The most important part of organizing a narrative may be deciding what to leave out. You can't explain every aspect of a story from beginning to end, and you're under no obligation to provide such details. You would only bore your reader and send wrong signals about what is important. The comic narrator of *Tristram Shandy,* an eighteenth century novel by Laurence Sterne (1713–68), promises to give a complete account of his entire life, but realizes—after spending a year writing three and a half volumes—that he has managed only to describe the day of his birth. His life is advancing faster than his ability to write: "as at this rate I should just live 364 times faster than I should write—It should follow . . . that the more I write, the more I shall have to write." Sterne's comic point is that no novel (or narrative) can pretend to be a thorough or logical account of a person's life—and thank goodness! Spend the greatest portion of your narrative describing those moments that mean the most to you and to your readers.

7 D

Pers Narr

Michael Minor, for example, begins his narrative with himself already stalking deer in the West Texas Highlands. He doesn't bore us by describing how he got in the wilderness or what he brought with him, nor does he clutter the ending of the story by assuring us that he got home safely. The story is about his tracking of the buck and that's what he concentrates on.

It may help you to visualize the structure of a narrative as several major incidents linked by transitions, with the key incident near the end, the climax.

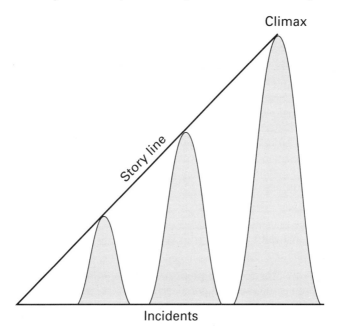

Narratives typically grow toward this instance of discovery or revelation the same way a movie builds to a high point near its conclusion. This major incident need not be a gaudy or action-packed moment—the equivalent of the tire-smoking car chase in the weak Hollywood script. It can be as simple as a word or gesture, if the writer has prepared for the event carefully. In Michael Minor's narrative, for instance, the climax of the story is less the shooting of the buck than the narrator's emotional reaction to his initiation into the brotherhood of hunters.

> (20) My soul filled with triumph when I finally stood over my buck, yet my glee was short-lived. For as the gallant beast looked up at me, I noticed his split abdomen and the entrails spilling out their testimony to my marksmanship. **A deep shame filled my breast.**
>
> (21) I stared into his eyes of green nickel and he blinked twice. They begged me to finish the job. I saw that his face was very old, very grey, and the ice of his breath hung to his whiskers like beads. **I wished him peace.**
>
> (22) **"Forgive me,"** I said, and pulled the trigger.

7 D

Pers Narr

It may help you organize the paper if you consider that all descriptions and incidents in the story should contribute to the main action. If, early in the narrative, you describe some feature of an airplane—let us say, an escape hatch—that hatch should play a key role later in the story. If a character's selfishness is the chief motive for an ugly incident, that self-centeredness ought to be revealed in little ways throughout the narrative, in petty actions or through bits of dialogue. If a character's appearance or reputation is a key element, be sure to plant those features in a reader's mind well before the conclusion. An effective narrative does not require a surprise ending or a twist; a more subtle organization is one in which the writer shows how a major action follows inevitably from a pattern of smaller incidents.

So in drafting a narrative, looking for the centers of action. They are often the moments you most enjoy writing about. (The rest of the story can sometimes seem like dull mortar necessary to set these bricks into place.) It may help you to work backward, to write the key moment and then to determine what is the minimum of narration that needs to precede it. Don't feel limited to one key event however. You may have a series of incidents to narrate, a sequence of actions that build toward a conclusion. That's fine. Just be sure that each incident is in the story for a purpose.

➤ **Consider your readers.** Narratives require shrewd assessments of audience. A good narrative, naturally, is written in language readers can understand, and at a pace that keeps them interested.

But there are other considerations—very straightforward ones—that a good many writers find troublesome. A good narrative, like a sound piece of journalism, has to answer those familiar questions: *who, what, where, when, how,* and *why.* But it can't provide them quite so directly or it ends up sounding, well, like a news article. It's important then in revising a narrative to determine whether you've supplied all the information critical to understanding a story, and even some that may not be, but readers expect to have anyway. Here's a checklist of factual details writers often fail to cover.

_____ Date of incident—how long ago?

_____ Location—especially name of town or school

_____ Name of characters—at least a first name

_____ Age of characters—told or clearly implied

_____ Relationship of characters, especially among relatives

Remember that you don't have to provide all these facts up front. Not until the ninth paragraph of "The Voices" does Mike Minor tell us how old he as when the incident in his narrative occurred. The mention of age is withheld until Minor raises the crucial theme of manhood initiation.

7 D

Pers Narr

(9)   I thought of the painting, I thought of the kill, the spear and the sun, the bloody bison. Those long-dead hunters would laugh if they could see me, I knew. And I believed they could. I could almost hear their scoffs at my quivering. No, I would not embarrass them today, **three days into my seventeenth year.** I would enter their clan with my kill, my initiation.

In similar fashion, you will need to supply other information as needed, depending upon the sophistication of your audience. Minor's essay provides two examples relating to the fall of snow. He doesn't assume that his audiences share the same hunting experiences he has, so, without making a big deal of it, he feeds readers the bits of lore they need.

(3)   I looked up and noticed the clouds, heavy with ice. "Dang it," I said, as I watched my shadow disappear completely. Perfect for a blizzard. **The first thing a deer does in inclement weather is bed down and the only way to find one then is to step on him** — and that is a dangerous proposition. I decided to hole up in one of the caves as the first flurry melted on my cheek.

(13)   Now I praised the storm; **it is easy to track over the white of snow.** I began to follow the drops, hurriedly, before the blizzard covered all traces.

Figuring out how much your reader needs to know isn't always easy, but it is one of the issues you wrestle with in tailoring a narrative for an audience.

➤ **Sweat the details.** Narratives often succeed or fail in the details. In general, you should be as specific as you can with people, places, things without being tedious; descend as low on the ladder of abstraction as you can sensibly go (see

Section 13A). Details should relate directly to the story, not stand as embellishments. In "The Voices," for example, Michael Minor gains authority in his second paragraph simply by using proper names where he might have used generic expressions:

{**Dull generic version**}   I jogged across the floor of **a draw,** wanting to

reach the riverbed before the sun cleared the peaks of the **moun-**

tains. I moved quickly to keep warm, pushing through the brush

and cactus. Everywhere **bushes and plants** assaulted my thighs,

their points just missing me.

{**Actual version**}   I jogged across the floor of **Downey Draw,** wanting to

reach the riverbed before the sun cleared the peaks of the **Sierra**

Orientals. I move quickly to keep warm, pushing through the

brush and cactus. Everywhere **the sotol and Spanish dagger** as-

saulted my thighs, their points just missing me.

Your use of details need not be splashy and attention-grabbing. Go for the subtle feature that builds a picture.

Why be abstract . . .	*When you could provide details?*
A big truck headed toward me.	An eighteen-wheeler rumbled toward me.
Tripping over her own tennis shoes . . .	Tripping over her own Reeboks . . .
. . . after finishing her cereal.	after finishing her Wheaties.
We entered the house,	We entered the upscale duplex,
Munching something, Kitty	Munching pork rinds, Kitty
Wearing a cap, Al	An Orioles cap shading his baldspot, Al
She brought us dinner.	She brought us ravioli and spumoni.
. . . to the sound of pleasant music.	to a quartet playing Mozart.

A good place to find memorable details is in your cultural experiences. We all bring divergent racial and ethnic mixes to a story, different upbringings, hometowns, religions, allegiances, alliances, and family histories. Let those elements contribute color to a story at the same time they prove that you know what you're talking about.

▶ **Give some life to the people in your narrative.** To readers, the character you describe in a narrative as "my best friend" or "a great person" or "my funny Aunt Rita" is only a shadow. Until you provide flesh-and-blood contours for the people in your story—perhaps through a thumbnail sketch, a habit of dress, or a sample of dialogue—readers won't understand who they are and why they act as they do. People propel the action in a narrative, so even minor characters deserve a writer's attention.

Don't, however, go overboard with the adjectives. The action of a narrative shouldn't come to a screeching halt while you provide a head-to-toe description three paragraphs long of your eccentric aunt. Instead, look for one or two characteristics that would enable a reader to recognize the character were he or she to walk into a crowded room—it can be a detail of dress, a physical swagger, a habit of speech.

> With eyes that turned instinctively away from people, Edna kept to herself mostly and spoke—when she had to—in a tinny, apologetic voice.

> He seemed bigger than he was, bounding down the court, his thick hair about as orange as the basketball.

Drop descriptive phrases into your narrative strategically, where they will make a difference in understanding who or what a person is like.

> Renee joined us at the table, **an austere pre-law student with fierce green eyes and a backpack stuffed with notebooks.**

7 D

Pers Narr

Give a longer description when a character warrants such attention—when, for example, knowing about a person's upbringing or family background reveals the motives for certain behaviors or when the description itself provides a kind of action and activity.

> Mr. Brumley was about what we expected from a football coach teaching history, big enough to scare us into silence, but brainless as a rocking chair. He could relate any event in American's two centuries to an athletic event—usually one from the past weekend. When a student got on his nerves, he would grab his pinky finger, fold it forward, and squeeze until the hand and arm went numb. I was so worried about my fingers I couldn't concentrate on history.

But remember that strictly functional descriptions, simple and direct, are often sufficient to give shape to a minor character.

> Bryan's father came in, **a fleshy man in his late thirties, always out of breath.**

> My boss, **robust and brisk,** ordered me to her office.

Look for opportunities to insert quick, luminous details that brighten sentences with an unexpected, but authentic insight.

> James, our pilot, was something of a chowderhead. I felt queasy knowing that my life was in his hands. **The tobacco stuffed in his lower lip** made him look droopy and vaguely deranged.

Describing characters well may force you to observe them yourself for the first time as others might see them. Who are these people? Why is Jim your best friend, and what is it exactly about Tarshia's dress and posture that makes her seem smart and self-confident? Don't be satisfied with the first word that comes to mind: remember that the more general your description is, the less likely a reader is to get anything out of it.

Why be general . . .	*When you could be specific?*
Acting irritated, the nurse . . .	With a Doberman growl, the nurse . . .
Gary's black hair	Gary's hair, black as cinders
a kind man, especially to kids.	our neighborhood's Saint Nick.
Bright eyes	Eyes like neon marbles

➤ **Give your characters a voice: use dialogue.** Dialogue adds vigor and authenticity to a narrative when it reveals character and moves the action along. There's no point in using dialogue to report basic facts or mention locations. Such attempts can sound like lines from a bad movie.

> "Well, here we are at the Grand Canyon at last," said Mike as we piled out of the van.

> "It took us nearly three days to get here and, gee, I'm tired," Stephanie replied. "That Victorian structure near the rim must be our hotel."

No one talks like that.

Think of dialogue as an element of characterization. Like a well-chosen incident or a description of a location, dialogue should seem purposeful. But that doesn't mean you can't use a lot of dialogue when the give-and-take between characters tells the story.

> "Give me the crescent wrench," I said to Stuart, slipping under his Escort to loosen the drain plug.

> "The what?"

> "The crescent wrench." He handed me a screwdriver.

> "Stuart," I said, crawling from under the car "have you ever changed your oil before?"

> He grinned sheepishly, knowing I wouldn't laugh, "I didn't even know I had oil."

The standard form for dialogue is to begin a new paragraph with each new speaker, but this convention is sometimes ignored. A writer might alternate quickly between speakers within a single paragraph to convey a sense of energy or activity. Or the speakers may not be defined clearly enough to warrant separate paragraphs.

> The section nearest first base exploded. "You're blind!" a raw-boned woman screamed from the first row, shaking a thin fist. "Send him back to Minnesota," a Detroit patron hollered. The umpire rocked on his heels serenely, knowing his call had been fair.

One caution about dialogue: don't be too ingenious in describing how characters speak their words. The term *said* can be repeated often without drawing too much attention to itself. An occasional variation makes sense, particularly when it accurately describes some feeling or emotion: Ellen *bellowed;* Celia *interrupted,* Jason *objected.* But don't feel obligated to find a new verb for each change in speaker, particularly in a long passage of dialogue. The variations can begin to seem contrived, even comic: Jack *articulated;* Ellen *retorted;* Sam *enthused;* Irene *expostulated.*

➤ **Pay attention to setting.** *Where* an action happens may determine not only the flavor of a narrative, but also aspects of characterization and style. Unfortunately, many writers don't appreciate how interesting their native environments are. If they were to write about a trip to Paris, Hawaii, or the Sahara, they would report intriguing details about landscapes, buildings, climate. But they ignore all those features in narrating an action in their own neighborhood, not realizing that, to some potential readers, Dime Box, Texas, Albany, New York, or Ashtabula, Ohio, might be as exotic as Delhi.

Remember, though, that descriptions in a narrative must serve a purpose. One important purpose is to create atmosphere. It may make a major difference that a street brawl takes place on a hot afternoon in July on an inner city street; you have a different story entirely if a gang fight breaks loose in an air-conditioned suburban health club. Consider the role the cold weather and snow plays in Michael Minor's "The Voices," or what the driving rainstorm contributes to the beginning of the following narrative.

> I couldn't see the road ahead, only a rain-glazed stripe I hoped was the center line. The van was steering like a bumper car, loose and slippery. Front tires must be hydroplaning, I figured.
>
> Lightning flashed and thunder exploded—near and hard—then crashed again, rattling the trim around the instruments. Double wipers labored across the windshield as raindrops—thick as oil—splattered, swirled, and hung on the glass momentarily before peeling off in sheets. Four o'clock in the afternoon, and dark as night.
>
> I was driving into a tornado.

7 E

Pers Narr

7 E   DRAFTING AND REVISING A NARRATIVE PAPER

When you have developed some feel for your personal narrative, start drafting it. If you find that the story tells itself, from beginning to end, let it—including in your draft as many incidents and as much detail as possible. You can always cut later. If the paper is slower in developing, vent any feelings that want to get out. You'll often have a keen sense of how the climax should build or what the dramatic confrontation in the story should include. Fine. Write that part, then gradually backfill. But get something on paper which you can then begin reworking and revising.

The following advice applies to a paper you write yourself or to a narrative you are asked to edit for a colleague.

In reviewing the draft of a personal narrative . . .

➤ **Assess the subject.** You may have to rely on gut instinct here, but ask whether it seems worth the effort. Is the story worth telling? If it isn't, be honest enough to consider another subject, or another aspect of the original narrative. It also may be the case that you aren't quite ready to tell a particular story yet; you may need to put several years between you and the events before you have the perspective to frame the narrative memorably.

Sometimes the initial version of a personal narrative reveals that a writer is really interested in a minor character or a relationship only implied in the draft. No problem; the first version has proved to be a "discovery draft," a valuable form of invention. Use a second draft to develop the theme or idea revealed by the first draft.

➤ **Assess the organization.** Does your narrative flow? Is its story line confusing? Does the tale start too slowly? Does it bog down? If so, mark those places in your draft where the action seems unclear or off the subject. Imagine yourself as a reader of the draft and pencil in the margins any questions that come to mind—issues that need to be explained or resolved for the narrative to make sense.

Respond to your feelings honestly. If a portion of a story gives essential information, but seems dull, admit it; mark that portion of the draft and consider ways that the necessary information might be given without halting the movement of the action. Put the information in a phrase, perhaps, or convey it through action or dialogue.

➤ **Check the opening.** Would you read the entire narrative if you weren't compelled to? Does the opening paragraph draw you into the story? Or does it just lay out background information without a hint of what's to come?

7 E

Pers Narr

If the opening is dull or confusing, look for another way to begin the narrative. Might a paragraph later in the narrative provide a more vigorous opening? Remember that a story can begin in the middle of things—background information can be reported in flashback. Use the technique to get a story moving.

➤ **Consider the ending.** The tone of the conclusion is critical: does a reader leave the narrative in the proper frame of mind? In most cases, less is better than more. Don't draw out all the conclusions or implications for a reader; let them do some thinking.

Many writers of narratives feel the obligation to conclude a piece by stating a moral or explaining what they learned from the incident. If the incident is told well, the moral and ethical lessons should be clearly implied. At all costs avoid sentences in the conclusion that begin "From this incident, I learned that . . ." or "The moral of this story is. . ." The problem is not with the lessons learned themselves, but with hammering the reader over the head with them.

➤ **Provide all the needed background information.** Look for any gaps in the story, particularly in time sequences. A careful reader should be able to reconstruct any progression of events where the passing of time is crucial. Don't begin an event in the morning, account for the passage of an hour or two, and conclude it in the dark of night. Readers will notice such gaffs.

Be sure to explain *who* the major characters are and *why* they do what they do. Mention their names too, especially if they are relatives. "My older sister" wears thin pretty fast.

➤ **Mark missed opportunities for details.** Look for all those places in a narrative where a more particular term might be unobtrusively substituted for an abstract or generic term. Don't clutter the text with meaningless detail, but give it texture and color with place names, product names, and proper nouns.

➤ **Mark missed opportunities for description and characterization.** Remember that even a small detail, collapsed into a single phrase, can bring a character to life. Use such constructions to add a bit of color to even minor characters in the narrative:

> Artie, **his jeans ripped and his eyes swollen from the fall,** still managed to . . . .
>
> **Dressed in somber gray and carrying a purse shaped like a small casket, the defendant** Mrs. Arroyo approached . . . .

➤ **Mark missed opportunities for dialogue.** Where might a little dialogue move the action forward more vigorously or enhance a reader's understanding of a character? Dialogue is easy to recreate, even when the exact words of a speaker aren't remembered.

In reading a draft, consider also the possibility of too much dialogue. Does a conversation ramble on without contributing much to the action? Are the important remarks sandwiched between unneeded courtesy expressions and filler? If so, cut.

7 E

Pers Narr

➤ **Check the setting.** Does the setting of the narrative contribute to the action? Could it do so more effectively? Can particular details of the setting be introduced—names of particular streets, buildings, and neighborhoods—to add authenticity and interest?

➤ **Check the style.** Does the tone of the paper match the subject? A humorous narrative can usually be lighter in tone and more full of slang and colloquial expressions than a more serious one, but no guidelines hold true in all cases. A very serious action, for example, might include dialogue full of street talk.

Good contemporary narrative does tend to be lean and vigorous—with an emphasis on strong subjects (people and real objects) and action verbs. For that reason, descriptions of setting and character should be brief and a part of the action. Make every word count.

What about obscenities? They become an issue in personal narratives more often than in other kinds of writing. Can you use an expletive or four letter word? The answer is usually *yes* if the word has genuine power in a particular setting—and if it is the word a character really used. The fact is that obscenities in public settings have become so routine that they have lost much of their impact. A writer who has to rely on them to sustain interest is working with pretty thin material.

➤ **Assess the authenticity of the narrative.** Does the paper seem like a faithful account of a real event? This can be a tough matter to determine. Michael Minor's "The Voices" acquires an almost mythical tone when the narrator begins describing the imaginary hunters watching him. Has a realistic hunting story turned into something else—the story of an inner event? Probably. And that would justify Minor's exploratory movement away from "just the facts, Ma'am."

If a piece strikes you as off the mark, unrealistic, or phony, revise it.

➤ **Edit carefully.** When you have a draft that meets your narrative goals, you can begin editing (see Section 5C for a thorough checklist). A few points peculiar to narratives are worth noting:

—Check the spelling of all proper nouns—especially names and places.

—Check the quotation marks used with dialogue. Remember to provide opening *and closing* quotation marks for all such passages.

—Check the paragraphing. Paragraphs in narratives tend to be relatively short. They should track the action and contribute to the pace of the story. Long paragraphs of background information should probably be revised and broken up.

—Check the title. Look for one that provides a focus for the paper without giving away the entire action. Titles that might be appropriate in an academic report may be too dull or factual for a personal narrative: "My Automobile Accident"; "Our California Vacation"; "The First Time I Got Drunk." Look fo, a title with a little color, resonance, or connections to contemporary ideas: "The Camaro that Flew"; "Big Sur and Little Sally"; "M.A.D.D. at Myself." Consider how the title Michael Minor uses for his story leaves the implications of the story rich and ambiguous—"The Voices"; consider how much duller the narrative would seem if it had been called "The Day I Shot a Buck and Became a Man."

8 Analyzing Cause and Effect

A Understanding cause/effect
B Examining a sample paper
C Choosing a topic
D Preparing and planning
E Drafting and revising

Terms you need to know

CAUSE. Any force, person, phenomenon, or other agency that brings about a change or enables some existing condition to continue. Causes may be direct or indirect, immediate or remote, obvious or hidden.

EFFECT. A specific and observable condition or change that follows from the action of some force or agency.

8 A UNDERSTANDING CAUSE AND EFFECT: EXPLAINING WHY

Perhaps you have read "The Charge of the Light Brigade," a poem by Alfred Lord Tennyson celebrating a doomed British cavalry charge that took place during the Crimean War (1853–56). Six hundred horsemen heroically, but mistakenly, rode into a valley ringed with cannon. As Tennyson puts it:

> Someone had blundered:
> Theirs not to make reply,
> Theirs not to reason why,
> Theirs but to do and die.

This silent allegiance to duty wins the soldiers in Tennyson's poem a hard-earned measure of glory. But who wants to emulate such behavior? People who refuse to ask *why*—in political or social situations especially—act blindly, just like the doomed warriors, "theirs not to reason why." To understand the world, writers need to ask the *why* question over and over again. Essays that attempt to answer *why* are described as studies of "cause and effect."

When done well, cause-and-effect analyses are among our culture's most powerful (and characteristic) operations; when managed poorly, causal analysis can lead to stereotypical thinking, prejudiced attitudes, and poor political judgments. If that sounds overstated, just consider how regularly political figures, news analysts, and ordinary people trace effects back to causes in order to dole out blame: liberals blame conservatives for the national debt; conservatives blame liberals for government bureaucracy; Third World nations link their economic woes to exploitation from the West; the Federal Aviation Administration cites "pilot error" as the cause of a jumbo jet disaster; parents finger administrators for the poor quality of their children's education; environmentalists blame everybody for the sad state of the ecosphere.

In some cases, we seek to understand "causes" in order to control their effects. Corporations routinely spend millions of dollars on consumer research to find out what motivates people to buy some products and not others; political consultants use the same tactics to identify and exploit trends among voters.

8 A

Cause/Eff

On other occasions, we recognize specific effects, but don't quite understand their causes. Such circumstances can be quite ordinary: the car won't start or the sink won't drain. To handle the repairs, we first need to find out *why*. In other cases, the effects are more complex and worrisome. We see cities fill up with homeless people and wonder what changes in our culture have led to this situation. We sense that our high school students know less about science and want to know why, despite massive funding of education, this should be so. We see young people succumbing to heart disease and wonder what brings on this problem? What could be done to prevent such effects? Can we alter or eliminate conditions that lead to them?

In still other situations we simply crave to know how different phenomena are related. What conditions fostered the blossoming of artistic talent in England during the reign of Elizabeth I? Why do birds build a specific type of nest and not any other? Why do left-handed people die at a younger age than right-handed people? Why is the universe shaped the way it is? All such inquiries—from the frivolous to the profound—spin off from the question, **why?**

Some cause-and-effect analyses	
Psychoanalysis	White papers
Apologies	Investigative reports
Excuses	Blue-ribbon commission reports
Historical analyses	Technical/scientific papers
Analyses of the news	Cross-examinations in court
Medical diagnoses	Autopsies
Sociology experiments	

Cause-and-effect analyses require both explanatory and exploratory writing processes. Identifying and describing either causes or effects (or both) is typically the first step in any such project: what is already known needs to be explained so that readers can agree that, "yes, something *has* happened and we need to know why," or "yes, these *are* the forces in place and we now need to anticipate what their effects might be."

The exploratory side of the analysis involves trying to identify the unknowns in either direction:

Effects ──────────────────────────────▶ Causes?

What forces have led to this situation or condition?

Causes ──────────────────────────────▶ Effects?

What are the likely effects if such forces continue to operate?

8 A

Cause/Eff

In both cases, the writer, using reason and imagination, will try to explain how different events or phenomena are connected. Yet two writers may interpret the same effect differently and trace it to incompatible causes:

- Poverty in America is caused by too *much* government control of private enterprise.

- Poverty in America is caused by too *little* government control of private enterprise.

That's because, to some extent, cause-and-effect analyses are persuasive: writers try to convince readers to understand, accept, and, perhaps, act upon their interpretations of events. Thus, both in reading and in writing cause-and-effect papers, you must look scrupulously at the evidence and think deeply about the situation. It is easy to be duped.

Places to Find Cause/Effect Analyses

In newspaper analytical pieces
In scholarly journals
In research articles
In the reports of government commissions and panels
In weather forecasts
In psychiatric reports
On radio call-in programs
In advice columns: Ann Landers, Dr. Ruth
In political campaign speeches
American Sociological Review
The Congressional Digest
Federal Reserve Bulletin
Foreign Affairs
Harper's
Organic Gardening
Prevention
Scientific American
Weekly Weather and Crop Bulletin
Fashion magazines: *Vogue, Cosmopolitan, Mademoiselle*

Finding a subject for a cause-and-effect analysis shouldn't be difficult but often is. Cause-and-effect papers should arise more from curiosity than an assignment, from the desire to understand some condition or activity in society. For most writers, tracing an effect back to its possible causes is easier than moving from cause to possible effects. You are moving from effect to cause when, for example, you notice that more college students than ever work part-time and begin speculating why that might be so. You are working from cause to possible effects when you sense a trend in society and then set about to consider what the future effects of such a trend might be: for example, you notice a nostalgia among consumers for simpler, low-tech products and then explore what the implications (if any) of the trend could be for politicians, businesses, governments, or private citizens.

8 B

Cause/Eff

Here are just a few of the many potential reasons for writing a cause-and-effect analysis:

- to explain why something happened;

- to consider what might happen as a result of certain trends or movements;

- to challenge accepted explanations for certain phenomena;

- to challenge stereotypical thinking;

- to affirm the validity of certain explanations in the face of new challenges;

- to explore the relationships between various causes and effects;

- to understand the complexity of political and social relationships;

- to overturn superstitions or simplistic explanations for complex phenomena;

- to undermine or question complex explanations for simple phenomena;

- to raise questions about values and cultural assumptions by examining their implications.

8 B   EXAMINING A SAMPLE ESSAY

Here is an example of a cause/effect analysis written by Michael Contreras when he was a freshman at the University of Texas at Austin. Michael also wrote the exploratory essay used as an example in the following chapter (9B). You may find it interesting to compare the serious tone of "Beware of the Dark Side" below with the lighter approach Michael takes in "Grackles," his essay in Chapter 9.

AUTHOR: Michael Contreras

AUDIENCE: His classmates in a Freshman English course.

ASSIGNMENT: Write a cause-and-effect analysis of some familiar behavior.

REQUIREMENTS: Length—about 750 words.

Beware of the Dark Side

(1)   There are many reasons people should not smoke--lung cancer, heart disease, emphysema, and the list just seems to grow. Every day another *one thousand* people fall victim to a disease caused by smoking; in the United States, this
deadly habit accounts for *one* out of every *six* deaths. According to former surgeon general C. Everett Koop, the average male smoker is *twenty-two times* more
likely to die from lung cancer than a non-smoker. Last year alone (1988), smoking was linked to *26,500 stroke deaths.* In light of such statistics widely circu-
lated to the public in newspapers and on television, why do millions of
Americans continue to smoke?

8 B

Cause/Eff

(2)   One reason is the influence of advertisements. Cigarette companies spend
millions of dollars in magazine advertisements alone. Billboards alongside every
major highway display cigarette slogans. One of the best-known cigarette campaigns is probably that presented by Marlboro. Marlboro's familiar ad displays a
rugged cowboy, "The Marlboro Man," lighting a cigarette after a difficult day on
the ranch in "Marlboro Country." This ad makes smoking look like a tough,
manly thing to do, encouraging men to smoke. Women also have many advertisements designed to convince them to try smoking. Virginia Slims' promotions
push the slogan, "You've come a long way baby" with a picture of a modern-day
woman next to a woman from the early 1900s, who had to hide her smoking. This
ad suggests that women's rights have come a long way and that smoking is a way
to exercise those rights. So advertisements get many people to try smoking; however, there is nothing quite like the experience of smoking to keep them hooked.

(3)   Smoking is an efficient and fast way to get a drug to the brain, and this
is a major reason people smoke. Many people with monotonous jobs find that
smoking allows the day to go along more easily because nicotine stimulates the
central nervous system. People also discover that smoking is extremely pleasur-
able and relaxing. Laboratory experiments have proven that large doses of nicotine have a depressant effect while smaller doses have a stimulant one. So smokers can actually control the way they feel at any given moment. For example, if
smokers feel tired and sluggish at the beginning of the work day, a cigarette
brings them back to life, allowing them to feel alert and awake. Unfortunately,
many people enjoy the stimulating and relaxing effects of smoking, unaware that
their bad habit is influencing others to smoke.

(4)   What it often comes down to is a case of monkey-see, monkey-do: people smoke because they observe other people doing it. Many parents, for example, do not realize that their smoking influences their children to imitate them. My mother has smoked for as long as I can remember. Consequently, I have always associated smoking with adulthood, as I am sure thousands of other children have. Once I began smoking, I noticed that many of my friends began to smoke-- not because their parents smoked, but because I smoked. There was an unintended peer pressure working between my friends and me. I never actually asked my friends to smoke, but my smoking was a silent way of conveying the message. Such an indirect and unintentional pressure is especially evident at teen parties where I have noticed that people who usually do not light up may try smoking. Parties often create an atmosphere where drinking and smoking seem to be the accepted things to do.

8 B

Cause/Eff

(5)   However, many people also smoke because it seems to be part of human nature to do what is bad for the body. Some people eat too much, causing them to become overweight and susceptible to heart disease, diabetes, and other conditions; other people drink alcohol, another habit that can create many health problems. Yet these problems are easy to ignore, at least for a while. Human nature also leads people to do extremely dangerous things--such as auto racing and cliff diving. Racing and cliff diving are sports that can result in death, but to avoid death is what makes the deed worthwhile. Smoking is an activity which resembles both a bad habit and a dangerous sport. Even though people may realize that smoking is bad, they don't care because human nature either ignores the dangerous effects or actually pursues them for the sake of excitement. Part of the fun in smoking comes in showing people that you aren't afraid of the risks. It's a way of thumbing your nose at a society that wants to make everything too clean, too healthy, and too safe.

➤ Analysis of Michael Contreras's "Beware of the Dark Side"

Purpose: This paper was written for an English course. How does that fact shape his purpose and the source of his evidence (chiefly, his own experiences)? What other kinds of evidence might Michael have used if this were a paper for a science or sociology class? Would you characterize this cause-and-effect paper as chiefly explanatory or exploratory?

Audience. Michael himself smokes. How does that fact affect readers of this analysis? Does Michael's smoking give him more or less credibility? Does it seem appropriate for Michael to use "I" so often in his analysis, or would the paper be more convincing if it were less personal?

Effects. What function do the statistics in the first paragraph have? What does Michael need to prove about smoking as a phenomenon to explain his curiosity about smoking?

Causes. Do any of Michael's rationales for smoking strike you as weak or farfetched? Why or why not? Which of the causal factors do you think is strongest? Most unexpected? What might you have liked to see him develop at greater length? Are you surprised by the bluntness of the conclusion? What causes of smoking might you add to this paper in a revision? Do you find that the title of the paper fits it: "Beware of the Dark Side"?

Language. In general, how would you describe the language of the paper—is it formal, informal, elaborate, plain? Where does the writing strike you as most effective? Least effective?

Transitions. Michael is careful to include transitions throughout the paper. Locate the key transitional words, phrases, and sentences and evaluate their effectiveness.

8 C

Cause/Eff

Reader's response. Did you find yourself convinced by "Beware of the Dark Side"? Does the analysis confirm any of your own experiences? What assumptions does the writer make about smoking? Do you have any sense that the writer is interested in quitting smoking? What does the story reveal about the writer's world and culture?

8 C TOPICS FOR CAUSE/EFFECT ANALYSES

> **The Basic Assignment**
>
> Write a cause-and-effect analysis in which you first identify some situation, activity, custom, or problem and then trace its various causes. Explore as many plausible explanations for the phenomenon as possible, but argue in favor of what you believe are the deepest, most significant causes.

➤ **Variations**

a. Look for a *deep* explanation for some familiar custom or fashion—the kind of thing people do all the time without thinking about it: visiting relatives at holidays; using cologne or perfume; voting for a particular political party; wearing ties; ignoring traffic laws; cruising the Dairy Queen on Friday nights. In selecting a topic, choose a phenomena with cultural implications that are wider or more significant than might be apparent upon first glance.

b. Analyze the way some important person or event had an unexpected or unusual impact on your life. Don't write a narrative, but a frank analysis in which you explain precisely how specific people or events in the past have shaped crucial dimensions of your life, personality, or career choice.

c. Select some popular brand of consumer product that is quite similar to its competitors, but much more successful. Explain its success in the broadest possible terms. Look for reasons that go beyond individual features and advantages of price. Why, for example, will people invest twice as much money in a foreign luxury car as in a domestic one? Why will they pay outrageous prices for certain brands of clothing or perfumes? Don't take this analysis lightly. Explore the deep reasons people have for choosing so-called "prestige" items.

d. Explain some phenomenon in sports—for example, why the popularity of soccer and competitive cycling has grown so slowly in the United States; why records in high jumping have progressed so dramatically; why athletes in many sports are now involved in weight training and body building; why salaries of professional athletes have risen so much in the last decade. Look into the subject deeply; don't be satisfied with the first reasons you come up with. Take sports seriously; our society does.

e. Form a writing group with three to five students to produce a cause-and-effect analysis of some social problem. If possible, form the group out of a common interest or concern to know *why:* why women seem to be paid less than men; why the high school dropout rate among Hispanics remains so high; why so few athletes seem to finish their degrees; why young men pay more for auto insurance than young women. Decide what data must be collected (and by whom) to prove that the situation *is* as you portray it. Then brainstorm possible explanations and research them, delegating the individual research problems to members of the team. Write up a group report summarizing your findings and possible conclusions. Allow for the possibility of dissenting opinions or minority reports—that is, papers from members of the research group that do not agree with the majority assessment of the situation.

f. Working in a group, select some neighborhood you know well—preferably one that is either notably prosperous or in obvious decline—and describe the social and economic forces causing noticeable changes in that community. Assign members of your writing group to interview people in the neighborhood—especially those who have been there for a while, such as the elderly, business people, clergy, and local government employees (police, postal workers, librarians). Get a feel for the forces shaping the area and then, after assembling your data and discussing its implications, collaborate in writing a paper to explain why the community seems to be changing. Be careful not to get bogged down in describing the situation; keep your focus on explaining the causes of the change. You might perform a similar, smaller-scale cause/effect analysis on a local institution: a business, community center, church, school, park.

g. If you have a job, explain why your place of employment is or is not thriving.

h. Get a copy of some recent issue of *The Gallup Report* or a similar journal that chronicles public opinion. Choose one set of data and write your own assessment of the numbers. Explain why people feel this way about such an issue. Explore the deep reasons for their feelings.

i. This assignment is for people who like to do research and have access to an ample library collection of magazines and newspapers. Pick some major political or social decision made in the recent past (five-to-twenty-five years ago) and then read heavily in the literature of the day—editorials, news analyses, commentaries, letters-to-the-editor—to get a feel for what people writing at the time of the decision predicted its outcome might be. Assess the accuracy of these writers' predictions. You might select, for example, commentaries on inflation or the adequacy of America's oil supply made during the Carter administration (1977–80) or predictions made about the likely results of the Reagan tax cuts in 1981. Or see what people were predicting for the Beatles during their explosive popularity in the mid-sixties. In your paper, assess the accuracy of the writers' cause/effect analyses. Pay particular attention to where the pundits went wrong and why. Because of the amount of research this assignment might involve, it might be a good project to develop with the help of one or two colleagues.

8 D

Cause/Eff

8 D   WRITING A CAUSE/EFFECT ANALYSIS

Americans, it is said, prefer easy solutions to complex problems; unfortunately, cause-and-effect analyses *can* be used to promote such quick-fix attitudes. No doubt you've heard simplistic cause-and-effect arguments like these from all points on the political spectrum:

> Rising pregnancy rates are the result of too little sex education. So let's increase funding for sex education and eliminate the problem.

> Rising pregnancy rates are the result of too much sex education. So let's end sex education and eliminate the problem.

In such cases, it's not so much that either side is completely wrong, as that each side understands only a part of the problem. Neither knows (or will acknowledge) the whole story.

More rarely, the problem with a causal analysis runs in the opposite direction: interested parties make a lingering problem seem insoluble by tying the cause-and-effect relationship in endless knots—until a real crisis strikes. For example, for at least two decades, the U.S. automakers claimed that high labor costs, investments in existing plants, American consumer tastes, and dozens of other factors prevented them from building small, efficient, and high-quality automobiles. It took an oil crisis and stiff competition from foreign manufacturers to shake the huge industry from its lethargy. Suddenly all those "causes" just seemed like excuses.

Anyone who has worked within a bureaucracy (whether a school, business, or government office) will recall similar situations—when dozens of objections prevented the solution of a festering problem. The factors contributing to the problem look so formidable that any solution seems unthinkable. You've heard the bureaucratic lament: "We can't possibly do that!"—can't, that is, until someone somewhere applies pressure at the right place, breaks the logjam, and resolves the problem. What happened? Well, either the time for change had come or the factors causing the problem weren't quite as complicated as they had been made to appear.

To examine causes and effects well . . .

➤ **Find a subject by identifying a situation that needs explaining.** This is a crucial but interesting step. You can manage it either by writing a paper about some phenomenon that is puzzling or by looking at a familiar situation in a new light.

In the first case, you might be puzzled by a new fad, fashion, trend, or phenomenon. You see the need to explore why so many people suddenly claim an interest in Third World music. Or you find it puzzling that, in your college neighborhood, apartment prices are still rising while real estate prices everywhere else in town are falling fast. You discover that a surprising number of classmates are thinking about entering the teaching profession or that voters in your town have unexpectedly elected someone from a non-mainstream political party to city council. In all these cases, the status quo has met something new—a blip on the chart that needs to be explained.

8 D

Cause/Eff

On the other hand, cause-and-effect papers can also be about the status quo. Take a habit as routine as wearing a baseball cap to class. No one thinks twice about it. Everyone knows that men wear caps to keep the sun out of their eyes or to hide bald spots. But are the obvious explanations for the habit adequate in this case? There's little glare in a classroom and most college men aren't bald yet. Why the caps? Do some guys wear them to keep from having to comb their hair in the morning? That's a plausible reason for the behavior, but hardly a convincing one. Any deeper causes? What do the ball caps represent? What do people associate with them? What sorts of guys wear them? What sorts of signals about dress and behavior do ball caps send? Do any women wear them?

These are all relevant questions when a familiar behavior becomes the object of scrutiny. Such analyses prompt writers to look closely at their cultural assumptions—to see them fresh, as if through the eyes of an outsider to whom the "why?" question might be genuinely puzzling.

➤ **List possible subjects.** You might begin this brainstorming session by captioning a sheet of paper "Why . . ."

Why . . .

do people grow old?
do teenagers rebel?
do people procrastinate?
hasn't a cure for cancer been discovered?
is the rate of Hispanic dropouts from high school so high?
has the divorce rate increased tenfold in this century?
did Bush defeat Dukakis in the 1988 presidential election?
is smoking increasing among women?
have student fees on campus increased five times faster than the rate of
    inflation?
is the British army in Northern Ireland?
did the Hula Hoop become so popular so quickly in 1958?
did NASA decide to build the Space Shuttle in its present configuration?
did Chrysler almost go broke in the late 1970s?
don't Americans vote?

do many doctors in the United States not feel comfortable recommending acupuncture?

do high school athletes experiment with steroids knowing that they are harmful?

do most people dislike opera?

do Americans eat so much meat?

➤ **Select a topic interesting to both you and your audience.** You obviously need a topic you either know a great deal about or can research easily enough. You also need a topic that fits your intended readers. For instance, an audience of structural engineers would already know why metal rusts, so a paper on the subject would be boring to them; a class of high school juniors, on the other hand, might be very interested in the chemistry that's causing the fenders of their Camaros to crumble. Some subjects may raise the curiosity of a general audience:

8 D

Cause/Eff

> When Americans think of fads, they recall the Hula Hoop—the national passion in 1958. Although the hoops were nothing more than simple rings of polyethylene tubing joined by wooden plugs and fastened by staples, everyone had to have one. According to Richard Johnson, author of *American Fads,* within six months after the phenomenon took off, sales of the hoop had reached $100 million in a depressed economy, and Americans everywhere—young and old—were competing to see who could keep the rings spinning around their waists longest. Stars like Dinah Shore and Art Linkletter endorsed it and the fad lasted a solid year. But what exactly made this plastic hoop the most famous fad ever?

➤ **Explore your subject to uncover both immediate and deep causes.** Immediate, obvious, or surface causes are those that present themselves to a writer (or reader) without much thought. They are either immediately apparent or generally accepted. Why did England and France go to war against Hitler in 1939? The immediate cause was obviously Hitler's invasion of Poland. Why did people flock in such numbers to see the film *Batman* in the summer of 1989? No doubt it was because of the hype that greased the movie's release.

Tracing deeper causes usually requires more thought, research, and analysis. Because they are less apparent, such causes must be presented in more detail and with greater evidence. So, in analyzing the deeper reasons for the Allies' response to Hitler's invasion of Poland, you might explore the economic, political, social, and historical conflicts between Germany and its European rivals. The deeper reasons for a moviegoer's response to *Batman* might be found in society's need to identify with a new kind of hero, one with a darker, less optimistic view of the world than, for example, Superman.

Fine. But how do you find these deeper reasons—particularly when obvious explanations seem adequate? You can begin by applying one of the strategies for developing a topic (see Section 3A); in particular, consider the journalist's questions:

Who?   **When?**
What?   **Why?**
Where?   **How?**

Think of these questions as inquiries about all the potential forces that might cause things to happen:

> **Who?** What people are responsible for this situation? Have particular individuals contributed to the existing effect? Should the effect be traced to the actions and beliefs of whole groups defined by gender, race, class, religion, profession, avocation, talent, and so on? For example, if you were to examine changes in high-jumping techniques, you would have to learn about individuals, including Dave Albritton and Dick Fosbury. An inquiry into the causes of the American Civil War, however, could lead you to explore the differences between entire social and economic classes—Northern industrialists and merchants and Southern farmers and plantation owners.

> **What?** Identify the forces operating to make something happen. These may be actual physical forces (the atmospheric conditions needed to form tornados); biological forces (cholesterol deposits on the walls of arteries); political forces (voter acceptance of higher taxes); or social forces (an increase in the proportion of elderly in the United States).

> **Where?** Consider how a location may be responsible for a condition or situation. When appropriate, think of location in broad, cultural terms: the West, the Middle East, the Orient, Eastern Europe. What forces—political, environmental, geographic—arise from these locations? Think of location, too, in more local terms: the neighborhood, the street, the factory, the school, the tenement, the mall, the corridor. How do physical environments shape a situation? Might the architecture of a building (or the architectural styles of an entire culture) explain some way of living or working? For example, the elimination of the plague in England has been traced to the demise, after the Great Fire of London, of buildings with thatched roofs—a construction feature that had provided an ideal environment for disease-bearing fleas.

> **When?** How does time affect or shape a situation? What intellectual trends occurring at a given historical moment might explain certain effects? You can treat time as a powerful historical force: tracing the roots of a particular phenomenon to 1968 (the core of the radical "sixties") would lead to different conclusions than if the same event belonged to 1958 (amidst the conservative "Eisenhower" era). The time element may also be a local event, something as commonplace as morning, noon, or night: time of day, for example, could be explored as a causal factor in the onset of heart attacks; they occur most frequently in the morning.

> **Why?** In a sense, this whole chapter is about *why*. But think of *why* as an inquiry into motives: who benefits or loses in a given circumstance? When you understand the motives of people involved in a situation, you've gone a long way toward explaining it. Consider all the basic human emotions and drives when assessing the causes of a situation: food, shelter, security, love, lust, greed, friendship, loneliness, pride, and so on.

> **How?** Think of this as the knowledge question: how do specific ways of thinking shape human actions? For example, what beliefs and values made it possible for Europeans to bring slavery to the Americas? What specific

technology made it possible to land people on the moon in 1969? What attitudes might lead to increasing racial tension in the 1990s?

Don't look for a single force to explain a complicated effect. You'll find that causes often interact. Even a person choosing to smoke probably does so for several reasons—a combination of peer pressure, parental example, the pleasures of smoking, the influence of advertising.

➤ **Consider how you will convince readers that a phenomenon or situation deserves attention.** This is also a crucial step, particularly when you select a topic which, at first glance, seems to need no explanation at all, like procrastinating or oversleeping in the morning. But even with a puzzling situation—let's say a sudden increase in traffic deaths in the campus area—you need to prove that a phenomenon exists before you can explore it. What is the normal rate of accidents? How significant is the increase in accidents? And perhaps most important, why should readers care?

8 D

Cause/Eff

Just claiming that something has happened isn't enough to make readers appreciate a phenomenon. You want to give the problem a *presence*—in effect, convince readers that a given situation is puzzling enough to merit a cause-and-effect study.

If, like Michael Contreras in "Beware of the Dark Side," you decide to explore why people smoke, you'll need to confront readers with some grim facts before they'll pay much attention. Statistics have a way of breaking through to people who believe they already know enough about a subject.

> . . . Every day another *one thousand* people fall victim to a disease caused by smoking; in the United States, this deadly habit accounts for *one* out of every *six* deaths. According to former surgeon general C. Everett Koop, the average male smoker is *twenty-two times* more likely to die from lung cancer than a non-smoker. Last year alone (1988), smoking was linked to *26,500 stroke deaths.* In light of such statistics widely circulated to the public in newspapers and on television, why do millions of Americans continue to smoke?

That last sentence hits home: *in light of such statistics.* People know that smoking kills—why do they *still* take the risk?

➤ **Organize the paper strategically.** The typical cause-and-effect paper will probably have two parts, whether you begin with an effect and work to explain possible causes,

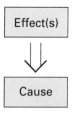

or begin with forces in operation and imagine their effects.

In either case, the first part typically serves as an extended introduction, explaining the existing situation. The bulk of the paper will then be concerned with interpreting the circumstances described in the first part of the essay. In the typical cause-and-effect essay, the second part will consist—as it does in Michael Contreras's paper—of a list of causes:

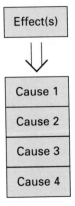

This arrangement is solid and simple, but still requires arranging the causes from the most obvious, specific, or non-controversial to the more subtle, abstract, and challenging ones.

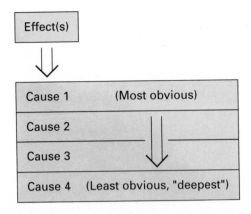

Quite often, a cause-and-effect paper discusses and refutes false causes—forces that seem important, but which prove irrelevant. Again, there are many ways of handling such refutations. Using the model below, you would dismiss unworkable causes until you reach the one explanation that seems plausible:

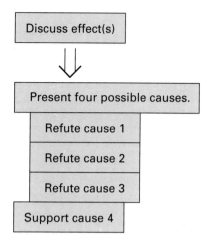

No abstract model of a cause-and-effect paper will suit every (or even most) cause-and-effect analyses. But be sure to work out some plan helpful to both you and your readers.

➤ **Research your subject.** The best insights in a cause-and-effect paper may come from unexpected insights or daring speculations. But don't rely only on speculation and cleverness in presenting your ideas. Back up your conjecture with data. Collect any information you will need at the library; find authorities to support or contribute to your paper. Present facts, figures, and information carefully. See Section 37B on library research for some suggestions.

8E   DRAFTING AND REVISING THE CAUSE/EFFECT PAPER

Before drafting your cause-and-effect paper, try freewriting. Use the freewriting exercise both to probe the soundness and logic of your analysis and to experiment with the form it may take.

When you begin the draft itself, convince your readers that your subject is important. You'll be able to do that easily when exploring the causes of homelessness or infant death syndrome. But the job may be tougher when handling topics that may, at first glance, seem lighter and less intense: professional wrestling; medical insurance for pets; bumper stickers. But these analyses, too, may help us understand our culture if they are shrewd and inventive.

In reviewing the draft of a cause/effect analysis . . .

➤ **Carefully evaluate the cause-and-effect relationships you have suggested.** When two events occur in sequence, it's tempting to assume that they are causally related—but often they are not. Such faulty connections (the result of the fallacy of **faulty causality**) are easy to see when simple or foolish: breaking a mirror doesn't cause seven years of bad luck; walking under a ladder doesn't bring disaster. But more serious causal misrepresentations might not be so obvious. An upturn in the national economy, for example, may or may not be related to some particular presidential decision or congressional action—yet politicians will be quick to suggest such a linkage.

Faulty causality can be much more dangerous when it leads to stereotyping people—simplistically attributing their successes or failures to their race, ethnicity, religion, gender, social or economic class, or physical traits. This does not mean that no conclusions can be drawn about the behavior of people in groups, but that such analyses must be undertaken with enormous care, scrupulous attention to facts, and great sensitivity to the many variables in human behavior.

In short, don't rush to judgment. Look carefully at your data, your logic, and your premises to be sure that any causal connections you make are, in fact, plausible.

8 E

Cause/Eff

▶ **Be sure you have presented causes, not just facts.** Writers sometimes confuse information with analysis. Providing facts is not the same thing as establishing causes—though facts can be made to serve a cause-and-effect analysis. Here's an example of a paragraph from a paper exploring why people drink and drive. The writer intends to explain why drivers risk driving while intoxicated, but places the emphasis on the facts of a DWI conviction. The result is confusion.

> People also need to take into account the tremendous fees that follow the criminal act of driving while intoxicated. For a first DWI offense, a driver in Texas faces a Class B misdemeanor, a fine not to exceed $1000, and up to eighty days in jail. A respected Austin law firm charges from $2500-3000 to a client who wishes to go to trial on a DWI charge and plead not guilty. If convicted and given probation, the driver pays $40 a month for two years to a probation officer . . .

Yet it's easy to shift the paragraph back to a study of causes by asserting the relationship between drunk driving and its serious consequences.

> Perhaps many people persist in driving drunk because they have never really tallied up the consequences of a DWI arrest. For a first DWI offense . . .

▶ **Check that you have stated causes clearly.** When you describe a cause, be sure you present it as a force that might actually do something; relate a cause to its effect using language as direct as the facts will allow. Here's an example of a paragraph lead-in that would leave most readers puzzling over *who* is doing *what* to *whom*. It's from an essay examining the causes of an increasing pregnancy rate among teenagers.

> The most evident and changeable factor in the pregnancy increase directly relates to the media.

If you examine the sentence, you won't actually find an explanation for the pregnancy rate, only the suggestion that some evident and changeable factor *relates* to the media. *Relates* is an ambiguous verb. In what sense is this factor connected to the media? Indeed, what is the factor? The topic sentence doesn't tell you. It needs to be revised to make the causal connection much more direct so that the paragraph which follows from it can have surer direction.

> The clearest blame for the increase in teenage pregnancies belongs
>
> to the national media--newspapers, magazines, films, and television--
>
> which are filled daily with articles that make teens believe that
>
> early sexual activity is both normal and healthy.

Wow! Quite an indictment. A reader might disagree, but at least he or she has something to disagree with—a causal connection stated clearly and directly. Who would react to the original version of the topic sentence in the same way?

8 E

Cause/Eff

➤ **Assess the organization. Work on the transitions.** Often, a reader will lose track of a subject because a writer gets a little careless in the body of an essay and begins hinting at ideas rather than spelling them out.

Here, for example, is a paragraph lead-in from the paper cited earlier examining the causes of a nationwide increase in teenage pregnancies.

> Other factors we must consider are social acceptance and pressure.

Notice that this key sentence doesn't even mention teenage pregnancies, nor does it explain how the vague terms *social acceptance* and *pressure* are related to the pregnancy rate. The writer knows precisely what she means, but needs to slow down a bit to share the details with readers.

> Other factors responsible for the increasing juvenile birthrate
>
> include a wider acceptance of teenage pregnancy among all classes
>
> and greater pressure on young girls to have sex early and often.

The revised topic sentence is better not because it is longer but because it gives readers something to anticipate in the remainder of the paragraph. The sentence raises tangible questions about cause and effect.

➤ **Consider the ending.** The conclusion of a cause-and-effect essay can be quite abrupt when you leave readers with such a thought-provoking idea that they are compelled to consider its implications. This is the case with the conclusion of Michael Contreras's piece on smoking.

> . . . Part of the fun in smoking comes in showing people that you
>
> aren't afraid of the risks. It's a way of thumbing your nose at a
>
> society that wants to make everything too clean, too healthy, and
>
> too safe.

The last sentence forces readers to think not only about smoking, but about a great deal more—about all those other potentially harmful behaviors people seem to indulge in despite noisy and repeated warnings. In fact, if Mr. Contreras is right, many anti-smoking, anti-drunk driving, and anti-drug messages may be having precisely the opposite of their intended effects. That's surely something to ponder!

In cases where you don't have such a provoking conclusion, you need to explore the implications of the analysis on your own. If you have discovered something significant about your subject, what should readers think or do next? What additional research or work becomes necessary as a result of your thinking? Spend a paragraph exploring such possibilities.

➤ **Check the style.** Check that the style of your analysis matches the seriousness of its subject matter. A cause-and-effect paper can be serious, comic, or anything in between. It's quite possible for a paper to begin quite humorously—consider that baseball cap analysis again—and move toward a more sober appreciation of a phenomenon.

Look carefully for transitions in these papers—words or phrases that show how separate ideas are related. Be sure that the transitions clearly signal the differences between obvious causes and deeper ones: (*the most obvious reason . . . a more subtle rationale for . . .*).

➤ **Edit carefully.** Edit only after you have a draft you like (see Section 5C for a thorough checklist). These points common to cause/effect analyses are worth noting:

—Check the accuracy of any dates you use.

—Check the paragraphing. Treat one idea at a time, one major cause (or effect) per paragraph.

—Check the title. Look for one that introduces the cause-and-effect relationship you intend to explore.

9 WRITING AN EXPLORATORY PAPER

A About exploration
B Examining a sample essay
C Choosing a topic
D Composing the essay
E Drafting and revising

9 A ABOUT EXPLORATION

You'd probably object if we described the essay as a neglected form of writing.

"Neglected! Why, I've been composing essays since the third grade. Just last month, I had to write a paper for my history class and I've got a psychology essay due next week, and a report coming up for a physics lab."

Well, those aren't the kind of essays we are describing now. In this chapter, we don't mean *essay* in its generic sense—as a synonym for term paper, article, written assignment, piece, or report. We're more interested in the root sense of the word, its derivation from a French verb *essayer,* which means "to try." An essay, as first practiced by the French writer Michel de Montaigne (1533–92), is a stimulating, sometimes playful, more often serious, investigation of an idea—an intellectual audition or "try out," a civilized (and civilizing) attempt to come to grips with a subject or a problem. It may be bare-bones simple or stylishly literary.

By its very nature, the essay demands risk. When attempting one, a writer often begins with no more than a feeling or an intuition—there's a subject inside that wants to be addressed, a problem that demands attention and voice, an irritating matter that won't leave the writer alone until peace has been made with it through language. Some exploratory pieces are systematically organized, so much so that we can outline at least one generic form of the exploratory essay. Others spin out an array of patterns, rich threads that surround ideas, arrange them in different ways, or suspend them at odd and unpredictable angles. Though an essay is almost by definition exploratory, we can imagine a continuum of types even here, from the paper that lays siege to a topic, picking it apart bit-by-bit, to one that makes a headlong assault upon a subject—"damn the torpedoes, full speed ahead."

125

> **Some examples of exploratory writing**
>
> | | |
> |---|---|
> | Sermons | Science fiction |
> | Proposals | Planning papers |
> | Public addresses | Journals |
> | Newspaper columns | Dialogues |
> | Humor/satire | |

Whatever its pace, the essay is a social form of writing. Indeed, a good essay breaks down the boundaries between private and public thinking. Though essays can be very personal, they are typically written for the ear of humankind—for the widest possible audience. With exploratory essays, writers take the risk of entering the world of public affairs, where ideas have stature and consequences, where words shape lives and societies:

9 B

Explor

> Authors communicate themselves to the world by some special and extrinsic mark; I am the first to do so by my general being, as Michel de Montaigne, not as a grammarian or a poet or a lawyer. If the world finds fault with me for speaking too much of myself, I find fault with the world for not even thinking of itself.
>
> —"Of Repentance"

> **Places to read essays**
>
> *Harper's* ("Notebook" section)
> *Newsweek/Time* (columns)
> *Ms.*
> *The New Yorker*
> *Esquire*

Here are just a few reasons for writing an essay:

- to understand human nature;
- to examine one's values;
- to explore one's own culture;
- to understand other cultures;
- to seek solutions to problems;
- to explore emotions;
- to understand people and institutions;
- to see the humor in things.

9 B   EXAMINING AN EXPLORATORY PAPER

Don't assume that exploratory essays must be profound or deeply serious. Montaigne's best pieces sparkle with wit. So does the following paper, which attempts to solve a "campus crisis." Notice that the tone is a bit playful and mocking—one possible pose of an exploratory piece.

AUTHOR: Michael Contreras, freshman at the University of Texas at Austin. (Michael also contributes an essay to Chapter 8.)

AUDIENCE: His classmates in a freshman English course.

ASSIGNMENT: Write an exploratory essay in which you attempt to solve a problem.

REQUIREMENTS: An in-class essay, written and revised during a three-hour final examination period. [And polished a bit for inclusion in this chapter.]

Grackles?

(1)   When I first arrived at the University of Texas at Austin to attend the summer session, I had never heard of a grackle. So when at our first orientation meeting my campus mentor Sharon warned me to beware of them, I didn't inquire what grackles were. I was afraid I'd seem like a stupid freshman. But eventually I got up the courage to ask the resident advisor in my dormitory, "What are grackles?" Chuckling to himself, he explained that they were the huge, noisy blackbirds perching all over campus, like extras from Alfred Hitchcock's The Birds. But it was not until the next day that I understood Sharon's warning.

(2)   I was walking along Speedway Avenue with my roommate to Gregory Gym when, suddenly, we were enveloped by a disgusting stench. Looking around, I noticed bird droppings covering the sidewalk, trees, cars, road--terrified pedestrians. I realized immediately that the University of Texas had a problem: thousands and thousands of squawking birds that roosted in its trees and deposited layers of filth on sidewalks, trees, cars, and roads. Back at the dorm, I asked Sharon why the university could not just kill the filthy grackles: let's put our campus' SDI research to practical use, I suggested. She told me that, unfortunately, the pests were protected by migratory laws and that Austin is considered a bird sanctuary. Sharon then narrated the sorry history of the university's attempts to rid the campus of grackles.

(3)   Some of the failed solutions were mere "scare tactics." One scare tactic involved placing in the trees alarm systems which played distressed grackle calls. This method did persuade the grackles to leave some trees, but only to fly to others without the alarms. The university would have had to put alarm systems in over 4,000 trees for this plan to work properly, an endeavor that would have required too much time and money. Then the university tried cannons which would boom at various times to scare the grackles away. Unfortunately this

method worked for maybe ten minutes after the guns had fired. Then the grackles would come back from wherever they were hiding. Finally, the university tried placing fake owls in trees around campus. Owls eat grackles and, at first, the fake owls did scare off the prey; but, after a while, the grackles figured out the owls weren't real. The failure of the "scare tactics" did not, however, end the University of Texas' campaign against the grackles.

(4)   UT decided if "scare tactics" did not work, maybe "tree tactics" would. One "tree tactic" involved cutting off small branches from all the trees on campus, the logic being that then the grackles would have nowhere to roost. But, rather predictably, the grackles took to sitting on larger branches. Another "tree tactic" was misting the foliage in cold weather. Unfortunately, the grackles did not seem to mind the cold water and the concrete underneath the trees became slippery due to the runoff from the water. Final score: Grackles 5, UT 0.

(5)   It distressed me to think that such a prestigious research university might not be capable of solving a simple grackle crisis. What, I had to wonder, is the present status of the struggle? Pathetic, I quickly learned--equal to surrender: a university maintenance crew hoses down the dirty sidewalks daily. But that means students and faculty continue to be pelted with bird droppings on their way to and from class, Speedway Avenue still stinks, and cars always leave parking lots plastered with filth.

(6)   The campus paper is currently suggesting that peregrine falcons might be encouraged to live in the UT tower. Such falcons eat other flying birds and the falcons would not have to eat too many grackles before those pesky birds realize they would be safer in the distant hills. The only problem with this approach is that peregrine falcons are endangered birds that live only in captivity now. So not only would the university have to buy the falcons, but it would also have to be sure no harm would come to them.

(7)   After considering all the past and present approaches to the problem I realized one thing--all of these solutions involve working against the grackles. As the old saying goes, "If you can't beat 'em, join 'em." I have a proposal that might work; it involves thinking like a grackle.

(8)   Grackles come to campus for reasons such as safety, food, and shelter. My proposal is to lure them away from the central campus area by providing ample food for them in more isolated parts, such as Waller Creek. This proposal would

9 B

Explor

require the cooperation of both UT administration and students: no food must be thrown on the ground to discourage grackles from coming to the heart of campus for goodies. UT must also make arrangements to have delicacies available around Waller Creek for the birds to consume--not just one type of food, but a variety of seeds, crickets, and grasshoppers to keep the birds happy. Seed and insects can't be too expensive, so the monetary investment would be minimal; in the long run, feeding the grackles would have to be cheaper than hosing the sidewalks daily. The only drawback to my proposal is that, admittedly, it may not work. Maybe the grackles will continue to leave their droppings along Speedway. (9)   I, however, do not think this will be the case. The squirrels around campus are friendly to humans only because humans have been friendly to them. Once the university community starts to show consideration towards the grackles, the grackles will no longer act like pests. The grackle problem has plagued the campus for years, but I truly believe that by working with the grackles instead of against them, The Birds may simply become a memory.

9 B

Explor

➤ **Analysis of Michael Contreras's "Grackles?"**

Author. What does this essay gain from being told from a first-person perspective: *I*? Where do you find Michael's personal "voice" most effective? How serious is he being in this paper? How do you know how seriously he wants to be taken? How would you characterize the author you meet in this paper—what adjectives would you use to describe him?

Audience. Is "Grackles?" written to a specific audience? Would any group of readers be offended by it? What is the effect of Michael's comment on SDI [Strategic Defense Initiative] research in paragraph two? Of his sports allusion, "Final score: Grackles 5, UT 0"?

Description of "the problem." Michael uses a narrative approach ("When I first arrived . . .") to introduce the grackle problem. Do you find that technique effective? What other approach might he have used? The problem Michael Contreras describes is a very local one. Does Michael make it sufficiently interesting to readers not affected by it? If so, how?

Assessment of previous solutions. Michael outlines at least five failed solutions to the grackle problem. Does he explain those solutions (and their failure) in sufficient detail? Why or why not?

New solution. Does the solution Michael offers to the grackle problem seem any less plausible than those already tried? How serious does Michael seem to be about his solution? Does he make a reasonable case for its feasibility? What factors might he be overlooking in making this proposal?

Reader's response. What do you find appealing in this essay? How would you describe the purpose of such a piece? How appropriate is humor in this paper? Can you imagine a more serious version of this paper?

9C CHOOSING A TOPIC

> **The Basic Assignment**
>
> In an essay, explore an aspect of human nature or culture that poses a problem of sorts. It may be a curious human foible or a serious societal dilemma that stimulates your thinking, but approach the subject with an open mind. Write about it with energy and spirit. If appropriate, make it a personal essay.

Variations

a. Identify some troubling problem in your world (school, town, club, work place, church) and try to find a solution. Explain the problem as clearly as possible, explain why current solutions haven't worked, identify new approaches, select the strategy you believe is most workable, and, finally, show why it is feasible. Be prepared to do some reading and research on this assignment. You may argue in support of a solution others have suggested before. Explain why you believe it offers the best hope for resolving the dilemma.

b. Explore an old saw or famous saying. Consider its meaning, its implications, its complications. Place it in a contemporary context. Does the saying make sense to you now or does it seem a pious substitute for original thinking? Be serious or playful or both. Here's a list of wise words from which you might choose your subject. Or check any dictionary of quotations. You'll find thousands of prompts.

- You don't need a weather man to tell which way the wind blows.

  —Bob Dylan

- Patriotism is the last refuge of a scoundrel.

  —Samuel Johnson

- There never was a good war or a bad peace.

  —Benjamin Franklin

- Nothing emboldens sin so much as mercy.

  —William Shakespeare

- Old people like to give good advice, as solace for no longer being able to provide bad examples.

  —La Rouchefoucald

- The only thing you find in the middle of the road are yellow stripes and dead armadillos.

  —Texas legislator

c. In a short essay, challenge some attitude or idea you have encountered lately that you don't like. What's leading people to think this way? What are the particular consequences of such thought? Be as descriptive and particular in your analysis as possible. Your tone may be serious or comic.

d. Spin an essay off common objects, activities, or phenomena: write about new-fangled watches, dog food ads, software manuals, election posters, videocamcorders, new age music, two-hundred-dollar jogging shoes—in short, any small thing that ticks you off and sets you thinking. For a model, you might listen to one of Andy Rooney's pieces on *60 Minutes.*

e. Identify a currently stable situation—personal or societal—and then explore what would happen if an element responsible for the stability were withdrawn. For example:

> —What happens if the cold war returns to Europe and the superpowers once again become adversaries?
>
> —What happens if inflation once again rises to double digits?
>
> —What happens if the Democrats lose control of the U.S. House of Representatives?
>
> —What happens if a major industry in your town shuts down?
>
> —What would you do if you were unable to attend college?

9 D

Explor

Direct this essay (even a personal one) to a wide and serious audience. Don't spend too much time narrating ("first I would . . . and then I would . . ."). Instead, consider the implications and ramifications of a rapid change in the status quo.

f. Sit down with a group of classmates in a comfortable location and talk about the world's problems. Let the conversation flow in any direction it takes, but keep it reasonably centered on serious public issues—matters that would concern people outside the immediate circle. Use that conversation as the springboard for a collaborative exploratory piece—a sort of "state of the world" paper representing the various points of view in the group.

9 D   PREPARING AND PLANNING AN EXPLORATORY PAPER

To write an exploratory paper, a writer needs imagination—the ability to see familiar things in new ways or new things in familiar ways. Too often, we regard this power as a force beyond rational control: a few people seem to command it naturally; the rest of us must be content to admire those who've got it. After all, creative writing is mainly for artists, right?

No, not at all. A little imagination can fuel almost every piece of writing—and we all wield the tools: words and ideas. If some forms of writing constrain us a bit, the exploratory essay certainly shouldn't. It invites a writer to slip the restraints of conventional thinking, to explore new relationships, to solve problems, even to create a few. Think of exploratory writing as imaginative nonfiction.

To write an effective exploratory paper . . .

➤ **Begin with a puzzle.** Throughout this text, we have described explanatory and exploratory processes of writing (see Section 2A). Obviously, the exploratory essay will evolve from an open-ended process of discovery. By definition it begins with a problem, a gap, an uncertainty. You might begin with an inner feeling that things aren't right in your world, or with hard evidence that a given situation—in school, at home, in the country—must change. But how? You don't have an answer initially, but you feel the need to think this issue through. That's an exploratory impulse.

Sometimes you'll just be amused by human nature—what we are, what we do, what we produce. How curious people seem sometimes. How odd. What can you say about that? Perhaps a child asks a simple but puzzling question—"Why do people cry?"—"What happens when people grow old?" You begin to wonder yourself. Sometimes a friend's chance remark makes you see everything in a new light. What prevented you from seeing things this way before? These are exploratory impulses, all of them.

➤ **Define the issue.** When the exploratory essay is actually about a problem, it's important to know what the problem is. Put the issue in words to understand where you are and what needs to be done. Indeed, you may find that the bulk of your essay will be about the problem—understanding and appreciating its complexities.

It may be tempting, sometimes, to portray a problem in terms simple enough to allow for an easy solution.

- Look at all these homeless people. Why doesn't the government just build them houses?

- We still have 5 percent unemployment. Let's stop illegal immigration and give the jobs they take to Americans!

- We've got too many drug users. We need to put them all in bootcamps busting rocks.

Solutions such as these are not so much wrong as inadequate—and they are so because a writer hasn't taken the time to wrestle with the problem, to understand the terms a good solution must meet.

When you finally have come to terms with those issues, you'll want to share them with readers. That's why exploratory pieces sometimes begin with rather direct statements about the nature of a problem. The following example of such an opening is from a draft by Ursalanett Clark.

> The issue at hand is the dwindling number of blacks who are
> seeking higher education. According to Black Enterprise
> (September, 1988), the percentage of black high school graduates
> entering college dropped from 35.5 percent in 1976 to 26.1 percent
> in 1985. What is preventing blacks from seeking higher education?

One of the main stumbling blocks for blacks may be money. A recent study by the United Negro College Fund (UNCF) and the National Institute of Independent Colleges and Universities in Washington, D.C., reveals that black students are growing more dependent on financial aid. Other reasons besides money that prevent blacks from going to college are their fears of racism, their decisions to join the military, or their involvement in drugs and crime. The enormous problem of blacks not seeking higher education must be dealt with immediately.

This opening spends little time discussing the problem of black enrollment in colleges since the initial statistics spell out its seriousness well enough. Instead, Ursalanett immediately begins suggesting a variety of contributing factors, each of them one piece in a complex puzzle.

9 D

Explor

➤ **Explore the problem.** Exploration requires imaginative thinking, some that you do on your own, some in conversation with others. Since exploration thrives on new ideas and perspectives, it is important to take risks and to ask "what if?" and "why not?" Two excellent techniques of invention for stimulating thinking are brainstorming and freewriting (Section 3A). Both get the mental juices flowing by lowering restraints on composing—you can write whatever comes to mind without worrying about grammar, organization, or style.

Exploration also needs the give-and-take only a second (and third and fourth . . .) voice can provide. The technical term for such an exploratory procedure is dialectic—an intellectual quest that deliberately poses one idea against its opposite to test and explore the nature of truth. If that sounds daunting, just think of dialectic in terms of the best late-night debate you've ever had, when ideas flew thick and fast between you and your friends, and the problems of the world seemed within your power to grasp and solve. That's the kind of stimulating discussion that you want to cultivate when you set about to write an essay.

If you can't find occasion to talk an issue out, you can enter another kind of intellectual conversation—that which occurs any time you read. Spend a few hours in the library.

➤ **Analyze current attitudes toward your subject.** Since exploratory papers can go off in any number of directions, it is difficult to describe a common approach: surprise is part of a fine essay. The last thing a reader wants is stale thinking.

Yet to avoid conventional thinking means that a writer must either describe or acknowledge the conventional view. In some cases, you'll need to explain in detail to readers what the current thinking on a subject is before you can show how your approach differs from the common wisdom. For example, an exploratory essay on education in the United States would need to portray how the writer views the current state of affairs—what's right and what's wrong (particularly the latter) about American schools before launching into new ideas and proposals.

Note that we emphasized *the writer's view* of the situation: authors and readers will often disagree about the nature of a problem or of the status quo. But agreement isn't necessary here—merely understanding. Indeed, quite often we are going to be most stimulated by writers we don't agree with. It's the dialectical principle again. But we need to know from the outset of a piece where the writer stands in relationship to current beliefs so we understand later the nature of his proposals or the focus of his critical energies.

In a rather light-hearted way, for example, Michael Contreras scolds the efforts of the University of Texas to solve its problem with grackles. The basic point underlying his criticism is that all of the administration's solutions have involved hostility to the birds—working against them. What makes his thinking new is the assumption that the university should work with the birds. Even Michael isn't sure his proposal will work, and, as readers, we may also have our doubts about his specific proposal. Yet, thanks to his essay, we understand both the nature of the old thinking he repudiates, and the basic principle that might stimulate innovative approaches.

9 D

Explor

➤ **Look at the subject in new and creative ways.** To do this, we'd suggest you just start writing. Putting words on paper doesn't *record* ideas; it *creates* them. As you start writing, you'll hear voices that have shaped your thinking: the opinions of authors you have read, the arguments of classmates you have talked to, the advice of teachers you have studied with, the prattle of slogans you have heard. All of these become part of your mental conversation, consciously or unconsciously, and help to shape the words you now choose to write down—language that represents yet another view on the subject, your view—at least for the time being.

Chances are you may not like what you have written the first time around. You may find yourself trapped in clichés that do not satisfy the exploratory impulse you began with. Well, write some more. Express your dissatisfaction on the page. Give *your* voice free rein—you can always come back and prune back any excesses.

Write dialectically. Force yourself to see an issue—whether serious or frivolous—from new perspectives.

Do you believe that we are spending too little on education? **Proposition:** we are spending too much on education.

Are you concerned that TV situation comedies are keeping children from reading? **Proposition:** sitcoms stimulate reading.

Are you worried that Americans can never resolve the abortion debate? **Proposition:** Americans don't need to settle the matter.

You don't have to accept any of these new ideas, but what harm can follow from pondering them for a paragraph or two?

➤ **Organize the essay as you see fit.** It's very difficult to suggest how an exploratory paper ought to be stitched together. The notion of voice is particularly important: if you develop a rapport with readers, your authorial voice can lead them through an essay, guiding them through difficult ideas confidently. A great many professional writers simply rely on this ability to chart a path for readers: they don't organize according to some pre-ordained pattern. They move readers from paragraph to paragraph by giving them a sense of direction and purpose:

> Let's look at this issue more closely because it's crucial to . . . .

> Now, if that really were the case, wouldn't it seem more logical to . . . .

> I can't agree, however, and find that . . . .

> . . . If only life were so simple. Unfortunately,

It takes confidence to guide readers through an essay that doesn't follow one of the patterns or sequences we've outlined in other chapters. But an exploratory essay just might have to avoid such patterns to embody the twists and turns of a complex idea. That's not to suggest that a writer is at liberty to confuse readers, but that some ideas just can't be handled by simple thesis/support or comparison/contrast patterns.

9 D

Explor

We can, however, outline a rough form for exploratory essays expressly intended to explore and perhaps solve problems. This pattern—one followed by Michael Contreras in his essay on grackles—is really just a sequence of considerations most authors have to address when facing any difficult situation. Each of the points below might be dealt with in one or more paragraphs.

The Problem
Current beliefs
Problem(s) caused by status quo
Crisis: need for solution

Alternatives (rejected)
Alternative 1 advantages/disadvantages
Alternative 2 advantages/disadvantages
Alternative 3 advantages/disadvantages

The Proposed Solution
Explanation of solution
Feasibility of solution
Disadvantages
Advantages
Implementation of solution

The first part of the pattern illustrates the need to describe a moment of crisis—an incident or common perception that explains why a writer is bringing an issue to public scrutiny. In Ursalanett Clark's essay on minority education, for example, a single sentence identifies the crisis that requires new and creative thinking.

> According to <u>Black Enterprise</u> (September, 1988), the percentage of
>
> black high school graduates entering college dropped from 35.5
>
> percent in 1976 to 26.1 percent in 1985.

We've got a problem and we've got to solve it—now.

9 D

Explor

The second part of the exploratory pattern steers the reader through various proposals for solving the problem, through what is in effect an inventory of possibilities. Since most of these ideas are going to be rejected (or perhaps furnish some part of the recommended solution), each one is studied carefully to expose both its advantages and limitations. What this section of the exploratory essay does is to assure readers that a writer has done his or her homework—that no plausible approach to the problem has been ignored.

The third part of this pattern proposes some solution. Any given essay may stress different facets of that solution, but clearly the first element is essential—an explanation of the solution. The writer needs to disclose what exactly should be done. To say something *should* be done is rarely enough; it's also important to explain that it *can* be done—that the solution proposed is feasible.

The writer may then want to discuss the advantages and disadvantages of a proposal. While exploratory essays often have persuasive aspects to them, a truly exploratory piece probably should be as frank about the weaknesses of an idea as its strengths. Readers need to feel that nothing is under wraps, that no "hidden agendas" guide the proposal. The paper can then conclude with a confident scheme for implementing change, for explaining how words become action.

➤ **Imagine an audience you'd want to talk to.** Not every exploratory essay is about a social problem. Sometimes the pieces address "human nature"—that endlessly puzzling phenomenon. Consider the way columnists like Erma Bombeck and Bob Greene ask us to consider our behavior in odd and intriguing ways. We laugh; we grimace; we groan. We do so because we feel comfortable enough to trust the writers; we enjoy seeing the world from their points of view.

To write like that, you've got to win the goodwill of audiences by projecting yourself into your writing. Consider how much you learn about the essayist Montaigne from this single famous line, as profound in its insight as it is simple and human:

> "When I play with my cat, who knows but that she regards me more as a plaything than I do her?"

It is a moment of confession, lively and conversational. Talk with your readers just as openly and honestly. Treat them as people you'd like to chat with. Be sure they understand how what concerns you also might concern them. And, don't be too formal. Include contractions, slang where appropriate, allusions to people, places, and things we all recognize. Let readers hear your voice.

9 E   DRAFTING AND REVISING AN EXPLORATORY PAPER

You can minimize the risks inherent in exploratory papers by drafting early, thereby giving yourself the time to probe a subject carefully and refine your ideas through several versions. But we want to be honest about this: you can sometimes produce a dazzling paper in the heat of the night. One draft. Gonzo writing. Tinkering with the piece too much may even ruin it. You see, the essay can be a devilish form: you work and work and produce only pencil tracks. Hours drift away and your time seems wasted. But your thoughts have been incubating, rising silently like a yeasted dough; you try one last time and suddenly, words start falling into place, ideas click, and the paper takes on a life of its own. You read your essay the next day and you can hardly believe you are so smart. Readers praise your directness and clarity, vigor and originality. You attribute the inspiration to caffeine.

9 E

Explor

To revise an essay . . .

➤ **Consult friends.** Exploratory pieces need attentive critics willing to speak their minds. Give your drafts to capable readers—those whose opinion you value and who might have a stake in the issue you are addressing. Be brave. Look for a reader who might not be sympathetic to your point of view. Ask him or her for a constructive reaction. What have you left out? What should you know? What have you misrepresented?

If you are lucky enough to have a group of writers to show your work to, observe whether your exploratory piece stimulates interest and talk. If it doesn't, ask your readers what you might do with the subject. (Trying a new topic is an option.) If the paper stirs up opinions, listen carefully to what's said and consider what you might convey from the conversation into the final version.

➤ **Don't feel trapped by your words.** When you've got some words on a page, it's tempting to stick with them. Resist that inclination unless you really are happy—not just content—with what you've created. In an exploratory piece, you'll sometimes have to trust your instincts. If something doesn't feel right to you, rework it until it does.

➤ **Check your explanation of the problem.** Exploratory papers that focus on problems often overestimate what readers know about a situation. Eager to get on with the essay, a writer begins discussing the "current economic situation" or the "dilemma of contemporary youth" without pausing to explain just what the economic situation or youth dilemma is. It may be necessary to run through the journalists' drill before heading deeper into a paper: who? what? where? when? how? why?

Remember to present the situation you are exploring as a *problem* if you see it that way. After all, your readers may not. Perhaps you intend to probe the dearth of talent among the current crop of rock musicians. That's fine, but will everyone appreciate what it is that's bothering you enough to write a paper on the subject? What's the problem if rock music *is* in a slump? Don't leave readers guessing.

➤ **Check the feasibility of any solutions you offer.** Good readers and editors usually won't let you get too far with an implausible solution. But don't count on them detecting your flaws. If your exploratory piece makes some suggestions, become your own toughest critic. If your solution will cost money, where will it come from? Have you taken the time to check? If your solution will ask people to change their behavior, have you provided sufficient motivation for such reform? If your solution won't be popular, how will you sell it to those who have to be influenced?

You need not resolve every practical issue in an exploratory paper—after all, the point of such an exercise is to give yourself room to think. But don't grow so open-minded that your brains fall out. Take responsibility for your proposals.

➤ **Check your conclusion.** Does it lead somewhere beyond the boundaries of the paper? It probably should. Consider the implications of your ideas and spell them out. Let readers see the importance of your thinking. Ursalanett Clark does this in the conclusion of her exploratory piece on African-American students in college.

> The black population in the United States is very large. If we can
>
> sustain the desire to learn and provide funds for black youth to
>
> receive a higher education, then our society as a whole will benefit.
>
> Who knows what great ideas are in the minds of these young
>
> people? They could very well be holding the key to a bigger and
>
> brighter future for the United States.

If your essay is more humorous and personal—let readers smile a bit at the end and reflect on human nature. Don't just drop them cold.

➤ **Edit carefully.** Edit only after you have a challenging draft (see Section 5C for a thorough checklist). Here are several points worth checking.

—If you use direct quotations or dialogue, handle them properly. See Section 34E.

—Work on the title. It should capture the spirit of your piece. The title of a humorous essay might parody the name of another piece. A serious essay can be more direct: Francis Bacon titled his great essays very simply "Of Studies," "Of Truth," "Of Marriage and Single Life."

10 Writing a Review or Evaluation

A Understanding evaluation
B Examining a sample paper
C Choosing a topic
D Preparing and planning
E Drafting and revising

Terms you need to know

CRITERIA. The standards according to which something is measured or judged. Some standards are concrete and measurable (weight, height, color, volume, accuracy); others are more abstract and subjective (persuasiveness, liveliness, beauty, honesty).

10 A UNDERSTANDING EVALUATION

Almost every day, you make snap judgments about dozens of things—movies, food, music, athletes, politicians, automobiles. In fact, you yourself may be the object of some on-the-spot evaluations: an acquaintance might comment snidely on your taste in clothes, or a captain choosing teams for a basketball game might eagerly pick you first. Such informal evaluations are not that far removed from the more conscious judgments you are expected to make in school or on the job. But, in these more formal situations, evaluations usually need to be supported with convincing evidence. Moreover, you often must commit such opinions to paper—a big difference because you obviously become more accountable when an opinion goes "on the record."

Occasions that call for judgments and evaluations are numerous. You may be asked to assess a person's work or achievements; to judge the quality of a performance, a product, or an idea; to compare persons, objects, performances, or ideas in order to make preferential judgments.

Some types of evaluation are relatively straightforward and conventional; they result from **explanatory** processes in which judgments are made according to well-established criteria. Deciding whether a particular major league baseball player belongs in the Hall of Fame, for example, is a matter of judging an individual's record against standards already set by generations of athletes. Other evaluative projects may be more **exploratory**—requiring the development of new

> **Some evaluations**
>
> | | |
> |---|---|
> | Restaurant reviews | Software reviews |
> | Movie reviews | Oscars |
> | Report cards | Nobel Prizes |
> | Job evaluations | Beauty contests |
> | Baking contests | Stock reports |
> | Personnel files | Letters of recommendation |
> | Elections | Environmental impact statements |

10 A

Eval

criteria of evaluation or refinements on traditional ways of valuing things. Consider how the process of evaluation changed in the art world at the turn of this century as painters moved from creating works that were realistic to those that were abstract. That movement required significant shifts in the criteria of evaluation used by critics (and the public) in looking at paintings and other works of art. At various points, both artists and critics had to take considerable risks in arguing for new standards of judgment.

What makes an evaluation or review effective, convincing, and fair? First, a writer needs to settle on criteria of evaluation suited to what is being examined. Once criteria of evaluation are in place, a writer looks to see exactly how well what is being evaluated measures up to the accepted criteria, weighing evidence that confirms the case. So a review has three basic parts: the criteria of evaluation, the evaluation itself, and the evidence.

Criteria of evaluation, as we have already suggested, are simply measures of quality—the standards we apply to decide how good something is. Criteria can be very simple or quite complex: a good photograph is "sharp"; a fine steak is "marbled"; a successful movie "represents the beliefs and styles of its time." Criteria of evaluation, however, are not always stated outright in an article, especially when reviewers can safely assume that most readers will agree with the standards being applied, for example, to a play, a book, a movie, a ballet, an athletic performance, a restaurant, and so on.

Criteria are more likely to be discussed and defended when readers either disagree with the standards ("You call that piece of trash *art!*") or don't know what they are ("Coefficient of drag? What does that have to do with a sports car?"). In such exploratory situations, a writer may need to explain the criteria in detail—a practice common in consumer magazines which rate various products. Or the reviewer might spend some time defending his or her standards, proving they are the best ones to apply even when they aren't terribly controversial.

To some degree, criteria are arbitrary. They are certainly influenced by historical circumstances; time and audience, for example, determine whether a particular fashion is deemed "attractive" or a government program "effective" (otherwise bustles and prohibition might still be in vogue). Nonetheless, in most situations, criteria can be found that are stable enough for reasonable people to agree upon—or at least to agree to disagree about.

Any time you go to a department store, for example, you are guided by dozens of subtle criteria, many of them dependent on still other variables—*price,* for example. For years, Sears has sold some items according to a "good, better, best" scale to help consumers identify the type of item most suited to their pocketbooks and *needs* (yet another factor in establishing criteria). Their "best" power drill might be just right for a carpenter or laborer, but too laden with features for the weekend tinkerer. For each shopper, the criteria of evaluation might be slightly different, though—in an absolute sense—one drill might be undeniably "the best," superior in materials, design, and versatility.

Places to find evaluations

In business and lifestyle sections of newspapers
In scholarly journals
In grocery stores
At county fairs
In auto showrooms
At political conventions
The American Spectator
Car and Driver
Chronicles
Consumer Reports
MACWORLD: The Macintosh Magazine
The New Yorker
New York Review of Books
Popular Photography
Prevention
The Times Literary Supplement
TV Guide
Video Magazine
The Wall Street Journal (stock market page)
Woman's Sport and Fitness

---

10 A

Eval

Standards of evaluation are sometimes created in the process of evaluation. Consider how ad agencies, through words and images, create a portrait of the ideal candidate—what a judge, governor, senator, or president ought to be like. To fit the "mold," a candidate is made to *seem* strong, decisive, patriotic, sensitive, warm, down-to-earth, honest, good-natured, intelligent, serious—all at the same time; one of George Bush's most successful ads during the 1988 presidential campaign rattled off his credentials while showing him surrounded by his grandchildren. Of course, political campaigns and advertising agencies don't operate in a vacuum. They watch how people respond; they study what voters seem to prefer in their candidates and in the candidates' ideas. Knowing that when we vote for a person, we've made some kind of judgment based upon criteria, campaign strategists make it a point to study our electoral decisions in order to predict and eventually shape how we'll behave in the voter's booth. Our preferences become the criteria of evaluation for future candidates.

Despite the importance of establishing criteria, the focal point of any review is the evaluation itself. Just as criteria vary in complexity, so do statements of evaluation. In explanatory evaluations, objects may simply be ranked, classified, graded, judged, or labeled (good/bad, effective/ineffective, sensitive/insensitive). This is the type of evaluation in place when a hotel is described as "four-star," a slab of beef as "prime," a movie as "two thumbs up."

Exploratory evaluations are usually more complex; their judgments may not be reducible to a simple ranking, a number of stars, or a single sentence. Evaluating a major book, a government policy, or a presidency, for example—or even a fine wine—may require many qualifications and whole series of separate, interrelated decisions. Such evaluations will usually depend upon observations which are obviously subjective or tentative. In many cases, exploratory judgments will be difficult and controversial.

Here are just a few of the many reasons for writing a review or evaluation:

- to praise or blame someone or something;
- to assess your own strengths or weaknesses;
- to explain why something has or has not worked well;
- to advise others in a purchase, course of action, or political choice;
- to seek a way of improving something by understanding both its strengths and weaknesses;
- to assess the competition.

10 B

Eval

10 B   EXAMINING A SAMPLE PAPER

Here is an essay by Luis Garcia, written when he was a freshman at the University of Texas at Austin. It shows how he handles an evaluative assignment. We've modified the essay slightly to update some of the references and rearranged one of the paragraphs, but most of the paper is exactly as Luis wrote it during a summer session freshman English class. Although Luis uses sources, he was not required to provide a *Works Cited* sheet for this essay—though one might have been helpful.

Papers by Luis Garcia also appear in the next two chapters—on proving a thesis and persuasion. We've included three essays by one student to enable you to see how Mr. Garcia approaches several different assignments. You'll find that each paper is distinctive, yet marked by characteristic habits of thought and style. See what similarities you can detect between Luis's essay in this chapter and those in sections 11B and 12B.

AUTHOR: Luis Garcia.

AUDIENCE: General educated audience: readers of periodicals like *Time* and *US News.*

ASSIGNMENT: Evaluate something you know well or can write about authoritatively.

REQUIREMENTS: Length: not specified.

No Competition

(1)   If Henry Ford could see the trouble the American auto industry is in now,

he probably would have never invented the assembly line. Foreign auto makers have left American companies in the dust. For years now, the Japanese car makers have been gaining sales in all segments of the market, at the expense of the Big Three U.S. car makers (General Motors, Ford, and Chrysler). According to the May 25, 1989, issue of The Wall Street Journal, the Big Three's overall U.S. car sales have dropped 10 percent in the first four months of 1989, while Japanese car companies have increased their sales in the U.S. by 6 percent. The reason is that domestic cars are falling short in comparison to Japanese-made cars. Many Americans opt to buy Japanese over domestic automobiles on the basis of better price, higher quality, and more service after the sale.

(2)   Certainly, one of the more important criteria for selecting a car to any potential buyer is the price. Although Japanese car companies face import tariffs and must compete against a weak dollar (which raises the price of foreign goods), they have been able to keep their products affordable by producing popular vehicles in the United States--notably the Honda Accord, which seems likely to displace the Ford Escort as the best-selling car sold in America. Shopping at any of the Japanese dealerships like Nissan, Honda, or Toyota, a person can find a wide selection of new automobiles well under the $14,000 price that Time cites as the average price of a U.S.-made car (July 31, 1989). Yet, ironically, Americans often prefer to spend more money on a Japanese-made car than on a cheaper American-made counterpart because of quality.

10 B

Eval

(3)   Americans have found that Japanese car companies do not sacrifice quality at the expense of the customer. According to the Consumer Reports 1989 Buying Guide Issue, Japanese cars on the whole are superior to American- and German-made cars in customer satisfaction based on repair and maintenance records. Buyers find that their Japanese-designed vehicles are delivered in near-perfect condition, with all body panels neatly aligned, all trim carefully screwed down, and all mechanical components functioning exactly as they should. In an interview in the October 17, 1989, issue of Business Week magazine, Nissan purchasing vice-president Robert Drake explains that "in most cases . . . the Japanese quality is better [than that of American cars]. But a lot of American companies don't feel that it's necessary to have every part in here [the car] that's good. If they've got a certain reject rate they think it's O.K." In order to make customers aware of their excellence, Japanese car makers have used effective advertising campaigns like Lexus's emphasis on perfection and Infiniti's sophisticated discussions of quality, harmony, and nature to build potential customers' confidence

in their cars. In contrast, American manufacturers must attract buyers through rebates and giveaways. As a result, more Americans are purchasing Japanese automobiles. Furthermore, because Japan leads in engine and transmission technology as well as building fuel-efficient cars, Americans know that they are getting more than they pay for when they buy Japanese-made cars.

(4)   If a buyer is not impressed by the price or quality of a Japanese car, then he or she will be impressed by the Japanese companies' continuous service after the sale. Unlike many of the American companies' "buyer beware" policy, the Japanese know that the secret to customer loyalty is providing efficient and adequate service after the sale. In an interview with the December 19, 1989, issue of <u>U.S. News and World Report</u> magazine, Tom Gauer, who compiles the J. D. Power customer satisfaction index, agrees that "As auto companies are beginning to reach parity in manufacturing quality, the battleground is shifting to quality of service." In addition to building cars that require far less maintenance and have fewer mechanical problems, Japanese companies insure better service on customer's cars by giving bonuses to those mechanics who do the best job. Coupled with future plans for 24-hour road service and free car rentals and hotel rooms if needed, the Japanese hope to ensure the loyalty of their customers.

(5)   Japanese cars, with their appealing designs, are not only satisfactory to the wallet but also to the senses. The Japanese companies' success in every aspect of the automotive market from mass-market vehicles to their new line of luxury sedans is due to the cars' surprisingly affordable prices as well as their quality and dependability compared to their domestic counterparts. Although most Americans would like to spend their money on domestic cars, they are not willing to support the U.S. automotive industry at their own expense. Buying American is no longer buying smart.

➤ Analysis of Luis Garcia's "No Competition"

Purpose. What different groups of readers might be interested in Luis' analysis and why? Do you think that Garcia's process of writing is chiefly explanatory or exploratory? Why do you think so?

Criteria. What specific criteria of evaluation does Garcia use in comparing Japanese cars to domestic cars? Are any other criteria of evaluation stated indirectly or implied? If you were to challenge any of Garcia's criteria for judging these vehicles, which would it be? Do you think any of the criteria Garcia uses needs to be explained more clearly? What other criteria might he have used to explain his belief that Japanese cars are better choices than American-designed products?

Judgment. Does this evaluation have a specific thesis sentence that expresses its author's point of view in the comparison? Does Garcia's judgment seem neutral and objective, or do his personal feelings intrude? Does Luis Garcia give any indication of special expertise in the field—what, if anything, qualifies him to judge automobiles? Should Garcia qualify his strong endorsement of Japanese cars? Why, or why not?

Evidence. What specific evidence does Garcia use to suggest that Japanese cars are built to higher standards than American-designed vehicles? Is that evidence convincing? Is there any point in the essay where you would like more evidence to support a point? What evidence used in the paper seems the strongest to you? The weakest?

Organization. Do you find the organization of this review clear? Why or why not? Does the writer connect ideas in a helpful way? Do you find the three-point organization of the paper too predictable? Can you suggest an alternative plan for the essay?

10 C

Eval

Reader's Response. Did reading "No Competition" affect your opinion of Japanese and American cars? As precisely as you can, explain why or why not. What evidence did you most respond to? What comment would you have made on a draft of this paper to improve the evaluation? How would you characterize the impression you have of Luis Garcia after reading this paper? Do you tend to trust his judgment or question it? Why or why not?

10 C   CHOOSING A TOPIC FOR AN EVALUATION PAPER

> **The Basic Assignment**
>
> **Evaluate some person, place, or thing you know well enough to judge both fairly and convincingly. Make sure it is an object about which both you and your readers might have a strong opinion—and over which you might disagree. Express a clear judgment and argue your case fully, with criteria and evidence provided as needed.**

➤ **Variations**

a. Reread a book (fiction or nonfiction; prose or poetry) you once were compelled to study in school and clearly remember *disliking*. After rereading the work, write an honest evaluation of it now that some time has passed and you are reading it from a different perspective.

b. If there is a notably unpopular building, work of art, or other controversial object in your immediate neighborhood, evaluate it as if you were writing for a professional journal of architecture, art, or whatever discipline fits the object you are assessing. Try to explain why the building or artwork is unpopular with the public. Make and explain your own independent judgment of the piece.

c. Evaluate a classic movie that you believe is overrated. Explain both its enduring popularity as well as your reasons for believing the film is less good than critics or general viewers believe it is.

d. Evaluate a movie or television series you believe is underrated. Explain what makes the production better viewing than most people think it is.

e. Working in a group, agree upon a movie or television program to review, and then spend some time exploring possible criteria for evaluating the work. Try to view it together. Then, working independently, freewrite about the show to expose and clarify your initial feelings about it. Then share and discuss your preliminary opinions with other members of the group. Try to come to a consensus about the film or TV program that can be expressed in a single group essay. You may find it difficult to accommodate all points of view in one paper, but don't allow the review to become just a list of opinions. If you find strong differences in the group, take time to discuss the reasons behind those disagreements and see if compromise is possible. If no consensus results, write more than one review.

10 C

Eval

f. Compare an original film and a remake (*King Kong*), a book and the film made from it (*The Hunt for Red October*), a film turned into a television series (*M*A*S*H*), or any two works whose stories come from the same source (*Romeo and Juliet* and *West Side Story*). Decide which of the two works you regard as the more successful and give the reasons for your judgment. Be quite specific in comparing the works. If necessary, do some background reading.

g. Working in a group, nominate a man or woman for the Presidency of the United States (or some other elected position). Explain why this person is especially well-suited for the job. This paper will be more interesting and challenging if you write in support of a public figure who is not routinely considered a presidential hopeful. But be sure the candidate your group nominates is someone of impressive stature with a record you can research (if necessary)—someone you genuinely believe would serve the nation well as its chief executive. In the course of your evaluation, be sure to define the criteria by which we should measure a President of the United States. Don't limit your potential candidates to politicians. Consider the possibility that good candidates may have distinguished themselves in other fields and endeavors—business, labor, sports, academics, the arts.

h. Write a paper in which you nominate someone as best-in-field: best tennis player in the world, best photojournalist, best chef, best quarterback. Pick a subject you know well enough to write about with some authority. Assume that your readers are not experts in the field—so it will be necessary for you to explain what your criteria of judgment are. Furnish plenty of detailed evidence to prove that the person you nominate is the best. Feel free to compare your candidate with other potential nominees.

i. Working in a group, have a little fun nominating someone or something as worst-in-field: worst science fiction movie; worst television series, worst actor, ugliest building in America, worst advertising campaign. Be careful to take time to agree on criteria of evaluation and give plenty of evidence to prove that whomever or whatever your group has selected really deserves the label of "worst."

j. If you own a car, camera, boat, VCR, stereo, or some other type of item routinely reviewed in enthusiasts' periodicals (*Motor Trend, Popular Photography,* and so on), read several such periodicals, observing how they create or explain criteria of evaluation and arrive at their judgments. Then review the product you own, modeling your evaluation after the professional ones. (The item you evaluate need not be brand new, but be sure to adjust your criteria to take into account its age and condition.) Write your review for the same audience that might read one of these magazines.

k. Very seriously and carefully, evaluate the person you consider to have been your most effective teacher, showing how that instructor helped you or others of a class to learn. In the course of this piece, think about the aims of education and the means by which learning can be enhanced.

l. Consider some particular social or political dilemma and evaluate one approach being taken to resolve it. You might examine a foreign policy decision (the United States' decision to restrict trade to country *X*), a social policy decision (providing condoms to high school students), or an ethical problem (stopping government support for pornographic works of "art"). Whatever you decide to do, be sure to *evaluate* an existing policy; don't just describe the situation or feel obligated to offer an alternative solution. What criteria would a good solution to the problem have to meet? How well does the existing approach meet those criteria?

10 D

Eval

10 D   PREPARING AND PLANNING A REVIEW OR EVALUATION

Evaluations go off track when writers presume that readers will agree with them. That's easy to do when a reviewer is dogmatic about a judgment or omits the specific evidence needed to support an opinion. The resulting review is awash with unsubstantiated claims and general terms like *good, awful, really fine, fantastic.* Just as bad are reviews that never get to the point; readers suspect the reviewer is making a judgment but darned if they can tell what it is. Both dogmatic and indecisive evaluations leave readers uninformed and uninterested.

To write an effective review . . .

➤ **Decide precisely what you are going to evaluate.** When the choice of topic is yours, begin with an object or area you know something about. If you know tennis, evaluate tennis players, rackets, tournaments, or clubs. If you are a good cook, check out restaurants, cooking utensils, food markets, or frozen cuisine. If you read voraciously, evaluate a novel or an author. Everyone is an expert on some subject. Learn to appreciate that expertise.

➤ **List general criteria that might be used in evaluating your subject.** At this stage, list all the criteria you can think of. If you were evaluating a play, for example, your list might include:

props	blocking	pace of action	interpretation of play
acting	lighting	starting on time	projection of voices
scenery	costumes	use of music	seating arrangement

If you were evaluating an automobile, your criteria might be:

handling	styling
acceleration	braking
fuel mileage	interior design
quality of construction	"feel"
reliability	price

➤ **Decide which general criteria apply specifically to your subject.** Which might be most useful in guiding you toward a judgment? If you already have a strong opinion about your subject, which of these criteria do you think you'll have to explain most comprehensively to your readers? Consider that your readers may know a good deal less about your subject than you do. Praising the *blocking* in a theatrical production won't get you anywhere if readers don't appreciate the technical meaning of the term and what exactly good blocking achieves on stage. Suggesting that a luxury car has a good interior design may mean to you a carefully engineered relationship between a vehicle's controls and its driver; to the average reader, it might be nothing more than comfortable seats.

10 D

Eval

➤ **Examine the criteria applicable to your subject more critically.** For each general criterion, define specific standards which you think your readers will accept or which you are willing to defend. Discard any criteria that don't provide reasonable grounds for assessment.

> **Criteria for acting in a play:**
>
> **good acting seems natural**
> **good acting is subtle**
> **good acting makes an audience forget the actor**
> **good acting interprets a character in a unique way**

> **Criteria for scenery in a play:**
>
> **effective scenery doesn't intrude on the action**
> **effective scenery highlights the action**
> **effective scenery creates an appropriate mood**
> **effective scenery looks realistic**

> **Criteria for quality of construction in a car:**
>
> **materials are rugged and handsome**
> **body seams are narrow and even**
> **surfaces are "finished": no bare metal or rough edges**
> **all components fit flush and are free of rattles**

➤ **Examine your subject in terms of the specific criteria you have listed.** For each criterion, list specific evidence that shows how your subject either meets or fails to reach that standard. Look for as much evidence as you can, and be specific.

Criterion: Good scenery doesn't intrude upon the action of a play.

Evaluation: The scenery in *Macbeth* kept getting in the way.

Evidence:

—Awkward platforms put Macbeth and his wife at different levels at crucial moments.
—Several actors almost collided with fake pillars.
—The scenes with the witches were too dark to see what the actors were doing.
—Part of scenery collapsed during the banquet scene.

10 D

Eval

Criterion: A fine sports/utility vehicle must have versatile four-wheel-drive capability.

Evaluation: The Jeep Cherokee offers a well-proven four-wheel-drive system.

Evidence:

—Driver can select part-time or full-time four-wheel-drive.
—Driver can shift into and out of four-wheel-drive while in motion.
—System uses a rugged solid front axle.
—System is compatible with anti-lock brakes.

➤ **After assembling the evidence, make a firm judgment about your subject** or decide whether your initial opinion is supported by the facts you have assembled.

The English Department's recent production of *Macbeth* is a failure.

The Jeep Cherokee is a practical vehicle for many drivers.

Then write a preliminary thesis statement that expresses your opinion in specific detail.

The English Department's recent production of *Macbeth* is a failure because of awkward staging, weak performances, and faulty conception.

Though capable of handling rugged off-road terrain, the four-wheel-drive Jeep Cherokee is also civilized enough for comfortable, day-to-day driving.

➤ **Consider possible objections to your opinion.** Few evaluations are totally one-sided. What contradictory arguments must you anticipate in your review? If necessary, refine your thesis.

The English Department's current production of *Macbeth* manages to avoid many clichés, but fails because of awkward staging, weak performances, and a basic misconception about the tragedy.

Although it lacks the sophistication of some European and Japanese all-wheel-drive sedans, the four-wheel-drive Jeep Cherokee wagon is civilized enough for comfortable, day-to-day driving and probably more rugged than its competitors.

➤ **Organize the paper carefully.** Prepare a scratch outline that explores and develops the judgment you have made. Be sure to find a place in your paper to acknowledge and deal with alternative points of view and opinions. In most cases, you will be more persuasive if you deal with potential opposition first and then present your own arguments. Put your strongest evidence where your readers will remember it best—near the end of the paper.

10 D

Eval

1. Describe what Shakespeare's *Macbeth* is about.
2. Admit that the play is so familiar that an original production is difficult to create.
3. Evaluate the staging.
4. Evaluate the acting.
5. Evaluate the basic conception of the production as a musical.
6. Conclude.

1. Explain the difference between all-wheel drive and four-wheel drive. Explain the market for such vehicles and the competitors in the field.
2. Admit that the Jeep Cherokee is not as mechanically refined as some competitors.
3. Argue that it is suitably refined and perhaps more rugged.
3. Evaluate the interior accommodations of the Cherokee.
4. Evaluate the ride and handling.
4. Evaluate the off-road capabilities.
5. Evaluate the ruggedness of the drivetrain.
6. Conclude.

The various components of an evaluative paper might follow one of the two designs shown on the next page. In the first, the criteria are discussed or defended separately before they are applied to the particular object of the paper; in the second pattern of organization, the criteria of evaluation are examined in the same part of the paper where they are applied. In this second design, the criteria might be discussed only briefly—in a sentence or phrase, as in Luis Garcia's paper above.

Whichever design is followed, it makes sense to build toward the strongest point. If you want readers to agree with your evaluation, be sure that the last argument you present is free of strong counterarguments and is supported by ample evidence. If, however, the judgment you come to is not a simple or unqualified one (and that's a legitimate outcome of an evaluative paper), let your conclusion reflect that complexity of the situation.

➤ **Define your evaluative terms as precisely as possible.** If necessary, describe what your expectations are in short sentences or a paragraph. Don't, for example, simply say that the movie should have "good action." Explain to your readers how they might recognize good action when they see it: what are its trademarks and characteristics?

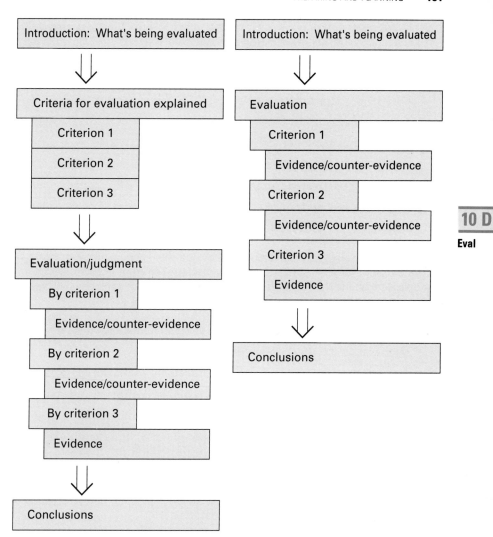

In the following paragraph from a review of Stephen King's novel *Misery,* the writer is fairly specific about her evaluative terms. For instance, she requires a novel to have a complex and challenging plot. So she complains when the storyline of *Misery* becomes predictable.

> Misery begins with an intriguing string of events, including graphic scenes such as Wilkes' dismemberment of her terrified prisoner with a rusting ax; the reader anticipates an exciting story loaded with exciting incidents. Unfortunately, Misery develops into an exaggerated "slasher movie" cliché, and the plot blunders unsuspensefully toward a disappointing climax.

In the essay reprinted earlier in this chapter, Luis Garcia is also quite specific about key terms. After citing a source that suggests that Japanese cars are generally of higher quality than domestic or European brands, he lists some specific elements that define quality from the point of view of buyers.

> According to the <u>Consumer Reports 1989 Buying Guide Issue,</u>
>
> Japanese cars on the whole are superior to American- and German-
>
> made cars in customer satisfaction based on repair and
>
> maintenance records. Buyers find that their Japanese-designed
>
> vehicles are delivered in near-perfect condition, with all body panels
>
> neatly aligned, all trim carefully screwed down, and all mechanical
>
> components functioning exactly as they should.

10 D

Eval

➤ **Use graphic examples.** Whatever you are evaluating—person, place, or thing—help the readers to see or understand it by placing it in front of them. Don't, for example, talk about the "comfortable" seats in a sports car; explain what type of seats they are and what exactly makes them appropriate for driving.

> The driving position is highlighted by firmly bolstered Recarro-
>
> style seats with adjustments in every direction, including the
>
> under-thigh and lumbar positions. Soft enough to make day-to-day
>
> cruising a pleasure, they also provide plenty of support in more
>
> spirited driving. The fabric grips tightly and the cushions don't go
>
> mushy in a turn; the belted driver stays put through the tightest
>
> curves.

An evaluation this detailed enables readers to see that you aren't making a snap judgment, but have thought hard about the subject. Your opinion is based on a careful assessment of many factors.

Why be general . . .	*When you could be specific?*
fine taste	smooth, buttery taste, like caramel
such a nice color	bluer than a summer afternoon
good photography	images alive with humor and originality
powerful motor	a torquey, 5-liter overhead cam V-8

➤ **Use comparison and contrast.** Sometimes the best way of explaining why something is good or bad is by showing it in relationship to its competitors. Be sure when you do a comparison or contrast that you compare comparable items—whether people, politicians, or consumer products. And be sure readers know what it is you are comparing.

Here's a rather elaborate example of a comparison from *Car and Driver* that shows how evaluating a single seemingly minor item can provide insight into the qualities of various automobiles. The passage is from an article trying to name the best luxury sedan of 1990.

Miës van der Rohe opined that God is in the details. With that in mind, we started looking beneath the surface of these cars, at details that normally escape notice. The editorial gaze finally settled on the trunk hinges. Every car has two of them, plus wiring that must jump from the body to the lid for various electrical devices.

On the Cadillac and the Jaguar, the hinges are straightforward metal stampings, painted body color, with the wiring routed alongside the arm. Just the basics, in other words.

On the Audi and the Mercedes, the hinge arms are made of tubing and the wire is routed within one of them. Still basic, but very tidy.

On the BMW and the Infiniti, the hinge arms are clad with black molded plastic that hides the wire. Extra effort expended there.

On the Lexus, the arms are beautifully formed stampings arranged so that the sheared edges of the metal are hidden, leaving only smooth radii for the eye to behold. Into the left-side arm is formed a deep groove running its full length. The wiring is routed inside the groove, and it is concealed by a black rubber welt. All you see are two elegant hinges, one showing an orderly, black seam. A sublime execution.

There are countless details in a luxury sedan. Lexus, particularly, seems to have lavished attention on every one of them.

Not surprisingly, the car with the most refined trunk hinges also ranked number one in the magazine's overall ratings.

Luis Garcia designs his entire evaluation as a comparison between Japanese and domestic vehicles. Each paragraph develops a new aspect of the comparison and some key sentences use contrast as a part of their structure:

> **Unlike many of the American companies' "buyer beware"**
>
> **policy,** the Japanese know that the secret to customer loyalty is
>
> providing efficient and adequate service after the sale.

> **Although most Americans would like to spend their money on**
>
> **domestic cars,** they are not willing to support the U.S. automotive
>
> industry at their own expense.

➤ **When appropriate, use tables, charts, and graphs.** When reviewing objects or products, you'll often need to gather data, make measurements, and do comparisons. Information of this kind is usually conveyed most efficiently to readers through visuals: pie charts, bar graphs, tables. Use them whenever you can, but consult a technical writing handbook (or a software manual) to learn how to construct them properly.

➤ **Look for models of the kind of review you are writing.** Despite adhering to a basic formula (criteria / evaluation / evidence), reviews take many forms. Art, movie, television, and music journals routinely include reviews. Newspapers typically cover the local restaurant scene, evaluate sports teams, and even assess politicians. Various consumer magazines evaluate all sorts of products. Notice

10 D

Eval

that Luis Garcia uses information from several consumer and business-oriented sources to add credibility to his evaluation: *Consumer Reports, Business Week, The Wall Street Journal.*

Whenever you are assigned to write a review, look for examples of comparable work in magazines, journals, newspapers, and pamphlets. Study these models to understand how other writers use criteria and evidence to arrive at judgments, but don't feel obligated to mimic any particular pattern.

➤ **Be tactful, yet honest.** Readers are counting on you to be forthright in your review. You will quickly lose your credibility and authority as a writer if you are either vicious on the one hand, or uncritical on the other. Reviewers needn't worry so much about being right or wrong as about making a strong case for whatever they've come to believe. It's more important that readers respect your opinion than agree with it.

So temper any tendencies to allow criticism to slide into abuse. In this paragraph from a review of an amateur production of *Macbeth,* the reviewer's critique of a nonprofessional actor steps beyond the bounds of good taste. The reviewer is enjoying himself too much, substituting attack for criticism:

> Nothing in the show could compensate for the sheer ineptness of Macbeth as played by Professor Sweno—the biggest ham since Hormel. Every word he spoke was accompanied by a gesture, every gesture by a twitch, every twitch by a leap, left or right, as if he were stomping roaches on the stage floor. In fact, Professor Sweno seems to have been counting syllables, delivering Shakespeare's iambic pentameter with a maddening regularity that defied both sound and sense. Instead of an ambitious thane, we got a mincing fool.

It *is* possible to be honest without being so cruel.

Compare this harsh evaluation with the cool, rational tone of Luis Garcia's concluding paragraph. He conveys a sense of regret that American cars aren't as good as they might be, at the same time explaining why many Americans are inclined to buy Japanese.

> (5)   Japanese cars, with their appealing designs, are not only satisfactory to the wallet but also to the senses. The Japanese companies' success in every aspect of the automotive market from mass-market vehicles to their new line of luxury sedans is due to the cars' surprisingly affordable prices as well as their quality and dependability compared to their domestic counterparts. Although most Americans would like to spend their money on domestic cars, they are not willing to support the U.S. automotive industry at their own expense. Buying American is no longer buying smart.

➤ **Convince readers that your evaluation is worth believing.** It is often said that everyone is entitled to an opinion, but judgments supported by facts and good reasons are more respected and powerful than naked opinions. In college especially, it makes sense to augment your personal evaluations with the authority of secondary sources—Luis Garcia, for example, builds his short paper from five different periodicals. If knowledgeable people or groups agree with your opinion of a book, political figure, or idea, incorporate their perspectives into your paper.

10 E   DRAFTING AND REVISING A REVIEW OR EVALUATION

Once they get rolling, many writers find evaluations less difficult to write than other kinds of papers. If you've picked a subject you feel strongly about and have the expertise to support your opinion, the ideas and arguments will come. Just imagine that someone has asked: "What do you think about . . . ?" Take it from there.

10 E

Eval

A great help in drafting an evaluation is a scratch outline touching on the major points in your projected paper. Also helpful are any materials you've gathered to buttress your judgment: lists of features; various facts and figures; relevant comparisons; quotations from experts. Not only can such materials be written into the paper at the appropriate points, but they'll help you see your subject from various angles.

In reviewing the draft of an evaluation or review . . .

➤ **Consider the other side of the argument.** After you have written the evaluation, put yourself in the shoes of someone who would disagree with it. Ask yourself how a director who you criticized might respond to your remarks, how a product engineer might explain a design flaw you slighted. Don't change your evaluation just to salve the feelings of those who might object to your opinion. But consider where in the paper some qualification of your judgment might make you look more reasonable, judicious, and fair. You may actually strengthen your paper by conceding one point or another. Here, for example, the reviewer of a production of *Macbeth* acknowledges that directing the play involves special difficulties. Although the remainder of the review will be highly critical of the production, the evaluation opens with a token of sympathy.

> . . . the very familiarity of *Macbeth* poses a problem for any contemporary director: what do you do to make a production new or different? One doesn't dare alter the special effects written into the play—including daggers that hover and woods that move. And when every child in the audience not only knows who murders whom, but can recite some of the best lines from memory ("Murder most foul!"; "Out, damned spot!"), a director is admittedly somewhat hamstrung.

> So Professor Bellona's current staging of *Macbeth* at least represents a brave attempt to produce a new version of the tragedy. . . .

➤ **Check your introduction.** Be sure the introduction provides some rationale for performing the evaluation. Why is it important for readers to understand that *Gone With the Wind* is a film worth seeing; that Jim Brown was a better fullback than Walter Payton; that your physics instructor is one of the most talented teachers you have ever met? Such an explanation need not be elaborate, but it is a necessary element of your paper. In many cases, your rationale will be keyed to a particular readership: "Anyone thinking about buying a _____ soon had better be aware of . . . ."; "Citizens voting this November should be willing to consider . . . ."

➤ **Check your evidence.** When you have a strong opinion about a subject, your confidence can blind you to the need to present enough evidence to convince skeptical readers. In the following passage, notice that the reviewer not only expresses an opinion about a production of *Macbeth,* but describes the show so readers "see" what the problems are.

10 E

Eval

> Professor Bellona moves the action of *Macbeth* out of darkened castles and blasted heaths and sets it in a Euro-style executive suite. Her characters, too, fit this new locale. Macbeth is now an ambitious corporate executive, sleek and polished, who has won his steely reputation by vanquishing enemies in the boardroom. Lady Macbeth is cold and ruthless too, more like one of the background singers in a Robert Palmer video than the mad Valkyrie of the typical production. Predictably, old king Duncan is the tottering founder of a giant industrial firm, thinking about passing on the reins of power to a younger generation.
>
> Unfortunately, this concept doesn't serve Shakespeare's noble tragedy well. The problems are most evident in the little things, those details of staging and stagecraft that establish the credibility of a performance. They all look and feel wrong in this jazzy, MTV nightmare. The famous "bleeding sergeant" of the first act clutches a briefcase while piteously delivering his account of a fierce battle. (Was he wounded, one wonders, by a flying fax machine?) Banquo does not die at the hands of Macbeth's hired assassins as in the original; instead he loses his family-owned business to corporate raiders. And Birnam Wood, when it finally comes to Dunsinane, looks suspiciously like a rubber plant from somebody's lobby. All these changes are hard to take seriously.

The tone of the passage is harsh, but the evidence seems to suggest that the reviewer has reasons for questioning the wisdom of updating *Macbeth.*

➤ **Expand vague evaluative terms.** Quite often, writers use evaluative terms that are too vague to be taken seriously.

Vague terms			
great	neat	bad	fine
nice	big	good	little

The whole point of writing an evaluation is to explain the feeling you have when you describe a book as *great,* a meal as *sensational,* or a resort as *nice.* The evaluation ultimately resides in the details. So every time you use a vague evaluative term in a draft, circle it, and ask yourself: what do I mean by _____ ? What exactly makes my subject _____ ? Then incorporate some of those specifications into the review.

Why write . . .	*When you could provide details?*
good material . . .	plush leather, soft as down.
a great idea . . .	an idea that influenced Jefferson . . .
large portions . . .	a 16-ounce steak and a plate full of . . .
nice music . . .	innovative, romantic orchestration,

Be skeptical of any evaluative expressions that begin with vague qualifiers such as *pretty, sort of, kind of, such a,* and *so.* In fact, the best advice might be to avoid such expressions entirely because they produce statements very difficult to assess: "The restaurant had *such a nice* atmosphere and served *so fine* a meal." A reader has to be puzzled. How nice an atmosphere did the restaurant have? Exactly how fine is "so fine"?

➤ **Qualify sweeping statements.** Can you support all the evaluative statements and judgments you make? Prudent qualifiers may help limit your liability.

Qualifiers	
most	some
many	sometimes
in many cases	in a few cases
almost	occasionally

Review your draft to see whether you have made any claims that need to be reined in a bit. A first draft is an appropriate place to express yourself enthusiastically; in the second draft, take another look.

It is possible to qualify judgments in such a way that one is seen as objecting not to a particular idea or concept, but to an individual execution of it. Here's an example of such an elaborate qualification from a now-familiar review of *Macbeth.*

> **There is nothing wrong,** per se, with setting Shakespeare to music. Verdi did it. So did Leonard Bernstein. **Such adaptations are fine when** they are written to explore new aspects of Shakespeare's dramas, not simply to try something different. Unfortunately, Professor Bellona seems to be using the music in her production just to increase box office revenues. **The problem isn't even** the music—which is, on balance, quite good; most of Frank Bacon's songs make you want to get up and dance. But . . .

➤ **Edit carefully.** Edit only after you have a draft you are satisfied with (see section 5C for a thorough checklist). Here are two particular points in evaluations and reviews worth checking.

> —Check the spelling of any proper nouns you use. Look especially carefully at the spelling and capitalization of brand names.

> —Check the title. Explanatory essays usually take fairly straightforward titles: CD Players: Are There Any Differences? Exploratory reviews may have more inventive titles. With reviews of books, movies, television programs, and films, you may need nothing more elaborate than a title that names the work being examined:

Review: Tom Clancy's *The Cardinal of the Kremlin.*

11 Proving a Thesis

11 A PROVING A THESIS

Simplest tasks often prove the most challenging. Most American students first hear about thesis statements and the need to support them in the earliest elementary school grades. What could be easier? Make a statement, prove it with at least three reasons and illustrations, add an introduction and a conclusion, and you've got a paper—the classic five-paragraph essay.

Introduction: Thesis
Argument 1 + examples/illustrations
Argument 2 + examples/illustrations
Argument 3 + examples/illustrations
Conclusion

If only life were so simple and ideas so eager to slide into convenient slots!

Unfortunately, just because three ideas can be lined up under an assertion doesn't mean that the statement has been proved. Far from it. Three or more reasons can be marshalled in favor of any proposition.

> Large doses of radiation must be beneficial to human health.
>
> • Atomic power produces useful energy.
>
> • Radiation powers satellites.
>
> • Radiation is used to cure cancer.

11 A

Thesis

The result of such a pattern of organization can be sheer nonsense; the "arguments" are related neither to the main point nor to each other. And, as above, they certainly don't prove the initial statement (radiation in large doses is good for people). Yet some writers believe that they have done their job when they have corralled ideas this way.

The five-paragraph essay structure *does* provide an organizational framework on which to hang ideas, so it may be a handy device for writers who aren't sure how to shape an idea. The pattern also reminds writers that any serious claim has to be supported by arguments, illustrations, and examples. Still, in practice, the five-paragraph structure too often becomes just a formula, a routine way of generating 500-word papers, not of discovering and structuring the best rationales for carefully formulated propositions. There's much more to proving a thesis than fitting ideas into slots.

Like other types of writing, proving a thesis can engage a full range of *explanatory* and *exploratory* processes. (See Section 2A for a discussion of these processes.)

The process of writing the paper will be mainly explanatory when you begin with a thesis you're confident you can prove: you know that materials supporting the hypothesis exist and you know where to look for them. Your job is to locate that information, record it, and then report it clearly and convincingly. Were you to explain, for example, how the British and Americans got involved in the War of 1812 or why automakers today use front-wheel drive in most small cars, you might need to do some research—in the library or in the labs of engineers. But you could be confident from the outset that you'd soon learn enough about the subject to assemble an authoritative, comprehensive, and convincing paper.

When you approach a more open-ended subject, you might actually write an essay in the special exploratory sense of that term discussed in Chapter 9, Writing an Exploratory Paper; in such a paper, you commit yourself to proving a thesis that offers few certainties. You actually begin with an *hypothesis,* a new idea that you want to test. But you realize from the start that the materials surrounding the issue—the people, the raw data, the printed sources—won't yield supporting evidence in a form you can readily use. You must rework and reshape the information in your sources—find new configurations and new lines of argument. When you begin the project, you can't be confident that you'll finally have a point to make, a thesis to demonstrate.

Let's say that because you suspect that homelessness in America can be attributed, at least in part, to a declining faith in the work ethic, you decide to write a paper examining (and defending) that hypothesis. You'll quickly discover that there's no simple source to refer to, no authoritative guide to the motives of human beings; if you intend to prove the thesis, you must *invent* the evidence— not make it up, but create it new from raw materials. When writing such an exploratory paper, chances are good you'll have to change or refine your thesis more than once as you learn more about the homeless. Yet, even after weeks of research and thinking, all you may be able to do is to suggest how homelessness and the work ethic *might* be related or how that relationship *might* be examined.

Well, that's fine. Not all ideas can be packed into neat thesis statements supported by rows of proofs; nature and society aren't that simple. The problem with the five-paragraph essay model is that the design can bully writers into making simplistic judgments. Don't let this happen to you. Sometimes a writer just has to admit that life is complicated.

11 A

Thesis

Some types of writing that support a thesis

Research papers	**Articles in journals**
Magazine reports	**Position papers**
Sermons on a "text"	**Some news articles**
Doctoral dissertations	**Supreme Court decisions**
Traffic ticket appeals	**Legal briefs**
Literary criticism	

Places to read articles that prove a thesis

The Christian Science Monitor (opinion page)
The Journal of Modern History
The New Republic
The Partisan Review
Psychology Today
Science
Scientific American
The Sewanee Review
Social Forces
The Utne Reader

Here are just a few reasons for proving a thesis:

- to tell readers something they don't know;
- to prove that something known *is* so;
- to disprove a false belief or assumption;
- to explain how something came to be;
- to enumerate the parts or elements of a situation;
- to explain how or why something occurred;
- to show how or why something works or doesn't work.

11 B EXAMINING A SAMPLE PAPER

Here is an example of a paper in which a writer works to prove a thesis. The paper is unusually serious in tone and hard-hitting in content, though we are uneasy with the stereotyping of the German and Japanese people implied in the first paragraph. Luis Garcia's ethnic background may have prompted him to write so strongly about Japanese activities during World War II: his mother is Chinese. So keep the historical circumstances of World War II in mind as you read this paper. We do think Luis's moving essay shows what happens when a writer uses an academic assignment to explore an idea with strong personal associations.

AUTHOR: Luis Garcia, freshman at the University of Texas at Austin. (Luis also contributes essays that appear in Chapters 10 and 12.)

AUDIENCE: His classmates in a Freshman English course.

ASSIGNMENT: Write a research paper supporting an argumentative thesis.

REQUIREMENTS: Length—about 1200 words.

11 B

Thesis

The Crimes of the Rising Sun

(1) In a Japanese textbook passage, a Japanese narrator relates a conversation
he overheard at a party of Southeast Asians. The passage reads in part:

"Which nation is the most cruel?"

"The Germans."

"No. No. The Japanese."

A Malaysian then recounts watching a Japanese soldier sticking his sword
through a Malaysian child in front of its mother (Chira "For" A5). This gross
display of injustice is only one example of the ruthless and inhumane campaign
the Japanese waged against opposing military forces and local civilian populations prior to and during World War II. After the invasion of Manchuria in 1931,
and to an increasing degree in 1937 when Japan declared war against China,
members of the Japanese army, navy, and government beat, tortured, raped, and
massacred Chinese by the thousands. When the Japanese declared war on the
rest of the world, many Allied prisoners of war, including U.S. soldiers, met similar fates. Although terms such as "concentration camp," "Holocaust," and "the
final solution" invoke nightmarish thoughts of German inhumanity and cruelty,
the Germans did not hold a monopoly on war crimes. Japanese war crimes,
though not as systematic, were just as atrocious as the Germans'--except for one
difference. Japanese war crimes are not widely known.

(2)   Part of the reason the Japanese mistreated their prisoners of war is that the Japanese felt that the POWs did not deserve treatment worthy of a soldier, for they had shamefully surrendered or allowed themselves to be captured. One instance of the Japanese mistreatment of POWs is the Bataan Death March. Approximately 70,000 American and Filipino prisoners captured in the Philippines were forced to march 55 miles to a prisoner camp on April 10, 1942. Starved and beaten, only 54,000 prisoners reached Camp O'Donnell (Britannica). According to Staff Sgt. Harold Feiner, who survived the march, "If you fell, you were dead. They bayoneted you right away. No bullshit! If you fell, bingo, you were dead" (Knox 138). The Japanese had no compassion for prisoners of war, nor did they abide by the provisions of the Geneva Convention of July 27, 1929, relative to the Red Cross and protection of POWs (Piccigallo 3).

11 B

Thesis

(3)   A direct violation of the Geneva Convention was the Japanese use of civilians and POWs as slave labor. In 1942, the Japanese forced POWs and civilians to build a railroad through the dangerous jungles connecting Burma and Thailand. More than 120,000 workers died in the jungle, 12,500 of whom were POWs. According to E. R. Hall, a survivor of the Thai-Burma railway project, "Some died on the job during the day and others, having the embarrassment of dysentery, fouled their bodies . . . while trying to work" (149). The Japanese felt that dying in the service of the Emperor was one way for prisoners to atone for the cowardice of allowing themselves to be caught (279).

(4)   One of the cruellest crimes the Japanese committed against civilians and POWs occurred at Unit 731. Once located in the present Chinese town of Ping-fan in Manchuria, Unit 731 was the testing ground for perfecting bacteriological warfare agents. From 1939 to 1945, at least 2,000 Chinese, Korean, Soviet, and Mongolian prisoners died at Unit 731 from deadly diseases, including anthrax, smallpox, the plague, and typhoid (McGill 32). Some victims were tied to stakes and then subjected to mustard gas until their bodily organs ceased to function (Monroe 27), while others were tied to stakes and then bombarded with "flea bombs." These bombs carried a flea-borne plague which fatally infected the prisoners (McGill 32). Unlike many Jews who died in the Holocaust, these prisoners of Unit 731 had to endure the agony of the slow death attributed to many of the diseases exposed to them by so-called Japanese "scientists."

(5)   While the Germans were killing innocent Jews, the Japanese were also committing heinous crimes against innocent civilians who stood in the path of

the rampaging Japanese Imperial Army. Whole populations of villages of Java, Kuala Lumpur, and the Southwest Pacific Islands were massacred (Piccigallo xii). The Filipinos suffered the greatest losses of innocent human lives. In the city of Manila alone, tens of thousands of innocent people were brutally killed, with thousands more tortured and raped (Reel 4). An elderly Chinese gentleman testified to witnessing three of his countrymen kneeling in front of a ditch that the Japanese had forced them to dig. According to the Chinese man:

> three Japanese soldiers with fixed bayonets advanced and thrust the bayo-
> nets into the bodies of the kneeling Chinese. When the bayonets were
> pushed through the victims, the soldiers kicked the bodies into the
> ditch. . . . Five yards away from us I saw a Japanese officer with a big saber
> in his hands. He went forward and he lifted his sword and cut the head off
> a Chinese. (Reel 3).

11 B

Thesis

In 1937, a similar event occurred in the Chinese city of Nanjing. Japanese troops brutally killed approximately 40,000 people, mostly women and children, and 100,000 more in the countryside (Chira E12). The Japanese had no mercy then and, apparently, have little remorse today.

(6) Although fifty years have passed since Hitler first implemented Kristall-nacht, the beginning of the Nazi campaign to exterminate Jews, Germany as well as the rest of the civilized world has yet to forget the horrors that occurred in Nazi concentration camps from 1938 until 1944. In fact, the Holocaust is even a growing subject in American school rooms (Berger A16). Yet in direct contrast to the experience of West Germany, where there were observances throughout the country to commemorate the 50th Anniversary of Kristallnacht, the Japanese choose to forget the events that occurred during the war (Chira E12). As a result, Japan's youth are growing up with a distorted view of the war. Many of the Japa-nese textbooks do not mention the cruel Japanese occupation of Korea or the slaughter of civilians by Japanese troops. Those textbooks that do contain pas-sages or lessons of Japanese brutality--such as the conversation at the beginning of this paper--are censored outright by ruling Japanese party politicians who do not want the truth to be known (Chira "For" A5). In one instance, a group of Japanese revisionist historians tried to change the number of innocent civilians killed in the "Rape of Nanjing" from approximately 200,000 to 20,000 (Hoyt 173). When questioned about the use of prisoners in testing of germ warfare agents, a press secretary in the Japanese Embassy in Washington replied, "The

Japanese government has no record of the biological tests which are said to have been conducted in China. . . . All the records of the wartime have been destroyed, so we don't know" (Monroe 27). The Japanese would simply like the world to forget their actions during World War II.

(7) Ironically, the Japanese wish has come true. With the exception of the Chinese and citizens of the South Pacific Islands, most people are unaware of the crimes Japan committed during World War II. In fact, although the United States participated in trying Japanese war criminals, it also did its part in condoning Japan's criminal actions. In the case of Unit 731, the United States Government gave Unit 731's senior members immunity from prosecution in return for their findings on germ warfare (Monroe 27). According to an internal American report written in December 1947, "Such information could not be obtained in our laboratories because of scruples attached to human experimentations" (McGill 32). The United States Government obviously placed little value on the lives of those Chinese, Soviet, Korean, and Mongolian POWs who died as guinea pigs.

(8) One of the reasons the Jewish Holocaust continues to be remembered and discussed is because of the statement it makes about the dangers of racism. But more importantly, the Holocaust is remembered and taught to future generations in order to remind people of the capacity humans have to perform acts of unspeakable evil. For this reason, Japanese war crimes during World War II should be remembered and the evils of such actions should be taught to future generations. Only then can people realize the effects of war and possibly stop future atrocities.

11 B

Thesis

Works Cited

"Bataan Death March." Encyclopaedia Britannica: Micropedia. 1985 ed.

Berger, Joseph. "Once Rarely Explored, the Holocaust Gains Momentum as a
    School Subject." The New York Times 3 October 1988, sec. A:16.

Chira, Susan. "Despite New Efforts, Japan Avoids Making Peace with War." The
    New York Times 25 December 1988, sec. E:12.

---"For Japanese, Textbook Drops a Lesson on War." The New York Times 5 Oct
    1988, sec. A:5.

Hall, E. R. The Burma-Thailand Railway of Death. Australia: Graphic, 1981.

Hoyt, Edwin P. Japan's War. New York: McGraw, 1986.

Knox, Donald. Death March. New York: Harcourt, 1981.

McGill, Peter. "A Cover-up for a Death Camp." Maclean's 20 May 1985: 32.

Monroe, Linda R. "Atrocities: Report Lists POW Experiments." L.A. Times 11 August 1988: 27.

Piccigallo, Philip R. The Japanese on Trial. Austin: U. of Texas P, 1979.

Reel, Frank A. The Case of General Yamashita. New York: Octagon, 1971.

➤ **Analysis of Luis Garcia's "Crimes of the Rising Sun"**

11 B

Thesis

Thesis: What is the thesis of this paper? What sort of proof does Luis Garcia have to provide to support such a thesis? Does he provide such evidence?

Audience. Luis has ethnic ties to China. How does that information influence your reading of his paper? How did you react to the charges he makes against the Japanese for their activities in World War II? Does your own ethnic or cultural background influence how you respond to the paper? Can you anticipate some objections to the paper from portions of the reading audience? Does Luis provide a convincing rationale for discussing an ethnically sensitive subject like this?

Organization. How would you describe the strategy of the paper—that is, how does Garcia arrange his information? Do the separate paragraphs seem related; if so, how or why? How do references to Nazi Germany and the Holocaust help to structure the paper?

Evidence. The paper is full of supporting evidence. Do you find that information convincing? Why or why not? What evidence do you find most memorable or convincing—that is, which provides the best support for the thesis? Do you find any of the evidence shocking or sensational? Should the paper include its graphic descriptions of torture and slaughter? Are any topics or facts omitted that you believe should have been mentioned?

Introduction. Explain the function of each sentence in the introductory paragraph, treating all the material preceding the first in-text note— (Chira, "For" A5)—as one sentence. How did you respond to this opening? Would you describe the opening as successful? Explain why or why not.

Conclusion. By the last paragraph, has Luis Garcia fulfilled the commitment he made in the first paragraph? How much of the concluding paragraph would you describe as summary? What else does the concluding paragraph do?

Reader's Response. If you had an opportunity to talk to Luis Garcia, what would you say to him about this paper? What more would you want to know? Can you think of any topic you might treat similarly? In what ways is this paper informative? In what ways is it persuasive? Do you find it easy to separate the informative and persuasive aspects?

11 C CHOOSING A TOPIC

> **The Basic Assignment**
> Write a paper in which you provide evidence to support some clearly stated and debatable assertion. Your assertion should concern an issue significant to you and (potentially at least) to your readers. Provide whatever rational evidence is suited to your subject: logical arguments, facts and figures, examples, illustrations, precedents.

11 C

Thesis

➤ **Variations**

a. Prove that some assumption or belief about you, about someone you know, or about an organization you belong to is—in fact—true. Provide ample evidence to support your contention, remembering to look for evidence that would persuade a skeptical outsider. For example, you might prove that you really are as clever as your friends believe you are; that your friend Sidney deserves her reputation for community service; that your fellow Democrats really are as concerned about social justice as they claim to be.

b. Prove that some widespread belief about you, someone you know well, or an organization you belong to is, in fact, a misconception. Examine possible reasons for the misconception and then provide evidence that shows that such a view is, in fact, a misrepresentation. For example, you might prove that you aren't as self-confident as you let on; that your brother Carl isn't as mechanically adept as he seems to be; that your fellow feminists really do have a sense of humor.

c. Demonstrate the influence that some person, thing, idea, or movement has had on the culture at large. For example, you might show that football is the perfect expression of American sporting attitudes; that rock and roll is a form of music that expresses more than just the feelings of teenagers; that American "First Ladies" have had a larger role in modern presidential administrations than most people realize. Remember that you aren't merely describing a situation, but proving that something is so. The burden of proof is on you, so be sure to furnish examples, illustrations, and strong arguments.

d. Working in a group, come up with a list of common assumptions, slogans, or clichés that express what might be described as "shared values" either in your local community or in society at large. Discuss each statement and examine evidence from within the community or culture which either supports or refutes the value expressed. Consider statements like the following.

• God helps those who help themselves.

• When the going gets tough, the tough get going.

- A mind is a terrible thing to waste.
- Everyone is entitled to his or her own opinion.
- All persons are created equal.
- A woman's place is in the home.
- Children should be seen—not heard.

Then have each member of the group write an essay demonstrating the truth or falseness of the statement as an expression of current community values. Be sure the statements you choose to explore are those that really might influence what people think and believe. Compare and discuss the essays both in draft and final versions.

e. Defend something you do to which other people might object—hunt, wear furs, eat meat, avoid meat, drive a foreign car, refuse to recycle. Provide a detailed and factual defense of your behavior, showing why or how it makes sense. Don't feel the obligation, however, to persuade others to follow your example.

11 C

Thesis

f. 50 Topic Ideas. The topic ideas below could be developed in various ways. If you have strong opinions about one of the subjects already—that is, your mind is made up and you want to convince others to adopt your position—then you are ready to write a persuasive paper. (See Chapter 12.) If you are less certain about endorsing a particular position, and more interested in learning what the facts might be, write a paper that develops and proves a thesis.

1. The U.S. needs / does not need to build a super-collider.
2. British actors are / are not better trained than American actors.
3. The effect of advertising on popular thinking is to _____ .
4. The establishment of a permanent space lab would _____ .
5. African art can be / cannot be interpreted effectively from a Western or Eurocentric point of view because _____ . (Also consider Indian, Native American, any Third World artistic or literary tradition.)
6. The consumption of alcohol (or another substance or drug) is / is not as harmful as popular belief suggests.
7. One of the greatest sports figures of the last decade (twenty-five years; fifty years; century) was _____ .
8. Antarctica should / should not be open to international mineral exploration.
9. "Modern" art (or name some particular artistic movement) has / has not contributed significantly to Western culture.
10. The Olympics should / should not have a permanent site in Greece.
11. What I.Q. tests actually measure is _____ .
12. Buying a foreign car does / does not hurt American workers.
13. Loving the opera is / is not a measure of cultural sophistication.
14. The salaries of professional athletes (or some other group) are / are not excessive.
15. Religion should / should not be studied in public universities.
16. Women and men do / do not behave differently in social (or _____) situations.

17. Darwin is / is not solely responsible for the theory of evolution.
18. One contribution of (film / television / poetry / novel / short story / drama / painting / sculpture / other) to contemporary culture is _____ .
19. Professional boxing should / should not be banned.
20. Eastern philosophies and religions do / do not have a significant impact upon the American cultural mainstream.
21. The business cycle can / cannot be controlled by precise management of the money supply.
22. The most important achievement of _____ (name a particular philosopher) was _____ .
23. Americans have / have not overreacted to various scares about possible cancer-causing agents (saccharine / alar / caffeine / cigarettes).
24. Marxist-style socialism has / has not been entirely discredited as a basis for a modern economy.
25. Cartoons play an increasing / decreasing role in American political discussion.
26. Exploiting natural resources (choose one: forests / minerals / fisheries / wetlands / oil fields / rivers) does / does not benefit the national welfare.
27. Americans should / should not support a free market trade policy— that is, a policy that does not restrict the importation of goods manufactured in foreign countries.
28. The veneration of saints in Christian tradition served to _____ .
29. Bio-engineering experiments should / should not be encouraged and regulated.
30. The value and contribution of small farms to American life has / has not been exaggerated.
31. Children's literature does / does not represent a significant field of study.
32. A knowledge of Chinese cultural traditions or history of China (explore some single aspect) illuminates current political / social events in this way: _____ .
33. Cats are smarter / dumber or better pets / worse pets than dogs.
34. The calendar is / is not in need of reform.
35. One effect of European colonial policies in (Africa / Asia / the Americas) was to _____ .
36. The value of endangered species (plants or animals) has / has not been exaggerated.
37. One effective way of improving (primary / secondary / undergraduate) education in the United States would be to _____ because _____ .
38. A popular misconception about psychology (or any other field) as a discipline or profession is _____ .
39. A person who is (or will be) regarded as essential to the development of the computer is _____ because _____ .
40. One function of the dance in (name a culture or country) is _____ .
41. As a principle of social organization, "class" can be seen influencing _____ in American culture.

11 C

Thesis

42. One function of choral music in western culture has been to
    _____ .
43. We know / don't know how to prevent heart disease.
44. Contemporary architecture is / is not successful, functionally and / or
    aesthetically.
45. The most important achievement of _____ (name a particular mu-
    sician or composer) was _____ .
46. A major achievement of ancient Egyptian culture is _____ .
47. In historical perspective, the circus has served as _____ .
48. The most important accomplishment of _____ (name a scientist)
    was _____ .
49. The most important achievement of _____ (name a politician or
    diplomat) was _____ .
50. In animals and plants, one of the functions of color is to _____ .

11 D   PREPARING AND PLANNING A PAPER THAT SUPPORTS A THESIS

You can't make a reasonable assertion about any subject until you know something about it. That's why some people catch a case of writer's block when asked
to prove a thesis: they expect inspiration to provide them with a fully articulated
thesis statement, something like this:

> Gothic cathedrals—with their solemn light-filled interiors, vast open
> spaces, soaring towers, and glorious windows—were perhaps the greatest
> artistic achievement of the European Middle Ages.

And they wait, and wait, and wait.

Such theses just don't appear. They are the end products of a writing
process—not the starting blocks. Think of a thesis and the arguments supporting
it as growing in tandem—the more you learn about a topic, the more refined the
thesis becomes. The more refined the thesis becomes, the more precisely a topic
can be researched or examined. During the composing process, you don't so
much prove a thesis as find it while you learn more about a subject.

To find and prove a thesis . . .

▶ **Find a subject area worth exploring.** Almost any subject can fit the bill if you
approach it with vigor and common sense. Common sense in this case means
thinking of a subject in terms of your audience and purpose.

A college audience provides many opportunities, but also makes special
demands. It invites you to write on virtually any topic, but demands that you
provide a sensible explanation for the choice. It supplies you with a platform for
your thoughts, but expects you to make good use of the forum. It invites you to
bring your own perspective to a topic, but suggests strongly that some points of
view are more appropriate than others.

You probably know, almost instinctively, that general subjects like pizzas, proms, or pets are likely to raise the eyebrows of your college instructors and many of your classmates; such topics don't seem serious enough for college-level papers. But let's say you were interested in how the traditional fast-food pizza was being revised to fit new American dietary preferences. Or you suspected that proms revealed as much about changes in male/female relationships as any other aspect of contemporary culture. Or you could show—in a comic, but thoughtful way—that people depended on pets for support they couldn't get as reliably from people. Might you develop interesting, college-level papers from such topics? Probably. That's because "interesting" in this case would describe a paper that challenged people to think in new ways—to find more than what they expected in simple things. So a "lowbrow" topic is not necessarily off bounds in a college course.

11 D

Thesis

Nor will a "serious subject" automatically win praise from college readers. Some writers rush to controversial issues like abortion, gun control, capital punishment, drugs, and euthanasia, thinking that the sheer weight of the topic will earn credit with readers. But such topics are notoriously difficult. They are either too complex to treat well in a short essay or too remote from personal experience to make a writer sound authoritative and confident. The resulting essays drone on earnestly, but without feeling or commitment—like sermons delivered (or heard) for the fourth or fifth time.

College readers, like most others, enjoy being challenged and surprised by topics. They appreciate the insider's point of view, the clever reversal of a traditional approach, the detailed introduction to a new phenomenon, or the exposé of what they supposedly knew well. Such readers prefer the specific to the abstract.

Why write about . . .	*When you could write about . . . ?*
the weather	the physics of tornados
television	the early days of TV journalism
pain	"phantom limb" pain
the problems of women	battered wives
the problems of men	inequalities in custody battles
sports	sports medicine

➤ **Understand the issues involved in the topic before formulating a thesis.** You can't know everything about a subject, especially at the outset of a project. But, whether you are involved in an explanatory or exploratory project, you probably should know at least as much about your subject as you can discover in an authoritative background source.

Talking about a subject with classmates and instructors can often help you appreciate what to do with it. Or reading two or three articles on the subject either in books or periodicals (see 37A Selecting a Topic for more advice about finding a topic). Get the lay of the land.

➤ **Do some research.** Once you have a subject area to explore or a question that intrigues you, learn even more about the topic. The best way, of course, is to research the subject in the library (see 37B Gathering Information). There's no getting around the fact that, in college, you'll usually find the support you need to defend a thesis in printed sources.

There will be times, however, when you'll find that proving a thesis requires that you do interviews, take surveys, perform experiments, observe people, study objects, or formulate shrewd arguments. Fine. Bringing a variety of proofs into a paper is one way of bolstering a position—showing, for example, that some course of action not only has the facts behind it, but also public opinion.

For explanatory papers, the journalist's questions (see p. 27) may provide a helpful method for locating material (or arguments) that you need to cover; for exploratory papers, a freewriting exercise, a looping exercise, or discovery draft (see p. 10) may be the best devices for homing in on a thesis you can support.

➤ **Formulate a tentative thesis.** Having a thesis to prove implies having a topic that provokes doubts: after all, what's the point in proving what is already widely known? Yet some of the best papers are written when a writer sheds new light on an aspect of a subject people *thought* they knew well.

11 D

Thesis

Even explanatory papers that provide new information often need to be given a little life, a spark. For example, an explanatory paper about syphilis that develops from the following thesis would provide neither writer or reader with much incentive to pursue the project.

The history of syphilis in western Europe is debated.

Nothing is at issue or at stake; what needs to be proved hardly seems worth the effort—even though it might be. Fortunately, it's easy to revise the thesis so that it provides the writer with an assertion to prove and the reader with an argument to follow.

While it is possible that syphilis was brought to Europe by Christopher Columbus on his return from the Americas, it is just as likely that the disease had infected the Old World as early as Biblical or Roman times.

Notice that this lengthier thesis now gives the paper a sense of direction and organization. (Without reading the paper, for example, you'd suspect that it will have two major divisions.)

You'll often want to use such an expanded thesis to provide readers with an overview of a paper. Recall that it is the thesis that makes a commitment to readers—one you later must fulfill (see Section 3E).

Here's another example of an elaborate thesis statement that points the way to a complex argument and makes a commitment:

If enacted into law, so-called "comparable pay" statutes would turn a vigorous American economy into an Eastern European-style basketcase **by creating** the equivalent of central economic planning in the United States, **by placing** the economy under the control of a new class of "experts" eager to dictate social policy, and **by disrupting** ordinary market mechanisms that today effectively guide the economy.

Such a comprehensive statement can only be the end product of a great deal of thinking and writing; a thesis this complex probably developed from a much simpler hypothesis, perhaps something no grander than this:

"Comparable pay" is a bad economic policy.

Notice that the expanded thesis uses a parallel structure to connect its three major subtopics, each of which could be developed at some length in a paper: *by creating; by placing; by disrupting.*

➤ **Gather evidence.** The kinds of evidence you can deploy to support a thesis are too varied to discuss in detail. In some cases, your support will be in the form of logical arguments—reasonable statements that make good sense to most readers.

> Repairing sturdy existing houses will often provide better homes for the poor than bulldozing older neighborhoods just to erect shoddy "low cost" public housing.

> Unless some reasonable cap is placed upon benefits, we won't be able to pay for social security much longer. Simply put, far more money will be leaving the social security fund than will be coming in.

Other forms of evidence available to a writer include:

- figures and statistics gathered from reliable sources;
- interviews and surveys;
- information gathered from reading;
- quotations from authorities (see Chapter 37 on Beginning Research).

Consider, for example, how effectively Luis Garcia combines paraphrase and direct quotation to support his contentions in this paragraph from his essay on Japanese war crimes:

> (2)   Part of the reason the Japanese mistreated their prisoners of war is that the Japanese felt that the POWs did not deserve the treatment worthy of a soldier for they had shamefully surrendered or allowed themselves to be captured. One instance of the Japanese mistreatment of POWs is the Bataan Death March. 70,000 American and Filipino prisoners captured in the Philippines were forced to march 55 miles to a prisoner camp on April 10, 1942. Starved and beaten, only 54,000 prisoners reached Camp O'Donnell (Britannica). According to Staff Sgt. Harold Feiner, who survived the march, "If you fell, you were dead. They bayoneted you right away. No bullshit! If you fell, bingo, you were dead" (Knox 138). The Japanese had no compassion for prisoners of war, nor did they abide by the provisions of the Geneva Convention of July 27, 1929, relative to the Red Cross and protection of POWs (Piccigallo 3).

➤ **Consider counterarguments and objections.** The point of demonstrating a thesis is to provide the best evidence to support a position. As you develop an argument, you may find that opposing positions are not without merit. A honest paper takes such contradictory views into account, either showing their limitations or acknowledging their merit. Indeed, it is the friction of alternative views that hones a thesis to razor sharpness—that guides it steadily toward language that is more accurate, sensitive, and defensible.

➤ **Arrange the arguments and evidence.** In recommending an organizational pattern for a paper that proves a thesis, it's hard to avoid the five-paragraph model discussed earlier. After all, an assertion *does* have to be supported with arguments, illustrations, and evidence. Papers that result from a chiefly explanatory process often will take a simple, straightforward shape:

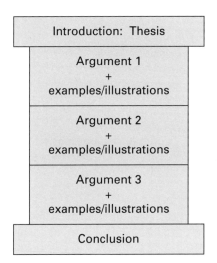

But even such papers can include significant digressions and variations. When you prove a thesis, you must almost always deal with the opposing arguments; if you don't address them, the paper will seem to evade key questions. Counterarguments inevitably make the structure of the paper more complex. Here's what the "basic model" might look like when counterarguments are added:

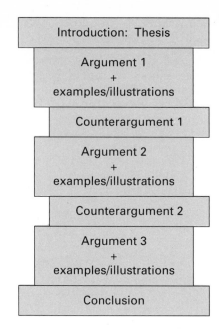

Notice that the physical structures of these models suggest that all the components of the essay would receive about the same treatment. This is a distortion: in practice, you would give your best points more attention—using all the examples and illustrations you need to make your case. Minor points would obviously get less coverage than major ones.

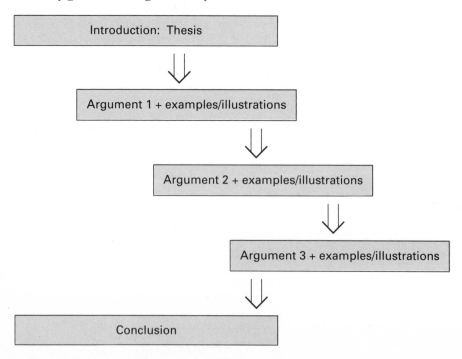

Papers that prove a thesis can be organized another way. This second kind of structure presents a series of related arguments which build upon each other—each new line of argument developing directly from the one before it. You cannot remove any portion of the argument without demolishing the whole structure.

This pattern of organization is potentially more complex than the earlier one because every part of the paper depends upon its connection with a previous part. But the cliché that a chain is only as strong as its weakest link applies here. The links between portions (or paragraphs) of the paper become especially important: a writer has to take pains to see that readers are following the evidence, understanding how it develops and where it moves. Transitional words and phrases must be carefully selected because the paragraphs do not relate directly back to a single thesis, but to other ideas within the paper—which do eventually trail back to the thesis.

Such structures have the advantage of greater flexibility, perhaps greater subtlety; the writer can take an argument in a variety of directions. But this effect is possible only if the transitions work well.

11 D

Thesis

➤ **Connect the ideas within paragraphs.** Whatever general pattern of organization is employed, it is also important to connect the ideas within the paragraphs, particularly since gaps between sentences are often harder to spot than those between larger components of a paper. For the sake of economy, writers often—and understandably—omit the connectors when taking notes or jotting down ideas. Unfortunately, they just as often fail to restore those connections when reporting the information on their own. The result can be paragraphs of related, but unrefined ideas:

> Physicians will usually perform artificial insemination only on married women. When a single woman wants a baby, she will often be rejected. Single parenthood, it is believed, is not good for a child.

Such a cluster of sentences furnishes little support for a thesis because it frustrates readers more than it informs them. Readers just about have to rewrite the paper to make sense of it. What the writer needs to do is make the connections more explicit, to spell out the relationships.

> Physicians will usually perform artificial insemination only on married women **who are having trouble conceiving naturally.** Believing that single parenthood is not good for a child, **doctors** will often reject a single woman who wants to have a baby **by this method.**

The concluding sentence of a paragraph can also function as a kind of connector. Not every paragraph requires a concluding statement that reinforces the thesis of the paper. But if, within a paragraph, you have furnished plenty of evidence, don't leave it up to readers—time and again—to reckon how that evidence supports your thesis. Make the connection yourself in a competent concluding sentence. Consider, for example, how Luis Garcia concludes a paragraph (6) describing Japanese attempts to cover up evidence of World War II crimes with a simple statement that immediately throws a bridge to the next paragraph:

> (6)   ...All the records of the wartime have been destroyed, so we
>
> don't know" (Monroe 27). **The Japanese would simply like the**

world to forget their actions during World War II.

(7) Ironically, the Japanese wish has come true. With the

exception of the Chinese and citizens of . . . .

➤ **Refine the thesis.** Most writers expect to reshape a thesis statement several times in the process of drafting and revising. In fact, it may be a sign that a paper is *not* going well if its thesis *never* changes: you may not have ventured far enough from your original assumptions to understand the topic adequately. Some revisions of a thesis may be cosmetic—a livelier verb, a more accurate adjective. Others will be redirections in the argument itself. To understand more about how a thesis develops, consult Section 38A, Refining a Thesis.

11 E

Thesis

11 E DRAFTING AND REVISING A PAPER THAT SUPPORTS A THESIS

A paper that supports a thesis can often be written in parts. That is, one piece of the evidence may fall into place sooner or more readily than others. So you may find it practical to write bits and pieces of the paper as you are assembling the information and roaming through sources. No rule says a draft has to be composed in the order in which it will eventually be read. Many writers compose the opening paragraph last—which makes perfect sense if it is to serve as a helpful introduction. If you do assemble the paper from separate parts, be sure to give extra attention to the connections between those parts. (See Chapter 15 on transitions.)

To revise a paper that proves a thesis . . .

➤ **Take a clear stand on an issue.** Vague thesis statements leave readers wondering what you are trying to say.

> Which side of the fence you stand on basically determines whether or not you favor special academic benefits for athletes.

> Today capital punishment is one of the most debated controversial issues in the United States; the moral crisis questions what is human and what is fair and justified.

What are these writers trying to prove? All that is clear from the first example is that people might disagree about academic benefits for athletes. Here's a possible revision of that thesis sentence, a new statement that makes a clearer commitment by taking a stand and supporting it with good reasons:

> Athletes in college programs should receive special academic counseling, course registration preferences, and tutoring because they contribute significantly to the reputation, spirit, and financial well-being of their schools.

The second thesis sentence (on capital punishment) may be even more confusing. It seems to be arguing what everyone already knows—that capital punishment is a difficult and complex issue. But even that point is not certain. If the writer wants to argue that it is not possible to take a stand on the issue, she might just say so:

> Capital punishment is such a difficult issue that I cannot find a compromise between the human side of the issue and the legal one.

We would then expect the writer to talk about each of these sides (*human* and *legal*), explaining what she means by them and showing the conflict between them. That wouldn't be easy, but then there's no reason to presume that writing a good argument will involve simple choices.

➤ **Check that the key ideas in a thesis are clearly related.** A thesis statement that lists arguments, but lacks a parallel structure may be a tip-off that a writer isn't sure yet how important ideas are related. Ideas are parallel when they are expressed in matching grammatical forms or structural patterns:

{**Parallel phrases**}   The forces of the Axis powers were steadily driven back **on the sea, in the air,** and **on the ground.**

Here's an example of a thesis that is confusing because its key elements don't have a single grammatical form and, so, don't seem related—even though they are. The thesis is from a paper about single women having children through artificial insemination.

> The process is simple, but it **requires a donor,** knowing the **legal aspect** and **problems** the mother and child will face.

The thesis asks readers to do all the work—to make the necessary connections between vaguely stated notions. The original version might be suitable in a rough draft, but the final version must be much more explicit if it is to lead readers into the paper.

> The process of *artificial insemination* is simple, but *a woman who wishes to use it to have a child* must **locate** a suitable donor, **understand** the legal aspects of such a reproductive technique, and **anticipate** problems both for herself and for her child.

Here, the parallel structure aligns the related ideas and places them in relationship to the key figure in the paper: the woman who wishes to have a child through artificial insemination.

➤ **Check the evidence you have provided for all key points.** You can't prove an assertion merely by stating it or contradicting it—no matter how confident you are of your views. You must take the time to analyze and argue. Consider these sentences from a paper on battered women:

> . . . A common belief in society today is that wives who put up with beatings over a long period time are probably masochists who come to regard the assaults as signs of love." **This is obviously not true.**

The second sentence, though based upon the writer's reading and probably an accurate statement, carries little weight as part of an argument or proof because it is presented as a mere assertion. In fact, the first sentence is not *obviously* false; if that were the case, the belief would probably not be so common. The writer needs to do more work, providing evidence and alternative explanations for why some wives do put up with long-term abuse. A paraphrase of or a quotation from the original source might provide all the clarification necessary to back up the assertion. But without this explicit discussion of the issue, readers are more likely to believe the myth than the writer's denial of it.

➤ **Qualify generalizations.** You'll have a much easier time proving claims that are limited in scope, whether such generalizations are in the thesis or supporting arguments. If you are writing about conditions in the United States, for instance, say so; don't assume that readers will assume national limits if you haven't specified them.

11 E

Thesis

> Throughout history, minorities have been barred from institutions of higher learning until the civil rights movement broke those barriers.

An audience of college classmates is especially likely to include international students:

> In the United States, minorities were barred from most institutions of higher learning until the civil rights movement of the 1960s broke those barriers.

Explain carefully at the beginning of an essay what you are writing about. If you start off lamely, you'll lose readers fast.

> In the past, it was a common belief that when a couple in love graduated from high school, they should get married and begin a family.

A statement this vague won't so much be questioned as ignored. It provides neither a specific era to discuss ("in the past" could be any time), nor a culture to understand ("it was a common belief"—among whom? why?). There's no topic here and, consequently, no idea for the writer to support or challenge. It's important that you set a frame for the discussion. Be precise and concrete. You can do that quickly and easily if you are sensitive to what your readers need to know. Here's a more successful example:

> In September, 1985, the wives of several U.S. Senators met with conservative parents' groups to form an organization critical of rock music—the Parent Music Resource Center (PMRC). This new group soon launched a campaign. . . .

Consider how weak the opening could have been if it began:

> Today, the lyrics of music have been challenged by groups of parents.

> **Phrases to avoid:**
>
> **Since the dawn of time . . .**
> **In today's society . . .**
> **Through the years . . .**
> **Throughout history . . .**
> **In the world in which we live today . . .**

▶ **Be sure you have cited authorities whenever you support assertions with figures or other data.** Don't expect readers to take your word for any claim that might be disputed and don't simply assume that you know what the facts are because you've heard some generalizations. All the following statements would need statistical backing if they were important to reinforcing a thesis:

> Since most minority students come from underprivileged homes that cannot afford to send children to college, more scholarships should be available for minority students than for white students.

> It is a scientific fact that a marijuana cigarette kills more brain cells than a night of free drinks on Bourbon Street.

> There is no evidence that capital punishment serves as a deterrent to crime.

> Student-athletes perform at the same academic level as students in the general population.

11 E

Thesis

▶ **Be careful not to advance an argument through questions.** As a way of focusing a discussion, a question can be useful, particularly when you have a reply ready.

> Should the brutality of a crime determine the severity of a criminal's punishment? Of course. That principle is essential to our whole criminal justice system . . . .

However, it is risky to pose a question and then leave it unanswered. An entire argument could collapse if readers answer it to themselves in ways you hadn't anticipated.

> Mr. Arafat is being taken seriously as a statesman now. Has the world really forgotten his terrorist activities already? Can a former terrorist be trusted in negotiations?

If readers recall any revolutionaries who were later accorded the status of national leaders and diplomats, then the argument folds—and that's not what the writer intended. It would be better in this case to control the argument through a careful statement of the key ideas.

> Mr. Arafat is being taken seriously as a statesman now. But his word cannot be entirely trusted in negotiations, for some say it is the word of an international terrorist.

▶ **Don't lose track of what you are talking about.** You need to reinforce your argument as the essay progresses so that readers see how each separate part of the paper supports the main idea. In a paper arguing that student athletes require special academic assistance, it would be important to keep the focus on athletes, especially several paragraphs after the initial statement of the position.

{**General**} If a person does not receive a good education, he or she will later become a burden to society and it will leave him or her with nothing at all to contribute to the working world. It is obvious that students, especially freshman, require these benefits to manage their academic and future careers.

{**Specific**} If a **student-athlete** does not receive a good education, he or she will later become a burden to society. **Without a solid education in some field,** the athlete will have nothing to contribute to the working world. It is obvious that **student-athletes,** especially freshman, require **academic counseling** to be sure they learn to manage their academic lives and future careers.

It is especially important to reestablish what it is you are trying to prove whenever you offer a new supporting argument. Unfortunately, writers sometimes think that just because they have stated a thesis clearly once, they aren't required to reinforce it. Readers are expected to understand. The fact is that they often won't—and they'll resent the sloppy and hurried impression that weak topic sentences can give.

11 E

Thesis

Here's the beginning of a paragraph deep in an essay supporting the thesis that certain government and history courses should be removed from the core curriculum.

Another aspect of what a waste government and history courses are
is time.

The writer's intentions are good. He gives readers a transitional signal (*Another aspect*) and a reminder of the general topic (*what a waste government and history courses are*), but both are vague and the new supporting idea is mysterious: *time*. What does time have to do with government and history courses? Whose time? A more careful topic sentence will have to move more slowly, spelling out ideas for readers. Here is one possible revision.

Eliminating the government/history requirement from the core curriculum has the added advantage of freeing six credit hours on students' crowded schedules, giving them the time for two more electives.

This version is longer, but that's because it quickly supplies information the writer would have add to the paragraph eventually. Why make readers waste their time getting to the point?

▶ **Edit carefully.** Edit only after you have a draft that satisfies the assignment (see Section 5C for a thorough checklist). Here are several additional points worth checking.

—If you have used sources, acknowledge them. Check with your instructor to determine whether you should use MLA or APA documentation form. See Sections 39B and 40B.

—If you use direct quotations, handle them properly. See Section 34E.

—Give your paper a clear and specific title, one that enables readers to identify more than just your general topic area. Don't be cute. Try to imagine how informative your title would seem if it were listed in an index or card catalogue.

—Check the spelling of all technical terms and all proper nouns.

—Doublecheck the accuracy of all figures and statistics you use. Be sure readers have accurate data.

12 PERSUASION

A Understanding persuasion
B Examining a sample paper
C Choosing a topic
D Preparing and planning
E Drafting and revising

Terms you need to know

RHETORIC. The art of finding, arranging, and presenting arguments and evidence so that an audience is moved to think or act in a particular way.

INVENTION. The process of finding arguments and evidence systematically.

12 A   UNDERSTANDING PERSUASION

Persuasive writing *begins with* belief. That's how it differs from proving a thesis (see Chapter 11). When proving a thesis, a writer begins with an hypothesis—a "what if?" proposition that does not necessarily reflect strong commitments, personal convictions, or political principles. If the evidence comes in against the hypothesis, the writer alters or refines the hypothesis until it agrees with the facts.

PROVING A THESIS
   (ARGUMENTATION/SCIENTIFIC DEMONSTRATIONS)

Facts/evidence ——————————— lead to ———————————▶ thesis/position

When persuading, a writer *begins with a commitment* to a position and then finds evidence and arguments to convince readers to share that belief. The success of a persuasive essay depends on whether the article moves readers to endorse or at least understand a writer's position.

PERSUASION
(POLITICAL/SOCIAL CONTROVERSY)

Commitment (thesis/position)——————— draws on ——————▶ facts/evidence

Some theorists hold that there are no differences between proving a thesis (some call it "argumentation") and persuasion; they maintain, for example, that all arguments are ultimately political, and that scientific writing merely conceals its political intentions under a facade of objectivity. Others counter that failing to distinguish between scientific and persuasive writing leads to distortions of reality—to attempts to bend facts to fit political designs.

12 A

Persuasion

We can't resolve such a deep conflict here, but we want at least to alert you to a distinction between

• a kind of scientific demonstration that attempts an accurate and comprehensive description, discussion, and analysis of the material facts (that's "Proving a Thesis," Chapter 11);

• a political kind of argumentation that provides guidance for decisions and action in the world of human affairs, where facts and evidence cannot be handled free of the entanglements of human emotions and personalities.

Both types of writing are legitimate and valuable. This chapter is about the second kind of writing, what we will call persuasion and what the classical tradition described as "rhetoric"—the end product of an art of persuasion.

Some types of persuasion	
Sermons	Fund appeals
Advertisements	Legislative debates
Political speeches	Sales pitches
Newspaper editorials	Appeals to a jury
Letters to the editor	

To many people, the term *rhetoric* has negative connotations. They associate rhetoric with the tricks of advertisers, or the empty words of politicians "mere rhetoric." Without a question, rhetoric and persuasion *are* concerned with using language to move men and women to do things that they might not have done without prompting. But persuasion itself is not a bad thing, else we would all be locked into rigid beliefs. In fact, one might argue that rhetoric is essential in democratic societies: persuasion thrives where the opinions of individual citizens matter. Without persuasive writing and speaking, we would have trouble making choices, whether we were voting, buying, or choosing sides in a debate.

Why don't we just argue facts? The simple answer is that people don't operate on the evidence of facts alone. If they did, would anyone smoke? The more complex response is that, in themselves, facts don't tell us much. They have to be interpreted to have any meaning, and such interpretations are always done by people living in communities with histories, customs, beliefs, and intellectual traditions—all of which affect the way "facts" are understood. Agreement about factual matters is not impossible, but neither is "agreement" or "consensus" a simple process of getting people to see things straight and true. Human nature is too complex (and too impatient) for scientific logic—something that the rhetorical tradition, from its earliest formulations in ancient Greece, has recognized.

Places to read persuasive articles

TV Guide
The New York Times Book Review
The Nation
National Review
Rolling Stone
Harper's
The Village Voice
Vital Speeches of the Day

---

12 B

Persuasion

These are just a few reasons for writing a persuasive paper:

- to judge a proposed action;
- to change the opinion of readers about some past action;
- to *persuade someone* to take action;
- to praise or blame someone for something;
- to change the opinion of people about someone's reputation;
- to argue against an accepted theory.

12 B EXAMINING A PERSUASIVE PAPER

Here is a persuasive paper written by a student just a few weeks after the Supreme Court of the United States in 1989 struck down a law that banned flag-burning.

AUTHOR: Luis Garcia, freshman at the University of Texas at Austin. (Luis also contributes essays to chapters 10 and 11.)

AUDIENCE: His classmates in a Freshman English course.

ASSIGNMENT: Write a persuasive essay that deals with an important political or social issue.

REQUIREMENTS: Length—about 500 words.

The Right to Burn

(1)   When the Founders wrote the Bill of Rights they probably never imagined

that the First Amendment would someday be used to defend the desecration and destruction of Old Glory herself. Yet in its recent ruling on the American's right to burn the U.S. flag, the Supreme Court found that the act of burning the flag is as fundamentally constitutional as the right to speak freely. According to the First Amendment,

> Congress shall make no law respecting an establishment of religion, or prohibiting the free exercise thereof, or abridging the freedom of speech, or of the press; or the right of the people peaceably to assemble and to petition the Government for a redress of grievances.

12 B

Persuasion

This amendment is the foundation upon which the United States was built. For this reason, the Supreme Court ruled in favor of the right to burn the American flag in order to preserve America's fundamental rights to freedom of speech and expression. According to Justice William J. Brennan, "The Government may not prohibit the expression of an idea simply because society finds the idea itself offensive or disagreeable." Although flag-burning is a deeply offensive and disrespectful act, a free society must preserve an individual's right of self-expression, and, consequently, must permit the burning of the American flag as an act of political dissent.

(2)   The flag plays different roles to different people. Those who oppose the Supreme Court's ruling see the flag more as an actual part of the country rather than just a symbol of the country's might and dignity. Any attack on the flag becomes an attack on the nation for which it stands. Obviously, the flag plays an important role in society: school children pledge their allegiance to the flag every day, soldiers are taught to honor and respect the flag, and America honors its dead on Memorial day by flying the flag at half-staff. To veterans, the flag represents patriotism and deserves respect and honor. In the patriot's eyes, if America is worth fighting for, then the symbol of that country is worth defending.

(3)   And yet, the same amendment that protects the veterans' views about the flag also protects the people who burn the flag in an act of dissent. Under the Constitution, the radical views that the flag is only a piece of cloth are as worthy of legal protection as those patriotic views that the flag embodies all the values and greatness of a country. According to conservative Supreme Court Justice Anthony M. Kennedy, "It is poignant but fundamental that the flag protects those who hold it in contempt." In fact, the more socially disagreeable a speech or an expression is, the more necessary Constitutional protection becomes. And important disputes are bound to arise because the United States is composed of many different groups, religions, ethnic communities, and races.

(4)   Yet part of America's uniqueness is in its citizens' diversity as well as in their Constitutional right to think and speak freely without fear of condemnation. But the freedom is not absolute and loses Constitutional protection when personal liberties infringe on the rights of others. In the United States, one may demonstrate freely against abortion, but may not physically prevent the act. One may smoke cigarettes, but may not force others around him to do so. In the same respect, the Supreme Court has ruled that the burning of the American flag is constitutional only in the limited form of dissent and ceases to be constitutional when such an act incites violence or is a case of vandalism. In other words, like all liberties, the right to burn the flag is not absolute.

12 B

Persuasion

(5)   Thus the dispute over flag-burning arises from the exact significance of Old Glory herself. The flag, according to the Supreme Court, is a symbol of freedom. Contradicting the veterans' view that the flag is an actual part of the country, the flag is only a symbol and does not play any role in the actions of the country. A flag does not bring America to war, nor does it embody the patriotism of a country. Poor policymakers bring a country to war and people reflect a country's patriotism.

(6)   Unfortunately, many legislators feel that the ruling is a grave mistake and they are already trying to amend the First Amendment making the burning of the flag unconstitutional. The foundation of this country is the Constitution. To alter the Constitution because of conflicting views is to undermine the basic structure upon which America was built. Nevertheless, the flag that ironically protects those who destroy it also protects the legislators' rights to try to amend the Constitution.

▶ **Analysis of Luis Garcia's "The Right to Burn"**

Thesis. What is the thesis of this paper? How would you characterize the tone of the thesis—forceful and aggressive; firm but controlled; tentative and weak? Cite phrases or complete sentences that demonstrate the dominant tone of the paper.

Audience. To what type of reader would Luis's paper appeal? What kinds of people might find the paper ineffective? What groups of people are specifically mentioned in the paper? Do you think people in those groups would at least listen to Luis Garcia's argument? Why or why not?

Organization. Briefly outline the arguments presented in the paper. Does the organization make sense to you? Why or why not? Examine the transitions between each paragraph. How effective are they? Can you think of any way to improve them?

Evidence. Why does Luis quote the first amendment to the U.S. Constitution in the first paragraph? Is the citation effective? What other kinds of evidence does Garcia use in the paper? Can you think of any evidence he might have used?

Reader's Response. If you were in agreement with Garcia's opinion even before you read "The Right to Burn," what in the paper strikes you as his strongest argument? If you opposed Garcia's position before reading the paper, did his essay change your point of view in any way? Why or why not? What do you regard as the weaknesses of the paper?

12 C   CHOOSING A TOPIC

> **The Basic Assignment**
>
> Identify some political, social, economic, or ethical position you hold strongly. Then choose an audience you would like to persuade to adopt your position and write a paper to accomplish this. Your position should concern an issue on which your readers are likely to have some opinions and knowledge.

➤ **Variations**

a. Respond to a newspaper editorial you disagree with either by writing a letter to the editor or a full column that might be published as a rebuttal. Explain your opposition to the editorial position taken by the newspaper and advocate a position of your own.

b. Address one of the following issues or questions in a persuasive paper. Argue your case to your classmates or another audience which you carefully specify.

1. Should the federal government fund abortions for the needy?
2. Should college students be allowed to design their own course programs?
3. Should students have the right to evaluate teachers?
4. Should affirmative action programs be abandoned or expanded?
5. Do campus racial or sexual harassment policies violate first amendment guarantees of free speech?
6. Should the U.S. adopt an amendment to the Constitution making English the nation's official language?
7. Should the U.S. commit itself to more extensive manned space flights—including missions to the moon again or to Mars?
8. Should tax money be used to fund the projects of artists, sculptors, musicians, and other artists?
9. Should a gay or lesbian couple be accorded the legal status of a family—and the right to family leave, shared pension funds, and so on?
10. Should preserving the environment take precedent over economic development in underdeveloped areas of the world?

c. As part of a class project, read about and then discuss a controversial political or social issue. As the discussion develops, try to define the two or three basic positions around which opinion seems to be coalescing. Then divide up into writing groups. Let two or three of the groups be made up of people who essentially agree about their positions on the issue; construct the remaining two or three groups out of individuals who don't see eye to eye on the matter. Let each group write a single persuasive essay advancing some position on the controversy. (Obviously, negotiation and compromise will be necessary in both groups, but more so in those groups where members begin with opposing views.) At the conclusion of the project, compare the papers and the writing process of those in the groups whose members agreed on the issue with those in groups made up of people who didn't agree at the outset. Draw some conclusions about the advantages and disadvantages of constructing a persuasive paper with the assistance of those who differ with your position.

12 D

Persuasion

12 D   PREPARING AND PLANNING A PERSUASIVE PAPER

Writing a persuasive piece may resemble proving a thesis: you develop a position, gather arguments to support it, and arrange your materials effectively. But persuasion is much harder: when you support a thesis successfully, people will smile appreciatively—"nice job," "really interesting thinking," "admirable work." If you then try to convince the same people to do something about the issue you've just argued, to *act* as well as to *understand,* well that's a different matter—"not sure," "asking a lot," "maybe next year." To persuade (rather than just prove), you may have to identify more with your readers, understand alternative positions, anticipate the strategies of those with whom you disagree, and deploy a wider range of arguments.

In persuasive writing, the audience is number one. Readers alone determine whether you fail or succeed: thumbs up; thumbs down. In one way, it's that simple. In another way it's not, because what may be a wonderful argument for one group of readers won't persuade another. So there's no such thing as a good argument in itself—it's good only if it works with specific readers. Your first task, then, is to identify those readers and consider how you're going to appeal to them.

Begin by asking yourself whether you are in a debate, that is, a situation in which you think of the person on the other side as an opponent. If so, you probably don't really expect to persuade him or her to your point of view—the lines are too strongly drawn. Rather you are arguing beyond your opponent to another group of readers whom you hope to persuade by demonstrating that the other side's arguments are weak and yours are convincing. Under such circumstances, you can mount an argument as you would a campaign or game plan. You can point out weaknesses on the other side, try to undermine their credibility, point out inconsistencies in their position, and hope to overwhelm them with your facts. Such strategies can work well with an audience whose vote you want, particularly if you're well prepared.

But suppose you hope to persuade someone who is close and important to you, a friend or business associate, someone whose opinion you value and whose cooperation you need. Then the situation changes. Now you must try to present your argument in ways that don't threaten or anger the person you're trying to persuade. You don't win arguments with people by making them hostile or by demeaning them. You only make them defensive and stubborn, and though you may think you have presented a stunning case against their point of view, you won't persuade them. They might quit arguing with you, but you haven't won their support.

To win over readers like these, you must appeal to common interests and accommodate their points of view. You can do that logically, but logic alone often won't move audiences to abandon cherished beliefs or to act in new (possibly expensive) ways. To accomplish that, you have to win readers' regard and trust. You have to show you respect them, understand their concerns, and are willing to compromise, if necessary, to come to a working agreement.

12 D

Persuasion

Your ability to persuade depends, to a great extent, upon your ability to understand people—their needs, their desires, their fears, and their hopes. We've talked about audiences elsewhere in this book; we urge you now to review that section (see pp. 14–17). As to finding and shaping arguments effective in moving both mind and heart, we've outlined below some strategies writers use. (We couldn't possibly list them all.) We think you'll find this material surprisingly interesting because, finally, it's about how people think and behave.

To write an effective persuasive paper . . .

▶ **Be sure you know what you are arguing.** To develop strong arguments in favor of your position, you'll need to understand the limits of your claim and the evidence required to support it. So the first step is simple: put your claim into words. State your position in one clear sentence. If you cannot do that, chances are you don't have a position to support.

Any statement of position you make this early in the process will be tentative: you may eventually need to refine the language and qualify the claims you are making. But you shouldn't have to wrestle with the basic terms of your argument. If you do, you probably don't know your subject well enough to write a compelling persuasive paper. Why should other people follow your lead when you don't know where you're going?

Luis Garcia may have begun drafting his essay on flag-burning (see above) with a thesis no more sophisticated than this:

Burning the American flag must be permitted as an act of political protest.

Such a statement would represent his position at the beginning of the writing process, before he has more fully explored the issues in the controversy. As he writes the paper, he refines his initial position and polishes his wording until he has a claim worthy of serious consideration—and capable of persuading.

Although flag-burning is a deeply offensive and disrespectful act, a free society must preserve an individual's right of self-expression, and, consequently, must permit the burning of the American flag as an act of political dissent.

But that simple, preliminary position was essential. Without it, Luis's process of writing would have lacked purpose.

▶ **Understand your audience.** An earlier section in this handbook (see Section 2B) deals with many of the general aspects of audience you need to appreciate in writing any paper. But we can outline a few considerations peculiar to persuasion.

First, consider how your readers define "happiness." Sound odd? It's not. To persuade people, you need to show them that the course of action you recommend will satisfy their general desire for happiness in this world. That's not to say that they must exit any persuasive piece you write smiling, but that they should appreciate how your argument contributes to their welfare and current concerns. Any number of factors—race, gender, religion, occupation, economic status, and political orientation—will influence a reader's definition of "happiness."

Obviously, the better you know your readers, the more precisely you can tailor your presentation to them. If your audience is quite general (as it often will be), then you must rely on cultural norms to guide your selection of arguments. In American society, for example, audiences will ordinarily respond well to appeals to hard work, fairness, justice, and democracy—even though many individuals within that larger group will object to particular items in the list. You can probably list values that appeal (or repulse) any specific audience you can name. If you don't know an audience well enough to understand its general values, you'll have a problem appealing to them.

When you know an audience well, you can then choose examples, illustrations, and allusions suited to that group. For example, allusions to classical music might work well with affluent, urban readers, but look pretentious to small-town business people. You also need to write in language suited to the audience. To see how language changes from audience to audience, just pick up a few magazines aimed at different age groups, professions, or economic groups. You'll find differences in the tone, style, organization, and vocabulary (in the professional magazines especially) of these pieces. The differences evident in the periodicals represent the adjustments writers must make to be "heard" by their readers. To be listened to in an academic setting, for example, you must master something called *college writing*. (See Chapter 6.)

When persuading, you must write in language your readers are willing to hear. For one thing, that means that you don't attack them. Few readers will continue to read something that they feel denigrates their ideas or suggests they're stupid. It also means that you show good judgment about how formal or informal you want to sound and how much specialized terminology you want to use. If you sound too distant or use too many unfamiliar terms, your readers won't stick around to read your conclusions.

Finally, consider the length your readers will tolerate. Whatever your approach, don't carry on beyond what your readers will willingly endure. The persuasive essay that drones on and on sounds like propaganda or harassment, so make your point, provide the evidence, highlight your conclusions, then leave the matter with your readers. Show them that you trust their judgment.

▶ **Review all the arguments you can think of to support your position.** In some respects, persuasion follows an explanatory writing process: many writers begin

12 D

Persuasion

a persuasive piece already knowing where they stand. But what is open-ended in persuasive writing is the process of "invention"—the discovery and creation of arguments in favor of your position.

In some cases, you'll know your arguments well enough to have rehearsed them. You may even feel a little like the politician delivering a "stump" speech for the twentieth time, but you can't afford to seem either bored or overconfident to readers. After all, the arguments will be new to them.

In most cases, you'll have to work to find arguments. Initially, just listing every idea you think of may be the most fruitful technique of invention. You'll discover that writing down one idea will often stimulate a second and third possibility. As always, don't be too critical at this early stage. Even weak arguments may suggest the framework of stronger ones. While you are at it, list counterarguments as well. Here is a sample list from a paper against capital punishment.

Argument	*Counterargument*
—life imprisonment without parole is more humane than capital punishment.	—life imprisonment often leads to release on parole.
—capital punishment is brutal; executions are often grisly.	—lethal injection is humane form of execution.
—killing the criminal can't undo the original crime, causes more suffering.	—justice requires "eye for an eye."
—no evidence that death penalty deters murder or serious crimes.	—evidence on deterrence isn't clear; benefit of doubt should be with potential victims of crime.
—justice is fallible: innocent person might be executed. No way to correct such an error.	—miscarriages of justice do not warrant abolition of death penalty.

If listing doesn't seem to work, try freewriting on your topic for ten or fifteen minutes (see Section 3A). Chances are the freewriting will start off slowly, but then gather steam.

When you have a preliminary sense of the lines of argument to follow, do some reading to learn even more about your subject. Such reading may help you find common ground with readers with whom you disagree. After all, you aren't going to move a hostile reader to understand your perspective by pointing out only where you differ or where *you* are right. Look for ideas that might develop into arguments about mutual values, shared premises, and common traditions. Explore the advantages of compromise; look for solutions that benefit all sides in a controversy. It's better to have your adversaries whisper "brother" or "sister" than cry "uncle."

But even when you have generated a wealth of ideas, you still aren't done. You now need to transform your knowledge and your arguments into persuasive energy—into the kinds of statements that move readers to appreciate your point of view. The remaining sections suggest ways of framing arguments powerfully.

➤ **Argue from definition.** Identify key terms in your argument and define (or redefine) them honestly, but in a way favorable to your position. Quite often, a definition can actually determine whether an argument is won or lost: was it murder or self-defense? Murder or mercy killing? Civil disobedience or vandalism? Such questions of definition are not trivial matters. Take definitions seriously. Weigh the meaning of every word.

Consider, for example, how crucial definitions of human life have been in arguments about abortion. Here, in a paper arguing for legal abortion, the definition of "person" proves critical:

> ...On the other hand, **science defines a person** as having the capacity to be aware, sense, reason, and make moral judgments. A fetus does not have these qualities until the development of the neocortex and central nervous system, which takes nineteen to twenty-two weeks. Therefore, a fetus cannot be considered a human being until almost five months into the pregnancy ....

12 D

Persuasion

If readers accept the definition offered, the argument flies.

As you might expect, arguments by definition can be countered by challenging the accuracy or authority of the definition in question—or any part of it. In the case above, opponents might home in on the undocumented assertion preceding the definition: "science defines." Whose science? Which scientists? At a minimum, the writer would need to cite a source for the definition offered—one that proves the scientific claim. More likely, opponents of abortion would attack the terms of the definition of "person" itself, pointing out that current version seems to exclude young children (who do not make moral judgments) from the category of persons: does the definition mean that an infant at three months does not possess a right to life? The writer offering the definition (and favoring abortion) would certainly want to refine "person" before using it as part of his argument.

Understanding that a given controversy stems from a problem of definition can be a first step toward resolving a conflict. For example, arguments over *who* ought to spend *what* to enhance public literacy might be less heated if people shared a common definition of **literacy.** Does it merely mean someone who can read or does it entail a wider conception of cultural understanding? When the definition of a critical term is made clearer, people sometimes discover that they have been debating matters about which they essentially agree.

➤ **Argue from fact.** Americans tend to favor arguments that use facts and figures, so if you can add the "weight of facts" to the case you're making, you'll strengthen that case. This is where it pays to do your homework. When you show that you've taken the trouble to gather evidence and statistics to support your claims, you'll improve your credibility.

If you make a factual claim—let's say that women, on the average earn only two-thirds as much as men—back it up. Backing it up involves more than just being able to cite a source; it means commanding the information behind the number—where does the fact come from, what does it involve, how reliable is it? But facts are worth the trouble: if you were writing a paper urging the adoption of comparable pay legislation, for example, the fact that women earn only a fraction what men do tips the balance of argument decidedly in your favor—if you can make that number stick.

When the facts seem to weigh against your side of an argument, challenge those items. Make your opponents show that they're valid and raise questions of your own—lots of them. Ask where the data came from and who interpreted them. The income figure cited above seems like damning evidence of job inequity. But what does the figure actually measure? Do the women in the study have the same years of service as the men, the same education, the same job skills? Better yet, counter with figures on your own: you might find statistics showing that—when economic and social factors are taken into account—women earn 96 percent of what men do. In some jobs, statistics show that women actually earn more.

12 D

Persuasion

When figures conflict (as in the average pay example), who is right? The writer who knows the subject best has anticipated challenges and has built rebuttals into any presentation of facts. Hard work pays off.

But facts can also be used to find common ground between opposing positions. Often enough you may find yourself able to refute the facts, but not the reality that goes along with them. What difference does it make to the deserving poor if the actual number of homeless is 3,000,000 or 300,000, you might ask. A compromise to assist the homeless might be an agreement to ignore the debate over numbers and to focus on the existing needs of displaced people.

▶ **Argue for the greater good; argue for the lesser evil.** More often than not, readers will see merit on both sides of an argument; after all, contradictory proposals can each offer a legitimate benefit. When that's the case, a good writer sees to it that his or her proposal is perceived as the *greater* good. In arguing for affirmative action programs, for example, you might admit than an ideal society would hire and promote people free of any considerations of race, ethnicity, and gender, but that, in the United States today, justice is better served by programs that deliberately promote the careers of certain minority groups—even at the expense of other groups. Such an argument offers historical justice as a greater good than fairness. But the argument can be turned around, using the same principle: while granting preference to minorities and women in hiring provides a type of compensation to social groups left behind in the past, affirmative action programs undermine a *greater good*—the establishment of a just society free of all biases. In this case, *both* lines of argument have merit and power. It's up to individual writers to sell their version of the "greater good."

Arguments that describe some course of action as the lesser of two evils can also be effective, particularly when urging readers to take some course of action they'd rather not. Such arguments might include the familiar ones for spending increased sums on prenatal care for expectant mothers or on job-training programs for high school dropouts. Such projects are always expensive, but neglecting such programs will almost certainly cost taxpayers even more: a healthy pregnancy is cheaper—in the long run—than dealing with the consequences of medical neglect; teaching an adolescent how to be a productive citizen is less costly than warehousing him or her in a prison. Taxpayers might prefer to spend no money at all, but the "lesser of two evils" approach effectively eliminates that as an option.

Once again, arguments about greater and lesser good hold the potential for compromise. You may discover a way of creating a win-win situation simply by admitting the merit in alternative positions: if each side in a dispute has virtues, combining the approaches (or portions of them) may even solve the problem. Each side gives a little ultimately to gain a great deal.

> **Argue from fairness and equality; expose the fallacy of fairness and equality.**
Perhaps the most dependable line of argument in America today is the appeal to fairness. The argument is hard to challenge because it appeals to a key concept of democratic government: equal treatment under law.

Because of its almost universal appeal, the fairness or equality argument occurs in circumstances that have nothing to do with law or government. In almost any situation, if you can show that people have been treated unfairly—or that they have been excluded from privileges others have enjoyed—you will find supporters for your case. For example, domestic manufacturers of products in competition with foreign products will often charge that, while the American market is wide open to all comers, the Japanese, Brazilians, or the Europeans place restrictions in their homelands on American goods or marketing. Thus the issue of "fairness" is used to argue for changing an imbalance: the foreigners should treat us the same way we treat them. Sounds unimpeachable.

Yet strong as the fortress of fairness is, it can be challenged in several ways. One tactic is to brand the fairness appeal as a smokescreen—the tactic of a group really more interested in privilege than equality. Another is to demonstrate that factors other than prejudice or unfairness are responsible for a "seeming" inequity. Such arguments may question whether "fairness" is the natural or desirable result in cases where individual talent, dedication, and labor play a part. In short, you advocate fairness at the starting gate, but not at the finish line.

Where fairness really does seem to be an issue—as in the case of trade practices—you might look for ways of denying that fairness tells the whole story. Foreign manufacturers, for example, often charge American companies with not doing their homework—not learning to speak the language or understand the cultural habits of foreign countries. Thus, the American failure to exploit these markets is portrayed more as the consequence of bad business strategies than the result of inequalities in trading agreements.

Notice that Luis Garcia shrewdly deploys the fairness argument in his essay on flag-burning in an effort to defuse the conflict. In a sense, he puts both patriots and flag-burners on the same side of the controversy, treated in the same way by the law.

> In the patriot's eyes, if America is worth fighting for, then the
>
> symbol of that country is worth defending.
>
> (3)   And yet, the same amendment that protects the veterans'
>
> views about the flag also protects the people who burn the flag in an
>
> act of dissent.

12 D

Persuasion

According to Mr. Garcia, protecting the first amendment proves to be the fairest way of guaranteeing everyone's rights. His essay concludes on that point exactly.

> Nevertheless, the flag that ironically protects those who destroy it
>
> also protects the legislators' rights to try to amend the Constitution.

➤ **Argue for the long-term good; argue for the short-term good.** If what you are proposing will have slow or deferred benefits, argue for the wisdom of appreciating the "big picture"—of thinking about one's kids or grandchildren rather than oneself. You can always portray a long-term benefit as more serious, substantial, and judicious than an immediate one. If, for example, you are opposed to building public housing projects, you might point out that, in the long run, market forces tend to produce better housing for all because the poor eventually move into residences built and designed for wealthier owners. Building low-cost ("cheap") public housing could then be identified as a "quick fix," one that finally won't solve the housing problem, but only will only create additional urban blight.

On the other hand, you might be the one favoring immediate action and commitment, while your opponents support a slow and steady approach, one that builds for the future at the expense of the present. In such a case, you stress the "critical" status of the current situation and, perhaps, list factors contributing to the "crisis." In your analysis, you portray the long-term position either as a luxury the current situation cannot afford or as yet another "delaying" tactic of the opposition. For example, if you support public housing, you might stress the need to shelter the dispossessed immediately; after all, the needy cannot wait for the "plodding corrective of market mechanisms that haven't worked very well to this point anyway."

Remember, though, that just hammering on your opponents will achieve little if you need their cooperation to accomplish something. When all sides in a controversy seem obsessed by the need to pursue their own agenda, it might be wise in an argument to urge everyone to step back for a broader perspective. Try to show that all parties are really moving toward similar goals—ecological health, fiscal soundness, ethical behavior—and suggest that those destinations might be more easily reached if you put aside angry politics and conflicts between personalities. You may accomplish more in your argument by playing it cool and allowing face-saving compromises all around.

➤ **Argue for the benefit of greater numbers; argue the special case.** Most courses of action benefit some people more than others. When your position seems to help many people, you can simply apply the weight of numbers to your argument.

> Building a cross-town highway through the Annandale neighborhood will ease traffic congestion for tens of thousands of motorists each day. The new highway would also reduce traffic accidents and injuries in what has become one of the most dangerous corridors in the city. The common good demands that a few property owners sacrifice their homes for this much-needed highway project.

It is somewhat harder to argue for a narrower group against the interests of the general public. But the key is to make the individual members of the public imagine themselves in the position of those likely to be injured by the public good.

Building a six-lane freeway through the heart of the historic Annandale neighborhood may save the motoring public a few minutes of commuter time. But it will cost many homeowners their homes, their property, and the community life they have spent a lifetime building. If the lives of a few citizens can be so drastically disrupted by the plans of the highway commission, who can feel safe in this city?

Luis Garcia uses precisely this tactic in explaining the need to protect dissent from the weight of majority opinion. He does it, however, by emphasizing how the Constitution ultimately protects everyone.

According to conservative Supreme Court Justice Anthony M.

Kennedy, "It is poignant but fundamental that the flag protects

those who hold it in contempt." In fact, the more socially

disagreeable a speech or an expression is, the more necessary

Constitutional protection becomes. And important disputes are

bound to arise because the United States is composed of many

different groups, religions, ethnic communities, and races.

12 D

Persuasion

Luis implicitly argues that everyone belongs to some group that may one day require the protection the First Amendment affords. Thus he advances his argument by showing that he appreciates the need to protect both majority and minority opinions. No one is left out.

➤ **Argue from the self-interest; argue against self-interest.** Unless readers understand how they benefit from a proposal, they aren't likely to act upon it. So explain exactly how readers might benefit from a proposal; be as specific as possible when you can cite real advantages. Quite often, however, a writer has to urge readers to look beyond self-interest, to act for the good of their institutions, posterity, nation, or world community. Such appeals are always difficult: try persuading Southerners to give up air-conditioning to save the ozone layer, or Northerners to stop burning coal to end acid rain. But even acting against self-interest can be made less painful. As they say, virtue is its own reward. Make readers who choose the "right course" feel good.

➤ **Argue from tradition and authority; argue against tradition and authority.** Some writers don't like to support arguments by appealing to long-standing traditions or authorities, yet such appeals make sense both logically and emotionally. Why take time to justify values, principles, and arrangements which readers will accept on the basis of an appeal to authority: "As Thomas Jefferson has said . . ."; "To use the argument originally put forth by Dr. Martin Luther King, Jr., . . ."; "For more than a century, people have agreed that . . . ?" Such arguments can be shortcuts for a writer—efficient ways of asking people to recognize and act upon their core values.

When readers have not considered their positions on an issue deeply, they may be willing to rely upon the opinion of a person or institution they trust—a former president, a distinguished artist, a famous writer, a competent journalist. Arguments from authority that stress familiarity, security, and continuity can win enormous support.

While authority can make readers feel secure, when a situation is particularly bad, an appeal to authority carries little weight: the situation clearly demands change. So, ironically, arguments against authority can be just as powerful as those that champion it. We admire the nonconformist, the rebel (with or without a cause), the David standing up to Goliath. Urging people to break with "stifling conventions," "outworn conventions" or "musty traditions" can have impact on any readers who like change and "progress."

You can sometimes move an argument toward compromise by looking for and citing an authority whom both sides admire. The well-respected person can thus serve as a sort of neutral third party in a squabble—someone to whom both sides can listen without feeling threatened or misrepresented.

12 D

Persuasion

▶ **Argue from precedents; argue against precedents.** Precedents are particularly important in legal arguments where lawyers and judges routinely look to previous decisions to determine how a new case ought to be decided. If something has been done in the past and has been accepted as either legal or traditional, it becomes a sort of defense for similar actions in the present. Luis Garcia, for example, combines an argument from precedent with an argument from analogy to acknowledge that all freedoms in American society have limits.

> ... freedom is not absolute and loses Constitutional protection when personal liberties infringe on the rights of others. In the United States, one may demonstrate freely against abortion, but may not physically prevent the act. One may smoke cigarettes, but may not force others around him to do so. In the same respect, the Supreme Court has ruled that the burning of the American flag is constitutional only in the limited form of dissent and ceases to be constitutional when such an act incites violence or is a case of vandalism. In other words, like all liberties, the right to burn the flag is not absolute.

Where the precedents of a given case weigh against your argument, you need to challenge them—to suggest that they are outdated or, perhaps, that they do not apply to the current situation. Look for differences between the previous situation or the current one either in the people involved, the numbers, the time, the historical circumstances, and so forth. If the precedent is a formidable one, suggest that it is time to break with the past.

▶ **Argue from feasibility.** Whenever you argue for a change in the status quo, it's important to prove that your proposal is workable—not the pie-in-the-sky scheme of a do-gooder. However, the burden of proof is with you, so gather the figures, furnish the plans, provide examples of comparable projects undertaken elsewhere. For example, let's say you are arguing in favor of building a convention center in your town. To do that, you'd have to suggest how the project would be paid for, how it will support its own operating costs, and how the community will benefit. You might cite the successes of other towns that have built convention centers.

If you find yourself opposing some scheme or project, you can simply reverse the feasibility tactics: you gather figures that suggest the project can't be managed (or show that your opponents' financing is based upon rosy economic projections). And you look for the examples where similar undertakings have failed. For example, advocates of legalized drugs have long made a feasibility argument: they question whether tougher laws and campaigns of education can ever control the scourge of drug use. In addition, they point to the high costs of the drug wars and to the similar failure of prohibition to curtail use of alcohol.

➤ **Argue from simplicity; argue from complexity.** When you can offer a simple proposal for solving a complex problem, you've got a real ace-in-the-hole argument. An "elegant" solution is admired both in rhetoric and mathematics. But make sure readers appreciate the brilliance of your solution—list its advantages and emphasize how easily it can be implemented.

12 D

Persuasion

When you need to oppose a proposal or idea that has the virtue of simplicity, show that either that the problem really is too complex to solve easily or that the simple solution isn't so elegant after all.

An example of an appealingly simple solution to a complex problem, consider the proposal to end the scourge of illicit drugs by legalizing them. If you are in favor of the idea, you'd emphasize how this action would eliminate the need for elaborate law enforcement measures, reduce tensions with foreign governments, end large-scale border patrols, and even provide a new source of tax revenues. A great many troublesome matters disappear once drugs are legalized: drug dealing, organized crime, drug testing. Simple? Well, if you are on the other side, you say "wait a minute. Not a simple at all. We've still got a nation full of drug users who need treatment and education. We still have to keep drugs out of the hands of children. We've got to set up a new bureaucracy to handle the drugs—to import them, check their quality, control their distribution."

And so the argument from "simplicity" rolls on.

➤ **Argue the emotional side; expose the emotional argument.** When you have a strong emotional case to make, don't be afraid to show it. People aren't computers: they are moved when an argument takes a human form. Moreover, such arguments are completely valid when any emotion generated is in proportion to the gravity of the subject. Fighting famine with pictures of starving children makes sense when relief must be mobilized quickly; opposing legtraps may require depicting the suffering of captured animals.

When you must oppose an emotional argument, you aren't helpless. Try to take control of your opponents' emotional appeals by pointing them out to readers as precisely that and exposing any excesses in the presentations. When you are up against a tough one, try placing the emotional situation in a larger context by suggesting equally compelling situations that might be hidden. For example, hunters who favored the harvesting of baby seals counterargued by suggesting that the livelihoods of entire communities depended upon the hunts. But don't underestimate the persuasive power of graphic, emotionally appealing images rendered in words or photographs. Sometimes their effect can't be overcome.

➤ **Extend the argument: where does the argument lead?** When you want to change a particular situation, project its consequences into the future. Let readers understand that what seems like a small problem now can only get worse—and here's how. Similarly, if you are opposed to a particular idea, trace its implications and suggest to readers what could happen if the action is taken. Use a "worst-case" scenario to show how a small program might grow into a bigger one, how one authorized intrusion into private life may lead to others, how buying one foreign product hurts the domestic economy in dozens of ways. Such arguments have real impact, particularly in pessimistic times.

> **Argue from comparison and analogy; attack comparisons and analogies.** You may be able to influence readers if you can suggest to them that a disputed issue resembles another more familiar and settled situation. Sometimes you can make the point quickly and memorably:

12 D

Persuasion

> We kick students out of the university who do not have a high enough GPA; there is no reason not to do the same with drug abusers, who deserve dismissal even more.

Sometimes the comparison or analogy requires more explanation. Let's say, for example, in writing a paper to oppose burning of the American flag, you want to argue that it is appropriate for the nation to respect its symbols. The desecration of a flag might then be compared with a related situation:

> Communities have long given special protection to objects of important symbolic value. In Austin, Texas, for example, a man was arrested in 1989 for poisoning the Treaty Oak, a magnificent tree that took root well before Columbus explored the Americas. The man accused of poisoning the tree was tracked, arrested, and indicted because the Austin community shared an interest in the Treaty Oak as an object worthy of special protection and veneration. Harming the tree was, in a real sense, a physical attack upon the entire community. If a tree, with its limited symbolism, can be protected by law, shouldn't the American flag, with its vastly greater symbolic importance—enjoy even stronger protection?

Remember, however, that a comparison or analogy makes a shaky basis for an argument because situations are almost never comparable in every respect. It's often easy to show that an analogy won't stand up to close analysis.

> It is tempting to compare burning of the American flag with the vandalism of other American symbols or monuments. Those who would offer special protection to the flag point out that we don't permit citizens to deface memorials: we would arrest and prosecute someone who damaged the Washington Monument or spray-painted the Vietnam War Memorial. But such analogies are not valid; acts of vandalism obviously differ significantly in motive from acts of political dissent. But even if a war memorial were damaged as a political gesture, the physical damage alone would merit prosecution because it is done to an irreplaceable object that belongs to the public. In such a case, it is the property damage that is illegal—not the political gesture. A burning flag, however, is a purely political act—an exercise of free speech—that damages no publicly-owned monument. More than likely, the flag burned is the property of the dissenter herself, so punishing such an act is necessarily a gesture of political repression.

▶ **Look for inconsistencies; reveal contradictions.** Spotting an inconsistency in arguments can be an effective strategy; in effect, you make the arguer take responsibility for his or her premises. To spot an inconsistency, look at the premise a writer uses and check whether that premise is followed throughout the paper. For example, a writer may oppose providing income tax breaks for families sending children to college on the grounds that the tax system shouldn't be used to shape social policy. Fine—that's a legitimate position. But what if she also favors tax breaks on home mortgages? That's certainly a law that shapes social policy. Given the initial premise, she can't have it both ways.

▶ **Control the connotations.** Choose your descriptive language carefully to enhance your position. This is tricky because name-calling and obvious bias do not work well in written arguments. But you can characterize both yourself and your opponents in language that is both fair and shrewd. Consider how terms in the abortion and affirmative action debates represent alternative ways of saying the same thing.

12 D

Persuasion

Positive connotations	*Negative connotations*
Pro-life	Pro-abortion
Pro-choice	Anti-choice
child	fetus
affirmative action	reverse discrimination
guidelines for job action	hiring quotas

▶ **Find ways to identify with an audience.** Don't alienate potential allies by assuming a lofty moral tone that suggests only you have special insight or sensitivity.

> Soon there will be no animals that people haven't either eaten, trapped, mutilated, or caged. And the sad thing is that no one will even care. Most people will go their way without even noticing that the skies are empty, the trees silent, the woodlands barren and lifeless.

The fact is that a great many people would care. By suggesting that they won't, you risk antagonizing exactly the people you are most likely to have success persuading. Moreover, you've led the argument off target: instead of focusing on animal rights, you have made human insensitivity the issue.

▶ **Limit your judgments.** Use qualifiers and transitional phrases to give readers the impression that your position is precise and sensible.

> in a few cases, perhaps . . .
>
> of course, not every . . .
>
> I am not arguing that . . .
>
> Do not think that I am advocating . . .
>
> While the argument may seem forced, in fact . . .

Avoid the mindless generalization that says to readers "this bozo is spouting nonsense."

Like Hitler, mankind has long favored a totalitarian society controlled by a patriarchal master race, and for thousands of years, man has killed, slaughtered, maimed, and conquered to get his way.

Such unsubstantiated, emotional diatribes simply cause readers to turn elsewhere for enlightenment.

➤ **Don't surrender.** You may find your faith in an idea shaken by your opponent's arguments. If so, do some good hard thinking. You *may* be wrong, and the appropriate move may be toward compromise. But consider, too, that you may just be temporarily routed by a good argument skillfully mounted. So don't give up too easily. In a democracy, persuasion means something only when all camps capably put forth their strongest arguments. In a sense, when you believe passionately in your cause, it is your obligation to maintain as stout an offense (and defense) as you can.

➤ **Organize shrewdly.** In persuasion, you use many of the organizing principles that apply when you "prove a thesis" (see Section 11A). You'll ordinarily want to assemble a series of strong arguments and to group them sensibly by subject or theme. You obviously need a compelling opening to invite readers into the paper, but your strongest argument and most compelling language should be saved until the end: you want readers to leave the paper remembering the most powerful rationale for your case.

The chart shows one possible arrangement for a persuasive paper.

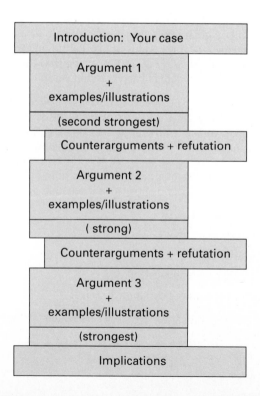

12 E   DRAFTING AND REVISING A PERSUASIVE PAPER

Draft your persuasive paper earlier enough to show it around, especially to readers you suspect won't agree with your basic position. Pay close attention to the feedback you receive and then modify the paper sensibly. Remember, however, that you'll never be able to satisfy every audience and that readers very hostile to your position may not accept even the ablest statement of your case.

Be particularly sensitive to any faults readers find in the structure of your arguments—that is, not in what you say, but in *how* you argue. If readers complain that arguments are inadequately or improperly developed, take action. Or if they point to any of the fallacies of argumentation discussed below, either reframe the argument or delete it.

When their complaints concern the substance of your argument, you need to be slower about revising. It is true that one measure of an argument is how successfully it wins converts to your side. But there also comes a point where modifying a position just to appeal to readers destroys the position itself. Don't refine your argument out of existence.

To revise a persuasive paper effectively . . .

➤ **Avoid the "to the person" fallacy.** It's a common tactic to attack an argument by undermining the integrity of those who support it. Carrying the argument "to the person" rather than to the facts is, however, considered a fallacy, a way of avoiding real issues. If you have raised questions about the people who oppose you—about their honesty, integrity, past associations—be sure those charges relate directly to the matter under discussion. If they don't, drop that line of reasoning.

Similarly, avoid name-calling. Irresponsible charges of *traitor, liar, fascist, racist, sexist,* and the like are hard to retract, and may boomerang on the ones making them. Name-calling may even generate sympathy for the person attacked.

So to attack the patriotism, intelligence, decency, or fairness of opponents without ample evidence is both unfair and potentially libelous. But even simpler stereotyping is often unfair; *chauvinist, women's libber, radical, reactionary, capitalist pawn, Mercedes marxist* are all terms that shouldn't be used as a substitute for deeper argumentation.

➤ **Avoid the "to the people" fallacy.** Arguments "to the people" usually involve blatant attempts to prey upon the fears and prejudices of large groups. When a course of action is characterized in a way that might arouse passions or make people act without thinking, the argument is vulnerable to this charge. In this category we might place attempts to frighten elderly citizens into buying medical insurance policies by exaggerating nursing home costs.

You would not, however, want to cut every appeal to emotion from a paper just to avoid a potential charge of emotionalism: arguments that stir the emotions are often both valid and effective. They are valid when an emotion illuminates an issue and makes a reader better able to grasp its complexity. However, when the emotion stirred seems out of proportion to the subject proposed (turning a local water rights issue into a question about patriotism), when the emotion blinds readers to complexities (framing trade problems in racist terms), when readers might regard the appeal as transparent or blatant (waving the flag to sell products), cut the argument.

▶ **Avoid the either/or fallacy.** Look carefully to see that you haven't overstated your argument or oversimplified the choices available to readers. If you've resorted to a simple dichotomy of "I'm right and you're wrong," you can be charged with the either/or fallacy, the error of reducing complex options to simple choices. All a critic has to do to undermine your position is to suggest that the discussion is naive or simplistic.

12 E

Persuasion

When you do believe it would be effective rhetorically to reduce the reader's choices to one obviously "good" course of action and one undeniably bad one, take some time in the paper to explain why other options have been rejected. You can handle such approaches quickly and dismissively: "We could do _____ , but it would only have the effect of . . . ." Then home in on the choices you think readers must actually face.

▶ **Avoid faulty causality.** This fallacy (also known as *post hoc, ergo propter hoc*) involves the assumption that two events are causally related because they follow one another in time. One could be guilty of the fallacy if one argued, for example, that the divorce rate increased in the last decade *because* the United States elected a divorced man as President. The rationale for asserting such a one-to-one correspondence would be highly questionable. What simplistic causal arguments tend to do is bury true or more interesting relationships. Divorce rates might be increasing for the same reason that voters didn't find Ronald Reagan's divorce a serious campaign issue: divorce is more tolerated now.

Faulty causality may also lead to perverse or distorted sorts of analyses. One could show, for example, that the more the United States has spent on education, the less effective its schools have become. It is tempting then to reverse the argument and to suggest that reducing funding ought to increase the quality of American schools. But if you argue this way, you're just playing with words—and once again avoiding the serious implications in the causal relationship observed: factors other than money must be diminishing the quality of American schools; just spending money won't automatically improve education. The lesson here is to be subtle in drawing causal relationships. Don't make yourself vulnerable to charges of oversimplification.

▶ **Avoid the false analogy.** Remember that any analogy—that is, any extended comparison between different things—eventually fails; the objects of comparison are, after all, not identical. Nevertheless, you need not abandon comparisons as a means of arguing since—within bounds—they so often make ideas easier to understand.

To protect your comparisons from charges of "false analogy," don't overextend them. A simile can be fun if it's quick and memorable:

Senator Harlow is like a pitcher who can't throw a strike.

Push it further and the analogy begins to seem ludicrous:

The more he talks about important issues, the farther he gets from the strike zone. He's high and outside on federal spending. He throws beanballs on medicare and social security. On defense issues, it's one wild pitch after another. In congressional debate, his opponents hit one long ball after another, driving the senator to an early shower. It's time voters called him out for good.

Avoid the analogy, like this one, so farfetched it evokes groans.

➤ **Avoid the red herring.** A red herring is any tactic designed to distract a reader's attention from the real issue. It's easy to go off track in a persuasive paper, to begin harping on your favorite concerns. But you become vulnerable to the red herring charge whenever you do stray; all the critical reader needs to deflate your argument is the simple question: "What's *that* got to do with anything?" If you can't show the connection simply and directly between your main point and any portion of your paper, cut the digression.

➤ **Avoid the faulty or hasty generalization.** Avoid any claims based on stereotypes or on evidence drawn from just a few cases. Such unsubstantiated arguments often stem from too great a faith in personal experiences. It is tempting to build arguments around what we have seen ourselves, but such personal knowledge often needs to be supplemented by other evidence. It might be appropriate to observe that some of the poor people you know don't work very hard or that a Japanese TV you own is a piece of junk; to generalize, however, about either *the poor* or *Japanese products* from your very limited sample of these groups would be improper.

➤ **Avoid stylistic excesses.** Some writers try to add energy to their persuasive papers by various stylistic and typographical devices. A device such as repetition *can* help readers remember the point you are trying to make, but repetition alone won't win an argument and may seem simply monotonous.

You won't win arguments either by emphasizing key points with capital letters, underlining, or exclamation marks. Such devices look childish, hysterical, or desperate.

➤ **Edit carefully.** Edit only after you have a draft you are satisfied with (see Section 5C for a thorough checklist). A few points worth noting:

—Check the accuracy of any facts you use.

—Identify your sources. Mention the names (and professions) of any authorities who stand with you—and be sure to spell their names correctly.

—Check the paragraphing. Use paragraphing to highlight your ideas. A key sentence may stand alone as a paragraph.

—Check the title. Find an inviting one.

STYLE

PART 3

Style comes from *choice;* it is the product of the many decisions about words and sentences that you make to suit your writing to your purpose. You decide what kind of words you will use, what the length and shape of your sentences should be, how you will begin and end, and how formal or casual you will be. The result is writing with a special voice and tone, writing that reflects you.

This section is a guide to some of the stylistic choices you can make. Because the subject of style is so large and the options for shaping language so numerous, we concentrate on what we regard as the major choices you can make to enhance style, those places where your writing will show significant improvement if you invest time and attention.

13 Making Paragraphs Work

A Achieving unified paragraphs

B Using different paragraph patterns

C Finding ways to reduce paragraph sprawl

D Improving paragraph appearance

Terms you need to know

PARAGRAPH. A paragraph is a group of sentences working together to

> develop a single idea,
> group related points,
> introduce a new point, or
> break up a piece of writing into readable chunks.

Paragraphs are marked by separations (indentations or double spacing between lines) that encourage readers to pause slightly as they read.

¶. A symbol meaning "paragraph." Editors and instructors insert the symbol where a new paragraph is needed in a paper. "No ¶" indicates that the writer should not begin a paragraph at that point.

Troubleshooting

Although decisions about paragraphs are not always easy to make, they're important to both readers and writers. For a reader, paragraphs break up a piece of writing into manageable chunks. For a writer, paragraphs provide a device for grouping related sentences and for dividing a large stretch of print into smaller sections that readers will find less intimidating and more readable.

To manage paragraphs well, you need to know how to handle two common paragraph problems. We term them *paragraph sprawl* and *bad paragraph appearance.* These two concepts cover considerable ground.

Paragraph sprawl is mainly an *internal* problem because it is a problem with the way a paragraph *works.* In a loose, sprawling paragraph, the sentences do not fit together tightly or focus on a central point; they lack unity. You have a problem with paragraph sprawl if the sentences in a paragraph go off in different directions, if you include several unconnected ideas in one paragraph, or if several sentences in a paragraph would fit into it just as well in one place as another.

Bad paragraph appearance is mainly an *external* problem because it is a problem with the way a paragraph *looks.* Paragraphs that look bad may be so long that they discourage readers and make it hard for them to separate the ideas being presented. They may also be so short that they chop writing into too many small parts, making it hard for the reader to see connections between the parts.

Learning to manage paragraphs well also means mastering the conventions of introductory and concluding paragraphs, which will be the topic of the next chapter.

13 A   PARAGRAPH UNITY

Troubleshooting

We don't speak in paragraphs the way we speak in sentences because, unlike sentences, paragraphs do not represent natural units of thought. Rather, they are divisions created by writers (or editors) to help readers by marking off units in printed or written material.

13 A

¶ Unity

Conventionally, textbooks define a paragraph as a distinct unit of writing dealing with a single idea. A neat definition, but unfortunately, when you are the writer, it's not always easy to decide what constitutes a paragraph or to know when you have written one. Nor is it always easy to decide where to break a paragraph and where to start a new one. Yet the decisions you make about paragraphs can significantly influence how readers respond to your work.

Readers will feel your work is out of control if your paragraphs seem to lack unity. That problem reflects what we have called *paragraph sprawl.* It usually occurs when a writer starts a paragraph by writing down thoughts as they occur rather than jotting down ideas in notes or an outline and then developing one idea at a time. The result is a paragraph like the following, filled with ideas but shapeless.

{**Sprawling**}   There are thousands of school districts across this country, reflecting widely different social, ethnic, and intellectual milieus. Yet students from all of these districts are admitted to college according to the dictates of nationwide placement examinations, the SAT and the ACT. Such examinations, which tend to reflect the biases of the people who write them, are economically efficient because they are easy to grade. But many students may not be exposed to the kind of intellectual and cultural material covered on these examinations. Various services around the country claim to be able to raise SAT scores by a significant number of points, but they are available only at a price. Smaller school districts may not be able to prepare students as adequately as larger districts. Test scores have leveled off in recent years, following a long period of decline. But how can scores from these tests really represent the achievements of four years of high school and the differences between what different students learn in Vermont, New York City, or rural Arkansas? These are problems.

The reader has trouble following the point of the paragraph because its sentences go off in several different directions instead of focusing on and developing one point. The following revised version eliminates much of the sprawl and makes the paragraph more readable and effective.

{**Focused**}   There are thousands of school districts across this country, reflecting widely different social, ethnic, and intellectual milieus. Yet students from all of these districts are admitted to college according to the dictates of nationwide placement examinations, the SAT and the ACT. Standardized examinations of this kind tend to reflect the biases of the people who write them, not the training of the students who take them. How, then, can scores from these tests reflect fairly the differences between what an affluent student learns in a private Vermont prep school, what a newly arrived Puerto Rican student achieves in a New York City public high school, or what a student from a farm community learns in a large consolidated rural high school in Arkansas?

Writers also produce sprawling paragraphs when they write several sentences that are all on a high level of generality. (See Section 17A on general and specific language.) Instead of making one general statement and then developing it with specific details or examples, they string together a series of generalizations. Even if all of them discuss the same main idea, they don't really develop that idea. For example:

Everyone is interested in preserving the quality of our environment and natural habitats. The beauty of nature is something almost everyone responds to. Respect for nature comes from a feeling we all share that the environment is something important to our own well-being today, and to that of our children and grandchildren tomorrow. Without a healthy environment, we will all find ourselves ravaged by disease and deprived of the beauties of nature. Unless we do something about the environmental crisis in our society today, we soon won't have a society to worry about.

13 A

¶ Unity

A paragraph like this leaves readers feeling frustrated and bored because they learn little from it. The paragraph lacks unity or direction. Any one of its sentences might provide the topic statement for a totally different paragraph, but the paragraph as a whole probably isn't worth salvaging—better to take one idea from it and start over.

Three particularly useful devices for controlling paragraph sprawl are *topic sentences, commitment and response,* and *downshifting.*

To eliminate paragraph sprawl . . .

➤ **Use topic sentences.** One good way to avoid paragraph sprawl and keep a paragraph tightly pulled together is to use a topic sentence that states your main idea clearly and directly. The topic sentence doesn't have to be the first one in the paragraph, although it often is, particularly in academic writing. Wherever it is, a topic sentence acts like a magnet around which related sentences cluster. Here is an example by a professional writer; the topic sentence is italicized.

For the foreseeable future Japan will be America's single most valuable partner because of what it can do in three areas. First is the U.S.-Japan military understanding, which prevents Japan from building as large an army as it would need on its own, leaves the United States as the reigning power in the Pacific, adds very little direct cost to the U.S. military budget, and prevents an arms race throughout Asia in which all countries would try to defend themselves against the Japanese. Second is finance: Japan has become America's financier, providing investment capital and covering much of the U.S. government's debt. Third is business: Japanese-American business relations provide technology, markets, talent, supplies and other essential elements to both nations' companies.

—James Fallows, "Containing Japan," *The Atlantic Monthly,* May 1989, 41.

Fallows summarizes his key claim in an opening topic sentence and goes on to explain and develop that claim in the following sentences.

Another name for this kind of sentence is *generative sentence* because it is a sentence that *generates* additional material on the original idea.

13 A

¶ Unity

In our culture boys play competitive games with clear rules and winners and losers. Boys learn to "depersonalize the attack," to compete against friends and cooperate with people they dislike. Team games teach boys emotional discipline—self-control rather than self-expression. Boys tend to practice adversarial relationships and organizational skills necessary to co-ordinate large groups. In contrast, girls most often play cooperatively in pairs, with no explicit goal, no end point, no winners. Girls' games reinforce nurturant skills, expressions of personal feelings, cooperation rather than competition. Girls *play* more than boys; boys *game* more than girls.

—Dana Jack and Rand Jack, "Women Lawyers: Archetype and Alternatives," in *Mapping the Moral Domain.* Ed. Carol Gilligan et al. Harvard University Press (Cambridge), 1988. 264-5.

The statement made in the first sentence *generates* more sentences; the writers cannot just drop their idea stating it. They must explain.

A writer can also lead up to a topic sentence, giving readers details that build their interest, and then summarize the content in one sentence. Here is another example from a professional writer; the topic sentence is italicized.

Felix is in his 20's and gangly. Heinrich is in his 40's, a solid block of a man who has survived three avalanches. He is one of a team of scientists at the University of Bern. With the big drills that he designed and built in the university machine shop, the Bern team brings up cylindrical cores of ice from hundreds of feet below the surface of Swiss glaciers, and from many thousands of feet down in the Antarctic and Greenland ice sheets. The ice holds an abundance of bubbles the size of seltzer fizz. *The bubbles hold a wealth of stories on themes that encompass the planet: the death of the fabled island of Atlantis; the history of the greenhouse effect; the cause of ice ages; scenarios of the Earth's climate in the next hundred years.*

—Jonathan Weiner, "Glacier Bubbles Are Telling Us What Was in the Ice Age Air," *Smithsonian,* May 1989, 78.

Not all paragraphs have topic sentences, nor do they need them. Some paragraphs are unified in other ways. We don't have any evidence that professional writers even think about whether they are writing topic sentences for their paragraphs. Nevertheless, student writers can use topic sentences to good effect when they want to write clear, well-developed paragraphs. Beginning a paragraph with a sentence that states your main idea will help you to stay focused on that idea and guide your development. Topic sentences work especially well to focus and control academic writing—analyses, reports, critiques, and so on; they can help you keep your writing organized and readable.

EXERCISE 13.1

Read the following opening sentences of paragraphs to decide which seem like potentially good topic sentences. Then choose one sentence and write a paragraph that develops it.

1. Americans like to pretend that they have no class system.
2. Some of the most startling new hair styles show up on young men.
3. Any good comedian is necessarily a shrewd judge of audience.
4. The first car to come around the curve was a Porsche.
5. Many educational critics claim that insipid textbooks smother children's interest in reading.

13 A

¶ **Unity**

➤ **Organize according to a commitment and response pattern.** The phrase "commitment and response" describes a simple concept: *making a promise to your reader and then keeping it.* It means raising your readers' expectations and then fulfilling them. Here is an example.

> *A young man might go into military flight training believing that he was entering some sort of technical school in which he was simply going to acquire a certain set of skills.*

[response]

Instead he found himself all at once enclosed in a fraternity. And in this fraternity, even though it was military, men were not rated by their outward rank as ensigns, lieutenant commanders, or whatever. No, herein the world was divided into those who had it and those who did not. This quality, this *it* was never named, however, nor was it talked about in any way.

—Tom Wolfe, *The Right Stuff* (New York: Farrar, Straus, & Giroux, 1979), 27.

Wolfe makes an opening commitment in this paragraph when he says "a young man might go into military flight training believing. . . ." His readers immediately expect him to explain why the young man's belief might be wrong, and he does, thus fulfilling his commitment.

Another form of this strategy is to begin a paragraph with a question. For instance:

[commitment]   [response]

Is Silicon Valley sliding toward retirement? America's electronics spawning ground still packs a powerful entrepreneurial punch, as witnessed by the debut last week of Apple's long-awaited portable Macintosh. Yet five decades after Bill Hewlett developed an oscillator in his Palo Alto garage, America's high-tech hothouse is going gray at its cutting edges.

—Peter Dworkin, "The Graying of Silicon Valley," *U.S. News and World Report,* October 2, 1989, 44.

The author commits himself to answer the question he opens with. Since this paragraph is the opening paragraph of an essay, it also serves as a commitment that forecasts what he is going to discuss in the complete article.

EXERCISE 13.2

13 A

¶ Unity

Underline the commitment statement in this draft of a paragraph written by Darwin Ferguson for an engineering magazine. Then go through the paragraph and cross out sentences that don't have anything to do with the opening promise.

> Anyone who has gone to an auto show lately would have to agree with the president of one of America's largest auto companies who recently said, "Americans want a lot of things in their cars, but economy and safety aren't high on the list." The number of convertibles and T-tops on display would underscore that statement, if nothing else. So does the great number of high-wheeled, open-top sports trucks even though tests have shown that some of them are unstable. The young people cluster in that part of the show. High-powered, high-speed cars like Corvette ZR-1s, Nissan 300 ZXs, and T-birds occupy a prominent place on the revolving platforms, and heavy, gas-consuming cars such as Lincoln Continentals, Jaguars, and BMW 735s are surrounded by throngs of admiring prospective purchasers. Smiling girls and music are everywhere—the last thing you hear mentioned is price.

EXERCISE 13.3

Working in a group with other students, discuss how you might develop paragraphs that begin with these commitments. Then each person should write a paragraph based on one of these first sentences.

1. Who doesn't recall the first time he or she tried to drive a car?
2. Many of today's best-selling items are things consumers didn't even know they wanted ten years ago.
3. For many young people today, becoming rich has become a consuming passion.
4. Students entering college are rarely prepared for learning in the fast lane.
5. When blue denim originated in France in the last century, it was used only as a sturdy material for work clothing.

➤ **Downshift to develop your paragraph with specific details.** *Downshifting* means developing a paragraph by writing sentences that move from a general statement to increasingly specific statements. The writer makes a broad statement or assertion in the first sentence and, in the following sentences, enriches and expands that statement by giving more details and concrete examples. Such paragraphs can move through several levels, rather like subdividing a topic into smaller and smaller details. For example, if we designate a sentence at the highest level of generality as 10, here is how a writer might develop that sentence by moving to lower levels of generality.

13 A

¶ **Unity**

> 10. There are signs, however, that girls are finding their way into the world of computing, despite its male bias.
>> 9. A large proportion of the current enrollment in college computing classes is female.
>>> 8. For example, at Mount Holyoke, a women's college, 50 percent of this year's graduates have used computers in their courses—up from 15 percent seven years ago.
>>>> 7. According to John Durso, professor of computer studies, the number of terminals available to Mount Holyoke students has increased from one to forty over the same period.
>>>> 7. "The basic course in computing, taught twice a year, had quadrupled in enrollment from 30 students seven years ago to 120 today."*
>> —Sara Kiesler, Lee Spoull, and Jacquelynne S. Eccles, "Second Class Citizens?" *Psychology Today*, March 1983, 47.

*The two sentences marked "7" are at the same level of generality.

Downshifting is a good cure for those paragraphs made up of several sentences all on the same level of generality. Here is an example of that kind of problem.

> The '80s may be remembered as the era when millions of people became obsessed with fitness. For most people, this was the decade in which they thought continually about how their bodies functioned. A preoccupation with one's body was a sign of the times. It was very fashionable to talk about how important it is to be fit.

This is a paragraph that doesn't go anywhere; it merely repeats the same generality four different ways, and that's not paragraph development. If, however, the writer starts with the main idea and develops it by downshifting to lower levels of generality and adding specific details, it can become interesting.

10. The 1980s may be remembered as the era when millions of people became obsessed with fitness.

   9. Ambitious young people took up aerobics and weightlifting as a flat belly and sloping shoulders became assets on the career ladder.

   9. Others took up running, and comparing marathon times became the approved cocktail party talk.

      8. Even the cocktail parties themselves were affected.

         7. The boss began drinking Perrier water instead of white wine, and the really strong stuff like martinis brought raised eyebrows from everyone.

            6. Smoking at any party made the offending culprit feel like a pariah.

EXERCISE 13.4

13 A

¶ Unity

Try plotting the levels of generality in the following paragraph. Mark the first level as "10" and work your way down until all sentences are accounted for. Remember that you may have more than one sentence at any level of generality. After you have diagrammed the paragraph, decide whether it should be revised to eliminate sprawl.

> The term "student" doesn't seem to mean the same thing at an urban commuter college and on the wooded campus of a large state institution like Pennsylvania State University or the University of Washington. At urban campuses, the students are all ages. In fact, most of them look closer to thirty or forty than to twenty. Many are even parents dropping off their children at the campus daycare center on their way to class. At a state university like Penn State, you rarely see a student who looks over twenty-five. To encounter a student walking with or carrying a child is unusual. Clothes are different too. At urban colleges, students are dressed like most of the other working people hurrying by because they too are working people, coming to campus after their jobs or before they go to work. At a state university, the costume is likely to be blue jeans or shorts and a T-shirt adorned with some slogan; shoes are Reeboks or Nikes, and a backpack adorns every shoulder.

EXERCISE 13.5

Develop a paragraph from one of these opening lines by downshifting through several levels of generality. Pair up with other students who have chosen to develop the same paragraph and compare your results.

1. The remote control on today's television sets, with its easy-to-use mute button, is changing the way people watch TV.
2. People are rarely neutral about country music [or opera].
3. *People* and *US* magazines, as well as those tabloids you see at every grocery check-out counter, reflect the U.S. public's preoccupation with celebrities.
4. The 1980s saw the beginning of a new era in salaries for sports figures.
5. Scuba diving is not a hobby one can take up casually.

> **TIP:** By now you may have noticed that these three devices for controlling paragraphs—topic sentences, commitment and response, and downshifting—resemble each other. If you have trouble figuring out which technique you're using or should use, don't worry about it. The label for what you're doing isn't particularly important. The principle behind it is.
>
> That principle is that, as you write, be sure to keep the contract you made with your readers. You give them signals about what to expect, and in order not to disappoint them, you have an obligation to follow through.

13 B

¶ Form

13 B   OTHER PARAGRAPH PATTERNS

Troubleshooting

Writers use many kinds of paragraph patterns, some of which may be useful for you to think about when you're writing. We don't know how many writers use these patterns consciously—perhaps the patterns just emerge in the process of writing because they so closely resemble typical thought patterns. Nevertheless, it is worth your time to know what the patterns are and how you can use them to develop your paragraphs. They parallel the organizational patterns already identified in Chapter 4. Here are those you are likely to find most useful.

Cause and effect   Classification
Comparison and contrast   Narration/process
Definition   Analogy
Illustration

To try out various paragraph patterns, consider . . .

➤ **Cause and effect.** In a paragraph explaining why or how something happened, you can begin with a statement of effect, then enumerate the causes, or you can give your causes first and conclude with the effect. Here is an example of the former pattern, written by Luke Scandino for an economics paper.

{**Effect**}   Yet another example of competition in the world market that

helped consumers occurred in the automobile industry.

{**Causes**}   By the mid-1980s, the prices of economy cars had risen substantially, with the smallest Japanese and American sedans bearing sticker prices that approached or exceeded five figures. American car companies claimed that the profit margins on cheap cars were too small to justify producing vehicles under $6000. Because of import quotas, the Japanese could export only a limited number of vehicles, so they understandably preferred to ship their more profitable luxury and sporty lines to America. As a consequence, a gap opened at the lower end of the automobile market, leaving room for manufacturers from third-world countries, with their reduced labor and production costs, to compete. They introduced to America some of the lowest-priced cars consumers had seen in years.

13 B

¶ Form

➤ **Comparison/contrast.** Similarly, a paragraph can be built quite naturally upon a *comparison and contrast* pattern. Here's an easy-to-follow paragraph from Luke's paper that sets up a comparison in the first sentence, discusses each item in alternating sentences, and concludes with a sentence that again compares both objects.

Two of the earliest and most publicized of these low-priced, third-world automotive imports were the Yugo and the Hyundai. The Yugo looked dated the day it arrived on American shores, not surprising since it was based on a twenty-year-old Fiat design. But the Yugoslavian sedan could claim one feature no other new car available in America offered: a sticker price under $4000. The Hyundai introduced to Americans was a brand new car, with a body styled in Europe and an engine based on Japanese technology. Not quite as cheap as the bare-bones Yugo, the Hyundai still managed to offer modern technology at old-fashioned prices. Both manufacturers established a beachhead in the American market within a year, the Hyundai's much larger than the Yugo's.

➤ **Definition.** Paragraphs of definition often work well in the introductory part of a paper that explains or argues. They're helpful in setting limits on establishing the meaning of a crucial term. For instance, here is one written by Stevie Mendelson for a health column for the college newspaper.

Aerobic exercise is exercise involving steady movement performed at a rate sufficient to reach a target heartrate substantially above the normal pulse and to sustain it at that rate for a prescribed period of time, at least twenty but preferably thirty minutes. For beneficial aerobic effect, an individual needs to maintain a target heart rate of approximately twice his or her normal heart rate. Steady rowing, swimming, bicycling, running, or brisk walking are aerobic activities. Golf, tennis, weight lifting, and other activities in which one rests frequently between periods of exertion are not. Aerobic exercise benefits the cardiovascular system and helps the body to burn calories.

➤ **Illustration.** A paragraph of illustration starts out with a general statement (or question) and develops it by furnishing examples that support or elaborate on the statement. Notice that this pattern is similar to downshifting.

> Gold is the universal prize in all countries, in all cultures, in all ages. A representative collection of gold artifacts reads like a chronicle of civilizations. Enameled gold rosary, 16th century, English. Gold serpent brooch, 400 B.C., Greece. Triple gold crown of Abuna, 17th century, Abyssinian. Gold snake bracelet, ancient Roman. Ritual vessels of Achaemenid gold, 6th century, B.C., Persian. Drinking bowl of Malik gold, 8th century B.C., Persian. Bulls' heads in gold . . . Ceremonial gold knife, Chimu, Pre-Inca, Peruvian, 9th century.
> —J. Bronowski, *The Ascent of Man* (London: Futura, 1981), 83.

13 B

¶ **Form**

➤ **Classification.** A writer develops a classification paragraph by first naming the subject to be classified, then explaining the system by which he or she is going to carry out the classification and giving examples to illustrate the various classes. In the following paragraph, the author begins with a question that shows how he is going to divide his topic, gives his authority for making that division, then names the first division, and gives examples to illustrate that division.

> You did not know that superstition takes four forms? Theologians assure us that it does. First is what they call Vain Observances, such as not walking under a ladder and that sort of thing. Yet I saw a deeply learned professor of anthropology, who had spilled some salt, throwing a pinch of it over his left shoulder; when I asked him why, he replied, with a wink, that it was "to hit the Devil in the Eye." I did not question him further about his belief in the Devil: But I noticed that he did not smile until I asked him what he was doing.
> —Robertson Davies, "A Few Kind Words for Superstition," *Newsweek,* November 20, 1978.

➤ **Narration/process.** One popular and simple way to control and develop a paragraph is to use a narrative to relate events in chronological order. You would probably use it instinctively in writing personal or historical accounts, but you can also use it effectively when writing reports that tell what happened or even in describing a process. For example, here is the narrative of a naturalist studying wolves.

> Quite by accident I had pitched my tent within ten yards of one of the major paths used by the wolves when they were going to, or coming from, their hunting grounds to the westward; and only a few hours after I had taken up residence one of the wolves came back from a trip and discovered me and my tent. He was at the end of a hard night's work and was clearly

tired and anxious to go home to bed. He came over a small rise fifty yards from me with his head down, his eyes half-closed, and a preoccupied air about him. Far from being the preternaturally alert and suspicious beast of fiction, this wolf was so self-engrossed that he came straight on to within fifteen yards of me, and might have gone right past the tent without seeing it at all, had I not banged my elbow against the teakettle, making a resounding clank. The wolf's head came up and his eyes opened wide, but he did not stop or falter in his pace. One brief, sidelong glance was all he vouchsafed to me as he continued on his way.

—Farley Mowat, *Never Cry Wolf* (Boston: Little, Brown, 1963), 54.

➤ **Analogy.** Writers who are explaining a concept they want to elaborate on or make vivid often turn to analogy to communicate better with their readers. One especially good use of analogy is to help readers understand a difficult concept by drawing an analogy between the known and the unknown, as physicist John Wheeler does in this paragraph. In the preceding paragraph, he has asked his readers to imagine they are flying over a city and see a domed stadium. Then he writes:

13 B

¶ Form

The domed-over stadium gives no evidence to the traveler of the crowd within. However, he sees the lines of traffic converging from all directions, becoming more and more tightly packed in traffic jams as they approach the center of attraction. A black hole whirling about, and being whirled about in orbit by, a normal star will also be the recipient of clouds of gas from this companion, with all the puffs and swirls that one can imagine from watching a factory chimney belch its clouds of smoke. This gas will not fall straight in. It will orbit the black hole in ever tighter spirals as it works its way inward, making weather on its way. It, like the traffic approaching the stadium, will be squeezed more and more.

—John Wheeler, "Black Holes and New Physics," *Discovery: Research and Scholarship at the University of Texas at Austin,* Winter 1982, 5.

EXERCISE 13.6

Use two of the paragraph patterns discussed and illustrated in the previous section to write paragraphs on one of the following topics.

1. A paragraph defining in detail a term you have learned recently; for instance, "substantial writing component course," "credit by examination," "computer-assisted instruction," or "tenure."
2. A paragraph explaining how to operate a machine you use regularly; for instance, a food processor, a jet ski, an off-road vehicle, or a computerized ticket machine.
3. A paragraph setting up a classification of your relatives at a family get-together, of the students in the lounge of your student union, or of the passengers you encounter every day on a bus or subway.
4. A paragraph narrating an incident that happened to you recently.
5. A paragraph that employs an analogy to explain the success or failure of a sports team you follow.

Read the following paragraphs and classify them into one of the paragraph development patterns discussed above. Then working with other students in a small group, compare your answers. If you have differences of opinion about your classification, analyze the examples to find out why you differ.

1. "In the seventeenth century," [Willie] Ruff continued, "when West Africans were captured and brought to America as slaves, they brought their drums with them. But the slave owners were afraid of the drum because it was so potent; it could be used to incite the slaves to revolt. So they outlawed the drum. This very shrewd law had a tremendous effect on the development of black people's music. Our ancestors had to develop a variety of drum substitutes. One of them, for example, was tap dancing—I'm sure you've all heard of that. Now I'd like to show you a drum substitute that you probably don't know about, one that uses the hands and the body to make rhythm. It's called hambone."
   —William Zinsser, *Willie and Dwike* (New York: Harper & Row, 1984), 4.

2. Self-help is a system of medicine addressed not to rare diseases treatable in hospitals but to the aches and pains of everyday life, treatable at home. Its central philosophy grows out of medical research and clinical observation borrowed from mainstream medicine, experience that indicates that many serious diseases can be avoided by treating the minor ones. The belief is that your aches and pains are important messages from your body, telling you to do something, to change something in your life so that you'll be more comfortable.
   —Hal Zina Bennett, *The Doctor Within* (New York: Clarkson N. Potter, 1981).

13 C

¶ **Focus**

13 C REDUCING PARAGRAPH SPRAWL

Troubleshooting

If your instructor or another reader says your writing seems choppy, you may need to control your paragraphs by using one or more of the following strategies for keeping paragraphs unified and tightly controlled.

To keep your paragraphs unified, try using . . .

➤ **Pointer words.** Set up a path for your readers to follow by putting in words like "first," "second," "next," "last," and so on.

> Kyle, a nonsmoker, argued eloquently before the University Senate that there were many reasons to oppose a campus-wide ban on smoking. **First,** such a policy unduly penalized an activity which, though obnoxious, was not, in fact, illegal. **Second,** enforcement of the policy might encourage insidious intrusions upon the privacy of students in their dormitory rooms and faculty in their offices. **Last,** a ban on smoking might set an

unfortunate precedent, leading to the elimination of other habits and activities certain groups regarded as similarly offensive or harmful: drinking alcohol or coffee, eating fatty foods, dancing, listening to rock music, or even driving a car.

➤ **Relationship words.** Connect sentences by using words like "consequently," "therefore," "nevertheless," "yet," and so on.

Opinion in the Clear Lake University Senate had generally favored the proposal to abolish smoking on campus. **However,** Kyle's arguments made some proponents waver as they considered the wider implications of their actions. What would happen, **for example,** if one group on campus, citing statistics on heart attacks, demanded a campus-wide ban on fast foods? The ban on smoking would provide a precedent for such a restriction.

➤ **Repetition.** Using one or two key words several times through a paragraph can tie it together effectively.

What makes smoking a social problem, not an individual one, Professor Upton argued, is the phenomenon of "**passive smoking.**" **Passive smoking** describes the inhalation of combustion by-products by **nonsmokers** living or working in the vicinity of smokers. Scientific studies suggest a **correlation** between certain health problems in **nonsmokers** and **passive smoking.** Because of this **correlation,** institutions must act prudently to protect their employees and residents from a possible health hazard.

➤ **Parallel structure.** Establishing a strong pattern of parallel sentence structure in a paragraph is an excellent way to tie it together.

Should smoking be banned because it imposes a health hazard upon individuals who do not smoke? Then **shouldn't drinking be similarly outlawed,** since alcoholism victimizes millions of families and drunk driving kills thousands of innocent people every year? **Shouldn't automobiles be banned** because they maim hundreds of pedestrians every day? **Shouldn't the printing of controversial books be halted** because they plant dangerous ideas in the minds of millions of readers every hour?

You will find more on transitions and achieving links *between* paragraphs in Chapter 15.

13 C

¶ **Focus**

EXERCISE 13.8

Examine the following paragraphs, identifying any hooks and transition words the writer has used to achieve unity. Put parentheses around devices and then try to read the paragraph without them. How is the paragraph hurt by removing the transitional words and phrases?

1. These things are known about Houdini. The same tireless ingenuity, when applied to locks and jails, packing cases and riveted boilers; the same athletic prowess, when applied at the bottom of the East River or while dangling from

a rope attached to the cornice of the *Sun* building in Baltimore—these talents account for the vast majority of Houdini's exploits. As we have mentioned, theater historians, notably Raymund Fitzsimons in his *Death and the Magician,* have carefully exposed Houdini's ingenuity, knowing that nothing can tarnish the miracle of the man's existence. Their accounts are technical and we need not dwell on them, except to say they mostly support Houdini's oath that his effects were achieved by natural, or mechanical, means. The Houdini problem arises from certain outrageous effects no one has ever been able to explain, though capable technicians have been trying for more than sixty years.

> —Daniel Mark Epstein, "The Case of Harry Houdini," in *Star of Wonder* (Shawnee Mission, Kan.: Overlook Press, 1986), 42.

2. In the face of nutritional ignorance, myths and downright quackery have gained a strong foothold. People lambaste "chemicals" in our foods and overlook the fact that major nutrients like fat and sugar are actually doing the most damage. Millions search for the elixir of youth in bottles of vitamins and minerals, cakes of yeast, or jars of wheat germ. The current interest in micronutrients—vitamins, minerals, and trace elements—has prompted many to conclude that haphazard eating habits and unbalanced menus can be compensated for by swallowing a pill or potion of concentrated nutrients. This is not true. It's comparable to giving a Lincoln Continental an occasional shot of premium gasoline to make up for the low-octane fuel you fill it with most of the time. Your body is a machine; it will run as well as its fuel allows.

> —Jane Brody, *Jane Brody's Nutrition Book* (New York: Bantam Books, 1982), 7.

13 D

¶ **Look**

13 D   IMPROVING PARAGRAPH APPEARANCE

Troubleshooting

You may not want to worry about how to divide your paragraphs when you are writing your first draft or even the second one. But when you prepare your paper for its public debut, you need to check on paragraph appearance. Printed material has a kind of body language that affects the way readers respond to it. In fact, the way an essay, article, or book looks affects the attitude a potential reader has even before he or she reads a word. If the print is small, close together, and goes on for long stretches unbroken by headings, spaces, or segments of dialogue, most readers will assume the subject matter is going to be difficult and the style stiff and not "reader friendly."

See if you can find an uninterrupted page of print in a book. Hold it away from you and just look at it, making no attempt to read the words. One message comes through quickly, doesn't it? That message is **I am hard to read.**

Why do we get that message? From our experience, for one thing. It's generally true that closely printed, unbroken prose with long sentences and long paragraphs usually deals with difficult topics, and it takes us longer to read and

comprehend the material. But we also respond negatively for another reason that we may not be as aware of. That is, our brains process information in chunks, so we like to have it presented to us in manageable units. If the unit is too long or looks too jammed with information, we react negatively and don't want to read it because we suspect we'll have trouble. Of course, a skilled and persistent reader can eventually work through long stretches of unbroken print and understand what is being said, but it's tough going, and most of us would rather avoid that kind of reading.

That's why readers are put off by paragraphs that are too long. It is also the reason writers need to consider breaking up their paragraphs frequently to help their readers. Your readers are much more likely to take a friendly attitude toward what you write if they see that your paragraphs are fairly short. How short is a "fairly short" paragraph? Probably no more than seven or eight sentences—fewer if possible.

We also have to caution you, however, about writing one- or two-sentence paragraphs. Many writers have a tendency—perhaps picked up from reading newspapers—to begin a new paragraph every few sentences, without much regard for content. If too many long paragraphs intimidate readers, too many short ones can distract them or make them feel that the content of a paper is trivial. Yet short paragraphs have their place, too, for emphasizing ideas.

13 D

¶ **Look**

To improve paragraph appearance . . .

➤ **Break up long paragraph blocks that look hard to read.** Of course, you shouldn't just chop up paragraphs arbitrarily to make your paper look more inviting. A paragraph is supposed to develop an idea, and it usually takes several sentences to do that. But often, after you write a paragraph and reread it, you can spot places where you can break it up. Here are the kinds of junctures where you can split up paragraphs. For instance, look for

- *Shifts in time.*   Look for spots where you have written words such as "at that time," "then," or "afterward," or have given other time signals.
- *Shifts in place.*   Look for spots where you have written "another place," or "on the other side," or have used words that point to places.
- *Shifts in direction.*   Look for spots where you have written "on the other hand," "nevertheless," "however," or have indicated contrast.
- *Shifts in emphasis or focus.*   Look for spots where you have shifted to a new point, perhaps used words like "another," "in addition," or "not only."

Here is an example of a long paragraph at the beginning of a student paper that, in revision, was broken into three shorter ones, each of which still develops a point effectively.

{**Original version**}

Fire Down Below

While I was in high school I had an unusual summer job working

as a chimney sweep's assistant. Even though chimney sweeps have

been around for hundreds of years, my partner and I were an odd sight. Clad in black tails and top hat, we would search out jobs in Chicago neighborhoods with lots of chimneys. We always generated an audience as we pulled up in front of someone's house in our old station wagon. In a cloud of soot, we would unload our chimney sweeping equipment and begin preparing for our ascent to the chimney top. At each job we organized our tools to avoid unnecessary climbing, the most dangerous part of our job. I often wondered what I was doing climbing on hot rooftops and risking my neck for a summer job. My partner tried to persuade me that chimney sweeps had a special significance in the world and that I was lucky to be welcomed into people's homes for their yearly sweep. In the past, chimney sweeping was an important industry because people burned considerably more wood and coal for heating and cooking than they do now. Ben Franklin wanted chimney sweeps to be public servants like policemen and firemen. My partner told me of youngsters in England who, like Oliver Twist, were kidnapped in the early 1800s and forced to be "climbing boys." Their job was to squeeze through large chimneys and scrape the walls clean. As the story goes, if a boy got stuck in a chimney, a fire would be lit under his feet to encourage him along.

13 D

¶ **Look**

{Revised paragraphing}

While I was in high school I had an unusual summer job working as a chimney sweep's assistant. Even though chimney sweeps have been around for hundreds of years, my partner and I were an odd sight. Clad in black tails and top hat, we would search out jobs in Chicago neighborhoods with lots of chimneys.

We always generated an audience as we pulled up in front of someone's house in our old station wagon. In a cloud of soot, we would unload our chimney sweeping equipment and begin preparing for our ascent to the chimney top. At each job we organized our tools to avoid unnecessary climbing, the most dangerous part of our job. I often wondered what I was doing climbing on hot rooftops and risking my neck for a summer job. My partner tried to persuade me that chimney sweeps had a special significance in the world and that I was lucky to be welcomed into people's homes for their yearly sweep.

In the past, chimney sweeping was an important industry because people burned considerably more wood and coal for heating and cooking than they do now. Ben Franklin wanted chimney sweeps to be public servants like policemen and firemen. My partner told me of youngsters in England who, like Oliver Twist, were kidnapped in the early 1800s and forced to be "climbing boys." Their job was to squeeze through chimneys and scrape the walls clean. As the story goes, if a boy got stuck in a chimney, a fire would be lit under his feet to encourage him along.

13 D

¶ Look

EXERCISE 13.9

Read the essay on chimney sweeps continued below, printed as a single paragraph, and decide how you would break it up. Use the symbol for new paragraph— ¶ —to indicate where you might start additional paragraphs in the essay. Then working with a small group of other students, compare your paragraphing breaks. If you don't agree about where paragraphs should oc-cur—and you probably won't since there are no absolute rules about para-graphing—discuss different people's reasons for their paragraphing decisions.

Because people today rarely consider having their home's chimney swept, we had to hustle to make any money, carefully explaining to potential customers why sweeping was necessary to remove creo-sote, a flammable, tar-like substance, from their chimney walls. Cleaning the creosote encourages proper drafts, removes foul odors from a house, and helps to avoid costly relining in the future if a chimney is heavily used. In our sales pitch, we also played on the fears of homeowners by warning them that a build-up of creosote could cause a chimney fire. Since average chimney fires cause $30,000–$40,000 in damage, most people proved eager to eliminate the fire hazard. After convincing the customer that they needed a sweep, we would begin the job. Standing on the chimney top, we pulled our brushes up from the ground with ropes. (Watching a mis-placed brush fall off the roof reminded me of the long trip down I would enjoy if I took a careless step over the edge.) We then selected a wiry brush of the right shape or diameter and forced it down the chimney with a snap-together fiberglass extension. The chimney would resist by expelling clouds of thick black smoke in our faces. Reaming the flues several times left us covered in filthy residue. While on the rooftop, we repaired any external damage to the chimney and tried to shake a few pounds of unwanted soot from our formal attire. Before we entered a customer's home for the second half of the job, the lady of the house almost invariably lined our pathway with newspapers and insisted we give our jackets a few more shakes. Inside the house, we covered the area around the fireplace with drop cloths the way a surgeon might surround an incision. I usually had the dirty job of donning a gas mask and climbing as far as possible into the fireplace. With a loud, high-powered vacuum in hand, I cleaned the fireplace, smokebox, and lower flue. As I worked, more clouds of black soot poured out of the chimney into the house. Cleaning up the house when we were done often proved as difficult as cleaning the chimney. Charging $45 for a two-story house and $55 for a three, we relied on additional revenue from reconstructing chimneys and selling chimney caps. A chimney cap is supposed to keep debris out of the chimney without blocking rising smoke. To encourage sales of caps, we kept a few dead squirrels in the wagon. Inside the house, we would convincingly pull one of the stiff critters from the fireplace at an appropriate moment. This trick of the trade worked especially well if we evoked a good shriek from one of the family members. Homeowners seemed to enjoy our visit far more than they would the plumber's or electrician's. People often shook our hands for luck, believing that chimney sweeps are bearers of good fortune. Romanticism aside, chimney sweeping is an interesting job. Few authentic sweepers are around anymore because most people don't consider having their chimney swept. This fact didn't worry my partner and me, however; we could always find jobs in a neighborhood where a chimney fire the past winter had destroyed a house.

—Robert Irmen

13 D

¶ Look

▶ **Reconsider short paragraphs.** Paragraphs can be too short as well as too long. A paragraph is, after all, supposed to develop an idea—that is, consist of a group of sentences that focus on and explain or illustrate a point. That's hard to do in one sentence. So if you use a series of one- or two-sentence paragraphs in your paper, you are either not developing your ideas sufficiently or you're chopping what should be a coherent unit into segments that are going to confuse your readers.

Sometimes, of course, short paragraphs work well, particularly when the writer wants to manage a transition, to emphasize a point, or to introduce a series. Here is an example of a single-sentence paragraph from a professional writer whose work is often praised.

> Tennis has become more than the national sport; it is a rigorous discipline, a form of collective physiotherapy. Jogging is done by swarms of people, out onto the streets each day in underpants, moving in a stolid sort of rapid trudge, hoping by this to stay alive. Bicycles are cures. Meditation may be good for the soul but it is even better for the blood pressure.
> As a people, we have become obsessed with Health.
> There is something fundamentally, radically unhealthy about all this. We do not seem to be seeking more exuberance in living as much as staving off failure, putting off dying. We have lost all confidence in the human body.
> —Lewis Thomas, "The Health Care System" in *The Medusa and the Snail* (New York: Penguin Books, 1981), 43.

You shouldn't be afraid to use one- or two-sentence paragraphs occasionally, but do so sparingly. When you do, think about how they are going to look and the message they will give your readers.

13 D

¶ Look

Finally, then, how long should a paragraph be? Of course, there is no simple answer. It depends on who your readers are, what you're trying to accomplish, what kind of writing you're doing, what kind of style you've chosen to write in, and other factors. When you're writing formal reports, term papers, or other kinds of academic papers, or a detailed history for a grant proposal, you can use some long paragraphs without creating problems. When you're writing an informal narrative, a brochure, or a process paper, short paragraphs work best. So, as with most decisions about writing, you have to consider your purpose and your audience when you edit for paragraph length.

14 Opening and Closing Paragraphs

A Opening paragraphs
B Closing paragraphs

14 A EFFECTIVE OPENING PARAGRAPHS

Troubleshooting

Opening paragraphs warrant special attention because they introduce you and your paper to the reader, and that first impression is important. Newspaper editors talk about the **lead** for a news story, the opening that has to catch the readers' attention and give them a strong signal about what to expect. The opening paragraph for whatever you write is your lead, the part of your paper that gets you off to a good or bad start with your reader. In writing you do outside of your classes, your first paragraph can even determine whether your reader will read what you have written. Remember, then, a first paragraph should do these things:

- Get your readers' attention and interest them in reading more.
- Announce or suggest your main idea without delay.
- Give your readers a signal about the direction you intend to take.
- Set the tone of your essay.

These are heavy responsibilities. That's why first paragraphs are so hard to write, but it is also why they are worth careful attention.

> **TIP:** Just because first paragraphs are so important in the final versions of papers, don't let yourself get stalled trying to write perfect openers. You can waste many hours getting one just right only to find that you have to change the opener later anyway. If you find yourself bogging down in your first paragraph, just write anything you can think of and go on. You can revise after you finish your first draft.

227

To write an effective opening paragraph . . .

➤ **Remember that different kinds of writing call for different opening paragraphs.** For some types of writing—for example, laboratory reports, grant proposals, or an environmental impact statement—certain kinds of opening paragraphs are standard. You may need to start with a statement of the problem to be discussed or a review of what others have written. In such cases, do find out what the typical pattern is and use it. In other kinds of writing, such as newspaper articles, reviews, critical analyses, personal experience papers, or opinion pieces, you have more choice and can try different approaches to write interesting opening paragraphs. In every case, you need to consider the impression you want to make, what kind of reader you're writing for, and the tone you want to set. Here are some approaches that writers rely on.

➤ **Make a commitment to your reader.** We have mentioned commitment and response before (see Section 13A) as an organizational strategy, but commitment can also serve you well in an opening paragraph. There you can use it in a variety of forms—an anecdote, a description of a situation, a statement of a problem, a narrative, even a question. Whatever shape it takes, a commitment introduces readers to a topic by promising to supply more information.

14 A

Opening ¶

Here is an example of an opening paragraph Connie Lim wrote for an article in the *Clear Lake Clarion*.

> This weekend a formidable competitor from the Clear Lake Chicago campus comes to town to ride in the annual 25 kilometer bicycle obstacle race around Lake Nittani. Marty Green, a veteran of other 25K races in Lincoln Park in Chicago, has honed his broken-field bike-riding skills on his job as a bicycle courier in the Chicago Loop and financial district. But he may not have the quadriceps to carry him over those steep hills at the west end of the lake. To find out how great a challenge he may give our local riders, I interviewed Marty yesterday.

Here Connie catches the attention of bicycle enthusiasts among her readers, signals them that she is going to write about an upcoming race, and *commits* herself to give them more information about what to expect in the race.

Here is a different kind of opening commitment for a paper Darwin Ferguson wrote in connection with his part-time job with an engineering firm.

> The Ruralia City Council hopes to start negotiations soon with the national Habitat organization, a group that enlists volunteers to work with local organizations to build housing for low-income groups. If they are able to get Habitat to agree to sponsor the construction of ten houses in Ruralia, two local citizens, Bruce Batson and Hilda Jones, have agreed to donate property, and several student organizations from Clear Lake College will provide volunteer labor. I would like to suggest a way that our firm, Jupiter Engineering Enterprises, can also contribute to this civic project.

Here Darwin gives his audience necessary background information, then commits himself to explaining his proposal.

EXERCISE 14.1

Draft an opening commitment paragraph that might begin an informal essay with one of these titles.

1. What Jobs Do for—or to—Teenagers
2. The Best (or Worst) Course You Can Take on This Campus
3. Who Is Going to Teach Today's Children?
4. The Tragedy of Teenage Pregnancy
5. Can You Really Work Your Way Through College?

If your instructor thinks it's a good idea, join with other students who have chosen to write on the same title and read your paragraphs aloud. Discuss which ones seem to work well and why.

➤ **Make a direct announcement of your intentions.** Sometimes you will do best to open your essay by simply telling your readers exactly what you are going to write about. Such openings work well for many of the papers you write in college courses, for reports that you might have to write on the job, for grant proposals, and for many other kinds of factual, informative prose. Here is an example of the first paragraph for a paper for a business course written by Luciano (Luke) Scandino, student at the Clear Lake—Chicago campus and student intern at a travel agency on LaSalle Street. Luke announces his topic directly and forecasts the main points he intends to cover.

14 A

Opening ¶

> Despite recent claims in *Business Week* and *The Wall Street Journal* that the travel agency business is overcrowded, two Clear Lake College students at the Chicago campus are doing well with their package trips to Mexican resort cities during college vacations. Their strategy for success combines three important ingredients: striking deals with dollar-hungry Mexican hotels, negotiating for blocks of cheap seats on airliners, and advertising heavily at low rates. This is how they did it.

For a more formal paper, you may want to write a particularly straightforward announcement in your opening paragraph. Here is the first paragraph of a chapter in a book by a professional writer.

> When Enrico Fermi, an Italian immigrant to the United States, and his colleagues triggered the world's first atomic pile in Chicago in 1941, science opened Pandora's box. Out of it came new ways of healing, new tools with which to study the structure of the universe, the potential for virtually free electric power—and the atomic bomb. Of all the developments of atomic physics, two possibilities affect our future more than any others: electricity produced by the fission process and annihilation by nuclear strike.
> —James Burke, *Connections* (Boston: Little, Brown, 1978), 45.

EXERCISE 14.2

Draft a "direct statement" opening sentence or paragraph for an article that would develop one of these titles.

1. What It Means to Live Below the Poverty Level: A Case Study
2. My Latest Experience with Computers
3. The Option Racket and Car Prices
4. The Result of No Pass/No Play Rules in High School
5. Some Good Jobs for College Students

➤ **Ask a question.** A third strategy for an opening paragraph is to pose a question that highlights a problem or piques readers' curiosity. Sometimes writers may elaborate on a single question, and sometimes they may raise several questions in an opening paragraph. Not only can questions provide a tantalizing lead-in, but they also make commitments. Here is an opening paragraph from an article written by Greta Ericson, co-owner of Wildflowers Good Health Cafe and Market, for the magazine *Hearty Health.*

14 A

Opening ¶

> What distinguishes the sensible, nutrition-minded shopper from the health-food nut? Sensible shoppers have come to a health food store because they know it will carry vegetables raised without pesticides, meat raised without hormone injections, lots of oat bran and brown rice, plus an assortment of whole-grain breads and cereals. He or she isn't looking for seaweed pills or macrobiotic miracles that will cure baldness or any other hereditary disaster. The health-food nut, on the other hand, has entirely different expectations.

Here, Ericson leads off with the central question she will answer in her article, assures the reader she has the experience to answer it, and commits herself to doing so in detail.

Here is another example, this time from a news magazine.

> What makes a good college? The question seems deceptively simple. However, for the millions of students and parents who each year hope to choose "the right school" from a seemingly endless list of colleges and universities, the answer rarely is simple.
> —"What's Behind the Rankings," *U.S. News and World Report,*
> October 16, 1989, 58.

EXERCISE 14.3

Working in small groups, write opening questions that might make good lead-ins for articles or essays on two of the following topics. Then compare and discuss your questions within the group.

1. A board of regents' proposal to ban student cars from the central campus and impose a student fee for shuttle buses.
2. The fact that only two of the twelve copying machines in the college library work.

3. The effects of television on salaries in professional sports.
4. The revelation that clerical workers at your college are paid less than custodians.
5. New designs in athletic shoes.

➤ **Focus on key facts.** Another good anchor for an opening paragraph is the statement of an important fact that clues the readers into what your topic is going to be and gives them the base of information that they need to continue with their reading. Such a statement of fact (or facts) becomes the take-off point for the essay. Here is how Sue Ellen Rizzo, writing an argument paper, focused on important facts in her opening paragraph.

> Every major industrial country in the western world except the
> United States has an extensive system of subsidized child care that
> assures working women their children will be adequately taken
> care of by qualified people. In Sweden, for example, every city and
> town has government-sponsored day-care centers, and in many
> countries, factories and corporations provide on-site care that al-
> lows women to visit their children during the day. In those compa-
> nies, absenteeism for both men and women is notably lower than it
> is in our system. Most of the business owners in Ruralia, however,
> still have a dinosaur mentality when it comes to establishing child
> care facilities.

14 A

Opening ¶

Here Sue Ellen has focused her opening paragraph on important information about child care policies in other countries and indicated that she is going to use that information to discuss problems with child care in Ruralia.

EXERCISE 14.4

Write down three important facts you could use as the hook for an opening paragraph. (Check an almanac if you can't locate or recall any pertinent statistics.) They might be statistics about divorce, the amount of money the nation spends on cat food, the number of homeless people in Santa Barbara, the amount spent on athletic scholarships in your college, or any other data that you find interesting. Or they could be statements such as "In 1986, at the age of thirty-one, Earl Campbell hung up his uniform and quit professional football." Be sure the facts you use are verifiable—not just biases or opinions. Draft an opening paragraph based on the most interesting of your facts.

➤ **Avoid "circling the field" or "wheel spinning."** In the struggle to get started, writers who can't think of anything to say sometimes string together generalizations that comment on the topic rather than get down to business. It's like a pilot circling the field, getting ready to land, or someone giving a car too much throttle while pulling away from a stoplight. There's a lot of noise, smoke, and wheel-spinning, but little forward movement. For example, here is a paragraph that returning student John Maynard Ringling wrote while trying to open a paper on how buying a computer had changed his study habits.

> In this modern complex world of today, computers play an important role in everyone's lives. There are more computers today than there have ever been before. Whether we like it or not, we are involved with computers. Computers today affect just about every area of our lives. So it is silly to say, "Oh, I'm too old to learn about computers."

All the sentences before the last one would bore the reader. They are filler, a wind-up to get to the point made in the last sentence. They're fine to work up momentum for a preliminary draft, but Ringling shouldn't waste his readers' time with them in a final version. He would do better to provide specific examples of computers becoming a part of his life. He might start with an anecdote about an encounter he had with a computer. For example:

14 A

Opening ¶

> I was an old-timer in a technical writing class full of nineteen- and twenty-year-olds when I discovered what I had been missing by resisting word processors. Most of my classmates were turning in second and third versions of reports they were composing on computers while I was still grinding out an erasure-scarred first draft on my old manual typewriter. For a while, I thought that my typewriter and I suited each other. We both worked kind of slow. Then I recognized that my thinking wasn't old fashioned—just my technology. I learned quickly how foolish I was being to say "Oh, I'm too old to learn about computers."

> **TIP:** Check the introductory paragraphs in a draft you have written to see if you're circling or spinning your wheels. Are you telling your readers more than they want to know? Will they start skimming to get to the point? If you suspect that might be the case, try starting the paper with the *second* paragraph. Quite often, a paper really begins there. Don't be afraid to cut your original introduction if it doesn't move quickly enough.
>
> Remember, though, that you haven't necessarily wasted your time writing a rambling paragraph in the first draft. Such paragraphs can help you break through a writing block and work up the momentum to get started.

14 B   EFFECTIVE CONCLUDING PARAGRAPHS

Troubleshooting

Concluding paragraphs are notoriously hard to write, harder, we think, than opening paragraphs and more resistant to standard solutions. About all we can say is that the concluding paragraph for a paper should give your readers the sense that you have brought the paper to a satisfactory conclusion, that you have left no loose ends or unanswered questions. You don't want your readers asking "Then what?" or "And so?" when they finish or looking on the back of the page to see if they have missed something. There are no simple prescriptions for achieving that important goal; however, we can suggest three patterns that make for satisfying endings.

To write an effective concluding paragraph . . .

➤ **Make a recommendation when one is appropriate.** Such a recommendation should grow out of the issue you have been discussing. This approach usually gives a paper a positive ending and closes off the topic. For example, here is a conclusion from a paper on nutrition written by Abel Gonzalez.

14 B

Closing ¶

> But even if you are an athlete who wants quick results, you should
> not go to extremes in trying to improve your overall nutrition.
> When you decide to change your eating habits, your motto should be
> "Eat better," not "Eat perfectly." By increasing carbohydrates and
> reducing fat in the diet, that is, by eating more fruits, vegetables, and
> whole grains and less whole milk and fat meat, you can improve
> your energy level rather quickly. You will also feel better, play better,
> and look better than you ever imagined.

EXERCISE 14.5

For an editorial for your college newspaper, draft a closing paragraph in which you make a recommendation about changing some college regulation. Some possibilities are having to pay tuition when you preregister months before the semester starts, not allowing "boom box" radios on campus, or requiring that a student must take twelve credit hours to be eligible for financial aid.

➤ **Summarize the main points you have made.** Sometimes you can bring your paper to an effective close by re-emphasizing your main points (though not in precisely the same words you have used before) and closing with a wind-up sentence. You want to be careful, however, not to write an ending that sounds forced, as if you were tying the paper up in red ribbon and sticking a bow on it. Here is the conclusion for Richard Wesley's English paper in which he argues convincingly that restaurant customers should tip their waiters even if they will never see them again.

> Anyone who has ever worked in a restaurant knows that all too often the food isn't hot, the salads are soggy, or customers have to wait thirty minutes for a steak that should take ten minutes. When that happens, it's easy to short-change a waiter by saying "The food wasn't good," or "I had to wait too long." But ask yourself, "Was it really the waiter's fault?" The bottom line is that tips are part of a waiter's pay, and if you don't tip, you've stolen part of his or her labor.

Here's a concluding paragraph from a professional writer and teacher of writers.

<table>
<tr><td>

14 B

Closing ¶

</td><td>

Ultimately every writer must follow the path that feels most comfortable. For most people who are learning to write, that path is nonfiction. It enables them to write about what they know or can observe or can find out. This is especially true of young people—they will write far more willingly about experiences that touch their lives because that's what interests them. Motivation is at the heart of writing. If nonfiction is where you do your best writing, don't be buffaloed into the notion that it's an inferior species. The only important distinction is between good writing and bad writing. Good writing is good writing, whatever form it takes and whatever we call it.

—William Zinsser, *On Writing Well,* 3rd ed., Harper and Row (New York), 1985. 57–58.

</td></tr>
</table>

➤ **Link the end to the beginning.** Another effective way to end your paper is to tie your conclusion back to your beginning in a way that makes a kind of frame for the paper and unifies it. Notice how the boldfaced words in the example below forge a connection between opening and closing paragraphs. These paragraphs are from a paper written by Jenny So for her "History of Astronomy" course.

Opening paragraph:

> In 1931 an event occurred in Holmdel, New Jersey, that was to turn the world of astronomy on its ear. **An electrical engineer named Karl Jansky** was trying to find out what was causing **the static** that was interfering with radio-telephone reception between the United States and Europe. What he found instead was that the heavens were broadcasting! The **"static"** was caused by radio waves reaching the earth from the center of our **Milky Way** Galaxy.

Closing paragraph:

If Karl Jansky had not stumbled onto the "static" in the **Milky Way** and thus led to the development of the radio telescope, we would probably still know nothing about quasars, one of the most astonishing discoveries of our day. And it is doubtful that *Jansky* himself ever fully realized what a powerful tool he had hit upon for investigating the secrets of our universe.

> **TIP:** Probably the most important thing to remember about closing a paper or essay is this: Stop when you're finished. If you have covered all your points and are reasonably well satisfied with what you've said, quit. Don't bore your reader by tacking on a needless recapitulation or adding a paragraph of pious platitudes.

14 B

Closing ¶

EXERCISE 14.6

Read the following closing paragraphs from professional articles. What features do you find in them that give the reader a sense that the author has brought his or her essay to a satisfactory close?

1. No one could wish for a more advantageous heritage than that bequeathed to the black writer in the South: a compassion for the earth, a trust in humanity beyond our knowledge of evil, and an abiding love of justice. We inherit a great responsibility as well, for we must give voice to centuries not only of silent bitterness and hate but also of neighborly kindness and sustaining love.
   —Alice Walker, "The Black Writer and the Southern Experience," in
   In Search of Our Mothers' Gardens. (New York: Harcourt Brace Jovanovich, 1983), 21.

2. Even as medical students attach the highest value to their science, they should never forget that it works best when combined with their art, and that their art is what is most enduring in their profession. Ultimately, it is the physician's respect for the human soul that determines the worth of his science.
   —Norman Cousins, "The Physician as Communicator," in
   The Healing Heart. (New York: W. W. Norton & Company, 1983), 137.

EXERCISE 14.7

Read the closing paragraphs from two papers you have written recently or that you are working on. What features have you used to bring your writing to a conclusion? What other strategies do you think you could use?

15 Transitions

A Diagnosing problems with transitions

B Improving transitions

Terms you need to know

TRANSITIONS. Connecting words and phrases that help readers move from one unit to the next in your writing. They hold a piece of writing together, bridging gaps, and linking sentences and paragraphs.

EXPLETIVE CONSTRUCTIONS. The words *there* and *it* used as lead-ins to sentences.

It is going to be a day to remember.

There were hundreds of spectators watching the demonstrators.

Troubleshooting

When you write, you take your readers on a journey, and you certainly don't want them to get lost. Unfortunately, if you give them any opportunity to do so, they usually will. They'll miss turns, go off in the wrong direction, or fall through gaps you have left. If that seems to happen to your readers frequently, it may be because they're not reading attentively, but it may also be that you're not making good connections within your writing. When your teacher tells you that you have problems with transitions or your readers say, "Hey, I'm lost," believe them. They need help, and it's up to you to give it to them.

First, ask yourself if you have pushed your readers in the right direction by composing a first paragraph that previews what you're going to say in your paper. That's an important first step in keeping them on track. (See Chapter 14 on opening paragraphs.)

Second, ask yourself if you're showing your readers the connections between sentences and paragraphs by inserting the hooks, links, and signs they need to point them the way you want them to go. The connections between your sentences may seem so obvious to you that it's hard to realize your readers can't see the links. This chapter will suggest how you can provide them.

15 A   PROBLEMS WITH TRANSITIONS

Troubleshooting

If your instructor tells you that your writing is choppy, you need to work on your transitions as you revise. Remember, though, that the best linking devices are *organizational* and *internal*. That is, the best way to produce the smooth, tightly unified writing that is the sure mark of a skilled writer is to establish patterns that run through a piece of writing and carry your readers along naturally. For example, you might use a cause and effect or a comparison/contrast pattern, or you might set up a problem/solution or question/answer pattern. You can also use repetition, parallelism, and balance in your sentences and paragraphs. (See Section 15B.)

But even with such patterns, you sometimes need to use *external* transitional terms, those visible hooks, links, and directional signals that keep readers moving from point to point. These are the principal transitions we discuss in this section.

15 A

Trans

To diagnose problems with transitions . . .

➤ **Pay attention to the types of sentences you are writing.** Do you frequently write series of mostly short, simple sentences with very few commas? Do you avoid complex sentences with clauses or introductory phrases? If so, you may be writing in a choppy, disconnected style because those omitted phrases and clauses provide the links between sentences. Without them, you may be doing little more than making a series of statements without showing how they connect. You need to show those connections, not leave it up to your reader to guess about them.

Here's an example of a paragraph where the sentence structures seem too simple to connect ideas significantly. All the sentences are fairly short with similar patterns and no commas. Although you don't get lost in the paragraph, the style is choppy and graceless.

{**Weak transitions**}   Ombudsman Hector Stavros's mother, Hilary Stavros, is fifty-eight years old. She is a passionate believer in exercise. She lives by what she preaches. She won a blue ribbon in the over-fifty division of the ten kilometer run last week. She swims a mile before breakfast every morning. She works out on the Nautilus machines. She walks two miles on a treadmill every other morning. While she walks, she listens to Mozart and Vivaldi on her Sony Walkman.

Here is a revised version with some sentences combined and others connected with transitional terms boldfaced.

{**Revised**}   Ombudsman Hector Stavros's mother, fifty-eight-year-old Hilary Stavros, is a passionate believer in exercise, **who** lives by what she preaches. Just **last week** she won a blue ribbon in the over-fifty division of the ten kilometer run. **Not only** does she swim a mile before breakfast every morning, **but** she works out on the Nautilus machines and walks two miles on the treadmill every other morning, listening to Mozart and Vivaldi **as** she exercises.

▶ **Check to see if you're using subordinate clauses in some sentences.** Do your sentences have few subordinate clauses with the typical dependent clause signals such as *although, if, since, because, so,* and *unless?* If so, you may not be clearly showing connections between your ideas.

{**Weak transitions**}   Ms. Stavros watches the exercise habits of her Chicago friends. They don't walk. They ride the bus and the El. When it snows, they take taxis. Most of them are pretty lazy. They are exhausted from just existing in Chicago. They claim they don't have the energy to exercise. She thinks their habits become a vicious cycle.

You get no sense of the connection of one idea to another in this paragraph. Here is a revised version that hooks ideas together by joining sentences and using terms that show subordination; the transitional terms are boldfaced.

{**Revised**}   **Since** Ms. Stavros has been watching her Chicago friends' exercise habits, she has decided most of them are pretty lazy. **Instead of** walking, they take a bus or the El, or, **in case of snow,** they take a taxi. They claim they don't have the energy to exercise **because** they are so exhausted from living in Chicago. Hilary thinks **such** habits become a vicious cycle.

▶ **Be suspicious of expletive constructions.** Do you tend to write a lot of sentences beginning with the strung-out constructions "There is," "It is," and "There are"? If so, you may be putting together groups of sentences that are weakly connected, and you may also be creating a monotonous rhythm in your paper.

{**Weak transitions**}   It is Hilary Stavros's belief that exercise is like money. It is good for almost everything. There are people who think that exercise makes you tired. That is true only when you overdo it, she points out. Most kinds of exercise actually give you energy. One of the best for that is Hatha Yoga. Another is stretching. Hilary takes stretching classes three times a week.

Again, you get little sense of the relationship between these sentences, and the repetitious patterns are boring. Here is the paragraph reworked with better sentence openings and stronger connections. Transitional terms are boldfaced.

{**Revised**}   Hilary Stavros believes that exercise, like money, is good for almost anything. **Although** some people think exercise makes you tired, she points out that's true only if you overdo it. **On the contrary,** most exercise actually gives you energy, particularly Hatha Yoga. **Another** good exercise is stretching, **which** Hilary does in a class three times a week.

▶ **Use frequent markers to show time and sequence.** Move your readers along from one part to another by putting in words like *once, when, ago, formerly, finally,* and *after;* you can also use *first, second, then, last,* and similar words to good effect. Time markers can be important links in your writing.

{**Weak transitions**}   Stavros was not always an athlete. She started ten years ago. She was a flabby woman who didn't know her biceps from her pectorals. She had hamstrings so tight she could hardly bend over. She had little soft pouches bulging over her belt. She had 30 percent body fat. Her breath was short. She could hardly walk up a hill.

The effect is choppy and disconnected. The reader has no help relating the ideas. Here is a revision with time markers and transition words boldfaced.

{**Revised**}   Stavros was not always an athlete. **When** she started exercising ten years **ago,** she was a flabby woman who didn't know her biceps from her pectorals **and whose** hamstrings were so tight she could hardly bend over. **With** 30 percent body fat, little pouches bulged over her belt. Her breath was **so** short she could hardly walk up a hill.

➤ **Check your drafts for connecting words of all kinds.** Does your writing lack those typical words that signal connections between ideas? Some of the more common ones are *and, but, or, too, moreover, consequently, nevertheless, therefore,* and *also.* If they're missing, the cracks in your writing are probably showing, and your writing will seem fragmented.

{**Weak transitions**}   Hilary's inspiration came from her son Hector Stavros. He was in poor condition. She got tired of looking at him falling onto the couch every day after work. He had very little energy. She realized he wouldn't be attractive to women. He might live at home the rest of her life. It was a frightening thought. One of them had to get out of the house on nights and weekends. Hector wasn't interested. It was up to her to act.

15 A

Trans

There is a gap after each period, with no strong links between the sentences. Here is the revision with connectives and links boldfaced.

{**Revised**}   Her inspiration came from her son, Hector Stavros, who was **also** in poor condition. He **too** had little energy. She realized he wouldn't be attractive to women **and** might live at home the rest of her life. **That** was a frightening thought. One of them had to get out of the house on nights and weekends, **but** Hector wasn't interested. **Thus** it was up to her to act.

> **TIP:** We suspect that for some writers, problems with transitions stem from worrying about how to punctuate sentences. They write simple sentences, but fail to connect them because they're not sure where to put commas or how to use semicolons. They're afraid that if they try to compose the more complex sentences they would like to use, their writing will become tangled. So they limit themselves to an immature and choppy style.
>
> If you think this might be your problem, we suggest that, at first, you forget about the punctuation in those complex or involved sentences. Just go ahead and write them. You can figure out how to fix them later, getting help if necessary from an instructor or writing lab. With most instructors, you'll get more points for expressing good ideas in interesting sentences than you will for having all your commas in the right places.

▶ **Check for gaps between paragraphs.** Major transitional problems are most likely to occur as you move from paragraph to paragraph. Unless you have set up a strong pattern that unifies your writing, you may need some device to link your paragraphs. It can be as simple as starting paragraphs with an appropriate transitional word. You can also use a key word at the end of one paragraph, then repeat it at the beginning of the next. Or you might end one paragraph with a question, then answer the question in the paragraph that follows. Whatever device you use, you are giving your readers signals that say, "Come this way."

One way of checking the transitions in a paper is to examine the beginnings and endings of paragraphs, reading them apart from the essay as a whole to see whether they still make sense. Here, for example, are the opening lines for paragraphs in an article about Hilary Stavros. Notice how after the opening sentence, each subsequent paragraph starts with a connecting term that links it to the previous paragraph. Linking words are boldfaced.

15 A

Trans

Opening line, first paragraph:

"Hilary Stavros grew up in a time when few women took sports seriously or even thought about exercise."

First line, next paragraph:

"**Now,** however, while most middle-aged people working out at health clubs are still men, a growing number of women are getting into the act."

First line, next paragraph:

"**Furthermore,** they aren't concerned only about their figures."

First line, following paragraph:

"**Additional evidence** that regular exercise has unexpected benefits for people over fifty comes from Wanda Latterstein, head of the physical education program at Clear Lake College."

First line, following paragraph:

"**Not only** does Latterstein's research show that older women in trained condition have better reflexes, but it also shows they do better on memory tasks."

First line, last paragraph:

"**Still,** the fact is that few women are willing to make the effort that Hilary has."

Linkages can also be made between the last line of one paragraph and the first line of the next, as in the following examples.

Key word at end of one paragraph:

"It took a week for Hilary to decide whether she should try running, rowing, swimming, or walking. By the end of the week, she had made a **decision,** one based on Chicago winters."

Word repeated in opening line of the next paragraph:

"Hilary's **decision** led her to the Lincoln Park Health and Fitness Center."

Question at the end of one paragraph:

"After she had checked out all the facilities and equipment, she had only one question for the fitness director: **When can I get a trainer to get me started?**"

Answer at beginning of next paragraph:

"**Hilary started with her trainer,** Sharon Sullivan, the next morning."

These examples represent only a few possibilities.

> TIP: Take special care that any paragraph that ends at the bottom of a page has a clear link to the paragraph at the top of the next page. If it doesn't, readers may get lost and think they've skipped a page.

15 A

Trans

EXERCISE 15.1

Rewrite the following paragraph, reorganizing and changing some sentences or adding signal words to improve transitions.

Chicago presents a challenge to exercisers. It's a great city for exercise in the summer and fall. There is a green belt along Lake Michigan. Boats on the lake make the scene interesting. Mostly the weather is pleasant. Winter brings a different story. There is snow and subfreezing weather four or five months a year. The winter wind off Lake Michigan can turn a runner to an icicle.

EXERCISE 15.2

Working with two or three other students, read over the following paragraphs, then diagnose the transition problems you find between and in paragraphs. Working together, rewrite some first sentences or last sentences in a way that would solve those problems.

The dangers of exercise are not only that one might injure one's back or pull a hamstring. True, people new to exercise need to guard against such injuries. No one wants to be a fallen weekend athlete, crippled on Monday morning from running a ten kilometer race or biking up a mountain on Sunday.

The newcomer to exercise can become a fanatic. In some ways, the atmosphere around a health and fitness club encourages fanaticism. At 6:00 A.M., the hard-core weight lifters and triathalon competitors are there sweating and puffing, but enjoying every minute of it. They look great and exude confidence. They seem to have their priorities straight—work-outs come before work.

The fitness craze can take over one's life. With aerobics, weight lifting, and stretching, it's easy to use up three hours a day before you know it. What happens to earning a living or to studying if one is a student? What happens to one's social life? Not only do exercisers have to go to bed early, but when they start to preach—and they usually do—nonexercising friends can quickly disappear.

15 B HOW CAN YOU STRENGTHEN TRANSITIONS?

Terms you need to know

DEMONSTRATIVE PRONOUN. A pronoun that points something out: *this, that, these,* and *those.*

RELATIVE PRONOUN. A pronoun that refers to a person, thing, or place: *who, which, where,* and *that.*

Troubleshooting

Once you have learned to diagnose your problems with transitions, you can use a variety of strategies to solve them. The concept that underlies all of them is this: Each sentence should leave a little trace or residue out of which the next sentence can grow. There should always be a reference, a hint, a repetition, a key word that links what you're saying with what's come before and what lies ahead. A plan of organization is the best tactic, of course. Here, however, we offer a few smaller-scale ways to establish connections between ideas.

To improve your transitions . . .

➤ **Accumulate a stockpile of the conventional transition words.** When you edit, check to see if you need to insert one or more of the traditional linking terms in order to firm up connections in your writing.

But be careful. Transitional words and phrases are not neutral. On the contrary, they give strong but diverse signals to readers. They say "turn here," "stop for a qualification," "notice the cause and effect," "here's something similar," or "here's something different." You cannot just use a transitional term at random; you have to be sure it gives the signal you want.

The most common transitional words and phrases are listed below according to their function.

likewise similarly in the same way	[showing similarity]
however instead nevertheless although in spite of on the other hand not only	[showing contrast]
moreover in addition to for example	[showing accumulation]
hence consequently therefore as a result of thus	[showing consequence]
because since for	[showing causation]
next subsequently after finally first, second, etc.	[showing sequence]

15 B

Trans

➤ **Repeat a key idea throughout a paragraph to establish a *motif* or central idea running through it.** An idea can be a key word plus variations. For example, if you are writing a paper about rockets, then rockets become a key idea that can be repeated through a variety of potential synonyms and connected terms: *missiles, boosters, launchers, launch vehicles,* and so on. Each word helps to establish a connection to the central topic. In the example below, the key theme of health is repeated through synonyms that include *well-being, physical condition,* and *vigor.*

On a nasty Monday night in January ten years ago, faced with another evening of Hector and pro football, Hilary Stavros left for the Lincoln Park *Health and Fitness Center.* She braved the icy streets primarily to improve her own *physical* and mental *health,* but also to safeguard Hector's *physical condition.* She was afraid she was going to kill him. But the results of that first visit ten years ago have been not only mental *health,* but also *physical,* emotional, and financial *vigor* for Stavros.

▶ **Use the demonstrative terms** *this, that, these, those,* **and** *such* **within sentences to tie ideas together.** Notice how the boldfaced words in the following example hook directly into the previous sentences.

> The change in Hilary has come about gradually, and she points **this** out frequently. Exercise won't turn a flabby woman over forty with 30 percent body fat into a triathalon champion with 18 percent body fat in a matter of months or even years. **That** kind of claim is ridiculous. **Such** achievement requires not only perseverance, but a major change in attitude.

▶ **Use relative pronouns to show links between sentences.** *Who, which, where,* and *that* are powerful words that link a descriptive or informative statement to something that has preceded it. Notice how the boldfaced words in this paragraph serve as links to other words and ideas.

> Hilary's first few weeks at the health club were exhausting but exhilarating. It was a place **that** challenged her, one **where** she could see healthy people **who** cared about themselves. The contrast of **these** people with Hector, **who** even then was being his couch-potato self at home, was encouraging.

▶ **Use parallel structures and downshifting (see Sections 13B and 13C) within a paragraph.** Ideas contained within parallel sentences automatically seem connected because they share similar patterns. Ideas that branch off from one another also seem tightly connected.

The following example employs both techniques. The first sentence states the topic of the paragraph: the difficulty of a fitness regimen. The next three parallel sentences downshift to develop that main idea. Finally, the last sentence downshifts again to enlarge on the fourth one, providing an illustration of the main point.

> The middle-aged woman who wants to become really fit **must embark** on a strenuous exercise and diet program that she may find distinctly unladylike. She **must join** the sweaty men at the health club at least an hour every day. She **must do** a series of exercises that require her to groan and puff. She **must change** her eating habits, trading in chicken salad and chocolate cheesecake for pasta and raw vegetables. At one point, Hilary Stavros felt that she had eaten enough carrots and lettuce to make her nose start twitching.

▶ **Use a semicolon to link two closely related statements.** Although many writers ignore this useful piece of punctuation, the semicolon signals a tight connection that says, "These groups of words go together." Often a semicolon can connect parts of a sentence more effectively than *and* or *also*. For more details about the semicolon, see Chapter 33.

> Hilary Stavros no longer worries about what guests will think of her chocolate soufflé; now her concern is how many push-ups and abdominal crunches she would have to do to counteract the soufflé.

> Hilary has the fervor of a convert; she realizes, however, that most of her friends don't want to hear her preach.

EXERCISE 15.3

Underline the transitional words and phrases in the following paragraph.

On that January night ten years ago when she walked through the snow to the Lincoln Park Health Club, Hilary Stavros never dreamed that today she would be famous. Yet she is now a well-known citizen in her part of Chicago, at least among the over-fifty group. Her book *Energy after Fifty* is on the best-seller list at many bookstores and is the next selection of the month for the national Golden Age Book Club. She also appears regularly on Chicago talk shows and has been asked to write a column for *Modern Maturity,* the magazine of the American Association of Retired People.

EXERCISE 15.4

Working with other students in a group, rewrite the following paragraph to improve the transitions.

It is unfortunate that Hector Stavros, Hilary's son, is not pleased with his mother. He is still a couch potato. Monday nights find him glued to the TV screen. He is watching football or reruns of <u>New-hart.</u> He complains that his mother should act her age. He hates to think about her in exercise clothes working out on Nautilus machines around all those men. What he really worries about is that she might meet some equally fit sixty-year-old widower. She might marry again. Hector could be out of a place to live. On hearing this, Hilary Stavros's only comment was, "Could be."

16 Kinds of Language

A Levels of language
B Meaning
C Dialects
D Sexist language

Troubleshooting

Few people would choose to use the same kind of language every time they write anymore than they would wear the same kind of clothes on every occasion. Most writers instinctively, often unconsciously, adapt their language to their audience and situation because they have developed a sense of what is appropriate; they know that what works on one occasion may not work as well on another. And just as the person with good clothes sense knows how to choose the right outfit to make the desired impression, skillful writers know how to select language to fit their needs. But to do that, they have to know what choices are available to them. The purpose of this chapter is to explain what some of those choices of language are.

16 A CHOOSING THE APPROPRIATE LANGUAGE LEVEL

Terms you need to know

FORMAL LANGUAGE. Language that is polite, impersonal, and conventional. Most academic, professional, and business writing is formal.

INFORMAL LANGUAGE. Language that is casual and personal. Informal language is still usually quite conventional in grammar and usage, though it uses contractions more regularly and makes use of vocabulary items that might seem more appropriate in everyday speech.

Troubleshooting

The answer to the question "How formal or informal should I be when I write my papers?" is "That depends." It depends on your writing situation. To make appropriate choices about the level of formality for a piece of writing, you have to ask yourself

- Who are my readers?
- What do they expect from me?
- What do I want to accomplish with this audience?

Only after you have an idea of the answers to these questions can you choose language that will work well for a specific writing situation.

Unfortunately, many writers assume that to impress professors, colleagues, or other demanding readers, they must adopt an excessively formal style. They think writing in an "academic style" means writing hard-to-read prose stuffed with big words and long, dull sentences—something so impersonal and dry that it reads as if it came from an insurance policy or a badly written textbook. So they turn out writing like this example that Brian McVicker wrote for the first draft of a paper in a psychology course.

> Neonate infants are believed to have the ability to relate visual
> sensory perception with motor function. The neonatal visual
> system is probably the most prefunctional of the senses at birth.
> Manifestly, this competence is not correlated with time outside the
> womb for in early months infants have the problem-solving ability
> that comes from linking sensory systems and motor activity. The
> observation that these subjects manifest visual preference for facial
> forms upholds the assumption that a connection exists between
> visual and motor activity.

16 A

Lang Lev

Brian was proud of this paragraph. It sounded impressive to him and he was disappointed when his readers complained that it was dull and difficult to read. Most readers, and particularly professors, who have to read a great many papers, want to be able to understand what they read. Thus both Brian's fellow students and his professor preferred this revision, which, though still formal, is much clearer.

> Observers now realize that newborn infants can coordinate sight
> and movement. In fact, vision seems to be the sense that is best-
> developed when babies are born for it is evident very early that they
> can solve problems that require linking vision and motor ability.
> The fact that they can recognize different facial expressions and
> respond to them supports this theory.

To be sure, there is something called *academic writing,* and it's useful to be able to shift into that style when you need to. But we think that mastering the conventions of academic writing is not primarily a matter of commanding a formal style and an intimidating vocabulary. Rather it is learning how professors want you to organize and present your ideas and what kind of support they expect for those ideas. They care far more about clear thinking and informed writing than they do about an elevated style (see Chapter 6).

When you write, you'll often find yourself shifting between various levels of formality, looking for the word, phrase, or expression that fits your writing situation and creates the tone you want. Such choices are tricky because we cannot make a simple, black/white classification of formal and informal language. You should think of levels of formality in language as a scale or a continuum that has very formal language—the stiff and intimidating language of a legal document—at one end and very informal language—slang and colloquialisms—at the other.

Levels of Language

Very formal

Legal Documents

Technical Reports

Scientific magazine articles

Major political speeches

Sermons

Newspaper editorials and columns

Popular magazine articles

Personal experience papers

Notes to friends

Very informal—colloquial or casual

Neither of the extremes on this scale concern us here since virtually no writing that students need to do requires them to be either very formal or extremely colloquial. It is, however, useful for you to know something about the general characteristics and uses of at least three of the intermediate levels.

To handle language levels appropriately . . .

➤ **Recognize formal writing.** Formal writing tends to have these characteristics:

Long sentences and long paragraphs
Abstract language
Impersonal tone—few personal references; few contractions

Little action and few strong, active verbs
Serious tone
Considerable distance implied between reader and writer

Writers who choose a formal style may do so for several reasons. First, they may be writing on a serious and complex topic, one for which a casual, personal style would not be appropriate. Second, they may be writing for a serious formal occasion, such as a public speech, and don't want their writing to sound too much like everyday speech. Or they may want to sound impersonal and not emotionally involved with their topic, so they adopt a style that distances them from their reader. For example, here is the opening paragraph from Darwin Ferguson's term paper for an environmental studies course.

> An inescapable fact of the world energy situation today is that fossil fuel resources are finite, and continued reliance on coal, gas, and oil for generating electricity is not viable. However, meeting future electricity needs requires raising public awareness about finding alternate options. The most important characteristics of these options will be flexibility, cost, and low risk. Three programs currently under investigation are a broader energy information program, cogeneration and small power production, and small renewable power production.

16 A

Lang Lev

This is a clear and informative paragraph that gets the reader off to a good start, but it's not much fun to read because of the formal language. Nevertheless, much of the writing done in Darwin's field of engineering sounds like this, and Darwin's professor wants her students to write this kind of formal prose.

➤ **Recognize moderately informal writing.** Although there are many kinds of moderately informal writing, and it occupies a considerable spread across the continuum, we find that it has these general characteristics:

Variety of sentence lengths
Short- to medium-length paragraphs
Mixture of abstract and concrete language
Some use of first and second person pronouns
Some use of contractions
Frequent action verbs
Variety of topics, from casual to serious
Little perceived distance between reader and writer

The writing in this book is an example of moderately informal prose; so is the work of newspaper columnists like Ellen Goodman and William Raspberry and most of the writing you may read in magazines like *Newsweek, Sports Illustrated,* or *Mademoiselle.* Most writing in *The New York Times* would be toward the high end of informal prose; writing in *TV Guide* would be at the low end of informal prose.

Writers who choose an informal style usually do so because, although their topics may be serious, they don't want to sound solemn. They want their readers to feel as if they are talking to them at a close and comfortable distance. An informal style seems more relaxed. Here is the opening paragraph from a paper on educational technology written for an education course by Stephanie Mendelson.

> In the last year, interest in preparing America for its high-tech future has exploded. The current scenario predicts that we will be a huge information society, and the current generation of youngsters will need to be perfectly at ease using computers. School districts are now scrambling to meet this need by adding computer courses to their curriculum. They're trying to make as many students as possible "computer literate." One of the major problems, however, is that too often the teachers in these schools have little training or experience with computers and certainly do not feel at ease themselves.

Here is another, more informal, example—the opening paragraph from a descriptive paper written by Luke Scandino for a campus magazine.

> When you think of tourism in Africa do you think of East Africa, especially big game safaris in Kenya and Tanzania? Most people do. What you and other potential visitors probably don't realize is that West Africa has treasures and wonders to equal, if not surpass, anything else on the African continent. Not only treasures and wonders, but mystery and adventure can be found in one country in particular—Mali, the land that is reached by the road to Timbuktu.

➤ **Recognize casual writing.** Casual writing tends to have these characteristics:

> Short- to medium-length sentences, short paragraphs
> High proportion of specific words and vivid language
> Many personal pronouns, references to people
> Frequent use of contractions
> Some slang terms and colloquial language
> Many lively action verbs
> Topics that may be light
> Very little distance between reader and writer

Writers who choose a casual style usually do so when their subject is popular or light, and they want their writing to give a fast-moving, breezy impression. They want to make their readers feel relaxed and very comfortable. Here as an example is the opening paragraph from a column written by Kyle Talbot for the sports page of *The Clear Lake Clarion*.

> Do you wish you could find a fun way to relax and sharpen your body and mind without making your checkbook wince? Ever think about tennis?

Probably so, but decided it cost too much and you wouldn't be that good anyway. Well, think again. With a little savvy about shopping at Good Will and a little luck in the bargain corner of Barney Meyers' Jock and Jogger Store, you can get started in tennis for less than $75.

Here is the opening paragraph from a feature article on drinking and driving for *The Clear Lake Clarion* by Rita Ruiz. (It's even more informal although notice that the topic is not light.)

You've been hittin' the books all weekend. A new guy from your chem class calls and wants to cruise out to the lake for a swim. He's kind of cute, so you go, picking up a couple of six packs along the way. The afternoon passes, and it's been fun. But now it's time to go home, and your date's had one too many. You're feelin' kind of buzzed yourself. What d'ya do?

Each of the students in the preceding examples chose the level of formality for his or her paper by thinking about the purpose of the paper and the audience who would read it. Darwin knew his professor wanted the impersonal and abstract tone of an engineering report—no personal pronouns, no contractions. Stephanie knew that her professor wanted a factual but not stuffy article on computers in the schools, one that might be printed later in a departmental newsletter. Luke wanted to be a little less formal in his article on Mali because he was writing for his fellow students and thought if the article sounded too much like a paper for a course, they wouldn't read it. Kyle wanted an informative but easy-to-read style for his tennis-playing readers so he chose to sound conversational and casual.

16 A

Lang Lev

Finally, Rita deliberately chose to write her article about drinking and driving in such an informal and colloquial style for two reasons. First she was writing for student readers of the college newspaper and felt a light, informal style would appeal to them. Second, she thought a colloquial style would sound less preachy, and she knows students don't like to be lectured to. She also knows, however, that such a style is much too informal for most papers.

EXERCISE 16.1

Working in a small group, decide how you would classify the levels of formality in these passages from two professional writers whose work appears in anthologies in freshman English courses. Discuss reasons for any differences.

1. One day last summer I had a vision near St. Paul's Chapel of Trinity Church. I had walked a lot of the length of Manhattan, and it seemed to me that a large part of my time had been spent stepping around men who stood in the gutter snapping imaginary whips. Strangers had approached me trying to sell Elavil, an antidepressant. As I stood on Broadway I reflected that, although I had grown to middle age seeing strange sights, I had never thought to see people selling Elavil on the street. Street Elavil, I would have exclaimed, that must be a joke! . . .

   In the morning, driving into Manhattan, the traffic had seemed particularly demonic. I'd had a peculiar exchange with a bridge toll taker who seemed to have one half of a joke I was expected to have the other half of. I didn't. Walking on Fourteenth Street, I passed a man in an imitation leopard-skin hat who was crying as though his heart would break. At Fourth Avenue I was offered the Elavil. Elavil relieves the depression attendant on the deprivation of re-refined cocaine—"crack"—which is what the men cracking the imaginary whips were selling. Moreover, I'd been reading the papers. I began to think that I was seeing stoned cops, stoned grocery shoppers, and stoned boomers. So it went, and by the time I got to lower Broadway I was concerned. I felt as though I were about to confront the primary process of hundreds of thousands of unsound minds. What I was seeing in my vision of New York as super-stoned Super City was cocaine in its role of success drug.

—Robert Stone, "A Higher Horror of the Whiteness: Cocaine's Coloring of the American Psyche," *Harper's,* December 1986, 49.

16 B

Den/Con

2. Biological evolution has been accompanied by increasing complexity. The most complex organisms on earth today contain substantially more stored information, both genetic and extragenetic, than the most complex organisms of, say, two hundred million years ago—which is only five percent of the history of life on the planet, five days ago on the Cosmic Calendar. The simplest organisms of Earth today have just as much evolutionary history behind them as the most complex, and it may well be that the internal biochemistry of contemporary bacteria is more efficient than the internal biochemistry of the bacteria of three billion years ago. But the amount of genetic information in the bacteria today is probably not vastly greater than that in their ancient bacterial ancestors. It is important to distinguish between the amount of information and the quality of that information.

—Carl Sagan, *The Dragons of Eden* (New York: Random House, 1977), 21.

EXERCISE 16.2

What level of formality do you think would be appropriate for writing done in each of these situations? In each case, consider what impression the writer wants to make and the distance he or she wants to maintain between reader and writer. Give reasons for your choice.

1. A letter to a representative or senator asking to be considered for a summer internship in his or her office.
2. A biographical statement to accompany an application for college.
3. A brochure promoting a student-organized ski trip.

16 B DENOTATION AND CONNOTATION: WHAT'S APPROPRIATE?

Terms you need to know

DENOTATION. The neutral or objective meaning of a term. Sometimes called the "dictionary meaning," the denotation of a word attempts to explain what a word means when separated from its emotional, political, or ethical associations.

Examples of denotative definitions:

1. *socialism:* a theory or system of social organization which advocates the vesting of ownership and control of the means of production, capital, land, etc. in the community as a whole.

2. *democracy:* a form of government in which supreme power is vested in the people and exercised by them or by their elected agents under a free electoral system.

These are straight forward definitions that seem to give "just the facts."

CONNOTATION. The meanings and associations a word has acquired over and above its dictionary meaning; its emotional overtones.

Troubleshooting

Connotative words are, inevitably, value words. Connotation has the power to evoke strong responses from readers because it taps into their emotions and senses, not just their intellects, and reminds them of experiences, beliefs, or traditions that are important to them. One specialist in communication, Richard Weaver, labels strong connotative language "God" words and "Devil" words; that is, words so powerful that they immediately evoke fiercely positive or negative reactions.

16 B

Den/Con

Connotations of words change over time. For instance, in the time of the eighteenth-century English author Jane Austen, the word "unexceptional" meant admirable; it described a person to whom one could take no exception. Now it means ordinary, not particularly worthwhile.

Connotations also change according with audiences. For one group of readers, "individualistic" is a favorable word, implying a free spirited, self-reliant person; to other groups, "individualistic" suggests an uncooperative person who is unconcerned about the general welfare.

The more sensitive to language you become, the more you'll feel that words sometimes shift meaning and change on you. You can't count on them to hold still, so it's often hard to determine when a word is denotative or connotative—and whether it's the right word to use in a certain situation.

That's hardly surprising. Language is so vital and dynamic that it is seldom possible to put words into strict categories. Thus rather than to say emphatically "This word is denotative and that word is connotative," we think it works better to set up a continuum, putting strict denotation at one end and extreme connotation at the other. By doing so, we create a yardstick on which we can arrange types of writing (next page).

At the denotative extreme of the yardstick, we would find language so flat, impersonal, and uninteresting that no one would read it unless absolutely necessary—for example, the language of an insurance policy.

The amount of loss for which the Company may be liable to the Insured under Section I shall be payable 60 days after Proof of Loss, as herein provided, is received by the Company and ascertainment of the loss is made either by agreement between the Insured and the Company expressed in writing or by the filing with the Company of an appraisal award as herein provided.

Denotative

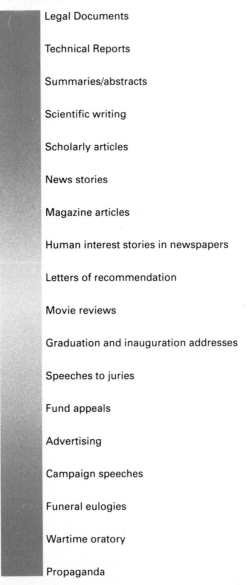

Legal Documents

Technical Reports

Summaries/abstracts

Scientific writing

Scholarly articles

News stories

Magazine articles

Human interest stories in newspapers

Letters of recommendation

Movie reviews

Graduation and inauguration addresses

Speeches to juries

Fund appeals

Advertising

Campaign speeches

Funeral eulogies

Wartime oratory

Propaganda

Connotative

At the connotative extreme of the yardstick, we would find language so emotional and inflammatory that most readers would feel insulted at the blatant assault on their senses and emotions. Most propaganda could be put in this category. For instance:

The bleeding heart do-gooders who are conniving to pass these laws want to grind freedom underfoot and allow despicable and depraved criminals to wander the streets of our cities terrorizing helpless citizens.

In between these two extremes, neither of which you are likely to encounter in your college reading or need to use in your college writing, falls a broad range of language for different kinds of writing. In the following sections, we make suggestions about the **degree** of denotation or connotation that's appropriate in a variety of writing situations.

To use different kinds of language effectively . . .

➤ **Know when to choose denotative language.** A contemporary astronomy textbook begins its chapter "Introduction to Astronomical Observations" like this:

> The comet was so horrible and frightful . . . that some people died of fear and others fell sick. It appeared as a star of excessive length and the color of blood; at its summit was seen the figure of a bent arm holding a great sword in its hand, as if about to strike. On both sides . . . were seen a great number of axes, knives, and spaces colored with blood, among which were a great number of hideous human faces with beards and bristling hair.
>
> —Ambrose Pare, physician, 1528

The authors of the textbook follow with this comment:

> The observation quoted above is clearly lacking in objectivity. Along with such famous observations as the one of Aristotle that women had more teeth than men (he couldn't have looked very hard), we would tend today to label such work as "unscientific." The rapid progress made in the twentieth-century physical sciences stems largely from a method of investigation in which the systematic and objective measurement of the phenomena of nature is the ultimate arbiter of truth. . . . It is only from the interplay between theoretical speculation and careful measurement that new knowledge is attained rapidly and efficiently.
>
> —William H. Jeffreys and Robert Robbins, *Discovering Astronomy*
> (New York: John Wiley & Sons, 1981), 14.

What the authors are criticizing is, in part, the language of the sixteenth-century observer; it is heavily connotative and inexact, reflecting hysteria and fear. Such language contradicts everything modern science stands for: "systematic and objective measurement" reported in clear, objective language. As scientists, Jeffreys and Robbins insist that to be scientific, knowledge must be communicated by *denotative* language.

Today, professionals in science, technology, law, medicine, and the academic world in general expect writing in those fields to fall heavily at the denotative end of the denotation/connotation scale. They value objective, factual writing that reports accurately and unemotionally—writing that informs but does not seek to bias. Here is a good example, written by an eminent physicist for a general audience.

> In every strategic defense system there are three main components. The first is the tracking and discrimination apparatus, the radars and optical sensors which are supposed to find and identify the targets. The second is

the data-handling system, which takes the information from the sensors and feeds it to the computers which launch and steer the interceptors. The third is the interceptor system, the rockets or other more exotic weapons which actually hit and kill targets. The first two jobs, discrimination and data handling, are by far the hardest part of the problem of defense. The third job, sending up an interceptor to kill a target once you know exactly where it is, is comparatively easy.

—Freeman Dyson, "Star Wars," in *Infinite in All Directions*
(New York: Harper & Row, 1988), 216.

Still on the denotative end of the scale but a little further toward the middle lies writing in disciplines such as history and sociology. It still focuses on information, but the writing is less objective. Authors tend to use more language that appeals to the senses and emotions, but they still retain an impersonal stance toward their material.

16 B

Den/Con

Hanoi awoke to a festive day on September 2, 1945. Young Vietnamese had worked overnight, bedecking drab buildings with lanterns and flowers, red flags and banners bearing nationalist slogans. Shops, offices, and schools had closed for the occasion as hundred of thousands of people converged throughout the morning on Ba Dinh Square, a large grassy field that lay beyond the handsome French residential district. Peasants in black pajamas and conic straw hats had flowed in from nearby villages to mingle with merchants and mandarins; Vietminh guerrillas, some armed with spears and machetes or primitive flintlocks, marched to the cadence of gongs and drums. Children scurried everywhere, and even Buddhist monks in saffron robes and black-gowned Catholic priests appeared, all for a single purpose—to see the mysterious Ho Chi Minh.

—Stanley Karnow, *Vietnam: A History* (Penguin Books, 1984), 17.

Here is an example from a book on the sociology of women.

Thus women not only define themselves in a context of human relationship but also judge themselves in terms of their ability to care. Women's place in man's life cycle has been that of nurturer, caretaker, and helpmate, the weaver of those networks of relationships on which she in turn relies. But while women have thus taken care of men, men have, in their theories of psychological development, as in their economic arrangements, tended to assume or devalue that care. When the focus on individuation and individual achievement extends into adulthood and maturity is equated with personal autonomy, concern with relationships appears as a weakness of women rather than as a human strength (Miller, 1976).

—Carol Gilligan, *In a Different Voice* (Cambridge:
Harvard University Press, 1982), 17.

Clustered toward the middle of the denotative/connotative scale we find various kinds of writing in which authors seek not only to inform but to persuade. They're still focusing on facts, but they also want to communicate their attitudes and emotions, so they use connotative language. We give only two representative examples from a broad spectrum of writing that fits into the category. The first is from a newspaper opinion column.

When I was in college, there was an infamous course known as Chem 20. Organic chemistry was the sieve into which was poured every premedical student in the university. But only those who came through it with an A or B could reasonably expect to get into medical school.

Chem 20, therefore, became a psychological laboratory of pre-med anxiety. Every class was a combat mission. Every grade was a life and death matter. It reeked of Olympian anguish and Olympic competitiveness. It taught people whose goal in life was the relief of pain and suffering that only the fittest, the most single-minded, would survive.
　　—Ellen Goodman, "The Chem 20 Factor," from *Close to Home* by Ellen
　　　　Goodman. Copyright 1979 by Washington Post Company.

The second example is autobiographical writing in which the author tries to convey his feelings. It falls further toward the connotative end of the scale than the Goodman excerpt does.

I stand there. I continue thinking about what she [my mother] has asked me [what is psychiatry?]—and what she cannot comprehend. My parents seem to me possessed of great dignity. An aristocratic reserve. Like the very rich who live behind tall walls, my mother and father are always mindful of the line separating public from private life. Watching a celebrity talk show on television, they listen for several minutes as a movie star with bright teeth recounts details of his recent divorce. And I see my parents grow impatient. Finally my mother gets up from her chair. Changing the channel, she says with simple disdain, "Cheap people."
　　—Richard Rodriguez, *Hunger of Memory* (New York:
　　　　Bantam Books, 1982), 184.

16 B

Den/Con

Finally, far toward the connotative end of the scale lies patriotic, religious, or ethical writing designed to move peoples' emotions and arouse their fervor and support. You can find stirring examples in the war speeches of Winston Churchill, the inaugural speech of John F. Kennedy, or the presidential speeches of Abraham Lincoln. No one, however, was a greater master of this form than Martin Luther King, Jr. Here is a brief passage from his "I Have a Dream" speech.

Let us not seek to satisfy our thirst for freedom by drinking from the cup of bitterness and hatred. We must forever conduct our struggle on the high plane of dignity and discipline. We must not allow our creative pro-test to degenerate into physical violence. Again and again we must rise to the majestic heights of meeting physical force with soul force. The marvel-ous new militancy which has engulfed the Negro community must not lead us to a distrust of all white people, for many of our white brothers, as evidenced by their presence here today, have come to realize that their destiny is tied up with our destiny and their freedom is inextricably bound to our freedom. We cannot walk alone.
　　—Martin Luther King, Jr., "I Have a Dream."

➤ **Choose denotative or connotative language according to your writing situation.**
The selection of examples given above can't begin to cover the range of denotative and connotative writing you will encounter in everything from technical journals at one extreme to political propaganda at the other, but we hope it will give you

an idea of how professional writers choose the denotative or connotative language that is appropriate to their situation and audience. You should make your choices in the same way.

When you are writing papers or reports for most of your academic courses, you should rely primarily on denotative language and use value words only when you want to make a judgment. In scientific and technical writing, case studies, and write-ups of statistical data, you should be especially careful to stay as objective as possible and avoid connotative language. When you are writing in the social studies, humanities, or fine arts, you can use connotative language a little more freely, particularly when you're writing criticism. Nevertheless, you should still show great restraint and stay near the denotative end of the scale. Professors expect objectivity, not bias, in papers for most college courses.

When you are doing other kinds of writing—perhaps business writing, an editorial or a review for a newspaper, a column for the newsletter of a church or social group, or an appeal for funds—you can move toward the center of the scale, mixing denotative and connotative language as seems appropriate for your purpose and your audience. Sometimes you may want to move far toward the connotative end of the denotative/connotative scale if you're writing on an issue about which you feel strongly and for an audience you think would be receptive to such language. But know your audience and use caution.

16 B

Den/Con

In the final analysis, you can make intelligent choices about using denotative and connotative language only if you are aware of your purpose and your audience. Words shift meanings according to their context, and what seems like the right word with one group of readers may prove to be exactly the wrong word with a different group.

> **TIP: Don't think of denotative and connotative language in terms of wrong or right. Even in academic writing, denotative language isn't always good just because it seems to be objective, and connotative language isn't always bad just because it appeals to the senses and emotions. In order to write effectively in a wide range of situations, you need to use both and to be able to move easily up and down the continuum.**

➤ **Avoid "whoopee" words in public writing.** There is a special group of connotative words that we call "whoopee" words—terms of exaggeration that are so overused they're virtually meaningless. Here are some of the more popular ones:

fantastic	unbelievable
sensational	fabulous
incredible	marvelous
terrific	tremendous
wonderful	devastating

These are hardly more than hackneyed buzz words, and they have little place in college writing except, perhaps, in dialogue.

EXERCISE 16.3

Copy two advertisements from magazines or newspapers and underline the connotative words. Compare the ads you choose with those chosen by some of your classmates and discuss what you think the ad writers are trying to achieve with connotative language.

EXERCISE 16.4

Analyze the following editorial from the *Clear Lake Clarion* to decide if connotation and denotation are used appropriately. If you think the language is not appropriate, rewrite the paragraph with more connotation or less connotation. If you think the language is appropriate, explain why.

> We believe it is crucial to consider whether changes should be made at the Clear Lake College Student Health Service. The County Medical Board recently inspected the decrepit facilities at the Student Health Service and charged that the X-ray machines had been bought in 1928 and the laboratory equipment was condemned as unsatisfactory two years ago but has not been replaced. The current head of the Health Service, Dr. Janet Salinger, received her license from Paducah Medical School in 1942 and has not taken any additional training since that time. Today, Dr. Salinger sees approximately fifty student patients a day and is running the Clear Lake Doc-in-a-Box Emergency Medical Service as an additional business.

16 C

Dialect

16 C   USING DIALECT APPROPRIATELY

Term you need to know

DIALECT. A spoken or written variation of a language.

Troubleshooting

A *dialect* is a spoken variation of a language. The written version of a language is generally standardized and uniform, but the dialects of different groups of people within the area in which that language is used are often quite different, sometimes radically so. In some places, such as India or parts of Africa, dialects of various groups and tribes vary so much that they cannot communicate with each other at all.

In the United States, our dialects cause fewer communication problems. New Yorkers can understand people from California, and someone who was born in Detroit usually has no real trouble understanding natives of Florida, although their accents may sound strange. Moreover, Americans travel and move so frequently that young people often partially lose their early speech patterns and adapt to those of their new regions. But we do have many different dialects in this country—southern dialect, northeastern dialect, midwestern dialect, African-American dialect, Creole dialect, to mention a few—and their marks are quite distinctive, enough so that foreigners whose command of English is sufficient to understand the announcers on television can have problems understanding southern or Texan dialect.

You may be an American who has a dialect markedly different from varieties considered "standard." Occasionally you may have problems when some of its features appear in your writing. Use this handbook and other resources to edit out those features so that your readers focus on the content of your writing instead of on features of your dialect. But just because you choose to get rid of those features doesn't mean you should abandon your dialect. Even though it may cause problems at times, it plays an important part in your life. Being bidialectal is often as much of an accomplishment as being bilingual. But all educated Americans also need to be able to use the standard written dialect of the United States, American edited English, so they can communicate easily with the millions of others who command it.

---

16 C

Dialect

To give dialects their due . . .

➤ **Recognize their uses and importance.** Dialects are important and useful to the groups that speak them. A dialect helps to hold a group together, gives it a sense of community and identity, and provides its members with a sense of being insiders. Those who belong to a dialect group feel comfortable with each other because it's reassuring to be around other people who "talk your language." Thus dialects act as a major source of strength within a group and, as such, should be appreciated and protected for personal communication between individuals within a particular dialect community. Usually such communication is spoken. Here, for example, is how Bret Easton Ellis represents the dialect of California youth in his novel *Less than Zero:*

> Julian looks really tired and kind of weak, but I tell him he looks great and he says that I do too, even though I need to get a tan.
> "Hey, listen," he starts. "I'm sorry about not meeting you and Trent at Carney's that night and freaking out at the party. It's just like, I've been strung out for like the past four days, and I just, like, forgot . . . I haven't been home. . . ." He slaps his forehead. "Oh man, my mother must be freaking out." He pauses, doesn't smile. "I'm just so sick of dealing with people." He looks past me. "Oh, shit, I don't know."
> —Bret Easton Ellis, *Less than Zero* (New York: Simon & Schuster, 1985), 47.

➤ **Acknowledge their limitations.** The problem with some dialects is that, when they show up in public writing—and that is what most of the writing you do in college and your profession will be—they can be misunderstood and misinterpreted. Items of vocabulary within a dialect may not be understood by those outside of it. Certain grammatical forms that are completely natural and logical within a community may be regarded as nonstandard by other users of the language.

For example, in this passage from her novel *The Bluest Eye,* Toni Morrison represents the dialect known as Black English.

> The onliest time I be happy seem like was when I was in the picture show. Everytime I got, I went. I'd go early, before the show started. They'd cut off the lights, and everything be black. Then the screen would light up, and I'd move right in on them pictures. . . . Them pictures give me a lot of pleasure, but it made coming home hard, and looking at Cholly hard.
> —Toni Morrison, *The Bluest Eye* (New York: Pocket Books, 1970), 97.

The passage shows the character Pauline's most private kind of communication, inner speech to herself.

Here is another example of private dialect in this personal letter between two characters in Larry McMurtry's *Lonesome Dove,* a novel about a cattle drive from Texas to Montana.

> Dear Ellie—
> We have come a good peace and have been lucky with the weather, it has been clear.
> No sign of Jake Spoon yet but we did cross the Red River and are now in Texas, Joe likes it. His horse has been behaving all right and neither of us has been sick.
> I hope that you are well and have not been bothered too much by the skeeters.
>
> Your loving husband,
> July
>
> —Larry McMurtry, *Lonesome Dove* (New York: Simon & Schuster, 1985), 386–387.

16 C

Dialect

In the letter, we read the disarming phrases of a man not comfortable expressing his feelings in words. The salutation and formal closing show that July knows the form a letter should take, but, since this is a private communication, the vocabulary and rhythms of his day-to-day speech dominate. We don't expect Ellie will criticize the comma splices July uses to link his ideas or his spelling of *piece* and *mosquitoes.* But we can easily imagine situations in which such writing would seem out of place and colloquial.

Letting your private dialect intrude into your public writing, then, is not so much "wrong" as it is inappropriate. When your readers find the marks of your personal language in writing that is directed toward a group of readers who don't share that dialect, they're going to feel that it doesn't belong there.

➤ **Use dialect when appropriate.** When can you use your dialect without its interfering with communication in standard English? First, you can use it in your private life among friends or others who share the dialect, either in conversation or letters. Second, you might also use it in a first, discovery draft where you are trying to get down ideas and reflections and don't want to make your task more difficult by worrying about the conventions of standard written English. In subsequent drafts, you can edit out dialect features. Finally, you might also use dialect in an anecdote you are adding to your paper to illustrate some point, or you could use it in dialogue that played a necessary part in a paper. Except for these instances, though, spoken dialect generally doesn't fit into the kind of public writing you'll be doing in college or business.

16 D   AVOIDING SEXIST LANGUAGE

Term you need to know

SEXIST LANGUAGE. Language that reflects prejudiced attitudes and stereotypical thinking about the sex roles and traits of both sexes, but most frequently about women.

Troubleshooting

Every writer today needs to learn how to identify sexist language in order to avoid it in his or her writing. The idea of sexist language may be new to you, and you may not understand why we are focusing on it and why you should take pains to avoid it. There are at least four good reasons.

- *Sexist language is often inaccurate and deceptive.* A little more than half the people in the United States are women, not men, and if you consistently write "he" and "him," you're going to be wrong a large part of the time. If you talk about a doctor or a physicist as "he," you are ignoring the facts that a third of today's medical students are women and women now get about one-fourth of the degrees in science.

- *Sexist language frequently annoys and alienates readers.* Most of the women in the United States are working women; half of all college students are now women. Such women make up an alert, intelligent, and powerful group of readers, and they're going to be impatient and often angry with writers they feel are stereotyping and patronizing them—or who are just so unaware that they don't think about what they are doing.

- *Sexist language can cause legal problems.* Because federal laws now prohibit discrimination on the basis of sex, anyone who is writing grant proposals, policy statements, or any of the other dozens of documents we all use must be sure not to use any language that could be considered discriminatory. To suggest that a scholarship or an award might be open only to "hims" or "hers" is to invite a lawsuit.

- *Sexist language perpetuates sexist attitudes and behavior.* Social scientists and linguists, as well as politicians, salespeople, and therapists, know that *language shapes thought.* What we say and write can limit how we think and behave. As long as we refer to all scientists and engineers and astronauts as "he," we will tend to think that women cannot (or should not) aspire to those professions; as long as we write "chair*man*," "states*man*," and "police*man*," we reinforce the tendency to think of people in power as men. And these thought patterns make it difficult to achieve an equitable society.

To identify sexist language . . .

➤ **Watch for the consistent use of the pronouns** *he* **and** *him* **as all-purpose pronouns to refer to people in general.** For example, "Everyone should remember *he* is a student," or "Any executive enjoys *his* bonus."

➤ **Check for the term** *man* **used as a catch-all term to refer to all people or all members of a group.** For example, "all *men* should vote regularly," or "the recession threw thousands of *men* out of work."

➤ **Learn to spot gender-specific pronouns and terms to refer to individuals in professions or roles that have been traditionally thought of as male or female.** For example, "a pilot must be licensed before *he* can fly," but "a secretary should think of *herself* as an administrator."

➤ **Watch for between-the-line implications that men and women behave in stereotypical ways.** For example, *talkative women, giggling girls, rugged men,* and *rowdy boys.*

To avoid sexist language . . .

➤ **Rewrite your sentences to substitute** *someone, anyone, person,* **or** *people* **for the terms** *man* **and** *woman* **used in a general sense.** For instance, instead of writing "the *man* who wants to be an astronaut . . . ," write *"anyone* who wants to be an astronaut." Instead of writing "the *girl* who hopes to be a dancer . . . ," write *"someone* who wants to be a dancer."

➤ **Identify people by occupation or role, not by sex.** For instance, *parent, student, naval officer, voter, consumer,* and so on are not gender specific. So instead of writing *"mothers* who are concerned about their children's health . . . ," write *"parents* who are concerned about their children's health." Instead of writing *"men* who want to do their own auto repairs . . . ," write *"owners* who want to do their own auto repairs." Notice that the second versions are also more accurate; fathers as well as mothers are concerned about their children's health, and some women car owners do their own repairs.

➤ **When you can, replace job-related terms that use the suffix** *man* **or** *woman* **with another, more accurate term.** For instance, write *police officer* instead of *policeman, mail carrier* instead of *mailman, custodian* or *janitor* instead of *cleaning woman,* and *business executives* instead of *businessmen.* Avoid terms like *poetess* and *waitress* when you can; *poet* and *waiter* can be used to refer to either sex.

➤ **Be careful not to stereotype men and women by assuming that they belong in what have traditionally been thought of as men's and women's occupations or roles.** For example, instead of writing *"men* who hope to become scholarship athletes . . . ," write *"men* and *women* (or *young people)* who hope to become scholarship athletes." Instead of writing *"housewives* who want to become better cooks . . . ," write *"people* who want to become better cooks" or *"anyone* who wants to become a better cook."

16 D

Sexist

➤ **Find strategies to avoid having to use the pronouns *he* or *him* alone unless the antecedent is clearly a male.** You can use plural nouns, reword your sentence to eliminate pronouns, use *he* and *she* alternately, or occasionally write *he or she*. (For a full discussion of ways to solve the problems of sexist pronouns, see Section 29D.)

> **TIP: You probably shouldn't worry prematurely about sexist language when you are writing your first or second drafts—it's a problem that you can wait to deal with until you get to the editing stage and are tinkering rather than making large-scale changes. After you have worked to avoid sexist language for a while, you will gradually become more conscious of the problem and will be less likely to use sexist language even in your first drafts.**

16 D EXERCISE 16.5

Sexist Rewrite the following sentences to eliminate sexist language. If necessary, refer to the section on sexist pronouns in Section 29D.

1. The professor who expects his students to respect him should not consistently come to class ill-prepared.
2. Athletes are guys used to suffering the slings and arrows of outrageous fortune.
3. Anyone who goes into campus politics should carefully consider his motives.
4. A woman who wants to avoid premature wrinkles should stay out of the sun.
5. Most of the patrolmen on college campuses lead calm lives writing parking tickets.
6. Fortunately, many graduate students at universities have working wives.
7. The high school music teacher who was trained at Clear Lake College may find some embarrassing gaps in her education.
8. Some of Illinois's most prominent businessmen graduated from the University of Chicago.
9. Any lawyer who thinks he can intimidate Darwin Ferguson will be in for a surprise.
10. Medical students are often young men who are either very money conscious or very nurturing types; in either case, they are nearly always bright.

17 Making Your Writing Clearer

A Be concrete and specific

B Make your writing visual

C Use actor/action sentences and active verbs

D Avoid bureaucratic prose

E Chunk your writing

Troubleshooting

When you're writing, remember that first prize always goes to clarity; whatever comes second—and experts probably couldn't agree on what that is—comes way down the line. After all, if your readers can't understand what you mean, they're not likely to admire your smooth writing or wonderful ideas.

Now a few talented souls may be naturally clear writers, just as a few lucky people in the world seem to have bodies that are naturally fit without having to work at it. But there aren't many people in either group. If you want to learn to write clearly or to develop a fit body, you have to care about results and be willing to work to get them. There are no quick fixes. But you can attain both goals by developing habits that, over a period of time, virtually guarantee impressive results. This chapter gives you the guidelines for developing such habits.

17 A BEING MORE SPECIFIC

Terms you need to know

ABSTRACT WORDS. Words that refer to qualities, ideas, attitudes, or beliefs that we cannot see, hear, or touch—words like *convenience, accountability, generosity, intolerance,* and *mysticism.* We can **conceive** of abstract qualities only in our minds so we often need examples to illustrate them.

CONCRETE WORDS. Words that refer to qualities or things that we can touch, smell, see, or hear—words like *purple, hot, computer, horse,* and *automobile.* We **perceive** the things that concrete terms refer to with our senses, and often we use these concrete terms to help illustrate and explain abstract terms.

GENERAL LANGUAGE. Language that makes broad statements without giving details or supporting examples.

SPECIFIC LANGUAGE. Language that refers to individual examples and details.

ANALOGY. An extended comparison between two things, usually between something familiar and something less well known. Analogies help a reader visualize what might be difficult to understand.

Your body is like a machine; if you use it often, maintain it, and provide it with high-quality fuel, you can expect it to function well.

Troubleshooting

Among the most frequent comments instructors make on papers are "Your writing is too general—you need to give specific details," and "Your language is too abstract—let's have some concrete examples." If you're getting responses like these to your drafts, you can improve your writing by learning how to combine abstract/concrete language and general/specific language.

To make your writing more specific . . .

➤ **Learn to combine abstract and concrete language.** When writing gets too abstract, it quickly becomes hard to understand. Abstract language transmits no images to our brains and gives us no examples with which to identify; therefore it takes longer for us to process and remember. That's why you have so much trouble with some of the material you have to read for your courses and with documents like insurance policies and legal descriptions.

It's possible, however, to use abstract language and still write clearly. You can do so by combining it with specific language and concrete examples that let your reader connect the intangible (abstractions) with the tangible (concrete examples).

Here's an example of a passage that's unnecessarily difficult to read because it's overloaded with abstract nouns. It's a paragraph from the first draft of a paper Mary McCrory wrote for her nutrition course. In it, she's reporting on some of her research on the problems of overweight people.

{Original} The **propensity** of overweight people to gain extra adipose tissue at holiday time is due to two **factors: greater susceptibility and responsiveness to food stimuli** and **poor compensatory regulation** of food intake. Such individuals seek **justification** for their **behavior** by citing the **pressures of hospitality** and the special **tastiness** of the food.
[abstract words boldfaced]

Mary's instructor and classmates told her the writing was hard to understand and that she needed examples to make her point. When they saw this revision, her classmates said, "That's more like it."

{Revision} **Overweight people** gain **weight** at **holidays** for two reasons: **they** like to eat more than **other people** do, and **they** have less self-control. **They** excuse their **overeating** by saying their **hosts** urge them to eat and, besides, the **food** is too good to refuse.

17 A

Clarity

You may have noticed that the writing in many textbooks, professional articles, and certain periodicals, such as the *Atlantic* or *The New York Times,* tends to be abstract. Often the writers for these publications or the stories being reported in them deal with complex and inherently difficult issues and must use abstract terms. Those who want particularly to get their ideas across, however, often find ways to enliven and clarify their writing with analogies and concrete, familiar references. Here is an example from, of all places, the Director of the Federal Budget.

> The sheer size of the [Federal] budget makes it seem like a monster. . . .
> Of course, monsters do not naturally invite examination. [Yet] On "Sesame
> Street" . . . there is a wonderful character known as Cookie Monster. As all
> monsters are, Cookie Monster is initially intimidating. His manner is
> gruff. His clumsiness occasionally causes damage.
> But quickly Cookie Monster comes to be seen as benign—indeed,
> downright friendly. He has a few bad habits. He cannot resist gobbling up
> anything and everything, especially cookies. . . Yet clearly, he means no
> harm. . . . The budget might be seen as the Ultimate Cookie Monster.
> —Richard Darman, quoted in *The New York Times,*
> January 25, 1990, 10.

17 A

Clarity

Get in the habit of checking your first drafts to see if they go along for several paragraphs without any interesting examples or references to help your readers grasp your ideas. If so, when you're doing the second draft look for ways you can use familiar examples or analogies to bring your writing down to earth and make it clear.

EXERCISE 17.1

Classify the words in this list into abstract and concrete, then compare your answers with those of another person in your class. Notice that you may not be able to agree on all the answers; words are not always easy to classify.

responsibility	sunshine	mockery
soldiers	racketeers	antiquity
admiration	convenience	antagonism
teenagers	video games	white water
inspiration	militarism	ambivalence

EXERCISE 17.2

Working in a group, discuss and experiment with ways you might use examples or comparisons like the Cookie Monster one above to write a readable and interesting paragraph on the suggested topics.

1. The influence of the SAT (Scholastic Aptitude Test) (or a comparable test) on college admission policies.
2. The increasing cost of getting elected to public office in the United States.
3. The complications of being a college student and a parent at the same time.

Below is a highly readable paragraph from a medical writer who is known for writing well. Working in a group with other students in your class, analyze the particular words and phrases that help to make the paragraph clear and readable.

> The worst thing that has happened to science education is that the great fun has gone out of it. A very large number of good students look at it as slogging work to be got through on the way to medical school. Others look closely at the premedical students themselves, embattled and bleeding for grades and class standing, and are turned off. Very few see science as the high adventure it really is, the wildest of all explorations ever taken by human beings, the chance to catch close views of things never seen before, the shrewdest maneuver for discovering how the world works. Instead, they become baffled early on, and they are misled into thinking that bafflement is simply the result of not having learned all the facts. They are not told, as they should be told, that everyone else—from the professor in his endowed chair down to the platoons of postdoctoral students in the laboratory all night—is baffled as well. Every important scientific advance that has come in looking like an answer has turned, sooner or later— usually sooner—into a question. And the game is just beginning.
> —Lewis Thomas, "Humanities and Science," in *Late Night Thoughts on Listening to Mahler's Ninth Symphony* (New York: Viking Press, 1983), 154.

17 A

Clarity

➤ **Use specific details and examples to clarify and expand on general statements.** As a writer, you have to make general statements; otherwise you would never be able to theorize or summarize, and you'd never rise above the level of the individual facts. But if you fall into the habit of writing too many generalizations and not following through on them with specific details and illustrative examples, you may quickly lose your readers.

One way to bring specific details into your writing is to downshift, a strategy explained earlier in Chapter 13. When you downshift, you move down from a high level of generalization to a series of increasingly specific statements. For example, here is a story from the Clear Lake College newspaper that downshifts by adding specific details.

Level 5. Marty Green's job as bicycle courier in the Chicago Loop would challenge even the most intrepid cyclist.

> **Level 4.** First, he has to weave his way through aggressive pedestrians who cross intersections at six different angles.

>> **Level 3.** Some are even capable of jabbing an umbrella at his wheels as he rides by.

> **Level 4.** He also has to dodge the pillars that hold up the El tracks,

>> **Level 3.** sometimes scraping paint off them as he skids past.

> **Level 4.** But the worst trials come in the winter.

>> **Level 3.** Not only does Marty brave 20° below weather as he makes his rounds,

>>> **Level 2.** but he doesn't let snow bother him.

>>>> **Level 1.** He's welded chains for his bike wheels!

EXERCISE 17.4

Working in a group with other students, develop these sentences by down-shifting with two or three more sentences that give specific details or examples.

1. If you are a cable television subscriber in the United States, you have an astonishing array of programs available.
2. A come-on ad for a new car may claim the price is $9995, but what it doesn't give are the costs of those options that are near-necessities.

17 B   HELPING YOUR READERS SEE YOUR POINT

Terms you need to know

METAPHOR. A figurative comparison between two things that does not use the words *like* or *as.* (When a comparison contains the words *like* or *as,* it is a simile; for example, "George is like a dinosaur on the football field.")

All the world's a stage.

Racism is a vicious disease.

Our first assignment was a breeze.

VISUAL WRITING. Descriptive or colorful writing that helps the reader visualize a person, image, or scene.

17 B

Clarity

Troubleshooting

Writing is more readable and interesting when it helps us to visualize something. That's because we live in a visually oriented culture in which television is immensely popular, and filmstrips and educational movies are common tools of instruction. Thus you will make your writing clearer if you can create pictures for your readers, make them *see* things. In this section, we suggest several ways to make your writing more visual and thus clearer.

To make your writing more visual . . .

➤ **Show something happening.** You can create a scene or drama; you can show action; you can describe a colorful picture or object—there are dozens of ways of showing ideas in action. Here is a visual example in which a writer clarifies a hard-to-grasp, abstract concept by showing something occurring. The visual elements are boldfaced.

> The distinction between Newton's and Einstein's ideas about gravitation has sometimes been illustrated by picturing **a little boy playing marbles in a city lot. The ground is very uneven, ridged with bumps and hollows. An observer in an office ten stories above the street would not be able to see those irregularities in the ground. Noticing that the marbles appear to avoid some sections of the ground and move toward other sections,** he

might assume that a "force" is operating which repels the marbles from certain spots and attracts them toward others. But another **observer on the ground would instantly perceive that the path of the marbles is simply governed by the curvature of the field.**

—Lincoln Barnett, *The Universe and Dr. Einstein* (New York: William Morrow, 1968), 84.

➤ **Add people.** Another way to add a visual element to your writing is to put people in it. Most of the issues and ideas we discuss do involve human beings after all, and your readers are more likely to understand what you are writing about if you bring those human beings into your writing. For example, here is an example of how the abstract discussion of an economic issue becomes clearer when the author puts people into it. This is a sample paragraph taken from the first draft of a paper written by Leona Maddox.

{**First draft**}   Although the federally funded student loan program makes a medical education accessible to low-income populations, the amount of debt incurred during the educational years has significant effects on the career choices available to those populations. Options such as fellowship programs or practices in inner-city communities are unfeasible for individuals with heavy indebtedness because large loan payments begin shortly after graduation.

Leona's writing group told her, "For heaven's sake, let's see some people. You're talking about human beings, not stethoscopes!" So she rewrote the paragraph:

{**Revision**}   Although many young people from low-income families can become doctors because of the federally funded loan program, they incur so much debt that they limit their career choices. A doctor who owes $70,000 or $80,000 on graduation, as many do, can't choose a research fellowship that pays only $30,000 a year or set up practice in the inner city when she must begin making big loan payments soon after she graduates.

Leona's group said "We like the change," when they saw the revision. Notice that when Leona put people in her sentence, other specific details also emerged.

➤ **Use metaphors and analogies.** You can also make your writing clearer by adding metaphors and analogies that help readers make connections with something they already know. Notice how the boldfaced metaphors and analogies work in these examples.

{**Example 1**}   Here, a Nobel prize-winning astrophysicist reinforces a necessarily abstract explanation with a familiar and concrete analogy.

17 B

Clarity

This technique [measuring the motion of a star] makes use of a familiar property of wave motion, known as the Doppler effect. When we observe a sound or light wave from a source at rest, the time between the arrival of wave crests at our instruments is the same time between the crests as they leave the source. On the other hand, if the source is moving away from us, the time between arrivals of successive wave crests is increased over the time between their departures from the source because each crest has a little farther to go on its journey to us than the crest before . . . Similarly, if the source is moving toward us, the time between arrivals of wave crests is decreased because each successive crest has a shorter distance to go. . . . **It is just as if a traveling salesman were to send a letter home regularly once a week during his travels: while he is traveling away from home, each successive letter will have a little farther to go than the one before, so his letters will arrive a little more than a week apart. On the homeward leg of his journey, each successive letter will have a shorter distance to travel, so they will arrive more frequently than once a week.**

—Stephen Weinberg, *The First Three Minutes* (New York: Basic Books, 1977), 9.

{**Example 2**}   I started this book as an account of **my own educational journey** from the high school vocational track **up through the latticework** of the American university.

—Mike Rose, *Lives on the Boundary* (New York: Free Press, 1989), 8.

17 B

Clarity

> **TIP: Remember, however, that abstract phrases and people-less writing may be appropriate when you are doing technical or scientific writing.**

EXERCISE 17.5

Working in a group with other students, discuss what writing strategies one could use to give a visual angle to articles on the following topics:

1. An editorial about the high cost of housing at your college
2. An article comparing various kinds of motorcycles
3. A guide to inexpensive restaurants close to your campus
4. An article about ways to combat racism on your campus
5. An article for potential buyers of car stereo systems

EXERCISE 17.6

Rewrite this paragraph from the draft of a paper written by Rita Ruiz for her sociology course. Replace some of the abstract language with sentences that include people.

The increasing addiction to drugs among the young female population is alarming to social agencies. Because the responsibility for child rearing has traditionally been assumed by women, any element that reduces their effective functioning will have an inevitable effect on the children. Manifestations of such effects are common today.

Working with other students in a group, try to create metaphors or analogies that would add a visual element to these sentences. For example, you might compare Coach Voorhees to a triumphant general returning from battle.

1. Coach Marie Voorhees returned in triumph from the Women's National Volleyball Playoffs yesterday, feeling justifiably exuberant as she got off the plane.
2. When she and the team left Ruralia last Friday, almost no one would have bet any money that there was a chance they would get beyond the first round.
3. In fact, their chances were rated so low that the team had trouble even finding the money for their plane fare since whoever figured out the volleyball budget of $850 obviously didn't anticipate any post-season travel.
4. But a surprisingly large group of fans turned out at the airport to help make up for the neglect Coach Voorhees's team had suffered this season.
5. What they learned to their surprise was that not only had the coach brought home a trophy and a national small college championship, she had also brought home an offer for a new and more profitable contract for herself.

17 C Clarity

17 C   MAKING YOUR WRITING MORE DIRECT AND EASIER TO READ

Terms you need to know

ACTOR/ACTION SENTENCE. A sentence in which the *subject* of the sentence is a person or thing who does an action and in which the *verb* is an action verb.

> **President Shade congratulated** the volleyball team.

VERB PHRASE. A cluster of words that acts as a verb.

> Their problems **are a reflection of** the sluggish economy.

ACTIVE VERB. A verb that shows an action taking place.

> Queen Boadicea **led** the revolt against Britain.

PASSIVE VERB. A verb form that shows the subject of the sentence receiving the action instead of doing it.

> Poodles **are said** to be unusually intelligent dogs.

Troubleshooting

If your instructor or your fellow students tell you that your writing is adequate but a little dull, you need to think about how you can liven it up. After all, you want people to enjoy what you write, not just plow through it because they have to. You'll find that one of the quickest remedies for dull writing is to revise your sentences so that a reader can immediately get an answer to two questions: *What's happening? Who's doing it?* They will get those answers if you arrange your sentences to put an actor/action relationship at their core and if you use direct, active verbs. In other words, quickly tell your readers what's going on and who's doing it.

For example, look at these flat and rather plodding sentences:

Bicycles are the mode of transportation for millions of Chinese.

It is a common occurrence to see two or three people on one bike.

When they are revised into actor/action patterns with active verbs, they become more interesting and easier to read.

Millions of Chinese ride bicycles.

One often sees two or three people on a single bike.

17 C

Clarity

To make your sentences clearer and easier to read . . .

➤ **Ask yourself "who or what is acting?" and make that person or thing the subject of your sentence.** Then find a verb that describes the action. These short examples show how much clearer your writing can be.

{**First draft**}   It is not unusual for a successful business enterprise to begin as a small operation on a college campus as a response to a student's need to earn his or her way through school.

{**Revision**}   Many a successful business began on a college campus when some student found a new way to work his or her way through school.

{**First draft**}   The pleasure of keeping up with new plays and art exhibits in Chicago is one of the advantages of attending college in the city.

{**Revision**}   Students at the Clear Lake College campus in Chicago enjoy the advantage of new plays and art exhibits in the city.

Naturally you wouldn't want to write all your sentences in actor/action patterns since often you need to write about concepts, theories, or processes that require abstract language. But you can probably use actor/action sentences more often than you realize—after all, even when you're writing about history, philosophy, or economics, you're still writing about people and what they do. You may want to wait until a second draft to adapt some of your sentences to an actor/action pattern, but if you work at it, eventually you can develop the habit of using this kind of sentence even in a first draft.

EXERCISE 17.8

Recast these sentences in actor/action patterns that show more clearly who is doing what to whom.

1. Sound Instincts, a local stereo store and campus meeting place for both students and faculty, is the brainchild of Christy Rasmussen, to whom the lack of a decent place to buy discs and tapes was astonishing when she arrived here from Minnesota to go to college five years ago.
2. Since the interest of Christy's partners (her parents) is baroque music, it's understandable that their daughter's interest in groups with names like "Microwave Katz," and "The Red Hot Chili Peppers" is baffling to them.
3. Nevertheless, the Rasmussens' faith in their daughter's business intuition and their secret conviction that the triumph of Mozart was inevitable in an educated community formed the basis of their decision to invest in Sound Instincts.
4. $75,000 was the sum Christy required for inventory and six months' rent, but what she hadn't anticipated was her parents' suggestion—along with another $50,000—for a separate coffee room with background music of Mozart and Haydn and a stock of classical, mostly baroque, discs and tapes.
5. Now the Coffee and Classics room is the domain of Ivor Rasmussen, the popular music section in the front is Christy's bailiwick, and the profits of Sound Instincts are rolling in, supported by family cooperation, confidence in Mozart, and good coffee.

17 C

Clarity

➤ **Favor active verbs over verb phrases, passive verbs, and "to be" verbs such as *is, are, were,* and so on.** Pay special attention to your verbs when you revise because those are the spots at which your readers are likely to lose track of your ideas. For example:

Why write	*When you could write*
put the emphasis on	emphasize
make a comparison of	compare
give permission to	allow
be knowledgeable about	know

The change will enliven your style.

Passive verbs, those verbs that conceal who or what is taking the action in a sentence, can also contribute to a plodding style and can even confuse your readers because they may lose track of who is doing what. For example,

{Original}   The grade **received** by Li Chang was low because the bibliography **was left out** of his research paper. (Who gave Li Chang the grade? Who left out the bibliography? The author? The typist? The copy center?)

{Revision}   Professor Collins gave Li Chang a low grade because the typist had left the bibliography out of his research paper.

{Original}   It is claimed that more poor research papers are caused by inattention to detail rather than by faulty documentation. (Who claims this? Who is inattentive to detail?)

{**Revision**} Many professors claim that students' inattention to detail causes more poor research papers than does faulty documentation.

In some kinds of writing, of course, you need passive verbs. For example, in a technical report, you may want to focus on the process and the result rather than on the individuals involved. You may also want to use passive verbs if you want your writing to sound impersonal. So passive verbs have their place, but you should use them sparingly. In quantity, they detract from good writing. (Also see Section 23E, Active and Passive Voice.)

Another culprit that detracts from a clear style is the *is* verb and all its relatives—*am, are, was,* and *were.* Such verbs are crucial to writing, of course; none of us could get along without them. But when you use them too often, you can drain the life out of your writing, and you risk having your readers get lost because a little *is* can almost disappear when it gets surrounded by phrases and clauses. For example, look at the improvement in the sample sentences when we replace forms of *is* with an active verb.

{**Original**} It **is** because of the way the nature of research **is** understood that the joy of discovery **is** unknown to most students.

{**Revision**} Most students never know the joy of discovery because they misunderstand the nature of research.

{**Original**} Once research **is** thought of as an exercise in reading articles in the encyclopedia instead of as searching for new knowledge, enjoyment of the task **is** unlikely.

{**Revision**} Few people will enjoy research if they think of it negatively as reading articles in the encyclopedia rather than searching for new knowledge.

17 C

Clarity

> **TIP: Watch out for sentences that begin with "It is . . . ,"
> "There is . . . ," "There are . . . ," or "There were. . . ."
> These phrases, called *expletive constructions,* can make
> your writing seem strung-out and monotonous. If you
> have several in a paragraph, find ways to rephrase the
> sentences when you revise.**

EXERCISE 17.9

Write sentences in which you use an active verb in place of the verb phrases listed below. For example, for a sentence that used the phrase "gave consideration to," your new sentence might read, "The referee considered putting on a crash helmet before going on the field."

1. "is in need of"
2. "have objections to"
3. "made a failure of"
4. "gave permission to"
5. "was knowledgeable about"

EXERCISE 17.10

Working as a group, read this paragraph and identify the passive verb forms. Check the definitions of passive and active verbs again if you feel it would help. Then work together to revise the paragraph by changing the passive verbs to active ones where you think it would improve the style.

> Brian McVickers was overwhelmed by the task he was faced with—writing a freshman research paper. His anxiety was brought on partly by wondering whether he had the skills that would be required to work in the college library and partly because he was riddled with doubts that any topic could be chosen that he wouldn't hate before the job was completed. He feared total writer's paralysis could be brought on by the double dilemma.

EXERCISE 17.11

17 D

Clarity

Rewrite the following sentences and substitute active verbs for the various *is* verbs. (Tip: Try redoing each sentence with a person or thing as its subject.)

1. The idea of having to write on an artificial topic that the author of some textbook thought would be good for him was a pain to Brian.
2. Brian's belief is that there is a need to connect writing with real-life activities when possible.
3. It was accidental that a topic turned up that was interesting to Brian.
4. The topic of bicycles is one that was of fascination to Brian when he was seven.
5. It is, however, such a huge topic that it was difficult for him to narrow it down to one of manageable size.

---

17 D   LIGHTENING BUREAUCRATIC PROSE

Terms you need to know

NOMINALIZATIONS. Nouns made by adding endings to verbs and adjectives: *acceptability, demystification, prioritization,* and so on. In this handbook, such words are called *heavy-duty* nouns.

PREPOSITIONAL PHRASE. The combination of a preposition and a noun or pronoun. The following are prepositional phrases: *on our house, above it, to him, in love, through them, by the garden gate.*

Troubleshooting

Writers in college and occasionally even in business sometimes tell us that they think their readers expect them to write stodgy, impersonal, and noun-heavy prose—in fact, some writers expect to be penalized if they don't write such indigestible stuff. Such suspicions might be true. Certainly, the material you read in some textbooks or scholarly articles is written in a noun-heavy, preposition-stuffed style, as are many insurance policies and bureaucratic memos. Here is an example of this style. (This kind of writing is sometimes called *jargon.*)

> It is of utmost importance to maintain the vitality of those institutions that serve society as instruments of continuity. Thus the stability of the country's institutions of higher education should be a high priority with the current administration. These institutions need predictability and reliability of financing and fewer regulations about federal grants. Actions of this kind would facilitate a welcome disentanglement of higher education and federal bureaucracy.

If you're absolutely convinced your reader expects this style—perhaps you have a professor or boss who also writes that way—go ahead and compose such mind-numbing, hard-to-read prose, but recognize that you are doing it to impress someone, not to communicate. Communicate it doesn't.

We believe that the majority of your readers, including professors, much prefer writing that is clear, lively, and pleasant to read. That is what both business executives and professors claim and what our own experience tells us. You will score more points with your readers if you clean out as many of those heavy-duty nouns and prepositional phrases as you can and substitute clear, straightforward sentences.

17 D

Clarity

To make your writing more direct and easier to read . . .

➤ **Reduce your use of heavy-duty nouns.** Heavy-duty nouns, also known as *nominalizations,* are all those nouns made by adding endings to verbs and adjectives. There are thousands of them in English, too many to list, but this sample will show you what we mean.

utiliz**ation**	interfer**ence**
maximiz**ation**	imprecise**ness**
specific**ity**	implement**ation**
valid**ity**	simplifi**cation**
prioritiz**ation**	comprehensibil**ity**

In other words, nominalizations are words created by adding suffixes—*-tion, -ity, -ance, -ence, -sion,* and others—to a verb or adjective. *Militant* becomes *militancy, accountable* becomes *accountability, specific* becomes *specificity,* and so on.

Such heavy-duty words can be useful, even necessary at times. Too many of them in writing, however, act as a thickening agent, like cornstarch or concrete. A few are fine, but when they begin to accumulate, they clog up your writing and make it hard to get through.

➤ **Reduce the number of prepositional phrases in your writing.** In a prepositional phrase, a preposition and a noun combine to show a relationship. Again, a few samples will refresh your memory.

to the limit	**for** the duration
with the exception	**of** the opinion
by the side	**against** the advice
above the average	**with** the proviso that
over the objections	**under** those conditions

Although prepositional phrases are unavoidable, if you overuse them, your writing will take on a monotonous rhythm—ta-tum, ta-tum, ta-tum—like the sound of tires slapping over expansion joints. When something you've composed seems especially dull, try underlining all the prepositional phrases to see if you have too many. If the underlining shows prepositional phrases clustered in your writing, you have detected one cause of your dull prose.

Unfortunately, heavy-duty nouns and prepositional phrases tend to attract each other, and when a writer gets in the habit of using both, the result can be dreary, lifeless writing. Here is an example of a passage made almost unreadable by too many heavy-duty nouns and prepositional phrases. The heavy-duty nouns are boldfaced, the prepositional phrases italicized, and a revised version is offered.

17 D

Clarity

{**Original**}   The **proliferation** *of credit cards among college students* is the result *of extensive marketing by banking institutions* who see college students *in terms of future profitability.* The **manifestation** *of such **promotions** at our college* is the recent placing *of credit card **applications** in prominent view at local restaurants,* convenience stores, and video shops. Such placement does not reflect **generosity** *toward students* or **misconceptions** *about their* current wealth. Rather it shows hopes *of their acquiring* the credit card habit *at an early age.*

{**Revision**}   More and more students are acquiring credit cards because banks promote credit cards so they will make money from those students in the future. For example, the local bank has been featuring card applications prominently at restaurants, convenience stores, and video rental places. They have done it not because they think students have a lot of money to spend, but because they want them to acquire the habit of buying on credit.

EXERCISE 17.12

Working with others in a group, revise these sentences to get rid of heavy-duty nouns and excess prepositional phrases.

1. The inaccessibility of registration materials at convenient locations has long been a problem for students in our college.
2. Apparently implementation of better procedures is beyond the capability of our administration.
3. Improvement is possible if the administration would move toward simplification of their system of distribution.
4. The reliability of the method employed by the IRS should act as a model for Clear Lake College's innovation in registration procedures.
5. In our opinion, Darwin Ferguson's proposal to institute utilization of the U.S. mails for distribution of registration materials, although radical in its approach, merits consideration.

17 E **MAKING YOUR WRITING MORE READABLE**

Troubleshooting

A piece of writing has its own "body language" that can make readers react to it positively or negatively. (See Section 13D on paragraph appearance.) If you jam so much information into one sentence or one paragraph that it looks long and forbidding, you risk repelling your readers. Their instinctive reaction may be, "Oh, that's too hard to read. I'm sure I won't understand it so I won't even try."

Even if readers are willing to try, you're likely to overload their mental circuits so they will have to go back and reread what you have written—not because your ideas are too difficult, but because you have tried to package too much in one unit. And if their circuits overheat too often, your readers will probably quit reading altogether.

To make your writing more readable . . .

➤ **"Chunk" your writing; break up sentences and paragraphs into manageable parts to make them easier to read.** When you divide up or "chunk" your writing, it becomes much easier to read, and your readers can process and remember the content more easily. Chunking is the principle behind dividing telephone numbers; instead of ten numbers jammed together in a long sequence that would overload a reader's memory, they are broken up into three units that the brain can process. If they weren't you'd have to deal with 2143280090 instead of 214-328-0090. And could you ever remember your social security number if it were not divided? The same principle applies to jamming too many words into one sentence or too many sentences into one paragraph. For example, look at this sentence.

17 E

Clarity

{**Original**}   Citing an instance in which a sixteen-year-old student was working forty-eight hours a week at Burger King in order to pay for a new car and simultaneously trying to attend high school full time, and claiming that the fast-food restaurants often pressure youngsters to work overtime on school nights, New York educators have recently proposed legislation that prohibits high-school students from working more than three hours on a night before school, limits the total amount of time they can work in one week to twenty hours when school is in session, and sets fines of up to $2000 per violation on employers who violate these regulations.

While not unreadable, the sentence is overloaded, and the writer risks losing readers before they get to the end. It would work better to break it up like this.

{**Revision**}   Educators in New York recently proposed legislation to limit the number of hours high-school students can work during the school year to three hours on school nights and no more than twenty hours during the week. As an example of why such laws are needed, the bill's sponsors cited the case of a sixteen-year-old high-school sophomore who was working forty-eight hours a week at Burger King to buy a new car. They also claim that fast-food restaurants frequently pressure employees to work overtime on school nights. Under the new law, employers could be fined up to $2000 per violation.

The sentences, while still not overly simplified, are much easier to follow.

You should also try to chunk long paragraphs by breaking them up into two or three small units. For examples, review Section 13D on paragraph appearance and the exercises that go with it.

EXERCISE 17.13

Reorganize the following sentences by breaking them into more manageable chunks.

1. The job a girl has in high school can play an important part in introducing her to new responsibilities, increasing her confidence in herself, and getting her used to the idea that she can earn her own way and doesn't have to spend the rest of her life asking someone else, usually a man, for spending money or always letting someone else make the final decisions about what she can buy.

2. Parents are often ambivalent about having their high-school youngsters work because almost inevitably it causes conflicts about whether their job or their schoolwork is more important, and although ideally one can always say that both are important and students have to learn to balance them, finding that balance often proves to be difficult, particularly when the parents cannot give their children the allowance that would allow them to have the clothes and privileges that their peers have.

3. Other conflicts can also arise, especially for parents and children who think it's important for young people to be involved in extracurricular activities such as sports, music, debate, and so on, but also think that it's important and somehow quintessentially American for young people to "earn their own money" and demonstrate the values of self-discipline, responsibility, and thrift, and, in addition, get good grades so they'll be able to get into the college they want to attend.

➤ **When you have a substantial amount of information to present, arrange it in a list.** Instead of writing overpacked sentences or paragraphs in which readers will get lost, organize the information for them by putting it into a list. For example, here is a paragraph from Gail Witliff's freshman English paper reacting to the new limitations proposed on working hours for high-school students.

{**Original**} Before passing the proposed law, New York legislators need to consider why so many students work. Most don't do it to buy new cars. Some other, more important reasons are that their jobs provide meals as well as money, they have to buy their own clothes, they contribute to household expenses, their jobs increase opportunities to meet people, their jobs meet requirements in Distributive Education, their work increases their self-confidence, and they need to save money for college.

After the third or fourth reason, the reader loses track of the argument. Notice how much easier it is to follow when Gail breaks the reasons down into a list.

{**Revision**}   Before passing the new law, New York legislators need to con-

sider why so many high school students work. They don't all do it to

buy new cars. Some other important reasons are these:

1. Jobs often provide meals as well as money.

2. Students often have to buy their own clothes.

3. Many young people contribute to household expenses.

4. Jobs increase opportunities to meet people.

5. Jobs meet requirements for Distributive Education.

6. Work increases young people's self-confidence.

7. Jobs help young people save money to go to college.

Breaking out information into a list like this takes more space, but pays off handsomely in readability.

17 E

Clarity

EXERCISE 17.14

What suggestions about "chunking" could you make to the author of these instructions for a personal computer to make them more readable?

You will find it easy to get started with your new personal computer. Unpack it from its case, saving all the styrofoam pads in which it is packed so that you may reuse them when moving your machine. Check to see that you have grounded electrical outlets at the location where you plan to plug the machine in. Set up your computer, being sure that you keep it well away from any magnets such as the ones that may be found in telephones. Place the printer near the computer, either on a printer stand to hold paper or on an edge that allows a space through which paper can feed. Plug the keyboard, mouse, and printer into the ports on the back of the computer, using the cables provided and following the icons printed over each port. Finally, attach the power supply cord to the computer and plug it into the grounded outlet. Turn on your machine.

18 Revising for Sentences That Work Better

A Revise to clarify tangled sentences

B Revise to fix derailed sentences

C Reorganize overloaded sentences

D Revise to make sentences parallel

When we speak casually with one another, all of us construct sentences just as naturally and easily as we put one foot ahead of another when we walk. Because we know instinctively how our native language works, we have no problem putting words together in understandable sentences. When we write, however, things get a little more complicated. Then we need to think more about how sentences work—the way the different parts match up, the patterns we can use, how they can be arranged and rearranged to do what we want them to do. That's what this chapter and the next ones are about.

As we do in other parts of the book, we'll deal with issues about sentences in order of their priority. In this chapter, we'll focus on the first priority in revising sentences: how you can make them clear. In the next chapter, we'll focus on how you can rewrite sentences to make them express your ideas more efficiently. In the third sentence chapter, we'll focus on some finer points about revising sentences: first, how you can make them more interesting, and second, how you can polish them.

> **TIP: Notice that in the chapter titles and subtitles and throughout the discussion of sentences we talk about *revising* sentences, not about writing them. That's important.**
>
> In most cases, we don't think it's practical to start out by thinking about what kind of sentence patterns you're going to write. Just start writing and put down sentences as they come to you. Sometimes you may write yourself into a tangle and have to delete something and start again, but for the most part, trust your natural sense of language to help you get down sentences that say what you mean and move along toward your goal. Before you make your sentences more interesting, it is important to make them clear. Wait until you have written at least a paragraph or two before you start to revise.

18 A   REVISING TO CLARIFY TANGLED SENTENCES

Terms you need to know

SENTENCE. A group of words that expresses an idea and is punctuated as a separate unit of writing.

CLAUSE. A group of grammatically related words that has a subject and a verb but is not a sentence.

INDEPENDENT CLAUSE. A clause that *could* act as a sentence if it were punctuated as one.

DEPENDENT CLAUSE. (subordinate clause) A clause that depends on a main independent clause to make sense and could *not* act as a sentence even with a period at the end.

PHRASE. A group of grammatically related words that does not include a subject and a verb.

Troubleshooting

Sometimes those who are reading drafts of your papers may tell you they get lost trying to follow your sentences. They may complain that the sentences are too complicated, that you've tried to do too much in one sentence, or just that they don't work—they don't know what's wrong. In such cases, there's not much point in trying to explain what you meant. You'll do better to reread the sentences that are confusing your readers and figure out how you can rewrite them and make them clearer. This section makes some suggestions.

18 A

Sent

> **TIP: You can untangle many snarled sentences by first looking for the subject of your sentence when you start to revise. Then, if possible, make that subject a person or thing, put it close to the front of the sentence, and put an active verb with it. Often the tangles will disappear. (See Section 17C on actor/action sentences.)**

Sentences may get tangled if . . .

➤ **The writer begins a sentence with a clause or phrase that the reader expects will connect to the subject of the sentence but doesn't.**

{**Tangled**}   When eating at the Blue Tuna on Dearborn Street, students from the Clear Lake—Chicago campus can be seen working there.

> (Readers expect the introductory clause "When eating at the Blue Tuna . . ." to give information about "students," the subject of the main sentence, but it doesn't.)

{**Possible revisions**}   When eating at the Blue Tuna on Dearborn Street, a customer can see many students from the Clear Lake—Chicago campus working there.

> A customer eating at the Blue Tuna on Dearborn Street can see many students from the Clear Lake—Chicago campus working there.

▶ **The writer starts with a dependent clause but does not connect it to an independent main clause.** Instead, he or she has combined two sentence fragments.

{**Tangled**}   If a person is energetic and a quick learner, expecting to make good tips at a Blue Tuna.

> (The second part of this combination is a phrase without a subject or a verb; it can't serve as the main clause of the sentence.)

{**Possible revisions**}   Anyone who is energetic and a quick learner can expect to make good tips at a Blue Tuna.

> People who are energetic and learn quickly can expect to make good tips at a Blue Tuna.

▶ **The writer doesn't keep track of the main subject of the sentence as he or she writes and forgets to put in a verb to complete the sentence.**

{**Tangled**}   Anyone who likes working at a place like the Blue Tuna, realizing that the restaurant business offers good job opportunities after college.

18 A

Sent

> (The reader keeps looking for a verb to go with the subject, "Anyone who likes working at a place like the Blue Tuna . . ." but doesn't find it. By themselves, *-ing* words can't act as verbs.)

{**Possible revisions**}   Anyone who likes working at the Blue Tuna should realize that the restaurant business offers good job opportunities after college.

> The restaurant business offers good job opportunities after college for anyone who likes working at a place like the Blue Tuna.

TIP: You can usually find several good ways to revise a faulty sentence. Don't assume that there's just one right way to write every sentence.

EXERCISE 18.1

Working with a group, consider why these sentences don't work. Then try to come up with a more effective version of each one.

1. If a young person would like to make a career of the restaurant business, many opportunities in college towns.
2. While working in the food business, a special appeal to it for many because it is so basic.
3. Among the practical reasons to work in restaurants, tips and free meals are usually easy to get.
4. In restaurants like the Blue Tuna, show business or food business is a question some critics ask.
5. A restaurant manager who sets up certain codes of dress which everyone who works there has to meet.

18 B   REDIRECTING DERAILED SENTENCES

Sometimes writers construct sentences that start off in one direction, then at a connecting place seem to "derail" and take off in a different direction.

➤ **When this happens, pinpoint the intersection where the sentence went wrong and set it going back in the right direction.**

{**Derailed**}   What made Truman Forbes want to get into the restaurant business, no one in his family had ever done anything so down-to-earth before.

(The sentence derails at the intersection after "business," and takes off in an unexpected direction because the writer hasn't shown a clear connection between the two ideas. To get it back on track, she needs to rethink her meaning—it's not clear.)

{**Possible revisions**}   Forbes wanted to get into the restaurant business although no one in his family had ever done anything so down-to-earth before.

Forbes wanted to get into the restaurant business precisely because no one in his family had ever done anything so down-to-earth.

{**Derailed**}   Since college students are intelligent and have lots of energy, and it's a good job for them at the Blue Tuna.

(Here the sentence derails at the comma after "energy" and goes off in another direction because the writer has given a confusing signal by connecting the two parts of the sentence with "and.")

{**Possible revisions**}   Since college students are intelligent and have lots of energy, jobs at the Blue Tuna are good jobs for them.

A job at the Blue Tuna is a good one for college students who are intelligent and have lots of energy.

EXERCISE 18.2

Working with other students in a group, decide what has gone wrong with the following sentences; then each person rewrite the sentences and, as a group, compare the revisions.

1. Clear Lake College students like to work at the Blue Tuna restaurant on Dearborn Street, but in some cases it doesn't always succeed.
2. When they hear the Great Blue Tuna striking the gong for dinner, and fresh blue aprons are worn to open the doors for the customers.
3. Chicago residents have always liked seafood restaurants, and when the Blue Tuna opened there, real excitement.
4. Like a character from Disney World, dressed in a blue fish suit wandering the restaurant, but it is a job that's boring.
5. Occasionally Truman Forbes himself in the blue fish suit, the boss walking around and talking to people but also checking on service.

EXERCISE 18.3

For each number below, write a straightforward sentence that stays on track and combines the two ideas given. For example, a sentence that combines the ideas of a successful restaurant and cost control might read like this: "If a restaurant is to succeed, everyone must think about good cost control."

1. Intelligent college students; good service in restaurants.
2. Good tips in a restaurant; congenial atmosphere.
3. Customers who come back to a restaurant; quality of service.
4. Cheerful service; influence of a restaurant manager.
5. What kind of service customers expect; the price of meals in a restaurant.

18 C REORGANIZING OVERLOADED SENTENCES

18 C

Sent

Troubleshooting

Long sentences aren't necessarily confusing sentences. If they're well-organized and written in a clear and lively style, they can work well. But you can run into trouble when your sentences get too long, particularly if you've overstuffed them with information. Thus, when you're revising, it pays to look carefully at sentences that run to more than about twenty-five words. You may find they're rambling and harder to follow than they need to be.

You can improve long, overloaded sentences if you . . .

➤ **Divide the material into two or three shorter sentences.**

{**Too long**}   The employee training program at the Blue Tuna chain of restaurants, a large and rapidly growing organization that promises to challenge the acknowledged giant in the franchise seafood business, the Red Lobster chain, may seem raucous and occasionally even juvenile in its manufactured enthusiasm, but employees who have graduated from it seem to know their business.

> (Not a terrible sentence, but it's too long—over fifty words—and someone reading it could quickly get lost.)

{**One possible revision**}   Employees who have graduated from the training program at the Blue Tuna chain of restaurants seem to know their business even though that program may seem raucous and juvenile at times. The large and rapidly growing Blue Tuna chain promises to challenge the Red Lobster franchise, the acknowledged giant in the franchise seafood business.

➤ **Keep introductory clauses and phrases brief.** They shouldn't overbalance the main part of the sentence or contain so much information that the reader gets lost. For example, here is an overly long sentence introduction that makes the sentence lopsided.

{**Overloaded**} **Having a family who thought it was wonderful that she was going to college but believed that the main reason a woman would spend four years getting a degree was so that she could get a prestigious professional job,** Martina Cabeza got nervous when she thought about telling them she might like to run a restaurant.

> (The important information in the long lead-in phrase overbalances the main part of the sentence.)

{**Possible revision**} Martina Cabeza got nervous when she thought about telling her family that she might like to run a restaurant. Although they thought it was wonderful that she was going to college, they believed the main reason a woman would spend four years getting a degree was to get a prestigious professional job.

▶ **Avoid writing sentences in which the subject of the sentence gets so long it dwarfs the verb that follows it.** When such long subjects are groups of abstract terms combined with a weak verb like *is* or *are,* they can be particularly confusing.

{**Inflated sentence subject**} The assumption, not common in this country but long held by many people in other cultures, that people who have a college education should never have to work with their hands is often a deterrent to bright young people in those cultures who seek nontraditional careers.

> (An inflated subject that is grammatically correct but leaves the reader scrambling to find the verb to go with it.)

{**Possible revision**} Although one doesn't encounter the belief often in the United States, many people in other cultures assume that educated people should never have to work with their hands. That attitude deters many bright young people in those cultures from going into businesses like catering or construction.

> **TIP: If the inflated, abstract style in the examples in this section sounds sophisticated to you and you think you'd like to try writing that way, think twice before you try to imitate it. It's a style that's hard to correct, and hard to read.**

EXERCISE 18.4

Revise these overloaded sentences to make them easier to read and to understand. You can divide them, reorganize them, and, if you like, trim out words that don't affect meaning.

1. Trainees in the Blue Tuna program are expected to have energy, enthusiasm, and a smile for every customer, be strong and agile enough to carry a heavily loaded tray through a crowded dining room without ever letting it tilt, memorize the entire menu of over 100 items as well as knowing what the "catch of the day" is every day, and continually improve their sales pitch to persuade customers to buy desserts and drinks.
2. Given the shrinking pool of eighteen-year-olds, it's perhaps surprising that so far the Blue Tuna restaurants and others like them continue to be able to find young people who will go through the demanding training programs, subject themselves to inspections, and work irregular shifts that often include late hours and overtime even though working at such a restaurant can, with good tips, pay very well indeed for waiters and waitresses who are bright, cheerful, and energetic.

18 D MAKING SENTENCES PARALLEL

18 D   **Terms you need to know**

‖ **Sent**   **PARALLEL SENTENCE.** A sentence in which clauses or phrases that are grouped together have a consistent pattern. These examples are parallel.

Martina had three priorities for her restaurant: the food **should be tasty,** the service **should be excellent,** and the prices **should be reasonable.**

As manager, she is responsible for **doing the buying, training the employees,** and **serving high-quality food.**

FAULTY PARALLEL STRUCTURE. A sentence or other unit of writing in which phrases or clauses that are grouped together don't show a consistent pattern. These examples are not parallel.

College students who work at restaurants are often **enterprising, cheerful,** and **with big appetites.**

Some managers like to hire college students but deplore **their practical jokes** and **they eat too much.**

Troubleshooting

Sentences can mislead your readers if parts grouped together aren't consistent—that is, they don't follow through in the same pattern in which they start out. When they don't, they are not *parallel.* The disrupted pattern jars the flow of the sentence.

The principle of parallel patterns is similar to that tested on aptitude tests in which you are shown several objects and asked to identify which one doesn't fit. When you are shown sketches of several different fruits but a potato is included, you know the potato doesn't fit. It isn't consistent; it's not *parallel.* Thus in a sentence, if you use two adjectives in a series, the third element should also be an adjective; otherwise it doesn't fit—it's not parallel. If you use two noun phrases of one pattern, the third noun phrase should be in the same pattern or it's not parallel.

To correct faulty parallelism . . .

➤ **If you know from past experience that you sometimes have trouble with parallel structure in your sentences, get in the habit of checking sentence patterns when you are revising.** Look for the part of the sentence that doesn't fit the pattern. You can also ask people who will be reading your drafts if they will watch for faulty parallelism.

Here are examples of how such patterns can go wrong and some suggested ways of fixing them. Both faulty and revised elements are boldfaced.

{**Faulty**}   When Tom Miller came to work at the Dearborn Street Blue Tuna, he showed **enthusiasm, energy,** and **having a good attitude.**

[The first two elements are nouns, but the third is a verb phrase.]

{**Parallel**}   When Tom Miller came to work at the Dearborn Street Blue Tuna, he showed **enthusiasm, energy,** and **a good attitude.**

{**Faulty**}   Tom was quick **to learn** the daily specials and not **getting** spots on his blue apron.

[The first part is an infinitive—*to learn*—but the second one—*getting*—isn't.]

{**Parallel**}   Tom was quick **to learn** the daily specials and not **to get** spots on his blue apron.

[Now both parts are infinitives.]

18 D

|| **Sent**

EXERCISE 18.5

Working in a group, read over these sentences and decide which ones have faulty parallel structure. Work together to revise those in which you find inconsistent or faulty patterns, making all the parts consistent or parallel.

1. On opening night at the Blue Tuna restaurant on Dearborn Street, Martina Cabeza called together all the waiters and waitresses to be sure that their shirts and slacks were pressed, their shoes shined, and without a spot on their blue aprons.
2. Martina knew that Tom Miller and Greg Corrigan had a bet on to see which one's customers would spend the most on drinks, order the most expensive items, and, of course, the biggest tip that would be left.
3. Early in the evening it looked as if Greg would win because of his skill in describing food, his talent for pushing Alaskan king crab legs ($19.95) and fresh Norwegian salmon ($17.50), and he could talk people into fancy desserts.
4. At nine o'clock, however, a happy group of fourteen sat down at one of Tom's tables and began to order exotic and expensive cocktails, double orders of king crab, and liked premium wines.
5. As Tom served the last of the expensive meals and fancy wine, he smiled

5. As Tom served the last of the expensive meals and fancy wine, he smiled hugely, lifted the tray high over his head, but, unfortunately, flipping it over to land right in the middle of the crowded table.

EXERCISE 18.6

Write three sentences with good parallel structure, incorporating the elements given below. Here is how one example might work:

Subject: A cook   three actions in preparing a meal

Sentence: Doing the best he could, the amateur cook fried the fish, warmed the bread, and took the dessert from the freezer.

1. Subject: traffic cop   three actions in ticketing a speeder
2. Subject: parent   three actions in complimenting a child
3. Subject: entertainer   two actions (full independent clauses) in perform-
                            ing for a crowd

19 Revising for Better Constructed Sentences

A Revising for better coordinated sentences

B Revising for better sentence subordination

C Revising to combine sentences

D Revising to correct faulty sentence predication

Troubleshooting

The traditional terminology we use to talk about organizing sentences—subordination, coordination, compound and complex sentences, and so on—makes the process sound terribly complicated. It isn't. You speak in well-structured sentences all the time without even thinking about what you're doing, and most of the time they turn out well. So don't worry too much about how to organize your sentences and don't assume that there are hard and fast rules about when you should use a compound sentence or a complex one. Nevertheless, when you learn a little more about the options you have for arranging and varying the elements of a sentence, you may write tighter, more effective sentences.

19 A REVISING FOR BETTER COORDINATED SENTENCES

Terms you need to know

COORDINATING CONJUNCTION. A word that links independent clauses in a sentence; for example, *or, and, yet, neither,* and *but.*

COORDINATION. The arrangement of sentence elements in a way that joins elements that are not dependent on each other.

Troubleshooting

If you write mostly short, simple sentences in your first drafts because you want to avoid worrying about punctuation problems, your writing may be choppy. Simple sentences are often clear and forceful, but when you write too many in a row, your reader can lose the connection between them. Thus in second drafts it's useful to look for ways to coordinate some of your simple sentences to tie ideas together and smooth out your writing.

To write better sentences . . .

➤ **Write coordinate (compound) sentences when you want to join two independent clauses that are closely related and about equally important.** When you join such clauses, even though they could work as sentences by themselves, you tell your reader to consider the separate points as parts of one main idea.

The most common words used to join coordinate clauses follow:

- The conjunctions *and, but, yet, or, for,* and *so.*

{**Example**} Rita Ruiz is a senior this year, so she plans to look for interviews for jobs at the job fair.

- The phrases *either . . . or, neither . . . nor,* and *not only . . . but also,* or a semicolon used alone.

{**Example**} Rita is the top student in her advanced economics class; her professor expects her to get several job offers.

- Joining (conjunctive) adverbs such as *but, nevertheless, however,* and *although,* if used with a semicolon.

{**Example**} Rita herself is confident she'll do well; however, she is worried about what to wear for her interviews.

Notice that different joining words give different signals, so be sure to pick the ones that do what you want them to. For example, *and, moreover, also,* and the semicolon show that you're joining ideas of the same kind.

For the last three years, Rita has worn boots, blue jeans, and flannel shirts to class; **moreover,** she openly jeers at the male students who wear ties to class.

> **TIP: Writing too many sentences in which clauses are joined by *and* makes your writing seem monotonous and amateurish. If you find you're overusing *and,* when you revise try to combine clauses to subordinate some of the clauses, redoing them as modifiers. You'll have more interesting sentences.**

But, yet, however, and *nevertheless* signal contrast between the two independent clauses of a coordinate sentence.

Professor Chase is the best-dressed woman on the faculty of the College of Business, **yet** Rita knows she is also greatly admired for her fine mind.

> **TIP: When you use *but, and, yet,* or *or* to join two independent clauses, be sure to put a comma *before* the joining word. (See Chapter 22 for punctuation in this kind of sentence.)**

The words *for, so,* or *thus* usually show cause and effect.

> Professor Chase acts as a consultant to several major Chicago banks **so** Rita knows her recommendation could be important.

Or, either . . . or, and *nor* signal that the clauses being joined are alternatives.

> Rita isn't willing to go into debt to buy a new wardrobe, **nor** does she want to borrow money from her brother.

EXERCISE 19.1

Redo the following sentences and join the independent clauses, using one of the conjunctions or joining adverbs given above in a way that shows a clear relationship between the ideas. Be sure to get the punctuation right!

{Example} Professor Chase gives good advice. Rita doesn't want to accept it. {Possible revision} Professor Chase gives good advice; however, Rita doesn't want to accept it.

19 B

Sent Sub

1. Some people like to think clothes are unimportant. Most surveys of how people react to others don't bear that out.
2. It can be a financial hardship for college students to buy clothes. Many of them have ingenious solutions to the problem.
3. Being well dressed is really a matter of adapting to the situation. It isn't always easy to predict what one's situation will be.
4. Almost everyone has suffered the embarrassment of being badly dressed on some occasion. Some occasions are more humiliating than others.
5. Most college students are not indifferent to the clothes they wear. One sees definite trends and fads on the average college campus.

---

19 B   REVISING FOR BETTER SENTENCE SUBORDINATION

Terms you need to know

SUBORDINATION. The arrangement of sentence elements in a way that makes one idea or clause dependent on the other.

SUBORDINATING CONJUNCTION. A word that links a subordinate (or dependent) clause to the main clause of the sentence; for example, *although, nevertheless,* and *however.*

Troubleshooting

In going over your first draft, you may realize or have another reader point out to you that in some sentences you haven't made your emphasis clear or haven't shown the relationship between the parts of the sentence. When that happens, look for places where you need to change or rewrite the sentence to subordinate one part to another.

To correct problems with sentence subordination . . .

➤ **Use signals to show that one clause is tied to and depends for its meaning on another clause.** You need a signal word to show relationships of time and contingency. The most common ways to signal subordinate clauses follow:

- The words *although, as, after, since, before, until, unless, when, while, if,* and *because;* words that begin relative clauses—*who, whoever, that, which,* and so on—can also signal a dependent clause.

- The phrases *so that, in spite of, in case of, no matter how, even though, if only,* and others.

Here are two examples.

Unless Rita decides to go on for a graduate degree, she must find a job.

While one is in school, it's easy to put off making career decisions.

➤ **Choose subordinating signals carefully to convey the meaning you intend.** Subordinating words give such strong messages that you need to be sure you put the right word in the right place. Notice the differences here.

Although Rita Ruiz was the top student in Professor Chase's class, no one paid much attention to her.

Until Rita Ruiz was the top student in Professor Chase's class, no one paid much attention to her.

One construction shows contrast; the other one shows causation.

Here is another example.

Since Professor Chase acts as a consultant, she brings practical experience to the classroom.

When Professor Chase acts as a consultant, she brings practical experience to the classroom.

➤ **Subordinate one part of a sentence to another so the most important idea will be emphasized.** Usually this means you should make the main independent clause carry the main point of the sentence and have a subordinate clause or clauses carry less important information. Otherwise you're likely to mislead your readers. For example:

{**Misleading subordination**}   Even though Professor Chase delivered a polished lecture on corporate mergers, she had forgotten her notes.
[The important point about Professor Chase gets lost here.]

{**Revised for better emphasis**}   Although she had forgotten her notes, Professor Chase delivered a polished lecture on corporate mergers.

{**Misleading subordination**}   Although Marya Chase's appearance has changed greatly since she wrote a successful book five years ago, people who have met her recently don't realize it.
[The important information gets lost.]

19 B

Sent Sub

{**Revised for better emphasis**}   Although people who have met her recently don't realize it, Marya Chase's appearance has changed greatly since she wrote a successful book five years ago.

➤ **Arrange some of your sentences with subordinate clauses to create more efficient sentences.** (You will find more on this strategy in the next section.)

{**Original**}   Professor Marya Chase was always an attractive woman. She tried to hide her good looks in graduate school. She feared some people would assume she wasn't bright.

{**Revision**}   Although Professor Marya Chase was always an attractive woman, in graduate school she tried to hide her good looks because she feared some people would assume she wasn't bright.

➤ **Avoid stringing too many subordinate clauses together.** You can overdo subordination in a sentence, and wind up with a sentence that incorporates so many ideas that the reader gets lost.

{**Too many clauses**}   Although Professor Chase herself dressed well, and although she believed graduate students should too, because she was sensitive to their tight budgets, she raised the issue of correct corporate dress discreetly.

{**Revised**}   Although Professor Chase herself dressed well and believed graduate students should too, she raised the issue of correct corporate dress discreetly because she was sensitive to their tight budgets.

19 B

Sent Sub

EXERCISE 19.2

Join the following pairs of sentences, making one a subordinate clause.

1. Some people claim that clothes aren't important. Others say people's clothes give messages about them.
2. Clothes do seem to matter less on college campuses than they do in other settings. Students' apparent indifference to clothes may be deceptive.
3. Some students depend on thrift stores for their wardrobes. The reason is not always lack of money.
4. Other students go to stores that advertise "vintage clothing," a fancy term for second-hand clothes. They are not necessarily looking for bargains as much as for funky clothes.
5. They thoroughly enjoy their expeditions to such stores. Often it's like taking a journey into the past.

EXERCISE 19.3

Working with other students in a group, read the following sentences and decide which sentences have too many subordinate clauses or in which sentences the subordination seems to emphasize the less-important idea. As a group, rewrite those sentences for better organization or better emphasis. Some may work well as they are.

1. Although Rita is not interested in being chic, she is a woman who wants to use the degree that she has worked hard to get and that she knows is her passport into the corporate world.
2. If she has to do so to make a good first impression, she will buy a new wardrobe.
3. But even though she has to put on the required skirt, blouse, blazer, and pumps, she doesn't intend to buy them brand new at outrageous prices.
4. While the most important thing is not to spend more than seventy-five dollars, quality is also a consideration.
5. As she lays out her rather complicated plan for solving her wardrobe problem, she begins to see her task as an interesting challenge.

19 C

Sent Comb

19 C REVISING TO COMBINE AND IMPROVE SENTENCES

Troubleshooting

When you reread sentences in your draft, you may notice that the information in some of them overlaps or that several short sentences in a row convey a "Dick and Jane" effect. Your instructor may also advise you that you would have tighter, more graceful sentences if you would combine some of them to get more information into fewer sentences. You can combine sentences in several ways.

To combine sentences effectively . . .

➤ **Look for places where you can put the information from one sentence into another one in the form of an introductory phrase or clause.** Sometimes you will find your sentences will sound better and be more economical if you find places where you can condense one sentence and use it as the beginning of the next one. For instance:

{**Original**} You may see some young men wearing ties in the halls of philosophy or English departments. You can be fairly sure they are book sellers.

{**Combined**} If you see young men wearing ties in the halls of philosophy or English departments, you can be fairly sure they are book sellers.

{**Original**} Men wearing ties do show up in English classes occasionally. They may turn out to be clandestine literature addicts from the College of Business.

{**Combined**} The occasional man wearing a tie in an English class may turn out to be a clandestine literature addict from the College of Business.

➤ **Look for places where the information in simple sentences overlaps; then see if those sentences can be combined through coordination or subordination.**

{**Original**}   The college years may be the best time for anyone to indulge a taste for wild styles. In college, both professors and students are used to seeing elaborate costumes. They may range from bib overalls and cowboy boots to black leather punk outfits.

{**Combined**}   The college years may be the best time to indulge a taste for wild style since professors and students alike are used to seeing costumes ranging from fringed jackets and cowboy boots to black leather punk outfits.

{**Original**}   At big urban universities, the mixture of styles can be particularly striking. One can see Indian women in sequined saris and Sikhs in turbans. One can also see Africans in colorful robes that stand out against the predominant blue jeans and denim jackets.

{**Combined**}   One can see a particularly striking mixture of styles at a big urban university where Indian women in sequined saris, Sikhs in turbans, and Africans in colorful robes stand out against the predominant blue jeans and denim jackets.

➤ **Look for sentences that can be compressed and put into another sentence as a modifier.**

{**Original**}   Smart women don't let so-called fashion experts dictate their choices. Those experts want women to spend money on trendy clothes. Such clothes are poor investments.

{**Combined**}   Smart women don't let so-called fashion experts persuade them to spend money on trendy clothes that are poor investments.

{**Original**}   Today's career women have minds of their own about fashion. They don't depend on dress-for-success books. They want good-looking and high-quality clothes. But they also want them to reflect their own tastes.

{**Combined**}   Today's career women, who have minds of their own about fashion and don't depend on dress-for-success books, want good-looking, high-quality clothes that reflect their own tastes.

> **19 C**
> **Sent Comb**

> TIP: Although sentence combining can be useful for smoothing out choppy writing and getting more information into your sentences, don't overdo it. If you try to condense too much material into one sentence, you can wind up with overstuffed, hard-to-read sentences like the ones we've used as examples of wordiness (see Section 18C). You can also lose track of your main point if you try to put too many sentences together.

EXERCISE 19.4

Combine into one or two sentences the separate elements listed. Remember you can combine the elements in several different ways.

1. Rita Ruiz is a bright young woman. She is planning ahead for her interview with New Horizons Enterprises. It is a young company. It has the reputation of being aggressive and willing to take risks. She might well be interested in working for the company.
2. The president of the company is a Cornell graduate. He is only 36 years old. He is already frequently mentioned in business journals. Some call him the "Wonder Boy" of Wall Street. They predict a brilliant future.
3. Rita began by going to the library. She checked the business indexes to see what the company's standing was. She checked their financial standing in Dun and Bradstreet. She checked the papers to see how much their stock was worth. She looked back to find out about their enterprises in the last year.
4. She learned from the research. She remembered what she had learned in Professor Chase's class. She began to have doubts about the company. Its financial standing looked inflated. The stock fluctuated too much for her taste. New Horizons Enterprises was involved in some shaky deals.
5. At the end of her stint in the library, she made up her mind. She cancelled the interview. She wanted nothing to do with Wonder Boy's company. She predicted that his future holds more indictments than glory.

19 D

Sent Pred

19 D REVISING TO CORRECT FAULTY SENTENCE PREDICATION

Terms you need to know

PREDICATE. The verb of a sentence, along with the components that accompany it—modifiers, complements, and auxiliaries.

> Rita **envisioned her career.**

> Professor Chase **told Rita about opportunities.**

COMPLEMENT. A word or phrase that follows a linking verb, completing its meaning. Complements can be nouns, pronouns, or adjectives.

LINKING VERBS. The verb *to be* and others like it that link or join the subject of the sentence and the modifier that describes that subject. Some common ones besides *to be* are *seem, appear,* and *feel.*

FAULTY PREDICATION. A mismatched subject/verb/complement combination in a sentence; with faulty predication, the subject and verb cannot logically go together or the verb and complement cannot work together. The boldfaced portions shown here illustrate the problem.

> Research **grants hope** to attract more applicants.
>> [Faulty because *grant* is an abstract term; it cannot *hope*.]

> Her **laziness is waiting** to be fired.
>> [Faulty because *laziness* is a personality trait; it cannot *wait* for something.]

TRANSITIVE VERB. A verb that takes a direct object; that is, it acts on someone or something and that object receives the action of the verb.

> Connie **struck** the desk.

> Mike **sabotaged** the truck.

Troubleshooting

If the people reading your drafts sometimes tell you that the parts of your sentence just don't fit together, that your verbs don't match what you join them with, they're talking about faulty predication. Such mismatched constructions are not always easy for writers themselves to see, but once they're identified, they're fairly easy to fix. When your readers show you sentences that don't work, here are some ways you can identify the problem and correct it.

To identify and repair faulty predications . . .

➤ **Look first for an impersonal or abstract subject used with an active verb.** Check the culprit sentence to see if you've paired an active verb with a subject that couldn't possibly do what the verb says it is doing. For instance:

{**Faulty**}   Professor Chase's taste in good clothes yearned for a better place to shop.

> [The sentence is faulty because *taste* is impersonal and abstract; it can't *yearn.*]

{**Acceptable**}   Professor Chase's pleasure in clothes moved her to seek out a better place to shop.

{**Faulty**}   Racks of look-alike clothes concentrate their attentions on bargain hunters.

> [The sentence is faulty because *racks of clothes* are inanimate and can't *concentrate* on anything.]

{**Acceptable**}   Racks of look-alike clothes are meant to draw the attention of bargain hunters.

➤ **Look for a sentence that has a subject and a linking verb but ends with a complement that can't complete the linking verb.** A linking verb gives the reader an equation sign; it says A = B. Thus the complement on the right side of the equation has to match logically with the word on the left side of the equation. For example:

{**Faulty**}   Rita's thriftiness is unwilling to spend money on new clothes.

> [The construction is faulty because *thriftiness* is an abstract term; it can't be *unwilling.*]

{**Acceptable**}   Rita was so thrifty that she didn't want to spend money on new clothes.

{**Faulty**}   The kind of clothes available from the Eddie Bauer catalog are mostly to ski and hunt.

> [The construction is faulty because *kind of clothes* on one side of the linking verb *are* can't be matched with the verb infinitives *to ski and hunt.*]

{**Acceptable**}   The kind of apparel available from the Eddie Bauer catalog are mostly skiing and hunting clothes.

19 D

Sent Pred

> **TIP: You are less likely to get into faulty predication tangles if you remember to start your sentences with concrete or personal subjects.**

➤ **Look for a subject plus transitive verb construction paired with an object that can't fit with the verb.** Transitive verbs (verbs that take an object) have to fit logically with the objects that come after them in a sentence. If they don't, they can confuse the reader. For example:

{**Faulty**} Being around the leaders in a field can exhilarate a young person's attitude.

> [The sentence is faulty because *exhilarate* can't take *attitude* as its object.]

{**Acceptable**} Being around the leaders in a field can exhilarate a young person.

> **TIP: When you use the phrase [*Something*] *is when . . . ,* you're lapsing into a predication error. For example,**
> "Bad taste *is when* you hurt someone's feelings."
> "Joint custody *is when* both parents have equal responsibility."
> **Although your readers are likely to understand what you mean, the construction is still nonstandard. To avoid the problem, don't use the phrase *is when* in a definition.**

---

19 D

Sent Pred

EXERCISE 19.5

Work with a group to rewrite the following sentences and untangle the faulty predication. You may find more than one way to revise any sentence.

1. Rita's college clothes have no suitability for business.
2. New clothes are a difficult decision for her.
3. Inflexible is not Rita's problem; she has a conviction to change.
4. Her first necessity is in the form of a loan.
5. Triumph was when she put on her new outfit.

20 Revising for More Polished Sentences

A Revising for more varied sentences

B Revising to add detail

C Revising for leaner sentences

D Revising for more stylish sentences

Troubleshooting

The most important job any sentence has is to communicate an idea clearly, and that should be your first priority when you're writing. But just as there is more to cooking than preparing wholesome and nutritious food, there's more to writing than crafting clear, straightforward sentences. You can also revise your sentences to make them more interesting, a pleasure to read because they are varied, skillfully arranged, and rich with detail.

20 A REVISING FOR MORE VARIED SENTENCES

Terms you need to know

SENTENCE COMPLEMENT. A word or phrase that follows a linking verb and completes its meaning. A sentence complement can be a noun, pronoun, or adjective.

> subject   l.v.   complement
> The Apollo Computer Enterprises is a new organization.

> subject   l.v.   complement
> The founders of the group are young and intelligent.

Troubleshooting

To avoid getting caught in punctuation or arrangement tangles, writers sometimes rely on just a few simple sentence patterns. The most reliable are the old standbys, S-V-O (Subject-Verb-Object) and S-V-C (Subject-Verb-Complement).

> subject verb   object
> S-V-O: Nancy booted up the computer.

301

subject   verb   complement

S-V-C: Nancy is a doctoral student.

These patterns are basic in English, and they work well. But you need to vary them occasionally to keep your writing from becoming monotonous. It's useful, then, to learn some other patterns that you can experiment with when you revise.

You can achieve more variety in your sentence patterns if you . . .

▶ **Change the usual sentence patterns by inverting the typical order and moving information.** See if you can reorganize the S-V-O or S-V-C patterns by putting the verb or complement at the beginning of the sentence or by turning a sentence into a question. You can also move information around within your sentences. For example, here is a paragraph from a student paper that is solid and clear but rather monotonous because most of the sentences have the same subject-verb pattern.

20 A

Sent Var

{**Original**}   The boots a person wears are too often considered a status symbol. People believe the more expensive the boots, the better the cowboy. Most often "urban cowboys" will sport the most expensive boots. They wear these to social events, on dates, and to dances, never setting foot on the ranch or farm. The true cowboy can be seen in old, dirty, well-worn boots most of the time. The true cowboy buys boots for durability.

Now let's change some of the sentence openings, and invert some patterns.

{**Revised for sentence variety**}   Too often, the boots a person wears become a status symbol. The more expensive the boots, the better the cowboy, some people seem to believe. But who really wears the most expensive boots? Often it's urban cowboys, who wear them to social events, on dates, and to dances, but never set foot on the ranch or farm. On the other hand, most of the time the true cowboy can be seen in old, dirty, well-worn boots. The true cowboy buys boots for durability.

Obviously you could find many other equally good ways to change sentence patterns to improve the paragraph.

Let's look at some ways patterns for individual sentences can be turned around. The originals are from student papers.

{**Original**}   Many sociologists concerned with the fairness of standardized tests have determined that the type of questions, if not their very wording, is biased in favor of higher-income groups.

{**Variation 1**}   Are standardized tests fair? Many sociologists concerned with such tests believe that the questions, and perhaps even their wording, are biased in favor of higher-income groups.

{**Variation 2**}   In judging the fairness of standardized tests, many sociologists who are concerned about them say that the test questions, and perhaps even their wording, are biased in favor of higher-income groups.

{**Original**}   The rock-and-roll protest songs of the sixties were the musicians' way of expressing their opinions and criticisms of political and social events.

{**Variation 1**}   In order to express their opinions and criticisms of political and social events, the rock-and-roll musicians of the sixties wrote protest songs.

{**Variation 2**}   In the sixties, the rock-and-roll musicians wrote protest songs as a way of expressing their criticisms and opinions of political and social events.

In neither of these examples are the variations necessarily *better* than the original. They're just different, and they show some of the many good options for crafting sentences.

➤ **Vary sentence length.** Another way to add variety to your sentences is to mix sentences of different lengths together in one paragraph. To some extent, of course, you'll consider who your readers are and what kind of writing you're doing when you decide how long your sentences should be. If you're explaining a process to an uninformed audience or writing for a very young audience, you'll want to write relatively short sentences. If you're writing on a complex topic for an educated and informed audience, your sentences will probably be longer.

Regardless of what kind of writing you're doing, however, when you revise, it's always a good idea to check sentence length. If you've written a group of consistently short sentences, your writing may seem choppy. On the other hand, if your sentences are somewhat longer but all about the same length, your writing may seem monotonous. You'll achieve a more graceful, interesting style by breaking up some of those sentences and varying the length.

20 A

Sent Var

Here is an example of a paragraph that is monotonous because all of the sentences are too nearly the same length.

{**Original**}   The birth of Apollo Computer Enterprises was one of those happy accidents. It started last year in the English department's computer laboratory at Clear Lake College's Chicago campus. Three of the founding partners were working in the lab and designing software for the English department writing courses. Two other partners-to-be were graduate assistants teaching writing and one was a professor. They all began to talk with each other about using computers to teach writing. They theorized that computers must represent the wave of the future in education. Thus did Apollo Enterprises come into being.

{**Revised for variety**}   The birth of Apollo Computer Enterprises was one of those happy accidents. It began as a brainstorm last year when three graduate students who were running the computer laboratory for the English department began designing software for the department's writing courses. As they started talking to two other graduate students and a professor who were teaching writing, an idea emerged. "Computers are going to transform teaching writing, and we need to be in on it," said Bernard. "Let's just do it." Thus did Apollo Enterprises come into being.

➤ **Remember the power of short sentences.** Occasionally vary the rhythms of your writing by writing short, direct sentences. They're good for catching your readers' attention at the beginning of a paragraph or for highlighting important points you don't want lost. Mixed with longer sentences, they can mark the confident writer, someone who wants to say what she means straightforwardly, without embroidery. Notice their good effect in these two examples.

It [the earthquake] began with a vague rolling sensation, accompanied by the tinkling of glass. Small household items fell and shattered. Then a sudden lurch moved homes, unearthed ancient trees and toppled bridges. Within 15 seconds the seizure stopped.

> —"When the earth rumbles," *U.S. News and World Report,* October 30, 1989, 38.

Although starting a new business is risky for anyone, it would seem particularly hazardous for graduate students who have spent most of their lives in school. But such young people also have invaluable assets. They have energy and enthusiasm. They see new opportunities. And they're confident they can do what no one else has ever done.

EXERCISE 20.1

20 A

Sent Var

Work out at least two ways to revise each of these sentences by changing the patterns.

1. The Apollo Computer Enterprises started from the work that graduate students were doing in the English department computer lab of Clear Lake College.
2. They were primarily interested in developing computer software that could be helpful to students in departmental writing classes.
3. They wanted to develop a program that would help students think about what they wanted to write in their papers.
4. They hoped they would be able to develop a program that would allow students to look at each other's drafts as they were writing them.
5. The graduate students accomplished almost everything they hoped for by the end of the spring semester.

EXERCISE 20.2

Read the following paragraph; then, working with a group of other students, decide what changes you could make in sentence patterns or sentence length that would improve the paragraph. Remember you can break up the sentences or move them around.

The graduate students were so enthusiastic about their Apollo project that they convinced themselves that they could carry a superhuman load of teaching, studying, and writing papers and still have time to do all the things they had to do to form a new company. But graduate students in English are also teaching writing courses, which means they have forty or more student papers to read and comment on virtually every week. Although that load handicapped them, it also acted as a great incentive to work on their computer system because they were convinced that once they perfected it, writing teachers would be able to spend less time responding to all those student papers and still do a good job.

20 B REVISING TO ADD DETAIL TO YOUR SENTENCES

Terms you need to know

APPOSITIVE. A group of words that gives more information about the word that it follows.

> appositive
>
> Talking head shows, *television programs on which the hosts interview celebrities or other people of special interest,* are becoming increasingly popular.

EMBEDDING. Increasing the amount of information in a sentence by adding a clause or phrase.

FINAL MODIFIER. A final phrase or clause that comes at the end of the sentence and gives additional information.

DOWNSHIFTING. Expanding a sentence by adding more specific details that are on a lower level of generality than the main statement of the sentence.

Troubleshooting

You may be writing papers that are clear and well focused, but your readers are asking for more details, telling you they think your papers could be much richer and more interesting. One way to make sentences more interesting is to expand them with specific details.

You can enrich your sentences if you . . .

➤ **Add details by embedding.** One way to enrich a sentence is to embed additional information by adding details at the beginning, in the middle, or at the end.

You can embed additional information at the beginning of a sentence by putting details in an introductory clause or phrase. For example:

{**Original sentence**}   Bernard surprises others in the group with his ability to overcome his reserve when a client needs special help.

{**Expanded through embedding an introductory phrase**}   Usually a reticent person, Bernard surprises others in the group with his ability to overcome his reserve when a client needs help.

You can embed additional information in the middle of a sentence by inserting an appositive clause or phrase that gives more details about somebody or something in the sentence. For example:

{**Original sentence**}   Professor Maynard wonders if the whole realm of computers isn't a young person's game.

{**Expanded through embedding an appositive**}   Professor Maynard wonders if the whole realm of computers, with its talk of expert systems, hypertext, and fuzzy logic, isn't a young person's game.

You can expand a sentence by giving additional details in a final modifier added at the end, usually after a comma. For example:

{**Original sentence**}   Many educators would be delighted to see computers come into the writing classroom because they know computers have special appeal for many young students.

{**Expanded through embedding a final modifier**}   Many educators would be delighted to see computers come into the writing classroom because they know computers have special appeal for many young students, particularly those already good at computer games.

▶ **Add details by downshifting.** We have discussed this strategy for making your writing more specific in two other places, Chapter 13 and Chapter 17. You can also use it to good effect within your sentences.

> **TIP: When you add details, you may not be sure whether you are embedding an appositive, adding a final modifier, or downshifting. It really doesn't matter whether you can label what you're doing. The point is, you're making your sentences richer and more interesting.**

20 B

Sent Dev

EXERCISE 20.3

Expand these sentences by adding an introductory phrase or clause. For example:

{Original} Computer-based writing instruction requires some special effort from both teachers and students.
{Expanded} Like any new system, computer-based writing instruction requires some special effort from both teachers and students.

1. Significant changes have begun to take place in many writing classes across the country.
2. Systems for tying all the individual computers in a computer classroom together have altered the way students behave in the classes.
3. An on-screen dialogue among students about the drafts of their papers is now possible.
4. Instructors using the system find that students who are reluctant to speak up in class will participate in these on-screen dialogues.
5. Writing instructors can now make student drafts appear on their computers at home and respond to those drafts on screen.

EXERCISE 20.4

Working with other students in a group, explore ways to expand these sentences by inserting an appositive with additional information somewhere in the body of the sentence. For example:

{Original} Writing multiple drafts of a paper is much easier when one writes on a word processor.

{Expanded} Writing multiple drafts of a paper, once a time-consuming chore, is much easier when one writes on a word processor.

1. Nancy and Bernard devised a special program for responding to student drafts.
2. The program offers an alternative to writing comments in the margins of papers.
3. Some students are nervous about this method at first.
4. Others like it immediately because it gets rid of the dreaded red pencil marks.
5. Some teachers resist this new method for responding to papers.

EXERCISE 20.5

Working with others in a group, explore ways to expand the following sentences by adding a final modifier at the end. For example:

{Original} Almost anyone who has used a computer for writing says he or she would never go back to a typewriter.

{Expanded} Almost anyone who has used a computer for writing says he or she would never go back to a typewriter, now considered obsolete technology.

1. A few months ago, the Apollo group began to think about the future of its program.
2. They were convinced that since it had succeeded at Clear Lake College, it could succeed at other colleges.
3. Virtually every college and university in the country has an extensive writing program.
4. Moreover, the faculty and administration of those same colleges and universities are eager to use computers with their students.
5. The combination is a natural for the Apollo group.

20 C

Sent Econ

20 C REVISING TO MAKE YOUR SENTENCES LEANER

Terms you need to know

REDUNDANT. A word or expression that is repetitious or unnecessary.

DOUBLING. Pairing two words that mean the same thing.

EMPTY MODIFIER. An adjective or adverb that repeats what is already stated in the word being modified: for example, ***end*** *result,* ***final*** *outcome,* ***desired*** *goal.*

SURPLUS INTENSIFIER. A word or phrase that is paired with another one but adds nothing to the first one's meaning; for example, *weather* ***activity,*** *point* ***in time,*** *consensus* ***of opinion.***

Troubleshooting

When your instructor and fellow students suggest that your writing is wordy or that you take too long to get to the point, check to see if you are using extra words and canned phrases that take up space but add nothing to your meaning. The writer and editor William Zinsser calls them "clutter," the clichés, pat phrases, and obvious comments that pad writing and keep it from being trim and crisp.

The bad news is that the war against clutter never ends. Professional writers know that those overstuffed phrases and pointless repetitions continually creep into their writing; the only remedy is to prune ruthlessly as you revise. The good news is that you can develop strategies to combat clutter. Used consistently, they will get the fat out of your writing and shape up your style.

To reduce wordiness, you can . .

➤ **Condense lead-in phrases.** To write clean, economical sentences, get rid of wheel-spinning expressions that pad and don't add. Ask yourself:

<table>
<tr><td>**Why write**</td><td>**When you could write**</td></tr>
<tr><td>in the event that</td><td>if</td></tr>
<tr><td>in light of the fact that</td><td>since</td></tr>
<tr><td>on the grounds that</td><td>because</td></tr>
<tr><td>regardless of the fact that</td><td>although</td></tr>
<tr><td>on the occasion of</td><td>when</td></tr>
<tr><td>at this point in time</td><td>now</td></tr>
<tr><td>it is obvious that</td><td>obviously</td></tr>
</table>

We are so accustomed to hearing these padded phrases that we forget they don't say anything; they do, however, clutter writing. For example:

{Wordy} **Regardless of the fact that** Helen isn't a member of the Apollo Group, she continues to attend meetings.

{Revised} **Although** Helen is not a member of the Apollo Group, she continues to attend meetings.

{Wordy} **In the event that** she has an opinion, she always gives it.

{Revised} **If** she has an opinion, she always gives it.

➤ **Seek out and destroy redundant, useless, and empty expressions.** When you are trying to streamline your sentences, keep a sharp eye out for those places where you have repeated yourself or where you have used double constructions or pointless modifiers. Look to see if you are

• **Doubling.** We have become so used to using some words in pairs that we forget they are synonyms; for example, "we *hope* and *trust*," "he shows *insight* and *vision*," or "it is *fitting* and *proper*."

• **Adding empty modifiers.** It's easy to fall in the habit of prefacing important words with adjectives or adverbs that are the equivalent of empty calories in food; they inflate your writing but contribute nothing because they only repeat the meaning already present in the word they're modifying.

Consider these examples: "I'm *completely* finished," "It was a *terrible* tragedy," "The *eventual* outcome was . . . ," and "She's *totally* exhausted." Such phrases can add emphasis in casual conversation but shouldn't appear in carefully edited writing.

• **Using surplus intensifiers.** The function of an intensifying word is to increase power. For instance, in the sentences "That chemical is *extremely* dangerous," and "She is *extraordinarily* talented," the italicized intensifiers serve a legitimate purpose. If, however, you add words that aren't needed to increase the power of the word you've paired it with, you're loading your writing with excess baggage.

Why write	*When you could write*
trading **activity** was heavy	trading was heavy
the papers were **of a confidential nature**	the papers were confidential
obstetrics is her **area of specialization**	her specialty is obstetrics
the banner was **blue in color**	the banner was blue

20 D

Sent Style

EXERCISE 20.6

Rewrite the following sentences to eliminate unnecessary words and phrases.

1. As Nancy and Bernard thought and pondered about the ultimate outcome of their plan to revolutionize completely how composition classes were taught, they became really excited.
2. They saw that the final result of their fresh and innovative idea could be that red ink would totally disappear from the writing classroom.
3. They could also see that old and venerable model of students hunched over their yellow legal pads chewing on a pencil would become obsolete and outmoded in the event that the electronic classroom became a reality.
4. "Unfortunately," Nancy pointed out, "I can also envision total disaster and absolutely furious students if the computer network crashes and burns, and twenty-four nearly finished drafts are erased at one time."
5. "In case of such a happening," said Bernard, "I am confident I have the ability to run faster than the students."

20 D REVISING FOR MORE STYLISH SENTENCES

Terms you need to know

BALANCED SENTENCE. A compound sentence that has two or more clauses having the same pattern. The clauses balance each other like the parts of an equation.

Romance requires infatuation; love requires respect.

A few people live by scripts they have written, but most live by the scripts others have written for them.

PARALLEL SENTENCE. A sentence containing two or more repetitions of the same pattern.

> "{Hitler} will find **no peace, no rest, no halting-place, no parley.**" (Winston Churchill)

> **By their need for flexible hours, by their willingness to work** for the minimum wage, and **by their naiveté about management tactics,** high school students enable fast-food restaurants to operate at a profit.

Troubleshooting

You may be writing well enough that your instructor or fellow students have few specific suggestions for improving your drafts, but they're saying, "See if you can make your sentences a little more polished and stylish," or "This is good, but you could fine tune it a little." Such comments don't help much in telling you what to do; you just have to tinker around, adding, pruning, rearranging, and editing. But that playing around with your sentences can be fun, and you could get some gratifying results.

20 D

Sent Style

You can polish and improve your sentences if you . . .

➤ **Highlight contrasting or similar points with balanced sentences.** Try reorganizing some of your sentences into the dramatic patterns of the balanced sentence. Notice how much more forceful and rhythmic the following sentences are when they are recast into balanced patterns.

{**Original**}   Nearly everyone in our culture takes computers for granted these days, but that doesn't mean they really understand what computers do.

{**Revised**}   Most people in our culture take computers for granted; few people understand what they do.

{**Original**}   Although the general public seems to believe computers are magic machines that can work miracles, those who really understand computers know they are limited machines.

{**Revised**}   Those who are awed by computers think they can work miracles, but those who understand computers know how limited they are.

➤ **Arrange the points in a sentence into parallel phrases or clauses that set up a pattern of repetition.** Although they resemble balanced sentences, parallel sentences are more flexible. They can go beyond showing contrast to building emphasis for an idea and setting up a rhythm in your writing. For even stronger emphasis, you can write a series of sentences that follow the same pattern. Here are examples of both strategies.

{**Original**}   The Apollo group faced the task of changing their enterprise from a project that seemed amateurish, limited, and specialized to a project that looked professional, comprehensive, and adaptable to a variety of teaching situations.

{**Possible revision**}   The Apollo group faced the task of changing their enterprise to a project that looked **not amateurish but professional, not special-**

ized but comprehensive, not limited but adaptable to a variety of teaching situations.

{**Original**} In their boldest move, they decided to go to a national conference on computers in writing and buy space to set up a booth where they would demonstrate their program. They had confidence in themselves and in their product. They also had confidence that the market was there and they could beat the competition.

{**Possible revision**} In their boldest move, they decided to go to a national conference on computers in writing and buy space for a booth where they would demonstrate their product. **They had confidence in themselves. They had confidence in their product. They had confidence in the market.** And **they had confidence** that they could beat the competition.

[Notice it's apparent that this repetition is purposeful, not careless.]

> **TIP: You will find additional strategies for polishing your writing in Chapter 17, "Making Your Writing Clearer?" Look especially at the sections on using metaphor and analogy and on making your writing more visual.**

20 D

Sent Style

EXERCISE 20.7

Working in a group, explore ways in which you could rewrite the following sentences as balanced sentences. Here is an example.

{Original} Although two members of the Apollo group had to stay in Chicago to mind the store, five members were heading for Atlanta in pursuit of fortune.

{Revision} Two members of the Apollo group stayed in Chicago to mind the store; five members headed for Atlanta in pursuit of fortune.

1. Liz and Professor Bates, who were staying at home, made the arrangements for the trip to Atlanta since the others were in a frantic, last-minute rush preparing the presentations they would give at the conference.
2. The van they were renting for the trip had to be a large one, big enough not only for the five people and their luggage, but also big enough to pack in the personal computers they were taking for their demonstrations.
3. Although Liz did a great job in negotiating a good rate for the van, she forgot to read the restrictions in fine print on the contract.
4. In Indiana, they discovered both good and bad news; it was true they weren't supposed to drive the van out of Illinois, but the good news was the rates were cheaper for an educational corporation.
5. Their discoveries had two consequences; they ate a little better because they were saving money, but Roscoe got indigestion because he worried so much about driving the van across state lines.

Working with other students in a group, rewrite the following sentences so each will be a parallel sentence with a repeated pattern. You can break some sentences into two or three sentences if you like. Here is an example.

{Original} Driving straight through, they got to Atlanta in thirty hours, with everyone exhausted but eager to get started and feeling both nervous and excited about the conference.

{Revision} Driving straight through, they got to Atlanta in thirty hours; everyone was **exhausted but eager to start, nervous but excited about the conference.**

1. As tired as they were, they went to their booth immediately to set up their tables and hang out the golden Apollo logo as well as unpack and connect the computers and lay out all the literature they had brought about Apollo.
2. They sent Roscoe off to get a shave and a nap because he was the one delegated to put on a suit and tie and take the first shift of talking to potential customers who might come by the booth.
3. About this time, anxiety attacks suddenly set in for everyone as they worried about whether anyone would show interest in their program, if the conference were poorly attended, or what if they proved to be wretched salespeople.
4. The next morning, however, they all looked wonderful and radiated confidence—Nancy looked competent but chic, Bernard came across as the articulate intellectual, while Professor Maynard played the role of scholar; well dressed and business-like, Roscoe kept track of customers, and Larry was in charge of keeping the computers running.
5. At the end of the conference at 6:00 P.M. on Saturday, weary but happy, they sat down to tally their results and found that their gamble had paid off because people in the profession now recognized their logo and more than fifty schools had signed up to get a demonstration disk of their program.

GRAMMAR
AND USAGE

Grammar and usage are the rules of the language game. Like the length of a football field or the number of outs in an inning of baseball, some rules and usages of grammar are relatively stable and unchanging. Other grammatical "conventions" are modified more often, like the size and weight of a baseball or the rules for tackling a quarterback.

What follows is not a comprehensive description of English grammar, but a sort of "playbook" describing problems you are most likely to encounter when writing—and ways to deal with them.

21 Mini-Grammar

A Parts of speech
B Common sentence problems
C Subject/verb agreement
D Verbals
E Pronoun problems
F Comma problems
G Semicolon problems
H Forgotten apostrophes
I *Its/it's* and *whose/who's*
J *Good/well* and *bad/badly*
K *Who/whom*
L Special concerns

Troubleshooting

Even experienced writers need to review key concepts once in a while. So this "mini-grammar" covers twelve areas many writers find troublesome. Subsequent chapters treat these areas in more depth, but you can use this section to brush up on some tricky points.

21 A   THE PARTS OF SPEECH

Terms you need to know

The eight traditional parts of speech are: *adjective, adverb, noun, pronoun, verb, conjunction, interjection,* and *preposition.* They are briefly defined below.

ADVERB. A word that modifies a verb, adjective, or another adverb.

> adverb   verb
> Bud **immediately** *suspected* foul play at the Hutton estate.

> adverb   adjective
> It seemed **extremely** *odd* to him that Mrs. Hutton should load a large burlap sack into the trunk of her Mercedes.

315

adverb   adverb

Mrs. Hutton replied **rather** *evasively* when Bud questioned her about the sack.

Some adverbs modify complete sentences.

adverb

Obviously, Mr. Hutton had been murdered!

An important type of adverb called a **joining** or **conjunctive adverb** links independent clauses. Conjunctive adverbs include *consequently, furthermore, however, likewise, meanwhile, moreover, nevertheless, therefore,* and similar expressions.

Jake was suspicious; **consequently,** he rejected the contract.

Alicia flew all night; **nevertheless,** she began the meeting as scheduled in New York.

ADJECTIVE. A word that modifies a noun or pronoun. Some adjectives describe the words they modify.

an *unsuccessful* coach   a *green* motel
the *lucky* one   a *sacred* icon

Such adjectives frequently have comparative and superlative forms.

the *fatter* cat   the *happiest* people
the *brighter* star   the *direst* prophecy

Other adjectives limit or specify the words they modify.

this adventure   *every* penny
neither video   *each* participant

Proper nouns can also serve as adjectives; in this form, they are called **proper adjectives.**

Italian marble   *African* sculpture
Cantonese cuisine   *American* enterprise

Another important kind of adjective is the **article:** which points either to a particular object (**definite article:** *the*) or to objects in general (**indefinite articles:** *a, an*).

NOUN. A word that names a person, place, thing, idea, or quality. In sentences, nouns can serve as subjects, objects, complements, appositives, and even modifiers. There are many classes of nouns: **common, proper, concrete, abstract, collective, mass,** and **count.**

common nouns: *automobile, dog, mailbox*

proper nouns: *Detroit, Picasso, U.S.S. Enterprise*

concrete nouns: *firecracker, Valentine, bench*

abstract nouns: *patriotism, charity, equality*

collective nouns: *jury, team, class*

mass nouns (things not counted): *oil, gelatin, knowledge*

count nouns (things counted): *beans, envelopes, pins*

Nouns can show number (singular or plural) and possession.

21 A

Prts Spch

Singular: *boy*

Plural: *boys*

Singular possessive: *boy's*

Plural possessive: *boys'*

VERB. The word or phrase that establishes the action of a sentence or expresses a state of being.

verb

The music **played** on.

verb

Turning the volume down **proved** to be difficult.

A verb and all its auxiliaries, modifiers, and complements is called the **predicate** of a sentence.

complete subject   predicate

The music played by David's band **would have rocked on all night.**

complete subject   predicate

Silencing the rock band **proved to be much more difficult than the neighborhood association had anticipated it might be.**

PRONOUN. A word that acts like a noun, but doesn't name a specific person, place, or thing—*I, you, he, she, it, they, whom, who, what, myself, oneself, this, these, that, all, both, anybody,* and so on. There are many forms and varieties of pronouns: **personal, possessive, relative, interrogative, intensive, reflexive, demonstrative, indefinite,** and **reciprocal.**

personal: *I, you, he, she, it, we, they*

possessive: *my, mine, yours, its, his, hers, theirs*

relative: *who, which, that*

interrogative: *Who? What? Which?*

intensive: You *yourself;* I *myself*

reflexive: Won't you help *yourself?*

demonstrative: *this, that, these, those*

indefinite: *all, each, every, some, any*

reciprocal: *one another, each other*

INTERJECTION. A word that expresses emotion or feeling, but that is not grammatically a part of a sentence. Interjections can be punctuated as exclamations (!) or attached to a sentence with a comma. Common interjections include: *oh, hey, wow, well, ouch.*

PREPOSITION. A word that links a noun or pronoun to the rest of a sentence. Prepositions point out all kinds of basic relationships: *on, above, to, for, in, out, through, by.* The combination of a preposition and a noun or pronoun results in a prepositional phrase. The following are prepositional phrases: *on our house; above it; to him; in love; through them, by the garden gate.*

CONJUNCTION, COORDINATING. The word *and, or, nor, for, but, yet,* or *so* used to link words, phrases, and clauses that serve equivalent functions in a sentence. That is to say, a coordinating conjunction could join two independent clauses or two dependent

21 A

Prts Spch

clauses; it would not link a subordinate clause to an independent clause. See *conjunction, subordinating.*

Oscar **and** Marie read the book.

Oscar liked the story, **but** Marie did not.

Neither repairing the roof **nor** improving the landscaping raised the value of the property, **but** the Huttons didn't care.

CONJUNCTION, SUBORDINATING. An expression such as *although, because, if, since, before, after, if, when, even though, in order that,* or *while* that relates a dependent (that is, subordinate) clause to an independent clause. Subordinating conjunctions introduce subordinate clauses.

dependent clause
Although *both Oscar and Marie began the book,* only Oscar liked it enough to finish it.

dependent clause
Oscar liked the story **even though** *no one else did.*

dependent clause
When *the movie version opened,* audiences rushed to see it.

CONJUNCTIONS, CORRELATIVE. Conjunctions that work together in pairs: *either . . . or; neither . . . nor; not . . . but; whether . . . or.*

---

21 A

Prts Spch

EXERCISE 21.1

Identify the part of speech of the boldfaced words. Identify the type of any nouns or pronouns bracketed (*count, mass, reflexive,* and so on).

(1) **The** influx of small, inexpensive (2) **European** cars (3) **into** the domestic automobile market in the late 1950s (4) **generated** a wave of (5) **panic** (6) **among** the major American manufacturers. In the fall of 1959, the companies responded with (7) **three** (8) **newly** designed American compact cars: the (9) **Falcon,** Valiant, and Corvair. The companies introduced (10) **these** cars enthusiastically, assuring (11) **themselves** (12) **that** these compacts (13) **would drive** the Volkswagens, Renaults, and Fiats (14) **back** into the Atlantic.

The Falcon from the (15) **Ford** Motor Company was the brainchild of Robert McNamara, (16) **future** Secretary of Defense in the (17) **Kennedy** Administration. The Falcon was a placid sedan with a drooping hood and pie pan taillights— (18) **neither** sophisticated nor pretty. (19) **It** was hardly the dream car Detroit had (20) **fondly** promised for decades; (21) **however,** Americans bought it in record numbers.

(22) **Chrysler's** entry, the Valiant, was the (23) **biggest,** fastest, and sportiest of the new American compacts. Bristling with (24) **pushbuttons** and adorned with a fake spare on (25) **its** fastback decklid, the Valiant proudly claimed to be "(26) **nobody's** kid brother."

Chevrolet introduced the Corvair, the most radical American design in a (27) **decade.** Air-cooled, rear-engined, tiny, and (28) **Spartan,** the Corvair captured the hearts of many sporty drivers. (29) **Despite** the Corvair's daring engineering and stylish appearance, Americans seemed to prefer the dowdy Falcon.

(30) **None** of (31) **these** American challengers, (32) **all** with six (33) **cylinder** engines, (34) **could match** the fuel economy of the Renaults or the (35) **quality** of the VW.

Check Your Answers: Parts of Speech

1. article
2. adjective (or proper adjective)
3. preposition
4. verb
5. abstract noun
6. preposition
7. adjective
8. adverb
9. proper noun
10. demonstrative pronoun
11. reflexive pronoun
12. relative pronoun
13. verb (or predicate)
14. adverb
15. proper noun
16. adjective
17. proper noun (used as modifier)
18. correlative conjunction
19. pronoun
20. adverb
21. conjunctive adverb
22. proper noun (possessive)
23. adjective (superlative form)
24. noun (count)
25. pronoun (possessive)
26. indefinite pronoun (possessive)
27. common noun (count noun)
28. proper adjective
29. subordinating conjunction
30. indefinite pronoun
31. demonstrative pronoun
32. indefinite pronoun
33. common noun (used as a modifier)
34. verb (predicate)
35. abstract noun

21 A

Prts Spch

Grammar Warmup

Underline or circle the correct answer.

You may want to use this exercise as a diagnostic quiz. In the sections that follow, answers to these items are identified by bracketed numbers next to various examples.

1. All autos meet safety standards(**,/;**) they are quite strict.
2. Carla quit the bar (**no punctuation/;**) she was about to be fired.
3. The company, as well as its employees, (**is/are**) eager to relocate.
4. The key to successful schools (**is/are**) capable teachers.
5. Everyone should keep (**his/their**) temper.
6. Do you agree with the figures supplied by (**they/them**) and Mr. Archer?
7. The dean spoke with Kent and (**me/myself**).
8. The presidents attending the memorial service were Nixon, Ford, Carter (**,/or no comma**) and Bush.
9. The university will reimburse you for travel and lodging (**,/;**) however, you are responsible for entertainment expenses.
10. The estimate is for refurbishing the (**mens/men's**) room.
11. The hot iron left (**it's/its**) grim outline on the silk shirt.
12. (**Whose/Who's**) on first?
13. Jason plays the tuba (**good/well**).
14. The program runs (**bad/badly**).
15. For (**who/whom**) are you writing the software manual?

21 B OVERCOMING COMMON SENTENCE PROBLEMS

▶ **Independent clauses cannot be joined by commas alone.** Such faulty punctuation produces a **comma splice.** Correct the comma splice by adding a coordinating conjunction, a semicolon, or by recasting the sentence.

comma splice

{Wrong}   All autos meet safety standards, they are quite strict.

{Right}   All autos meet safety standards, **and** they are quite strict.

{Right}   All autos meet safety standards; they are quite strict. {1}

{Right}   All autos meet safety standards **that** are quite strict.

Independent clauses must be joined by a conjunction, a semicolon, or, more rarely, a colon. If one of these linking devices is not in place, the sentences are **run-on.**

run on

{Wrong}   Carla quit the bar she was about to be fired.

{Right}   Carla quit the bar **because** she was about to be fired.

{Right}   Carla quit the bar; she was about to be fired. {2}

In most cases, a complete sentence requires both a subject and verb. A sentence lacking either or both of these components is called a **fragment.**

{Fragment}   The Mustang was a hit with the public. **From its first day on the market.**

{Corrected}   The Mustang was a hit with the public from its first day on the market.

{Fragment}   **Lee Iacocca having conceived of the Mustang as a personal car rather than a real sports car.**

{Corrected}   Lee Iacocca conceived of the Mustang as a personal car rather than a real sports car.

21 C

Subj/Vb

21 C UNDERSTANDING SUBJECT/VERB AGREEMENT

Singular subject + Singular verb form

Herb	invests.
She	saves.

Plural subject + Plural verb form

Consumers	invest.
They	save.

➤ **Subjects joined by *and* are plural except after *each* and *every* and with certain phrases.**

> The building *and* its landscaping **are** too expensive.
>
> Every manager *and* executive **is** on the plane.
>
> {Rock *and* roll} is my favorite music.

➤ **Subjects are unaffected by *along with, in addition to, as well as, together with*.** Such phrases usually fall between commas.

> The *company,* as well as its employees, **is** eager to relocate. {3}

➤ **When subjects are joined by *either . . . or* and *neither . . . nor,* the verb agrees with the subject closer to it.**

> Neither the company nor its *employees* **are** eager to relocate.
>
> Neither the employees nor the *company* **is** eager to relocate.

➤ **Some subjects can be either singular or plural—or both.** When in doubt, consult a dictionary.

> The *jury* **ponders** its decision.   [*jury* treated as singular]
>
> The *jury* sit just inches from the prosecutor's table.   [plural]

➤ **When a sentence begins with *here* or *there,* the verb still agrees with the subject—which usually trails after it.**

> There **is** a *reason* for her action.
>
> There **are** *reasons* for her action.

➤ **Keep your eye on the real subject. It controls the verb.**

> The *key* to successful schools **is** capable teachers. {4}

21 D

Verbals

21 D DEALING WITH VERBALS

➤ **When a verbal phrase proves to be a fragment, attach it to an independent clause or make the phrase a complete sentence.**

{**Wrong**}   The actors bowed to the audience. **Knowing that their show was a success.**

{**Right**}   The actors bowed to the audience, **knowing that their show was a success.**

{**Right**}   The actors bowed to the audience. **They knew that their show was a success.**

➤ **Infinitives are verbals that consist of a verb preceded by *to: to strive, to seek, to find, to yield*.** Many careful readers object to split infinitives—in which a word or phrase splits the *to* in an infinitive from its verb.

{**Split infinitive**}   The mission of the Starship *Enterprise* was **to boldly go** where no one had gone before.

{**Corrected**}   The mission of the Starship *Enterprise* was **to go boldly** where no one had gone before.

{**Split infinitive**}   Words fail **to adequately describe** the genius of her design.

{**Corrected**}   Words fail **to describe** the genius of her design **adequately.**

21 E   MANAGING PRONOUNS

> Singular pronouns refer to singular words, plural pronouns to plural.

> **Singular referent + Singular pronoun**

The **carton** was full when I closed *it*.

> **Plural referent + Plural pronoun**

The **cartons** were full when I closed *them*.

{**Singular reference**}   An **American** always assumes that government agencies will help *him or her* when trouble strikes.

{**Plural reference**}   **Americans** always assume that government agencies will help *them* when trouble strikes.

> Use a dictionary to determine whether an indefinite pronoun *(each, everyone, none, someone, few, many)* is singular or plural.

Each of the candidates has *her* own ideas.

Everyone should keep *his* temper. {5}

Many contributed *their* finest efforts.

Exactly what a pronoun refers to should usually be evident.

{**Vague**}   The plant is new, efficient, and conveniently located. Workers especially liked **this.**   [What is *this*?]

{**Clearer**}   The plant is new and efficient. Workers especially liked the convenient location.

> Use the objective form of a pronoun after a preposition. (The objective form can't be used as a subject.)

{**Wrong**}   Do you agree with the figures supplied **by** *they* and Mr. Archer?

{**Right**}   Do you agree with the figures supplied **by** *them* and Mr. Archer? {6}

{**Wrong**}   Just **between** *you* and *I,* the grade seems unfair.

{**Right**}   Just **between** *you* and *me,* the grade seems unfair.

➤ **Avoid sexist pronoun usage.**

{Sexist}   None of the engineers was satisfied with **his** work.

{Nonsexist}   None of the engineers was satisfied with **his or her** work.

➤ **Don't use a reflexive pronoun to make a sentence sound more formal.**

> ### Reflexive pronouns
>
> **Reflexive pronouns are created when *-self* is added to personal pronouns: *myself, yourself, himself, ourselves, themselves.***

{Wrong}   Mary and **myself** drafted the proposal.

{Right}   Mary and **I** drafted the proposal.

{Wrong}   The dean spoke with Kent and **myself.**

{Right}   The dean spoke with Kent and **me.** {7}

➤ **Use a reflexive pronoun only when a subject and object refer to the same person.**

Ms. Lentz had only **herself** to blame for the error.

21 F

Commas

21 F   MANAGING COMMAS

> **Commas ordinarily signal a pause or minor sentence interruption.**

➤ **Don't join complete sentences with commas.**

{Wrong}   The valve leaked under pressure, the seal was faulty.

{Right}   The valve leaked under pressure. The seal was faulty.

➤ **Use a comma before coordinate conjunctions: *and, but, for, so, or, yet.*** (Can be omitted when clauses are very short.)

Oil prices rose, **but** gasoline prices at the pump remained stable.

Joel was easy prey, **for** anyone could pull the wool over his eyes.

➤ **Most writers (except journalists) use a comma before the last item in a series.**

The presidents attending the memorial service were Nixon, Ford, Carter, and Bush. {8}

Alice ordered a Bloody Mary, two gin and tonics, and three rum and Cokes.

➤ **If a phrase modifying a noun can be removed from a sentence without changing the meaning substantially, it is enclosed by commas.** If the clause is essential to the sentence, no commas surround it.

{**Compare**}

The satellite, **which resembled a trash can,** was placed in orbit.

The satellite **that was launched today** belongs to the U.S. Army.

{**Compare**}

Last night's presentation, **which dealt with business ethics,** led to prolonged discussions.

The presentation **that dealt with business ethics** has been cancelled.

{**Compare**}

Zircons, **which are synthetic stones,** resemble diamonds.

Diamonds **that are synthetically produced** are less flawed than natural stones.

➤ **Don't forget to use a comma after most introductory phrases.**

Despite having a formidable temper, Dr. Collet was liked by most of her colleagues.

In fact, our experiment supports previous research.

21 H

Apost

21 G UNDERSTANDING SEMICOLONS

> Semicolons are stronger pauses than commas, but weaker than periods. Avoid semicolons unless you are confident about how to use them.

➤ **Use a semicolon before *however, therefore, consequently, moreover,* and *nevertheless* when what follows such terms could stand alone as a complete sentence.**

The university will reimburse you for travel and lodging; **however,** you are responsible for entertainment expenses. {9}

Profitability must be increased; **consequently,** overhead and maintenance must be reduced.

21 H REMEMBERING TO USE APOSTROPHES

➤ **Don't forget the apostrophes in most possessive forms.**

> **possessive**
> **The possessive form of a noun or pronoun indicates ownership, and is usually shown by** *'s.*

{**Wrong**}   The estimate is for refurbishing the **mens** room.

{**Right**}   The estimate is for refurbishing the **men's** room. {**10**}

{**Wrong**}   The **chief-of-staffs** arrest embarrassed the firm.

{**Right**}   The **chief-of-staff's** arrest embarrassed the firm.

➤ **Don't forget the apostrophes in contractions.**

{**Wrong**}   The source of the seepage **cant** be determined.

{**Right**}   The source of the seepage **can't** be determined.

{**Wrong**}   Wont the car start?

{**Right**}   Won't the car start?

21 I   GETTING *ITS/IT'S* AND *WHOSE/WHO'S* RIGHT

➤ *Its* **is a possessive form.**

The hot iron left **its** grim outline on the silk shirt. {**11**}

➤ *It's* **is the contraction for** *it is.*

It's not certain who approved the purchase.

➤ *Whose* **is a possessive form.**

Whose teammate is on first base?

➤ *Who's* **is the contraction for** *who is.*

Who's on first? {**12**}

21 J

Good/Well

21 J   GETTING *GOOD/WELL* AND *BAD/BADLY* RIGHT

➤ **Both** *good* **and** *well* **can describe a person or thing.** Consider the difference between these sentences.

Carla is **good.**	*Jason is* **well.**
Carla feels **good.**	*Jason* feels **well.**
Carla looks **good.**	*Jason* looks **well.**
Carla smells **good.**	

➤ However, only *well* can describe an action.

    Jason *smells* **well.**   [Describes his capacity to smell.]

{**Wrong**}   The program *runs* **good.**

{**Right**}   The program *runs* **well.**

{**Wrong**}   Jason *plays* the tuba **good.**

{**Right**}   Jason *plays* the tuba **well.** {13}

➤ Only *bad* can describe a person or thing. Consider these sentences.

    Carla is **bad.**   *Jason* feels **bad.**
    Carla looks **bad.**   *Jason* smells **bad.**

➤ Only *badly* can describe an action.

    Jason *smells* **badly.**   [He has a poor sense of smell.]

    Jason *feels* **badly.**   [He has a poor sense of touch.]

{**Wrong**}   The program *runs* **bad.**

{**Right**}   The program *runs* **badly.** {14}

{**Wrong**}   Jason *plays* the tuba **bad.**

{**Right**}   Jason *plays* the tuba **badly.**

21 K

Who/Whom

21 K   GETTING *WHO/WHOM* RIGHT

➤ The basic rule is use *who* when the word is a subject; use *whom* when the word functions as an object.

{**Subject**}   **Who** wrote this letter?

{**Object**}   **Whom** did you fire?

{**Object of prep.**}   **For whom** are you writing the software manual? {15}

➤ If you can't tell subject from object, use *who* in most situations, except immediately after prepositions—where you should use *whom*. Even when wrong, you won't sound awkward.

{**Technically wrong**}   **Who** are you taking with you?

{**Right**}   **Whom** are you taking with you?

{**Technically wrong**}   The deficit will increase no matter **who** we elect President.

{**Right**}   The deficit will increase no matter **whom** we elect President.

{**With prepositions**}   **To whom** did the memo refer? **For whom** is the report intended?

21 L | SPECIAL CONCERNS

➤ **Sentences may begin with *and* or *but*. But the resulting sentences must be complete.**

> There was strong objection to the proposal by every member of the board and by others outside the corporation as well. **But** the motion finally passed.

➤ **Sentences may end with prepositions—especially when avoiding a preposition leads to an awkward construction.**

{**Compare**}   This is the sort of English up **with** which I will not put!
—Winston Churchill

> This is the sort of English I will not put up **with!**

➤ **But some sentences that end with prepositions *are* awkward—and should be rewritten.**

{**Compare**}   Pollution is a problem we should all be concerned **with.**

> We should all be concerned **with** pollution.

➤ **Contractions are an element of style, not grammar.** They are a way of controlling the level of formality. Contractions can be appropriate even in academic writing.

{**Compare**}   If you cannot meet our expectations, we shall discuss the problem.

> If you can't meet our expectations, **we'll** discuss the problem.

21 L

Spec

22 Subject-verb Agreement

A Subjects, singular/plural, and simple/compound
B Indefinite pronouns as subjects
C Collective nouns as subjects
D Subjects separated from verbs
E Subjects hard to identify

Terms you need to know

SUBJECT. A word or phrase that names what or whom a sentence is about. The subject ordinarily performs the action described by the verb in a sentence.

subject
The *fights* continued.

subject
These disturbances of the peace threatened the neighborhood.

A **compound subject** consists of two or more subjects performing the action of the same verb:

1st subj. + 2nd subj. verb
Citizens and police alike **want** crime to end.

VERB. The word or phrase that establishes the action of a sentence or expresses a state of being.

verb
The violence **escalated.**

verb
Protecting residents **proved** difficult.

The **predicate** of a sentence is a verb and all of its auxiliaries, modifiers, and complements.

complete subject | predicate
The violence between warring youth gangs **threatened the welfare of the entire neighborhood.**

subject | predicate
Not *one week* **has passed without an instance of arson or injury related to gang violence.**

AUXILIARY VERB. (also called **helping verb)** A verb, usually some form of *be, do,* or *have,* that combines with other verbs to show relationships of tense, voice, mood, and so on. All the italicized words are auxiliary verbs: *has* seen; *will be* talking; *would have been* going; *are* investigating; *did* mention; *should* prefer.

LINKING VERB. A verb, often a form of *to be* (*is, are, was, were, will be*), connecting a subject to a word or phrase that extends or completes its meaning. Common linking verbs are *to seem, to appear, to feel, to taste, to look,* and *to become.*

Mrs. Gorski **feels** angry.

PERSON. A way of classifying personal pronouns in sentences:

First person: the speaker—*I, we.*

Second person: the one spoken to—*you.*

Third person: the person or thing spoken about—*he, she, it, they.*

All nouns are in the third person: *bread, Akron, Mrs. Thatcher.*

NUMBER. The form a word has or takes to indicate whether it is singular or plural.

singular	thug	his	this
plural	thugs	their	these

PREPOSITIONAL PHRASE. The combination of a preposition and a noun or pronoun. Prepositions link a noun or pronoun to the rest of a sentence in order to show many kinds of basic relationships: *of, with, to, for, in.* The following are prepositional phrases: *of the proposals; with a few allies; to all members; in love.*

Sing/Pl

22 A AGREEMENT: SUBJECT SINGULAR/PLURAL OR SIMPLE/COMPOUND

Troubleshooting

Subjects and verbs in a sentence *agree in number;* the verb form may change depending on whether a subject is singular or plural.

The most important change occurs when a third person singular subject (for example, *he, she, it, Irene)* takes a verb in the present tense. In such cases, an *-s* or *-es* is added to the base form of the verb.

Third person, singular, present tense: Irene complains**.**
He complains**.**
She complains**.**

(To determine the base form, imagine a *to* before the verb: to *complain;* to *decide;* to *rule.)* The base form of the verb alone is used with all subjects except those in the third person singular.

First person, singular, present tense: I complain.

Second person, singular, present tense: You complain.

First person, plural, present tense: We complain.

Second person, plural, present tense: You all complain.

Third person, plural, present tense: They complain.

Verb forms also change to reflect agreement in tenses that require auxiliary verbs. That is because two important auxiliaries—*to have* and *to be*—are irregular. (*Irregular* means that they show agreement by more than just an additional -*s* or -*es* in the third person singular.)

I have	we have
you have	you have
he/she/it **has**	they have

To be changes more often, in both the present and past tenses.

I *am*	we are	I **was**	we were
you are	you are	you were	you were
he/she/it **is**	they are	he/she/it **was**	they were

To choose a correct verb form in the third person, you must know whether the subject of a sentence is singular or plural. Sometimes it isn't easy to tell, especially with constructions that seem to form compound subjects—which usually *are* plural.

To be sure subjects and verbs agree in number . . .

➤ **When a subject is linked to another noun by expressions such as *along with*, *as well as*, or *together with*, pay attention only to the subject.** The verb agrees with the subject, not with the second noun, which is usually the object of a prepositional phrase. In the following sentence, for example, a singular subject *Augie* is tied to another possible subject *a few allies* by the expression *together with*. Despite the nearness of the plural noun *allies*, the subject remains singular.

> sing. subj.   plural noun   verb
> *Augie,* **together with** a few liberal *allies,* **resists** the law-and-order demands of the Myrtle Hill Neighborhood Association.

The same principle holds when a plural subject (*neighbors*) is linked to a singular noun (*Mrs. Gorski*).

> plural subj.   singular noun   verb
> *The neighbors,* **along with** *Mrs. Gorski,* **favor** vigilante tactics to control the gangs.

➤ **Treat subjects joined by *and* as plural in most cases.**

> subject   +   subject   verb
> *Mrs. Gorski* **and** *her neighbors* **blame** Myrtle Hill's problem on poor enforcement of drug laws.

> subject + subject   verb
> But *Augie* **and** *the police* **believe** the problem is more complicated.

However, some subjects joined by *and* actually describe a single thing or idea. Treat such expressions as singular.

subject   verb

Peace and quiet **is** what all the neighbors want.

"Peace and quiet"—like "gin and tonic," "rock and roll," and similar expressions—really expresses one idea.

Similarly, when a compound subject linked by *and* is modified by *each* or *every,* the verb takes a singular form.

subject +   subject   verb

Every *resident and shopkeeper* in Myrtle Hill **has** an opinion.

subject +   subject   verb

Each *store owner and* ***each*** *member* of the association **intends** to speak his or her mind.

However, when *each* follows a compound subject, usage varies.

The angry resident and the irate shopkeeper *each* **have** their opinions.

The angry resident and the irate shopkeeper *each* **has** his or her opinion.

➤ **When subjects are joined by** *or, neither . . . nor,* **or** *either . . . or,* **be sure the verb (or its auxiliary) agrees with the subject closer to it.** Study these examples to understand how this guideline works. The arrows point to the subjects nearer the verbs.

plural   singular ↵

Neither the neighbors nor Augie **is** eager for trouble.

singular   plural   ↵

But *either Augie or his neighbors* **are** likely to hire a lawyer.

→ singular   plural

Does ***Augie*** *or the neighbors* know a lawyer?

→   plural   singular

Do *the* ***neighbors*** *or Augie* know a lawyer?

plural   plural ↵

Lawyers or **lawsuits cost** lots of money.

singular   singular   ↵

Compromise or ***cooperation*** **costs** much less.

The rule holds when one or both of the subjects joined by *or, either . . . or,* or *neither . . . nor* are pronouns: the verb agrees with the nearer subject.

↵

Neither *she* nor *we* **admit** to an opinion about the dispute.

↵

Neither *we* nor *she* **admits** to an opinion about the dispute.

↵

Neither *Kyle* nor ***I*** **have** any news.

↵

Neither *I* nor ***Kyle*** **has** any news.

22 A

Sing/Pl

Notice that when both subjects are singular, the verb may change to reflect a shift from a first person subject (*I*) to a third person subject (*Kyle*).

If a construction feels awkward, it can be revised—usually by making the verb plural or rewriting the sentence.

{**Awkward**}   Neither *you* nor *I* **am** bothered by the gangs.

{**Better**}   Neither *I* nor *you* **are** bothered by the gangs.

{**Better**}   *We* **are** not bothered by the gangs.

♦ FINE TUNING ♦

1. When subjects linked to expressions such as *as well as, along with,* or *together with* sound awkward with a singular verb, consider joining the subjects with *and* instead.

{**Slightly awkward**}   *Augie,* as well as his neighbors, **considers** a compromise possible.

{**Better**}   *Augie and his neighbors* **consider** a compromise possible.

2. Treat titles as singular subjects.

Franco Zeffirelli's *Romeo and Juliet* **remains** a popular film.

Streamers **is** a play about the Vietnam War.

22 A

Sing/Pl

EXERCISE 22.1

Decide which verb in boldface is correct.

1. The meeting of the Myrtle Hill neighborhood association (**promise/ promises**) to be explosive.
2. The association's officers, seated at a table near the front of the room, (**review/reviews**) the minutes of the previous meeting.
3. As soon as the meeting begins, Mrs. Gorski and her allies (**present/ presents**) their plan for an armed Citizens' Patrol to curb drug traffic in Myrtle Hill.
4. Augie, as well as other wary residents, (**sit/sits**) patiently in the audience, waiting for a chance to debate the suggestion.
5. "Common decency and the right of citizens to walk unmolested in their neighborhood (**demand/demands**) an end to gang violence," Mrs. Gorski argues.
6. Augie disagrees, observing that "neither I nor Mrs. Gorski (**is/are**) trained to deal with drug criminals."
7. "And," Augie continues, " I doubt that either the neighbors or Mrs. Gorski (**has/have**) considered the legal consequences of acting outside the law."
8. "Law and order (**is/are**) still legal in this country," Mrs. Gorski observes sarcastically.
9. Mrs. Gorski and Mr. Burtinelli (**agree/agrees**) that neither local businesses nor the association (**is/are**) helpless to deal with the problem.
10. Citizens at the crowded meeting (**expect/expects**) some effective action.

22 B AGREEMENT: INDEFINITE PRONOUNS AS SUBJECTS

Term you need to know

INDEFINITE PRONOUN. A pronoun that does not refer to a particular person, thing, or group: *all, any, each, everybody, everyone, one, none, somebody, someone,* and so on.

Troubleshooting

Some indefinite pronouns—words like *each, every, none,* and *any*—can seem both singular and plural. Selecting a verb to agree in number with such a pronoun can be quite difficult.

> *Each* **(has/have)** strong ideas about curbing the violence in Myrtle Hill.
>> [**has** is correct]

> *None of the officers* **(has/have)** a workable solution for the problem.
>> [**has** is correct]

To be sure verbs agree with indefinite pronoun subjects . . .

➤ **Use the chart below (or a dictionary) to determine whether the pronoun is singular, plural, or variable.** Then select an appropriate verb form.

Singular	Variable, S. or Pl.	Plural
anybody	all	few
anyone	any	many
each	either	several
everybody	more	
everyone	most	
nobody	neither	
no one	none	
somebody	some	
someone		

The most troublesome indefinite pronouns are probably *each* (which is singular in academic writing) and *none* (which varies, but is *usually* singular). Other indefinites, such as *either* and *neither,* are also difficult because they are treated as singular in formal and academic writing, but handled as plural in much day-to-day language. These examples follow academic form.

Each **believes** strong action needs to be taken.	[singular]
Nobody **knows** what the association will do.	[singular]
None of the arguments **is** easy to dismiss.	[variable]
None but the brave **are** at the meeting.	[variable]
Many in Myrtle Hill **hope** to take action.	[plural]
Few **intend** to watch their neighborhood decline.	[plural]

EXERCISE 22.2

Decide which verb in boldface would be correct in academic writing.

1. At the Myrtle Hill neighborhood meeting, several of the people **(discuss/ discusses)** a TV program about robberies in a similar residential area.
2. Everybody **(seem/seems)** to have seen the same show.
3. Most of the program **(was/were)** about a Neighborhood Watch established by the residents.
4. Most of the residents **(was/were)** involved in the surveillance.
5. None of the residents **(find/finds)** the proposal unworkable.
6. None but the least conscientious **(is/are)** likely to object to establishing such a program in Myrtle Hill.
7. Unfortunately, nobody in the group **(is/are)** willing to propose the Neighborhood Watch as an alternative to a more aggressive Citizens' Patrol.
8. Everybody **(expect/expects)** someone else to speak in public.
9. Few **(has/have)** the confidence to oppose Mrs. Gorski.
10. All of them **(wish/wishes)** the others would speak.

22 C AGREEMENT: COLLECTIVE NOUNS AS SUBJECTS

22 C

Coll N

Term you need to know

COLLECTIVE NOUN. A noun that names a group: *team, choir, band, orchestra, jury, committee, faculty, family.*

Troubleshooting

Collective nouns used as subjects may be either singular or plural, depending on how you treat them in a given sentence or passage. At times, you must decide which of two acceptable versions of a sentence you prefer.

> The *Mihalik family* **believes** that *its* business is threatened by drug pushers on street corners.
>> [subject treated as singular]

> The *Mihalik family* **feel** that *their* business is threatened by drug pushers on street corners.
>> [subject treated as plural]

To be sure verbs and collective nouns agree in number . . .

> ➤ **Decide whether a collective noun used as a subject acts as a single unit (the *jury*) or as separate individuals or parts (the *twelve* members of the jury). Then be consistent.** If you decide the subject is singular, be sure its verb is singular. If the subject is plural, the verb should also be plural.

{**Singular**} The legal *committee* **expects** to determine the feasibility of Mrs. Mihalik's Citizens' Patrol.

{**Plural**}   The legal *committee* **raise** their hands to vote.

You will usually have fewer problems if you treat collective nouns as singular subjects. Notice how awkward the following sentences seem because the collective nouns are treated as plural forms.

The *family* **feel** that their interests are in jeopardy.

The *committee* **seem** unable to make up their minds.

Revise sentences like these either by making the collective subjects singular or more clearly plural.

{**Singular**}   The *family* **feels** that its interests are in jeopardy.

{**More clearly plural**}   The *members of the committee* **seem** unable to make up their minds.

The following chart may help you manage other collective subjects:

Subject	*Guideline*	*Examples*
Measurements	Singular as a unit; plural as individual objects.	*Five miles* is a long walk. *Five more miles* are ahead of us. *Six months* is the waiting period. *Six months* have passed.
Numbers	Singular in expressions of division and subtraction. Singular or plural in expressions of multiplication and addition.	*Four* divided by *two* is two. *Four* minus *two* leaves two. *Two* plus *two* is/are four. *Two* times *two* is/are four.
Words ending in *-ics*	School subjects are usually singular.	*Physics* is a tough major. *Economics* is a useful minor. *Linguistics* is popular today.
	Other *-ics* words vary; check a dictionary.	His *tactics* are shrewd. *Athletics* are expensive. *Ethics* is a noble study. Her *ethics* are questionable. *Politics* is fun. Francie's *politics* are radical.
data	Plural in formal writing; often singular in informal writing.	The *data* are reliable. The *data* is reliable.
number	Singular if preceded by *the;* plural if preceded by *a.*	The *number* has grown. A *number* have left.
public	Singular as a unit; plural as individual people.	The *public* is satisfied. The *public* are here in great numbers.

22 C

Coll N

EXERCISE 22.3

Determine whether the collective subjects in the following sentences are being treated as singular or plural. Then select the appropriate verb form.

1. The Officers Committee **(adjourn/adjourns)** to a smaller room to make its recommendation while the general public **(wait/waits)** in the church hall, twiddling their thumbs.
2. A majority of the committee **(is/are)** uncertain about their own opinions, so they discuss the issue at length.
3. Members of the Officers Committee **(agree/agrees)** that the legalities of the situation **(support/supports)** the establishment of an armed Citizens' Patrol, but that the ethics of such a proposal **(is/are)** debatable.
4. Data furnished by Mrs. Mihalik **(show/shows)** that the public always **(feel/feels)** safer after a patrol has been established in its neighborhood.
5. While the committee argues, the number of people in the main hall **(has/have)** actually increased.

22 D AGREEMENT: SUBJECTS SEPARATED FROM THEIR VERBS

Troubleshooting

22 D

Sep'd

Subject-verb agreement errors often occur when subjects are separated from their verbs by modifying words or phrases. Nouns nearer the verb can mistakenly seem like subjects.

> *Augie,* encouraged by his *allies* and a few interested police *officers,* **(suggest/suggests)** an alternative to a Citizens' Patrol—a Neighborhood Watch program.

Subject-verb agreement difficulties also arise when the subject of a sentence is an indefinite pronoun modified by a prepositional phrase. In cases like these, you have to pay attention both to the pronouns and the modifying phrases before choosing a verb.

> *Each* of the *proposals* **(has/have)** strong points.

To avoid disagreement between separated subjects and verbs . . .

▶ **Be sure that a verb agrees in number with its real subject, not with other words that may stand between the subject and the verb.** Modifying words or phrases often separate subjects and verbs, but such a separation does not change the subject-verb relationship.

subject   modifying phrase
Augie, encouraged by his allies and a few interested police *officers,*

verb
suggests an alternative to a Citizens' Patrol—a Neighborhood Watch program.

In the example above, the verb remains singular because its subject is singular. The plural nouns *allies* and *officers* have no bearing on subject-verb agreement.

It is easy to mistake such nouns or pronouns for subjects because, standing closer to the verb than the subject does, they seem to determine its number. Remember that the phrase between the subject and verb only describes the subject; it is not the subject itself.

> subject   modifying phrase
> The *neighbors,* including the owner of the sporting goods store, *Mrs.*
> verb
> *Gorski,* **believe** that Augie's suggestion of a Neighborhood Watch in Myrtle Hill might work.

➤ **Remember that if a pronoun is always singular (see the chart on p. 388), it remains singular even if it is modified by a phrase with a plural noun in it.** Confusion is especially likely when the subject of a sentence is an indefinite pronoun such as *each, everyone, all,* and *none* followed by a prepositional phrase. *Each,* for example, is usually singular in academic usage, even when followed by a prepositional phrase (though this convention is not observed in general usage):

> subject   verb
> *Each* of the ***proposals*** **has** strong points.

When the indefinite pronoun varies in number (words such as *all, most, none, some)*, the noun in the prepositional phrase determines whether the pronoun (and consequently the verb) is singular or plural.

22 D

Sep'd

{**Noun in prepositional phrase is singular**}   *All* of the ***controversy*** **is** about methods, not motives.

{**Noun in prepositional phrase is plural**}   *All* of the ***arguments*** **are** sincere.

If the indefinite pronoun is more clearly plural, so is the verb.

> ind. pron.   verb
> A *few* in the ***audience*** **expect** that nothing will be done.

EXERCISE 22.4

Choose the correct verb for academic writing.

1. The members of the Officers Committee, locked in discussion within the conference chamber, **(ignore/ignores)** the sounds of discussion coming from the main hall.
2. Each **(feel/feels)** the obligation to weigh the facts of the proposal carefully.
3. But the committee members, especially the chair, Velma Johnson, **(decide/decides)** it is time for a decision.
4. All of the committee members, eager to serve the public, **(vote/votes)** to support Ivan's suggestion for a Citizens' Patrol.
5. The officers, a proud group that feels it has done its duty, **(march/marches)** into the main hall with the decision.

22 E AGREEMENT: SUBJECTS DIFFICULT TO IDENTIFY

Term you need to know

EXPLETIVE CONSTRUCTIONS. The words *it* and *there* used as sentence lead-ins.

> **It is** going to be a day to remember.
>
> **There were** hundreds of spectators watching the demonstrators.

Troubleshooting

Occasionally you may simply lose track of a subject because the structure of a sentence is complicated or unusual. One such situation involves sentences or main clauses beginning with *here* and *there*. Another involves singular subjects tied to plural nouns by linking verbs. In either case, the verb choice can be baffling.

To be sure subjects and verbs agree in number . . .

➤ **Don't lose track of your subject in expletive constructions. When a sentence begins with *here* or *there*, the verb still agrees with the subject—which usually trails after it.**

>   verb   subject
> {Singular subject}   Here **is** a surprising *turn* of events.

>   verb   subject
> {Plural subject}   In the main hall, there **are** already *calls* for decisive action.

➤ **Don't be misled by linking verbs.** A linking verb agrees with its subject even when a singular subject is linked to a plural noun.

>   sing. subj.   l.v.   pl. noun
> The best *tribute* to the spirit of compromise **is** the concrete ***proposals*** coming from the residents.

>   sing. subj.   l.v.   pl. noun
> A *key* to the neighborhood's success **is** its concerned ***citizens.***

The same is true when a linking verb connects a plural subject to a singular noun, but such sentences sound normal and don't ordinarily raise questions of agreement.

>   pl. subj.   l.v.   sing. noun
> The many concrete *proposals* **are** a ***tribute*** to the spirit of compromise.

➤ **Don't be misled by inverted sentence order.** When a verb comes before its subject, the verb still agrees in number with that subject. Such structures occur most often in questions.

>   verb   subject
> **Have** their *deliberations* inspired other efforts?

verb   subject

Also involved **is** the *chairperson.*

➤ **Don't mistake singular expressions for plural ones.** Singular terms such as *series, segment, portion, fragment,* and *part* usually remain singular even when modified by plural words.

> A *series* of questions **is** posed by a lawyer in the crowd.

> A substantial *portion* of Myrtle Hill's citizens **is** determined to reclaim their neighborhood from thugs.

The words *majority* and *amount* do not fall under this guideline; they can be either singular or plural, depending upon their use.

> The *majority* **rules.**   [*majority* treated as singular]

> A *majority* of townspeople **endorse** strong measures against drug users and pushers.   [*majority* treated as plural]

◆ **FINE TUNING** ◆

One of the subtlest subject-verb agreement problems occurs within clauses that include the phrase *one of those who.* In academic English, the verb is plural because its subject is plural.

> Augie is one of those politicians who never **seem** [not **seems**] discouraged.

To understand the situation more clearly, rearrange the sentence:

> Of those politicians *who* never **seem** discouraged, Augie is one.

Now watch what happens if you add the word *only* to the mix.

> Augie is the only one of the politicians who **seems** eternally optimistic.

Why is the verb singular here? The subject of the verb *seems* is still the pronoun *who,* but its antecedent is now the singular pronoun *one,* not the plural *politicians.* Again, it helps to rearrange the sentence to see who is doing what to whom.

> Of the politicians, Augie is the only one who **seems** eternally optimistic.

Notice that the sentence makes little sense if arranged this way:

> Of the politicians who **seem** eternally optimistic, Augie is the only one.

22 E

Difficult

EXERCISE 22.5

Choose the correct verb.

1. The chair of the Officers Committee **(pound/pounds)** a gavel at the podium to restore order.

2. There **(is/are)** grumbles from the crowd, but the group **(take/takes)** their seats.
3. A portion of the audience **(ignore/ignores)** the call for order, but soon most of the citizens **(is/are)** willing to listen to the committee.
4. Surprised by the meeting's harmony **(is/are)** many people who had expected only loud disagreement.
5. "**(Do/does)** the good people of this neighborhood prefer a Neighborhood Watch to a Citizens' Patrol?" Velma Johnson, spokesperson for the officers, **(ask/asks)**.
6. The reply **(is/are)** a string of strong "yeas" and a few "nays."
7. Mrs. Gorski speaks: "I am one of those people who **(object/objects)** most strongly to violence in our neighborhood."
8. "But apparently I am not the only one of these citizens who **(recognize/ recognizes)** that we should cooperate with our local police force. I withdraw my proposal for a Citizens' Patrol."
9. "**(Do/Does)** anyone want to make a motion in support of a Neighborhood Watch program?" Velma Johnson asks.
10. Augie Burtinelli **(do/does)** and a large majority quickly **(approve/approves)** the proposal.

22 E

Difficult

23 Verb Tense, Voice, and Mood

A Verb tenses

B Tense consistency in sentences

C Tense consistency in longer passages

D Irregular verbs

E Active and passive voice

F Subjunctive mood

Terms you need to know

TENSE. That quality of a verb that expresses time and existence. Tense is expressed through changes in verb forms and endings (*see, seeing, saw; work, worked*) and through the use of auxiliaries (*had seen, will have seen; had worked, had been working*).

VOICE, ACTIVE AND PASSIVE. Verbs that take direct objects—that is, transitive verbs—can be either in **active** or in **passive voice.** They are in active voice when the subject in the sentence actually does what the verb describes.

        subject   action

Professor Bellona **invited** Frank to write a score for the play.

They are in passive voice when the action described by the verb is done *to* the subject.

  subject   action

Frank **was invited** by Professor Bellona to write a score for the play.

See Section 23E for more details about active and passive voice.

23 A VERB TENSES

Troubleshooting

Choosing the right form of some irregular verbs can be tricky (see Section 23C below), but most writers have little trouble finding the tense they need. Even complicated forms usually fall into place easily. Yet some writers use only the simplest verbs—even when a slightly more complex form might better express a relationship between two actions.

341

{**Vague**}   Frank **was** reading the play an hour when he **dozed** off.

{**More precise**}   Frank **had been reading** the play an hour when he **dozed** off.

Writers need to have a clear sense of how to handle the various forms and tenses of English verbs.

To manage verb tenses effectively . . .

▶ **Know the tenses and what they do.** Below is a chart of English tenses, past, present, and future in the active voice. (See also the more complete "Anatomy of a Verb" on pp. 359–360.)

What It Is Called	What the Tense Looks Like	What It Does
Past	I *answered* quickly.	Shows what has happened in the past at a particular time.
Past progressive	I *was answering* when the alarm went off.	Shows something happening in the past at the same time something else happened in the past.
Perfect	I *have answered* that question often.	Shows something that has happened more than once in the past.
Past perfect	I *had answered* the question twice when the alarm went off.	Shows what had already happened before another event, also in a past tense, occurred.
Present	I *answer* when I must.	Shows what happens or can happen now.
Present progressive	I *am answering* now.	Shows what is happening now.
Future	I *will answer* tomorrow.	Shows what may happen in the future.
Future progressive	I *will be answering* the phones all day.	Shows something that will continue to happen in the future.
Future perfect	I *will have answered* all the charges before you see me again.	Shows what will have happened by some particular time in the future.
Future perfect progressive	I *will have been answering* the charges for three hours by the time you arrive at noon.	Shows a continuing future action that precedes some other event also in the future.

23 A

Tense

These, of course, are only the basic verb forms in the active voice. Verbs look more complicated when they are in the **passive voice** (see also Section 23C).

As you can see in the following chart, the various forms of the passive are sometimes constructed with the aid of **auxiliary verbs** such as *will, be,* and *have.*

Other auxiliary verbs can be used to indicate possibility, necessity, permission, desire, capability, and so on. Such **modal auxiliaries** include *can, could, may, might, should, ought,* and *must.*

> Frank **can** write music.
>
> Frank **might** write music.
>
> Frank **must** write music.

What It Is Called	*What the Passive Looks Like*
Past	I *was invited* to her party last year.
Past progressive	I *was being invited* by Alicia when the phone went dead.
Perfect	I *have been invited* to many of her parties.
Past perfect	I *had been invited* to this one, too—or so I had assumed.
Present	I *am invited* to everyone's parties.
Present progressive	I *am being invited* now! That's Alicia calling, I'm sure.
Future	I *will be invited* tomorrow. Wrong number.
Future perfect	I *will have been invited* by this time tomorrow. You'll see.

▶ **Use perfect tenses appropriately.** Some writers avoid the perfect tense in all its forms. The result can be sentences less precise than they might be.

{**Vague**} Professor Bellona could not believe that Professor Sweno actually **asked** her to assist him in producing *Macbeth.* [simple past]

{**Precise**} Professor Bellona could not believe that Professor Sweno **had** actually **asked** her to assist him in producing *Macbeth.* [past perfect]

The perfect tenses enable a writer to show exactly how one event stands in relationship to another in time. Learn to use these forms; they make a difference.

{**Simple past**} The last three Shakespeare productions **failed** to win large audiences, threatening the future of the annual drama festival.

{**Past perfect**} Because the last three Shakespeare productions **had failed** to win large audiences, the future of the annual drama festival was now in jeopardy.

◆ **FINE TUNING** ◆

An appropriate choice of tense will sometimes depend upon the tense of a verbal phrase (see Section 24A). For example, participles—which are verb forms used as modifiers—have both present and present perfect forms.

Present	*Present perfect*
admitting	having admitted
considering	having considered

The present participle may show that something is happening at the same time as the action of the verb in the independent clause.

23 A

Tense

pres. participle

Admitting the need to enliven the shows to attract a larger audience,

independent clause

Professor Sweno still **seemed** cool to the idea of a musical version of *Macbeth*.

The present perfect may show that something has happened before the action of the verb in the independent clause.

pres. perfect participle

Having considered Professor Bellona's suggestion for several days,

independent clause

Dr. Sweno finally **agreed** to allow Frank Bacon to write some tunes for *Macbeth*.

EXERCISE 23.1

Replace the verb forms in parentheses below with more appropriate tenses. You may need to use a variety of verb forms (and auxiliaries), including passive and progressive forms. Treat all five sentences as part of a single paragraph.

1. On the Monday after he **(agree)** to write music for the spring Shakespeare festival, Frank had lunch with Drs. Bellona and Sweno to discuss *Macbeth*.
2. Professor Sweno explained that he would be **(present)** *Macbeth* as a musical only because the drama festival **(need)** to attract as large an audience as possible.
3. Professor Bellona confessed it **(be)** her idea to perform *Macbeth* as a musical to add some life to the aging work. "People who attend our show **(experience)** something remarkable."
4. Professor Sweno **(look)** worried when Professor Bellona mentioned "our show," but he **(agree)** that his department could not afford to lose money again on the Shakespeare play, or it **(spell)** an end to the spring festival entirely.
5. "If it takes a little music to save future productions—well, that is just the price we **(pay)**."

EXERCISE 23.2

For each verb in parentheses, furnish the tense indicated. Use active voice unless passive is specified.

1. After his lunch with Drs. Bellona and Sweno, Frank retired to his room to read Shakespeare's *Macbeth*, the play for which he **(agree—perfect)** to write a score.
2. In the tragedy, three witches tell Macbeth that someday he **(rule—future)** Scotland.

3. Macbeth quickly explains to his wife, the ambitious Lady Macbeth, what the witches (*promise*—**past perfect**) earlier that day.
4. Lady Macbeth, even more ambitious than her husband, immediately (*devise*—**present**) a plot to murder King Duncan that very night and then (*convince*—**present**) her husband to do the horrid deed.
5. Even though the plot succeeds, and Macbeth becomes king, the new ruler fears that he (*challenge*—**future, passive voice**) by other ambitious men.
6. For the witches also (*prophesy*—**past perfect**) that the children of Banquo (*be*—**future**) kings.
7. Macbeth decides that both Banquo and his son Fleance (*eliminate*—**future, passive voice with modal auxiliary "must"**).
8. And so one murder (*lead*—**present**) to another until the thanes of Scotland, angered by Macbeth's bloody rule, (*conspire*—**present**) to remove the tyrant and his wife from the throne.
9. Macbeth is finally slain by Macduff, whose wife and children earlier in the play (*slaughter*—**past perfect, passive voice**) at Macbeth's orders.
10. "Gruesome stuff," Frank (*mutter*—**past**) to himself after closing his heavy edition of Shakespeare.

23 B CONSISTENCY OF TENSES IN SENTENCES

Term you need to know

PARALLEL STRUCTURE. A sentence arrangement that gives related words, clauses, and phrases an identical or similar pattern. The shared pattern reinforces the notion that these ideas are in some way related or equivalent.

> The college's marching band
> > **played** out of tune,
> > **marched** out of step, and
> yet **maintained** straight faces.

Troubleshooting

Verbs that serve the same subject often share the same verb tense and form. When they don't, sentences may be hard to read. The problem is often caused by faulty parallelism.

When a single subject is followed by one or more verbs . . .

➤ **Check that verbs are comparable in form.** Don't shift the tenses or forms of parallel verbs needlessly. In the following example, the verbs describing Dr. Bellona's action shift from past tense to past progressive tense without a good reason. They lack parallelism.

{**Lack of parallelism**}   Dr. Bellona **explained** to Frank that she knows he is a gifted musician and **was asking** him to write music for the spring Shakespeare production.

Subject	*Verb*
Dr. Bellona	explained
	was asking

The sentence reads more smoothly with the verbs made parallel in form.

{**Revised for parallelism**}   Dr. Bellona **explained** to Frank that she knows he is a gifted musician and **asked** him to write music for the spring Shakespeare festival.

Subject	*Verb*
Dr. Bellona	explained
	asked

Of course, changes in verb tense within a sentence are appropriate when they indicate obvious shifts in time.

> Currently, Frank **is scoring** the first scene, and soon **will be writing** the lyrics.

> Within a few days he **will have written** musical themes for the minor characters, and then **will compose** a noisy dance number for the banquet scene.

---

23 C

In Pass

EXERCISE 23.3

Correct any problems in tense consistency in the following sentences. The verbs are in boldface.

1. Frank **erased** three bars of a song, **gets** up to sharpen his pencil, and **hits** the mute button on the TV remote control.
2. Frank's mother **boasted** to all the relatives that her son had been asked to write a musical and **was telling** everyone she could reach.
3. Frank's father **wants** his boy to be a doctor and **is hoping** he may still **go** to medical school and **will make** something of himself.
4. Frank soon **will be speaking** to his father and **describe** his plans to go to New York after he graduates.
5. He **expects** his father **will object,** but **is hoping** he **won't.**

---

23 C   TENSE CONSISTENCY IN LONGER PASSAGES

Troubleshooting

Almost anything you write will incorporate past, present, and future perspectives. But writers are sometimes inconsistent about their choice of tenses in longer passages; they confuse their readers by pointlessly switching from tense to tense. Such shifts are best avoided.

To keep verb tenses consistent . . .

➤ **Establish a dominant point of view.** The following paragraph shows what can happen when verb forms shift inappropriately.

> Frank Bacon, a music major, **was surprised** when Diana Bellona, an ambitious young professor (and fencing coach), **summons** him to her office. Although **he had taken** a drama course from her when he **was** a freshman, he **had not done** well and never **expects** to see her again. He **wasn't** much of a fencer either, so he **has** no idea why he **is called** to her office. She **smiled** when he **walked** in and **asks** him to have a seat. Frank **was feeling** uneasy, as if he **did** something he **shouldn't have,** but **didn't know** what.

The passage sounds confusing because it jumps between two time frames. The first presents Frank's story as if it were happening at the present moment: Professor Bellona *summons* Frank; she *asks* him to sit down. But the second time frame in the passage presents events as if they have already happened: Frank *was surprised;* Professor Bellona *smiled* when he *walked* in. A revision is needed. Here is the passage with the action occurring consistently in the past.

> Frank **was surprised** when Diana Bellona, an ambitious young professor (and fencing coach), **summoned** him to her office. Although **he had taken** a drama course from her when he **was** a freshman, he **had not done** well and never **expected** to see her again. He **wasn't** much of a fencer either, so he **had** no idea why he **had been called** to her office. She **smiled** when he **walked in** and **asked** him to have a seat. Frank **felt** uneasy, as if he **had done** something he **shouldn't have,** but **didn't know** what.

The same passage may also be narrated as if Frank's appearance in Professor Bellona's office is occurring in present time. Notice, however, that this shift does not simply put all verbs in the present tense.

> Frank **is surprised** when Diana Bellona, an ambitious young professor (and fencing coach), **summons** him to her office. Although **he had taken** a drama course from her when he **was** a freshman, he **had not done** well and never **expected** to see her again. He **wasn't** much of a fencer either, so he **has** no idea why he **has been called** to her office. She **smiles** when he **walks** in and **asks** him to have a seat. Frank **feels** uneasy, as if he **has done** something he **shouldn't have,** but **doesn't know** what.

23 C

In Pass

EXERCISE 23.4

Revise the following paragraph to make the tenses more consistent. You may find it helpful to emphasize the present tense throughout the passage—but not every verb ought to be in the present. (Specific events in a literary work are usually described in the present tense: After Macbeth *kills* King Duncan, he *seizes* the throne.) Verbs have been boldfaced for your convenience.

(1) *Macbeth*, one of Shakespeare's most popular plays, **is** also one of his shortest; almost all of Shakespeare's other tragedies **were** at

least a thousand lines longer. (2) To explain this difference, some scholars **have been arguing** that the existing text of *Macbeth* **has been** a version shortened for stage production. (3) Others **are claiming** that the tragedy **was written** especially for King James I, who **preferred** short plays. (4) Whatever the explanation for its brevity, the drama **moved** like a predator on the stage, charging breathlessly through its first three acts. (5) In a matter of moments, it **portrays** rebellion, assassination, and murder most foul. (6) The smoke of a battle **has** barely **cleared** when Macbeth **encountered** three witches who **promise** him the throne of Scotland. (7) Almost immediately, his wife **persuades** him—against his good conscience—to act, and he **has murdered** King Duncan while the old man **sleeps.** (8) But Macbeth **will sleep** no more; the play **gives** him little respite until after he **murders** his friend Banquo. (9) Only in the fourth act **did** the pace slacken, but the action **rose** again in the fifth toward an intense and violent conclusion. (10) If *Macbeth* **left** audiences asking for more, it **may be** because it **offers** just a little less.

23 D   IRREGULAR VERBS

Terms you need to know

PRINCIPAL PARTS OF A VERB. The three basic forms of a verb from which all tenses are built: *infinitive, past,* and *past participle.*

INFINITIVE. The base form of a verb, what it looks like when preceded by the word *to: to walk, to go, to choose.*

PAST. The simplest form of a verb to show action that has already occurred: *walked, went, chose.*

PAST PARTICIPLE. The form a verb takes when it is accompanied by an *auxiliary verb* to show a more complicated past tense: *had* **walked,** *will have* **gone,** *would have* **chosen,** *was* **hanged,** *might have* **broken.**

REGULAR VERBS. Verbs that form their past and past participle forms (see immediately above) simply by adding *-d* or *-ed* to the infinitive.

Infinitive	*Past*	*Past Participle*
talk	talk*ed*	talk*ed*
coincide	coincide*d*	coincide*d*
advertise	advertise*d*	advertise*d*

IRREGULAR VERBS. Verbs that do not form their past and past participle forms (see Principal parts of a verb) by adding *-d* or *-ed* to the infinitive. They change their forms in various ways; a few even have the same form for all three principal parts. Irregular verbs are very common.

Infinite	Past	Past Participle
burst	burst	burst
drink	drank	drunk
arise	arose	arisen
lose	lost	lost

AUXILIARY VERBS. Verbs, usually some form of *be, do,* or *have,* that combine with other verbs to show various relationships of tense, voice, mood, and so on. Auxiliaries are sometimes called *helping verbs.* Auxiliary verbs described as **modal** are used to indicate possibility, necessity, permission, desire, capability, and so on. Such modal auxiliaries include *can, could, may, might, should, ought,* and *must.*

Troubleshooting

At one time or another almost everyone stumbles over verb forms: is it *drove* or *driven, swam* or *swum, hung* or *hanged?* Since the English verbs used most often tend to be irregular, we gain command over most of these forms quickly. But certain verbs are persistently troublesome. With such verbs, you may need help.

To be sure the form of an irregular verb is correct . . .

➤ **Consult a dictionary or check the following list of irregular verbs.** The following list of troublesome irregular English verbs gives you three forms: (1) the present tense, (2) the simple past tense, and (3) the past participle. (The past participle is used with auxiliary verbs to form verb phrases: *I have ridden, I had ridden, I will have ridden.*)

Most problems occur in distinguishing between the past tense and the past participle (*wore, worn; lay, lain*). As you will discover from the list, sometimes these forms will be identical (*brought, brought.*) And sometimes there may be more than one acceptable form (*dived, dove*). Your safest bet, when in doubt, is to check the list. Errors in verb form irritate readers.

23 D

Irreg

Present	Past	Past Participle
arise	arose	arisen
bear (carry)	bore	borne
bear (give birth)	bore	borne, born
become	became	become
begin	began	begun
bite	bit	bitten, bit
blow	blew	blown
break	broke	broken
bring	brought	brought
burst	burst	burst
buy	bought	bought
catch	caught	caught
choose	chose	chosen
cling	clung	clung

Present	*Past*	*Past Participle*
come	came	come
creep	crept	crept
dig	dug	dug
dive	dived, dove	dived
do	did	done
draw	drew	drawn
dream	dreamed, dreamt	dreamed, dreamt
drink	drank	drunk
drive	drove	driven
eat	ate	eaten
fall	fell	fallen
find	found	found
fly	flew	flown
forget	forgot	forgotten
forgive	forgave	forgiven
freeze	froze	frozen
get	got	got, gotten
give	gave	given
go	went	gone
grow	grew	grown
hang (a person)	hanged, hung	hanged, hung
hang (an object)	hung	hung
know	knew	known
lay (to place)	laid	laid
lead	led	led
leave	left	left
lend	lent	lent
lie (to recline)	lay	lain
light	light, lit	lighted, lit
lose	lost	lost
pay	paid	paid
plead	pleaded	pleaded
prove	proved	proved, proven
ride	rode	ridden
ring	rang, rung	rung
rise	rose	risen
run	ran	run
say	said	said
see	saw	seen
set	set	set
shake	shook	shaken
shine	shone, shined	shone, shined
show	showed	showed, shown
shrink	shrank, shrunk	shrunk
sing	sang, sung	sung
sink	sank, sunk	sunk, sunken
sit	sat	sat
slide	slid	slid
speak	spoke	spoken
spring	sprang, sprung	sprung
stand	stood	stood

23 D

Irreg

Present	*Past*	*Past Participle*
steal	stole	stolen
sting	stung	stung
swear	swore	sworn
swim	swam, swum	swum
swing	swung	swung
take	took	taken
tear	tore	torn
throw	threw	thrown
wake	waked, woke	waked, woken
wear	wore	worn
wring	wrung	wrung
write	wrote	written

The glossary in the back of the handbook treats various troublesome verbs, including some in the list above, in greater detail. Check the entries for *can/may; get/got/gotten; lay/lie; sit/set;* and so on.

EXERCISE 23.5

Choose the correct verb form from the choices in parentheses. In some cases, you may want to consult the glossary for assistance.

1. Taking a seat in a cluttered office, Travis nervously asked Professor Sweno, "**(Can/May)** I audition for a part in *Macbeth?*"
2. "You might, had you **(shown/shone)** talent of any kind," said Avery Sweno. "But given my low personal regard for wrestlers like you, I'd sooner be **(hanged/hung)** than allow one to audition for *Macbeth.*"
3. At these remarks, Travis **(rose/risen)** to his feet.
4. "**(Set/Sit)** down, please, before you break something," Professor Sweno warned. He seemed to **(bear/borne)** a grudge against the student.
5. Travis **(shook/shaked)** with anger.
6. He pulled a resumé out of his pocket and **(sat/set)** it before Professor Sweno.
7. "I have **(got/gotten)** plenty of acting experience in summer stock; I even **(did/done)** Shakespeare once," said Travis.
8. "The company must have **(fell/fallen)** on hard times to recruit an actor as bulky as you," Professor Sweno replied.
9. "I was **(chose/chosen)** over a dozen other actors for the part of Orlando— the wrestler in *As You Like It.*"
10. "That may be, but you have not yet **(proved/proven)** your ability to me, Mr. Beckwith. The real question is have you ever **(sang/sung)** on the stage before?"

23 E

Voice

23 E ACTIVE AND PASSIVE VOICE

Terms you need to know

TRANSITIVE VERB. A verb that takes a direct object. In a sentence with a transitive verb, the subject acts upon someone or something—the object; without this object to receive the action, the sentence sounds incomplete.

subj.   verb   object

{Transitive}   David **set** the music on the stand.

[You can **set** *something*.]

INTRANSITIVE VERB. A verb that does not take a direct object. This means the action of an intransitive verb does not pass on to someone or something; the sentence is complete even without an object.

{Intransitive}   I **slept** well.

[You cannot **sleep** something. *Well* is an adverb describing how you slept.]

David **sat** down.

[You cannot **sit** *something*.]

VOICE. Transitive verbs can be either in **active** or **passive voice.** They are in active voice when the subject in the sentence actually does what the verb describes.

subject action

Kyle **managed** the advertising.

They are in passive voice when the action described by the verb is done *to* the subject.

subject   action

The advertising **was managed** by Kyle.

23 E
Voice

Troubleshooting

Although passive voice is often necessary, many writers use it too often. By eliminating passive constructions, you can often turn vague sentences into stronger, more lively ones. Active sentences usually are more economical than passive ones. The action moves more directly from subject through verb to the object. To revise effectively, you need to recognize passive voice and—when appropriate—know how to make passive verbs active.

To change a passive verb to an active one . . .

➤ **Identify the passive verbs.** In a sentence with a passive verb, the subject doesn't perform the action. Instead, the action is *done* to the subject; the object switches to the subject position.

subject   action

Jenny **was selected** by Professor Bellona to be stage manager for *Macbeth.*

subject   action

She **had been nominated** for the job by Travis.

Passive verbs are always formed with some form of *be* + the past participle.

be + past participle

The van **had been wrecked** by Sister Anne.

be + past participle

The accident **was caused** by faulty brakes.

Of course, not every sentence with a form of the verb *to be* is passive, especially when *be* is used as a linking verb.

> She **was** unhappy that the damage to the van **had been** so great.

Nor is every sentence with a past participle passive. Perfect tenses, for example, use the past participle.

> Sister Anne **had driven** for ten years without an accident.
> [past perfect]

To identify a passive verb form, look for **both** the past participle *and* a form of *be*.

> The van **had been loaded** with flats and props for *Macbeth* when it **was wrecked.**

➤ **When you have identified a passive form, locate the word in the sentence that actually performs the action. Make it the subject.** When you revise the sentence this way, the original subject usually becomes the object. Notice that the revised version is a few words shorter than the original.

{**Original—passive**} Jenny **was selected** by *Professor Bellona* to be stage manager for *Macbeth*.

{**Revised—active**} Professor Bellona **selected** *Jenny* as stage manager for *Macbeth*.

Not every passive verb can or should be made active. Sometimes you simply don't know who or what performs an action.

> Hazardous road conditions **had been forecast** the morning Sister Anne ventured out. To make things worse, oil **had been spilled** at the intersection where her accident occurred.

> She **had been assured,** however, that it was safe to drive.

> The van **had been loaded** with flats and props for *Macbeth* when it **was destroyed.**

In this last example, you might revise the second verb, but leave the first alone.

> The van **had been loaded** with flats and props for *Macbeth* when Sister Anne **destroyed** it.

Passive verbs are useful constructions when *who* did an action may be less important than *to whom it was done*. A passive verb puts the *victim* (so to speak) right up front in the sentence where it gets attention.

> *Sister Anne* **was featured** on the TV nightly news.

> *She* **was interviewed** by several reporters.

The passive is also customary in many expressions where a writer or speaker may choose to be vague about assigning responsibility.

> Flight 107 **has been cancelled.**

> The check **was lost** in the mail.

When you need passives, use them. But most of the time, you can improve a sentence by changing a passive construction to an active one. (See Section 17C.)

23 E

Voice

> **EXERCISE 23.6**

Underline all the passive verbs in the following sentences; then revise those passive verbs that might be better stated in the active voice. Some sentences may require no revision.

1. Students working on Professor Sweno's production of *Macbeth* began to fear that the show had been cursed by the ghost of Banquo.
2. It was bad enough that the lead in the show had been given by Professor Sweno to a nervous student prone to laryngitis.
3. But then strange things had occurred.
4. Macduff's nose was broken in practice by a collapsing set.
5. Francie Knipstein was arrested by Officer Klinkhamer on her way to dress rehearsal because she looked "suspicious" in her Lady Macbeth costume.
6. Some of Frank Bacon's music was accidentally shredded by Professor Bellona's secretary.
7. The stage curtains had been singed by the witches' smoking cauldron.
8. In one rehearsal, Macbeth's head had even fallen off a pike and rolled into the audience.
9. And the entire cast had been infected by lice in the costumes rented by Professor Bellona.
10. Just as legend had it, the Scottish play had been cursed!

23 F

Mood

> **EXERCISE 23.7**

Select a paragraph you have written and underline all the passive verbs. Then rewrite the paragraph, making passive verbs active whenever such a revision makes a sentence livelier and more economical.

23 F SUBJUNCTIVE MOOD

Term you need to know

MOOD. A term used to describe how a writer intends a statement to be taken: either as a fact (the **indicative** mood), as a command (the **imperative** mood), or as a wish, desire, supposition, or improbability (the **subjunctive** mood). Mood is indicated by a change in verb form.

Indicative: The director **was** careful.

Imperative: Be careful!

Subjunctive: If the director **were** more careful . . .

Troubleshooting

Even if you don't know what the subjunctive is you are probably using it correctly at least half the time. You employ the subjunctive mood whenever you say *God bless* [instead of *blesses*] *you* or use the expressions *If I were* [not *was*] *you* or *As it were* [not *was*]. In English, subjunctive verb forms survive mainly in habitual expressions like these. Where employing the subjunctive requires a deliberate choice, it is fading from usage, replaced by the more familiar indicative forms. Still, using the subjunctive correctly where English preserves it is not especially difficult; indeed, the subjunctive is one of those points of grammar more troublesome to explain than to employ.

The subjunctive is used to express ideas that aren't factual or certain or to state wishes or desires. The subjunctive also appears in clauses following statements of request, demand, suggestion, or recommendation. In the abstract, you may find these occasions hard to recognize; in practice, they are easy to spot.

To use the subjunctive . . .

➤ **Identify situations where the subjunctive might be used.** The subjunctive is often used

- In statements that express wishes.

I wish it **were** [not **was**] bedtime.

Would he **were** [not **was**] here!

- In *if* clauses that describe situations that are contrary to fact, hypothetical, or improbable.

If Travis **were** [not **was**] a wealthy actor, he'd drive a Cadillac Allanté.

If Jenny **were** [not **was**] to call, Travis would pretend not to hear the phone.

If it **were** [not **was**] to rain, Professor Sweno would move the meeting indoors.

- In *that* clauses following verbs that make demands, requests, recommendations, or motions. These sentences will often seem formal or legalistic.

Professor Sweno demanded *that* his cast **be** silent.

"I ask only *that* all actors **give** their best in the performance," he said.

"It is necessary *that* you all **be** at the dress rehearsal tomorrow."

After Sweno left, Travis moved *that* the crew **send** their director a basket of figs.

- In certain common expressions.

Be that as it may	**Come** what may
As it **were**	Peace **be** with you

➤ **Select the subjunctive form of the verb.** As the examples above suggest, forms of the subjunctive are relatively simple. For all verbs, the present subjunctive is simply the base form of the verb—that is, the present infinitive form without *to.*

Verb	*Present subjunctive*
to be	be
to give	give
to send	send
to bless	bless

23 F

Mood

The base form is used even in the third person singular where you might ordinarily expect a verb to take another form.

> It is essential that *Connie* **have** [not **has**] her lines memorized by tomorrow.

> Sweno also insisted that *Travis* **be** [not **is**] on time for rehearsal.

For all verbs except **be,** the past subjunctive is the same as the simple past tense.

Verb	*Present Subjunctive*
to give	gave
to send	sent
to bless	blessed

For *be,* the past subjunctive is always *were.* This is true even in the first and third person singular, where you might expect the form to be *was.*

{First person}   I wish I **were** [not **was**] the director.

{Second person}   Suppose *you* **were** the director.

{Third person}   I wish *she* **were** [not **was**] the director.

EXERCISE 23.8

23 F

Mood

In the following sentences, underline all verbs in the subjunctive mood.

1. Just days before the opening night of *Macbeth,* Diana Bellona received a terse message from Professor Sweno: "It is essential that you be in my office at 2:00 P.M. today."
2. "If I were a betting woman," the ambitious Professor Bellona thought to herself, "I'd guess that Sweno is about to put me in charge of the production of *Macbeth.*"
3. And just as Professor Bellona suspected, Professor Sweno insisted at the meeting that she take over as director of the spring drama festival.
4. "You see," he explained, "Our Macbeth is down with laryngitis again. It is necessary that he be replaced immediately."
5. "If only he were less prone to throat infections! I have no choice."
6. "But where will you find a new Macbeth only days before the play opens? Far be it from me to criticize your decision, but if I were you, I'd cancel the event immediately."
7. "I wish it were possible," said Professor Sweno. "But come what may, the show must go on."
8. "But if I were to become director, what problems would that solve?" asked Professor Bellona.
9. "It is necessary that you take over as director," Avery Sweno explained, "because—I will play Macbeth!"
10. "If I were you," he continued, "I'd be thrilled at the prospect of directing."

EXERCISE 23.9

Write five sentences that include verbs in the subjunctive mood. Underline the subjunctive verbs and their subjects and then write another sentence with the verb (and same subject) in the indicative mood. For example:

{**Subjunctive**}   I wish *Thalia* **were** more careful with my camera.

{**Indicative**}   *Thalia* **was** careful with my camera.

ANATOMY OF A VERB: *to pay*

Principal Parts

Infinitive: pay
Past tense: paid
Past participle: paid

Tense

Present: I pay
Present Progressive: I am paying
Present Perfect: I have paid

Past: I paid

Past Progressive: I was paying
Past Perfect: I had paid

Future: I will pay
Future Progressive: I will have been paying
Future Perfect: I will have paid

Voice

Active: I pay
               you paid
               he will pay

Passive: I am paid
               you were paid
               he will be paid

Mood

Indicative: I pay.

Imperative: Pay!

Subjunctive: I suggested that he pay me.

Person/Number

First person, singular:	**I** pay
Second person, singular:	**you** pay
Third person, singular:	**he** pays
	she pays
	it pays
First person, plural:	**we** pay
Second person, plural:	**you** pay
Third person, plural:	**they** pay

Nonfinite forms

Infinitives: to pay [present tense, active voice]
to be paying [progressive tense, active voice]
to have paid [past tense, active voice]
to have been paying [past progressive tense, active voice]

to be paid [present tense, passive voice]
to have been paid [past tense, passive voice]

Participles: paying [present tense, active voice]
having paid [past tense, active voice]

being paid [present tense, passive voice]
paid, having been paid [past tense, passive voice]

Gerunds: paying [present tense, active voice]
having paid [past tense, active voice]

being paid [present tense, passive voice]
having been paid [past tense, passive voice]

23 F

Mood

24 Verbals

A Verbals

B Verbals and sentence fragments

C Split infinitives

Terms you need to know

VERBALS. Verb forms that act like nouns, adjectives, or adverbs. The three kinds of verbals are **infinitives, participles,** and **gerunds.**

INFINITIVE. A verbal that can be identified by the word *to* preceding the base form of a verb: *to seek; to find.* Infinitives also take other forms to show aspects of time and voice: *to be seeking; to have found; to have been found.*

PARTICIPLE. A verb form used as a modifier. The present participle ends with *-ing.* For regular verbs, the past participle ends with *-ed;* for irregular verbs, the form of the past participle varies.

GERUND. A verb form used as a noun: *smiling, biking, walking.*

24 A WHAT ARE VERBALS?

Verbals are verb forms that act like another part of speech (nouns, adjectives, adverbs). Like verbs, they can express time (present, past), take objects, and form phrases. The three types of verbals are infinitives, participles, and gerunds.

Infinitives act as nouns, adjectives, and adverbs.

{**Infinitive as noun**}   **To direct** a play is not easy.   [subject of the sentence]

{**Infinitive as adjective**}   Travis had many lines **to learn.**   [modifies the noun *lines*]

{**Infinitive as adverb**}   Travis smiled **to ease** the pain.   [modifies the verb *smiles*]

An infinitive can also serve as an **absolute,** that is, a phrase, standing alone, that modifies an entire sentence.

> *To make* a long story short, opening night recalled the sinking of the *Titanic.*

In some sentence constructions, the characteristic marker of the infinitive—*to*— is deleted.

The cast and crew purchased aspirin to help them **[to] deal** with the disastrous reviews.

Participles serve only as modifiers and take various forms, depending on whether the verb they are derived from is regular or irregular. Here are the participle forms of two verbs:

perform (a regular verb)	**Participles**
Present, active:	performing
Present, passive:	being performed
Past, active:	performed
Past, passive:	having been performed
write (an irregular verb)	**Participles**
Present, active:	writing
Present, passive:	being written
Past, active:	written
Past, passive:	having been written

(For the forms of some irregular past participles, check the list of irregular verbs on pp. 349–351.)

24 A

Verbals

As modifiers, participles may be single words.

Smiling, Brian McVicker left the auditorium to write his review.
[participle modifies Brian]

But participles often take objects, complements, and modifiers to form verbal phrases. Such phrases play an important role in structuring sentences.

Writing *his review,* Brian smiled at his own cleverness.

The actors, ***knowing*** *they had worked hard,* celebrated despite their dismal show.

Like an infinitive, a participle can also serve as an **absolute,** that is, a phrase, standing alone, that modifies an entire sentence.

*All things **considered,*** the actors didn't regret their efforts.

Because most **gerunds** end in *-ing,* they look exactly like the present participle.

{**Gerund**}   **Smiling** contributes to good mental health.

{**Participle**}   A **smiling** critic, however, is dangerous.

The important difference, of course, is that gerunds function as nouns while participles act as modifiers. Gerunds usually appear in the present tense, but can take other forms.

Having been treated unfairly angered Brian.
[Gerund in past tense, passive voice acting as subject of the sentence]

Being asked to write the review was an opportunity Brian wouldn't have missed.

     [Gerund in present tense, passive voice]

Gerunds have many functions.

{**Gerund as subject**}   ***Being*** *objective* now posed a problem for Brian McVicker.

{**Gerund as object**}   He enjoyed ***reviewing*** *movies and plays.*

{**Gerund as appositive**}   Brian needed to resist his great weakness, ***writing*** *scathing reviews.*

                                 subject   complement

{**Gerunds as subject and complement**}   *Reviewing* was ***seeing*** *things critically.*

EXERCISE 24.1

Identify the boldfaced words or phrases as infinitives, participles, or gerunds.

1. Professor Bellona sighed, **regretting** all her **misfired** schemes for enlivening Shakespeare's classic tragedy, *Macbeth.*
2. **Identified** in the program as the director of *Macbeth,* she was now completely associated with the **failed** show.
3. **To have expected** otherwise had been naive on her part.
4. It seems that she was no better at **directing** than Professor Sweno was at **acting.**
5. **To be** charitable, his performance in the **leading** role had been almost bearable, **evoking** only a few catcalls and hisses.
6. His **singing** of Frank Bacon's tunes was another matter entirely.
7. But Professor Sweno's performance wasn't the only cause for laughter. One of the witches, **tripping** over a riser, had fallen into the bubbling cauldron.
8. **To make** matters worse, the audience thought the **tripping** and **disappearing** into the pot were part of the show and applauded.
9. "**Seeing** *Macbeth: The Musical* is **believing** it" the **advertising** posters for the show had proclaimed.
10. Professor Bellona was inclined now **to disbelieve** it.

    24 B

    Frags

24 B VERBALS AND SENTENCE FRAGMENTS

Troubleshooting

An important difference between verbs and verbals is that the verbals alone cannot make phrases into complete sentences. For that reason, verbals are sometimes described as **nonfinite** (that is, unfinished) verbs. A complete sentence requires a **finite** verb—a verb that changes form to indicate person, number, and tense.

{**Nonfinite verb—infinitive**} **To have found** security . . .

{**Finite verb**} I have **found** security.

{**Nonfinite verb—participle**} The actor **performing** the scene . . .

{**Finite verb**} The actor **performs** the scene.

{**Nonfinite verb—gerund**} **Directing** a play . . .

{**Finite verb**} She **directed** the play.

A verbal phrase standing alone is a sentence fragment.

> Brian now had an opportunity for revenge. ***Having been criticized*** *in the past by Professors Sweno and Bellona.*

Occasionally, such constructions are appropriate.

> Avery Sweno loved the theater—every bit of it. **Coaching the actors. Blocking the scenes. Designing the sets. Acting.** It made life worthwhile.

But in academic writing, fragments usually need to be edited.

To turn a verbal phrase into a complete sentence . . .

➤ **Attach the verbal phrase to a complete sentence or make the phrase itself a complete sentence.** Quite often, a comma, colon, or dash is adequate to join a verbal phrase to an appropriate sentence.

{**Fragment**} Brian now had an opportunity for revenge. ***Having been criticized*** *in the past by Professors Sweno and Bellona.*

{**Revised**} Brian now had an opportunity for revenge, ***having been criticized*** *in the past by Professors Sweno and Bellona.*

{**Fragment**} **To be fair to the actors.** That was more important than getting even.

{**Revised**} **To be fair to the actors**—that was more important than getting even.

Turning the verbal phrase into a sentence will also repair the fragment.

{**Fragment**} The actors celebrated despite their wretched opening night performance. **Knowing they had done their best.**

{**Revised**} The actors celebrated despite their wretched opening night performance. **They knew they had done their best.**

EXERCISE 24.2

In the following passages, correct any verbal phrases that are sentence fragments. Defend any fragments you think are appropriate.

1. Professor Bellona preferred not to think about the reviews. Considering what they were likely to say.
2. Other matters were on her mind. Helping Professor Sweno. Encouraging the cast. Making the show really work.
3. She admitted to herself that *Macbeth* had been fun. Especially working with the young actors.

24 B

Frags

4. She had learned a lot from Professor Sweno. How to cast the roles, how to block a scene well, how to delegate authority to crew members.
5. To make *Macbeth* a hit. That would be her goal now.
6. Having Lady Macbeth dance during the banquet scene. That was probably a mistake.
7. In fact, several of the musical numbers needed to be cut. To improve the pace. Provided that the cuts didn't offend Frank Bacon.
8. Frank deserved plenty of credit. Having written a great deal of good music in a very short time.
9. But some of the musicians and singers Frank had to work with weren't very talented. To be honest.
10. Still, the show had potential. To be a hit.

24 C SPLIT INFINITIVES

Term you need to know

SPLIT INFINITIVE. An infinitive interrupted by an adverb: to *boldly* go; to *really* try.

Troubleshooting

Infinitives cause few difficulties. One problem, though, is quite famous: the matter of the **split infinitive.** According to some writers, it is incorrect to separate the *to* in an infinitive from its verb. Split infinitives are, however, such common constructions in English that many writers use them without apology. Here are some guidelines to help you through this minor, but troublesome point.

To avoid splitting an infinitive . . .

➤ **Check that no words separate the *to* in an infinitive from its verb.** If a sentence sounds awkward because a word or phrase splits an infinitive, move the interrupter.

{**Split infinitive**}   Brian's intention in his review was *to, the best he could, warn* other audiences about the play.

{**Revised**}   Brian's intention in his review was **to warn** other audiences about the play *the best he could.*

Revise any split infinitives that cause modification problems. In the following sentence, for example, *only* seems to modify *describe* when it should refer to *the worst parts.*

{**Confusing**}   Brian intended *to only describe* the worst parts of *Macbeth: The Musical.*

{**Clearer**}   Brian intended *to describe* only the worst parts of *Macbeth: The Musical.*

Consider too, whether a word dividing an infinitive is needed at all. Where the interrupting word is a weak intensifier that adds nothing to a sentence (*really, actually*), cut it.

{**Weak intensifier**}   Brian found it possible to **really** enjoy plays and movies that were excruciatingly bad.

{**Intensifier cut**}   Brian found it possible to enjoy plays and movies that were excruciatingly bad.

But in many situations, split infinitives are neither awkward nor confusing, so revising them won't necessarily improve a sentence.

{**Split infinitive**}   Words fail *to adequately **describe*** the incompetence of the acting.

{**Revised**}   Words fail *to **describe*** *adequately* the incompetence of the acting.

In academic and business writing, it's probably best to keep *to* and the verb together because some readers do object strongly to violations of the rule. Many of them would rather split a gut than an infinitive.

EXERCISE 24.3

Find the split infinitives in the following sentences and revise them. Decide which revisions are necessary, which optional. Be prepared to defend your decisions.

24 C

Split Inf

1. Brian McVicker decided to immediately tear up the first draft of his review after he read it.
2. He had allowed his personal feelings toward Professors Bellona and Sweno to too much intrude upon his professional judgment.
3. After all, it was a reviewer's responsibility to always strive for fairness.
4. His problem was how to really convey how bad the show was without seeming to only be responding to his personal feelings.
5. To viciously attack the entire show because of a personal vendetta would be to unfairly criticize many hard-working students.
6. But to too enthusiastically endorse *Macbeth* would be to badly, almost criminally, misrepresent the show.
7. Brian decided to carefully rework his entire evaluation.
8. His original intention was to only comment on what was wrong with the play conceptually.
9. But in writing his revision, he found it necessary to actually describe acting and staging problems that would be all too obvious to anyone watching the play.
10. To do that meant writing a tough, but fair evaluation.

25 Plurals, Possessives, and Articles

A Plurals

B Possessive nouns and pronouns

C Possessives before gerunds

D *A* or *an*

Terms you need to know

NOUN. A word that names a person, place, thing, idea, or quality. In sentences, nouns can serve as subjects, objects, complements, appositives, and even modifiers.

PRONOUN. A word that acts like a noun, but doesn't name a specific person, place, or thing—*I, you, he, it, they, who, this, whose,* and so on.

CASE. The form a noun or pronoun takes to indicate its function in a sentence. Nouns have two cases: the **possessive** form to show ownership and the **common** form to serve all other uses. Pronouns have three forms: **subjective, objective,** and **possessive.**

ARTICLES. The words *the, a,* and *an* used before a noun. *The* is called a **definite** article because it points to something specific: *the* book; *the* church. *A* and *an* are **indefinite articles** because they point more generally: *a* book; *a* church.

25 A PLURALS

Troubleshooting

Most plurals in English are formed by adding *-s* or *-es* to the singular form of the noun.

demonstration → demonstration**s**

picture → picture**s**

dish → dish**es**

Yet adding *-s* or *-es* causes spelling complications in words ending in *y, o, um, us,* or *f.*

Singular		*Plural*
turkey	→	turkey**s**
video	→	video**s**
curriculum	→	curriculum**s**/curricul**a**
bus	→	bus**es**/bus**ses**
chief	→	chief**s**

Some English words use the same form for both singular and plural meanings; others seldom appear in singular form.

Singular/ *Plural*	*Almost Always Plural*
athletics	scissors
mathematics	trousers
spacecraft	headquarters
Sioux	cattle

A substantial number of words—many borrowed from foreign languages—are simply irregular. You couldn't reliably predict what their plurals would be.

Irregular

man → m**en**	goose → g**ee**se
ox → ox**en**	child → child**ren**
mouse → m**ice**	fungus → fung**i** (fungus**es**)

Also troublesome are the plurals of compound words and of figures. In short, plurals merit your careful attention.

25 A

Plurals

When you are unsure about a plural . . .

▶ **Check the dictionary.** Most college dictionaries provide the plural forms of all troublesome nouns. If your dictionary does not give a plural form for a particular noun, assume that it forms its plural regularly, with *-s* or *-es*.

You may eliminate some trips to the dictionary by referring to the following guidelines for forming plurals. But the list is complicated and full of exceptions. So keep that dictionary handy.

▶ **Add *-s* to most nouns.**

demonstration → demonstration**s**
picture → picture**s**

▶ **Add *-es* when the plural adds a syllable to the pronunciation of the noun.** This is usually the case when a word ends in soft *ch, sh, s, ss, x,* or *zz.* (If the noun already ends in *e,* you add only *s.*)

dish → dish-**es**
glass → glass-**es**
bus → bus-**es** or bus-**ses**
buzz → buzz-**es**
choice → choic-**es**

➤ **Add -s when a noun ends in *o* and a vowel precedes the *o*; add -es when a noun ends in *o* and a consonant precedes the *o*.** This guideline has exceptions. A few words ending in *o* even have two acceptable plural forms.

Vowel before o *(add -s)*	*Consonant before* o *(add -es)*
video → videos	hero → heroes
rodeo → rodeos	tomato → tomatoes
studio → studios	veto → vetoes

Exceptions (add -s)	*Two acceptable forms*
banjo → banjos	cargo → cargos/cargoes
nacho → nachos	no → nos/noes
soprano → sopranos	motto → mottos/mottoes
piano → pianos	zero → zeros/zeroes

When in doubt about a word ending in *-o,* check a dictionary.

➤ **Add -s when a noun ends in *y* and a vowel precedes the *y*.** When a consonant precedes the *y,* change the *y* to an *i* and add *-es.*

Vowel precedes the y *(add -s)*	*Consonant precedes the* y *(add -es)*
attorney → attorneys	foundry → foundries
Monday → Mondays	candy → candies
boy → boys	sentry → sentries

An exception to this rule occurs with proper nouns. They usually retain the *y* and simply add *-s.*

25 A
Plurals

Proper names ending in y *(add -s)*	*Exceptions to the exception*
Gary → Garys	Rocky Mountains → Rockies
Nestrosky → Nestroskys	Smoky Mountains → Smokies
Germany → Germanys	Westerly wind → Westerlies

➤ **Check words ending in *f* or *fe*.** Some form plurals by adding *-s,* some change *f* to *-ves,* and some have two acceptable plural forms.

Add -s to form plural	*Change* f *to -ves in plural*
chief → chiefs	leaf → leaves
belief → beliefs	wolf → wolves
roof → roofs	knife → knives

Two acceptable forms
elf → elfs/elves
hoof → hoofs/hooves
scarf → scarfs/scarves
wharf → wharfs/wharves

➤ **Check multisyllabic words ending in *us* preceded by a consonant.** Some form plurals by changing *us* to *i.* But notice that even these may have a second, regular plural.

Change us *to* i

focus → fo*ci*/focus**es**
cactus → cac**ti**/cactus**es**
syllabus → syllab**i**/syllabus**es**

▶ **Check multisyllabic words ending in *um* preceded by a consonant.** Some form plurals by changing *um* to *a.* These often have a second, regular plural.

Change um *to* a

addendum → addend**a**
curriculum → curricul**a**/curriculum**s**
medium → medi**a**/medium**s**

▶ **Check compound words.** The last words in most compounds are pluralized.

dishcloth → dishcloth**s**
bill collector → bill collector**s**
housewife → housewi**ves**

However, the first word in a compound is pluralized when it is the important one. This is often the case in hyphenated expressions.

father-in-law → father**s**-in-law
chief-of-staff → chief**s**-of-staff
woman-of-the-year → wom**en**-of-the-year
passer-by → passer**s**-by

25 A

Plurals

Naturally, there are exceptions:

love-in → love-in**s**
sit-in → sit-in**s**
thirty-year-old → thirty-year-old**s**

Words that end with *ful* ordinarily add *-s* to the end of the whole word, though some dictionaries accept *s* added to the syllable before *ful.*

handful**s** [or hand**s**ful]
tablespoonful**s** [or tablespoon**s**ful]
cupful**s** [or cup**s**ful]

▶ **Check letters, abbreviations, acronyms, figures, and numbers.** These constructions usually form their plurals by adding either *-s* or *'s*. The *'s* is used where adding an *-s* without the apostrophe might cause a misreading.

three **e's** and two **y's**
several of the **I's** in the paper
twenty **V.I.P.'s**   [used because of the periods in the abbreviation]

Quite often, though, the apostrophe is left out, especially when it might mistakenly indicate possession.

3 mins.   the SAT**s**
42 lbs.   five CRT**s**

In many cases, either form of the plural is acceptable.

the 1960s/the 1960's
8s/8's
two *s/two *'s

EXERCISE 25.1

Form the plurals of the following words. Use the guidelines above or a dictionary as necessary.

basis	gas	soliloquy
duo	loaf	zero
tooth	alkali	mongoose
alumnus	datum	heir apparent
moose	Oreo	court-martial

EXERCISE 25.2

Form the plurals of the boldfaced words in the passage below. Use the guidelines on plurals above or a dictionary as necessary.

1. George Ericson prepared three **espresso** and two **mocha** and then sat with his
   wife, Greta, and her friends on one of the comfortable **sofa** at the back of his
   health food store.
2. The friends were Greta's **classmate** in a philosophy course she was taking at
   the college.
3. Their almost daily after-class **symposium** in the Ericsons' store usually began
   with debates and **cross-examination** of various **theory, phenomenon,** and
   problems introduced in the course, but almost always ended with Greta la-
   menting the passing of the **1960.**
4. "Where are the **Bob Dylan** and **Joan Baez** of your generation?" she would
   inevitably ask.
5. "All you kids care for these days," George would add, "is getting **A** and **B.**"

25 B
Possess

25 B POSSESSIVE NOUNS AND PRONOUNS

Term you need to know

POSSESSIVE CASE. The form a noun or pronoun takes to show ownership: *Greta's, hers,*
the students', the pride of the nation. Sometimes the possessive shows a similar
relationship, not exactly like ownership: *the day's labor, the city's destruction, the*
governor's approval.

Troubleshooting

Many writers mistakenly omit the apostrophe before or after an *s* that indicates ownership. As a result, their possessives look like plurals: *Gretas opinion, the students concern, the days labor.* Despite a trend to eliminate the apostrophe in some expressions (*mens room, Macys*), the apostrophe to indicate the possessive is necessary.

Even when you remember to mark the possessive, problems may arise with positioning the apostrophe (Ross*'s* or Ross*'* handball?), with possessives of plurals (the hostesses*'* or the hostesses*'s*?), or with joint possession (George*'s* and Greta*'s* shop or George and Greta*'s* shop?). Sometimes you must choose between the two possible forms of the possessive (the book*'s* spine or the spine *of* the book?).

Forming the possessive of pronouns can cause major problems, too. Unlike nouns, personal pronouns never take an apostrophe, yet look as if they might.

The problem is **theirs**.   [not their's]

Be sure you know **its** measurements.   [not it's]

All of the issues are addressed in detail below.

To form the possessive . . .

▶ **Add an apostrophe + *s* to most singular nouns and to plural nouns that do not end in *s*.**

Singular Nouns	*Plurals Not Ending in* s
dog**'s** life	geese**'s** behavior
that man**'s** opinion	women**'s** attitude
the NCAA**'s** ruling	children**'s** imaginations

Singular nouns that end in *s* or *z* may take either an apostrophe + *s* or the apostrophe alone. Use one form or the other consistently throughout a paper.

Ross**'s** handball or Ross**'** handball
Oz**'s** wizard or Oz**'** wizard
Goetz**'s** play or Goetz**'** play

The apostrophe alone is used with singular words ending in *s* when the possessive does not add a syllable to the pronunciation of the word.

Texas**'** Independence Day
Jesus**'** words

▶ **Add an apostrophe (but not an *s*) to plural nouns that end in *s*.**

hostesses**'** job	senators**'** chambers
students**'** opinion	Smiths**'** home

▶ **Indicate possession only at the end of compound or hyphenated words.**

president-elect**'s** decision
fathers-in-law**'s** Cadillacs
The United States Post Office**'s** efficiency

25 B

Possess

> **Indicate possession only once when two nouns share ownership.**

> Greta and George**'s** health food store
> Voorhees and Goetz**'** project

But when ownership is separate, each noun shows possession.

> Greta**'s** and George**'s** educations
> Voorhees**'** and Goetz**'** homes

> **Use an apostrophe + _s_ to form the possessive of living things and titled works; use _of_ with nonliving things.** This guideline should be followed sensibly. Many common expressions violate the convention and many writers simply ignore it.

Take apostrophe + s	_Take_ of
the dog**'s** bone	the weight **of** the bone
Professor Shade**'s** taxes	the bite **of** taxes
Time**'s** cover	the attractiveness **of** the cover

Use _of_ whenever an apostrophe + _s_ might be awkward or confusing.

{**Confusing**}   The **student** sitting next to Greta**'s** opinion was radical.

{**Revised**}   The opinion **of the student** sitting next to Greta was radical.

In a few situations, English allows a double possessive, consisting of both the _'s_ and _of._

> That suggestion **of** George**'s** didn't win support, although an earlier one did.

> An opinion **of** Greta**'s** spurred another argument.

> **Do not use an apostrophe with personal pronouns.** Personal pronouns don't take an apostrophe to show ownership: _my, your, her, his, our, their, its._ Constructions such as _her's, his',_ or _their's_ don't exist. The forms _it's_ and _who's_ are contractions for _it is_ and _who is_ and shouldn't be confused with the possessive pronouns _its_ and _whose_ (see also Section 28G).

> **It's** an idea that has **its** opponents in arms.

> **Who's** to say **whose** opinion is right?

Indefinite pronouns—such as _anybody, each one, everybody_—do form their possessives regularly: _anybody's, each one's, everybody's._

25 B

Possess

EXERCISE 25.3

Decide whether the forms boldfaced in the passage below are correct. Revise any you believe are faulty.

1. "That expression **of your's** is all wrong," Abel Gonzalez replied to **Greta's** assertion that the main concern **of most students'** was getting high grades.
2. Abel continued. "We care about the **society's** problems as much as students did in the **1960s'.** We just don't thumb **our nose's** hypocritically at our

parent's generation while enjoying **it's** benefits. Our protests aren't paid for by **someone elses** labor."

3. **Greta and George's** tempers flared.
4. "Hypocrites! This reminds me of *King Lear's* plot where ungrateful children abuse their **elders** generosity," George said with excessive drama. "**Its** a shame!"
5. Sue Ellen Rizzo, a student **of Georges** generation, tried to calm things down. "Mr. **Gonzalez'es** opinion is no more extreme than **your's,** George."

---

25 C POSSESSIVES BEFORE GERUNDS

Term you need to know

GERUND. A verb form used as a noun: *eating, biking, walking.* (See Section 24A.)

> **Eating** oat bran contributes to good health.
>
> Greta and George enjoy **recalling** the sixties.

Troubleshooting

Nouns (or pronouns) often precede gerunds. When they do, you must decide whether the noun or pronoun will be possessive or not.

25 C

Gerund

noun gerund

{Noun without possessive}   The customers jumped at the **shelf** *collapsing* in the health food store.

poss. noun   gerund

{Noun with possessive}   The customers jumped at the **shelf's** *collapsing* in the health food store.

> Guidelines are the best help in deciding when to use the possessive.

When a noun or pronoun precedes a gerund . . .

➤ **Use the possessive form in formal or academic writing; use the common (nonpossessive) form in informal situations.** Note that this guideline does *not* apply to proper nouns or to pronouns.

Academic Writing	Informal Writing
Possessive + gerund	**Regular + gerund**
the **student's** *arguing*	the **student** *arguing*
the **owner's** *complaining*	the **owner** *complaining*

➤ **Use the possessive form in *both* formal and informal writing when the word preceding the gerund is a proper noun or a pronoun.**

proper noun   gerund

Students had little respect for **George's** *whining* about the
sixties.   [not *George*]

pronoun gerund

They hissed **his** *acting* like a radical.   [not *him*]

➤ **Use the common form of the noun even in formal writing in the following
situations.**

- When the subject of the gerund is modified by other words.

Abel admitted that he enjoyed the thought of **George,** the respectable
storeowner, *being* arrested at Woodstock.
> [not *George's*]

- When the subject of the gerund is either plural or collective.

But the "**elders**" *going* to rock festivals and love-ins was a phenomenon he
could not imagine.
> [not *"elders'"*]

The **quartet** *playing* folk music in the health food store was a quaint idea.
> [not *quartet's*]

- When the subject of the gerund is abstract.

But to the students, **nostalgia** *getting* out of hand was George's problem.
> [not *nostalgia's*]

25 C

Gerund

♦ **FINE TUNING** ♦

When you want to emphasize the noun preceding the gerund rather than the
action described by the gerund, use the common form with nouns and the **object**
form with pronouns. Compare these versions.

{**Emphasis on noun**}   Abel couldn't imagine **George** *resisting* arrest for littering
at Woodstock.

{**Emphasis on gerund**}   Brian couldn't imagine **George's** *resisting* arrest for littering at Woodstock.

EXERCISE 25.4

Select the appropriate form for the nouns or pronouns used before gerunds
in the passage below. Gerunds are italicized. Assume the passage is written
for an academic audience.

1. **(George/George's)** *remembering* Woodstock was the hot topic at the **(coffee-house/coffeehouse's)** *gathering* of Greta's classmates.
2. Francie thought **(George/George's)** *pretending* not to remember **(Greta/Greta's)** *bailing* him out of jail was amusing.
3. "I was counting on **(his/him)** *being* broke," Greta said.

4. George, however, did not appreciate **(Mrs. Mihalik/Mrs. Mihalik's),** one of his regular customers, *reminding* Greta that George was still usually broke.
5. **(He/His)** *forgetting* to repay her for several years only made the situation more comic.

25 D IS IT *A* OR *AN*?

Troubleshooting

English has only one form for its definite article: ***the.*** So you cannot choose a wrong form: *the* argument, *the* European, *the* house, *the* historic day. But the indefinite article has two forms: *a* and *an.* Some writers think that they should simply use *a* before all words that begin with consonants and *an* before all words that begin with vowels. In fact, usage is just a bit more complicated, as a few examples show: *an* argument, *a* European, *a* house, *an* honorable person.

To choose between *a* or *an* . . .

➤ **Use *a* when the word following it begins with a consonant *sound;* use *an* when the word following it begins with a vowel *sound.*** In most cases, it works out so that *a* actually comes before words beginning with consonants, *an* before words with vowels.

Initial consonants	*Initial vowels*
a **b**oat	an **a**ardvark
a **c**lass	an **E**gyptian monument
a **d**uck	an **i**gloo
a **f**inal opinion	an **o**dd event
a **h**ouse	an **u**tter disaster

But *an* is used before words beginning with a consonant when the consonant is silent, as is sometimes the case with *h.* It is also used when a consonant itself is pronounced with an initial vowel sound (F → *ef;* N → *en;* S → *es*) as often happens in acronyms.

Silent consonant	*Consonant with a vowel sound*
an **h**our	an *F* in this course
an **h**eir	an SAT score
an **h**ors d'oeuvre	an X ray

Similarly *a* is used before words beginning with a vowel when the vowel is pronounced like a consonant. Certain vowels, for example, sound like the consonant *y,* and in a few cases, an initial *o* sounds like the consonant *w.*

Vowel with a consonant sound
a **E**uropean vacation (*eu* sounds like *y*)
a **u**nique painting (*u* sounds like *y*)
a **o**ne-sided argument (*o* sounds like *w*)
a **U**-joint (*u* sounds like *y*)

EXERCISE 25.5

Decide whether *a* or *an* ought to be used before the following words or phrases.

1. _____ L-shaped room
2. _____ hyperthyroid condition
3. _____ zygote
4. _____ X-rated movie
5. _____ Euclidean principle
6. _____ evasive answer
7. _____ jalapeno pepper
8. _____ unwritten rule
9. _____ unit of measure
10. _____ veneer of oak
11. _____ EPA investigation
12. _____ euphemistic expression
13. _____ aerobic exercise
14. _____ NASA engineer
15. _____ jellyfish
16. _____ OK from the editor
17. _____ Syrian import
18. _____ D – grade
19. _____ idiosyncrasy
20. _____ FBI investigation

25 D

A/An

26 Pronoun Reference

A Unspecified pronoun reference

B Ambiguous pronoun reference

C Vague use of *this, that, which, it*

Terms you need to know

PRONOUN. A word that stands in for and acts like a noun, but doesn't name a specific person, place, or thing—*I, you, he, she, it, they, whom, who, what, myself, oneself, this, these, that, all, both, anybody,* and so on.

There are many varieties of pronouns: **personal, relative, interrogative, intensive, reflexive, demonstrative, indefinite,** and **reciprocal.** See the Glossary for details about each type.

ANTECEDENT. The person, place, or thing a pronoun stands in for: *He = Frank; they = the bodybuilders in Sam's Gym.* The antecedent is the word you would have to repeat in a sentence if you couldn't use a pronoun.

REFERENCE. The connection between a pronoun and the noun it stands for. This connection should be clear and unambiguous.

26 A PRONOUN REFERENCES UNSPECIFIED

Troubleshooting

You have a problem with pronoun reference if readers can't find a specific word in your sentence that could sensibly replace the pronoun you are using.

> Brian liked to study rocketry though he had never seen **one** in his life.

Rocketry seems to be the word the pronoun *one* refers to, but the sentence doesn't read well if you make the substitution.

> Brian liked to study rocketry, though he had never seen **rocketry** in his life.

To make the sentence clear, replace the pronoun with a noun.

> {**Revised**}   Brian liked to study rocketry though he had never seen **a rocket** in his life.

376

In cases like this, you cannot leave a reader guessing. Pronouns shouldn't be used unless they have obvious antecedents.

To be sure your sentences are clear . . .

➤ **Revise a sentence or passage to eliminate vague pronouns.** Ask yourself whether another word in the sentence could be put in the place of the pronoun. If no word can, replace the vague pronoun with a specific word or phrase.

{**Confusing**}   Passengers had been searched for weapons, but **it** [?] did not prevent the disaster.

{**Revised**}   Passengers had been searched for weapons, but **this precaution** did not prevent the disaster.

When a word that might stand in for the pronoun is possessive, you may have to rewrite the entire sentence.

{**Vague**}   As for **women's** view of *Dirty Dancing,* **they** are either repulsed by *Dirty Dancing* or intrigued by its hero.

{**Revised**}   **Women** are either repulsed by *Dirty Dancing* or intrigued by its hero.

EXERCISE 26.1

Revise or rewrite the following sentences to eliminate vague pronouns. Treat the sentences as a continuous passage.

26 B

Ambig

1. Mr. Ransom loved to assign research in his history class, although he had never written one himself.
2. He encouraged students to write serious papers about oddball subjects because it stimulated their creativity.
3. In the opinion of some of Dr. Ransom's colleagues, they seemed like busy-work or contrived exercises in documentation.
4. Students often wrote twenty pages or more about the Empress Josephine's hosiery or George Washington's wooden teeth, but it taught them how much information about culture could be embedded in the tiniest historical artifact.
5. Had Dr. Ransom a less critical attitude toward his students' talents, he might have been extremely impressed by it.

---

26 B AMBIGUOUS PRONOUN REFERENCES

Troubleshooting

You have a problem with pronoun reference when a pronoun could refer to more than one antecedent.

> When Doris talked to Tiffany that noon, **she** did not realize that **she** might be resigning before the end of the day.

> When the rain started, we pulled out an umbrella, which was under the seat, and opened it. **It** dampened our spirits for a while, but we decided to stick **it** out.

In the first sentence, it is not clear who is resigning; in the second, **it** might be the umbrella or the rain. Such ambiguities must be clarified by making it possible for pronouns to refer to only one term.

To keep your pronoun references precise . . .

➤ **Revise a sentence to eliminate confusing or ambiguous antecedents.** You can usually make a confusing sentence clearer by replacing the pronouns with more specific words or by rearranging the sentence. Sometimes you have to do both.

{**Revised**}   When **they** talked to each other at noon, **Tiffany** did not realize that **Doris** might be resigning before the end of the day.

{**Revised**}   We pulled out and opened the **umbrella** stowed away under the seat. The **rain** dampened our spirits for a while, but we decided to **stay for the entire game.**

EXERCISE 26.2

26 C

This/That

Revise the following sentences to eliminate ambiguous pronoun references. Treat the sentences as a continuous passage. Several versions of each sentence may be possible.

1. Francie could hardly believe that Richard and Kyle had decided to room together. She doubted whether it would last since it was rare that they would agree about anything.
2. If you asked Richard to describe Kyle, he would say that he was a sly, ultra-conservative, Buick-driving, commie-bashing Republican, and then he would laugh.
3. Ask Kyle about Richard, and he would say that, while he wouldn't engage in gossip, he was sure he had links with the KGB.
4. When Richard dated Francie, Kyle would usually hide the keys to his car to be sure Francie was safe.
5. He didn't consider him a safe driver.

---

26 C   VAGUE REFERENCES WITH *THIS, THAT, WHICH,* AND *IT*

Troubleshooting

Your readers may be confused if you use the pronouns *this, that, which,* or *it* to refer to ideas and situations you haven't named or explained clearly in your sentence or paragraph. You expect readers to understand what *this* is—and they often do, especially in spoken English. But in written English, you should be more specific. This problem is one best explained through an example.

Readers find constructions such as the following confusing or imprecise.

The novel is filled with violence, brutality, and refined language. I especially like **this.**

Readers can't tell whether you like violence, brutality, or refined language—or all three. The *this* in the second sentence could refer to any one of those terms or to all of them. Vague references of this sort need to be clarified.

To avoid vague references . . .

➤ **Revise a sentence or passage to make it clear what *this, that, which,* or *it* means.** When a reader might mistake what a ***this* or *that*** means, you can usually remedy the problem by inserting an imaginary blank space after the pronoun (*this* _____ ? or *that* _____ ?) and filling it in with a word or phrase that explains what *this* or *that* is.

The novel is filled with violence, brutality, and refined language. I especially like **this** _____ ?

Now fill in the blank.

{**Revised**}   The novel is filled with violence, brutality, and refined language. I especially like **this** *combination of toughness and grace.*

Here's another example:

The influx of new residents brings growth, new business, talented people, heavier traffic, and large-scale housing developments. Mayor Carter is responsible for **this.**

Insert an imaginary blank space after *this* and fill it in.

{**Revised**}   The influx of new residents brings growth, new business, talented people, heavier traffic, and large-scale housing developments. Mayor Carter is responsible for **this** *sudden population increase.*

When the unclear pronoun is *which* or *it,* you must either revise the sentence or supply a clear and direct antecedent.

The Supreme Court acted decisively on the Gideon case after the accused had spent time in a Florida jail for a crime he had not committed, **which** (?) is typical of American justice.

When you face a confusing pronoun like the *which* here, you need to understand what sort of problem the vague word is causing your readers. In this sentence, readers can't tell *what* is typical of American justice. Revise the sentence to relieve the confusion. Several alternatives are possible, depending upon your meaning.

{**Revised**}   After the accused had spent time in a Florida jail for a crime he had not committed, the Supreme Court acted on the Gideon case **with the decisiveness typical of American justice.**

{**Revised**}   The Supreme Court **typified American justice** when it acted decisively on the Gideon case **only** after the accused had **already** spent **long months** in a Florida jail for a crime he had not committed.

26 C

This/That

Here's another example, with *it* as the vague pronoun:

> While atomic waste products are hard to dispose of safely, **it** remains a reasonable alternative to burning fossil fuels to produce electricity.

What is the alternative to burning fossil fuels? Surely not *atomic waste products.* The *it* needs to be replaced by a more specific term.

{Revised}   While atomic waste products are hard to dispose of safely, **nuclear power** remains a reasonable alternative to burning fossil fuels to produce electricity.

♦ **FINE TUNING** ♦

1. Don't use a pronoun to refer to the title of your paper or a word or phrase in a title.

All the World's A Stage

This is how a character in Shakespeare's *As You Like It* compares reality to the illusion of theater . . . .

Consider the title as separate from the rest of the paper.

All the World's a Stage

In Shakespeare's *As You Like It*, a character compares reality to the illusion of theater. . . .

2. In academic writing, avoid using *they* or *it* without antecedents to describe people or things in general.

{Vague}   In Houston, **they** live more casually than in Dallas.

{Revised}   In Houston, **people** live more casually than in Dallas.

3. Don't let a pronoun that is not possessive refer to a word that is possessive.

{Inaccurate}   Seeing **Rita's** car, Hector waved at **her.**

{Revised}   Seeing **Rita** *in her* car, Hector waved at **her.**

4. Avoid sentences in which a pronoun merely repeats the obvious subject.

{Repetitious}   The **mayor,** our favorite politician, **he** lost the election.

{Revised}   The **mayor,** our favorite politician, lost the election.

26 C

This/That

EXERCISE 26.3

Decide whether a reader might find the boldfaced pronouns unclear. Revise the sentences as necessary.

1. Kyle and Richard decided to collaborate on their history library assignments, preparing one paper for both of **their** classes, dividing up the labor, and producing a first-class research effort, **which** was against school policy.
2. Kyle was especially enthusiastic. He enjoyed doing research and poring through reference books and indexes in the library, although he had not written **one** since high school.
3. **It** suddenly occurred to Richard that **their** paper might also fulfill Francie's history assignment, so he decided to bring **her** in on **it.**
4. Francie had some qualms initially, but if Richard were involved, well, she'd do **it.** And she did.
5. However, soon after turning in the paper, Francie felt that her teacher was casting accusatory glances her way, although he didn't actually make **one.**

26 C

This/That

27 Pronoun Agreement

A Lost antecedents
B Agreement problem with *or, nor, either . . . or, neither . . . nor*
C Agreement problem with collective nouns
D Agreement problem with indefinite pronouns

Term you need to know

AGREEMENT. Pronouns and their antecedents are said to be in agreement when singular pronouns stand in for singular nouns (*his* surfboard = *Richard's* surfboard) and plural pronouns stand in for plural nouns (*their* surfboard = *George and Martha's* surfboard).

27 A DO YOU HAVE PROBLEMS WITH LOST ANTECEDENTS?

Troubleshooting

Pronouns and nouns are either singular or plural. You would ordinarily use a singular pronoun (such as *she, it, this, that, her, him, my, his, her, its*) when referring to something singular and a plural pronoun (such as *they, these, them, their*) when referring to plural things.

You have a problem with **pronoun agreement** when you use a singular pronoun to stand in for a plural noun (or its **antecedent**) or a plural pronoun to stand in for a singular noun (or its antecedent).

In most cases, you will have no difficulties with pronoun agreement when the pronoun and its antecedent are close together and when the antecedent is clearly either singular or plural.

plural   plural   sing.

The **football players** gathered **their** equipment while **Coach Rhoades**

sing.
looked for **his** car.

But sometimes, words and phrases that come between pronouns and their antecedents cause a kind of misdirection. A writer loses track of the real antecedent and, mistakenly, gives the pronoun the wrong number, as in the following example.

382

sing.

Even though the typical **student** enjoys a lively social life, parties, and

plural   plural

athletic events, our survey found that **they** also work hard on **their** schoolwork.

The plural pronouns *they* and *their* incorrectly refer to a singular noun, *student*. The mistake probably occurs because the writer thinks of a survey as involving more than one student. Consider, too, the possibility that the plural words *parties* and *athletic events* make the writer forget about that singular antecedent, *student*. The simplest way to be sure that pronouns and antecedents agree in this sentence is to make *student* plural.

plural

Even though typical **students** enjoy lively social lives, parties, and

plural   plural

athletic events, our survey found that **they** also work hard on **their** schoolwork.

Errors of this kind are among the most common in writing.

To be sure pronouns and antecedents agree . . .

➤ **First, identify the antecedents of any troublesome pronouns. Then be sure that singular pronouns refer to singular antecedents and plural pronouns to plural antecedents.** Here's an example:

sing.

An **American** always takes it for granted that government agencies will

plural

help **them** when trouble strikes.

Since *American* is singular and *them* is plural, revision is necessary to make pronoun and antecedent either consistently plural or consistently singular.

plural

{**Revised—first version**}   **Americans** always take it for granted that government

plural

agencies will help **them** when trouble strikes.

sing.

{**Revised—second version**}   An **American** always takes it for granted that

sing.

government agencies will help **him** or **her** when trouble strikes.

➤ **Keep pronouns consistent in number throughout a passage.** Don't switch back and forth from singular to plural forms of pronouns and antecedents. The following paragraph—with pronouns and antecedents boldfaced—shows this common error.

{**Inconsistent**}   One reason some **teenagers [pl.]** quit school is to work to support **their [pl.]** families. If **he or she [sing.]** is the eldest child, the **teen**

27 A

Antec

[sing.] may feel an obligation to provide for the family. So **they [pl.]** look for a minimum wage job. Unfortunately, the **student [sing.]** often must work so many hours per week that **they [pl.]** cannot give much attention to schoolwork. As a result, **he or she [sing.]** grows discouraged and drops out.

To correct such a tendency, be consistent. Treat the troublesome key term—in the passage it is *teenager*—as either singular or plural, but not both. Notice that making such a change may require adjustments throughout the passage.

{**Consistent**}   One reason some **teenagers [pl.]** quit school is to work to support **their [pl.]** families. If **they [pl.]** are the eldest children, such **teens [pl.]** may feel an obligation to provide for their families. So **they [pl.]** look for minimum wage jobs. Unfortunately, these **students [pl.]** often must work so many hours per week that **they [pl.]** cannot give much attention to schoolwork. As a result, **they [pl.]** grow discouraged and drop out.

EXERCISE 27.1

Revise the following sentences wherever pronouns and antecedents do not agree in number. You will have to change other words, too—possessive pronouns, verbs, nouns. For clarity, you may even want to replace some pronouns.

27 B

Or, Nor

1. Professor Ransom's typical class was conducted using the Socratic method, but they weren't always successful.
2. In the Socratic method, a teacher leads a student through a series of questions to conclusions that they believe they have reached without the teacher's help.
3. Dr. Ransom would ask leading questions, but the cleverer students in his class would answer it in a way that the professor hadn't anticipated.
4. For example, when Dr. Ransom asked questions about Senator Joseph McCarthy and McCarthyism, his students replied to it with an answer about Charlie McCarthy—Edgar Bergen's dummy.
5. Dr. Ransom sometimes wondered whether the typical student in his classes would recognize the Liberty Bell if it fell on them.

---

27 B   AGREEMENT PROBLEMS WITH *OR, NOR, EITHER . . . OR, NEITHER . . . NOR*

Troubleshooting

Quite often, writers have problems with pronoun agreement simply because they aren't sure whether the word or phrase a pronoun refers to is singular or plural—especially when a pronoun refers to more than one antecedent. When antecedents are joined by *and,* it is usually apparent that the pronoun should be plural.

plural   plural

When **Richard** *and* **Francie** finished their research, **they** celebrated.

But when the antecedents for a pronoun are nouns joined by *or, nor, either . . . or,* or *neither . . . nor,* the choice of a pronoun can become difficult.

Neither Brazil nor Mexico will raise **(their/its)** oil prices.

Either poor **diet or** long, stress-filled **hours** in the office will take **(its/their)** toll on the business executive.

To be sure pronouns agree with antecedents joined by *or, nor, either,* and *neither* . . .

➤ **Examine pairs of nouns joined by *or, nor, either . . . or, neither . . . nor* to determine which one of the following guidelines applies to your sentence.**

- When both nouns in the pair are singular, a pronoun referring to them should be singular.

                                  sing.
Neither Brazil nor Mexico will raise **its** oil prices.

- When both nouns joined by *or* are plural, a pronoun referring to them should be plural.

                                  plural
Players or managers alike may file **their** grievances with the commissioner.

- When one noun is singular, and one noun is plural, the pronoun should agree in number (and gender) with the noun nearer to it—except when the resulting sentence sounds awkward.

         sing.   plural   plural
Either poor **diet** or long, stress-filled **hours** in the office will take **their** toll on the business executive.

                     plural   sing.   sing.
Either the long, stress-filled **hours** in the office or poor **diet** will take **its** toll on the business executive.

Pronouns also agree in gender with the nearer antecedent when two nouns are joined by *or.*

         masc.   fem.   fem.
Either a **priest** or a **nun** will escort you to **her** office.

         fem.   masc.   masc.
Either a **nun** or a **priest** will escort you to **his** office.

Here's a third example, with yet a further complication.

Neither the **students** nor the **professor** wanted to recalculate **(her/their)** numbers.

Students is plural; *professor* singular. The pronoun is nearer to *professor,* so it should be singular.

27 B

Or, Nor

       plural   sing.   sing.
{Revised}   Neither the **students** nor the **professor** wanted to recalculate **her**
    numbers.

Notice, however, that it would be easy to assume from this revised sentence that
only the numbers of the professor were being talked about—and not those of the
students as well. The sentence might need to be revised if a different meaning
were intended.

       sing.   plural   plural
{Revised}   Neither the **professor** nor the **students** wanted to recalculate **their**
    numbers.

EXERCISE 27.2

In the sentences below, select the appropriate words in parentheses.

1. Neither Professor Ransom nor his honor students had bothered to confirm
   (his/their) flight from Chicago's O'Hare Airport back to Ruralia International
   after their field trip to the Art Institute.
2. Either the ticket agents or a flight attendant working the check-in desk had
   misread **(their/her)** computer terminal and accidentally cancelled the group's
   reservations.
3. The students and their faculty advisor had to make up **(their/his) (minds/
   mind)** quickly about arranging transportation back to school.
4. Neither Francie nor Kyle relished the thought of spending **(her/his/their)**
   money on yet another expensive ticket.
5. Wandering around in the vast terminal, Francie located a discount airline
   willing to fly either the students or their luggage back to **(their/its)** destina-
   tion cheaply.

27 C

Coll N

27 C   AGREEMENT PROBLEMS WITH COLLECTIVE NOUNS

Troubleshooting

Agreement problems occur frequently with pronouns that refer to nouns describing groups or collections of things: *class, team, band, government, jury.* These
so-called **collective** nouns can be either singular or plural, depending on use.

> The **orchestra** played **its** heart out.

> The **orchestra** arrived and took **their** seats.

A pronoun referring to a collective noun should be consistently either singular
or plural.

To handle references to collective nouns . . .

➤ **Identify any *collective* noun in a sentence to which a pronoun refers.** Decide
whether to treat that noun as a single body (the *jury*) or as a group of more than

one person or object (the twelve members of the *jury).* Then be consistent. If you decide to treat the word as singular, be sure pronouns referring to it are singular. If you decide it is plural, all pronoun references should be plural.

> The **jury** rendered **its** decision.

> The **jury** had **their** photographs taken frequently during the trial.

In most cases, your sentences will sound more natural if you treat collective nouns as single objects. Notice how awkward the following sentence seems because the collective noun is treated as plural.

> The **band** are unhappy with **their** latest recordings.

Sentences like this can be improved either by making the collective nouns more clearly plural or by making them singular.

> The ***members of the band*** are unhappy with **their** latest recordings.

> The **band** is unhappy with ***its*** latest recordings.

EXERCISE 27.3

In the following sentences, select the appropriate words in parentheses. Be prepared to defend your answers.

1. Mr. Ransom's **class** boarded the ancient aircraft and took **(its/their)** seats, eager to get home after **(its/their)** field trip, but suspicious of the charter Francie had arranged.
2. Kyle recognized the plane as a Ford trimotor, designed in the 1920s and part of a dwindling **fleet** that had enjoyed **(its/their)** best days long ago.
3. The students were followed onto the plane by the aircraft's **crew** carrying **(its/their)** equipment, including what looked like a rubber dinghy and parachutes.
4. "This plane is practically a flying museum," Kyle said to a **pool** of students wagering **(its/their)** spare change on how many miles the craft would taxi before taking off.
5. "All we need is an **orchestra** to play the saddest song **(it/they) (knows/know)** on kazoos as this tin goose plunges into Lake Michigan," said Richard.

27 D

Indef P

27 D AGREEMENT PROBLEMS WITH INDEFINITE PRONOUNS

Troubleshooting

A troublesome and common agreement problem involves references to pronouns described as **indefinite.** Common indefinite pronouns include *everyone, anybody, anyone, somebody, all, some, none, each, few, most.* It is not always easy to tell whether one of these indefinite words is singular or plural.

> **Everyone** should have **(his/their)** ticket in **(his/their)** hand.

> **None** of us intended to leave **(her/our)** place in line.

Yet a decision usually has to be made before a pronoun can be selected.

To handle problems with indefinite pronouns . . .

➤ **Use the chart below or a dictionary to determine whether an indefinite pronoun or noun in your sentence is singular, variable, or plural.** (The list is *not* exhaustive; refer to a dictionary, if necessary.) The chart reflects formal and academic usage.

Singular	Variable, S, or PL.	Plural
anybody	all	few
anyone	any	many
anything	more	several
each	most	
everybody	none	
everyone	some	
everything		
nobody		
no one		
nothing		
somebody		
someone		
something		

27 D

Indef P

➤ **If the indefinite word is regarded as singular, make any pronouns that refer to it singular.**

> sing.   sing.
> Did **anybody** misplace **her** notes?

> sing.   sing.
> **Everyone** should keep **his** temper.

> sing.   sing.
> **No one** has a right to more than **his or her** share.

Using singular pronouns in these cases may seem odd at times because the plural forms occur so often in speech and informal writing.

{**Informal**} **Each** of the candidates has **their** own ideas.

{**Informal**} We discovered that **everyone** had kept **their** notes.

But in academic and professional writing, you should still respect the principle of consistent agreement between pronouns and antecedents.

{**Revised—formal**} **Each** of the candidates has **his or her** own ideas.

{**Revised—formal**} We discovered that **everyone** had kept **his or her** notes.

In a few cases, however, the singular indefinite pronoun does take a plural referent, even in formal and academic writing.

> sing.   plural
> **Nobody** was late, were *they?*

sing.   plural

Everybody had plenty of money, and *they* were willing to spend it.

sing.   plural

Because **each** of the students arrived late, Dr. Ransom gave *them* a stern lecture on punctuality.

➤ **If the indefinite word is usually plural, make any pronouns that refer to it plural.**

plural   plural   plural

Several of the aircraft had to have **their** wings stiffened. **Few,** however,

plural

had given **their** pilots trouble.

➤ **If the indefinite word is variable, use your best judgment to determine which pronoun fits the sentence better.** In many cases, words or phrases modifying the pronoun determine its number.

var.   plural   var.

All of the portraits had yellowed in **their** frames. **Some** will be restored

plural

to **their** original condition.

var.   sing.   var.

All of the wine is still in **its** casks. **Some** of the vintage is certain to

sing.

have **its** quality evaluated.

27 D

Indef P

None is considered variable because it is regularly accepted as a plural form in much writing and speech. However, in formal writing, you should usually treat *none* as singular. Think of *none* as meaning *not one*.

None of the women is reluctant to speak **her** mind.

None of the churches has **its** doors open.

➤ **Rewrite any sentences that leave the reference of a pronoun unclear.** You can get into problems when a possessive pronoun referring to two antecedents doesn't explain clearly who owns what.

Neither Greta nor George is willing to sell **(his/her/their)** house.

What a reader needs to know is whether Greta and George own a single home (in which case **their house** would be appropriate) or two separate houses (in which case **his or her house** is probably the best choice). Often it makes sense simply to rewrite the sentence entirely to avoid confusion.

Neither Greta nor George is willing to sell **the house they jointly own.**

Greta **won't sell her** house and George **won't sell his.**

Fortunately, sentences with potentially confusing antecedents and pronouns usually make better sense when they are part of a paragraph or full document than when they are examined alone.

◆ FINE TUNING ◆

Person is a singular noun, not a plural one. Don't use *they* to refer to *person*.

{**Incorrect**}   If a **person** watches too much television, **they** may become a couch potato.

{**Revised**}   If a **person** watches too much television, **he or she** may become a couch potato.

EXERCISE 27.4

Select the correct word or phrase in parentheses. Indicate when either answer might be considered correct.

1. "Anybody can fly a plane like the Ford trimotor if **(they are/he or she is)** coordinated," claimed Kyle, enjoying the bumpy ride home after the day's field trip to Chicago.
2. "But not everyone is willing to risk **(his or her/their)** **(life/lives)** trying," Richard replied.
3. When Professor Ransom suggested that someone might want to write **(his or her/their)** research paper on the Ford trimotor, all of the students threw **(his or her/their)** safety cards at him.
4. Several of the students spent most of the flight with **(his or her head/their heads)** bowed in prayer.
5. All of them showed **(his or her/their)** nervousness in one way or another.
6. Everybody had been eager to leave Chicago, but **(he or she/they)** all had doubts about ever flying an unknown commuter airline again.
7. Almost everyone was enjoying **(his or her/their)** trip in the vintage aircraft, but **(he or she/they)** would have been reluctant to admit **(his or her/their)** feelings.
8. The plane flew so slowly and so low that nobody felt as nervous as **(he or she/they)** might have in another aircraft.
9. Francie was grateful when somebody up front shouted that **(he or she/they)** could see the lights of Ruralia in the distance.
10. Most of the students would make it home in time to spend **(his or her/their)** evening working on **(his or her research project/their research projects)**.

27 D

Indef P

EXERCISE 27.5

Review sections 27A–D. Then, in the following passage, look for pronouns that do not agree in number with their antecedents. Make whatever corrections are necessary. Sometimes you will need to change only a word; in other cases, you will need to revise the entire sentence.

1. "I'm sure everyone has done their own work," Mr. Ransom said as he returned the history term papers.
2. "If you have any problems with the essays or my comments on them, feel free to discuss it with me."

3. Francie cringed at his implied accusation—and his grammar. Why had she allowed Richard and Kyle to involve her in their scheme to write one paper for three different classes?

4. She was the one with a conscience who felt obligated to tell all. Either the boys or she had to admit their dishonesty and face the consequences.

5. Each would have to take their medicine—even if it meant an F.

6. The bell rang and Francie watched as the class left its seats, leaving her alone with Mr. Ransom.

7. Somebody returned for their textbooks left under a seat, but the interruption lasted only a second. She had to speak.

8. "Mr. Ransom?" she began, "Does a teacher remember what it was like when they were in college?"

9. "No one remembers everything they did, but almost all can recall some of his trials and tribulations," Mr. Ransom replied, rubbing his forehead thoughtfully.

10. Francie gulped, then spoke. "Mr. Ransom, I didn't write my paper myself. All my courses had its term paper due on the same day, so I got a little desperate. You remember how it was. None of us is perfect."

27 D

Indef P

28 Pronoun Case

A Case: subject/object/possessive
B Pronoun case after prepositions
C Pronoun case in comparisons
D Pronoun case after linking verbs
E Choosing between *who* and *whom*
F Possessive pronouns
G *Its* or *it's*

Terms you need to know

CASE. The form of a pronoun: **subjective** (or **nominative), objective,** or **possessive.**

SUBJECTIVE (NOMINATIVE) CASE. The form a pronoun takes when it is the subject of a sentence or a clause: *I, you, she, he, it, we, they, who.* A pronoun is also in the subjective case when it follows a linking verb as a **predicate nominative:** It is *I;* It was *they* who cast the deciding votes.

OBJECTIVE CASE. The form a pronoun takes when something is done to it: Elena broke *them;* Buck loved *her.* This is also the form a pronoun takes after a preposition: [to] *me, her, him, us, them, whom.* The subjective and objective forms of the pronouns *you* and *it* are identical.

POSSESSIVE CASE. The form a pronoun takes when it shows ownership: *my, mine, your, yours, her, hers, his, its, our, ours, their, theirs, whose.*

PERSONAL PRONOUN. A pronoun that refers to particular individuals, things, or groups: *I, you, he, she, it, we, they.*

PREPOSITION. A word that links a noun or pronoun to the rest of a sentence. Prepositions point out many basic relationships: *on, above, to, for, between, beyond.* The combination of a preposition and a noun or pronoun and its modifiers is called a **prepositional phrase:** *on our house; above it; to him; in love.*

28 A PRONOUN CASE: SUBJECT/OBJECT/POSSESSIVE

Troubleshooting

Some personal pronouns (and *who*) change their form according to how they are used in a sentence. They have one form when used as a subject (*he, they, who*),

392

another when used as an object (*him, them, whom*), and a third when they show ownership (*his, theirs, whose*). In most situations, writers are able to select the appropriate form (or **case**) without even thinking about their choices.

Whose book did **she** give to **him**?

They were more confident of **their** victory than **we** were of **ours.**

But at other times, selecting the right case is no easy matter. The correct pronoun choice may sound or look wrong.

To be sure you are using the right pronoun form (case) . . .

➤ **Use the chart below to select subjective forms when pronouns act as subjects, objective forms when pronouns act as objects (especially in prepositional phrases), and possessive forms when pronouns show ownership.**

Subject Forms	Object Forms	Possessive Forms
I	me	my, mine
we	us	our, ours
you	you	your, yours
he	him	his
she	her	her, hers
it	it	its, of it
they	them	their, theirs
who	whom	whose

You are most likely to have a problem selecting the correct case when faced with a pair of pronouns. The second pronoun is usually the troublesome one.

28 A

S/O/P

You and **(I/me)** don't have an effective partnership.

The pronouns here are both part of the subject. So you should select the subjective form of the *I/me* pair—which is *I.*

But even if you didn't recognize the need for a subject form, you could still make the right choice by imagining how the sentence would read if you dropped the first pronoun. With only one pronoun in the sentence, you can usually tell immediately what the correct form should be.

Me don't have an effective partnership.

I don't have an effective partnership.

Given this choice, most people will select the correct pronoun—*I.*

{**Revised**}   **You** and **I** don't have an effective partnership.

This simple but effective technique works with many confusing pairs of pronouns or even a noun/pronoun combination.

            noun   pron.
As for **my sister** and **(I/me?),** we chose not to attend.

Dropping the noun phrase *my sister* makes it clearer that the pronoun you select must be the object of the preposition *for.* Checking the chart above, you see that the objective form of *I/me* is *me.*

{**Revised**}   As for **my sister** and **me,** we chose not to attend.

Sentences in the passive voice pose a special problem.

(He/Him) and **(she/her)** were carried out on stretchers.

In this sentence, the verb *were carried* is passive, but the pronouns are the subjects of the sentence and, consequently, in the nominative case: *he/she.* This time, if you try the deletion technique, you will run into a complication.

{**1st version**}   **He** were carried out on stretchers.

{**2nd version**}   **Him** were carried out on stretchers.

Neither version seems correct. That's because of the change from a plural subject or object (*he/him* + *she/her*) to a singular one. To figure out the right pronoun, you have to adjust the sentence to a singular form.

{**1st version**}   **He** was carried out on a stretcher.

{**2nd version**}   **Him** was carried out on a stretcher.

Now the correct version is more obvious. Notice that the need to change the verb in itself indicates that the pronoun should be in the subjective form. You can now write the final version.

{**Revised**}   **He** and **she** were carried out on stretchers.

---

28 A

S/O/P

♦ **FINE TUNING** ♦

1. There is an exception to the guideline that pronouns in the subjective case take a subject form: when a pronoun is the subject of an infinitive phrase (*to be, to seek, to employ*), it takes the objective case.

infinitive phrase

The corporation expected **him** *to hire more minorities.*

infinitive phrase

The coach ordered **them** *to look sharp.*

To hire more minorities and *to look sharp* are infinitive phrases. *Him* and *them* are the subjects of those phrases, even though both are in the objective case.

2. When a pronoun is followed by a noun that describes or explains it (technically, the noun or noun phrase is called an **appositive**), the pronoun and noun both share the same case.

appositive

We *lucky sailors* missed the storm.   [Subject]

appositive

The storm missed **us** *lucky sailors.*   [Object]

You may run into a problem when a pronoun in a prepositional phrase is followed by an appositive noun. The proper form for the pronoun is the objective case, even though it may sound odd to the ear.

The New Yorkers decided to join with **us** *Texans* in supporting the legislation in Congress.

We Texans may sound more correct, but *we* is the subject form and should not be used after the preposition *with.* Another example follows.

For **us** *engineers,* the job market looks promising.

When in doubt about the proper form of the pronoun, read the sentence without the appositive.

28 B PRONOUN CASE AFTER PREPOSITIONS

Troubleshooting

Pronouns that are the objects of prepositions are almost always in the objective case. Difficulties with case are rare when a single pronoun closely follows its preposition.

Come **with me** now.

You would never say *Come with I now.*

But add another pronoun or noun after the preposition, and you may suddenly have doubts about the correct form.

Come **with** Travis and **(I/me)** now.

28 B

Prep

To be sure you are using the right pronoun form . . .

▶ **Use the objective case when pronouns are the object in a prepositional phrase.**
Again, difficulties are most likely to arise when the preposition takes two objects.

prep. object   object
Come **with (I,me)** and **Travis** now.

prep.   object object
Just **between you** and **(I/me),** the answer is "yes."

A quick glance at the chart of pronoun forms on page 393 shows that the object form of *I/me* is *me.*

In some cases, you can reach the same conclusion by deleting the object causing no difficulty and considering the alternatives.

{**1st version**}   Come **with I** now.

{**2nd version**}   Come **with me** now.

In this case, the deletion makes it clearer that version 2 is correct, and so the full sentence can be restored.

{**Revised**}   Come **with me** and Travis now.

EXERCISE 28.1

Select the correct pronoun from the choices offered in parentheses.

1. In Francie's opinion, neither **(she/her)** nor the guys had acted with good sense in collaborating on a paper without consulting their instructors first.
2. It was likely, however, that Dr. Ransom would now accuse **(she/her)** and **(they/them)** of scholastic dishonesty.
3. Francie was convinced that **(she/her)** and **(they/them)** had collaborated in order to do a better job.
4. Dr. Ransom and Dean Rack might take good intentions into account, but, with **(they/them),** who could be sure?
5. "You and **(I/me)** will just have to face the music," Francie told Richard and Kyle who frowned at **(she/her).**

28 C   PRONOUN CASE IN COMPARISONS

28 C

Compar

Troubleshooting

Expect problems with pronoun case when writing a comparison that includes *than* or *as* followed by a pronoun. You'll recognize this familiar difficulty immediately.

> I am taller **than (him/he).**

> Politics does not interest me as much **as (she/her).**

To select the right pronoun after *than* or *as* . . .

➤ **Expand the comparison into a full sentence and then decide what the appropriate pronoun form should be.**

> I am taller **than (him/he).**

Complete the comparison by assuming that the verb *is* follows the pronoun.

> I am taller **than (him/he)** *is.*

The correct pronoun form is now more obvious. The pronoun functions as the subject of the verb *is.*

{Revised}   I am taller **than he.**

Another example.

> She is far more active in the organization **than (me/I).**

Now expand the comparison.

> She is far more active in the organization **than (me/I) am.**

{Revised}   She is far more active in the organization **than I.**

Here is an example with *as.*

Politics does not interest me as much **as (she/her).**

Expand the comparison.

Politics does not interest me as much **as** it interests **(she/her).**

In this case, the expanded comparison shows that the pronoun could be the object of the verb *interests.* Hence, the objective form is necessary.

{**Revised**}   Politics does not interest me as much **as her.**

Sometimes a sentence can be expanded two ways, with the pronoun you select having an important effect on what the sentence means.

Shawn treats Connie better **than (I/me).**

{**1st version**}   Shawn treats Connie better **than I** *do.*

{**2nd version**}   Shawn treats Connie better **than he** *treats* **me.**

Both versions make sense, but the meanings are much different. You can avoid a misreading by adding a verb after *than* + the pronoun.

Politics does not interest me as much **as (she/her).**

{**1st version**}   Politics does not interest me **as much as it interests her.**

{**2nd version**}   Politics does not interest me **as much as she does.**

28 D

Link V

EXERCISE 28.2

Select the correct pronoun from the choices offered in parentheses.

1. Although Richard was as involved in the research paper collusion case as Francie, he felt somewhat less worried about the mess than **(she/her).**
2. Why did Francie feel more worried than **(he/him)** or even Kyle, who had conceived the joint project?
3. Perhaps because Francie was better informed than **(they/them)** about the definition of collusion?
4. In any case, Francie would sooner implicate herself than **(they/them),** even though Kyle and Richard were no less guilty than **(she/her).**
5. Kyle suspected that Richard liked Francie better than **(he/him);** Richard, however, believed that Francie liked Kyle better than **(he/him).**

28 D   PRONOUN CASE AFTER LINKING VERBS

Terms you need to know

LINKING VERB. A verb, often a form of *to be,* that connects a subject to a word or phrase that extends or completes its meaning. Common linking verbs are *to seem, to appear, to feel,* and *to become.*

Wolfgang Rack **is** Dean of Humanities.
He **seems** tired.

SUBJECT COMPLEMENT. A word or phrase that follows a linking verb, completing its meaning. Subject complements can be nouns, adjectives, or pronouns.

subj.   l.v. subj. comp.
Tiffany Shade is **president.**   [noun.]

    subj.   l.v. subj. comp.
The president is **she.**   [pron.]

subj.   l.v.   subj. comp.
President Shade appears **confident.**   [adjective.]

Troubleshooting

Many writers have problems deciding what the case of a pronoun ought to be after forms of *to be*. Which is correct?

It is **(I/me)**?

That is **(she/her)**?

This is **(he/him)**?

In academic English, the pronoun in these cases is treated as a subject complement in the subjective case: *I; she; he.* But exceptions are permitted: both *It is I* and *It is me* are considered acceptable.

28 D

Link V

To select the right pronoun after a linking verb . . .

➤ **In most cases, use the subjective case.**

The director was **(he/him).**

{**Correct**}   The director was **he.**

Here are other examples.

It will be **(she/her)** who will write the script.

{**Correct**}   It will be *she* who will write the script.

You are **(who/whom)**?

{**Correct**}   You are **who?**

➤ **Use the objective case when it sounds more natural.**

It is **me.**   That's **her.**

EXERCISE 28.3

Review sections 28A–D. Select the correct pronoun from the choices in parentheses. Use the form appropriate to academic writing even where the pronouns occur in dialogue.

1. "Which one is Dean Rack?" Francie inquired. "That is **(he/him)** in the back office, the bald man looking stern. The situation sure looks bleak for **(we/us)** students," said Kyle.
2. An unctuous secretary approached the students and said, "The Dean is expecting three students. I presume you are **(they/them)**?"
3. "That's correct," said Kyle. "**(We/Us)** three are **(they/them)**."
4. Soon Kyle and Richard were sitting glumly in one corner of the Dean's paneled office, Francie in another. Both **(she/her)** and **(they/them)** knew why the Dean had summoned **(they/them)**.
5. For the guys and **(her/she)** alike, this was a dark day. Yesterday, Francie had admitted to Professor Ransom that two other students had worked with **(she/her)** on the term paper she turned in for his history class.
6. While Francie was no more responsible than Kyle or Richard for the actual collusion, the guys were doing an expert job of making her feel more responsible than **(them/they)**.
7. Kyle, adjusting his glasses, was doing his best to stay calm even while his dream of law school seemed to be drifting away. "Don't feel bad, Francie. You don't have any more experience with this kind of situation than **(I/me)**. **(We/Us)** over-achievers don't expect to end up in Deans' offices."
8. "Just between you and **(I/me)**," Kyle continued, smiling a little, "don't you think that Richard is really the one at fault?"
9. Francie thought a moment: "If anyone can talk himself and **(us/we)** out of a mess like this, it's got to be Richard. Let's blame him."
10. "Come on, you guys. You're better at winning sympathy than **(I/me)**," said Richard. "Besides, do you want me to go to the Rack alone?"

28 E

Who/Whom

28 E   CHOOSING BETWEEN *WHO* AND *WHOM*

Term you need to know

DEPENDENT CLAUSE. A phrase containing a subject and verb that cannot stand alone as a sentence.

> **Whomever we nominate** is likely to be elected.

Troubleshooting

In spoken English, the distinction between *who* and *whom* (or *whoever/whomever*) has just about disappeared. In written English, however, many readers still expect the distinction to be observed, despite the problems it can cause.

To choose correctly between *who* and *whom* . . .

➤ Select the subjective form *(who)* when pronouns act as subjects and the objective form *(whom)* when pronouns act as objects— especially in prepositional phrases.

{**Subject form**}   **Who** wrote this letter?
{**Object form**}   You addressed **whom**?
     To **whom** did you write this letter?

The problem, of course, with *who/whom* is figuring out whether the word is acting as a subject or an object. Both versions of some troublesome sentences are likely to seem acceptable.

> **Who** did you address?
>
> **Whom** did you address?

To select the correct form, you need to identify the subject and the object.

object   subj.

{**Correct**} **Whom** did you address?

If you can locate the verb, you can usually figure out who is doing what to whom.

> **(Who/Whom)** are you taking on the tour?

The verb is *are taking.* The doer of the action is clearly *you: you are taking.* The person receiving the action, then, is the object form of *who/whom: whom.*

{**Correct**} **Whom** are you taking on the tour?

Be careful with sentences containing passive verbs, where the subject remains in the subjective case (*who*) even though it does not actually perform the action described by the verb.

{**Correct**} **Who** was accused of collusion by Professor Ransom?

So far, so good. But what happens when *who/whom* (or *whoever/whomever*) is part of a **dependent clause**—that is, when *who/whom* is the subject or object of a clause that is, itself, the object of another sentence? Now, this may sound far-fetched, but constructions of this kind are quite common. The phrases italicized below are clauses within full sentences.

> The system rewards **(whoever/whomever)** *works hard.*
>
> The deficit will increase no matter **(who/whom)** *we elect President.*

In these situations, *who/whom* takes the form it would have in the dependent clause, not in the sentence as a whole. In the first example, the correct version would be the following if you omitted *works hard.*

> The system rewards **whomever.**

Whomever is the object of the verb *rewards.* But when the clause is added, the case of the pronoun changes.

> The system rewards **whoever** *works hard.*

Whoever is now the subject of the clause *whoever works hard.* Here is a second example.

> The deficit will increase no matter **(who/whom)** *we elect President.*

Who/whom here is part of a clause: we elect *whom* President.

{**Correct**} The deficit will increase no matter **whom** *we elect President.*

28 E

Who/Whom

> **TIP: When you can't recall all the fine points of *who/ whom* (or can't consult your handbook), play it safe by using *who* in most situations—except immediately after a preposition. After a preposition, use *whom: to whom; for whom, with whom.* Using *who* in all other circumstances will mean you are technically incorrect whenever the word is acting as an object. But *who* misused as an object usually sounds less stodgy than *whom* misused as a subject.**
>
> > {*Who* misused as an object} You addressed *who?*
> > {*Whom* misused as a subject} *Whom* wrote this letter?

EXERCISE 28.4

Decide which of the pronoun forms in parentheses is correct.

1. Dean Rack looked like a man **(whom/who)** wouldn't trust a nun with a prayer.
2. He glared at the boys, and then at Francie. "**(Whom/Who)** would like to explain this plagiarism accusation to me?"
3. "We're guilty as sin," Francie blurted out with heart-rending contrition. "I've already confessed to Dr. Ransom, my history teacher, to **(who/whom)** you've probably spoken, that my friends and I collaborated on a paper for our classes."
4. "May I assume," asked the Dean, "that these young men here, with **(who/ whom)** you wrote the questionable essays, are your friends?"
5. "They might be," said Francie wistfully, "though a person can never really be too certain **(who/whom)** her friends are."

28 F

Possess

28 F POSSESSIVE PRONOUNS

Terms you need to know

POSSESSIVE PRONOUN. The form a pronoun takes when it shows ownership: *my, mine, your, yours, her, hers, his, its, our, ours, their, theirs, whose, anyone's, somebody's.*

PERSONAL PRONOUN. A pronoun that refers to particular individuals, things, or groups: *I, you, he, she, it, we, they.*

INDEFINITE PRONOUN. A pronoun that does not refer to a particular person, thing, or group: *all, any, each, everybody, everyone, one, none, somebody, someone,* and so on.

CONTRACTION. A word shortened by the omission of a letter or letters. In most cases, an apostrophe is used to indicate the deleted letters or sounds: *it is = it's; they are = they're; you are = you're.*

Troubleshooting

The most common way of showing ownership in English is to add an apostrophe + *s* to a noun: Sarah*'s* book; the dog*'s* owner. The familiar *'s* is not, however, used with **personal pronouns** (and *who*)—and this exception confuses some writers who are inclined to add an *'s* to personal pronouns that don't require it. This inclination is also responsible for one of the most common of all mechanical errors in English: mistaking the possessive pronoun *its* for the contraction *it's*. *Its/it's* is the subject of Section 28G to follow.

The possessive forms of **indefinite pronouns** can be troublesome as well. Some indefinite pronouns take the apostrophe + *s* to indicate ownership, but others do not.

To be sure you are using the right possessive pronoun . . .

▶ **Remember that personal pronouns do not require an apostrophe to show ownership.** This is true whether the possessive pronoun comes before or after a noun.

<table>
<tr><td>**Before the noun**</td><td>**After the noun**</td></tr>
<tr><td>That is *my* book.</td><td>The book is *mine*.</td></tr>
<tr><td>That is *your* book.</td><td>The book is *yours*.</td></tr>
<tr><td>That is *her* book.</td><td>The book is *hers*.</td></tr>
<tr><td>That is *his* book.</td><td>The book is *his*.</td></tr>
<tr><td>That is *our* book.</td><td>The book is *ours*.</td></tr>
<tr><td>That is *their* book.</td><td>The book is *theirs*.</td></tr>
<tr><td>What is *its* price?</td><td>What is the price *of it*?</td></tr>
<tr><td>*Whose* book is this?</td><td></td></tr>
</table>

▶ **Remember that while some indefinite pronouns can form the possessive by adding *'s*, others cannot.** Among the indefinite pronouns that cannot add *'s* to show possession are the following:

<table>
<tr><td>**Indefinite pronoun**</td><td>**Form of the possessive**</td></tr>
<tr><td>*all*</td><td>the opinion *of all*</td></tr>
<tr><td>*any*</td><td>the sight *of any*</td></tr>
<tr><td>*each*</td><td>the price *of each*</td></tr>
<tr><td>*few*</td><td>the judgment *of few*</td></tr>
<tr><td>*most*</td><td>the dream *of most*</td></tr>
<tr><td>*none*</td><td>the choice *of none*</td></tr>
</table>

Indefinite pronouns ending in *-body* or *-one* can form the possessive with *'s* or with *of.*

<table>
<tr><td>**Indefinite pronoun**</td><td>**Forms of the possessive**</td></tr>
<tr><td>**anybody**</td><td>**anybody**'s opinion
the opinion of **anybody**</td></tr>
<tr><td>**someone**</td><td>**someone**'s hope
the hope of **someone**</td></tr>
</table>

▶ **Remember that the possessive of *who* is *whose*.** Don't mistake *whose,* the possessive, for *who's*—the contraction for *who is* or *who has.*

Whose teammate is on first base?   [possessive form]

Who's on first?   [contraction]

♦ **FINE TUNING** ♦

1. Deciding whether to place a possessive pronoun before or after a noun is often a matter of style. Some combinations are simply awkward.

His and **their** projects were selected for the science fair.

The teaching assistant was curious about **her** and **my** ideas.

In cases like this, try other ways of expressing ownership.

His project and **theirs** were selected for the science fair.

Their projects were selected for the science fair.

The teaching assistant was curious about **her** idea and **mine.**

The teaching assistant was curious about **our** ideas.

2. *Whose* usually refers to living things; *of which* to nonliving objects. Use *whose,* however, in any sentence where *of which* seems awkward.

It is a land the people **of which** are splendid but the natural wonders **of which** aren't.

{**Revised**}   It is a land **whose** people are splendid but **whose** natural wonders aren't.

28 G

Its/It's

28 G   SPECIAL PROBLEM: *ITS* OR *IT'S*

One of the most common errors in writing is to use the contraction *it's* (which means *it is* or *it has*) where the possessive form *its* is required—and vice versa.

{**Wrong**}   **Its** unlikely that the aircraft will lose **it's** way in the dark. **Its** equipped with radar.

{**Right**}   **It's** unlikely that the aircraft will lose **its** way in the dark. **It's** equipped with radar.

{**Wrong**}   The van lost **it's** hubcaps while parked on the street. **Its** a shame that neighborhood thefts have increased.

{**Right**}   The van lost **its** hubcaps while parked on the street. **It's** a shame that neighborhood thefts have increased.

The apostrophe makes the contracted form—*it's*—look suspiciously like a possessive. And the possessive form—*its*—sounds like a contraction. But don't be fooled. The possessive forms of a personal pronoun never take an apostrophe, while contractions always require one.

{**Possessive form**}   The iron left **its** grim outline on the silk shirt.

{**Contraction**}   **It's** a stupid proposal.

Even without a rule, chances are you can tell *its* from *it's* when you have to. If you consistently misuse *its/it's,* circle these words whenever they appear in your work, and then check them. It may help if you always read *it's* as *it is.* Eventually you will eliminate this error.

Don't even imagine that such a construction as *its'* exists.

EXERCISE 28.5

Circle all occurrences of *its/it's* in the following passage and correct any errors.

1. "Its only recently come to my attention that scholastic dishonesty is occurring on this campus," said the Dean to Kyle, Richard, and Francie.
2. "It's been the policy of this school to encourage its students to be self-policing when it comes to plagiarism and the like," he continued.
3. "Its easy to see how some students might abuse such a policy, but in the long run I believe its in the best interests of a college to make it's students face their own consciences."
4. "However, many in the administration now believe it's time for sterner measures," Dean Rack continued.
5. "When an institution puts its name on a diploma, its got to be sure that any student who receives that certificate has earned it."

28 G

Its/It's

EXERCISE 28.6

Review sections 28F–G. Identify and correct any pronoun-related errors in the sentences below. Possible trouble spots are italicized, but not all the words and phrases italicized contain errors of possession or pronoun form.

1. "Now, exactly *whose* responsible for this collusion of *your's?*" Dean Rack asked Francie, Kyle, and Richard as he thumbed through their papers.
2. Kyle explained to Dean Rack how the three *of them* had decided to form a team—*it's* purpose to compose collaboratively the best essay in the least time.
3. Dean Rack slowly returned *everybodys* papers.
4. "These papers are each of *your's?*" he asked, and the three students nodded apologetically.
5. "Then, would one of you explain to me why three supposed plagiarists would each turn in a completely different paper?" The students looked up, *theirs* eyes proclaiming "*Its* a miracle!"

29 Other Pronoun Issues

A Reflexive/intensive pronouns

B Choosing between *that* and *which* and *who*

C Using *I, you, one, we*

D Nonsexist usage

29 A REFLEXIVE AND INTENSIVE PRONOUNS

Terms you need to know

REFLEXIVE/INTENSIVE PRONOUNS. The pronoun forms created when *-self* is added to singular personal pronouns and *-selves* to plural personal pronouns: *myself, yourself, herself, himself, itself, oneself, ourselves, yourselves, themselves.*

These words are **reflexive** in sentences like the following where both the subject and object of an action are the same person or things.

subj.   obj.
They took **themselves** too seriously.

They are **intensive** when they modify a noun or other pronoun to add emphasis.

noun
Warren himself admitted he was guilty.

pron.
I never vote **myself.**

Troubleshooting

Writers sometimes use reflexive pronouns—especially *myself*—inappropriately, thinking that intensive forms are somehow more correct or formal than simple personal pronouns. Other writers use the nonstandard forms *hisself* or *theirselves.*

To handle reflexive/intensive pronouns correctly . . .

➤ **Don't use a reflexive pronoun to make a sentence sound more formal.** The basic pronoun form is adequate.

{**Nonstandard**}   The gift is for Matthew and **yourself.**

{**Revised**}   The gift is for Matthew and **you.**

Use the pronoun reflexively only when the subject and object in a sentence refer to the same person or thing.

> subj.   obj.
> **Maggie** rediscovered **herself** in her painting.

> subj.   obj.
> **Corey** had only **herself** to rely on.

Problems occur most often with the form *myself* when used in place of a more suitable *I* or *me.*

> subj.   obj.
> {**Nonstandard**}   **Cate and myself** wrote the lab **report.**

Here, the subject and the object of the sentence are not the same. The simple subject form—*I*—suffices.

{**Revised**}   Cate and **I** wrote the lab report.

Compare the sentence above to a similar one using *myself* correctly as an intensive pronoun.

> I wrote the lab report **myself.**

29 A
Rflx/Int

➤ **Use intensive pronouns where emphasis is needed.**

> The gift is for **you yourself.**

> The **residents** did all the plumbing and wiring **themselves.**

➤ **Never use the forms *hisself* or *theirselves* in writing.** The correct forms for writing are *himself* and *themselves.*

{**Wrong**}   Lincoln wrote the memo **hisself.**

{**Corrected**}   Lincoln **himself** wrote the memo.

{**Wrong**}   They saw **theirselves** on television.

{**Corrected**}   They saw **themselves** on television.

EXERCISE 29.1

Correct any problems with reflexive or intensive pronouns in the sentences below.

1. Kyle tried to explain why the supposedly plagiarized paper he had turned in hisself might differ from Francie's and Richard's.
2. "I myself made a few changes in the paper Francie gave me," Kyle began.
3. Richard spoke next: "I know that Kyle and myself weren't completely happy with the paper Francie gave us, so I changed mine a little too."

4. "Me, too," Francie explained. "I wrote our collaborative version myself based on the materials Richard and Kyle had given me, but even they theirselves would admit that their work had gaps, so I made a few changes."
5. Dean Rack, scratching hisself on the forehead, now looked more amused than angry. "Let's see," he said, "You, Francie, wrote one version of a paper for Kyle and Richard and one version for yourself, while Kyle and Richard both wrote separate versions for theirselves, too?"

29 B   CHOOSING BETWEEN *THAT* AND *WHICH* AND *WHO*

Troubleshooting

You may recall a rule requiring the use of *which* before nonrestrictive clauses, and *that* before restrictive clauses. Nonrestrictive modifiers add information to a sentence, but aren't essential to its meaning.

{**Nonrestrictive clause**}   My car, **which is a station wagon,** sustained little damage.

Restrictive modifiers are essential to the meaning of a sentence because they specify the word they modify.

{**Restrictive clause**}   The car **that hit me** rolled into the ditch.

Yet in reading you may also have encountered writers who use *which* both restrictively and nonrestrictively. What *is* the correct form, and when is *who* an appropriate alternative to *which* and *that*?

29 B

Which

To decide between *that, which,* and *who* . . .

➤ **Understand that both restrictive and nonrestrictive clauses may begin with which.** A clause introduced by *that* will almost inevitably be restrictive. No commas are used around such clauses.

The concept **that intrigued the shareholders most** involved profit sharing.

The report **that I wrote** recommended the concept.

Context and punctuation, however, determine whether a *which* clause is restrictive or nonrestrictive. If the clause is restrictive, no commas separate it from the rest of the sentence; if nonrestrictive, commas enclose the clause.

{**Restrictive clause**}   The car **which hit me** rolled into a ditch.

{**Nonrestrictive clause**}   The car, **which hit me,** rolled into a ditch.

{**Restrictive clause**}   The concept **which intrigued the shareholders most** was the simplest one.

{**Nonrestrictive clause**}   The concept, **which intrigued the shareholders a great deal,** was quite simple.

Since many readers will hold you to the traditional rule, it makes sense to maintain the distinction between *that* and *which* if you understand it clearly.

➤ Use *who* rather than *that* or *which* when modifying a human subject.

{**Inappropriate**}   The woman **that** waved was my boss.

{**Better**}   The woman **who** waved was my boss.

EXERCISE 29.2

Decide between *that/which/who* in the following sentences. Add commas where needed.

1. Kyle was the student {**that/which/who**} seemed most likely to get both into and out of trouble.
2. The excuses {**that/which/who**} he offered for his behavior usually strained credibility.
3. His wallet {**that/which/who**} he lost about once a month was stuffed with traffic citations {**that/which/who**} remained unsettled or unpaid.
4. The citations {**that/which/who**} he received regularly usually involved creative driving—{**that/which/who**} the police preferred to describe as reckless.
5. The reason {**that/which/who**} Kyle was rarely in serious trouble was that he could usually charm his way out of situations {**that/which/who**} would baffle the average student.

---

29 C

29 C   **USING *I, YOU, ONE, WE***

I/One

Troubleshooting

Many writers are unsure when—if ever—they may use *I, we,* or *you* in professional or academic writing. Some teachers and editors effectively outlaw *I* or *you* in all but personal essays. As a result, students retreat to the passive voice ("it is believed"), to awkward references to self ("this writer"; "the author of this piece") or to the pronoun *one.* These strategies for avoiding *I* and *you* can make academic papers sound awkward or unduly formal.

Pronouns do, in fact, change the relationship between writer and reader. They aren't, however, interchangeable, nor is it easy to formulate strategies to explain which pronouns to use in every situation. However, you may find the following suggestions helpful.

When setting the tone for a paper . . .

➤ Use *I* whenever it makes sense for you or your opinions to appear in an essay. In general, avoid *I* in scientific reports and expository essays where your identity or your personal opinions are likely to be unimportant to readers.

I **learned** through a survey I **did** that students who drive a car on campus are more likely to have jobs than those who do not.

{**Revised**}   **A survey showed** that students who drive a car on campus are more likely to have jobs than those who do not.

However, when you find that avoiding *I* makes you resort to an awkward passive verb, use *I* instead.

It is felt that the play is too long.

If you believe the play is too long, say so.

{**Revised**}   **I believe** the play is too long.

You can often eliminate an awkward passive without using *I*.

{**Revised without *I***}   The play is too long.

The same advice—to use *I* sensibly—applies when you find yourself concocting words or phrases just to avoid the pronoun.

In the opinion of this writer, federal taxes should be lowered.

{**Revised**}   **I believe** federal taxes should be lowered.

{**Revised without *I***}   Federal taxes should be lowered.

The experience of this researcher suggests that the research design itself is flawed.

{**Revised**}   **I am convinced** that the research design itself is flawed.

{**Revised without *I***}   The research design itself is flawed.

Some editors and teachers simply will not allow *I* in academic and scientific writing. When writing for them, respect their rules. However, most writers today recognize that using *I* is both natural and sensible, even in formal prose.

29 C

I/One

➤ **Use *we* whenever two or more writers are involved in a project or when you are writing to express the opinion of a group.**

When **we** compared our surveys, **we** discovered the conflicting evidence.

We believe that City Council has an obligation to reconsider its zoning action.

Or use *we* to indicate a general condition.

We need better control of our medical care systems in the United States.

Avoid *we* or *us* as a chummy way of addressing your reader. When introducing a paper or handling a transition, don't make it sound as if you are taking readers on a grand tour of Europe.

Now that **we** have completed our survey of mental disorders, let **us** turn to . . .

In most academic writing, *we* used this way sounds pompous.

➤ **Use *you* whenever it makes sense to speak to your readers personally or when you are giving orders or directions.** *You* sounds direct, cordial, and personal. Consequently, when using *you* in academic writing, be sure you really want readers included in what you are discussing.

{**Inappropriate**}   A recent student government survey suggested that **you** will cheat in two courses during your college career.

This sentence is too personal; it seems to implicate the reader directly in scholastic dishonesty.

{**Revised**}   The student government survey suggested that **most students** will cheat in two courses during their college careers.

Also, be sure that when you write *you,* you aren't describing an experience that would be handled better from first-person (*I*) or third-person (*he, she, they*) points of view.

{**Inappropriate**}   **You** are puzzled by the nature of the ghost when **you** first read *Hamlet.*

{**Revised**}   **Some people** are puzzled by the nature of the ghost when **they** first read *Hamlet.*

▶ **Use *one* when you want to express a thought that might be yours, but which should be understood more generally.** *One* is often useful for conveying moral sentiments or general truths.

Consider the terror of not knowing where **one's** next meal is coming from.

Reading Dostoevsky, **one** senses the depth of the Slavic soul.

Notice that *one* here gives the sentence more authority than it would have if *one* were replaced by *I* or *you.*

29 C

I/One

Sentences with too many *ones,* however, may seem like the butlers of British comedy—sneering and superior.

{**Pompous**}   **One** can never be too careful about maintaining **one's** good reputation, can **one?**

In most cases, *you* or an appropriate noun sounds better and less formal than *one,* especially when giving directions.

{**Wordy**}   If **one** is uncertain about the authority of **one's** sources, **one** should consult a librarian in the reference room.

{**Revised**}   If **you** are uncertain about the authority of ***your*** sources, consult a librarian in the reference room.

▶ **Whatever pronoun forms you use, be reasonably consistent.** Don't switch pronouns in the middle of a sentence or paragraph. Problems are most likely to occur with the indefinite pronoun *one.*

{**Nonstandard**}   **One** cannot know what **their** future holds.

Here the pronoun shifts incorrectly from *one* to the plural form *they.* Several revisions are possible.

{**Revised**}   **One** cannot know what **his or her** future holds.

{**Revised**}   **People** cannot know what **their** futures hold.

{**Revised**}   **One** cannot know what the future holds.

You may shift between *one* and *he* or *she,* as the example above demonstrates. You may also want to change the pronoun to make a sentence sound less stuffy.

{Formal} When **one** turns on a political program these days, **one** is likely to see liberals and conservatives hotly debating the issues.

{Revised} When **you** turn on a political program these days, **you** are likely to see liberals and conservatives hotly debating the issues.

EXERCISE 29.3

Are the boldfaced pronouns or other expressions appropriate in the sentences below? Change any that you think are either awkward, unduly formal, or inconsistent. In some cases, you may have to rewrite entire sentences.

1. "Let **us** read from the opening paragraphs of each of your papers," Dean Rack said to Francie, Kyle, and Richard. "Shall **we** begin with yours, Richard?"
2. [Richard's opening paragraph] **I** don't know who invented the water clock, but **I** think the ancient Egyptians were the first to use it with any degree of sophistication. The advantage of the water clock over the sundial was that **you** could measure time at night; the disadvantage was that **you** might wake up in the morning with a frozen timepiece. . . .
3. [Kyle's opening paragraph] In some respects, the modern world began with the invention of the mechanical clock. Let **us** look at three inventions that made the mechanical clock possible, the escapement, the pendulum, and the balance spring. It is the opinion of **this writer** that we do not understand adequately the relationship between these important inventions. . . .
4. [Francie's opening paragraph] **One** can never know what will make **them** a success. Did the Jesuit missionary Matteo Ricci ever imagine that clocks, not religious fervor, would help to gain him access to the Chinese emperor in the sixteenth century? **You** wouldn't expect the sophisticated Chinese to be impressed by what amounted to little more than a European toy—but **they** were. **This paper** will review how Europe's invention of the mechanical clock made Ricci's missionary exploits possible.
5. The Dean put the papers down on his desk. "**One** hardly knows what to think when **one** encounters work of this sort, does **he? You** all wrote on the same general subject, but **you** didn't write the same paper. **One** is led to wonder, is this collusion, or isn't it?"

29 D

Nonsex

29 D NONSEXIST USAGE

Troubleshooting

What happens when you need to use a pronoun, but don't know whether it should refer to a man or a woman?

Each of the editors walked to **(his/her)** car.

Until recently, you would have been expected to use a masculine pronoun (*he, him, his*) in any such situation on the grounds that when you are talking about *man*kind you are also thinking about *woman*kind.

{**Sexist**}   Each of the editors walked to **his** car.

But, in fact, such male-only constructions exclude women from more than just grammar.

{**Sexist**}   A **Senator** gets to choose **his** own staff.

{**Sexist**}   The chair**man** has not completed **his** correction of the report.

Applied rigorously, the male-only rule leads to all sorts of distortions, some even humorous—as in this sentence taken from an actual paper.

One common myth teenagers believe is that a **person** cannot get pregnant the first time **he** has intercourse.

English has a second-person singular form that includes men and women alike: *you.* But, unfortunately, the third-person singular forms are either male (*he, him, his*), female (*she, her, hers*), or neuter (*it, its*). And *it* just doesn't work as a substitute for a person.

To avoid sexist pronouns . . .

➤ **Assume that all professions may include both men and women.** Remember that members of either sex may belong to almost every profession or group—students, athletes, coal miners, truckers, secretaries, nurses. Then let your language reflect that diversity. Obviously, you should acknowledge the inevitable exceptions.

Each of the nuns received an award for **her** valor.

None of the NFL quarterbacks received a payment for **his** appearance at the benefit.

But in situations where you cannot assume that members of a group will all be male or all female, be sure your language accommodates both sexes. You can do that in several ways, listed below.

➤ **Use the expressions *he or she, him or her,* or *his or her* instead of the pronoun of either sex alone.**

{**Sexist**}   Every secretary may invite **her husband.**

{**Revised**}   Every secretary may invite **his or her spouse.**

Unfortunately, *he or she* expressions—as well as variations such as *he/she* or *s/he*—can be awkward and tiresome when they occur more than once in a sentence. In many cases, you'll want to try another strategy for avoiding sexist usage.

➤ **Change a singular reference to a plural one.** Because plural pronouns do not have a specific gender in English, you can often avoid the choice between *he* or *she* simply by turning singular references into plural ones.

{**Sexist**}   **Every** secretary may invite **her husband.**

{**Revised**}   **All** secretaries may invite **their spouses.**

Here's a second example:

{**Tiresome**}   Before **he or she** leaves, **each** member of the band should be sure **he or she** has **his or her** music.

{**Revised**}   Before leaving, **all** members of the band should be sure **they** have **their** music.

Notice that this version eliminates the first *he or she* entirely.

➤ **Cut the troublesome pronoun.** The preceding example shows that, in some cases, you can simply cut the feminine or masculine pronoun from a sentence. Here are more examples:

{**Original**}   **Anybody** may bring **his or her** favorite record.

{**Revised**}   **Anybody** may bring **a** favorite record.

{**Original**}   **Nobody** should leave until after **he or she** has signed the guest book.

{**Revised**}   **Nobody** should leave until after signing the guest book.

{**Original**}   **Each** should keep a record of **his or her** losses and gains in weight.

{**Revised**}   **Each** should keep a personal record of losses and gains in weight.

This option is useful, but not always available.

➤ **Use *he* and *she* alternatively.** You can try to balance references to males and females in a particular article. This does not mean arbitrarily shifting gender with every pronoun. In most cases, pronouns can be varied sensibly and naturally within chunks of prose—between paragraphs, for example, or between the examples in a series. Handled skillfully, the shift between masculine and feminine references need not attract a reader's attention. Avoid varying pronoun gender within individual sentences.

> Dean Rack knew that any student could purchase **his** term papers through mail-order term paper services. If **he** could afford the scam, a student might construct **his** entire college career around bought papers, even designing **his** course schedule to fit the kinds of work the so-called research services perform.

> Yet Rack also believed that the typical plagiarist was not so grossly dishonest and calculating. **She** tended to resort to such highly unethical behavior only when **she** believed an assignment was beyond **her** capabilities or **her** workload was excessive. Then **she** tended to panic.

➤ **Use a plural pronoun with indefinite pronouns formerly considered singular.** Although this pronoun/referent disagreement—very common in speech—is gaining limited acceptance in writing, be warned that most readers still consider such forms simply wrong.

> **Every skier** took **their** turn on the ski slopes.

Technically, *every skier* is singular and thus requires a singular pronoun: *his or her.*

Everybody took **his or her** turn on the ski slopes.

Revise the following sentences to eliminate any pronouns that might be considered sexist. Treat all examples as if they occurred in written English—even when the pronouns in question occur in dialogue.

1. Francie spoke. "Well, Dean Rack, it looks as if each of us wrote his own paper after all."
2. "None of us is as good a writer or a researcher as he thinks he is," Richard observed, "yet apparently each of us believed he could do a better job than our collaborators."
3. "Like Francie," Richard observes, "I thought I could improve on the topic Kyle originally researched and Francie wrote up, but I didn't want to hurt him or her."
4. Francie sighed, "I guess each of us realized that a good student ultimately has to rely on his own strengths."
5. Kyle spoke last. "I did the same thing. I was going to write on the problems a timekeeper in ancient Egypt would have had keeping his calendar accurate, but ended up writing about water clocks instead."
6. "So, it seems," said the Dean, "that I have a case of collusion in which each writer chose his or her own topic, did his or her own research, and turned in his or her own paper."
7. "What ought a Dean do when he is faced with such a complication?" Rack asked.
8. Kyle smiled broadly and suggested that the Dean give each of the three students the warning he richly deserved and then dismiss the case.
9. Rack agreed, lecturing sternly for almost fifteen minutes about scholastic dishonesty. Then he ordered them to rewrite his or her paper and to do a month of cafeteria duty, washing dishes.
10. Each student took his punishment like a man.

30 Sentence Boundaries: Fragments, Comma Splices, and Run-ons

A Sentence fragments

B Minor sentences

C Comma splices

D Run-on sentences

Three of the most troublesome and common of sentence problems are the fragment, the comma splice, and the run-on. These faults in sentence structure occur so frequently in writing that we believe they merit a chapter of their own. As you'll see, all three problems arise from confusion about what the dimensions or boundaries of a sentence are. Once you gain a feel for what a sentence does, you are less likely to write one that doesn't do its job adequately.

30 A. SENTENCE FRAGMENTS

Terms you need to know

SENTENCE FRAGMENT. A group of words that does not fully express an idea even though it is punctuated as a sentence. It may also be called a "broken sentence."

{**Fragment**} Since David had never driven a really good car.

VERBALS. Words or phrases derived from verbs but which act as nouns, adjectives, and adverbs. The three kinds of verbals are **infinitives, participles,** and **gerunds.**

GERUND. A verb form used as a noun: *walking, disagreeing, writing.*

INFINITIVE. The *to* + *a verb* that is the base of any verb: *to eat, to swim, to demonstrate.*

PARTICIPLE. A verb form used as a modifier.

Grinning, the cat walked off.

The mouse, much **relieved,** went in the other direction.

APPOSITIVE. A word or phrase that stands next to a noun and modifies it by restating or expanding its meaning.

Groupies, **those insatiable fans who surround many rock stars,** are flattering but troublesome.

Troubleshooting

You may be getting your drafts or final papers back with "fragment" marked in the margins or with the warning that you're writing incomplete sentences and need to work on the problem. If so, you need to spend time figuring out what is going wrong because sentence fragments can confuse or distract your readers. They can also make you look like a careless writer. This section will show you how to identify sentence fragments or broken sentences and how to fix them or avoid writing them in the first place.

To eliminate fragments . . .

➤ **Check that you have not tried to make a dependent or subordinate clause stand alone as a sentence.** Dependent clauses—clauses that start with words like *although, because, if, for,* and *thus*—won't work as sentences by themselves even though they have a subject and a verb.

{**Fragment**}   If a rock group has a hit record.

{**Fragment**}   Because a tricky name seems to help a new group.

These are fragments or broken sentences—that is, parts of a sentence left suspended in air and needing something else to finish them. By themselves, they leave the reader puzzled, waiting to find out what they should be attached to. Such fragments can usually be repaired by linking them to another sentence. For example, the previous fragments have been attached to independent clauses to make full sentences.

<table>
<tr><td>**30 A**</td></tr>
<tr><td>Frag</td></tr>
</table>

{**Complete sentence**}   If a rock group has a hit record, it may break into the
> big time.

{**Complete sentence**}   Because a tricky name seems to help a new group, David
> chose something novel to call his band.

> Here are some additional examples showing the dependent clause fragments or broken sentences in boldface.

{**Fragment**}   David Barrett, manager and leader of Microwave Katz, has accepted
> the latest gift from his fan club. **Although its members prefer to think of
> themselves as supporters of the arts.**
>> [The clause starting with *although* has been broken off from *fan club* and doesn't make
>> sense by itself.]

{**Fragment eliminated**}   David Barrett, manager and leader of Microwave Katz,
> has accepted the latest gift from his fan club, although its members prefer
> to think of themselves as supporters of the arts.

{**Fragment**}   **Even though they have spiked hair, wear leather, and roar through
> town on noisy motorcycles whenever they get bored.** The group has bank
> accounts that make them respectable in Ruralia.
>> [The clause beginning with *Even though* goes on so long that at first it seems like a
>> sentence, but it can't be; it's an introductory phrase that requires a statement to
>> complete it.]

{**Fragment eliminated**}   Even though they have spiked hair, wear leather, and roar through town on noisy motorcycles whenever they get bored, the group has bank accounts that make them respectable in Ruralia.

EXERCISE 30.1

Write full sentences that correctly incorporate these sentence fragments.

1. Even if a rock band isn't very talented.
2. Because there is so much money to be made in the music business.
3. Although the major rock stars are usually guitarists.
4. When *Rolling Stone* reviews a new record.
5. Since an amateur group often has minimal musical equipment.

➤ **Check to see that you have not tried to make a relative clause or appositive phrase stand alone as a sentence.** Words like *who, which, that,* and *where* frequently signal the beginning of a relative clause that must be connected to the main part of a sentence to make sense.

{**Fragment**}   He was just plain David Barrett. **Who never expected to own a coveted sports car.**

Another sort of construction that often turns into a sentence fragment is the appositive. When such phrases are separated and made to look like sentences, you get sentence fragments. Here is an example with the fragments in boldface.

{**Fragment**}   Barrett's fan club bought him a handsome 1963 Corvette Sting Ray. **The most timeless of all Corvette designs.**

> [The phrase starting with *the* is punctuated as a sentence, but it lacks a verb and doesn't express a full idea by itself.]

{**Fragment eliminated**}   Barrett's fan club bought him a handsome 1963 Corvette Sting Ray, the most timeless of all Corvette designs.

30 A

Frag

EXERCISE 30.2

Write full sentences that incorporate these sentence fragments derived from relative clauses or appositives.

1. A car that any connoisseur would appreciate.
2. Which was a gift that would impress anyone.
3. A hobby that certainly isn't for the poor.
4. Who is the favorite among the local fans.
5. Which had never happened to him before.

➤ **Check to see that you have not mistaken a verbal for the verb in a sentence.** Verbals (see Section 24A and B) are tricky constructions that can easily mislead a writer into mistaking a phrase for a sentence. Verbals look like verbs, but they really act as nouns, adjectives, or adverbs. For instance in the phrase "to look at something," *to look* is the infinitive of the verb, but it doesn't act as a verb. In the phrase "running for office," *running* is a gerund, not a verb. In the phrase "recognizing his weakness," *recognizing* can be a noun or an adjective, but it can't be a verb. To eliminate fragments caused by verbals, it helps to remember that

- An *-ing* word by itself can never act as the verb of a sentence. It must have an auxiliary word such as *have, is, were.*

- An infinitive, such as *to run, to go,* and so on, can never act as the verb of a sentence.

Here are examples of how verbals cause sentence fragments. The fragments are boldfaced.

{**Fragment**}   When Barrett's fan club drove the Corvette up and parked it in front of his house, the usually talkative songwriter suddenly fell silent. **Feeling unworthy of that handsome split-window coupe.**
> [The boldfaced portion does not include a verb and cannot act as a sentence.]

{**Fragment eliminated**}   When Barrett's fan club drove the Corvette up and parked it in front of his house, the usually talkative songwriter suddenly fell silent, feeling unworthy of that handsome split-window coupe.

{**Fragment**}   **To hear the rumble of the 327 V-8.** That was magic.
> [The entire boldfaced portion is an infinitive phrase acting as a noun and shouldn't be punctuated as a sentence.]

{**Fragment eliminated**}   To hear the rumble of the 327 V-8 powering the machine was magic.

Write full sentences incorporating these sentence fragments derived from verbals or verbal phrases.

1. Given all the trouble he had caused the neighbors.
2. Never realizing those crazy fans had so much money.
3. Considered an outrageous luxury by most people.
4. Believing that it would make his career even better.
5. To see if there had been some mistake.

➤ **Check to see that you have not treated a disconnected phrase as a sentence.** Sometimes—particularly in advertising copy—a phrase with no subject or verb is punctuated as a sentence.

> The classic Corvette Sting Ray. **Muscular and powerful. Timeless design. Above all, performance.**

Such constructions are not always puzzling, but they're out of place in most academic or professional writing.

Turning a disconnected phrase into a full sentence usually requires adding a subject or a verb (sometimes both), depending upon what has been omitted from the phrase. Here is an example of disconnected phrases causing sentence fragments. The fragment is boldfaced.

{**Fragment**}   David buffed the fingerprints away. **Absentmindedly. With his new lambswool sweater.**

> [The prepositional phrase—*with his new lambswool sweater*—can be joined to the end of the sentence. *Absentmindedly* needs to be attached to what it modifies: *buffed*.]

{**Fragment eliminated**}   David, absentmindedly buffed the fingerprints away with his new lambswool sweater.

> **TIP: We know all these references to verbals, appositives, infinitives, gerunds, and so on are enough to make your eyes glaze over. Don't worry if you can't remember these terms or don't know which kind of fragment you've written. Just check your writing for sentence fragments when you revise, and eventually you'll develop a fragment detector that will tell you when a group of words doesn't have all the parts it needs to be a sentence. And keep in mind that when you are doing academic, professional, and business writing, you need to be more careful not to write fragments than you'd have to be if you were writing advertising copy, or fiction. See the next section on minor sentences.**

30 A

Frag

EXERCISE 30.4

Write full sentences that incorporate these fragments derived from disconnected phrases.

1. One of the fastest cars in town.
2. Never again.
3. Without looking back.
4. Not in his lifetime.
5. Awesome. Eye-catching.

EXERCISE 30.5

Rewrite the following sentences and eliminate any sentence fragments.

1. Although Barrett's neighbors thought they were used to almost anything. The next day they were startled to see a long, covered object in his carport with only a glimpse of white sidewall tires showing at the bottom.
2. As they watched, Barrett came out of the house in white overalls. Carrying two large plastic buckets of warm water and a basket full of car-care products.

3. Putting down the buckets and basket, he reached into his pocket. Drawing out a chamois.
4. The neighbors were consumed with curiosity about his preparations. Doing things ahead of time being very uncharacteristic of David the musician.
5. At last Barrett approached the Corvette. Half-dazed. Lost in admiration of so renowned a vehicle.

30 B   MINOR SENTENCES

Term you need to know

MINOR SENTENCE. A group of words that does not have all the usual parts of a sentence but can act as a sentence because it expresses an idea fully.

minor sentence
Is an old car an obsolete car? **Not always.**

minor sentence
Not in my back yard. That's the slogan of many groups opposing rock concerts.

Troubleshooting

When students in writing classes become concerned about avoiding sentence fragments, they begin to notice how often fragments appear in newspapers or certain magazines. Inevitably they ask, "How can those writers get away with using fragments when we can't?" For example, this paragraph might appear in a specialized car magazine.

> Some classic car buffs are fanatics. No moderation. No control. When they restore a car, they'll go to any extreme to see that it's perfect. Total authenticity. That's their goal.

It does make one wonder. Are sentence fragments considered wrong at some times but not at others? The answer is "Yes." It depends on the writer's purpose and on the audience.

Certain kinds of fragments can be classified as **minor sentences**—that is, phrases or groups of words that don't have all the traditional components of a sentence but effectively convey a full idea. Such sentences appear frequently in many informal essays, magazine pieces, and advertisements. For example:

> Do such obstacles mean that amateur auto detailers are doomed to failure? Not necessarily. Persistence and luck. If they have those, they can achieve their goal.

So writers can sometimes use fragments effectively when writing for certain purposes. For instance, they may want to achieve a quick pace or a staccato effect in their writing, they may want to create a series of images, or they may want to give their writing a very casual tone. One way to accomplish these goals is to use a series of sentence fragments.

The classic car connoisseur with a good eye can always recognize a master's work. The gleaming, immaculate finish. The authentic hood ornament. The perfectly restored hubcaps and manufacturer's insignia.

The problem is that both minor sentences and deliberate fragments can look just like the fragments many readers consider major errors. Thus it's a good idea to use minor sentences cautiously in most writing.

To avoid problems with minor sentences . . .

➤ **Use them sparingly.** Minor sentences and deliberate fragments should not appear regularly in any formal or academic writing, and certainly not in a research paper, report, job application letter, or literary analysis. You might use them in narratives, journal pieces, humorous essays, or personality sketches.

➤ **Be sure readers understand that they are deliberate.** Careful readers who think that fragments or minor sentences are accidental rather than used for some specific effect may object to them, thinking the writer doesn't understand sentence structure. If you do want to use fragments occasionally, think first what your purpose is in using them and who your readers are. For readers who you know are conservative about grammar, don't use fragments. For other readers, be sure you have some special reason for using them. You don't want minor sentences to look like careless accidents.

In the following passage, for example, Kyle Talbot, writing a sketch of David, deliberately uses a series of minor sentences and effective fragments to achieve the upbeat, rapid pace he wants to convey in his portrait.

> One would think that anyone as sharp as David Barrett wouldn't be overwhelmed by a car. **Any car. Not so.** But then a Corvette Sting Ray is not just any car. It's a cult item. **An icon. A grunting, pulsing emblem of America. Something every car nut worthy of his or her tachometer would kill for.** So no wonder David was overwhelmed. **And distracted from his music.**

30 C

CS

EXERCISE 30.6

Working with other students in a small group, find advertisements that use minor sentences and deliberate fragments. Rewrite them to eliminate all incomplete sentences. Then assess the difference between the original ad and the revised versions. Why do you think the writers used these fragments?

30 C   COMMA SPLICES

Term you need to know

COMMA SPLICE. The punctuation error of using a comma to join two groups of words, each of which could be a sentence by itself. May also be called a *comma fault*.

Being a member of a fan club is a gratifying experience, it is comparable to being in a football booster club.

Troubleshooting

If the mark *CS* or *comma fault* is decorating the margins of your papers all too often, and you can't figure out what you're doing wrong, it is worth your time to find out what a comma splice is and how to fix one when it appears in your writing. Look at this example of a comma splice:

David's fans showed great insight about his tastes, they couldn't have chosen a better gift for him.

Notice that the groups of words on each side of the comma could stand alone as sentences. When that happens, you know you have a comma splice.

▶ **To avoid comma splices in your writing, it may help to recall that the comma is a weak mark of punctuation.** Therefore, a comma doesn't work well to mark the strong pause needed to separate two groups of words when each one could be a sentence by itself.

When a comma in the middle of a sentence takes the place of a semicolon or a conjunction, it can also hide the relationship between the two parts of a sentence. As a result, the reader doesn't know if the writer wants to show that the two parts are closely connected, or if the writer wants to contrast the parts or show that one is less important than the other. For instance, see how confusing this sentence could be.

30 C

CS

David is an outstanding musician, he has no formal training in music.

Does the sentence mean that "David is outstanding *because* he has no training"? Or does it mean that "David is outstanding *although* he has no training"? The comma splice causes the problem.

Here are examples of typical kinds of comma splices.

{**Comma splice**}   David carefully put the buckets of warm water on the ground, he began to lay the cleaning tools on a table beside the car.
[Two independent clauses that need to be merged.]

{**Comma splice**}   He was supposed to be at rehearsal in thirty minutes, nevertheless, he continued to tinker with the car.
[This illustrates a frequent mistake: using a comma before *nevertheless* or *however* in a compound sentence. You need a semicolon.]

> **TIP: Only very short independent clauses, usually in threes, should be joined by commas.**
>
> **I came, I saw, I conquered.**
> **He ate, I paid, we left.**

To fix comma splices . . .

➤ Substitute a semicolon for the comma.

{Comma splice}   As David cleaned his car, every sponge, Q-tip, toothbrush, toothpick, and pipe cleaner was laid out in one neat row, every linen towel, chamois square, cotton ball, and silk handkerchief was laid out in another row.

> [The separation between these two closely related independent ideas gets lost among the commas that are separating items in the series.]

{Comma splice eliminated}   As David cleaned his car, every sponge, Q-tip, toothbrush, and pipe cleaner was laid out in one neat row; every linen towel, chamois square, cotton ball, and silk handkerchief was laid out in another row.

➤ Substitute a period for the comma.

{Comma splice}   Like a surgeon going to work, David began to wash one square inch of the car at a time, by the end of the morning he had finished the hood and one fender.

> [These two independent clauses should have a stronger separation to emphasize their difference.]

{Comma splice eliminated}   Like a surgeon going to work, David began to wash a few square inches of the car at a time. By the end of the morning, he had finished the hood and one door.

➤ Keep the comma, but insert a conjunction such as *but, and,* or *or* after it.

{Comma splice}   The reason his progress was so slow was that he probed each door crevice with a Q-tip or a toothpick, after he finished a section, he polished it to a high shine first with a linen towel and then with a silk handkerchief.

> [These two independent clauses need a strong separation to stress that they are in a sequence. The comma doesn't provide that separation.]

{Comma splice eliminated}   The reason his progress was so slow was that he probed each door crevice with a Q-tip or a toothpick, **and** after he finished a section, he polished it to a high shine with a linen towel and then a silk handkerchief.

➤ Make one of the clauses a dependent, subordinate clause.

{Comma splice}   David untangled himself from a squatting position, he balanced his buckets and basket in his hands.

> [The two clauses of the sentence are not equally important so the first one should be changed to a subordinate clause, and the comma retained.]

{Comma splice eliminated}   As David untangled himself from a squatting position, he balanced his buckets and basket in his hands.

30 C

CS

EXERCISE 30.7

Working with a group of other students, identify which of the following sentences have comma splices and correct them.

1. Not many fan clubs can afford gifts of fancy cars, the members are generally too young.
2. Usually fans content themselves with just being enthusiastic and loyal, they love shouting and applauding loudly.
3. They had taste, they had class, they had money.
4. David's fans were devoted, they thought he hung the moon.
5. Not all Ruralia residents appreciate rock music, however, nearly all the college students are ardent supporters of Barrett's group.

EXERCISE 30.8

Working with another student, look at these sentences and decide which have comma splices; then work out some ways to correct the problem.

1. The parents of the young people in David's fan club were perpetually astonished at their children's behavior, nevertheless, they tried to understand their fanaticism.
2. Wearing ear plugs, two of the more adventuresome parents actually attended a concert, afterward they were more astonished than before.
3. Both of them admitted that Microwave Katz gave a dynamic, energetic performance, they knew in their hearts that rock groups today just didn't measure up to the bands of their days, Jefferson Airplane, the Supremes, the Strawberry Alarm Clock.
4. They wanted to stay on good terms with their children, therefore, they were careful not to make any comparisons.
5. Finally, Lucinda's parents realized that the last thing she wanted was for them to like her music, that would take all the fun out of it for Lucinda.

30 D

Run-on

30 D RUN-ON SENTENCES

Term you need to know

RUN-ON SENTENCE. A sentence in which two independent clauses are joined without the necessary conjunction or punctuation. May also be called a **fused sentence.**

Troubleshooting

You may see *run-on* or *FS* (for *fused sentence*) in the margins of your papers and not understand what you are doing wrong. The symbol indicates a problem that is the opposite of a comma splice; that is, there is no punctuation at all between two independent clauses, and the reader can't tell how they should be separated. If your instructor has told you that you need to be careful about run-on sentences, you should habitually check any long sentence. See if you have run together two or more sentences that should be separated. If so, you have a punctuation problem that is easily fixed.

{**Run-on**}   Barrett's fans thought locating the 1963 Corvette Sting Ray would be a major job they never dreamed Walter Toth would be able to find one for them.

{**Rewritten**}   Barrett's fans thought locating the 1963 Corvette Sting Ray would be a major job. They never dreamed Walter Toth would be able to find one for them.

{**Run-on**}   The price they paid for the car is a well-kept secret speculation is that it was about the same as a brand new Lexus.

{**Rewritten**}   Although the price they paid for the car is a well-kept secret, speculation is that it was about the same as a brand new Lexus.

To eliminate run-on sentences or phrases . . .

➤ **Insert a period between fused sentences.**

{**Run-on**}   After four days of cleaning, waxing, and polishing, Barrett was finally satisfied with his Corvette he agreed with his neighbors that it could not have looked any better if it had belonged to Bruce Springsteen.

> [The sentence needs to be broken after *Corvette* so as not to confuse the readers. Adding a period makes a natural separation.]

{**Run-on eliminated**}   After four days of cleaning, waxing, and polishing, Barrett was finally satisfied with his Corvette. He agreed with his neighbors that it could not have looked any better if it had belonged to Bruce Springsteen.

30 D
Run-on

➤ **Insert a semicolon between two independent clauses that have been run together.** A semicolon suggests that the ideas in the two sentences are closely related.

{**Run-on**}   David's whole life now revolved around his Sting Ray he could think of nothing else.

> [The two clauses are closely related but need to be separated to show they are separate ideas. A semicolon separates the sentences, but preserves a relationship between them.]

{**Run-on eliminated**}   David's whole life now revolved around his Sting Ray; he could think of nothing else.

➤ **Make one of the independent clauses subordinate to the other.**

{**Run-on**}   The only problem was that while David "detailed" his 'Vette, his business manager, Maxwell Maverick, had to cancel three concerts for Microwave Katz Barrett had completely lost interest in his group.

> [The sentence needs to be rewritten to show the relationship between the two independent clauses.]

{**Run-on eliminated**}   The only problem was that while David "detailed" his 'Vette, his business manager, Maxwell Maverick, had to cancel three concerts for Microwave Katz **because** Barrett had completely lost interest in his group.

> ## EXERCISE 30.9

Working with a group, rewrite these sentences to eliminate punctuation problems that create run-on sentences.

1. Desperate, Maxwell Maverick racked his brain to find a way to get David to forget his car he knew they would all go broke unless he did something drastic.
2. Early on the morning of the seventh day of Barrett's addiction to the Corvette, Maverick called Lucinda Leverage, president of Barrett's fan club he spoke with her urgently for fifteen minutes.
3. At 10:15 that same day, Lucinda's bank issued a stop-payment order on a check from Lucinda Leverage to Walter Toth's Used Sport Cars at first Toth was outraged but after Lucinda talked to him, he approved her strategy.
4. At 11:00, a wrecker from Walter Toth's garage appeared before Barrett's house the red Corvette disappeared down the driveway David was so shocked he was speechless.
5. At 9:00 that night, Barrett gyrated once again with Microwave Katz on the stage of the Ruralia Coliseum in the first row stood Lucinda Leverage, waving a set of keys.

30 D

Run-on

31 Modifiers

Terms you need to know

ADVERB. A word that modifies or gives information about verbs, adjectives, other adverbs, and sometimes an entire sentence.

ADJECTIVE. A word that modifies or gives information about nouns and pronouns. Adjectives can modify only nouns and pronouns, nothing else.

LINKING VERB. Forms of the verb *to be*—for example, *is, are, was,* and *am*—and others like it that *link* the subject to a modifier that describes it. Some other common linking verbs are *seem, appear,* and *feel.*

MODIFIER. A word, phrase, or clause that gives information about another word, phrase, or clause. Writers use modifiers to make important qualifications in their writing, to make it more accurate, and sometimes to give it color and depth.

ABSOLUTE. A phrase that modifies a sentence, but doesn't modify any specific word in it. An absolute usually acts as a comment on the main clause and could easily be changed into a subordinate clause.

absolute

Given the way political campaigns work, Janice Hayes knew she needed to get broad support for her child care proposal.

absolute

Everything considered, she decided child care was an issue important to faculty, staff, and students in an urban college.

ABSOLUTE ADJECTIVE. An adjective like *perfect, unique, dead,* or *equal* that cannot have degrees. One cannot be *less equal* or *more dead.*

427

31 A USING PREDICATE ADJECTIVES

Term you need to know

PREDICATE ADJECTIVE. An adjective that follows a linking verb and gives more information about the subject of the sentence. The linking verbs are *is, are, was,* and other forms of *to be* plus verbs like *seem, feel,* and *look.*

predicate adj.

Political campaigns are often **expensive.**

predicate adj.

A good candidate feels **confident.**

Troubleshooting

Are you sometimes unsure which word to select to follow pesky linking verbs like *seem, feel, become,* and *look?* Are you supposed to say "I feel bad" or "I feel badly"? If that's your dilemma, you have plenty of company—this is a tricky area. We suggest that as your first step toward solving the problem, figure out which word in the sentence you want to modify. If that word is the subject of the sentence, then the word you need to complete your verb should be a predicate adjective, not an adverb ending in *-ly.*

31 A

Pred Adj

To handle predicate adjectives correctly . . .

▶ **Remember that only adjectives, not adverbs, can modify a noun.** If you are going to complete the verb of a sentence with a word that you want to link with the *subject* of that sentence, you need to use an adjective because you are modifying a noun. In the following examples, the first version of the sentence shows the incorrect adverb modifier; the second version shows the correct form.

{Incorrect} Janice feels **enviously** of the child-care facilities at the college her sister attends.

> [The modifier describes *Janice,* a noun, so it should be an adjective.]

{Correct} Janice feels **envious** of the child-care facilities at the college her sister attends.

{Correct} Janice thinks **enviously** of the child-care facilities at the college her sister attends.

> [Now the modifier describes *thinks,* a verb, so the adverb form is correct.]

{Incorrect} Janice feels **hopefully** about getting a better system at the Clear Lake—Chicago campus.

> [The term modifies *Janice,* a noun, so it must be an adjective.]

{Correct} Janice feels **hopeful** about getting a better system at the Clear Lake—Chicago campus.

▶ **Learn to manage *well* and *good.*** Among the trickiest modifiers are *good* and *well. Good* is always an adjective; *well* is usually an adverb, but sometimes it too can be an adjective. No wonder writers sometimes get confused about which one they should use. Here are some quick guidelines. See also Section 21J.

- Use *good* after a linking verb when you want to link the modifier to the subject. For example,

Jasper Hayes looks **good.**

His scholastic record is **good.**

He feels **good** about being a father.

- But when you are referring to someone's state of health, you should use *well* to finish the linking verb.

Most college students feel **well** in spite of, not because of, their eating habits.

- Except in very casual conversation with your close friends, it's not a good idea to use *good* as an adverb. For example, don't write:

The system doesn't run **good.**

Most jobs in child care don't pay **good.**

Instead, write:

The system doesn't run **well.**

Most jobs in child care don't pay **well.**

31 B

Adj Pos

EXERCISE 31.1

In these sentences, replace the boldfaced modifier with a better one.

1. Janice and Jasper feel **sadly** when they think about having to put their son, John, in a child-care center five miles away.
2. They have read about on-site college child-care systems in other countries that seem to work **good.**
3. They want to look as **well** as possible in the eyes of John's grandparents.
4. John acts **suspiciously** when he hears his parents talking about taking him to school with them.
5. Janice anxiously asked Jasper, "Do you think John feels **badly**?"

31 B PLACING ADJECTIVES CORRECTLY

Troubleshooting

Most adjectives precede the noun or pronouns they modify. The noun acts like a magnet, drawing the adjective to it: *red* Corvette, *outstanding* athlete. Sometimes, however, you can confuse your readers by putting an adjective in a place where its meaning is ambiguous. You're most likely to do that when two nouns appear together in a sentence so that it's not clear which noun the adjective goes with. Check to see that your adjectives are next to the noun or phrase they modify. For example:

{**Ambiguous**}   Janice knew she needed the enthusiastic administration's endorsement.

> [*Enthusiastic* attaches itself to *administration* instead of *endorsement*.]

{**Clarified**}   Janice knew she needed the enthusiastic endorsement of the administration.

To place adjectives effectively . . .

➤ **Relocate adjectives that are potentially confusing or ambiguous.** You may have to read your sentences carefully to appreciate how they might be misread. Better still, get a friend to read over your paper and point out places where your readers might get confused.

{**Ambiguous**}   The old representative's records were revealing.

> [Does *old* go with *congressman* or with *records*?]

{**Clarified**}   The representative's old records were revealing.

{**Ambiguous**}   The colorful student's clothes created a sensation.

> [Does *colorful* go with *student* or with *clothes*?]

{**Clarified**}   The student's colorful clothes created a sensation.

31 B

Adj Pos

➤ **Consider placing adjectives after the word or phrase they modify.** You can often make a sentence more graceful or readable by placing adjectives after a noun or pronoun. Notice how moving the adjectives enlivens the sentence in the second example:

> College president Mortimer Coates is a **frumpily dressed, absentminded** bachelor.

> College president Mortimer Coates is a bachelor, **frumpily dressed** and **absentminded.**

EXERCISE 31.2

Rearrange the adjectives in each of these sentences to make the sentences clearer or more effective. You could do it in several ways.

1. Janice and Jasper wanted to find a forceful women's group to help them plan their strategy.
2. Intelligent child care was to be the center of their campaign.
3. They saw the negative president's attitude as something they needed to work on.
4. Janice also sensed some old-fashioned regents' biases about the glory of being a stay-at-home mother.
5. She thought their stuffy patriarch's attitudes were out of date.

31 C   PLACING ADVERBS CORRECTLY

Troubleshooting

Adverbs are generally easier to work with than adjectives because they're flexible and can take several different positions in a sentence. For example:

> Janice and Jasper made their plans **carefully,** talking **softly** between themselves.

> **Carefully** Janice and Jasper made their plans, **softly** talking between themselves.

> Janice and Jasper **carefully** made their plans, talking between themselves **softly.**

But because adverbs are so flexible, it's also easy to get them in an inappropriate place, particularly if the sentence has two verbs and the adverb might modify either one of them. The result may be a confusing or ambiguous sentence.

> Analyzing an argument effectively improves it.
> [Does *effectively* go with *analyzing* or *improves?*]

Bad/badly

From an episode of NBC-TV's *Cheers,* first aired December 18, 1986. The patrons of the bar are watching a videotape of Diane attempting (with little success) to dance ballet.

DIANE
(oblivious to taunts)
Ever since I was a child I wanted to dance so badly.

NORMAN
It looks like you got your wish.

To position adverbs accurately . . .

➤ **Check to see that you have placed your adverbs so that your reader can't get confused about which words they modify.** Sometimes you may want to ask a friend to help you double-check for misplaced modifiers. For example:

{Adverb misplaced}   Hearing people talk **quickly** Janice realized that they had underestimated the appeal of their project.
> [The reader doesn't know whether *quickly* goes with *talk* or realized.]

{Adverb repositioned}   Hearing people talk Janice **quickly** realized they had underestimated the appeal of their project.
> [A comma after *talk* in both sentences would also help.]

▶ **Be sure the adverbs *almost* and *even* are next to the words they modify.** These common words are adverbs that can cause confusion in a sentence. Notice the ambiguities they cause in the following sentences because they are misplaced.

{**Adverb misplaced**}   Jasper and Janice **almost** knew every one of the young
        student parents would be interested.

> [Putting *almost* next to *knew* instead of *every* confuses the meaning.]

{**Adverb better placed**}   Jasper and Janice knew **almost** every one of the young
        student parents would be interested.

{**Adverb misplaced**}   They **even** figured young singles would be on their side in
        this issue.

> [*Even* could modify *figured* here, but it really goes with *young singles*.]

{**Adverb better placed**}   They figured **even** young singles would be on their side
        in this issue.

▶ **Place the adverb *only* directly before the word you want it to modify in a sentence.** The word *only* has one specific meaning: "this one and no other." Unfortunately, writers tend to let *only* drift around in sentences, slipping into positions where it can be confusing. Here are some examples.

{**Confusing**}   Janice **only** knew one group who actively opposed the idea of on-
        campus day care.

> [Could be misinterpreted to mean that Janice was the only person who knew a group
> opposed to on-campus day care.]

31 C

Adv Pos

{**Clearer**}   Janice knew **only** one group who actively opposed the idea of on-
        campus day care.

{**Confusing**}   The Coalition Against Higher Tuition group **only** thought about
        what the project might cost.

> [Could be misinterpreted to mean the group never thought about anything except the
> cost of the day-care center.]

{**Clearer**}   The Coalition Against Higher Tuition group thought **only** about what
        any project would cost.

EXERCISE 31.3

Rewrite the sentences to clarify them and to avoid misinterpretation.

1. Some experts think keeping a child at home unnecessarily deprives them of social contacts.
2. They even think that a few hours a week in day care is good for most children.
3. Older pediatricians, however, think automatically children get sick at day-care centers.
4. They only recommend the sheltered at-home care their own children had years ago.
5. Having a child unexpectedly disrupts one's college career.

31 D DOUBLE NEGATIVES

Term you need to know

DOUBLE NEGATIVE. A statement in which a second negative word unnecessarily repeats a negative already in the statement.

John **don't** like **no books** with snakes in them.

Troubleshooting

Although sentences that say *no* in two different ways can make good sense and be emphatic, you probably already know that they're nonstandard English and will jolt your readers' sense of good usage. So if you do lapse into them occasionally when you're writing drafts, you can get rid of them when you revise.

To avoid double negative constructions . . .

➤ **Check to see that you don't have two *no* words in the same sentence or independent clause.** In addition to *no,* look for such words as *not, nothing, nobody,* and *never.* If you find you've doubled them, you can usually just drop or alter a single word.

{**Double negative**}   Good day-care centers **don't never** hire untrained workers.

{**Corrected**}   Good day-care centers **never** hire untrained workers.

{**Double negative**}   John **doesn't** want **no help** tying his shoes.

{**Corrected**}   John doesn't want **any** help tying his shoes.

➤ **Don't mix the negative adverbs *hardly, scarcely,* or *barely* with another negative word or phrase.** If you do, you will have a sentence with a double negative, not considered standard English. Here are some examples of such faulty English usage.

{**Double negative**}   When Jasper realized what broad appeal a campus day-care center would have, he **couldn't hardly** wait to get organized.

{**Corrected**}   When Jasper realized what broad appeal a campus day-care center would have, he **could hardly** wait to get organized.

{**Double negative**}   He figured there **wouldn't be scarcely no** groups that would oppose it.

{**Corrected**}   He figured there **would be scarcely any** groups that would oppose it.

31 D

Doub Neg

> **TIP:** Avoid using the word *irregardless.* It's actually a double negative because the prefix *ir-* means *no* (*irreverent, irresponsible*) and so does *regardless.* The term is considered nonstandard.

EXERCISE 31.4

Rewrite any of the sentences that contain double negatives to eliminate the problem. Not every sentence is faulty.

1. Some unaware souls don't hardly know that many students have small children.
2. Jasper reasons that President Coates never sees no children around his part of campus.
3. That's understandable since there is scarcely any space for them.
4. The Clear Lake—Chicago campus can't hardly accommodate a large day-care center.
5. But Jasper isn't going to let nothing stand in his way.

31 E ADVERB FORM

Troubleshooting

Do you get confused about the difference between words that look like adjectives—for instance, *slow* and *tight*—and their obvious adverb forms *slowly* and *tightly,* wondering why it seems to be all right to say "drive slow" or "tie it tight" instead of "drive slowly" and "tie it tightly"? That's hardly surprising. These are among those common English words that have two forms, either of which can be correct in certain situations.

To choose the better adverb form . . .

➤ **Consider what kind of tone you want in your writing.** Many adverbs have both short and long forms.

slow/slowly	tight/tightly
quick/quickly	rough/roughly
fair/fairly	deep/deeply

{**Examples**}

The Redskins play rough.	She treats him roughly.
Connie drives slow.	Connie drives slowly.
Darwin thinks quick.	Darwin thinks quickly.
Richard plays fair.	Richard plays fairly.
Close that door tight.	Close that door tightly.

In most cases, the short form of the adverb sounds more casual and colloquial than the long form. Consequently, in most academic and business situations, you'll do better to use the *-ly* form. For example, if you were writing these sentences in a report, you would use the long form.

> Janice thought **deeply** about what she should do. She wanted all the parties involved to be treated **fairly.**

➤ **Use the adverb form ending in -*ly* in most writing situations.** Here are some examples that show the colloquial and formal usages.

{**Colloquial**}   Janice and Jasper worried **considerable** about how President Coates was going to react to their proposals for a campus day-care center.

{**Standard**}   Janice and Jasper worried **considerably** about how President Coates was going to react to their proposals for a campus day-care center.

{**Colloquial**}   He didn't always think **deep** about practical matters.

{**Standard**}   He didn't always think **deeply** about practical matters.

> **TIP: We can't give you a fixed rule for deciding when you should use the short form of these adverbs. You will have to decide on the basis of the situation in which you are writing. If you have real doubts, you're probably better off using the long form.**

EXERCISE 31.5

Working with a group of other students, discuss the following sentences and decide what the problems are. Then replace nonstandard adverb forms with appropriate ones.

1. Janice and Jasper were real surprised when more than 500 students showed up in response to their classified ad in the campus paper.
2. Some of them had already made placards that showed they took the issue serious.
3. A number of them quick came up to Janice.
4. Several had brought children who were crying loud.
5. Jasper could see that he needed to plan careful to organize this energy.

31 F

Mispl Mod

31 F   DO YOU HAVE PROBLEMS WITH MISPLACED OR DANGLING MODIFIERS?

Terms you need to know

DANGLING MODIFIER. A modifying phrase that doesn't seem connected to any other word or phrase in a sentence.

MISPLACED MODIFIER. A modifying word or phrase that is ambiguous because it isn't clear what it modifies.

Troubleshooting

Words tend to act as magnets to any modifier that comes near them; they pick up meaning whether or not that is what the writer intended. If you write a sentence with a modifying adverbial or adjectival phrase that is *not* next to the word it should modify, your sentence is going to derail. Two forms of this problem are **misplaced modifying phrases** and **dangling modifiers.** For example:

{**Misplaced modifying phrase**}   **Being short of money,** the plan by the university had to be inexpensive.

> [It is *the university,* not *the plan,* that is short of money.]

{**Correction**}   **Being short of money,** the university needed an inexpensive plan.

A dangling modifier occurs when a writer composes a sentence with a modifying phrase but doesn't supply anything in the sentence it could sensibly modify. As a result, the phrase just hangs there with nothing to modify. For example:

{**Dangling modifier**}   **Before deciding on a strategy,** a date has to be chosen by the committee.

> [The boldfaced phrase doesn't apply to anything in the main part of the sentence.]

{**Corrected**}   **Before deciding on a strategy,** the committee will have to choose a date.

To eliminate misplaced or dangling modifiers . . .

➤ **Be sure that an introductory modifying phrase is followed by the word it modifies.** Ask yourself who or what does what the modifying phrase refers to. (Usually the word or phrase modified will be the subject of the sentence.) Then make any necessary revisions. Sometimes you will have to supply a word that the introductory phrase can modify. In other cases, the whole sentence may have to be rearranged.

31 F

Mispl Mod

{**Misplaced modifier**}   **Never having married,** child care doesn't concern President Coates.

> [The underlined phrase doesn't describe *child care,* the noun closest to it; it describes *President Coates.*]

{**Revision**}   **Never having married,** President Coates is unconcerned about child care.

{**Misplaced modifier**}   **Sensing a groundswell of support,** the proposal for a campus day-care center was endorsed by the editors of the *Clarion.*

> [The boldfaced phrase doesn't describe *proposal;* it describes *the editors.*]

{**Revision**}   **Sensing a groundswell of support,** the editors of the *Clarion* endorsed the proposal for a campus day-care center.

➤ **Supply a word for a dangling modifier to modify.** This often means rewriting the entire sentence since you must usually add a word or phrase that the sentence alludes to but doesn't actually include. For example:

{**Dangling modifier**}   **On coming back to school,** baby-sitters aren't easy to find.

> [There is nothing in the sentence for *On coming back to school* to modify. In this case, the sentence has to be revised to include a subject.]

{**One possible revision**}   **On coming back to school,** young parents may have a hard time finding baby-sitters.

> **TIP: You are less likely to get yourself in a tangle with modifiers if you write actor/action sentences. When you use people as the subject of your sentences, it's easier to keep modifiers under control. See Section 17C.**

♦ FINE TUNING ♦

Some introductory modifying phrases may look like misplaced modifiers but are actually what we call **absolute modifiers;** that is, they are complete in themselves, serving only to give additional information about the sentence of which they are a part. Writers find such absolute modifiers useful so it's important to learn to distinguish them from faulty constructions.

absolute
Given the circumstances, no single person was to blame for the lack of child care on campus.

absolute
To be quite honest, the president had too many other things on his mind to be concerned.

To distinguish an absolute modifier that does work from a misplaced or dangling modifier that doesn't work, see if you could convert the absolute modifier to a subordinate clause. For instance, the two sentences above could be rewritten.

31 F

Mispl Mod

If all circumstances are considered, no one person was to blame for the lack of child care on campus.

If we are quite honest in our criticism, the president had too many other things on his mind to be concerned.

If you can do this, your absolute works. You can also ask yourself, "Is there any possible confusion here? Does the sentence make sense?" If you are satisfied that it does, the modifier is probably all right.

EXERCISE 31.6

Rewrite these sentences, placing modifiers in appropriate positions. Not all of the sentences need to be revised.

1. Trying to think about everything that would be involved, an example of a good tax-supported day-care center was needed.
2. Running around frantically, the search for a dramatic example began.
3. After going to the library, the perfect example surfaced.
4. To be honest, Janice hadn't expected such luck.
5. Considered among the finest in the country, she found a day-care center run by the local company, Metrotech, Inc.

31 G COMPARATIVES AND SUPERLATIVES

Terms you need to know

COMPARATIVE AND SUPERLATIVE. Adjectives and adverbs can express three different levels or degrees of intensity—the positive, the comparative, and the superlative. The positive level describes a single object, the comparative ranks two objects, the superlative three or more.

Positive	*Comparative*	*Superlative*
cold	colder	coldest
angry	more (less) angry	most (least) angry
angrily	more (less) angrily	most (least) angrily

Troubleshooting

Two problems typically arise with comparisons and superlatives. The first is using a superlative form when comparing only two objects.

> Jasper was the **tallest** of the two men.   [should be *taller*]

> Janice was the **most talented** of the two writers.   [should be *more talented*]

A less frequent error involves doubling the comparative and superlative forms, using both the ending (*-er; -est*) and *more* and *most*.

> That was the **most unkindest** cut of all.   [should be *most unkind* or *unkindest*]

Except for these two problems, you can usually just trust your ear when you use the comparative forms for adverbs and adjectives. As a general rule, you add *-er* and *-est* endings to one syllable adjectives and adverbs but put the comparative terms *more* and *most* before words of two or more syllables.

To avoid problems with comparisons . . .

➤ **Be sure to use the comparative, not the superlative, form when you are comparing two items.** That means using an adverb or adjective with an *-er* ending or modified by *more* or *less*.

{**Faulty comparison**}   John was the **smartest** of the two children.
> [*Smartest* is the superlative, not the comparative, form.]

{**Revised**}   John was the **smarter** of the two children.

{**Faulty comparison**}   Celeste, the other child, was the **most imaginative,** although that wasn't always good.
> [*Most imaginative* is the superlative, not the comparative, form.]

{**Revised**}   Celeste, the other child, was the **more imaginative,** although that wasn't always good.

➤ **Use the superlative form when comparing more than two objects or qualities.** In most cases when you compare three or more things or qualities, you need to use *-est* adjectives or adverbs or preface the modifiers with *most* or *least*.

Given a choice of several toys, Celeste would choose the one that was the **most** challenging.

Of all the children at his day-care center, John was the **liveliest.**

➤ **Avoid doubling the comparative or superlative forms.** You'll confuse your reader if you use two comparative forms in the same phrase. When you have compared something once, that's enough. For example:

{**Confusing**}   Jasper was **more stricter** as a parent than Janice was.

{**Clear**}   Jasper was **stricter** as a parent than Janice was.

{**Confusing**}   Of all the students on campus, Janice was the **most angriest** about the day-care dilemma.

{**Clear**}   Of all the students on campus, Janice was the **angriest** about the day-care dilemma.

EXERCISE 31.7

Write sentences in which you use the appropriate forms of comparison for the situation given.

1. Janice and Jasper couldn't decide which was the (**tough**) _____ problem they had to solve, President Coates's indifference or the lack of available space on campus for day care.
2. But they agreed that the situation at Clear Lake—Chicago was the (**bad**) _____ they had seen.
3. Their plan was to locate the (**desirable**) _____ site on campus for the day-care center.
4. They hoped to buy it _____ (**cheaply**) than the market value.
5. They would have to negotiate with either Dean Manning or President Coates, and they needed to figure out which would be the _____ formidable opponent.

31 H

Abs Adj

31 H   ABSOLUTE ADJECTIVES

Term you need to know

ABSOLUTE ADJECTIVE. An adjective like *perfect, unique, dead,* or *equal* that cannot have degrees. Logically, one cannot be *less equal* or *more dead.*

Troubleshooting

Occasionally someone may complain that, "You can't say 'most unique' or 'most perfect.' That just doesn't make sense!" Well, such expressions do make sense—certainly we understand what they mean. But technically, that person is right, and careful writers avoid such phrases.

A few words express qualities that can't logically be compared; for instance, *unique* means the only one of its kind, so it doesn't make sense to say *more unique; perfect* means without any faults, so it doesn't make sense to say *less perfect. Equal* means exactly the same, so logically we shouldn't say something is *more equal* any more than we should say it is *more empty.*

To handle absolute adjectives correctly . . .

➤ **Don't add qualifiers to words that already express an absolute, something that cannot be compared or compromised.** In conversation, of course, we frequently use such expressions, but in writing, it's a good idea to avoid using comparatives with the following words: *unique, perfect, singular, empty, equal, full, definite, complete, absolute,* and, of course, *pregnant.*

Thus it's not good usage to write, "Janice thought it was the *most perfect* model she had ever seen," or "The building is *emptier* at night than in the morning." A model is either perfect or less than perfect. A building is either empty or someone is in it.

EXERCISE 31.8

Working with other students in a group, read over these sentences and decide which ones have faulty modifiers. Confer to decide how any problems with modifiers might be solved.

1. By putting posters up all over campus, Jasper invited everyone who was interested in getting a university child-care center on campus to meet in front of the administration building for the most unique rally of the year.
2. When he arrived at the meeting at 5:30, the lawn in front of the president's office was the fullest anyone had ever seen.
3. Some people were carrying signs that showed how completely definite they were about wanting a child-care center for students.
4. When President Coates came out of his office, he thought the gathering was most singular.
5. He had thought that no college had facilities that were more perfect than those at Clear Lake College.

---

31 I   TOO MANY MODIFIERS?

Troubleshooting

Mark Twain once said, "About the adjective—when in doubt, don't use it." That's usually good advice for adverbs too. When you intend a passage to be colorful and descriptive, it's easy to get carried away and overdo the modifiers, laying on descriptive words like chocolate frosting. But remember how you groan inwardly when you encounter excessive description. You may enjoy it at first, but then your mind starts to hydroplane over the sparkling passage, thinking "I don't need to know this," or "This is overwritten." For example:

> Janice learned that the new child-care facility that Metrotech, Inc., had built was absolutely first class. It was superbly planned, remarkably roomy and spacious, imaginatively decorated with colorful, sparkling murals, and very competently staffed by highly trained and extremely conscientious people.

It's too much description. You stand a chance of losing your way among all those adjectives and adverbs.

Furthermore, when you use too many modifiers, you're *telling* your readers about something rather than *showing* it to them, and that's not good writing. People don't want to be told everything; they'd rather *see* it. For instance, instead of writing:

> The students looked as if they thought the rally was lots of fun. They were in high spirits and having a marvelous time.

You could write:

> Milling around in front of the president's office, the students laughed, twirled their signs like cheerleaders, and occasionally swung children up on their shoulders.
>
> [Instead of depending on adjectives and adverbs, this sentence uses active verbs to create a picture.]

To keep modifiers under control . . .

➤ **Believe in the modifiers you select.** Choose them for what they say, not how they sound. If you find yourself embroidering your writing with adjectives like *shimmering* and *magnificent* or adverbs like *savagely* and *egregiously,* be sure those are the words that best suit your subject. (See also our reminder about whoopee words in Section 16B, page 258.) For example:

> {**Overblown modifiers**}   Jasper thought it would be a **magnificent** triumph to be able to say he had changed the **antiquated, miserably inadequate** child-care situation at the Clear Lake—Chicago campus.
> [Such strong modifiers overstate the point and clutter the sentence.]

➤ **Cut out those pale but overused adverbs *definitely, terribly, very, really, actually,* and *so* as much as possible when you edit.** They are fuzzy intensifiers that seldom add significant information to your papers and can irritate your readers. For instance:

> {**Overloaded with fuzzy intensifiers**}   Janice **definitely** hoped that their rally would **really** improve child care at Clear Lake College. She wasn't **terribly** optimistic, however, because she had heard **so** many complaints before and **very** little had **actually** come of them.

The writing is stronger if you cut the boldfaced words.

31 I

Mod Prob

> ### EXERCISE 31.9

Working with two other students, read over these sentences and decide where they have too many modifiers. Remember, though, you don't have to get rid of every adjective or adverb. Be selective. Have each person rewrite three sentences to eliminate excess modifiers and fuzzy intensifiers and then get together again to compare notes.

1. But to Janice and Jasper's great astonishment, their little impromptu rally had an amazing impact on President Coates.
2. Six months before, a fabulously wealthy and terribly generous Clear Lake alumna, Mrs. Millicent Meriwether, had given her really fine house across from the campus to the college, specifying that it must be used for some student-related service, which she would support if she thoroughly approved of it.
3. Now that the students had gotten President Coates's attention, he felt terribly sad that these fine, upstanding young college students didn't have a place for child care when he had a dreadful white elephant of an obsolete mansion he would be happy to get rid of.
4. What better use for the sumptuous Meriwether house and inaccessible money than for a modern, state-of-the-art child-care center, he thought, particularly since it was beginning to sink in on him that it's terribly fashionable these days to have really liberal views about child care.
5. "Starting this very day, I'm going to launch a full-scale, all-out, intensive campaign to get the regents to give their unqualified endorsement to establishing the Meriwether house as the Clear Lake College Day-care Center, making it a facility of unprecedented high quality," he declared.

32 Commas

A Commas that don't belong
B Commas that separate
C Commas that enclose
D Commas that link

Function

The central fact about a comma is that it is an interrupter, a signal to pause. Think of a comma as a kind of stop sign at a juncture or minor intersection in a sentence, placed there to keep words from running into each other. It isn't as strong a stop sign as a semicolon, which marks a major intersection (one that warrants a traffic light instead of just a sign), and it's certainly not as strong as a period, which marks the end of the sentence (rather like a police officer at an intersection). But it does make readers pause momentarily when they come to it. For that reason it's just as important not to put in commas when they aren't required as it is to insert them when they are needed to mark separations.

It's important to know the guidelines for placing commas, but the truth is that knowing all the rules isn't necessarily going to solve all your comma problems. Ultimately, you have to develop a *feel* for commas, a sense of when you should interrupt the flow of your sentences and when you shouldn't. That requires you to think about the sense and structure of a sentence, not just stick commas in according to a formula. You need to think about the punctuation your readers need to make sense of a sentence. It will also help if you stop occasionally to observe how an author uses commas in an article or story you are enjoying and analyze why the commas are placed where they are.

➤ Major Uses

- To separate parts of a sentence to avoid confusion in the meaning.
- To mark off parts of a sentence that give information but are not necessary to the main idea.
- To mark off words like *and, but, yet,* or *for* when they join independent clauses.
- To set off introductory phrases and clauses when they are long enough to cause confusion.
- To set off interrupting or contrasting elements in a sentence.
- To break up long sentences that might otherwise be hard to read.
- To mark off items in a series.

➤ **Other Uses**

- To separate items in dates.

Sue Ellen and Renaldo were married on February 14, 1978.

- To mark off units in an address.

The Rizzos used to live at 17 Coleridge Place, Kubla Khan Estates.

- To separate proper names from titles and degrees that follow the names.

Renaldo Rizzo, M.D.

- To separate units of three within numbers.

4,110   99,890   5,325,777

- To follow the salutation in personal letters.

Dear Dr. Rizzo,

- To introduce quotations or follow them.

"Don't tell me he can't be held responsible," bellowed Judge Carver.

- To mark pauses for someone who is reading material aloud.

32 A   COMMAS THAT DON'T BELONG

32 A

,

Troubleshooting

If you are nervous about the rules for using commas, you may resort to inserting them where they *might* belong even though you're not sure why. That system doesn't work very well. Your readers don't want to be moving along in a sentence and run into a comma that disrupts a train of thought.

If your instructor says you're using too many commas, check commas when you're editing and ask yourself why you have used them. Don't depend on rules alone, however; rather, ask yourself, "Do I need a punctuation mark here?" Every comma in a sentence should be placed there for a reason: to mark a pause, to set off a unit, to keep words from running together, or for any of the other purposes listed at the beginning of this chapter.

COMMA PROBLEM 1:
Unnecessary interrupting commas

> **Unnecessary comma**
>
> Although, Sue Ellen Rizzo is thirty-one, she is an undergraduate student at Clear Lake College.

> **Unnecessary comma**
>
> What happened, is that at nineteen she dropped out of college to put her husband through medical school.

> **Unnecessary comma**
>
> **Ten years later, she found herself, without a college degree or a husband but with a nine-year-old son, Rodney.**

➤ **Diagnosis**

At each of the marked places in these sentences an unnecessary comma interrupts the flow of thought and makes readers skid to a stop when they should be moving along smoothly. They expect a comma to mark off part of a sentence *for some reason* and get confused when they can't figure out what the reason is. Here is an explanation of the problems.

1. The word *although* introduces a subordinating clause: *Although Sue Ellen is thirty-one, . . . Although* can't be separated from the rest of the clause and still have it make sense. Therefore a comma doesn't belong.

2. *What happened* is the subject of the sentence so it can't be separated from the verb *is* with a comma. Compare these sentences.

subject   predicate
Sue Ellen is determined to complete her education.
   [No comma should come between subject and predicate.]

subject   modifying phrase   predicate
Sue Ellen, who just turned thirty-one, is determined to complete her education.

32 A

,

   Now the commas belong where they are placed, since they set off a phrase that isn't an essential part of the subject or predicate.

3. Here the comma causes an interruption that confuses the meaning. The writer doesn't mean "Sue Ellen found herself," but "Sue Ellen found herself without a college degree or a husband. . . ."

➤ **Solution**

In all the sentences discussed, the unnecessary commas interrupt units of thought that shouldn't be divided.

> **Comma eliminated**
>
> **Although Sue Ellen Rizzo is thirty-one, she is an undergraduate student at Clear Lake College.**

> **Comma eliminated**
>
> **What happened is that at nineteen she dropped out of college to put her husband through medical school.**

> **Comma eliminated**
>
> **Ten years later, she found herself without a college degree or a husband but with a nine-year-old son, Rodney.**

➤ **Additional Example**
In each sentence, the boldfaced comma should be eliminated.

> Sue Ellen says it was quite a shock to find herself with an enormous house and little money**,** for maintaining it. She says that she had never aspired to be a woman**,** who had a career of her own.

Notice that if you read these examples aloud, you would not ordinarily pause at the places marked by the commas. Coming on them unexpectedly is like encountering a stop sign in the middle of a block. You slam on the brakes expecting an intersection, but then find there isn't one.

> **TIP: When you are drafting and revising, gamble on using too few commas rather than too many. Sentences with commas inserted where they are not needed are often more distressing to a reader than those with a few commas omitted.**

32 A

'

> **EXERCISE 32.1**

Working in a group, analyze these sentences to see if all the commas are needed. Then work together to rewrite sentences to get rid of commas that cause awkward interruptions. Notice that some of the commas are necessary.

1. Sue Ellen's principal problems, are coming from having to move out of her neighborhood because of her son, Rodney.
2. He is reputed to be, very bright, but he has a Mephistophelean imagination.
3. Granted, some of his escapades have shown, that, like the kids in *Weird Science,* he has creative genius.
4. However, some of Sue Ellen's neighbors in Kubla Khan Estates, her home right now, have complained, that he is a budding juvenile tyrant.
5. The only one, who is unconcerned is Rodney.

COMMA PROBLEM 2:
Comma splice

> **Comma splice**
>
> **Two years ago, Sue Ellen returned to college, she knew an education had to be her first goal.**

➤ **Diagnosis**

Your instructor may warn you that a **comma splice** is occasionally showing up in your writing. That is, you're joining two independent clauses in a sentence with a comma instead of a conjunction or a semicolon, and you're confusing your reader by not signaling a strong enough stop or by not putting in the joining term they need. See Section 30C for a more complete discussion of comma splices and how to get rid of them.

➤ **Solution**

You could simply replace the comma with a punctuation mark that provides a more complete stop—a semicolon.

> **Comma splice eliminated**
>
> **Two years ago, Sue Ellen returned to college; she knew an education had to be her first goal.**

Or you could rearrange the sentence like this.

> When Sue Ellen returned to college two years ago, she knew an education had to be her first goal.

➤ **Additional Example**

{**Comma splice**}   She thought courses like philosophy and English would be difficult for her, she has done well in them.

{**Comma splice eliminated**}   She thought courses like philosophy and English would be difficult for her, but she has done well in them.

COMMA PROBLEM 3:
Unnecessary comma with phrases joined by *and, or,* **or** *but*

> **Unnecessary commma**
>
> **At nineteen, Sue Ellen thought you went to college, or you got married.**

➤ **Diagnosis**

The two phrases in the sentence fit together so closely that there shouldn't be a comma to interrupt them.

➤ **Solution**

Get rid of the comma and let the parts of the sentence flow freely.

> **Comma eliminated**
>
> **At nineteen, Sue Ellen thought you went to college or you got married.**

32 A

,

COMMA PROBLEM 4:
Unnecessary commas around modifiers that are essential to the meaning of the sentence

---

Unnecessary commas

Some things Sue Ellen learned, as an unpaid wife and mother, changed her mind about getting a college degree.

Husbands, who say they don't want their wives to work, don't sound so wonderful anymore.

➤ **Diagnosis**

Here the writer has put commas around parts of the sentences that are essential to their meaning. Without the information in those sections (called **essential modifiers or restrictive modifiers**), the main clauses lose their point. In the first sentence, the modifier *as an unpaid wife and mother* has to be there for the subject to work. In the second sentence, the whole restrictive clause has to be there or the sentence doesn't work. Thus the parts marked off by the commas are not interrupters; they shouldn't be separated from the rest of the sentence.

➤ **Solution**

Just get rid of the commas so the reader reads straight through the sentence without confusing interruptions.

32 A

,

Commas eliminated

Some things Sue Ellen learned as an unpaid wife and mother changed her mind about getting a college degree.

Husbands who say they don't want their wives to work don't sound so wonderful anymore.

See Section 32B in the next part of this chapter for more discussion of using commas with essential (restrictive) and nonessential (nonrestrictive) modifiers.

EXERCISE 32.2

Rewrite these sentences to eliminate comma splices or commas that set off essential modifiers, those that are necessary to the meaning of the sentence. You can change the punctuation, add joining words, or reorganize the sentences.

1. Sometimes it is difficult to tell the difference between imaginative, creative children and rebellious, mischievous brats, it can depend on who is describing them.

2. Sue Ellen would like to think Rodney is just mischievous, and will improve with time, she is afraid she can't wait to find out.
3. His father thinks Rodney is a boy, who would be perfect to star in a movie version of O'Henry's "The Ransom of Red Chief."
4. In that well-known story, two amateur outlaws kidnap a young boy and hold him for ransom, their scheme backfires because the boy is smarter than they are.
5. The movie *Ruthless People,* starring Bette Midler, was a takeoff on that plot, probably many people didn't know the origin of the story, or the original author.

32 B   COMMAS THAT SEPARATE

Troubleshooting

If you find commas a mystery and hope you can remember most of the rules you need to keep them straight, don't despair. You have a lot of company. Putting commas where they belong is not an exact science, but it's a skill worth developing because commas give your readers important signals.

In this and following sections we'll give you some guidelines you can refer to when you need them, but, more important, we'll try to explain why you need to use commas. That's what you need to understand. The crucial point to remember is that commas are separators that are used to keep words from running into each other and confusing readers.

> **TIP: When you edit, watch for sentence openings that use clauses beginning with one of the common subordinating words, words like *although, if, when, because,* and *however.* Check to see that you have put a comma after the clause to separate it from the main part of the sentence.**

COMMA PROBLEM 5:
Commas after introductory subordinate clauses or long introductory phrases

> **Comma missing**
>
> **Although Rodney seems cherubic at first glance he excels in creating havoc.**

➤ **Diagnosis**

The comma has been left out after an introductory subordinate clause. When you forget to put a comma after an introductory subordinate clause, your readers are likely to slide past the place where the main idea of the sentence begins and stop in confusion. They have to go back and reread from the beginning to understand your sentence. In the example above, the reader may run right through the intersection between *glance* and *he,* wonder whether the phrase *at first glance* goes with the part before or after it, and then have to reread the sentence.

➤ **Solution**
Insert a comma after "glance."

> **Comma inserted**
>
> **Although Rodney seems cherubic at first glance, he excels in creating havoc.**

COMMA PROBLEM 6:
Commas to mark off phrases

> **Missing comma**
>
> **Considering the time required for psychoanalysis the only choice Sue Ellen has is to outwit Rodney.**

➤ **Diagnosis**
The sentence needs a comma between *psychoanalysis* and *the* to keep the reader from running right through the intersection between the two words. Without a comma, the reader may think *the only choice* goes with the introductory phrase. With a comma, the reader pauses and grasps the meaning immediately.

➤ **Solution**
Insert a comma at the intersection after the introductory clause. Notice that you are again setting off a nonessential part of the sentence with commas.

> **Comma inserted**
>
> **Considering the time required for psychoanalysis, the only choice Sue Ellen has is to outwit Rodney.**

➤ **Additional Example**
If Sue Ellen turns her back, she may soon find Rodney walking along the edge of the roof and dropping water bombs on passersby.

EXERCISE 32.3

Insert commas in these sentences where needed.

1. After conferring with her ex-husband Sue Ellen realized he wasn't going to be much help in controlling Rodney.

32 B

,

2. If Rodney were his patient Dr. Rizzo might have some solutions but as a father he was as frustrated as Sue Ellen, his ex-wife was.
3. Unless Sue Ellen gets Rodney under control she will not be able to move into student housing she can afford.
4. Considering that other children in the student housing compound might imitate Rodney it's possible Sue Ellen could have trouble with her neighbors.
5. Yet if she isn't able to get into student housing Sue Ellen will not be able to continue her education.

COMMA PROBLEM 7:
Commas to mark contrasts

> **Missing comma**
>
> Sue Ellen's primary requirement in a house is economy not glamor.

➤ **Diagnosis**
A comma is needed to set off a contrasting element in the sentence. The reader needs a fairly strong pause after *economy* to feel the shift of ideas; therefore, the intersection requires a comma.

➤ **Solution**
Add a comma.

> **Comma added**
>
> Sue Ellen's primary requirement in a house is economy, not glamor.

➤ **Additional Examples**

For Sue Ellen, getting into student housing is a necessity, not a whim.

Student housing residents welcome well-behaved youngsters, but not the likes of Rodney.

32 C

,

32 C   COMMAS THAT ENCLOSE

Terms you need to know

ESSENTIAL MODIFIER. (restrictive modifier) A modifying phrase or clause giving a description necessary to understanding the sentence that contains it. Essential or restrictive modifiers can't be removed from a sentence without changing or reducing its meaning significantly.

The boy **who hijacked the police cruiser** was Rodney.

NONESSENTIAL MODIFIER. (nonrestrictive modifier) A phrase or clause adding information about something in the sentence but not absolutely necessary to its basic meaning. A nonessential modifier can be removed from a sentence without radically altering its meaning.

> The police officers, **who seemed more embarrassed than angry,** found their vehicle on a used car lot.

APPOSITIVE. A noun or noun equivalent that follows a noun and gives information about it. Appositives are nearly always nonrestrictive modifiers.

> appositive
>
> Ike Cannon, **neighborhood-watch coordinator,** thinks Rodney will either be a genius or a terrorist.

Troubleshooting

If you wonder why you need to put commas around some parts of a sentence, the answer is for clarity. One of the useful things commas do is to chunk information into manageable segments. (See Section 17E on chunking for clarity.) In this section, we'll discuss using commas to enclose parts of sentences in a way that shows how they fit into the whole sentence.

COMMA PROBLEM 8:

32 C

,

Commas enclosing modifying phrases—nonessential (or nonrestrictive) vs. essential (or restrictive) modifiers

> **Missing comma**
>
> Rodney particularly excels at kidnapping the neighborhood dogs no matter how large they are and holding them for ransom.

▶ **Diagnosis**

Here, a nonessential (nonrestrictive) modifier is not marked off by commas. The modifying phrase *no matter how large they are* is an interrupting phrase that is not essential to the main idea; therefore it needs to be set off by commas.

▶ **Solution**

Mark off with commas that part of the sentence that can be omitted without changing the essential meaning.

> **Comma inserted**
>
> Rodney particularly excels at kidnapping the neighborhood dogs, no matter how large they are, and holding them for ransom.

However, when a modifying phrase is essential to the meaning of the sentence, it should *not* be set off with commas. Such a modifier is called essential or restrictive. For example:

It's true, of course, that a boy **who is a showman at such an early age** seems destined for success in America.

The boldfaced restrictive modifier is essential to the meaning of the sentence; without it, *destined for success in America* makes no sense.

➤ Additional Example

{**Nonessential modifier**}   Last winter, he captured a Doberman pinscher, **one of those dogs that normal people are afraid of,** and demanded a ransom of two Madonna albums and a CD player.

{**Essential modifier**}   Some observers say that Rodney is just imitating people **who were heroes in the days of Social Darwinism.**

An appositive (a noun or noun equivalent that follows a noun and gives additional information about it) is usually a nonessential modifier. Thus, you should be particularly careful to set appositives off with commas. For example:

appositive

Rodney's mother, **the long-suffering Sue Ellen,** has gotten so she hates to hear a knock at the door.

appositive

When his father, **now a child psychiatrist,** learns of Rodney's latest exploit, he grinds his teeth and worries about lawsuits.

32 C

,

There are, however, also essential (or restrictive) appositives that follow a noun and give information that is necessary. Such modifiers should not be set off by commas. For example:

appositive

Sue Ellen reflected that Dr. Rizzo **the student** was quite a different person

appositive

from Dr. Rizzo **the psychiatrist.**

To set *the student* and *the psychiatrist* off with commas, and thus indicate they could be separated from the sentence, would make the sentence confusing.

> **TIP:** You can't always make a quick decision about which modifiers are essential and which are not. When you're editing and are in doubt, check to see if the skeleton of the sentence—the main statement in it—makes sense by itself. If so, you need commas around the modifier. If the skeleton of the sentence doesn't make sense by itself, leave out the commas.

COMMA PROBLEM 9:
Commas surrounding other kinds of interrupting words and phrases

> **Missing commas**
> It's true however that Rodney can be lovable at times.

> **Missing commas**
> His mother at any rate loves him.

➤ **Diagnosis**

There are no commas around *however* or *at any rate* to indicate they are interrupting words or phrases. Again, the reader tends to run through the sentence intersection because there is no signal.

In both writing and speaking, we all use many qualifying words and phrases that give strong signals in a sentence even though they don't contribute directly to their meaning. The most common ones are adverbs like *however, nevertheless, moreover, therefore.*

We also use many interrupting phrases that don't contribute directly but affect the tone and pace of our writing. Typical ones are *of course, in any case,* and *under the circumstances.* Such phrases should usually be set off by commas, although increasingly you may find them unmarked in informal writing.

32 C

,

➤ **Solution**

Insert commas before and after the interrupting word and phrase.

> **Commas inserted**
> It's true, however, that Rodney can be lovable at times.

> **Commas inserted**
> His mother, at any rate, loves him.

➤ **Additional Example**

Sue Ellen realizes, of course, that Rodney's inappropriate behavior has to be controlled.

EXERCISE 32.4

Working with two or three other students, discuss these sentences to decide which modifiers are essential and which are not; then fix the sentences that need to be changed.

1. Child psychiatry a fairly new branch of medicine has only imperfect answers for many juvenile problems.
2. Sue Ellen thinks it is possible to distinguish between a boy who is daring and ingenious and one who is imaginative but destructive.
3. As a loving parent Sue Ellen wants to do the right thing for her child when she can figure out what that thing is.
4. The fact is however that she is in charge, and she can't wait indefinitely for a solution.
5. Dr. Rizzo the parent has misgivings that wouldn't occur to Dr. Rizzo the child psychiatrist.

COMMA PROBLEM 10:
Commas after linking (or conjunctive) adverbs

Missing comma

The upshot of Rodney's misbehavior is that Sue Ellen may not be able to leave Kubla Khan Estates; consequently the Kubla Khan Neighborhood Association has decided to sponsor a contest to help Ms. Rizzo.

➤ **Diagnosis**
A comma is missing after the strong signaling adverb *consequently* in the sentence. A comma is needed because words of this kind—*consequently, nevertheless, however, therefore,* and so on—are interrupters that mark a shift or contrast in a sentence. Putting a comma after them sets them off.

32 D

,

➤ **Solution**
Insert a comma after *consequently.*

Comma inserted

The upshot of Rodney's misbehavior is that Sue Ellen may not be able to leave Kubla Khan Estates; consequently, the Kubla Khan Neighborhood Association has decided to sponsor a contest to help Ms. Rizzo.

32 D   COMMAS THAT LINK

Troubleshooting

Though commas usually mark separations, they can also signal that certain groups of ideas belong together. When commas come before linking words, for instance, they tell readers that the ideas will continue. The stop isn't as full as it would be if it were marked by a semicolon or period. Similarly, commas that mark off and separate items in a series help readers understand that those items belong together.

COMMA PROBLEM 11:
Commas before linking words such as *and, but, yet,* and *or* when those words (conjunctions) come between independent clauses

> **Missing comma**
>
> The aim of the contest is to figure out how to control Rodney and so its judges will be Rodney's mother and two child psychologists who live in Kubla Khan Estates.

➤ **Diagnosis**
The comma is missing before the linking term *and.* A comma would help emphasize the break between the two clauses.

➤ **Solution**
Insert a comma before the *and.*

> **Comma inserted**
>
> The aim of the contest is to figure out how to control Rodney, and so its judges will be Rodney's mother and two child psychologists who live in Kubla Khan Estates.

32 D

,

➤ **Additional Examples**

The judges are looking forward to the contest, but at least one of the psychologists is dubious.

That psychologist, Mary Pearl Carver, is a mother herself, so she knows first-hand how irrepressible a nine-year-old boy can be.

> **TIP: Be especially careful not to insert the comma after the conjunction that joins independent clauses.**
> {Incorrect} Rodney's father remembers what a happy hellion he was as a child and, so he knows how intoxicated Rodney must be with his power. {Correct} Rodney's father remembers what a happy hellion he was as a child, and so he knows how intoxicated Rodney must be with his power.

EXERCISE 32.5

Rewrite the following sentences, adding commas where they are needed to link ideas, and moving those that may be misplaced.

1. In spite of Dr. Carver doubts about the success of the contest have not been expressed by any other neighbors.
2. So the Neighborhood Association will go ahead with plans for the contest; however the group does not have the money to award a prize for suggesting how to cope with Rodney.
3. At first they thought they might have to abandon their plans but, a thoughtful citizen stepped forward.
4. Rodney's father Dr. Renaldo Rizzo has announced that he will donate a prize but it must provide incentive to draw suggestions from harried parents who are worried about their children.
5. Of course Dr. Rizzo also hopes that he will get some ideas for dealing with his young patients yet, he doesn't want to make that motive obvious.

COMMA PROBLEM 12:
Commas to mark a series

> **Commas missing**
>
> So the "Let's Help Rodney Move" contest kicks off on Monday amidst excitement anticipation and high hopes.

➤ **Diagnosis**

There are no commas to mark off the words in the series *excitement, anticipation, and high hopes*. Again, commas are needed to mark a pause for the reader and to keep the words in the series from colliding.

32 D

,

➤ **Solution**

Add commas after all but the last word in a series of three or more items.

> **Commas inserted**
>
> So the "Let's Help Rodney Move" contest kicks off on Monday amidst excitement, anticipation, and high hopes.

In most cases, it is best to use a comma before the conjunction that signals the end of a series (usually either *and* or *or*).

Dr. Rizzo has consulted the works of Freud, Jung, Adler, and other psychiatrists who have theorized about children's problems.

Some editors, however, allow the comma before the conjunction at the end of a series to be omitted.

➤ **Additional Example**

All proposals submitted must be humane, legal, and relatively inexpensive.

♦ **FINE TUNING** ♦

Use commas to mark off *coordinate* adjectives in series—that is, adjectives that all modify the same noun they precede. For example:

Rodney is an **intelligent, conniving, daring** child.

Notice that these adjectives could be switched around without affecting the sense of the sentence. It could read *daring, intelligent, conniving child* just as well as the other way around. Here's a second example.

Sue Ellen is a **frazzled, tired,** and slightly **frantic** mother.

These adjectives could also be switched around with no problem.

However, when you have an adjective modifying another adjective, the words are *noncoordinate,* and you couldn't switch them around without changing the meaning. In that case, you shouldn't use commas between the adjectives. For example:

It's a tribute to Sue Ellen's **natural good** humor that she doesn't complain.

> **TIP: In recent years, many editors have advised their writers not to overpunctuate. That's good advice. If you put commas in every single place that the conventional guidelines recommend, you may end up with choppy sentences that make the reader stop every few words. Instead of trying to remember every comma rule, use common sense about how your sentences *sound* and put commas where the rhythm and sense of a passage call for them.**

32 D

,

EXERCISE 32.6

Rewrite these sentences, inserting commas where they are needed. If necessary, consult the section on "Other Uses" of commas on page 444 for guidance.

1. Some of the contest proposals for the reform of Rodney were imaginative but not sensible legal or practical.
2. For instance Tong Chai proposed that Rodney be sent to Hampstead England to work with the famous dog trainer, Barbara Woodhouse, noted for her book *No Bad Dogs.*
3. Finally out of the 100 proposals emerged one to which both the judges and Sue Ellen were able to say "This sounds like it might work."
4. When the time came for the judges to announce their decision suspense was high.
5. Everyone agreed that the judges had been courageous confident and perhaps naive to take on the responsibility in the first place.

EXERCISE 32.7

Working with a group of other students, read over these sentences from which most commas have been removed. For each sentence, add commas and then compare your version of the passage with someone else's. Note those places where you disagree about the need for a comma.

1. At the last minute a team Lawrence Butcher and Greta Ericson combined their skills for the "Let's Help Rodney Move" contest to draft the prize-winning proposal an imaginative yet practical idea.
2. To the judges' satisfaction Butcher and Ericson proposed to combine a sugar-less diet with Kung-fu martial arts to de-energize Rodney and at the same time give him an outlet for his aggressive competitive but at heart fun-loving nature.
3. Enthusiastically the contest winners predict that unless one of Rodney's Kung-fu partners maims him within three years the Rizzo youth will be calm happy and the holder of a black belt.
4. The beauty of the plan as they outline it is that it will keep Rodney away from his terrorist activities for three years at least and if he works hard make him appreciate the value of self-control and discipline.
5. Rodney however responded to the proposal by releasing every cat and dog from the Ruralia animal shelter reversing every street sign in his neighborhood and toilet-papering the yards of the judges.

32 D

,

33 Semicolons and Colons

A Semicolons

B Colons

Terms you need to know

CLAUSE. A group of related words with a subject and verb. Clauses can be independent or dependent. An independent clause can stand alone as a complete sentence.

> Whenever it could, **the Film Society held its meetings at a renovated art deco theater.**

A dependent clause cannot, however, stand alone as a sentence.

> **Whenever it could,** the Film Society held its meetings at a renovated art deco theater.

CONJUNCTIVE ADVERB. A word such as *however, therefore, nevertheless,* and *moreover* used with a semicolon to link complete sentences.

> Maggie knows that Sean regrets the damage his film crew did to her bowling alley; **nevertheless,** she intends to sue.

COORDINATING CONJUNCTION. The words *and, or, nor, but, for, yet,* and *so* used to join independent clauses or similar grammatical items.

> Sean apologized profusely, **so** Maggie has forgiven him.

33 A
;

33 A   SEMICOLONS

➤ Function

A semicolon is a stronger pause than a comma, but a weaker pause than a period. Think of a semicolon as a connector or an addition sign, joining related ideas. Or picture a semicolon as the center point on a balance because semicolons usually come between items of equal grammatical weight.

> **independent clause; independent clause**
>
> ▲

phrase; phrase

▲

item in a list; item in a list; item in a list

▲ ▲

Wes Craven directed *A Nightmare on Elm Street;* he later made the terrifying *The Serpent and the Rainbow.*

[semicolon separates complete sentences]

Professor Newcombe's course taught the basics of film production, including how to write treatments, outlines, and scripts; how to audition and cast actors; and how to edit.

[semicolons separate a series of phrases that contain commas]

We rented cassettes of *Baby, It's You; Star Trek IV: The Voyage Home;* and *Twilight Zone—the Movie.*

[semicolons separate equivalent items in a list]

➤ **Major Use**

—Use a semicolon to join independent clauses closely related in thought. The semicolon tells us to read the linked clauses as a pair. See Problem 1 below. For example:

Films focus on action and movement; plays emphasize language and thought.

➤ **Other Uses**

—Use a semicolon to join independent clauses that appear to be connected by words or phrases such as *however, therefore, nevertheless, nonetheless, moreover, consequently,* and so on. (Words such as these are called **conjunctive adverbs,** but they do not actually link sentences. They require a semicolon.) See Problem 2.

Sean had no trouble persuading friends to help him with his Film 101 project; **moreover,** he had more actors for the movie than parts.

—Use semicolons to mark off items in a series of phrases that would ordinarily be separated by commas—except that they already contain commas. See Problem 3.

The characters in Sean's film included Marcello, a rich industrialist from Milan; Master Laurence, a professor of comparative literature tortured by dark thoughts, a spendthrift wife, and gambling debts; and Maria, a temperamental, dark-haired actress trying to find financial backing for *Acid Grapes,* a film she has written about the wine industry in Germany.

—Use semicolons to separate clauses, phrases, or series that might be confusing if commas alone were used to mark boundaries. These phrases often contain punctuation marks other than commas. See Problem 4.

33 A

;

Sean's favorite films included *Airplane!; Come Back to the 5 & Dime Jimmy Dean, Jimmy Dean; M*A*S*H;* and *Plan 9 from Outer Space.*

SEMICOLON PROBLEM 1:
Comma used where a semicolon is needed

> **Comma splice**
>
> **Sean was a natural director, he enjoyed giving orders.**

> **Diagnosis**

This is a comma splice. A comma has been used where a semicolon is needed. A semicolon alone is strong enough to join two independent sentences, but a comma can link them only with the help of coordinating conjunctions—*and, but, for, yet, or, nor,* and *so.*

> **Solution**

Replace the comma with a semicolon.

> **Semicolon inserted**
>
> **Sean was a natural director; he enjoyed giving orders.**

33 A

;

> **Additional Examples**

Though a terrible actress, Charnelle was a gifted screenwriter; she knew how to create original characters. Charnelle's script had energy and intelligence; she was sure the actors would love their parts.

SEMICOLON PROBLEM 2:
Semicolons needed before conjunctive adverbs

> **Comma splice**
>
> **Sean cast Alicia in the title role, however, he preferred Lynda for the part.**

> **Diagnosis**

Here is another comma splice. A comma has been mistakenly used before a conjunctive adverb—*however*—where a semicolon is required. This is a common punctuation problem.

> **Solution**

Replace the comma with a semicolon.

> **Semicolon**
>
> Sean cast Alicia in the title role; however, he preferred Lynda for the part.

➤ **Additional Examples**

Lynda was the better actress; **however,** Alicia knew several people who might be willing to finance Sean's production.

Sean had a tight budget; **nevertheless,** he hoped to produce a professional-looking film.

♦ **FINE TUNING** ♦

Frequently Used Conjunctive Adverbs		
consequently	however	furthermore
hence	meanwhile	moreover
nonetheless	otherwise	rather
therefore	thus	then

A semicolon comes before the conjunctive adverb when it begins an independent clause, and a comma follows it.

33 A

Sean's film was a parody of all European movies; **however,** his chief inspiration was Fellini's *La Dolce Vita.*

But when the conjunctive adverb appears in the middle of an independent clause, it is preceded and followed by commas.

Sean's film was a parody of all European movies; his chief inspiration, **however,** was Fellini's *La Dolce Vita.*

When in doubt about the punctuation, check what happens when you capitalize the conjunctive adverb and put a period before it. If the conjunctive adverb **begins** an independent clause, the new version will make sense—and you may use a semicolon before the conjunctive adverb.

{**Original**}   Sean's film was a parody of all European movies; **however,** his chief inspiration was Fellini's *La Dolce Vita.*

{**Test version**}   Sean's film was a parody of all European movies. **However,** his chief inspiration was Fellini's *La Dolce Vita.*

If the adverb is in the middle of an independent clause, your attempt to create two independent clauses usually won't work—and you cannot use a semicolon before the adverb.

{**Original**}   The chief inspiration for Sean's parody of European movies, **however,** was Fellini's *La Dolce Vita.*

{**Test version**}   The chief inspiration for Sean's parody of European movies. **However,** was Fellini's *La Dolce Vita.*

➤ **Additional Example.**
(Compare the versions. Both are correct.)

{**Version one**}   Most of Sean's cast hadn't seen *La Dolce Vita;* **in fact,** they had never even heard of Federico Fellini.

{**Version two**}   Most of Sean's cast had, **in fact,** never seen *La Dolce Vita* or even heard of Federico Fellini.

SEMICOLON PROBLEM 3:
Complex lists

> **Confusing commas**
>
> **Sean's expenses included the cost of renting lights, costumes, and sound equipment, film and film-processing fees, duplication costs for scripts, contracts, and other paperwork, and money for miscellaneous props.**

33 A

➤ **Diagnosis**
The items within the list of Sean's expenses need to be separated. But since some of the items actually contain commas (*renting lights, costumes, and sound equipment*), using more commas makes the sentence hard to follow.

➤ **Solution**
Replace the commas between the series items with semicolons, since semicolons mark stronger pauses than commas do.

> **Semicolons replace commas**
>
> **Sean's expenses included the cost of renting lights, costumes, and sound equipment; film and film-processing fees; duplication costs for scripts, contracts, and other paperwork; and money for miscellaneous props.**

➤ **Additional Examples**

Charnelle's script included a dream sequence staged at the Lindstrom bowling alley; a scene at a health spa, using Sam's Gym as a location; and a midnight swimming episode to be filmed at Crystal Lake.

Sean decided that Alicia Bell, tall and charismatic, would play Maria, the sophisticated and hot-tempered Italian actress; Sue Ellen Rizzo, a single parent returning to school for a business degree, would play the ruthless

Celeste; and Travis Beckwith would take the role of Marcello because no
one else wanted the part.

Semicolon Problem 4:
Clearer boundaries needed

> **Confusing commas**
>
> Sean wanted Charnelle to include allusions in her
> screenplay to *Divorce: Italian Style, And the Ship Sails
> On,* and *400 Blows.*

➤ **Diagnosis**
The commas are potentially confusing because the items they separate contain
punctuation (:) or confusing connectives (*and*). Semicolons would provide
sharper boundaries between items.

➤ **Solution**
Replace the commas with semicolons.

> **Replace commas with semicolons**
>
> Sean wanted Charnelle to include allusions in her
> screenplay to *Divorce: Italian Style; And the Ship Sails
> On;* and *400 Blows.*

33 A

;

➤ **Additional Example**
The sound track for Sean's parody would include the overture from Wag-
ner's *Tannhäuser;* the Supremes' "Stop in the Name of Love!"; Bob Dylan's
"Rainy Day Women #12 & 35"; and Rogers and Hart's "Glad to Be
Unhappy."

Semicolon Problem 5:
Semicolon used where a comma is needed—between a phrase and an
independent clause or a dependent clause and an independent clause

> **Incorrect semicolon**
>
> Never having seen a foreign film; Travis wasn't really
> sure what Sean's parody was about.

➤ **Diagnosis**
A semicolon has been used to separate a modifying phrase (*Never having seen a
foreign film*) from an independent clause. This is a surprisingly common error.

➤ **Solution**

Separate these items with a comma.

> **Replace semicolon with a comma**
>
> **Never having seen a foreign film, Travis wasn't really sure what Sean's parody was about.**

Remember that a semicolon joins items that are equivalent:

> independent clause + independent clause;
> phrase + phrase;
> item in a list + item in a list.

So a semicolon would also be incorrect between a prepositional phrase and an independent clause or between a dependent clause and independent clause.

{**Wrong**} Sean found himself going over his budget; in the finest tradition of the greatest Hollywood directors.

{**Right**} Sean found himself going over his budget in the finest tradition of the greatest Hollywood directors.

{**Wrong**} Because he loved having his picture taken; Travis accepted the role of the vain Marcello.

{**Right**} Because he loved having his picture taken, Travis accepted the role of the vain Marcello.

33 A

;

SEMICOLON PROBLEM 6:
Semicolon used where a colon is needed—to introduce a quotation or a list

> **Incorrect semicolon before quotation**
>
> **At rehearsal one afternoon Alicia wondered aloud; "Do European students parody American films?"**

> **Incorrect semicolon before a list**
>
> **The film crew was amazed by the props Francie had located; an art deco sofa, a working Victrola, and the bumper from a 1954 Mercedes.**

➤ **Diagnosis**

A semicolon cannot introduce a quotation. Nor may it precede a list—though it may separate items within a list (see Problem 3).

➤ **Solution**

Direct quotations should be introduced by commas or colons.

> ### Replace semicolon with a comma
> **At rehearsal one afternoon Alicia wondered aloud, "Do European students parody American films?"**

Lists may be introduced by colons, commas, or—more rarely—dashes.

> ### Replace semicolon with a colon
> **The film crew was amazed by the props Francie had located: an art deco sofa, a working Victrola, and the bumper from a 1954 Mercedes.**

When a list is not so explicitly introduced, a comma or no punctuation at all should suffice.

{Wrong} Francie spent hours at antique stores; browsing shops, looking for treasures, haggling over prices.

{Right} Francie spent hours at antique stores, browsing shops, looking for treasures, haggling over prices.

♦ FINE TUNING ♦

1. In most cases, a comma is strong enough to join a pair of independent clauses linked by a **coordinating conjunction** (such as *and, but, for, yet*).

   The cast and crew for Sean's film were all amateurs, **yet** they worked almost as hard as professionals.

But a semicolon is sometimes used when the independent clauses are lengthy and contain punctuation themselves. The semicolon acts like a traffic signal, letting you know the difference between a brief stop (comma) and a major intersection (semicolon).

   The cast and crew for Sean's film were amateurs, from Charnelle, the scriptwriter, developing her first screenplay to Enrique, the electrician, trying to figure out how to illuminate a lake at night; **but** they all worked so hard that Professor Vorhees, the faculty supervisor on the project, decided to give them course credit for the production.

2. Placing semicolons between very short independent clauses can seem like punctuation overkill.

{With semicolons} Travis picked up costumes; Alicia arranged transportation; Francie gathered props.

When such clauses are short and closely related, they can be separated by commas.

{With commas} Travis picked up costumes, Alicia arranged transportation, Francie gathered props.

3. Don't use a semicolon to link independent clauses that are only loosely related as a way to build complex sentences. Be sure that thoughts separated by a semicolon belong together. Piling up semicolons in sentence after sentence can make writing seem stiff and needlessly complex.
4. Semicolons ordinarily fall outside quotation marks.

Travis decided to read "The Raven"; Poe was his favorite writer.

EXERCISE 33.1

Combine each group of sentences into a single sentence with at least two independent clauses. Join those independent clauses with a semicolon. Edit the sentences as necessary, cutting, adding, or rearranging words and phrases.

1. Federico Fellini is considered one of the cinema's greatest directors. Many Americans, however, have never seen any of his movies.
2. The heyday of the modern Italian film occurred in the 1950s. Fellini made a series of classic movies during this decade. The films included *La Dolce Vita*, *La Strada*, and *8½*.
3. French directors of the 1950s drew intimate sketches of everyday life. The Italians, on the other hand, portrayed the post-war European landscape in bold symbolic terms.

33 A

;

4. Fellini's films were particularly heavy with symbols. For example, *La Dolce Vita* opens with helicopter pilots waving at girls in bikinis. The pilots are airlifting a statue of Christ over the city of Rome.
5. As Fellini's reputation spread, his films grew more lavish. Many critics, however, still prefer his earliest works to later films. His later films include *The Clowns, Fellini Roma,* and *Fellini Satyricon.*

EXERCISE 33.2

Use semicolons to arrange the following clauses, phrases, and bits of information into complete sentences. You may have to add some words and ideas.

1. The action in mad-killer movies like *Friday the 13th.* Jason skewers two teenagers making love. Jason splits the skull of a camper. Jason drags a midnight skinny-dipper down to a watery grave. Jason drills an ice pick into a camp counselor's brain.
2. Strange titles of Bob Dylan songs. "Subterranean Homesick Blues" "It's Alright, Ma (I'm Only Bleeding)" "Love Minus Zero/No Limit" "Don't Think Twice, It's All Right" "I Shall be Free—No. 10"
3. Items in E. D. Hirsch's list of everything Americans should know. carbon-14 dating. *Veni, vidi, vici.* "Doctor Livingstone, I presume." "Yes, Virginia, there is a Santa Claus."

4. Exceptionally long movie titles. *Alice Doesn't Live Here Anymore. They Shoot Horses, Don't They? Jo Jo Dancer, Your Life Is Calling. The Effect of Gamma Rays on Man-in-the-Moon Marigolds. Close Encounters of the Third Kind: The Special Edition.*

EXERCISE 33.3

Revise the following sentences, adding or deleting semicolons as needed. Not all semicolons below are incorrect. You may have to substitute other punctuation marks for some semicolons.

1. Maggie Lindstrom had promised Sean he could use her bowling alley as a set if he made a film, however, she hadn't really expected his project to get off the ground when she made the offer.
2. Suddenly one Saturday morning they were all there; the director, crew, actors, and interested spectators all arriving simultaneously.
3. Maggie was mustering the courage to ask how long all this would take; when Sean strode up to her and asked; "Would you like to be in the movie?"
4. "We just need someone to serve drinks behind the counter during the scene, no acting talent is required," Sean said.
5. Maggie; however, didn't care, she was going to be a star!

---

33 B COLONS

➤ **Function**
A colon works like a strong directional signal. Think of it as two small arrows pointing in the same direction or a pair of eyes gazing at a particular spot.

➤ **Major Uses**
• Use a colon to direct a reader's attention to an example or explanation. See Problem 1 below.

> Sean faced a major problem in filming his parody: a cast who didn't take direction well.

• Use a colon to direct a reader's attention to a list. See Problem 2.

> The scene called for a variety of camera angles: a wide angle shot, an over-the-shoulder shot, a close-up, and a moving shot.

• Use a colon to direct a reader's attention to a significant remark or conclusion.

> Sean soon discovered the major ingredient in successful filmmaking: hard work.

• Use a colon to direct a reader's attention to a quotation or dialogue.

> After a tough morning of shooting and reshooting, Sean began to question Irving Berlin's line: "There's no business like show business."

➤ Other Uses

• Use a colon to join two complete sentences when the second sentence illustrates or explains the first.

> Making a film is like writing a paper: it absorbs all the time you'll give it.

• Use colons to separate numbers in various ways.

> 12:35 P.M.   Matthew 3:1

• Use a colon to punctuate the salutation in a business letter.

> Dear Sir: Dear Mr. Ebert:

• Use a colon to separate title from subtitle.

> *A Nightmare on Elm Street 3: Dream Warriors*

• Use a colon to separate place of publication from publisher or year from page numbers in various MLA bibliography entries.

> New York: Harper, 1991
>
> 4 July 1991: 154–63

COLON PROBLEM 1:
Unnecessary colon

33 B

> **Colon misused**
>
> **Shoestring budgets have produced many financially successful films, such as: *Flashdance, Breaking Away, Friday the 13th,* and *Halloween.***

➤ Diagnosis

The colon is not needed. Colons are not usually required after *such as, for example,* and *that is.* In fact, colons are stand-ins for such expressions. Colons are often used, however, after phrases that more specifically announce a list: *including these, as follows, such as the following.*

➤ Solution

Remove the colon. No additional punctuation is needed.

> **Colon eliminated**
>
> **Shoestring budgets have produced many financially successful films, such as *Flashdance, Breaking Away, Friday the 13th,* and *Halloween.***

➤ Additional Example.
(Compare the versions.)

{**Version one—with a colon**}   Sean intended to trim his production budget by cutting out some frills: special lighting equipment, rental costumes, and lunches for the crew.

{**Version two—without a colon**}   Sean intended to trim his production budget by cutting out some frills, such as special lighting equipment, rental costumes, and lunches for the crew.

{**Version three—with a colon**}   Sean intended to trim his production budget by cutting out some frills such as these: special lighting equipment, rental costumes, and lunches for the crew.

COLON PROBLEM 2:
Misused colon

> **Colon misused**
>
> **Sean's favorite directors were: Hitchcock, Carpenter, Antonioni, Fellini, and Pollack.**

➤ **Diagnosis**
Ordinarily, a colon is used to introduce a list chiefly when the list follows a complete sentence. This guideline is somewhat flexible. But in the example above, there is no need to interrupt the sentence by placing a colon after the linking verb.

33 B

➤ **Solution**
Remove the colon. No additional punctuation is needed.

> **Colon eliminated**
>
> **Sean's favorite directors were Hitchcock, Carpenter, Antonioni, Fellini, and Pollack.**

➤ **Additional Example.**
(Compare the versions.)

{**Version one—with a colon**}   The filmmakers Charnelle admired most were a diverse group: François Truffaut, Mel Brooks, Alain Robbe-Grillet, and David Lean.

{**Version two—without a colon**}   The filmmakers Charnelle admired most were François Truffaut, Mel Brooks, Alain Robbe-Grillet, and David Lean.

♦ FINE TUNING ♦

1. Colons and semicolons are not interchangeable, but you can use both pieces of punctuation in the same sentence. A colon, for example, might introduce a list of items separated by semicolons.

Charnelle, the writer of the film, gave the character of Marcello three options: remarriage to his fourth wife, the CEO of a nuclear waste disposal company; a potentially lucrative, leveraged buy-out of Fiat; or total bankruptcy.

2. Don't separate a preposition from its object(s) with a colon—or any other punctuation mark.

{**Wrong**}   By the end of a week of shooting, the students had filmed in: a bowling alley, a funeral home, a police car, and a locker room.

{**Right**}   By the end of a week of shooting, the students had filmed in a bowling alley, a funeral home, a police car, and a locker room.

[colon cut]

3. Don't introduce short quotations with colons. A comma or no punctuation mark at all will suffice. Compare the following sentences.

Dirty Harry said "Make my day!"
As Dirty Harry said, "Make my day!"
Sean recalled Dirty Harry's memorable challenge: "Make my day!"

[colon *is* appropriate here because it directs attention to a particular comment]

4. Colons ordinarily fall outside quotation marks (see Section 34E, Problem 2).

Francie decided to play "I Got You Babe": Cher was her favorite singer.

5. Don't use more than one colon in a sentence. A dash (see Section 34A) can usually replace one of the colons.

33 B

{**Problem**}   Almost every film critic agrees on this point: Orson Welles is responsible for one of the greatest films of all time: *Citizen Kane.*

{**Solution**}   Almost every film critic agrees on this point: Orson Welles is responsible for one of the greatest films of all time—*Citizen Kane.*

EXERCISE 33.4

Revise the following sentences, adding or deleting colons as needed. Not all colons below are incorrect.

1. At long last, the crew is ready to film the concluding scene: the midnight swim at Crystal Lake.
2. At the lake on a dark evening, Sean explains to his cast that in the final scene, the decadent Europeans, recognizing the folly of their lives, throw all their worldly goods into the lake, including: their jewels, their furniture, and their clothes.
3. "Then they plunge into the lake themselves, this midnight swim becomes the symbolic absolution that ends my film," Sean explained.
4. Alicia, Richard, Sue Ellen, and Travis all have the same question, "What are these decadent Europeans wearing while they are absolving themselves symbolically?"

5. Sean sighed impatiently, "They are wearing a great deal, their sorrow, their pain, their guilt, their grief, their corruption."

EXERCISE 33.5

Review Sections 33A–B. Revise the following sentences, adding or deleting semicolons and colons as necessary. Not all the punctuation below is incorrect.

1. "And their clothes?" asks Sue Ellen; who feels silly enough already: standing by a lake at midnight in the shabby garb of an avant-garde painter.
2. Sean admits that he may have failed to mention that his movie ends with a nude scene, however, he promises to film it as discreetly as possible.
3. Several weeks later the film premieres in the college auditorium, it is; in fact, a smashing success.
4. At the party after the premiere, Professor Voorhees tells Sean that she was especially impressed by the symbolic richness of the last scene where the decadent socialites throw everything that had been tormenting them into Crystal Lake; their jewels, their music, their alcohol, their director.
5. "Not until that final moment," Professor Voorhees explained, "when you are flung into the water; screaming like a scalded cat; stripped of your pretensions and your clothes; did I realize that the film was really a statement about: a filmmaker's struggle to create art. Bravo! Have you ever seen Fellini's *8½*?"

33 B

34 Sentence Markers

A Dashes

B Hyphens

C Parentheses

D Brackets

E Quotation marks

F Ellipses

G Italics

H Slashes

34 A DASHES

➤ Function

Used alone, a dash attaches one idea to another more vigorously than a comma would. Used in pairs, dashes highlight words or phrases by separating them from the rest of a sentence. Think of dashes as sparks of energy in a sentence, arcing from idea to idea.

➤ Major Uses

• Use a dash to join a phrase to the end of a sentence. The phrase might furnish an example, an illustration, or a summary. Or it might add a surprise, a contradiction, or an exception to the sentence. Like colons, dashes point to ideas. But where colons provide formal introductions, dashes introduce unanticipated guests.

> Late one February night, a tired group of juniors from Clear Lake College agreed to Drayton's suggestion that he arrange their spring break trip—a minor decision no one thought much about.

> Several weeks later, a travel agent delivered the students their airline tickets—to Cleveland, Ohio.

• Use a dash to insert an idea into the middle of a sentence. The interruption might be an example, an explanation, an illustration, an observation, an amplification, or a contradiction. In any case, the interrupting phrase, surrounded by dashes, could be lifted out of the sentence without affecting its overall sense.

Connie, Richard, Francie, Kyle, Travis, and Charnelle—everyone for whom Drayton had purchased a nonrefundable ticket—demanded an immediate explanation.

Drayton assured them that Cleveland had many attractions—a world class art museum, a great symphony, colorful ethnic neighborhoods—to make their spring break memorable.

➤ Other Uses

- Use a dash to show an interruption, especially in dialogue.

"When—perhaps I should say *if*—we arrive in Cleveland, what are we going to do there in March in the cold?" Connie asked at a gathering called to discuss the vacation crisis.

Travis sputtered, "My buds are cruising to Aruba, Cozumel, Antigua, and Padre Island, and I'm supposed to tell them I'm going—I can hardly believe it—to Cleveland?"

- Use a dash to set off items, phrases, or credit lines.

The Indians, the Browns, the Cavaliers—Cleveland boasted a complete slate of professional sports franchises.

Participants at the meeting agreed
    —to beg the airlines for a refund
    —to tell no one where they were going
    —to consider suitable measures for dealing with Drayton.

"I promise that your vacation in Cleveland will be the most memorable and rewarding of your entire lives."

                                              —Drayton Washington

34 A

- Use a dash to mark off questions and answers.

Q.—Did you understand fully the consequences of buying a nonrefundable ticket?

A.—To be honest, we did.

DASH PROBLEM 1:
Typing a hyphen where a dash is required

> **Hyphens used instead of dashes**
>
> Drayton promised his friends-on his word of honor-that he had an excellent reason for planning their trip to Cleveland.

➤ Diagnosis

Hyphens {-} have been typed where dashes are intended. Typed dashes are made up of two unspaced hyphens {--}. No space is left before or after a dash.

➤ **Solution**
Replace the hyphens with dashes.

> **Dashes replace hyphens**
>
> **Drayton promised his friends—on his word of honor— that he had an excellent reason for planning their trip to Cleveland.**

DASH PROBLEM 2:
Too many dashes

> **Too many dashes**
>
> **Francie—the incurable optimist of the group—suggested that more aggressive tactics—constant phone calls, letters to the editor, radio talk show appearances, picketing—might persuade the airline to give them their money back.**

➤ **Diagnosis**
The dashes cause confusion. Dashes are vigorous pieces of punctuation that should be used cautiously—one pair of dashes per sentence.

34 A

➤ **Solution**
Replace some of the dashes with commas.

> **Some dashes eliminated**
>
> **Francie, the incurable optimist of the group, suggested that more aggressive tactics—constant phone calls, letters to the editor, radio talk show appearances, picketing—might persuade the airline to give them their money back.**

➤ **Additional example**

{**Too many dashes**}   While Drayton argued that a vacation in Cleveland—which was his hometown—might open his classmates' eyes to new experiences— new people, different cultures, unusual neighborhoods—Travis reminded them of spring breaks they had enjoyed in the past—on sunny beaches in exotic, southern locales.

{**Revised**}   Drayton argued that a vacation in Cleveland—his hometown—might open his classmates' eyes to new experiences, new people, different cultures, and unusual neighborhoods. Travis, however, reminded them of spring breaks they had enjoyed in the past—on sunny beaches in exotic, southern locales.

EXERCISE 34.1

Add and delete dashes as necessary to improve the passage below.

1. After a full week of heated debate, Drayton began to convince his friends, one by one, first Charnelle, then Travis, then Connie, that a trip to Cleveland might be a unique way to spend spring break.
2. Their agreement to make the trip in March led—almost inevitably—to additional questions—for example, where would they be staying?
3. Drayton's friends never a suspicious group suddenly realized that he had said nothing about a hotel.
4. Evasion, allusions to livable quarters, a few half-muttered syllables that's all Drayton was willing to say at first about the lodging he had arranged.
5. His friends now committed to the trip considered that it might be best not to ask any more questions they might not like the answers.

34 B   HYPHENS

➤ **Function**
The hyphen, a humble but much-used mark, either divides syllables or links words. You might want to visualize these marks as hinges that make things glide smoothly.

➤ **Major Uses**
• Use a hyphen to divide words at the ends of lines when you run out of space. (However, both the MLA and APA style manuals now discourage breaking words at the end of lines. Also, if you are using a word processor, "word wrap" will eliminate most divided words.)

When you do need to divide words, here are some guidelines for hyphenation.

1. When you must divide a word at the end of a line, break it only at a syllable. If you are unsure about a syllable break, check a dictionary. Don't guess.

   fu-se-lage   vin-e-gar-y
   lo-qua-cious   cam-ou-flage

2. Never divide a word of one syllable or let a single letter dangle at the end of a line. Divisions like the following would be either wrong or inappropriate.

   mo-uth   cry-pt   cough-ed
   o-boe   e-clipse   i-dea

3. Never strand a letter or two at the beginning of a new line. Divisions like the following would be inappropriate.

   Ohi-o   clump-y   flatfoot-ed
   log-ic   oversimpli-fy   yo-yo

4. Don't leave a syllable at the end of a line that might be read as a complete word. The following sentence might be misread at first because of faulty division.

Nothing could deter Alicia in her pursuit of a management degree.

5. Don't hyphenate contractions, numbers, abbreviations, or initialisms at the end of lines. The following divisions would be inappropriate.

would-n't	250-000,000	NA-TO
U.S.-M.C.	Ph.-D.	NB-C

6. Divide compound expressions between words, not syllables.

space-ship	post-modern	hind-quarter

7. Divide expressions that contain hyphens at the hyphen—but don't add a second hyphen!

{**Wrong**} Last night, thieves robbed Anson's well-
-known music shop.

{**Right**} Last night, thieves robbed Anson's well-
known music shop.

• Use a hyphen to link compound words and expressions. Hyphens join words together in a variety of situations, but the conventions guiding their use are complicated. Sometimes you'll have to rely on instinct—or a dictionary. Here are some guidelines to sharpen your instincts.

34 B

1. Use hyphens when you write out numbers from twenty-one to ninety-nine. Fractions also take hyphens, but only one hyphen per fraction.

twenty-nine	two-thirds
one forty-seventh of a mile	one-quarter inch
two hundred forty-six	

2. Check a dictionary to be sure which compound expressions are typically hyphenated. Usage may vary. Here are some words that do take hyphens.

mother-in-law	son-in-law	great-grandmother
three-D	walkie-talkie	water-skier

Note, however, that many compounds do not take hyphens.

hitchhiker	evildoer	yearbook
selfsame	shoofly pie	motorcycle

3. Hyphens are often used when modifiers before a noun work together.

a **sharp-looking** suit   a **seventeenth-century** vase
a **stop-motion** sequence

If placing a comma between the modifiers or removing one of them changes the meaning of the phrase, then the modifiers probably should be linked by a hyphen.

a blood, curdling yell   →   a **blood-curdling** yell
a well, known artist   →   a **well-known** artist
a blue, green tint   →   a **blue-green** tint

However, hyphens are not used with adverbs that end in -*ly*. Nor are they used with *very*.

a sharply honed knife   a quickly written note
a bitterly cold morning   a very hot day

4. Hyphens are usually not required when compound modifiers follow a noun.

The artist was well known.
The scream was blood curdling.

➤ Other Uses

• Use a hyphen to link prefixes and suffixes to base words.

  pre-Columbian   governor-**elect**

• Use a hyphen to create compound phrases.

  Students resented the **holier-than-thou** attitude in Connie's editorials.

• Use a hyphen to prevent words from being misread.

  The students discovered that they would be spending spring break not in a hotel but in a **co-op**.

34 B

HYPHEN PROBLEM:
Faulty division of words at the end of a line

> **Faulty division**
>
> While other students packed suntan oil, towels, and beac-
> hballs, Drayton and friends tried to locate boots, blanke-
> ts, and ice-skates.

➤ Diagnosis
Words at the end of typed lines are divided in the wrong places.

➤ Solution
Divide the words between syllables. Check a dictionary if necessary.

> **Correct division**
>
> While other students packed suntan oil, towels, and beach-
> balls, Drayton and friends tried to locate boots, blan-
> kets, and ice-skates.

♦ FINE TUNING ♦

Sometimes a word or phrase may have more than a single hyphenated modifier. These suspended modifiers look like the following.

> Charnelle expected her vacation wardrobe to accommodate **cold-, cool-,** and **wet-weather** days.

> Connie, on the other hand, selected her apparel to suit **high-** and **low-**fashion occasions.

EXERCISE 34.2

Most people guess at syllable division when they divide words. Should they consult a dictionary instead? Try your hand at dividing the following twenty words into syllables. Then check your divisions against a dictionary. Tally up the number you get exactly right and enter it in the formula below for figuring your percent correct. Can you afford to rely on your best guesses?

Word	Right	Wrong
1. malfeasance	_____	_____
2. Aleutian	_____	_____
3. baboon	_____	_____
4. cooperate	_____	_____
5. measles	_____	_____
6. separate	_____	_____
7. zoology	_____	_____
8. flamingo	_____	_____
9. dyslexia	_____	_____
10. faucet	_____	_____
11. writing	_____	_____
12. mischievous	_____	_____
13. revelation	_____	_____
14. parabola	_____	_____
15. oceanographer	_____	_____
16. license	_____	_____
17. junior	_____	_____
18. hemorrhage	_____	_____
19. grabbed	_____	_____
20. novice	_____	_____

number right _____ x 5 = _____% correct

34 B

EXERCISE 34.3

In the following sentences, indicate which form of the words or punctuation marks in parentheses is correct. Use a dictionary if necessary. Treat the sentences as part of a single passage.

1. Local citizens have a **(once in a life-time/once-in-a-lifetime)** opportunity to-day to secure a priceless resource for their children tomorrow.
2. A large, wooded parcel of land is about to be turned into a shopping mall by **(real-estate/realestate)** speculators and **(pinstripe suited/pinstripe-suited)** investors **(—/-)** the tract of land bordering Crystal Lake.
3. The forest provides a haven for **(wild-life/wildlife)** of all varieties, from **(great horned owls/great-horned owls)** to **(ruby throated/ruby-throated)** hummingbirds.
4. Do we really need more **(video stores/video-stores),** more **(T shirt/T-shirt)** shops, more **(over priced/over-priced)** boutiques, and junk food restaurants?
5. Let's work to stop this **(recently-proposed/recently proposed)** assault on our environment. Call your **(City-council/City Council)** representatives today and tell them that you are opposed to further development at Crystal Lake.

34 C   PARENTHESES

➤ Function

Both parentheses and brackets act as enclosures. Parentheses are used more often than brackets and more generally—usually to show when something needs to be separated from the rest of a sentence or paragraph. Parentheses lack the snap of dashes; instead, they quietly contain an extra bit of information, a comment, or an aside. Brackets, on the other hand, are used only in a few specific situations (see Section 34D).

34 C

( )

➤ Principal Use

• Use parentheses to separate material from the main body of a sentence or paragraph. This material may be a word, a phrase, a list, even a complete sentence.

> The flight to Cleveland was quick **(only about ninety minutes)** and uneventful.

> Yet the students suspected that there was something odd about Drayton's carry-on items **(several fix-it manuals, a power drill, a small tool kit).**

> The students landed at Cleveland Hopkins Airport early **(11:20 a.m.)** and by noon were in a cab headed for their lodging. **(Drayton had handed the cabbie an address.)** The weather was gloomy, cold, and damp.

➤ Other Uses

• Use parentheses to insert examples, directions, or other details into a sentence.

> The note to the cabdriver included an address **(107 E. 97 St.).**

> If you get lost call the school **(346-1317)** or the church office **(471-6109).**

• Use parentheses to highlight numbers or letters used in listing items.

> Drayton realized that he could **(1)** tell his friends there in the cab what he was up to, **(2)** wait to tell them until after they had arrived at the co-op, or **(3)** direct the cabbie to return to the airport immediately.

Misplaced punctuation

Faulty punctuation

The neighborhood was run-down and littered. (Some houses looked as if they hadn't been painted in decades).

Faulty punctuation

On the corner was a small church (actually a converted store.)

➤ **Diagnosis**

The periods are misplaced. When a complete sentence standing alone is surrounded by parentheses, its end punctuation belongs inside the parentheses. However, when a sentence concludes with a parenthesis, the end punctuation for the complete sentence falls outside the final parenthesis mark.

➤ **Solution**

Move the periods. (See also the Fine Tuning section below.)

34 C

( )

Punctuation corrected

The neighborhood was run-down and littered. (Some houses looked as if they hadn't been painted in decades.)

Punctuation corrected

On the corner was a small church (actually a converted store).

◆ **FINE TUNING** ◆

1. If parentheses enclose a full sentence within another sentence, it begins without capitalization and ends without punctuation.

   Drayton pointed out a building on Woodhill Road where they would be lodging **(they glared at him),** led them into the lobby **(no one said a word),** and urged them to smile **(it was, after all, spring break).**

2. No punctuation is needed to introduce parentheses within a sentence. However, if necessary, a phrase in parentheses may be followed by a comma.

Although resigned to spring vacation in Cleveland **(Drayton had, after all, promised them the most memorable vacation of their lives),** the students were unprepared for the bleakness of the co-op.

3. Parentheses are used around in-text notes when using MLA or APA documentation. See Chapters 39–40 for details.

EXERCISE 34.4

Add parentheses as needed to the following passage. Pay special attention to punctuation and capitalization; you may have to change some marks.

1. As the students registered at the desk, they were greeted in turn by a minister Drayton seemed to know him, a kindly couple from Georgia, three more students including a young woman from Sweden, and an airline flight attendant, all dressed in work clothes.
2. Reverend Ike, wondering why this new group of volunteers looked so bewildered surely Drayton hadn't led them to expect luxurious accommodations, welcomed them warmly.
3. Ike's crew about ten men and women, all told carried ladders, hammers, cans of paint, drills, and lumber.
4. Drayton's companions turned on him angrily as soon as Reverend Ike's crew marched out of the lobby into the street. The wind was howling and a light snow had begun to fall. Kyle and Travis backed Drayton into an overstuffed chair it had a broken spring while Connie and Francie waved travel brochures at him.
5. An explanation it had better be a good one, too, Drayton realized was now required.

34 D

[ ]

---

34 D   BRACKETS

➤ **Function**
Like parentheses, brackets are enclosures. But they have fewer and more specialized uses. Brackets and parentheses are usually *not* interchangeable.

➤ **Principal Use**
• Use brackets to insert comments or explanations into direct quotations. You cannot change the words in a direct quotation, but you can add remarks to them by using brackets.

> Drayton pulled a newspaper article from his jacket and spoke to his friends, "This **[the newspaper piece]** is the reason you are spending spring break in Cleveland."

> "It explains a volunteer program called 'Home Front.' Ike Cannon **[the minister the students had met in the lobby]** organized it to rebuild run-down housing in the inner cities."

➤ Other Uses

• Use brackets to clarify situations where parentheses fall within parentheses. When possible, avoid parentheses within parentheses. If you cannot, the inner set of parentheses should become brackets.

> The house the students were assigned to work on had barely escaped a condemnation order (City of Cleveland **[order no. 34209]**).

• Use brackets to acknowledge or highlight errors that originate in quoted materials. In such cases the Latin word *sic* ("thus") is enclosed in brackets immediately after the error. See Chapter 38, page 569 for additional details.

> The sign over the co-op cash register read "We don't except **[sic]** checks for payments."

BRACKET PROBLEM:
Parentheses used instead of brackets

> **Parentheses mistakenly used instead of brackets**
>
> "This (the newspaper article) is the reason you are spending spring break in Cleveland."

34 E

➤ Diagnosis
Your typewriter may not have keys for brackets!

➤ Solution
Leave a space where the brackets should appear and draw them in after you have typed your paper. But don't forget.

> **Brackets drawn in**
>
> "This [the newspaper article] is the reason you are spending spring break in Cleveland."

34 E QUOTATION MARKS

Terms you need to know

DIRECT DISCOURSE. The actual words of a speaker or writer. Enclose all direct discourse in quotation marks.

> "I can barely hammer a nail straight," Travis muttered.

INDIRECT DISCOURSE. The substance of what a speaker or writer has said, but not the exact words. Indirect discourse is not surrounded by quotation marks.

> Travis muttered that he could barely hammer a nail straight.

➤ Function
Quotation marks—which always occur in pairs—highlight whatever appears between them. Conventionally, double marks (" ") are used around direct discourse and titles. Single marks appear (' ') with quotations or titles inside quotations.

➤ Principal Uses
• Use quotation marks to signal that you are quoting word-for-word from printed sources. Notice the capitalization and punctuation before and after the quotations in the following examples.

> "Heroism," says Ralph Waldo Emerson, "feels and never reasons and therefore is always right."

> Emerson reminds us that "Nothing great was ever achieved without enthusiasm."

> "Next to the originator of a good sentence is the first quoter of it," writes Emerson.

For more details about punctuating quotations, see Quotation Problems 1–3. For details about how to introduce direct quotations, how to tailor quotations to your sentences, how to handle long quotations, and how to quote from poetry, see Section 38D.

• Use quotation marks to indicate dialogue. Quotation marks enclose the exact words of various speakers. When writing extended dialogue, you ordinarily start a new paragraph each time the speaker changes.

> Drayton was insistent: "It's better to spend spring break providing a homeless family with a decent place to live than roasting ourselves on a noisy, crowded beach in Cozumel."

> "Dost thou think because thou art virtuous there shall be no more cakes and ale?" Francie replied, finally making use of a quotation she had memorized in a Shakespeare class.

> "Huh?" said Travis.

However, when dialogue is provided not for its own sake, but to make some other point, the words of several speakers may appear within a single paragraph.

> Drayton was confident that his friends eventually would see his point. "They'll come around," he thought. "They always do." And Connie, for one, was beginning to soften. "Spring break in Cancun last year wasn't so great," she admitted to herself. "What did it get me—sunburn, lost credit cards, a black eye, and stomach flu?"

• Use quotation marks to cite the titles of short works. These ordinarily include titles of songs, essays, magazine and newspaper articles, TV episodes, unpublished speeches, chapters of books, and short poems. (Longer works appear in *italics*.)

> "Love Is Just a Four Letter Word"—title of a song

> "Love Is a Fallacy"—title of an essay

➤ Other Uses
• Use quotation marks to draw attention to specific words. Italics can also be used in these situations. See Section 34G.

34 E

" "
' '

Travis wondered just what Drayton meant when he used the term "vacation."

● Use quotation marks to signal that you are using a word ironically, sarcastically, or derisively.

After the students had registered at the co-op, the clerk at the desk directed them to their "suites"—bare rooms crowded with bunks. A bathroom down the hall served as the "spa."

QUOTATION PROBLEM 1:
Periods and commas go inside quotation marks

> **Period and comma misplaced outside quotation mark**
>
> Down a corridor lined with antiwar posters, the students heard someone humming "Blowin' in the Wind". "This must be what the 60s were like", Charnelle said.

➤ Diagnosis
Both the period and comma are incorrectly placed outside the quotation marks. Commas and periods are always placed *inside* a closing quotation mark. The only exception is when a special reference is used—for instance, when a sentence ends with a page number in parentheses:

Hitchcock claims, "The sequence was never filmed" (21).

➤ Solution
Move the period and comma inside the quotes.

> **Period and comma relocated inside quotation mark**
>
> Down a corridor lined with antiwar posters, the students heard someone humming "Blowin' in the Wind." "This must be what the 60s were like," Charnelle said.

QUOTATION PROBLEM 2:
Colons and semicolons go outside quotation marks

> **Colon misplaced inside quotation marks**
>
> Travis nicknamed the co-op "Bleak House:" he complained about the sagging mattresses, noisy radiators, and broken blinds.

34 E

" "
' '

> **Semicolon misplaced inside quotation marks**
>
> **Connie found herself humming "If I Had a Hammer;" she'd like to have used one on Travis.**

➤ **Diagnosis**

Both the colon and semicolon are incorrectly placed inside the quotation marks. Colons and semicolons always go *outside* a closing quotation mark.

➤ **Solution**

Move the colon and semicolon outside the quotation mark.

> **Colon relocated outside quotation marks**
>
> **Travis nicknamed the co-op "Bleak House": he complained about the sagging mattresses, noisy radiators, and broken blinds.**

> **Semicolon relocated outside quotation marks**
>
> **Connie found herself humming "If I Had a Hammer"; she'd like to have used one on Travis.**

➤ **Additional Examples**

Kyle claimed to be "an expert carpenter": he had worked on construction jobs during the summer.

A billboard described Cleveland as "the greatest location in the nation"; however, Travis had his doubts.

34 E

66 99
6 9

QUOTATION PROBLEM 3:
Placement of question marks, exclamations, and dashes varies

> **Punctuation misplaced outside quotation marks**
>
> **When Kyle saw the house the students were to repair, he muttered "Good grief"! He turned to Drayton and said "Do you really think we can turn that into livable housing"? Drayton began to answer: "I'm pretty sure that"—but his foot went through a floorboard.**

> **Punctuation misplaced inside quotation marks**
>
> **Who was it that said "hard work never killed anybody?" Travis would have liked to teach him or her a lesson in "the Puritan ethic!"**

➤ **Diagnosis**

The closing punctuation is misplaced. Question marks, exclamation points, and dashes can fall either inside or outside quotation marks, depending on the context. They fall inside the closing quotation when they are the right punctuation for the phrase inside the quotes, but not for the sentence as a whole. They fall outside the closing quotation mark when they are the appropriate mark for the complete sentence.

➤ **Solution**

Move the punctuation inside or outside the closing quotation mark according to the guidelines above.

> **Punctuation relocated inside quotation marks**
>
> When Kyle saw the house the students were to repair, he muttered "Good grief!" He turned to Drayton and said "Do you really think we can turn that into livable housing?" Drayton began to answer: "I'm pretty sure that—" but his foot went through a floorboard.

> **Punctuation relocated outside quotation marks**
>
> Who was it that said "hard work never killed anybody"? Travis would have liked to teach him or her a lesson in "the Puritan ethic"!

34 E

66 99
6 9

♦ **FINE TUNING** ♦

1. Don't use quotation marks to mark clichés. Highlighting a tired phrase just makes it seem more fatigued.

   Working around electrical fixtures made Francie more nervous than **"a long-tailed cat in a room full of rocking chairs."**

2. Use quotation marks very sparingly to indicate irony or sarcasm. The technique loses its punch quickly.

   Travis called upstairs to Kyle to report a little **"problem"**; he'd just connected a waterline to the stove.

3. Don't put the title of your paper between quotation marks on the title page or first page.

   {**Wrong**}   "Rescuing American Cities: What Government Can't Do"

   {**Right**}   Rescuing American Cities: What Government Can't Do

4. When the words of one speaker extend beyond a single paragraph, do not place a quotation mark at the end of the first paragraph or at the end of any other paragraph until the very end of the quotation. However, each new paragraph *begins* with a quotation mark, as shown below.

"Let's see," Travis wondered, "if I attached the water line to the stove, what did I connect the gas line to?

"Of course, I might have forgotten to hook the gas line up to anything, in which case this kitchen would be filling up with explosive vapors.

"Or since there's a bathroom right next to the kitchen, I might have run the gas line into the . . . oh, no!"

EXERCISE 34.5

Rework the following passage by adding or deleting quotation marks, moving punctuation as necessary, and indenting paragraphs where you think appropriate.

Much to the students' surprise, their "labor" at the house being repaired by the Home Front organization attracted the attention of the local "media", complete with camera crew. (Travis hummed This Land Is Your Land whenever a TV camera pointed in his direction.) A reporter interviewed Drayton, who claimed that his friends had insisted on joining him on the project once he described the good work being done. This house means more to us than volleyball on the beach ever could he said. If more students dedicated just a little of their time to social projects, what couldn't we accomplish? Did you have any qualms about coming to Cleveland in March? the reporter asked, turning to Travis. He replied that, frankly, he'd rather be snorkeling in the Cayman Islands. But Kyle interrupted. I think we all had doubts about this. Drayton never did! Charnelle interjected. As I was trying to say, Travis continued, I'd rather be snorkeling, but that's the whole point. Things get out of kilter when people always do what they want rather than what they should. Charnelle was shocked. Travis, you really do have a heart! Travis blushed like a "bride".

EXERCISE 34.6

Write a passage of dialogue in which you extend the reporter's interview in Exercise 34.4. Or create a dialogue on a subject of your own.

34 F ELLIPSES

➤ Function
The three spaced periods that form an ellipsis mark indicate a gap in a sentence. Either you have left something out or you want an idea to seem to trail away.

➤ Principal Use
• Use ellipses to indicate that material has been left out of a direct quotation. This material may be a word, a phrase, a complete sentence, or more.

{**Complete passage**}   In *Walden* (1854), Henry David Thoreau describes his forest in spring: "Early in May, the oaks, hickories, maples, and other trees, just putting out amidst the pine woods around the pond, imparted a brightness like sunshine to the landscape, especially in cloudy days, as if the sun were breaking through the mists and shining faintly on the hillsides here and there."

{**Passage with ellipses**}   In *Walden* (1854), Henry David Thoreau describes his forest in spring: "Early in May, the oaks, hickories, maples, and other trees . . . imparted a brightness like sunshine to the landscape . . . as if the sun were breaking through the mists and shining faintly on the hillsides here and there."

➤ Other Uses

• Use ellipses to indicate any gap or pause in a sentence, not necessarily in quoted material.

Travis was sure he could repair the faulty fusebox . . . until it began shooting sparks.

• Use ellipses to suggest an action that is incomplete or continuing.

At the limits of his patience, Reverend Ike began counting under his breath, "One, two, three . . . ."

34 F
● ● ●

ELLIPSIS PROBLEM:
Spacing and punctuation before and after the ellipsis marks

Be sure to handle ellipses properly, especially when typing or using a word processor. An ellipsis is typed as three spaced periods (. . . not ...). Spacing is important, too. Here are four guidelines for placing an ellipsis.

• When an ellipsis mark appears in the middle of a sentence, leave a space before the first and after the last period.

most governments . . . are sometimes

• If a punctuation mark occurs immediately before the words you are cutting, you may include it in your edited version if it makes your sentence easier to read. The punctuation mark is followed by a space, then the ellipsis mark.

It is excellent, . . . yet this government

• When an ellipsis occurs at the end of a complete sentence, the end punctuation of the sentence is retained in the edited version, followed by a space, followed by the ellipsis. No gap is left between the last word in the sentence and its original end punctuation.

The people can act through it. . . .

• When a parenthetical reference follows a sentence that ends with an ellipsis, leave a space between the last word in the sentence and the ellipsis.

Then provide the parenthetical reference, followed by the closing punctuation mark.

the right to revolution . . ." (102).

♦ FINE TUNING ♦

If you want to leave a line or more out of a poem, type a full line of spaced periods.

{Original}

> Life's a crock, or so they say;
> Crocks are mud wrung dry as hay;
> Hay's a grass grows fast as weeds;
> Weeds are life drawn out of seeds.
>   —Travis Beckwith

{Line deleted}

> Life's a crock, or so they say;
> Crocks are mud wrung dry as hay;
>
> . . . .
> Weeds are life drawn out of seeds.

34 F
● ● ●

EXERCISE 34.7

Add ellipses to the following narrative. Try to place at least three ellipsis marks at various points in the passage. Be sure that the passage is still readable.

Within a week, the dilapidated Victorian house being restored by the Home Front volunteers began to look livable again, its exterior sheathed in gleaming siding, its gables restored, its gutters rehung, its roof reshingled. Even the main staircase, down which Travis had tumbled several times, knocking out the railings, had been rebuilt. Travis made a number of mistakes during the project, including painting several windows shut, papering over a heating register, and hanging a door upside down, but even Reverend Ike praised his conscientiousness. Francie had proved her worth by sanding away layers of paint and varnish accumulated over almost six decades to reveal beautiful hardwood floors that would have looked right in an executive suite. Connie contributed her organizational talents—the same ones that had earned her the editorship of the student paper—to keep the volunteers supplied with the raw materials, equipment, and advice they needed to make their jobs run smoothly. The volunteers worked from seven in the morning to seven at night, occasionally pausing to talk with neighbors from the area who stopped by with snacks and lunches, but laboring like mules until Reverend Ike pulled up with the van to drive them back to the co-op. Even a sagging mattress looked good, Travis willingly admitted, after a full day of sawing, pounding, and painting.

34 G   ITALICS

> **Function**

Italics, like quotation marks, draw attention to a title, word, or phrase. But they are even more noticeable because italics change the way words look. In a printed text, italics are *slanted letters*. In typed or handwritten papers, italics are signaled by underlining the appropriate words. In either case, italicized words get noticed.

> **Principal Use**

—Use italics to set off a title. Some titles and names are ordinarily italicized; others appear between quotation marks. The list below explains which is which.

Titles Italicized

books	*Bonfire of the Vanities*
magazines	*Time*
journals	*Written Communication*
newspapers	*The New York Times*
films	*Casablanca*
TV shows	*The Tonight Show*
radio shows	*All Things Considered*
plays	*Measure for Measure*
long poems	*Paradise Lost*
long musical pieces	*The Mikado*
albums	*Rattle and Hum*
paintings	the *Mona Lisa*
sculptures	Michelangelo's *Pietà*
ships	*Titanic*
	U.S.S. *Saratoga*
trains	the *Orient Express*
aircraft	*Enola Gay*
spacecraft	*Apollo 11*
software programs	*MacWrite*
	Pagemaker 3.1

Titles "In Quotations"

chapters of books	"Lessons from the Pros"
articles in magazines	"What's New in Moscow?"
articles in journals	"Vai Script and Literacy"
articles in newspapers	"Inflation Heats Up"
sections in newspapers	"Living in Style"
TV episodes	"Cold Steele"
radio episodes	"McGee Goes Crackers"
short stories	"Araby"
short poems	"The Red Wheelbarrow"
songs	"God Bless America"

Neither italics nor quotation marks are used for the names of **types** of trains, ships, aircraft, or spacecraft.

DC-10	Boeing 727
space shuttle	Atlas Agena
Trident submarine	

Neither italics nor quotation marks are used with titles of major religious texts, books of the Bible, or major legal documents.

the Bible	the Koran
Genesis	Exodus
1 Romans	the Declaration of Independence
the Constitution	the Magna Charta

➤ Other Uses

• Use italics to set off foreign words or phrases. Foreign terms that haven't become an accepted item of English vocabulary and scientific names are given special emphasis.

> Connie nearly fainted when Travis described his coworkers as *les bêtes humaines.*

> Staring out the window, Francie was convinced that she had spotted the first *Turdus migratorius* of spring.

However, the many foreign words absorbed by English over the centuries should not be italicized. To be sure, check a recent dictionary.

crèche	gumbo
gestalt	arroyo

Common abbreviations from Latin also appear without italics or underscoring.

etc.	et al.
i.e.	viz.

34 G

italics

• Use italics (or quotation marks) to emphasize or clarify a letter, a word, or a phrase.

> According to Drayton, when most people talk about *social concerns,* they really mean *higher taxes.*

> Does that word begin with an *f* or a *ph?*

♦ FINE TUNING ♦

1. You can use italics to highlight words you intend to define in a sentence.

"A *fascist,*" Travis complained, "is apparently anyone who doesn't agree with you, Connie."

2. You can italicize words to indicate where emphasis should be placed in reading.

"That may be how *you* define fascist," she replied.

> **EXERCISE 34.8**

Indicate whether the following titles or names in boldface should be italicized, in quotation marks, or unmarked. If you don't recognize a name below, check an encyclopedia or other reference work.

1. Launching a **Titan III** at Cape Canaveral
2. **My Fair Lady** playing at the **Paramount Theatre**
3. Watching **I Love Lucy**
4. Sunk on the **Andrea Doria**
5. Returning **A Farewell to Arms** to the public library
6. Playing **Casablanca** again on a **Panasonic** video recorder
7. Discussing the colors of Picasso's **The Old Guitarist**
8. Assigning Jackson's **The Lottery** one more time
9. Picking up a copy of **The Los Angeles Times**
10. Whistling **Here Comes the Sun** from the Beatles' **Abbey Road**
11. Reading **On the Town** in **The Washington Post**
12. Riding on **The City of New Orleans**
13. Working with **Wordstar** on an **IBM-PC**
14. Settling in for an evening with Puccini's **Madame Butterfly**
15. Photocopying **Trouble in Silicon Valley** from a recent issue of **Time**
16. Trying to remember Thomas Wyatt's sonnet **Farewell, Love**
17. Writing a paper about the **Edsel**
18. Rereading **The Grand Inquisitor** from Dostoevsky's **The Brothers Karamazov**
19. Quoting a paragraph from **Gulliver's Travels**
20. Spending an afternoon at the **Hirshhorn Museum** in **Gucci** shoes

34 G

italics

> **EXERCISE 34.9**

Add quotation marks and italics (underlining) to the following passage as needed. Remember that titles that require quotation marks take single quotations (' ') when they occur within a passage of dialogue already enclosed by double quotations (" ").

1. Heading for Cleveland Hopkins Airport in a van, Travis read the sports page of The Plain Dealer while Connie leafed through a copy of Time.
2. The other students were as pensive as Rodin's The Thinker, especially Drayton.
3. "Well," Francie sighed, "when our friends back at school flaunt their tans, we'll be able to display our blisters, n'est-ce pas?"
4. Let's skip the mumbo jumbo and get right to the heart of the matter," Charnelle said. "Drayton, I hate to admit it, but we all had a great time—the crème de la crème of spring vacations."
5. "You took us into a decaying inner city neighborhood, lodged us in a co-op that looked like a set from Apocalypse Now, and worked us hard enough to violate every provision of the Bill of Rights, but we ended up feeling like heroes from the Odyssey."

6. "It didn't hurt," Travis admitted, "to see ourselves on The Nightly News."
7. "And despite all the hours we spent restoring that old house," Kyle noted, "we heard the Cleveland Symphony play Beethoven, spent an afternoon at the Western Reserve Historical Society Museum, toured the Cleveland Clinic, and visited the site of the Rock and Roll Hall of Fame."
8. "Let's not lose track of who the real heroes are," Drayton reminded them as they lugged their bags into the terminal, "the people working hard to save their own neighborhoods."
9. As the students rode the Boeing 737 home, Travis hummed Blowin' in the Wind, Connie read A Farewell to Arms, and Kyle and Francie shared a copy of USA Today.
10. Drayton and Charnelle looked over an article entitled American Volunteers Help Poor in Central America; they were already planning their next spring adventure.

34 H   SLASHES

➤ Function
The slash indicates a division. It is a rare piece of punctuation with specific functions.

➤ Major Uses
● Use a slash to divide lines of poetry quoted within sentences. When you quote more than three lines of poetry, you simply indent the passage ten spaces.

> . . . But as King Lear wanders the heath in the horrible storm, he realizes for the first time how much the poor in his kingdom must endure:
>> Poor naked wretches, wheresoever you are,
>> That bide the pelting of this pitiless storm,
>> How shall your houseless heads and unfed sides,
>> Your looped and windowed raggedness, defend you
>> From seasons such as these?

Fewer than three lines are handled like regular sentences in a regular paragraph, with slashes used to divide the individual lines of poetry. A space is left on either side of the slash.

> Only then does Lear understand that he has been a failure as a king: "O, I have taken / Too little care of this!"

● Use a slash to separate expressions that indicate a choice. In these cases, no space is left before or after the slash.

either/or	he/she	yes/no	pass/fail
win/lose	s/he	on/off	right/wrong

Such expressions are more accepted in technical and scientific fields than they are in the humanities. Many people prefer "he or she" to "he/she" and find "s/he" unacceptable.

• Use a slash to indicate fractions when typing. Use a hyphen to attach a whole number and a fraction. Again, no spaces are left between the numbers, slashes, and hyphens.

2/3   2-2/3   5-3/8

EXERCISE 34.10

1. Write a sentence in which you quote fewer than three lines from the following passage from *Romeo and Juliet* in which Juliet warns Romeo to leave her bedchamber before he is discovered by her parents. She hears the lark, herald of the morning:

> *Juliet.* It is, it is. Hie hence, be gone, away!
>   It is the lark that sings so out of tune,
>   Straining harsh discords and unpleasing sharps.
>   Some say the lark makes sweet division;
>   This doth not so, for she divideth us.

2. Write sentences in which you use the expressions *either/or, pass/fail,* and *yes/no.*

34 H

/

35 Sentence Endings

A Periods
B Question Marks
C Exclamation Marks

35 A PERIODS

➤ **Function**
Periods say "That's all there is." They terminate sentences and abbreviations.

➤ **Major Uses**
- Use periods to end statements.

    A national environmental group decided to give Connie an award.

- Use periods to end indirect questions and many commands.

    Journalists sometimes wonder whether they have any influence with the public at all.

    Make the airline reservations immediately.

Strong commands are punctuated with exclamation points.

➤ **Other Uses**
- Use periods to punctuate abbreviations.

    abbr.   anon.   Cong.   Natl.
    rpt.   sing.   pl.   pp.

Not all abbreviations require periods. When in doubt, check a dictionary.

    NASA   HEW   GPO   GOP

- Use periods to express decimals.

    0.01 $189.00   75.4%

♦ **FINE TUNING** ♦

1. If a statement ends with an abbreviation, the period at the end of the sentence is not doubled.

497

Connie invited Kyle, Richard, and Francie to join her in Washington, D.C.

> However, the period at the end of the abbreviation is retained if the sentence is a question or exclamation.

Had any of the four ever been to Washington, D.C.?
Their flight departs at 6 A.M.!

> 2. If an abbreviation occurs in the middle of a sentence, it retains its period. The period may even be followed by another punctuation mark.

Though she had not yet earned her B.A., Connie's prospects looked bright.

35 B QUESTION MARKS

➤ **Function**
Question marks terminate questions.

Did the flight arrive on time?

➤ **Principal Uses**
—Use question marks to end direct questions.

Did they arrive at National Airport or at Dulles? When?

➤ **Other Uses**
—Use question marks to indicate uncertainty about dates, numbers, or statements.

Francis Marion (1732?–1795) is an American hero.

QUESTION MARK PROBLEM:
Punctuating the indirect question

Unnecessary question marks
Drayton wondered whether Connie had ever been to Washington before? He asked her if she might check some records for him at the National Archives?

➤ **Diagnosis**
These sentences have been mistakenly punctuated as questions because they seem to have questions within them. But look more closely and you'll discover that what looks like a question really is the completion of a statement: *Drayton wondered* [what?]; *he asked* [what?]. Such statements are called **indirect questions.** Compare these versions.

{**Indirect question**}   Drayton wondered whether Connie had been to Washington before.

{**Direct question**}   Drayton wondered, "Had Connie been to Washington before?"

➤ **Solution**
Punctuate indirect questions as statements.

> **Question marks omitted**
>
> **Drayton wondered whether Connie had ever been to Washington before. He asked her if she might check some records for him at the National Archives.**

♦ FINE TUNING ♦

1. A sentence that begins with a statement but ends with a question is punctuated as a question.

The flight to Washington had been smooth, but would the rest of the trip be as uneventful?

Don't confuse this sort of construction, however, with indirect questions. (See above.)

2. Direct questions that appear in the middle of sentences—usually surrounded by parentheses, quotation marks, or dashes—are immediately followed by question marks.

"Is that the FBI Building?" Connie asked the driver.

"No, it's the Commerce—or is it the Internal Revenue Service?—building."

3. Remember that question marks are placed outside quotation marks except when they are part of the quoted material itself.

Which federal building bears the motto "Equal justice under law"?

The clerk at the Hilton asked, "Do you have reservations?"

For a more detailed explanation, see Quotation Mark Problem 3, pp. 487–488.

35 C

!

35 C   EXCLAMATION MARKS

➤ **Function**
Exclamations add emphasis. They are vigorous marks with the subtlety of a red Corvette or a yellow dinner jacket.

➤ **Principal Use**
—Use exclamation marks to express strong reactions or commands.

They don't have our reservations!

EXCLAMATION MARK PROBLEM:
Too many!

> **Too many exclamations**
>
> This hotel cannot hold rooms past 6:00 P.M. without a guaranteed reservation! Reservations can be guaranteed by credit card only! We strongly recommend guaranteed reservations for all guests planning to visit Washington! Thank you!

➤ **Diagnosis**

Too many exclamation points. Save exclamations for those occasions—rare in academic and business writing—when your words really deserve emphasis.

➤ **Solution**

Revise to eliminate the exclamations. Replace some with periods.

> **Some exclamation marks removed**
>
> This hotel cannot hold rooms past 6:00 P.M. without a guaranteed reservation. Reservations can be guaranteed by credit card only! We strongly recommend guaranteed reservations for all guests planning to visit Washington. Thank you.

35 C

!

◆ **FINE TUNING** ◆

1. Don't use a comma or other punctuation mark after an exclamation in the middle of a sentence.

{**Wrong**}   "Please check your records again!," Connie demanded.

{**Right**}   "Please check your records again!" Connie demanded.

2. Don't use more than one exclamation point.

{**Wrong**}   Don't shout!!!

{**Right**}   Don't shout!

EXERCISE 35.1

Edit the following excerpt from Connie's letter to Charnelle, adding, replacing, and deleting periods, question marks, exclamation points, and any other marks of punctuation that need to be changed.

1. Charnelle, I made a fool of myself!!!
2. There I was in the lobby of the Washington Hilton, practically screaming at this polite young clerk behind the desk while Kyle, Richard, and Francie—can you guess how assertive they were being—rummaged through the luggage looking for the slip confirming our reservations!
3. I asked the clerk would he please call the manager? He said that he was the reservations manager, but would I like him to call the general manager.
4. "Of course, do it immediately!," I said, trying to look like an experienced traveller who doesn't deal with flunkies!
5. He asked if I would mind stepping aside until the general manager arrived?
6. Just then, what do you think Kyle found. The reservation slip!!!
7. Without looking at it, I hurled it down on the desk and said, "What do you think of that"?
8. He smiled politely and said, "Ma'am, you have two guaranteed rooms reserved".
9. "What did I tell you," I interrupted?
10. "At the Carroll Arms on First St.".

EXERCISE 35.2

Write five more sentences completing the dialogue between Connie and the reservations manager. Try to use exclamation points and question marks as well as periods.

35 C

!

36 Capitalization, Apostrophes, Abbreviations, and Numbers

A Capitalization
B Apostrophes
C Abbreviations
D Numbers

36 A CAPITALIZATION

Terms you need to know

PROPER NOUN. A noun that names some particular person, place, or thing: *Geoffrey Chaucer, Ohio, Lincoln Memorial.* The first letter in proper nouns is capitalized.

PROPER ADJECTIVE. An adjective formed from a proper noun: *Chaucerian, Ohioan.* The first letter in a proper adjective is capitalized.

Troubleshooting

Capitalization is required for proper names, for the first words in many expressions, and for titles. The following sections will guide you through the conventions of capitalization. When you are not sure whether an individual word needs to be capitalized, check a dictionary. Don't guess.

To be sure your capitalization is right . . .

➤ **Capitalize proper nouns according to the guidelines offered below for persons, places, and things.**

PERSONS

1. Names of people and characters. Capitalize names and initials.

William F. Buckley   Anzia Yezierska
J. Hector St. Jean Crèvecoeur

2. Titles before names. Capitalize titles that precede names.

Dean Rack   President George Bush
Justice Rehnquist   Uncle Miltie

3. **Titles after names.** Don't capitalize titles that follow names unless they refer to a person individually.

Wolfgang Rack, a **d**ean at Clear Lake College
Wolfgang Rack, the **D**ean of Liberal Arts

Don't capitalize the titles of relatives that follow names.

Anthony Pancioli, Cathy's **u**ncle

Exception. Capitalize any academic titles that follow a name.

Doris Upton, **Ph.D.**   Hector Stavros, **M**aster of **A**rts

4. **Titles without names attached.** Don't capitalize minor titles when they stand alone.

a **c**ommissioner in Cuyahoga County
a **l**ieutenant in the Air Force
the first **p**resident of the club

Exceptions. Prestigious titles are regularly capitalized even when they stand alone. Lesser titles may be capitalized when they clearly refer to a particular individual or when they describe a position formally.

President of the United States
the **P**resident
the **C**hief **J**ustice of the Supreme Court
the **P**ope
Secretary of **S**tate
the **C**hair of the Classics Department

5. **National, political, or ethnic groups.** Capitalize them.

Kenyans	**C**hicano	**C**hinese
African **A**mericans	**S**ocialists	**C**aucasian
Communists	**D**emocrats	**A**ustralians

Exceptions. Titles of racial groups, economic groups, and social classes are usually not capitalized.

blacks   whites
the proletariat   the knowledge class

6. **Businesses, unions, organizations, clubs, schools.** Capitalize them.

Time, Inc.	National **R**ifle **A**ssociation
The Ohio State University	Teamsters

7. **Religious figures, religious groups, sacred books.** Capitalize them.

God	**C**atholics	**B**uddha
the **B**ible	the **K**oran	Judaism

Exceptions. The terms *god* and *goddess* are not capitalized when used generally. When *God* is capitalized, pronouns referring to *God* are also capitalized.

The Greeks had a pantheon of **g**ods and **g**oddesses.
The **G**oddess of **L**iberty appears on our currency.
The priest praised **G**od and all **H**is works.

8. Academic ranks (freshman, sophomore, junior, senior, graduate, post-grad). Do not capitalize them in most situations.

The college had many fifth-year seniors.
The freshman dormitory was a dump.
The teacher was a graduate student.

> **Exceptions.** Capitalize academic ranks when these are referred to as organized bodies or institutions.

A representative of the **S**enior **C**lass
The **F**reshman **C**otillion

PLACES

9. Names of places or words based on place names. Names of specific geographic features: lakes, rivers, oceans, and so on. Capitalize them.

Asia	**O**ld **F**aithful
Asian	the **A**mazon
the **B**ronx	the **G**ulf of **M**exico
Lake **E**rie	**D**eaf **S**mith **C**ounty
Washington	the **A**tlantic **O**cean

36 A

Cap

> **Exceptions.** Don't capitalize compass directions unless they name a specific place or are part of a place name.

north	**N**orth **A**merica
south	the **S**outh
eastern Ohio	the **M**iddle **E**ast

10. Names of buildings, structures, or monuments. Capitalize them.

Yankee **S**tadium	**H**oover **D**am
the **A**lamo	the **G**olden **G**ate
Trump **T**ower	**I**ndianapolis **S**peedway

THINGS

11. Abstractions. Capitalize abstractions (love, truth, patriotism, and so on) when you discuss them as concepts or give them special emphasis, perhaps as the subject of a paper.

What is this thing called **L**ove?
The conflict was between **T**ruth and **F**alsehood.

> **Exception.** There is no need to capitalize abstractions used without special emphasis.

Travis had fallen in love again.
Either tell the truth or abandon hope of rescue.

12. **Names of particular objects—including ships, planes, automobiles, brand-name products, events, documents, musical groups.** Capitalize them.

S. S. *Titanic*	Boeing 747
Ford Taurus	Eskimo Pie
Super Bowl XXV	the Constitution
Rolling Stones	Cleveland Symphony

> **Caution.** In public and business writing, it is important not to violate the right to brand names or trademarks, even familiar ones. Names such as **Kleenex**, **Frigidaire**, and **Xerox** should be capitalized because they refer to specific, trademark-protected products.

13. **Periods of time: days, months, holidays, historical epochs, and historical events.** Capitalize them.

Monday	the Reformation
May	World War II
Victorian Age	Bastille Day
Fourth of July	Pax Romana

> **Exception.** Seasons of the year are usually not capitalized.

autumn   winter   spring

14. **-*Isms.*** Terms ending in -*ism* are not capitalized unless they name specific artistic, religious, or cultural movements. When in doubt, check a dictionary.

socialism	capitalism	monetarism
Impressionism	Vorticism	Romanticism
Judaism	Catholicism	Buddhism

15. **School subjects and classes.** Subject areas are not capitalized unless the subject itself is a proper noun.

biology	chemistry	physics
English	Russian history	French

> **Exceptions.** Specific course titles are capitalized.

Biology 101   Chemistry Lab   English 346K

16. **Acronyms and initialisms (see 36C, pp. 511–513).** Capitalize all the letters in acronyms and initialisms.

NATO	OPEC	SALT Treaty
DNA	GMC	MCAT tests

> **Exception.** Don't capitalize familiar acronyms that seem like ordinary words. When in doubt, check a dictionary.

radar   sonar   laser

36 A

Cap

> **TIP: Many writers fail to capitalize words that name na-
> tionalities or countries—words such as *English, French,*
> or *American.***
> {Wrong} Kyle has three english courses.
> {Right} Kyle has three English courses.
> {Wrong} Brian drives only american cars.
> {Right} Brian drives only American cars.
> **When proofreading, be sure that you capitalize any
> words taken from the names of countries.**

➤ **Capitalize the first word in a sentence.**

Naomi picked up the tourists at their hotel.

What a great city Washington is!

➤ **Capitalize the first word in a direct quotation that is a full sentence.**

Richard asked, "Where's the Air and Space Museum?"

"Good idea!" Connie agreed. "Let's go there."

Don't use a capital when a quotation merely continues after an interruption.

"It's on the Mall," Naomi explained, "not far from the Hirschhorn Gallery."

36 A

Cap

➤ **Capitalize titles.** Here are the rules.

> **Titles**
>
> **Capitalize the first word.**
> **Capitalize the last word.**
> **Capitalize all other words except**
>   —articles (*a, an,* and *the*),
>   —prepositions under five letters,
>   —conjunctions under five letters,
> **unless they are the first or last words.**

The Cardinal of the Kremlin
The Capitalist Revolution
"How Cruel Is the Story of Eve"

Articles and prepositions are capitalized when they follow a colon as part of what is usually a subtitle.

King Lear: *An Annotated Bibliography*

➤ **Capitalize the first word in a line of quoted poetry.** Don't capitalize the first letter in a line where a poet has used a lower case letter. Compare these pronouns.

Sumer is ycomen in,
Loude sing cuckoo!
Groweth seed and bloweth meed,
And springth the wode now.
Sing cuckou!

"The Cuckoo Song"

Ida,
ho, and, Oh,
Io!
spaces
with places
tween 'em.

T. Beckwith, "Travels"

♦ **FINE TUNING** ♦

1. Always capitalize the pronoun *I* and the exclamation *O*. Don't capitalize *oh* unless it begins a sentence.
2. Don't capitalize the first word of a phrase that follows a colon unless it is part of a title:

They ignored one item while parking the car: **a** no-parking sign.

Marilyn: The Untold Story

Don't capitalize the first word of a sentence that follows a colon **unless you** want to give that sentence unusual emphasis, as in the following **example:**

The phrase haunted her: **Y**our car has been towed!

3. Don't capitalize the first word of a phrase in parentheses, but do capitalize the first word in a full sentence in parentheses when it stands alone.

They gazed at the spot (**on** 7th St.) where their car had been parked.

"We were in the museum only a few minutes," said Kyle. (**T**hey had actually toured the exhibits for several hours.)

4. Don't capitalize the first word of a phrase or sentence enclosed by dashes.

Naomi's car—**a** brand new Plymouth Acclaim—had been parked **next** to a "no parking" sign.

Her Acclaim—**s**he couldn't believe it—was now in the hands of the police.

5. Observe the conventions of letter writing. Salutations and closings must be capitalized correctly. See Chapter 45.

36 A

Cap

EXERCISE 36.1

Review the following sentences, capitalizing as necessary.

1. Four students—two of them seniors, two juniors, all pursuing b.a.'s or b.s.'s—and not one had read the stern warning printed on the sign by district of columbia police: cars parked illegally will be towed.

2. Even washington-native Naomi, their ph.d. tour guide, had not seen the sign when they pulled up to the empty parking space suspiciously near the national air and space museum.
3. "I intend to write the president about this," Kyle muttered. "after all, i voted for the man." (he hadn't.) "or maybe I'll write senator Smith, or my aunt Roberta, an under-secretary of something or other."
4. "Please, o please, why not write queen Elizabeth and lady Di and be done with it?" Francie snorted.
5. Richard declared, "if you ask me, towing someone's car smacks of marxism. You expect this sort of thing in leningrad or beijing, not in the shadow of the Washington monument in the home of democracy and free enterprise."
6. While her friends jabbered, Naomi dug through her purse, finding her visa card, her nra membership certificate, and her amnesty international pledge, but no driver's license.
7. "They'll probably throw me in the bastille and I won't be out until thanksgiving," she thought.
8. She sighed, "I've learned my lesson: read signs carefully."
9. "Perhaps we should just follow the instructions—'If towed, call 471-2255' —printed on the bottom of the sign," Connie suggested, gazing placidly down the mall toward the capitol building.
10. "According to my *Guide to sights and services in Washington,* the nasa building is just down the street. We can find a phone there."

---

36 B

Apostrophes

EXERCISE 36.2

Capitalize the following titles.

1. *a history of western music*
2. "thoughts on the present state of american affairs"
3. *the spring of civilization: periclean athens*
4. *walden, or life in the woods*
5. *of a fire on the moon*

---

36 B APOSTROPHES

Troubleshooting

The problem with apostrophes is that writers often forget to put them where they belong. Yet one important function of apostrophes is to indicate that letters have been left out of a word or phrase. In forming contractions, the letters omitted are usually obvious.

> can't—can**not**   it's—it **is**
> you're—you **are**   who's—who **is**

A second use of apostrophes is to form possessives. Forgetting to insert an apostrophe in a contraction or possessive causes problems. Leaving the apostrophe out of the contraction *it's,* for example, turns the word into a possessive form, *its.*

Apostrophes are sometimes used to indicate the plurals of numbers, symbols, some abbreviations, and individual letters or to signal the omission of the century marker in dates: *1's, 2's, M & M's, "Summer of '69."*

Finally, apostrophes are occasionally employed by writers creating dialogue that mimics speech. The apostrophes, again, indicate words or syllables typically left out by speakers of some dialects.

To use apostrophes correctly . . .

> **Place them in contractions where letters have been omitted.**

should not—shouldn't   cannot—can't
had not—hadn't   have not—haven't
of the clock [never used]—o'clock

Contractions are used not because they have fewer letters, but because they are spoken more quickly and sound less formal. Contractions change the tone of what you are writing from black tie to jeans.

You **will** enjoy the movie.   **Cannot** you join us?
You'll enjoy the movie.   **Can't** you join us?

The apostrophe is not optional in a contraction. Leaving it out can alter the meaning of a word or create a misspelling.

it's—its   won't—wont   you're—youre

The *it's/its* problem is an especially tricky one. See Section 28G, for a discussion of *it's/its*.

36 B

Apostrophes

> TIP: Many readers object to contractions in academic and professional writing. For this reason, consider your audience carefully before using contractions.

> **Place apostrophes as needed to form the possessives of nouns and some pronouns.**

Kyle's report   Travis' poems
the Rhoades' daughters   everyone's opinion

Personal pronouns do not require an apostrophe to show ownership.

mine   yours   hers
his   ours   theirs

For a more thorough explanation of possessive nouns and pronouns, see Section 25B on possessive nouns and pronouns and Section 28F on possessive pronouns.

> **Place apostrophes as needed to indicate the plurals of numbers, symbols, individual letters, abbreviations, words used as *words*, and dates.**

2's and 3's   three $5's
two .45's and a .22   two &'s

five A's	two B.A.'s
three *the*'s and four *an*'s	1960's

The apostrophe is often omitted, especially when the 's might be mistaken as a possessive.

3600 rpm**s.**	the ACT**s**
42 lb**s.**	the CEO**s**

In many cases, either form of the plural is acceptable.

the 1980**s**/the 1980**'s**
10**s**/10**'s**

Whichever form you use, be consistent. For more details and an exercise, see Section 25A.

♦ FINE TUNING ♦

1. Apostrophes are sometimes used to replace the first two numbers in a date.

   "Summer of '69"   Spirit of '76   '64 Mustang

   However, in academic and professional writing, use the complete date (1776) unless the contraction is part of a familiar expression, such as "Spirit of '76."

2. You may occasionally write or read passages of dialogue in which apostrophes indicate letters characteristically dropped by speakers.

   . . . airline passengers all over America began to hear that awshuckin' driftin' gone-fishin' Mud River voice coming from the cockpit. . . . "Now, folks, uh . . . this is the captain . . . ummmm. . . . We've got a little ol' red light up here on the control panel that's tryin' to tell us that the landin' gears're not . . . uh . . . lockin' into position. . . ."
   —Tom Wolfe, *The Right Stuff*

36 B

Apostrophes

EXERCISE 36.3

Add or delete apostrophes and revise spelling as necessary in the following sentences.

1. The five stranded tourists searched in vain for a Federal Office open after five oclock where they might use a phone.
2. "Its youre fault, Kyle," said Francie, realizing she hadnt yet lay'd blame on anyone for the fiasco.
3. "The fault isnt Kyles or anybody elses," said Naomi.
4. "Lets just find a shop that has a public phone."
5. Wandering a block or so off the Mall, they found a drugstore that looked like a relic from the 50s.

6. As she dropped dime's into the public phone, Naomi asked if anyone recalled the number she was supposed to dial.
7. "All I remember," said Connie, "is that its got two 2s and two 5s."
8. "Thats a big help," groaned Naomi.
9. Richard smiled. "The first three numbers were 471, so lets give 471–2255 a try."
10. To everyones surprise, they reached a pleasant clerk: "If you're cars been towed, youd best get down to the traffic office right now."

36 C ABBREVIATIONS

Terms you need to know

ABBREVIATION. A shortened version of a word or phrase, usually consisting of part of the original word or phrase and usually punctuated with a period: *Rev.*—Reverend; *Mr.*—Mister.

ACRONYM. A single word created by joining the first letters in the words that make up the full name or description. Acronyms are pronounced as single words: *NATO*—*N*orth *A*tlantic *T*reaty *O*rganization; *NASA*—*N*ational *A*eronautics and *S*pace Administration; *MADD*—*M*others *A*gainst *D*runk *D*riving.

INITIALISM. A single word created by joining the first letters in the words that make up the full name or description. Unlike acronyms, however, initialisms are pronounced letter by letter: *IRS*—*I*nternal *R*evenue *S*ervice; *VIP*—*v*ery *i*mportant *p*erson.

36 C

Abbrev

Troubleshooting

Abbreviations, acronyms, and initialisms make writing some things a bit easier and quicker. Writers do have to be careful about when to use abbreviations and their kin. Many conventional abbreviations (*A.M.; P.M.; Mrs.; Mr.; Dr.; BC; AD*) are suited to every occasion. Other abbreviations, acronyms, and initialisms are appropriate on forms, reports, and statistics sheets, but not in more formal writing. Some of these issues are discussed below.

Deciding when abbreviations need to be punctuated and capitalized can also be difficult, particularly since practices vary. Is it *Tsps.* or *tsps.; N.A.S.A.* or *NASA?* The boxes below offer some helpful guidelines.

Use abbreviations, acronyms, or initialisms . . .

➤ **For titles, degrees, and names.** The following titles and degrees are ordinarily abbreviated.

Mr.	Mrs.	Ms.
Dr.	Ph.D.	D.D.S.
LL.D.	M.A.	M.S.
Jr.	M.D.	C.P.A.

Give credit for degrees either before or after a name—not in both places. Don't, for example, use both *Dr.* and *Ph.D.* in the same name.

{**Wrong**}   **Dr.** Katherine Martinich, **Ph.D.**

{**Right**}   **Dr.** Katherine Martinich
Katherine Martinich, **Ph.D.**

Abbreviations for academic titles often stand by themselves, without names attached.

Professor Martinich received her **Ph.D.** from Illinois, her **M.S.** from UCLA, and her **B.S.** from St. Vincent College.

Other titles are normally written out in full; they may be abbreviated only when they precede a first name or initial—and then chiefly in informal writing. In most cases, use the full, unabbreviated title.

President Bush	Pres. George Bush
Senator Gramm	Sen. Phil Gramm
Secretary Dole	Sec. Elizabeth Dole
Professor Upton	Prof. Doris Upton

Never let abbreviated titles of this kind stand alone in a sentence.

{**Wrong**}   The **gov.** agreed to debate the **amb.** at the invitation of the **prof.**

{**Right**}   **Governor** Cuomo agreed to debate **Ambassador** Kirkpatrick at the invitation of **Professor** Doris Upton.

36 C

Abbrev

Notice that titles attached to proper names are ordinarily capitalized.

Initials are suitable abbreviations for given names; don't abbreviate names in other ways unless such abbreviations are nicknames. Periods do not follow nicknames.

Dean Wolfgang Rack	George Ericson

{**Wrong**} Dean **Wolf.** Rack	{**Wrong**} **Geo.** Ericson
{**Acceptable**} **W.** Rack	{**Acceptable**} **G.** Ericson

➤ **For technical terms.** Abbreviations are often used in professional, governmental, scientific, military, and technical writing. When you are writing to a non-technical audience, write out any unfamiliar term in full the first time you use it. Then provide parenthetically the abbreviation you will use in the rest of the paper.

DNA	UHF	EKG
SALT	GNP	LEM
P.M.G.	SOP	SDI
START	kW	SAT

Governor Cuomo and Ambassador Kirkpatrick debated the effects the **Strategic Defense Initiative (SDI)** would have on the **Gross National Product (GNP).**

Punctuating Abbreviations, Acronyms, and Initialisms

1. Abbreviations of single words usually take periods: *abbrev.; vols.; Jan.; Mr.*
2. Initialisms are now commonly written without periods: *HBO; AFL-CIO; IRS.* You may still use periods with these terms, but try to be consistent with your usage.
3. Acronyms ordinarily do not require periods: *CARE; NATO; MIRV.* Acronyms that have become "regular" words never need periods: *radar; sonar; laser; scuba.*
4. Periods are usually omitted after abbreviations in technical writing unless a measurement or other item might be misread as a word without the period: *in.*
5. Use three periods consistently or none at all in terms such as the following.

m.p.g.	or	*mpg*
r.p.m.	or	*rpm*
m.p.h.	or	*mph*

Capitalizing Abbreviations, Acronyms, and Initialisms

1. Capitalize abbreviations of words that would themselves be capitalized if written out in full:

Saint Joan—*St.* Joan	Mister Roberts—*Mr.* Roberts
98°Fahrenheit—98°*F.*	General Motors—*GM*
U.S. Navy—*USN*	University of Toledo—*UT*

2. Don't capitalize abbreviations of words not capitalized on their own.

pound—*lb.*	minutes—*mins.*	miles per hour—*mph*

3. Capitalize most initialisms: *IRS; CRT; UCLA; NBC; EPA.*
4. Always capitalize *B.C.* and *A.D.* Printers ordinarily set them as small caps: B.C.; A.D.
5. You may capitalize *A.M.* and *P.M.* but they now ordinarily appear in small letters: *a.m.; p.m.* Printers ordinarily set them as small caps: A.M.; P.M.
6. Don't capitalize acronyms that have become ordinary words: *sonar; radar; modem.*

36 C

Abbrev

▶ **For agencies and organizations.** In some cases, the abbreviation or acronym regularly replaces the full name of a company, agency, or organization.

FBI	IBM	MCI	AT&T
AFL-CIO	GOP	PPG	MGM
A&P	BBC	NCAA	MTV

▶ **For months and days.** Dates are not abbreviated in most writing. Write out in full the days of the week and months of the year.

{**Wrong**}   They arrived in Washington on a **Wed.** in **Apr.**

{**Right**}   They arrived in Washington on a **Wednesday** in **April.**

Abbreviations of months and days are used primarily in notes, lists, forms, and reference works.

▶ **For time and temperatures.** Abbreviations that accompany time and temperatures are acceptable in all kinds of writing:

43 B.C.	A.D. 144	1:00 A.M.	4:36 P.M.
13°C	98°F	143 B.C.E.	

Notice that the abbreviation B.C. appears after a date, but A.D. usually before one. Both expressions are always capitalized.

▶ **For weights, measures, times.** Technical terms or measurements are commonly abbreviated when used with numbers, but written out in full when they stand alone in sentences. Even when accompanied by numbers, the terms usually look better in sentences when spelled out completely.

28 mpg.	3 tsps.	40 km.	450 lbs.
50 min.	30 lbs.	2 hrs.	

Naomi didn't care how many **miles per gallon** her Acclaim got. She just wished it hadn't been towed so many **kilometers** from where she stood. They had already lost **fifty minutes** locating a phone.

36 C

Abbrev

The abbreviation for number—*No.* or *no.*—is appropriate in technical writing, but only when immediately followed by a number.

{**Not**}   The **no.** on the contaminated dish was **073.**

{**But**}   The contaminated dish was **no. 073.**

No. also appears in footnotes, endnotes, and citations.

▶ **For places.** In most writing, place names are not abbreviated except in addresses and in reference tools and lists. However, certain abbreviations are accepted in academic and business writing.

USA	USSR
UK	Washington, D.C.

All the various terms for *street* are written out in full, except in addresses.

boulevard	road	avenue	parkway
highway	alley	place	circle

But *Mt.* [for *mountain*] and *St.* [for *saint*] are acceptable abbreviations in place names when they precede a proper name.

Mt. Vesuvius	**St.** Charles Street
[but not Rocky Mts.]	

In addresses (but not in written text), use the standard postal abbreviations, without periods, for the states.

Alabama	AL	Montana	MT
Alaska	AK	Nebraska	NE
Arizona	AZ	Nevada	NV
Arkansas	AR	New Hampshire	NH
California	CA	New Jersey	NJ
Colorado	CO	New Mexico	NM
Connecticut	CT	New York	NY
Delaware	DE	North Carolina	NC
Florida	FL	North Dakota	ND
Georgia	GA	Ohio	OH
Hawaii	HI	Oklahoma	OK
Idaho	ID	Oregon	OR
Illinois	IL	Pennsylvania	PA
Indiana	IN	Rhode Island	RI
Iowa	IA	South Carolina	SC
Kansas	KS	South Dakota	SD
Kentucky	KY	Tennessee	TN
Louisiana	LA	Texas	TX
Maine	ME	Utah	UT
Maryland	MD	Vermont	VT
Massachusetts	MA	Virginia	VA
Michigan	MI	Washington	WA
Minnesota	MN	West Virginia	WV
Mississippi	MS	Wisconsin	WI
Missouri	MO	Wyoming	WY

36 C

Abbrev

➤ **For certain expressions preserved from Latin.**

> i.e. [*id est*—that is]
> e.g. [*exempli gratia*—for example]
> et al. [*et alii*—and others]
> etc. [*et cetera*—and so on]

In most writing, it is better to use English versions of these and other Latin abbreviations. Avoid using the abbreviation *etc.* in formal or academic writing.

➤ **For divisions of books.** The many abbreviations for books and manuscripts (*p., pp., vols., ch., chpts., bk., sect.*) are fine in footnotes or parenthetical citations, but don't use them alone in sentences.

{**Wrong**}   Richard stuck the **bk.** in his pocket after reading **ch.** five.

{**Right**}   Richard stuck the **book** in his pocket after reading **chapter** five.

♦ FINE TUNING ♦

1. The *ampersand* (&) is an abbreviation for *and*. Do not use it in formal writing except when it appears in a title or name: *Road & Track*.
2. You may use symbols in technical and scientific writing—%; +; =; ≠; < >—but in other academic papers, spell out such terms. The symbol most likely to cause a problem is %—*percent*.

{**Acceptable**}   Connie was shocked to learn that **80%** of the cars towed belong to tourists.

{**Preferred**}   Connie was shocked to learn that **80 percent** of the cars towed belong to tourists.

3. You can use a dollar sign—$—in any writing as long as it is followed by an amount. Don't use both the dollar sign and the word *dollar.*

{**Right**}   "Just how many **dollars** is this going to set us back?" Naomi wondered.

{**Wrong**}   "The fine for parking in a towing zone is **$125 dollars.**"

{**Right**}   "The fine for parking in a towing zone is **$125.**"

{**Right**}   "The fine for parking in a towing zone is **125 dollars.**"

4. The abbreviations *Co., Corp., Bros., LTD,* and *Inc.* in corporate names appear only when the companies themselves use them in their official correspondence, advertising, or other public materials.

Philip Morris Inc.

Lennox Industries, Inc.

EXERCISE 36.4

36 C

Abbrev

Read the passage below, abbreviating where appropriate or expanding abbreviations that would be incorrect in academic or professional writing. Check the punctuation for accuracy and consistency. If you insist on periods with acronyms and initialisms, use them throughout the passage.

1. Leaving the Peoples Drugstore, Naomi, Kyle, Connie, Francie, & Rich. hailed a cab cruising slowly down the ave.
2. "It's nearly 6:00 Pm," Connie sighed. "If we don't recover Naomi's car soon, I'll be late for my Environmental Heroism Awards banquet at the Vfw Hall in Alexandria, VA."
3. "No problem. There's a better than 99% chance I'll get you there on time," said Ransom E. Bullet, P.H.D. of College Pk, Maryld., a cabbie who clearly liked to talk.
4. "You see, we just take Constitution Ave. down past the F.b.i. Building, ease onto the 12th Street Expressway, cruise by the Dept. of Agri., and follow I-395 till we get to the George Washington Mem. Pky, which will take us right into Alexandria, VA."
5. Naomi, irritated by the delay, thrust a slip of paper at the cabbie. "Cut the DC tour baloney. Just take us to this address."
6. "You sure this is where you want to go—ma'am?" Ransom asked.
7. "What's the matter, doesn't the good dr. know where it is?" she asked.
8. The six of them in the Chevy made a slow U-turn in the street and stopped at the curb just a few ft. from the drugstore, a ride of no more than ten secs.
9. "That'll be $2 dollars," said Ransom Bullet smiling wickedly.
10. Naomi looked at the address on the building next to the Peoples Drugstore, Inc., then at the st. sign: "We've just hired a cab to take us to the bldg next to the one we were in!"

36 D   NUMBERS

Terms you need to know

CARDINAL NUMBERS. Numbers that express an amount: *one, two, three.*

ORDINAL NUMBERS. Numbers that express a sequence: *first, second, third.*

Troubleshooting

Numbers can be expressed either through numerals or through words.

1	one
100	one hundred
1/4	one-fourth
0.05%	five hundredths of a percent

Deciding which to use depends on the kind of writing you are doing. Technical, scientific, and business writing tends to employ numerals. Other kinds of writing rely more on words. The guidelines and charts will help you figure out which form to use.

Basic guideline

Write out numbers you can express in one or two words. Use numerals for more complicated numbers.

one	fifteen	twenty
twenty-one	fifty-nine	one hundred
one thousand	ten million	fifty billion
101	115	220
1021	59,000	101,000
1001	10,000,101	50,306,673,432

This guideline has variations and exceptions discussed below.

---

36 D

Num

To be sure your numbers are right . . .

▶ **Don't begin a sentence with a numeral.** Either spell out the number or rephrase the sentence so that the numeral is not the first word.

{**Wrong**}   **32** people were standing in line at the parking violation center.

{**Right**}   **Thirty-two** people were standing in line at the parking violation center.

Sentences may, however, begin with dates.

1989 was the year Naomi's driver's license had expired.

▶ **Combine words and figures when you need to express large round numbers.**

100 billion	432 million
2.3 billion	103 trillion

But avoid shifting between numbers and figures within a sequence of numbers. If you need numerals to express one of several numbers in a series, express all the other numbers in numerals as well—even if they might ordinarily be set down in words.

> Kyle considered that there must be **800,000** people in Washington, **50,000** parking spaces, and only **150** tow-away zones.
> [You might ordinarily write *50,000* as *fifty thousand.*]

➤ **Use numerals when comparing numbers or suggesting a range.**

> A blackboard at the traffic office listed a **$50** fine for jaywalking, **$100** for speeding, and **$125** for parking in a towing zone.

> The students' in-pocket cash reserves ranged from a high of **$76** to a low of **$1.43** and some bubblegum.

➤ **Use numerals for dates, street numbers, page numbers, sums of money, and various ID and call numbers.**

July 4, 1776	1860–1864
6708 Beauford Dr.	1900 East Blvd.
p. 352	pp. 23–24
$2749.00	43¢
Channel 8	103.5 FM
PR 105.5 R8	SS# 111-00-1111

Don't use an ordinal form in dates.

{**Wrong**}   May 2**nd,** 1991

{**Right**}   May 2, 1991 *or* 2 May 1991

➤ **Use numerals for time with A.M. and P.M.; use words with *o'clock*.**

> 2:15 P.M.   6:00 A.M.   six o'clock

➤ **Use numerals for measurements, percentages, statistics, and scores.**

35 mph	13°C	5′ 10″
75 percent	0.2 liters	5.5 pupils per teacher
2-1/2 miles	Browns 42—Bears 7	15%

♦ FINE TUNING ♦

1. In large figures, commas separate thousands, millions, billions, and so on. Commas are omitted, however, in dates, after street numbers, and sometimes in four-digit numbers.

$1,700,000	4,342 parking spaces
4,453,500,000 protons	1988
1205 Sophia Gate	7865 Hershey's Kisses

36 D

Num

2. You form the plural of numbers by adding -*s* or '*s*.

five 6**s** in a row   five 98**'s**

See Section 25A for more on plurals.
3. In most cases, ordinal numbers are spelled out: *first, second, third, fourth,* and so on.
4. Just in case you need one, here's a table of Roman numerals.

Roman Numerals

1	i	12	xii	60	lx		
2	ii	13	xiii	70	lxx		
3	iii	14	xiv	80	lxxx		
4	iv	15	xv	90	xc		
5	v	20	xx	99	xcix		
6	vi	25	xv	100	c		
7	vii	29	xxix	200	cc		
8	viii	30	xxx	300	ccc		
9	ix	40	xl	400	cd		
10	x	49	xlix	500	d		
11	xi	50	l	1000	m		

EXERCISE 36.5

36 D

Num

Decide whether numbers used in the following sentences are handled appropriately. Where necessary, change numerals to words or words to numerals. Some expressions may not need revision.

1. 9:00 p.m. had come and gone before Connie crept into the VFW Hall where more than 500 formally attired members of the Spirit of Seventeen Seventy Six Society had gathered to honor her and 6 other recipients of its Environmental Heroism award for Nineteen Ninety-one.
2. Exhausted, Connie crept to a seat reserved for her at the main table and listened as the President of the three hundred thousand member society proclaimed the virtues of the 1st, 4th, and tenth Amendments to the Constitution.
3. All Connie could think of were the fines levied upon her and her friends, including $125 dollars for illegal parking, seventy-five dollars for towing, and another 35 dollars for Naomi's failure to present a valid driver's license.
4. Then the 5 of them had been driven in a two-ton government van crowded with fourteen other angry citizens 3/4 of a mile to Georgetown to a depot for towed cars, only to discover that Naomi's Acclaim was 5 miles away at a 2nd city depot near RFK stadium.
5. Still, she was proud to be at the head table, even though she looked as if she hadn't washed in three days and the camera from Channel six was pointing right at her.
6. "1 day we'll laugh about this," Kyle had kept saying as the crowded van bumped noisily toward RFK stadium and it became more obvious that Connie would be late for her 8 o'clock banquet.

7. While Kyle was wrong about things 1/2 the time, on this occasion Connie was sure he was ninety-nine percent right.
8. Connie *was* amused that she and her companions had been able to persuade a $6,000,000,000 investment company not to build a seven hundred and forty thousand square foot shopping center in their tiny town, but had been helpless in the face of a 2-bit traffic law in the nation's capital.
9. "And that, my friends, is America," the long-winded speaker concluded after nearly seventy minutes, pounding a 5-pound gavel to signal the presentation of the environmental heroism awards.
10. 500 people awoke with a start and Connie Lim soon found herself accepting a fourteen carat gold medal and waving from the podium to 4 weary, penniless, but cheering friends at the back of the hall.

PART 5

THE **RESEARCH** PAPER

PART 5

This section explains how to write a college-level research paper. Chapter 37 covers basic research procedures—using card and online catalogs, searching indexes, assessing source materials. In recent years, the computer has reshaped many basic research tools; even if you believe you know the library, you may want to review Chapter 37 to be sure your information is up-to-date. Chapter 38 reviews the process of writing the research paper itself, from finding a topic to proofreading the final version. Don't be daunted by the size of this chapter; you'll find practical advice here for writing a successful research paper. Chapter 39 explains the form of documentation most commonly used in humanities courses—MLA. Chapter 40 covers the form preferred in the social sciences—APA documentation.

37 Beginning a Research Paper

    A Selecting a topic
    B Gathering information
    C Keeping track of information
    D Avoiding plagiarism

Terms you need to know

EXPLANATORY WRITING. Writing that explains or presents ideas, theories, or data. Explanatory writing usually focuses on facts or events; the writer's goal is to present information clearly and effectively. Explanatory writing tends to be fact-centered.

EXPLORATORY WRITING. Writing that explores, reflects on, or speculates about concepts, ideas, or experiences. The writer often discovers content while writing and may not have a specific goal when he or she starts. Exploratory writing tends to be idea-centered and speculative.

Troubleshooting

Much of the writing done in school or on the job involves some kind of research. Whether exploring the life of an African novelist, describing the motion of the planets, or compiling a corporation's annual report, you need to know how to gather information and how to present it well. Doing research—that is, discovering what is unknown, or applying what is already known to new situations—is an activity our society values. It is not busywork or an elaborate game played with footnotes and bibliographies.

Admittedly, the conventions of academic research assignments can be challenging to learn, but they are the skills serious researchers use to channel the vast streams of information flowing through our research libraries, laboratories, schools, and businesses. Research is really about gathering and using information responsibly and creatively.

Yet there are also various kinds of research. You know you are using information differently when you consult an encyclopedia to recall the date that Jamestown was founded, summarize a book about the consequences of topsoil erosion, explain why the mice in an experiment mastered their maze so quickly, or compare conflicting articles on the morality of abortion. To appreciate such differences, you may want to review the distinctions drawn in Chapter 2 between *explanatory* and *exploratory* writing.

37

Instinctively, many of us think of research papers as **explanatory** writing, which involves reporting *known* information in a satisfactory, often conventional, form. Let's say that in a history class you are asked to write a report on the career of William Pitt the Younger, a Prime Minister of England during the Napoleonic era. You expect to rely entirely on sources for this paper since you may know very little about Pitt when you begin and expect to contribute nothing new to the existing body of knowledge. Your role is largely that of a retriever of information. The paper might briefly chronicle Pitt's life from birth to death, recount some single major event in his political career, or discuss his personal life. But any such paper would be essentially a report, an explanatory assignment.

But consider for a moment the value of an explanatory assignment. We know that people are more likely to remember and use information when they put it into writing. So explanatory research clearly has value from an educational perspective. Doing a competent explanatory report takes far more skill than may be evident at first glance. Your report on Pitt, for example, would require sifting through and evaluating what is known about an important historical figure in order to present a portion of that data to readers in a form they can use. You must furnish necessary background, define unfamiliar terms, and explain a complicated historical, political, and social context.

To understand the value of explanatory writing, consider the kinds of explanatory writing and research you rely upon daily: the newspaper, the encyclopedia, your favorite magazine, the directions in a computer manual, the brochure describing something you intend to buy. Whenever you rely on written information, you are counting on someone else having done a respectable job with his or her explanatory research. Your obligation is to do the same—and it is a responsibility to be taken as a serious intellectual challenge.

Other types of research fall more clearly into the **exploratory** camp: papers that go beyond the material facts immediately available to press into the heart of a controversy or problem. An exploratory research effort involves what some might regard as the essence of research—seeking new knowledge. Our impulse these days is to think of such a pursuit as uniquely scientific, involving controlled experiments, complex laboratories and equipment, and hefty research grants. Basic research of this kind is important, but exploratory work need not be so formal, nor confined to the scientific disciplines.

Any time you bring sources into a creative *conversation,* you are performing a type of exploratory research. Because neither the world nor information is static and unchanging, genuine research is done whenever existing ideas are reshaped to fit new situations. When you begin research on a controversial subject, chances are you don't begin with the issue neatly settled in your mind. You use books to explore the background of the issue—what the major participants in the debate have already written. You use the powerful tools now available in most libraries to search the most recent literature for the present state of the controversy. You sift, compare, contrast, examine parallel controversies, analyze, compute facts and figures, test ideas. Only then may you feel justified in drawing tentative conclusions.

What you have achieved through this sort of exploratory research—and it can happen in any discipline—is more than just a review of existing materials. When you have done an effective job, your work will extend the debate on an issue and have real consequences. Let us say, for example, you decided to explore the issue of sexual harassment. The subject could be approached usefully from an explanatory perspective as a recitation of definitions, illustrations, examples, and personal histories. Or you could do exploratory research into the nature of the problem: what are the causes and effects of harassment? In doing such an exploration, you are liable to become involved with the social and legal complexities of sexual harassment.

Your research might motivate and prepare you to join a campus committee concerned with establishing a university or college policy on harassment. You are ready to join that body because of the conclusions you have reached from a thorough and professional review of the issue. What you then contribute to the discussion is not just opinion either. It's **expertise** gained through responsible learning. Good research can have these sorts of consequences—or others. Many people choose entire careers as the result of papers they have written that opened them up to the possibilities in a discipline or subject area. Exploratory research has a degree of unpredictability to it because it involves both the subject and a researcher in the possibility of change.

37 A   SELECTING A TOPIC

Troubleshooting

For many writers, the most difficult part of doing a research paper can be choosing a subject. Yet the importance of a good topic can be overestimated: in and of themselves, topics aren't simply good or bad. What makes the difference is treatment—that is, how well you fit any topic idea to your assignment, your readers, and your abilities. Finding a good subject is not a matter of chance or luck. It involves, instead, deciding what you want to achieve and then carving out a path to that goal.

A first step is determining what is manageable. Assigned, for example, to write a 1500 word essay on a subject in contemporary history, you may be so worried about meeting the required length that you gravitate toward subjects as massive as the Holocaust, the U.S. space program, the American auto industry, or modern literary discoveries. But topics like these have hundreds of aspects that can be explored in thousands of ways. Dealing with a huge subject commits you either to writing a book or to narrowing your interests to something more suitable to a 1500–2500-word attempt.

To narrow a subject, you may want to look for an angle or a hook—an idea that grabs and holds an audience. The point seems so simple: a research paper should convey information that surprises readers. Just tossing around a topic idea should arouse curiosity, questions, objectives, or enthusiasm: How does acupuncture work? What did the Voyager spacecraft discover about Neptune? Why exactly did Chrysler almost go broke in the late seventies? Have scholars finally identified the "Dark Lady" of Shakespeare's sonnets?

Finding an angle on a subject can transform a research paper from a mere *assignment* to what it should be—an *investigation* as exciting for the writer as for the reader. Your initially vague interest in the space program might become a more focused explanatory study of the Voyager mission to Neptune, leading to a report on the bizarre terrain of Neptune's moon, Triton. Or speculation about the deeper implications of space exploration may initiate an exploratory paper that attempts to defend the expenditure of billions of tax dollars on interplanetary adventures.

Put simply, when you have the opportunity to choose the subject of your research paper, follow your inclinations and instincts. You will write a better paper if you like what you are researching. If your topic is assigned, well, that's life—sometimes you simply have to work with what you are given.

To select a topic for a research paper . . .

➤ **Size up the assignment carefully.** Be sure you understand what you are being asked to do. Read or listen to the assignment carefully, particularly to certain key words. Are you expected to analyze, examine, classify, define, discuss, evaluate, explain, compare, contrast, argue, prove, disprove, persuade? Each of those words means something a little different. Each gives you an idea of how to approach your subject—even how to organize it.

Analyze. Examine. Break your subject into its parts or components. Discuss their relationship or function.

Classify. Define. Place your subject into some larger categories. Distinguish it from other objects in those categories. What are its significant features? What makes it unique or recognizable?

Discuss. Talk about the problems or issues your subject raises. Which issues are the most significant? What actions might be taken? Look at the subject from several points of view.

Evaluate. Think about the subject critically. What criteria would you use to judge it? How well does it meet those standards? Is it *good, effective, successful, unsuccessful?* How does it compare to other similar subjects?

Explain. Show what your subject does or how it operates. Provide background information on it. Put your subject in its context so that readers will understand it better.

Compare. Show how your subject resembles other things or ideas.

Contrast. Show how your subject differs from other things or ideas.

Argue. Come to a conclusion about your subject and explain why you believe what you do. Use evidence to persuade others to agree.

Prove. Provide evidence in support of an idea or assertion.

Disprove. Provide evidence to contradict or undermine an idea or assertion.

Persuade. Provide good reasons for someone to think or act in a particular way.

Once you know what your assignment requires, appraise the length of the paper you are expected to produce. Be realistic about how much you can accomplish in five typed pages (roughly 1200 words), eight typed pages (2000 words), ten pages (2500 words), and so on. Your worry shouldn't be finding enough to write, but deciding what you can say within a given length. In general, the shorter the assignment, the sharper the focus of your essay will have to be. But even lengthier essays—say twenty pages—will require a narrowed subject supported by significant research.

▶ **Explore several topic areas.** Topic areas are big subjects that offer many directions for exploration. Here are just a few examples.

anorexia	the Holocaust
reverse discrimination	homosexuality
the U.S. auto industry	child abuse
rain forest destruction	ocean pollution
symphony orchestras	quasars
the aging U.S. population	science fiction
consumer fraud	nature photography
artificial intelligence	amateurism and the Olympics
African-American poetry	computer viruses
tax reform	the family farm

You begin with such general topic areas when you have no specific subject assigned. Select areas that intrigue you—not topics you vaguely suspect your teacher prefers. Treat yourself to an idea you won't mind exploring for several weeks.

Avoid stale topics: don't be one of a half a dozen students submitting essays on gun control or capital punishment—unless you are sure you can press a new vintage from the old grapes. But be wary, too, of topics drawn from today's newspapers or magazines. They may be fresh and exciting, but the indexes and bibliographies researchers rely on can't always keep up with the evening news. You may quickly exhaust your leads and resources in researching what happened last week. Finally, don't try to resuscitate an old paper—something you wrote in high school or in a previous college class—unless you are so eager to know more about its subject that you will, in effect, produce a new essay.

37 A

Topic

▶ **Read in that topic area.** Select the topic area you find most promising and do some selective background reading. Background reading does three things:

- it confirms whether you are, in fact, interested in your topic;

- it surveys the main points of your subject so you can begin narrowing it;

- it suggests whether the resources of your library or community will support the topic you want to explore in the time available.

It will also help you decide whether to approach your paper from an explanatory or exploratory perspective. Will your paper on the U.S. automobile industry provide an explanatory comparison of the differences in design philosophy between General Motors and the Ford Motor Company—an interesting subject that you could explore by gathering data, reading interviews, and surveying some historical accounts of the companies? Or do you wonder what role the U.S. auto companies play in shaping American popular culture—a more ambiguous and open-ended exploratory subject that might lead you to explore topics as different as music, architecture, city planning, and color palettes? Your preliminary reading will help you decide.

The most efficient sources for preliminary reading are encyclopedias, beginning with any that deal specifically with a particular field or subject. The more specialized the encyclopedia, the more authoritative its coverage of a subject area is likely to be. If you check the reference room of your library, you will find specialized encyclopedias covering all the major disciplines and majors. Here are just a few.

Doing a paper on	*Begin by checking*
American History	*Encyclopedia of American History*
Anthropology, economics, sociology	*International Encyclopedia of the Social Science*
Art	*Encyclopedia of World Art*
Astronomy	*Encyclopedia of Astronomy*
Computers	*Encyclopedia of Computer Science*
Crime	*Encyclopedia of Crime and Justice*
Economics	*Encyclopedia of American Economic History*
Ethical issues in life sciences	*Encyclopedia of Bioethics*
Film	*International Encyclopedia of Film*
Health/Medicine	*Health and Medical Horizons*
History	*Dictionary of American History*
Law	*The Guide to American Law*
Literature	*Cassell's Encyclopedia of World Literature*
Music	*The New Grove Dictionary of American Music*
Philosophy	*Encyclopedia of Philosophy*
Physics	*The Encyclopedia of Physics*
Political Science	*Encyclopedia of American Political History*
Psychology, psychiatry	*International Encyclopedia of Psychiatry, Psychology, Psychoanalysis and Neurology; Encyclopedia of Psychology*
Science	*McGraw-Hill Encyclopedia of Science and Technology*
Social Sciences	*Encyclopedia of the Social Sciences*

37 A

Topic

If no such specialized encyclopedia is available or if the specialized volume proves too technical for your level of knowledge, move to one of the more familiar general encyclopedias.

The Encyclopaedia Britannica
Colliers Encyclopedia
Encyclopedia Americana

Reading about the general topic should provide you with enough perspective to select a narrower subject. If, after reading about a subject, you find that it does not interest you or is too big a challenge, choose another general subject area and explore it. When you have found an area you think is workable, start narrowing your topic.

▶ **Narrow the topic to a preliminary thesis or hypothesis. Find a question to answer.** You can't stay with a general subject for too long without wasting time. Even a relatively focused general subject—for example, rock and roll in the 1980s—would be too large to explore randomly. You need to identify a single aspect of the subject worth extended study. For example, rather than worry about an entire decade of rock and roll music, you could focus on one or two artists who seemed to have a great impact during the period, or you might ask why pop tunes from the 1960s suddenly became all the rage in the late 1980s. Narrowing the subject this way will make your use of card catalogs, tables of contents, and indexes easier: rather than look under rock and roll, you search for Madonna, U2, or "Golden Oldies."

Any subject you choose at this stage is going to be preliminary: it will be shaped and reshaped by the reading and research you do later. What you may have initially is no more than a question or issue to guide your work.

Why do women have keener senses of smell than men?

How were the Nazis able to conceal the Holocaust?

What did *Voyager* discover about Neptune's moon, Triton?

What makes people abuse children?

How do scientists explain acupuncture?

Why did Chrysler almost go broke in 1979?

> **TIP: Focusing your topic will make you more confident about writing a successful paper and save hours of reading. It is an essential step for most writers. Don't go on to the next step—finding sources—until you have a tentative thesis or a question to answer.**

37 A

Topic

EXERCISE 37.1

1. Working with a group, compile a list of materials you have read recently that could be considered the results of explanatory research. Remember that explanatory research provides relatively straightforward information. Identify both the sources and any particular facts you drew from them.
2. In a group, discuss examples of exploratory research you have encountered recently. Exploratory research writing often involves proving or disproving something; you are more likely to detect an adversarial or argumentative slant in exploratory research than in explanatory materials.
3. Decide whether the following essay titles are more likely to describe an explanatory or an exploratory research project.
   a. "Buddhist Shrines in China"
   b. "The Political Consequences of Global Warming"
   c. "Hannibal and the Punic Wars"
   d. "Why Bilingual Education Programs Are Failing"
   e. "The Management Structure of IBM"

> ### EXERCISE 37.2

Below is a list of general topic areas. Alone or in a group, list a series of questions a writer might explore to develop one or two of the topics. Remember that any one question might furnish sufficient material for a complete essay. (If necessary, review Section 3C for advice about generating questions about a topic.)

Sample:

> **General topic**—White-collar crime.

> **Narrowing questions**—What is white-collar crime? What kinds of crimes are classified as white collar? Who is typically involved in white-collar crime? How are white-collar crimes detected? How are they punished? What is the economic impact of white-collar crime? How successful is law enforcement in stopping white-collar crime?

Topics:

Hypnosis	State lotteries
Child abuse	Rock and roll
Heredity	Sports and health
Racism	Immigration
Movies	Pesticides
Lyme disease	Capitalism

> ### EXERCISE 37.3

37 B

Sources

Use the list of encyclopedias (both specialized and general) in Chapter 49 to determine which reference works you might use to begin a research project in the following topic areas.

1. The Grand Old Opry
2. Supercomputers
3. The Battle of Bunker Hill
4. The properties of crystals
5. Yuri Gagarin

6. Building the A-Bomb
7. Planetary motion
8. Anxiety and depression
9. Education in American grade schools
10. The Watergate Affair

37 B GATHERING INFORMATION

Term you need to know

CD-ROM. (COMPACT DISK—READ ONLY MEMORY). A storage device for personal computers that records large quantities of information on a compact disk. CD-ROMs are now often used in libraries to give patrons direct access to data bases such as ERIC or PsycLit.

Troubleshooting

Efficient research is systematic, strategic, and comprehensive. It demands at the outset some effort to lay the groundwork for a project. But it means, in the long run, spending the least amount of time finding the best, fullest, and most authoritative sources. More important, good research habits are dependable: they produce results every time you need them.

Unfortunately, many would-be researchers simply ramble to the card catalog in their library, look up a subject, copy down the first few works listed under an appropriate heading, and then go off to the stacks, hoping that the books they've listed will get them started. This method seems easy at first, even natural. But it leads to complaints that the library "doesn't have any books on my subject" or "all the books I need are checked out." What follows is a "no excuses" approach to research.

To find information on your subject . . .

➤ **Use the card catalog efficiently.** Begin researching your subject by examining your library's basic holdings in your subject area. Whether the library has a regular card catalog or a computerized file, find out how subjects are listed. In many libraries, subject catalogs are kept separate from author/title listings.

Most subjects are cataloged following categories established by the Library of Congress. So you may need to examine the Directory of the Library of Congress (often called the *Subject List*) to determine how your topic is handled in the card catalog and to accumulate a list of related subject headings. These headings will tell you where in the catalog to look directly for your topic or for subjects related to it. The subject headings list, for example, will often include a main heading and suggestions for locating broader topics (labelled *BT*) and narrowed topics (*NT*).

Inspect the cards in your topic area. If your subject is a large one, the cards will be broken down into subcategories. Look for the category most relevant to your working thesis or question. Then scan books on your topic by title and date. For many subjects, the most recent volumes may be the most valuable. Make a bibliography card (see p. 544) for any titles that look immediately useful. Note whether any of the books listed in the card file either is, or contains, a bibliography. A bibliography on your subject can provide much pertinent information.

A catalog card itself carries plenty of information. If you examine it closely, it will tell you:

- the call number and library location of a book;
- author, title, publisher, and date of publication of a book;
- the number of pages and physical size of a book;
- whether a book is illustrated;
- whether a book contains a bibliography and index;
- what subject headings a book is listed under.

This information may help you decide whether a given book is worth examining. (Computerized catalogs may offer fewer details about the books listed.)

37 B

Sources

➤ **Author card**

```
HD
9710       Iacocca, Lee A.
U52            Iacocca: an autobiography/Lee Iacocca
I25        with William Novak.—Toronto; New York:
UGL        Bantam Books, c1984. xv, 352 p., [16] p. of
           plates: ill.; 24 cm.
           Includes index.
           ISBN 0-553-05067-2

               1. Iacocca, Lee A. 2. Automobile industry
           and trade—United States—Biography. 3.
           Businessmen—United States—Biography. I.
           Novak, William. II. Title
```

➤ **Title card**

```
HD         Iacocca
9710
U52        Iacocca, Lee A.
I25            Iacocca: an autobiography/Lee Iacocca
UGL        with William Novak.—Toronto; New York:
           Bantam Books, c1984. xv, 352 p., [16] p. of
           plates: ill.; 24 cm.
           Includes index.
           ISBN 0-553-05067-2

               1. Iacocca, Lee A. 2. Automobile industry
           and trade—United States—Biography. 3.
           Businessmen—United States—Biography. I.
           Novak, William. II. Title
```

37 B

Sources

Learn to make intelligent judgments about the materials entered in a catalog. Don't just copy down the titles on the first five or six cards. Look through the stack and compile a working bibliography of the most promising sources. Aim for a dozen or so to get you started.

Computerized online catalogs, where available, allow for greater flexibility, speed, and creativity in a search of materials. Because computerized catalogs are easy to update, they may reflect the actual state of a library collection better—even indicating what books are checked out, lost, or otherwise unavailable. Because the terminals for an online catalog can be located anywhere in a library, they are easier to consult than bulky card files. Finally, because online catalogs store their entries in computer files, you can search a collection in a great variety of ways—by author, title, author/title, key word in a title, subject, or even call number.

➤ **Subject card**

```
HD          Iacocca
9710
U52         Iacocca, Lee A.
I25            Iacocca: an autobiography/Lee Iacocca
UGL         with William Novak.—Toronto; New York:
            Bantam Books, c1984. xv, 352 p., [16] p. of
            plates: ill.; 24 cm.
            Includes index.
            ISBN 0-553-05067-2

               1. Iacocca, Lee A. 2. Automobile industry
            and trade—United States—Biography. 3.
            Businessmen—United States—Biography. I.
            Novak, William. II. Title
```

➤ **Subject card**

```
            AUTOMOBILE INDUSTRY AND TRADE—
HD          UNITED STATES—BIOGRAPHY.
9710        Iacocca, Lee A.
U52            Iacocca: an autobiography/Lee Iacocca
25          with William Novak.—Toronto; New York:
UGL         Bantam Books, c1984. xv, 352 p., [16] p. of
            plates : ill.; 24 cm.
            Includes index.
            ISBN 0-553-05067-2

               1. Iacocca, Lee A. 2. Automobile industry
            and trade—United States—Biography. 3.
            Businessmen—United States—Biography. I.
            Novak, William. II. Title
```

37 B

Sources

➤ **Locate suitable bibliographies.** You will save time if you can locate an existing bibliography—preferably an annotated one—on your subject. Bibliographies list books, articles, and other materials that deal with particular subjects.

- **Complete bibliographies** attempt to list all the major works in a given field or subject.

- **Selective bibliographies** usually list the best known or most respected books in a subject area.

- **Annotated bibliographies** briefly describe the works they list and may evaluate them.

- **Annual bibliographies** catalog the works produced within a field or discipline in a given year.

➤ **Subject card**

```
HD          BUSINESSMEN—UNITED STATES—
            BIOGRAPHY.
9710
U52         Iacocca, Lee A.
I25           Iacocca: an autobiography/Lee Iacocca
UGL         with William Novak.—Toronto; New York:
            Bantam Books, c1984. xv, 352 p., [16] p. of
            plates : ill.; 24 cm.
            Includes index.
            ISBN 0-553-05067-2

              1. Iacocca, Lee A. 2. Automobile industry
            and trade—United States—Biography. 3.
            Businessmen—United States—Biography. I.
            Novak, William. II. Title
```

thorough list of sources, both books and articles, than will a run through the card catalog. To determine whether a bibliography has been compiled on your subject, first check *Bibliography Index* in the reference room of your library. Chances are, however, that you may not locate a bibliography precisely on your subject area; instead, you may have to rely on one of the more general bibliographies available in almost every field. The professor of your course or the reference librarian should be able to suggest an appropriate volume. Only a few of the many bibliographies in specific disciplines are listed below.

37 B

Sources

Doing a paper on	*Check this bibliography*
American History	*Bibliographies in American History*
Anthropology	*Anthropological Bibliographies: A Selected Guide*
Art	*Guide to the Literature of Art History*
Astronomy	*A Guide to the Literature of Astronomy*
	Astronomy and Astrophysics: A Bibliographic Guide
Classics	*Greek and Roman Authors: A Checklist of Criticism*
Engineering	*Science and Engineering Literature*
Literature	*MLA International Bibliography*
Music	*Music Reference and Research Materials*
Philosophy	*A Bibliography of Philosophical Bibliographies*
Psychology	*Harvard List of Books in Psychology*
Physics	*Use of Physics Literature*

➤ **Locate suitable periodical indexes.** While you can find the books you need for a research paper in the card catalog, you won't find articles listed there. Yet, for many subjects, magazine stories and journal articles are likely to contain the most up-to-date and concise information. You shouldn't undertake any college-level research paper without examining the periodical literature on your topic.

Fortunately, articles on your subject can be traced through any number of periodical indexes, both printed and computerized, some general and wide-ranging, others more specialized and sophisticated. Indexes—which are usually located in the reference room of the library—list where you can find articles written about a given subject during a given period of time.

As with any reference tool, you should read the front matter of a printed index to be sure you are using it properly and understand its coverage and limitations. In addition, the front matter will help you decipher the entries in a periodical index—which may seem like a code until you learn what all the abbreviations mean.

The printed index you are most likely to have used is the *Readers' Guide to Periodical Literature.* It directs you to articles on many topics in many popular magazines. Another such general tool is *Magazine Index.* But for many college papers, you will almost certainly want to consult more specialized and powerful indexes. As with bibliographies, there are guides to periodical literature in every major academic field and many are now computerized (see next section). The list below is just a sampling of the printed indexes available. Check with the reference room librarian for the most helpful reference work in your topic area.

Doing a paper on	*Check this periodical index*
Anthropology	*Anthropological Literature: An Index to Periodical Articles and Essays*
Art	*Art Index*
Biography	*Biography Index*
Business	*Business Periodicals Index*
Computer Science	*Computer Literature Index*
Education	*Education Index*
Film	*Film Literature Index*
Humanities	*Social Science & Humanities Index; Humanities Index*
Literature	*Essay and General Literature Index*
Music	*Music Index*
Philosophy	*The Philosopher's Index*
Psychology	*Psychological Abstracts*
Public Affairs	*Public Affairs Information Service*
Science	*General Science Index*
Social Science	*Social Science & Humanities Index; Social Sciences Index*
Technology	*Applied Science and Technology Index*

37 B

Sources

▶ **Do a computer search.** Perhaps the most intriguing new tools available to the library researcher are computerized indexes and data bases. Although searching some data bases requires a librarian's assistance, most CD-ROM indexes can now be accessed easily enough by anyone who can punch a few keys. Like printed indexes, computerized data bases store information by author, title, and subject on articles published in various periodicals. But a computer index has several distinct advantages:

- It can be updated constantly.
- It can be searched quickly and creatively.
- It can provide a printed record of any search.

Since a typical data base search begins with the key words in your subject, it helps to have a thesis in mind when you start. So write out your topic idea or thesis sentence and underline the important words in it—those that might appear in the titles of other articles on the subject.

{**Tentative thesis 1**}   The mechanism by which <u>acupuncture</u> relieves <u>pain</u> is not precisely known.

In this first example, *acupuncture* is clearly the main focus and probably the best search word. But since acupuncture is related to the relief of pain, journal articles on *pain* might also include references to acupuncture. *Mechanism* is not underlined because it is too general a term to lead to information about acupuncture. Here's a second example.

{**Tentative thesis 2**}   Lee <u>Iacocca</u> saved the <u>Chrysler Corporation</u> from bankruptcy in 1979–80 by important <u>changes</u> in structure and management.

Here, the two obvious key words are *Iacocca* and *Chrysler. Bankruptcy* might seem too general a term to use for a search. But consider the importance of the date: *bankruptcy* and *Chrysler* are terms that would likely appear together often in the titles of articles written in 1979–80, so that a search that permits you to link key words (as some data bases do) might produce exactly the references you are seeking if the data base covers 1979–80.

37 B

Sources

> After you have searched key words in the thesis itself, consider other related terms. For the first thesis, you might search terms (or pairs) such as *anesthesia, painkillers, medicine/Chinese, medicine/alternative;* for the second, additional key search terms might include *automobile, automobile/industry, automobile/ management,* and *bail-out.* The more you use computerized indexes, the better you will become at finding search words to explore a topic. Fortunately, computer indexes in the library are almost always accompanied by detailed instructions and user's guides.

> Some indexes can search by only one key word at a time. More sophisticated indexes can perform what is termed **Boolean** searching; this process narrows the scope of a search by linking key words. For example, if your thesis included three key terms, you could search for articles whose titles linked all three, thus homing in on very specific topics.

{**Tentative thesis 3**}   The building of a permanent <u>base</u> on the <u>moon</u> should be <u>NASA's</u> next goal.

{**Tentative subject 4**}   <u>Drugs</u> seem to play a role in many cases of <u>child abuse.</u>

A Boolean search looks for those titles that contain all the key terms.

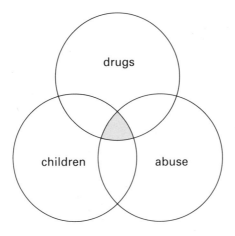

The range of the search can be expanded by directing the computer to look for synonyms of the key terms.

base, settlement, camp, station
drugs, narcotics, cocaine, marijuana
child, children, kids, youngsters

Refinements of this technique in some data bases enable researchers to look for selected combinations of words, particular clusters of letters, multiple word endings *(abuse, abuses, abused, abusing),* or to search within specific fields (only in selected journals, specific dates, particular authors, and so on). You can command great amounts of information by learning to use the key data bases in your field effectively.

When you have the information you need on the screen, you can then direct the computer to print out that information. In effect, you have created a personalized bibliography on your topic.

It is important to remember, however, that data bases often duplicate the information in printed indexes. When the machine is down or there is a line in front of the data base terminal, you may need to consult more traditional reference tools. Also remember that data bases often cover only periodicals from the last decade or so. For earlier material, you may have no choice but to consult a printed index.

Listed below are some useful computerized indexes; more are becoming available all the time.

37 B

Sources

Need information from/about	*Check this data base or computer index*
Astronomy	*INSPEC*
Business	*ABI/INFORM; Info Trac*
Contemporary events	*NewsBank*
Contemporary periodicals	*Academic Index; Info Trac; PAIS*
Economics	*PAIS*
Education	*ERIC*

Need information from/about	Check this data base or computer index
General information	*Wilsondisc* (covers same material as *Reader's Guide*)
Humanities	*Info Trac*
Literature	*MLA Bibliography*
Mathematics	*MATHFILE*
Psychology	*PsycLit*
Public Affairs	*PAIS (Public Affairs Information Service)*
Social Science	*Info Trac*

➤ **Check citation indexes.** Citation indexes tell you where a given work is mentioned again *after* it has been published. Using a citation index, you can trace the influence a particular article or author has had on a field. Indexes are arranged by author, item, and subject. While you may not need to use a citation index for your early college papers, you should know that these interesting tools exist. Three important citation indexes are the *Science Citation Index,* the *Social Sciences Citation Index,* and the *Arts and Humanities Index.*

➤ **Consult collections of abstracts.** Many disciplines now publish collections of abstracts that summarize major research articles in a given area. These abstracts can help familiarize you with major research issues or provide precise accounts of long research essays. Your librarian can direct you to any suitable collection of abstracts in your area of research.

➤ **Consult dictionaries of biography.** Quite often in preparing a research project, you will need to find information about famous people, living and dead. There are dozens of sources to help you in the reference room. Good places to start are *Biography Index: A Cumulative Index to Biographic Material in Books and Magazines, Bio-Base, Current Biography,* and *The McGraw-Hill Encyclopedia of World Biography.* There are also various *Who's Who* volumes, covering living British, American, and world notables, and volumes on African Americans, women, politics, and fashion. Deceased figures may appear in *Who Was Who.* Probably the two most famous dictionaries of biography are the *Dictionary of National Biography* (British) and the *Dictionary of American Biography.* More specialized dictionaries cover scientists, authors, architects, scholars, and so on. Here are some helpful sources.

37 B

Sources

If your subject is in	Check this source of biographical info
Art	*Index to Artistic Biography*
Education	*Biographical Dictionary of American Educators*
Film	*The Filmgoer's Companion*
Journalism	*Journalist Biographies Master Index*
Medicine	*Dictionary of American Medical Biography*
Music	*The New Grove Dictionary of Music and Musicians*
Politics	*Politics in America*
Psychology	*Biographical Dictionary of Psychology*
Religion	*Dictionary of American Religious Biography*
Science	*Dictionary of Scientific Biography*

If your subject is	*Check this source of biographical info*
African	*Dictionary of African Biography*
African American	*Dictionary of American Negro Biography*
Asian	*Encyclopedia of Asian History*
Australian	*Australian Dictionary of Biography*
Canadian	*Dictionary of Canadian Biography*
Female	*Index to Women; Notable American Women*
Hispanic	*Chicano Scholars and Writers: A Bibliographic Directory*
Islamic	*The Encyclopedia of Islam*

➤ **Check guides to reference books.** The reference room in most libraries is filled with helpful materials. But how do you know what the best books are for your needs? Consult one of these guides to reference books.

Bell, Marion V., and Eleanor A. Swidan. *Reference Books: A Brief Guide,* 8th ed.

Murphey, Robert W. *How and Where to Look It Up: A Guide to Standard Sources of Information.*

Sheehy, Eugene P. *Guide to Reference Books,* 9th ed.

Walford, Arthur. *Guide to Reference Material,* 3rd ed.

Also useful in some situations are indexes that list all books currently available (that is, books that are in print), their publishers, their prices. Updated frequently, such volumes include:

Books in Print;

Paperbound Books in Print;

Cumulative Book Index.

37 B

Sources

➤ **Locate statistics.** Where do you go to find the figures or statistics you need to support or counter an argument? Begin with the *World Almanac* for basic numbers on everything from population to sports. If your focus is on the United States, check out *Statistical Abstract of the United States,* or *Historical Statistics of the United States.* For information about the world, examine *The Statesman's Yearbook,* the *National Intelligence Factbook,* the *UN Demographic Yearbook,* or the *UNESCO Statistical Yearbook.* For business figures, check the *Handbook of Basic Economic Statistics,* the *Survey of Current Business,* or the *Dow Jones Irwin Business Almanac.* Also useful for surveys of opinion is the summary of Gallup Poll findings called *Gallup Poll: Public Opinion 1935–1971.*

➤ **Check news sources.** Sometimes you'll need information from newspapers. If you know the date of a particular event, you can usually locate the information you want. If your subject isn't an event, you may have to trace it through an index. Only a few papers are fully indexed; the one newspaper you are most likely to encounter in most American libraries is *The New York Times,* usually available on microfilm. *The New York Times Index* provides chronological summaries of articles on a given subject. Since the printed version of the *Times* index takes several months to arrive in a library, you may need to use the *Academic Index* data base for more recent events. *Academic Index* keeps several months of the *Times* on file. A second American paper with an index is *The Wall Street Journal.*

Another useful reference tool for current events—available since 1982 in computer format—is *Newsbank,* an index of more than 100 newspapers from across the country keyed to a microfiche collection. You can use *Newsbank* to present a sampling of journalistic coverage and opinion on major issues and notable people. *Facts on File* summarizes national and international news weekly; *Editorial Research Reports* gives background information on major problems and controversies. To report on what editors are thinking, examine *Editorials on File,* a sampling of world and national opinion.

➤ **Check book reviews.** To locate reviews of books, refer to *Book Review Digest, Book Review Index,* or *Current Book Review Citations. Book Review Digest* does not list as many reviews as the other two collections, but it summarizes those it does include—a useful feature.

➤ **Consult experts.** Sometimes people are the best sources of up-to-date and authoritative information. If you can discuss your subject with an expert (without being a nuisance), you'll add credibility, authenticity, and immediacy to a research report. If you are writing a paper about an aspect of medical care, talk to a medical professional. If exploring the financial dilemmas of community theaters, try to interview a local producer or theater manager. If writing about problems in the building industry, find a builder or banker with ten minutes to spare. Handle any interview professionally.

- Write or telephone your subject for an appointment and make it clear why you want the interview.
- Be on time for your appointment.
- Be prepared: have a list of questions and possible follow-ups ready.
- Take careful notes, especially if you intend to quote your source.
- Double-check direct quotations, and be sure your source is willing to be cited on the record.
- If you plan to tape the interview, get your subject's approval before turning the machine on.
- Promise to send the authority you interview a copy of your completed paper.
- Send a thank-you note to an expert who has been especially helpful.

➤ **Write to professional organizations.** Almost every subject, cause, concept, or idea is represented by a professional organization, society, bureau, office, or lobby. If you have time (you'll need lots of it), write to an appropriate organization for information on your topic; ask for pamphlets, brochures, tracts, leaflets, reports, and so on. The *Encyclopedia of Associations,* published by Gale Research, can be your source for addresses. Also remember that the U.S. Government publishes huge amounts of information on just about every subject of public interest. Check the *Index to U.S. Government Periodicals* or the *Monthly Catalog of United States Government Publications* for listings.

37 B

Sources

TIP: Do you recall the difference between primary and secondary sources? *Primary sources* are the materials on a topic upon which subsequent interpretations or studies are based, anything from first-hand documents, such as poems, diaries, court records, and interviews, to research results generated by experiments, surveys, ethnographies, and so on. When using a primary source, you look at the subject in its raw shape, before others have commented on it or influenced you.

Materials that provide interpretation and commentary are called *secondary sources.* Such works would include most encyclopedias and reference volumes, as well as books and articles that expand upon primary records. In the humanities, a novel would be a primary source and the book interpreting it a secondary source.

In the sciences, an article reporting the results of original experiments on IQ might be a primary source, while a book using that information to draw conclusions for admissions examinations to college would be a secondary source. Research papers should draw upon primary materials as much as possible, looking either at raw data or the results of original research. However, secondary sources are not necessarily less "good" than primary works; for many topics, the only sources available will be those that interpret existing data.

➤ **Prepare a working bibliography.** As you move through the card catalog, the bibliographies, the indexes, the interviews, and so on, list all your prospective sources on separate index cards (3″ x 5″ cards are ideal) so that you can add, delete, and alphabetize entries quickly. These cards form your preliminary working bibliography—a private data base on your subject.

37 B

Sources

If you have found only a dozen or so potential printed sources, you will probably have time to locate and examine all of them. But if you've found several dozen or more (which is easy to do if you use computerized indexes that provide print-outs), you'll have to decide which sources to pursue first. You may wonder whether you have enough information to make decisions about your materials when all you have are bald bibliographic entries, but you probably do. For each item in your working bibliography:

• *Check the title.* How close does it come to approximating your topic or addressing the question you are asking?

• *Check the author.* Is he or she an authority in this area? Did you come across the author's name in your preliminary reading? Does the author have credentials to write in this field?

• *Check the source.* Who is publishing this information? If a book, do you recognize the publisher? Is it an academic press (that is, one affiliated with a college or university)? If a periodical, is the article in a scholarly journal? A popular magazine? Which kind of publication will give you the perspective on the subject you are seeking?

- *Check the depth of coverage.* Is the piece long enough to give you the information you need, or is it simply an overview or a brief news item?

- *Check the date.* Is this source recent enough to reflect the latest research?

Rank the sources in the order of their apparent usefulness, and then begin locating and examining them. If some of your early sources don't pan out, drop down further in your list until you find the materials you need.

EXERCISE 37.4

For each of the three thesis ideas below, list sources of information named in this chapter that you might consult in researching a paper. Then identify sources you might use to explore a topic of your own.

1. Eleanor Roosevelt (1884–1962) was among the most influential women of the twentieth century.
2. Third-world countries with capitalist systems develop more rapidly than those with socialist economies.
3. A human mission to the planet Mars is unlikely before the end of the twentieth century.

37 C   KEEPING TRACK OF INFORMATION

37 C

Notes

Terms you need to know

SUMMARY. In note-taking, just the key ideas or gist of a source in a researcher's own words. Summaries tend to be short and do not attempt to outline an entire source.

PARAPHRASE. In note-taking, a statement that lists both the main ideas and key supporting points in the order they occur. The notes are in the researcher's own words. Paraphrases are usually longer and more detailed than summaries.

DIRECT QUOTATIONS. In note-taking, the exact words used in a source. The researcher copies the quoted material exactly as it appears—word for word—and places it between quotation marks.

Troubleshooting

After you have found all your printed sources, you have to read and evaluate them. And somehow, you have to keep track of *what* you have read and *where* so that you can locate and use the information when you actually write your paper.

For many writers, keeping track of what they've read may be more difficult than finding the material in the first place. Initially, at least, it seems easier to rely on luck and memory than system and strategy to get the right information in the right slots.

You know the scenario. Library books of all sizes clutter every corner of your desk, stuffed with slips and markers. The book you need most disappears under your roommate's bed, never to be seen again. You dutifully copy the names of two dozen articles from various indexes, and then promptly misplace the list. That perfect quotation for the opening of your paper disappears too, along with a sheet of paper listing its source. In the meantime, you photocopy a dozen pages of a helpful article, but—when you sit down with it two weeks later to write the paper—you can't cite the piece because the page numbers got cut off by the copier. As you try to write, your desk becomes a junkyard of scrap paper, borrowed books, photocopies, scattered notes, and lists of important details that don't quite make the same sense they did when you wrote them down. Sound familiar?

Most people drop at least one pass while writing a research paper. But a little forethought and planning can smooth the process and forestall major problems. As with finding sources systematically, keeping track of information efficiently requires front-end work. The reward for a careful start-up comes near the conclusion of a research project—when you are most pressed for time. Then you discover that you have an accurate "Works Cited" list, comprehensive notes, and all the page numbers you need for accurate documentation. Who could ask for anything more?

To keep track of research data efficiently . . .

➤ **Keep an accurate set of bibliography cards.** For every source you examine— whether it ends up in the final paper or not—make a complete bibliography card, one source per card. Don't keep bibliographical information on sheets of paper. You can't shuffle items entered on a list, rearrange them, or enter new ones alphabetically. And paper lists tend to get lost. So when you start a research project, *buy a stack of cards,* preferably 3″ x 5″.

Each bibliography card should contain all the information you will need to record one source in the *Works Cited* or *References* list at the end of the paper. Be sure to include a library call number or location (current periodicals may not have call numbers) in case you have to look the source up a second time.

37 C

Notes

Also consider assigning a code number to identify each separate source. Then when you begin taking notes from a source, put the special number for that source on those notes instead of tediously recopying all the information already on the bibliography card: author, title, publisher, date. The code number will tell you exactly where the notes are from. For example, a note card using information from Brock Yates' *The Decline and Fall of the American Auto Industry* (listed below) would bear code 1.

Here's the bibliographical information you need for some basic sources.

For a book:

- Call number/location in the library.
- The code number you have assigned this source (#1).
- Name of author(s), last name first, followed by a period.
- Title of work, underlined, followed by a period.
- Place of publication, followed by a colon.

- Publisher, followed by a comma.
- Date of publication, followed by a period.

> HD   1.
> 9710
> U52
> Y38
> 1983
> Undergrad. Lbry
>
> **Yates, Brock W. The Decline and Fall of the Ameri-
> can Auto Industry. New York: Empire-Harper,
> 1983.**

For an article in a scholarly journal:

- Call number/location.
- The code number you have assigned this source.
- Name of author(s), last name first, followed by a period.
- Title of work, followed by a period and between quotations.
- Name of the periodical, underlined.
- Volume number, followed by the date in parentheses, and a colon.
- Page or location, followed by a period.

37 C

Notes

> Undergrad. Lbry   2.
> Reading Room
>
> **Robinson, Jay L. "Literacy in the Department of
> English." College English 47 (1985): 482–98.**

For an article in a popular magazine or newspaper:

- Call number/location.
- The code number you have assigned this source.
- Name of author(s), last name first, followed by a period.
- Title of work, followed by a period and between quotations.
- Name of the periodical, underlined.
- Date, month, and year of publication, followed by a colon.
- Page or location, followed by a period.

```
Main. Lbry                                          3.
Reading Rm.


Vitullo-Martin, Julia. "Chrysler in Chaos: Is the
    Company Beyond Repair?" Saturday Review
    19 Jan. 1980:
    22-25.
```

For the exact *Works Cited* or *References* form of any bibliography card entry, check the MLA or APA form charts (Chapters 39 and 40). If you cannot record the source precisely according to form (you may not have your handbook with you), at least copy all the information needed to transform the card into a correct *Works Cited* or *References* entry when the time comes. If your bibliography cards *are* accurate, compiling these lists will require that you do no more than type up the notes in alphabetical order.

37 C

Notes

➤ **Keep a set of note cards.** You should put your research notes on cards for the same reasons you use cards to keep track of bibliographical information: they are neat, stackable, and can be shuffled. While 3″ x 5″ slips are fine for bibliography entries, larger cards may be more practical for notes.

Each note card should have four components:

- a code number to identify what source is being used;
- a heading to identify the kind of information on the card;
- the actual information itself;
- page numbers accurately locating the information in the source.

> Vitullo-Martin, "Chrysler in Chaos" **3/1**
>
> **Chrysler's critics**
>
> Many critics—including Ralph Nader—blamed Chrysler's problems on gross mismanagement. Vitullo sums up their arguments this way: "For years Chrysler made reckless decisions at every turn: building big cars when Americans wanted little cars, producing gas guzzlers right before the gas shortage hit and persisting with them long after, and manufacturing inefficient and unattractive cars when consumers were insisting on efficiency and style." (p. 22)

Above is a sample note card from source 3.

➤ **Summarize or paraphrase your sources carefully.** Take the kind of notes appropriate to your subject and your research material. A **summary** captures the gist of a source or some portion of it, boiling it down to a few words or sentences. A **paraphrase** will usually run longer than a summary because it is more faithful to the structure of a source, listing major and relevant minor points in their original order and with approximately the same emphasis.

Summarize any articles that support your thesis, but do not provide new information; paraphrase the more crucial materials—those that cover key issues, provide essential information, or supply significant details. Practically speaking, the distinction between summaries and paraphrases is less important than simply knowing how to take notes that accurately record all the information you'll need. You'll usually find yourself switching between summary and paraphrase. Some of the information may be so important you will even want to copy it word-for-word from the source, marking it clearly as a **direct quotation.**

37 C

Notes

> 938.03
> G235r
> Level 3
>
> **6**
>
> **Garnett, Samuel J. Classical Struggles: The Greeks and War.** Chicago: Rhoades, 1969. 360 pp. Index.

Let's say that you are writing a history paper about the invasion of Greece by the Persian monarch Xerxes in 480 B.C. You locate a book on Greek military history by Samuel J. Garnett entitled *Classical Struggles: The Greeks and War,* published by Rhoades Publishing in Chicago, 1969. Your bibliography card for the book might look something like the sample card at the bottom of page 546.

A check of the index in *Classical Struggles* leads you to the following pages that deal with your topic.

218

a continuing Asiatic challenge to the sovereignty of the Greek city states.

The Persian Wars

The Greek defense of Eastern European civilization against the Persian armies of Xerxes has traditionally been depicted as a David versus Goliath struggle. In the fifth century B.C., approximately 110,000 Greeks—so the legend has it—managed to stop an invasion by 1,700,000 Persians, thereby thwarting Xerxes' ambition to annex the Greek homelands to his already sprawling empire. The Hellenic victory over the invading Persians was illustrious, but the armies that faced each other in this conflict were never as unequally matched as some Greek historians would have readers believe.

The Persian monarch Darius first invaded Greece in 490 B.C. in an attempt to end Greek influence in the Aegean area, but his forces suffered a humiliating defeat at the Battle of Marathon. Enraged, Darius planned a more massive invasion that would crush the Greeks under a combined land and sea assault. Darius died before his attack could be launched, but relatives and counselors persuaded his reluctant son Xerxes to continue the military venture. Preparations for the attack were elaborate. A bridge was built across the Hellespont to expedite troop movements; channels were cut to protect the Persian navy from storms;

37 C

Notes

219

supplies were gathered along the projected route of the army's march from Asia into Europe.

Historians are unsure about the precise size of this army. The Greek scholar Herodotus is responsible for the figure of 1,700,000 men, a number now widely regarded as unacceptably high. More reputable estimates place the number of Xerxes' troops at approximately 210,000, which would still represent a formidable power. In fact, size would prove to be one of the Persians' major tactical problems. An army this large necessarily moved slowly, hampered by poor communications and the need to find large supplies of food in unfriendly territories.

A second difficulty Xerxes faced stemmed from the composition of his army. Aside from the Persian contingents and an elite force known as the Immortals, most of Xerxes' grand army consisted of conscripts from various parts of the empire—in effect, unwilling soldiers from captured nations. Moreover, these men were poorly armed, despite the earlier Persian experience of losing at Marathon in part because of the superiority of Greek weapons. In general, Greek foot soldiers were much better armed and armored than their Persian counterparts. (Xerxes did possess a superior cavalry.)

Herodotus also provides an exaggerated estimate for the size of the Persian navy, offering a

220

figure of 1207 ships. But even a more realistic estimate of 600–800 triremes gives Xerxes a fleet considerably larger than any the Greeks would have been able to assemble. Just as important, Xerxes had in his service the finest sailors in the world, the Phoenicians. Yet maneuvering a force this large in unfamiliar waters would prove a task too challenging for the Persians.

The Persian ships were constructed for speed and built high for the positioning of archers. The opposing Greek navy—which numbered approximately 400 ships—were low and built stoutly to withstand the ramming strategies favored by Greek sailors. Unlike the Persians, the Greeks preferred to board enemy ships and to engage in hand-to-hand combat, the technique best-suited for battle in tight quarters, where the advantage of superior numbers counted for less.

Battle of Thermopylae

The Persians marched easily through northern Greece in the summer of 480 B.C., following a strategic Greek withdrawal from the passe of Tempe.

37 C

Notes

A short summary of the pages would suffice if you found this source less useful than some others. The summary would remind you what *Classical Struggles* covered and would help you later if you needed more details about the military problems Xerxes faced.

Garnett, Classical Struggles— 6

(pp. 218–220). Although Xerxes had fewer men in arms than the Greek historian Herodotus claimed (219), he did have a larger army and navy than the Greeks. However Xerxes' invading force faced disadvantages in logistics, morale, armaments, and naval tactics.

If, however, you found information worth recording in detail, you might paraphrase its basic argument and then record important facts and figures. In the sample notecards below, notice that:

• the material is entirely in the researcher's own words—except for one clearly marked quotation;

• the material is arranged to highlight important information;

• each important fact is accompanied by a page number;

• the paraphrase is selective—material on Darius and the Battle of Marathon is omitted since it may not contribute to a paper on Xerxes's war effort.

Garnett, Classical Struggles 6/1
(pp. 218–219)

Xerxes' army
Persian invasion force numbered far less than the 1,700,000 claimed by Greek historian Herodotus (219); actual force was approx. 210,000 (219) versus the Greeks' 110,000 (218).

Xerxes' difficulties:
—Size of Xerxes' army made communications and supply difficult. (218)
—Troops, from all parts of the Persian empire, made loyalty doubtful. (218)
—Persians less well-armed than Greeks though cavalry was better (219).

---

37 C

Notes

Garnett, Classical Struggles 6/2
(pp. 219–220)

Xerxes' navy
Persian navy numbered approx. 600–800 ships—fewer than the 1207 claimed by Herodotus; Greeks had 400 ships. (220)

Comparisons:
—Persian navy included Phoenicians: "the finest sailors in the world" (220)
—Speedy Persian ships built high for archers. (220)
—Sturdier Greek ships built for ramming and hand-to-hand struggles (220).
—Greeks would have advantage in home waters, tight seas. (220)

Garnett, Classical Struggles   6/3
(p. 219)

Troubles with Xerxes' troops
"A second difficulty Xerxes faced stemmed from the composition of his army. Aside from the Persian contingents
...:... most of Xerxes' grand army consisted of conscripts
from various parts of the empire.... Moreover, these men
were poorly armed, despite the earlier Persian experience
of losing at Marathon [in 490 B.C.] in part because of the
superiority of Greek weapons. In general, Greek foot soldiers were much better armed and armored than their Persian counterparts. (Xerxes did possess a superior
cavalry.)"

You may, of course, incorporate direct quotations into a paraphrase, as in card
6/3 above. Or you may prefer using a separate card whenever you borrow the
exact words of a source. In such cases, be sure to copy the quoted material word-
for-word. Record the page number of the quotation. If your quotation extends
beyond a page, indicate the page break with a slash. Mark any omissions with
ellipses; place explanatory words between brackets.

• **Record page numbers for all material.** You will eventually have to cite page
numbers for all ideas and quotations you find in your sources. So, to save yourself
trips back to the library, take the time to carefully record the page numbers for
all critical information—especially quotations.

• **Try to record only one major point per card.** Don't crowd too much information onto a single slip. Later when you use the cards to help organize your paper,
you'll find it much easier if you can move ideas, arguments, statistics, and quotations independently—even if they come from the same source. If you crowd
three or four ideas onto a single card, they are locked together, unless you later
waste time recopying them.

• **Write on only one side of a note card.** Information on the flipside of a card is
easily forgotten. Moreover, you won't be able to lay out your cards in a tentative
outline—as sort of a flow chart—if you use two-sided cards. Writing on both
sides is a false economy.

• **Write your notes legibly in ink.** Always take notes that are legible enough for
someone else to read. Be especially careful in recording numbers and dates. It is
easy to reverse figures or to write one number that looks like another. Use ink for
notes because pencil tends to blur quickly and become illegible.

• **Photocopy passages you know you will quote from directly and extensively
(see below).** Since most libraries are equipped with copying machines, it makes
sense to copy your most important information. Be sure, though, that your copies

37 C

Notes

are complete and legible (especially page numbers and words near the spine of books). Record all bibliographical information directly onto the material so you don't forget where a photocopied article came from. Highlight passages you expect to refer to later or quote. Keep your copies in a folder.

---

from Classical Struggles
(source 6)

220

Pers. navy → figure of 1207 ships. But even a more realistic estimate of 600–800 triremes gives Xerxes a fleet considerably larger than any the Greeks would have been able to assemble. Just as important, Xerxes had in his service the finest sailors in the world, the Phoenicians. Yet maneuvering a force this large in unfamiliar waters would prove a task too challenging for the Persians.

The Persian ships were constructed for speed and built high for the positioning of archers. The opposing Greek navy—which numbered approximately 400 ships—were low and built stoutly to *Gr. navy* → withstand the ramming strategies favored by Greek sailors. Unlike the Persians, the Greeks preferred to board enemy ships and to engage in hand-to-hand combat, the technique best-suited for battle in tight quarters, where the advantage of superior numbers counted for less.

Battle of Thermopylae

The Persians marched easily through northern Greece in the summer of 480 B.C., following a strategic Greek withdrawal from the passe of Tempe.

---

37 C

Notes

37 D AVOIDING PLAGIARISM

Term you need to know

PLAGIARISM. Representing the words or ideas of a source as your own.

Troubleshooting

Most students understand that it is wrong to buy a paper, to let someone else revise a paper, or to submit someone else's work as their own. This kind of activity is simply dishonest, and most institutions have procedures for handling such scholastic dishonesty when it occurs.

But many students do not realize that taking notes carelessly or documenting sources inadequately may also raise doubts about the integrity of a paper. Such concerns are easily avoided if you take good notes (see Section 37C) and follow the guidelines discussed in this section. In fact, you will find that time spent carefully thinking about the ideas in your sources and then trying to state them in your own words pays off later when you sit down to write a draft. When you can explain complex material in your own terms, you gain an authority over a subject that enlivens every paragraph you write about it.

To avoid plagiarism . . .

➤ **Acknowledge all direct or indirect uses of anyone else's work.** Suppose, for example, that in preparing a research paper on the life of Beethoven, you come across the following passage from page 540 of *A History of Western Music* by Donald Jay Grout.

> The years up to 1815 were, on the whole, peaceful and prosperous for Beethoven. His music was played in Vienna, and he was celebrated both at home and abroad. Thanks to the generosity of patrons and the steady demand from publishers for new works, his financial affairs were in good order, despite a ruinous devaluation of the Austrian currency in 1811; but his deafness became a more and more serious trial. As it caused him to lose contact with others, he retreated into himself, becoming morose, irascible, and morbidly suspicious even toward his friends.

37 D

Plag

If you decide to quote all or part of the selection above in your essay, you must use quotation marks (or indention) to indicate that you are borrowing the writer's exact words. You must also identify the author, work, publisher, date, and location of the passage through a documentation. If you are using MLA documentation, the parenthetical note and corresponding *Works Cited* entry would look like this.

> While Beethoven enjoyed prosperity and success through 1815, his deafness continued to grow until he became "morose, irascible, and morbidly suspicious even toward his friends" (Grout 540).

Works Cited

Grout, Donald Jay. *A History of Western Music.* 3rd ed. New York: Norton, 1980.

You must use *both* quotation marks and the parenthetical note when you quote directly. Quotation marks alone would not tell your readers what your source was. A note alone would acknowledge that you are using a source, but would not explain that the words in a given portion of your paper are not entirely your own.

You may need to use the selection above in *indirect* ways, borrowing the information in Grout's paragraph, but not his words or arrangement of ideas. Here are two acceptable *summaries* of the passage on Beethoven that report its facts appropriately and originally. Notice that both versions include a parenthetical note acknowledging Grout's *A History of Western Music* as the source of information.

> Donald Jay Grout reports that Beethoven's life was prosperous in Vienna but, after 1815, his deafness became a major problem affecting his mental attitude and his relationship with friends (540).

> Beethoven, enjoying a steady demand for his work and a measure of prosperity, was relatively untroubled by the Austrian monetary problems of 1811 (Grout 540).

Without documentation, both versions above might be considered plagiarized even though only Grout's ideas—and not his actual words—are borrowed. You must acknowledge ideas and information you take from your sources unless you are dealing with **common knowledge** (see p. 558).

➤ **Summarize and paraphrase carefully.** A proper summary or paraphrase of a source should represent your own work and employ your own language (as in the last two examples above). But some writers mistakenly believe that they can avoid a charge of plagiarism just by changing a few words in a selection they are borrowing. They are wrong. The following passage based on Grout's original would be considered plagiarism—with or without a parenthetical note—because it simply takes the source's basic words and ideas and varies them slightly.

37 D

Plag

> The years to 1815 were mainly quiet and prosperous for Beethoven. His music was played a lot in Vienna, and he was famous both at home and abroad. Because of the goodness of patrons and the steady demand from music publishers for new works, his financial affairs were sound, despite a terrible devaluation in 1811 of the Austrian currency. Unfortunately, his deafness became a growing problem. As it caused him to lose contact with others, he retreated into himself, becoming depressed, irritable, and morbidly suspicious even toward his friends (Grout 540).

When you take notes, be sure to put the ideas you consider worth recording into your own words. Read the source, identify the key ideas, and then try to restate them in writing without looking directly at the source. When you are done, check to see that your version is accurate, yet does not come too close to the wording or sentence structures of the original. When you do quote material word-for-word, place such borrowings between direct quotations. Don't, however, hesitate to record facts, figures, and dates directly—along with the appropriate page numbers. See Section 37C for sample note cards that suggest how all these matters can be handled easily.

If you have any questions about how well you are handling source materials, check with your instructor or librarian.

38 Writing a Research Paper

A Refining a thesis
B Organizing a research paper
C Documenting a research paper
D Handling quotations
E Combining information from sources
F Writing a first draft
G Revising and editing a research paper
H Checking the form of a research paper

38 A   REFINING A THESIS

Troubleshooting

As the previous chapter suggests, finding material on almost any research topic is easy. But what do you do with that information once you have it? For many writers, developing a significant thesis—an idea that brings all that information to a point—is a more difficult challenge. Especially in explanatory essays that report facts, it is easy to rely too much on thesis statements that simply break a big research topic into parts.

38 A

Thesis

> Child abuse is a serious problem with three major aspects: cause, detection, and prevention.
>
> The most prevalent types of white-collar criminals are people who work in business, the military, and the government.
>
> The environmental crisis involves pollution of the water, the land, and the air.

These are shopping lists more than thesis statements.

The writers of these statements have good rhetorical intentions: the research paper is divided into such simple parts to assure comprehensiveness and clear organization. But such theses tend to deaden almost any subject by preventing readers (and, in most cases, the writer) from appreciating how the different aspects of the topic might be related—how a particular cause of child abuse, for example, might suggest a method of prevention or why white-collar crime in the government poses a threat to the work ethic. When issues are simply listed, no serious question is likely to be raised that readers might find intriguing.

To be sure your thesis is effective . . .

➤ **Make sure you have a point to make.** All the while you are reading and taking notes, you should be testing your preliminary thesis.

- Is it a substantial issue?
- Is it a debatable issue?
- Does the issue affect my readers?
- Will my readers understand how the issue affects them?

Questions like these are normal in the early stages of composing a research paper.

➤ **Focus on problems and conflicts.** Challenge yourself in your reading and research to develop a point that might be surprising or unconventional.

{**Tentative thesis**}   Students who read extensively may perform no better on achievement tests than those who read hardly at all.

You may find that the point you are pursuing cannot be sustained by the evidence. If that's the case, you have learned something and can explain your discovery in an intriguing way.

{**Final thesis**}   While some of us might like to believe that students who read extensively perform no better on achievement tests than those who read hardly at all, it's not true.

➤ **Ask basic questions about your topic, particularly *how* and *why*.** Get to the heart of a matter in defining a topic. Examine issues that matter.

{**Lifeless**}   Child abuse is a serious problem with three major aspects: cause, detection, and prevention.

{**Challenging**}   The charge of child abuse sometimes serves the interest of political groups eager to have the government define the relationship between parents and children.

{**Lifeless**}   The most prevalent types of white-collar criminals are people who work in business, the military, or the government.

{**Challenging**}   White-collar crime is rarely punished severely because—down deep—many people admire the perpetrators.

{**Lifeless**}   The environmental crisis involves pollution of the water, the earth, and the air.

{**Challenging**}   To save the global environment, citizens and nations may ultimately have to make sacrifices greater than those experienced during war.

➤ **Refine your thesis in light of your reading.** Your thesis statements are likely to seem like shopping lists if you commit yourself too quickly to topics without allowing reading and writing to shape and reshape the focus of a paper. You *do* want to narrow the scope of your research, but be prepared to refine and reshape a thesis idea until it says something interesting and important.

The author of one of the sample research papers in this handbook (see pp. 608–623) constructed seven distinct thesis statements while developing, drafting,

38 A

Thesis

and revising his paper. Adopting the general topic of "Problems in the American Auto Industry," James Balarbar began with a vast, overly ambitious idea, which he gradually winnowed to a precise and challenging hypothesis. The more he learned about his subject, the more focused he became and the more refined his thesis became.

{**Thesis 1**}　Chrysler nearly fell into bankruptcy in 1979 because of increased production costs, poor sales, and management difficulties; however, a change in the management placed the company back on its feet.

{**Thesis 2**}　Lee Iacocca saved Chrysler with his changes in its management and his strong leadership.

{**Thesis 3**}　Chrysler's near-bankruptcy was largely due to its poor and disorganized management.

{**Thesis 4**}　The weak and disorganized former management of the Chrysler Corporation nearly threw the company into bankruptcy with its automobile sales bank practice and its ventures into the foreign market.

{**Thesis 5—first draft**}　The sales bank, which displays the disintegration between the management, manufacturing, and sales, was a major cause in Chrysler's near downfall.

{**Thesis 6—second draft**}　A major cause of Chrysler's near-bankruptcy was a concept called "the sales bank," which illustrates the disintegration between the management, manufacturing, and sales. Although this method of conducting business was designed to better the company, it actually drained the company of its finances as well as its credibility.

{**Thesis 7—final version**}　A major cause of the Chrysler Corporation's near-bankruptcy in 1979–80 was a concept called "the sales bank," which exemplified the lack of coordination between the company's management, manufacturing, and sales divisions.

➤ **Finally, make a commitment.** As you can tell from James Balarbar's sparring with a thesis, sooner or later you have to commit to a topic idea. It may not be the best point, or the most profound subject, or the most memorable topic in your class—but it is yours, and you still have time to pound it into shape. Don't be shy about asking your instructor and classmates what they think of your idea. Get second and third opinions. An outsider may see an exciting side to your subject that you have missed.

38 B

Org

So you needn't rush into a topic, but don't expect a great notion to drop from the sky either. As you approach the first draft, you should have a reasonable idea of what you want to write. You may end up arguing something different, but you need to start somewhere.

38 B　ORGANIZING A RESEARCH PAPER

Troubleshooting

The basic principles of organization explained in Chapter 4 apply to research papers. But because of their greater length, research papers may require more conscious structuring than shorter essays. You may even need to use divisions and headings when a paper extends beyond eight or ten pages. In shaping the paper, keep your readers in mind; they'll appreciate your efforts to connect ideas.

To organize a research paper . . .

➤ **Make scratch outlines for the whole essay and for smaller parts of it.** Working from a plan, even a rough one, is usually easier than writing without any direction at all, especially with explanatory papers. Begin by flipping through your note cards. Stack them, arrange them, rearrange them until their facts and ideas start to fall into place. Then, with the cards as a guide, make a scratch outline for the whole essay—nothing elaborate, just your thesis, followed by the four or five major subpoints.

Put your thesis on the page in front of you as a reminder of your commitment to readers. Then check to see how each of your main points helps to explain or support that thesis. Consider the order of your subpoints. Would a reader understand why your first point comes before your second one, and the second before the third, and so on? If not, do you *have* a good reason for the order you selected? If so, how can you help your readers appreciate your strategy? If not, you may want to redraw your original scratch outline.

It may help if you ask yourself what your readers need to know first about your subject. Where does this background information lead? What ideas do you want your readers to be thinking about at the end of the essay? How can you get them there?

➤ **Be flexible.** Don't tie yourself to an original plan. You cannot resolve all problems of organization before you begin writing. Ideas have a way of following their own paths once they start moving. So don't hesitate to modify your original scratch outline while drafting an essay. And as you work through that draft, keep making tentative outlines for sections or paragraphs of the essay. These interim outlines needn't be complicated (or neat). Think of them as working papers, the scaffolding that surrounds an essay while it is under construction. Draw up several at a time to test your options; don't feel committed to any of them. And toss them out as soon as you invent something better.

38 C

Doc

38 C   DOCUMENTING A RESEARCH PAPER

Terms you need to know

COMMON KNOWLEDGE. Facts, dates, events, information, and concepts that belong generally to an educated public.

DOCUMENTATION. The evidence you provide a reader to support an idea or fact you present in a research paper. Documentation usually directs readers to printed sources of information: books, articles, tables of statistics, and so on. But it may also cite interviews, software, films, television programs, and other nonprint media. Various systems for handling documentation have been devised. Presented in this handbook are systems used by the Modern Language Association **(MLA)** and the American Psychological Association **(APA).** Most examples in this handbook follow MLA form.

PARENTHETICAL DOCUMENTATION. A form of documentation that places information about sources between parentheses right in the body of an essay itself instead of in **footnotes** or **endnotes.** With a few exceptions, parenthetical notes have replaced the older footnote and endnote systems.

FOOTNOTE/ENDNOTE DOCUMENTATION. A form of documentation that places information about sources outside the body of an essay, either in notes at the bottom of a page or in a list of notes at the end of a paper. Raised numbers (^{3}) appear in the text, keyed to the individual notes. Parenthetical documentation has generally replaced footnotes and endnotes, except for occasional **content notes** used to explain some point in the essay more fully and **bibliographic notes** employed to give readers facts about the sources used in preparing the essay.

WORKS CITED (MLA). An alphabetical list of the works used in preparing a research essay. The list is called **Works Cited** if it consists only of materials actually mentioned in the essay itself and **Works Consulted** if it also includes materials examined in preparing the paper, but not actually noted in the body of the essay.

REFERENCES (APA). The APA equivalent of the MLA *Works Cited* page.

Troubleshooting

You acknowledge the sources in a research paper so that readers can judge the quality, credibility, and originality of your work. Your citations let them know how thorough and up-to-date your investigation of a topic is and what they should read for more information.

Writers often find it difficult to decide what exactly has to be supported by documentation. Do you credit every fact, figure, and idea that appears in a paper? If a subject is new to you, doesn't that mean that virtually every sentence will have to include a citation? When does documentation become excessive?

Sometimes you need to provide readers with information that is, strictly speaking, not a part of your essay or argument. How do you do that without distracting the reader from the main body of your report? Is it scholarly to have lengthy explanatory footnotes in an undergraduate research paper—or just fussy?

38 C

Doc

To document a paper adequately . . .

▶ **Provide a source for every direct quotation.** A direct quotation is any material repeated word-for-word from a source. Most direct quotations in a college research paper require some form of parenthetical documentation—that is, a citation of author and page number (MLA) or author, date, and page number (APA).

{**MLA**}   It is possible to define literature as simply "that text which the

community insists on having repeated from time to time intact"

(Joos 51–52).

{**APA**}   One researcher questions the value of attention-getting essay

openings that "presuppose passive, uninterested (probably uninter-

esting) readers" **(Hashimoto, 1986, p. 126).**

You should also give credit for any diagrams, statistics, charts, or pictures in your paper that you reproduce from a source.

You need not document famous sayings, proverbs, or Biblical citations, but you should identify the author of any quotable phrase you include in your paper. A simple credit line is often enough for quotations used at the beginning of a paper or at chapter divisions.

> I remember your name perfectly, but I just can't think of your face.
> —William Archibald Spooner

➤ **Provide a citation for all ideas, opinions, facts, and information in your paper that you acquire from sources and that cannot be considered common knowledge.** In preparing a research paper, you need to record both what you have learned and where you learned it. In writing the paper, you'll use parenthetical notes to identify those portions of your essay that are based on the work of other authors. You'll also use these references to add authority and credibility to your assertions. The forms for parenthetical notes differ from discipline to discipline; two major systems—MLA and APA—are explained in Chapters 39 and 40.

Many writers aren't sure what they must document in a research paper and what information they can assume is **common knowledge**—which does not require a note. The difficulty increases when writing on an unfamiliar subject. In such a case, everything in a paper is borrowed, in one way or another, from a book, article, encyclopedia, or other source. Is it necessary to document every fact, concept, and idea since they are, indeed, someone else's material?

To answer this question, begin with the definition of common knowledge: facts, dates, events, information, and concepts that belong generally to an educated public. No individual owns the facts about history, physics, social behavior, geography, current events, popular culture, and so on. You may need to check an encyclopedia to find out that the Battle of Waterloo was fought on June 18, 1815, but that fact belongs to common knowledge. You don't have to cite a source to assert that Neil Armstrong was the first man to land on the moon, that Charlie Chaplin was a famous comedian, or that the Protestant Reformation was both a religious and political movement.

38 C

Doc

But if our culture shares a body of common knowledge, so does each discipline. And in writing a paper on a particular subject, you may also make some assumptions about common knowledge within a field. When you find that a given piece of information or an idea is shared among several of the sources you are using, you need not document it. If, for example, you were writing a paper on anorexia nervosa and discovered that most of your authors define the condition in approximately the same way and describe the same five or six symptoms, you could talk about these basic facts without providing a credit for every one. (You might, however, want to quote a particular definition of the condition from one of your sources.) Experts on anorexia nervosa know what the condition is and does. What the experts know collectively constitutes the common knowledge within the field about the subject; what they assert individually—their opinions, studies, theories, research projects, and hypotheses—is the material you must document in a paper.

➤ **Provide a citation for all ideas, opinions, facts, and information in your paper that your readers might want to know more about or might question.** The discussion above suggests that you do *not* have to document laboriously every fact and idea in a research paper just because it is new to you or your readers. Your strict responsibility is to credit material that is not—so far as you can tell—common knowledge in your topic area.

But you should ordinarily go somewhat beyond your strict responsibilities, anticipating where readers might ask the questions: *Is this true?* or *Who says so?* The more controversial your subject, the more you may want to provide documentation even for material that might be considered common knowledge within a discipline. Suppose, for example, you are writing a paper about witchcraft and make some historical assertion well-known by scholars within the field, but liable to be surprising or suspect to nonspecialists—for example, that the witches of western Europe were *not* the followers of ancient pagan religions. If you are writing to the audience of nonspecialists, you should certainly provide documentation for the historical assertion. If you are writing to experts on witchcraft, however, you would not have to cite sources for what they would consider basic information.

➤ **Provide content notes as needed, but sparingly.** Both major systems of documentation—MLA and APA—have done away with footnotes and endnotes for routine citations of sources. MLA, however, preserves **content notes** located in a list at the end of a paper (immediately after the body of the essay and before the *Works Cited* page). They are identified in the paper itself by superscript numbers at the end of a sentence.

        . . . the matter remains undecided.[3]

Content notes might be used:

- to discuss a point made in the text,
- to furnish a definition,
- to provide an explanation for a statistic or calculation,
- to expand upon what is said in the body of the essay,
- to acknowledge assistance, grants, and support.

In general, if the discussion of an idea is important enough to merit a lengthy note, it probably belongs in the body of the essay itself. Even short content notes can be distracting, especially if they are numerous. Rely on content notes only when you absolutely need them: that is, when the information is essential to understanding your paper, yet would interrupt the flow of the essay if inserted within the text itself.

MLA also permits **bibliographical notes.** Like content notes, bibliographical notes are identified by raised superscript numbers and located in a list at the end of a paper. (An essay that contains both content and bibliographical notes would combine them in a single list and number them, consecutively, from the beginning of the essay.) Bibliographical notes are used:

- to evaluate sources,
- to direct readers to other sources,
- to list multiple sources when necessary,
- to name a work or edition that will appear many times in parenthetical citations.

38 C

Doc

Sources (books, articles, newspapers) mentioned in a content or bibliographic note are also listed on the *Works Cited* or *References* page. Here are notes from the sample MLA research paper reproduced in the next chapter. The first is both a content and bibliographic note, the second a content note only.

> ¹Lee Iacocca joined Chrysler in November 1978 after Henry Ford II
>
> removed him from the Presidency of the Ford Motor Company. See
>
> Iacocca 120–53; Moritz and Seaman 196–97.
>
> ²According to Stuart Reginald, within his first year as President of
>
> Chrysler, Iacocca had abolished the sales bank: "Come hell or high
>
> water, we are never going to do it again!" (15)

> **TIP: Content and bibliographic notes are relatively rare in undergraduate essays. Use them whenever your paper needs the extra explanations they provide, but don't get carried away. Notes can distract readers.**

➤ **Provide dates, identifications, and other information to assist the reader.** When writing a research paper, particularly on a topic from history, philosophy, literature, drama, art, communication, government, or law, you will do readers a service if you date important events, major figures, and works of literature and art. Also be careful to identify any individuals readers might not recognize.

> After the great fire of London (1666), the city was . . . .

> Henry Highland Garnet (1815–82), American abolitionist and
>
> radical, . . .

> *Pearl* (c.1400), an alliterative elegy about . . . .
>> [The *c.* before the date stands for *circa,* which means "about"; see pp. 605–606 for a list of other abbreviations common in documentation.]

When quoting from literary works, provide information readers would need to locate any lines you are citing. For novels, you should supply page numbers; for plays, give act/scene/line information; for long poems, provide line numbers and, when appropriate, division numbers (book, canto, or other division). Examples of literary citations are given in Chapter 41.

38 D

Quotes

38 D   HANDLING QUOTATIONS

Troubleshooting

Some writers want to treat direct quotations like electronic modules: plug them in at the appropriate spots in the circuit board and the device should operate. Unfortunately, quotations don't work that way. You have to select them purposefully, introduce them intelligently, and tailor them to fit your language. Don't regard quotations as easy substitutes for your own words. If you do, you are misusing them. The last thing a research paper should be is a patchwork of quotations. If yours looks that way, you've got a problem.

To handle quotations effectively . . .

➤ **Select them well.** Every direct quotation in a paper should be there because it contributes something to the piece that your own words could not. You may want to use a quotation:

• **as a focal point for a paper.** Here James Balarbar, author of the sample research paper on pp. 608–623, uses a quotation early in his essay to describe a company plagued with management problems. This is the first paragraph of his paper.

> The old Chrysler Corporation is an excellent example of how not to run a business. Its management was shortsighted and disorganized; its method of conducting business, completely unorthodox. In fact, according to Lee Iacocca, chairman of the newly reformed company, **"Chrysler didn't really function like a company at all. Chrysler in 1978 was like Italy in the 1860's—the company consisted of little duchies, each one run by a prima donna. It was a bunch of mini-empires, with nobody giving a damn about what anyone else was doing"** (152).

• **as a representative statement of an opinion or idea.** In this opening paragraph, Travis Beckwith quotes a woman's complaint to summarize an attitude he sees in youth today.

> The elderly woman just shakes her head as three teenage boys roll noisily past on skateboards, hooting and hollering, nearly running her off the sidewalk before dashing into a crowded street. Horns blow and brakes squeal. **"Kids,"** the dignified lady sighs. **"They think they'll live forever."** She's right. Most young people take terrible and unnecessary risks with their lives and abuse their health wantonly, thinking that the shadow of human frailty can never fall on them.

• **as an assertion of facts.** Here in his research paper on the safety of nuclear plants, Darwin Ferguson uses a quotation to report a surprising fact.

> Despite the accident at the Chernobyl power station, many people still believe that nuclear power plants are inherently less life-threatening than fossil fuel plants. Roger Starr, for example, makes

38 D

Quotes

this point about the dangers of nuclear radiation: **"The radioactive discharges at the gates of a nuclear power station are so minor that, in one year, someone living next to a nuclear station would be exposed to no more extra radiation than on a single flight from New York to California and back, at altitudes partly above the atmosphere that filters out cosmic radiation"** (373).

• **as a voice that adds authority** or color to an assertion you have made. Francie Knipstein, for example, calls upon the eminent British political theorist Edmund Burke to second a point she wishes to make about critics of contemporary society:

> One sometimes gets the impression that certain self-proclaimed political leaders on campus spend much of their time looking for grievances to exploit or reasons to be offended, either in current events or in past history. Yet such tendencies are nothing new. Edmund Burke (1729–97), the great British legal scholar and parliamentarian, made the same charge against the political extremists of his day. In *Reflections on the Revolution in France,* Burke complains that such people—in this case, "atheistic libellers" of the Church—"find themselves obliged to rake into the histories of former ages (which they have ransacked with a malignant and profligate industry) for every instance of oppression and persecution which has been made by that body or in its favor, in order to justify . . . their own persecutions and their own cruelties."

• **to show a diversity of opinion.** Here, physicist Freeman Dyson, author of *Infinite in All Directions,* quotes another scientist in order to disagree with him on the relationship of knowledge and values.

38 D

Quotes

> . . . But as soon as we mention the words "value" and "purpose," we run into one of the most firmly entrenched taboos of twentieth-century science. Hear the voice of Jacque Monod, high priest of scientific rationality, in his book *Chance and Necessity:* **"Any mingling of knowledge with values is unlawful, forbidden."**
> Monod was one of the seminal minds in the flowering of molecular biology in this century. It takes some courage to defy his anathema. But I will defy him and encourage others to do so.

• **to clarify a point.** Tom Callahan, writing in *American Way* about the U.S. Army's remarkably successful recruiting slogan, uses the words of Craig Reiss, an advertising expert, in examining the campaign. Here the quotation from Reiss is lengthy enough to require indention.

> Be All You Can Be started in 1981 when studies showed that young people were most interested in learning technical skills and being personally challenged. Explains Craig Reiss of *Advertising Age* magazine:
>
> > **The army's approach to advertising changed with the end of the [Vietnam] war and the decline of the effectiveness of the bachelor's degree to get you job skills and an entry-level position. They began**

to use technology in their ads to position themselves as a big high-tech training school. That proved to be very effective because what else can you do in a peacetime army? You really can't use the emotional argument that you have to join to defend the country.

- **to demonstrate the complexity of an issue.** In an article in *National Review* entitled "Getting Warmer?" Jane S. Shaw and Richard L. Stroup quote statistician Andrew R. Solow on the issue of global warming to explain a technical point. Note that the direct quotation is followed immediately by an indirect quotation from the same source.

> Assuming, however, that the global warming trend is real, could CO_2 be the cause? If so, says Solow, we should be seeing much warmer temperatures than we have seen so far. **"For example, for the planet to warm by 2°C in the next hundred years, the average rate of warming would have to be four times greater than that in the historic record."** Greenhouse warming is expected to be greatest at high latitudes and more rapid in the north than in the south, but this pattern hasn't appeared either, he says.

- **to emphasize a point** or make it memorable. Here Paul Johnson in *Intellectuals* quotes Karl Marx to suggest that the political philosopher's physical ailments may have contributed to his jaundiced view of European culture.

> . . . He rarely took baths or washed much at all. This, plus his unsuitable diet, may explain the veritable plague of boils from which he suffered for a quarter of a century. They increased his natural irritability and seem to have been at their worst while he was writing *Capital.* **"Whatever happens,"** he wrote grimly to Engels, **"I hope the bourgeoisie as long as they exist will have cause to remember my carbuncles."**[45] The boils varied in numbers, size, and intensity, but at one time or another they appeared on all parts of his body. . . .

You may have noticed that many of these sources do not include in-text notes or footnotes to document their sources. Full documentation is more likely to appear in scholarly work—such as Johnson's *Intellectuals*—than in a magazine such as *Advertising Age.*

38 D

Quotes

➤ **Never use a quotation as a way to avoid writing.** Quotations should not be devices for padding your paper. Nor should you rely on them to say something you could have said competently in your own words. Respect your sources. Don't turn them into the academic equivalent of junk food restaurants—where you dine without paying attention to what you are eating.

➤ **Frame all direct and indirect borrowings in some way.** Readers should understand when the words or ideas in your paper aren't your own. To be sure they do, acquire the habit of routinely introducing or framing borrowed words and ideas. While quotation marks or indentions help identify direct quotations, these typographical devices don't tell a reader who wrote a passage, why it is significant, or in what relationship it stands to the rest of an essay. And, of course, indirect borrowings are not surrounded by quotation marks at all. So short introductions, attributions, or commentaries are needed to orient readers to what they are reading.

Such frames on the material can *precede, follow,* or *interrupt* the borrowed words or ideas. The introduction need not even be in the same sentence as the quotation; it may be part of the *surrounding* paragraph. Here are some ways that material can be introduced.

{Frame precedes borrowed material}

In one report to earth, the first [Skylab] crew crossed chili off their eating schedule. **Every time they opened a container of it, there was an explosion of food:** "Great goblets of chili go flying all over; it's bad news."
—Douglas Colligan

{Frame follows borrowed material}

"One reason you may have more colds if you hold back tears is that, when you're under stress, your body puts out steroids which affect your immune system and reduce your resistance to disease," **Dr. Broomfield comments.**
—Barbara Lang Stern

{Frame interrupts borrowed material}

"In principle," **says John Kert,** "dolphins can spell a word as fast as we can say it. . . ."
—Kevin Strehlo

"Whatever happens," **he wrote grimly to Engels,** "I hope the bourgeoisie as long as they exist will have cause to remember my carbuncles."
—Paul Johnson

{Surrounding sentences frame borrowed material}

Even taste is affected by zero-g. "Body fluids migrate to your upper body, and you end up with engorged tissue around the nasal passages and ear," **explains Gerald Carr, who was commander of the third and longest (eighty-four days) Skylab mission.** "You carry with you a constant state of nasal and head congestion in a weightless environment. It feels pretty much like you have a cold all the time."
—Douglas Colligan

If so, says Solow, we should be seeing much warmer temperatures than we have seen so far. "For example, for the planet to warm by 2°C in the next hundred years, the average rate of warming would have to be four times greater than that in the historic record." Greenhouse warming is expected to be greatest at high latitudes and more rapid in the north than in the south, but this pattern hasn't appeared either, **he says.**
—Jane S. Shaw and Richard L. Stroup

{Borrowed material integrated}

The study concludes that a faulty work ethic is not responsible for the decline in our productivity; quite the contrary, the study identifies "a widespread commitment among U.S. workers to improve productivity" and suggests that "there are large reservoirs of potential upon which management can draw to improve performance and increase productivity."
—Daniel Yankelovich

38 D

Quotes

Most borrowings in your research paper should be attributed in similar fashion. Either name (directly or indirectly) the author, speaker, or the work the passage is from, or explain why the words you are quoting are significant. Many phrases of introduction or attribution are available. Here are just a few examples.

President Bush **claimed** that " . . .
One expert **reported** that " . . .
The members of the board **declared** that " . . .
Representatives of the airline industry **contend** that " . . .
Marva Collins **asserts** that " . . .
Senator Nunn **was quoted** as saying that " . . .
"The figures," **according to** the GAO, "are . . .

Other verbs of attribution include the following:

accept	affirm	add	admit
allege	argue	believe	confirm
disagree	posit	deny	emphasize
insist	mention	propose	reveal
say	state	think	verify

Vary these terms sensibly. You needn't change the verb of attribution with every direct quotation.

➤ **Tailor quotations to fit the focus of your paper or argument.** Occasionally, only part of a long quotation may suit your purpose. Or a word or phrase crucial to understanding an idea may not appear in a passage you intend to quote. In such cases, you may need to use ellipses, brackets, or the expression *sic*.

• **Use ellipses (. . .) to indicate where you have cut material from direct quotations.** Ellipses might be used, for example, to trim the lengthy passage below if a writer quoting from it wanted to focus primarily on the oldest portions of the biblical text. The ellipses would tell a reader where words, phrases, and even whole sentences have been cut.

38 D

Quotes

{Original passage}

The text of the Old Testament is in places the stuff of scholarly night-mares. Whereas the entire New Testament was written within fifty to a hundred years, the books of the Old Testament were composed and edited over a period of about a thousand. The youngest book is Daniel, from the second century B.C. The oldest portions of the Old Testament (if we limit ourselves to the present form of the literature and exclude from consid-eration the streams of oral tradition that fed it) are probably a group of poems that appear, on the basis of linguistic features and historical allu-sions contained in them, to date from roughly the twelfth and eleventh centuries B.C. . . .

—Barry Hoberman, "Translating the Bible"

{Passage as cut for use in an essay}

Although working with any part of an original scripture text is difficult, Hoberman describes the text of the Old Testament as **"the stuff of schol-**

arly nightmares." He explains in "Translating the Bible" that while **"the entire New Testament was written within fifty to a hundred years, the books of the Old Testament were composed and edited over a period of about a thousand. . . . The oldest portions of the Old Testament . . . are probably a group of poems that appear . . . to date from roughly the twelfth and eleventh centuries B.C. . . ."**

When ellipses occur in the middle of a sentence, leave a space before the first period and after the third one. (Remember that the periods themselves are spaced.)

> "We the people of the United States . . . do ordain and establish this constitution for the United States of America."

When they occur at the end of a sentence or passage, place the first period immediately after the last word, and add a fourth period to mark the end of the sentence.

> "These are the times that try men's souls. The summer soldier and the sunshine patriot will, in this crisis shrink from the service of his country. . . ."
>
> —Thomas Paine

The same form (four periods) is employed when entire sentences or paragraphs are omitted.

Occasionally ellipses appear at the beginning of quoted sentences to indicate that an opening clause or phrase has been omitted. Three spaced periods precede the sentence, with a space left between the third period and the first letter of the sentence. Any punctuation occurring at the end of the clause or sentence preceding the quotation is retained.

38 D

Quotes

> "The text of the Old Testament is in places the stuff of scholarly nightmares. . . . the books of the Old Testament were composed and edited over a period of about a thousand [years]."
>
> —Barry Hoberman, "Translating the Bible"

You needn't use an ellipsis, however, every time you break into a sentence. The quotation in the following passage, for example, reads more smoothly without the ellipsis.

> In fact, according to Lee Iacocca, ". . . Chrysler didn't really function like a company at all" when he arrived in 1978.

> In fact, according to Lee Iacocca, "Chrysler didn't really function like a company at all" when he arrived in 1978.

Whenever you use ellipses, be sure your shortened quotation still accurately reflects the meaning of the uncut passage.

● **Use square brackets [ ] to add necessary information to a quotation.** Sometimes, for example, you may want to explain who or what a pronoun refers to, or you may have to provide a short explanation, furnish a date, and explain or translate a puzzling word.

Some critics clearly prefer Wagner's *Tannhäuser* to *Lohengrin:* "the well-written choruses **[of Tannhäuser]** are combined with solo singing and orchestral background into long, unified musical scenes" (Grout 629).

And so Iacocca accepted Chrysler's offer: "We agreed that I would come in as president but would become chairman and CEO **[Chief Executive Officer]** on January 1, 1980" (Iacocca 145).

But don't overdo it. Readers will resent the explanation of obvious details. If, for example, most of your prospective readers would know that the Battle of Hastings was fought in 1066, the explanation would be unnecessary.

• **Use [sic] to indicate an obvious error copied faithfully from a quotation.** Quotations must be copied accurately, word-by-word from your source—errors and all. To show that you have copied a passage faithfully, place the expression *sic* (the Latin word for *thus* or *so*) in brackets one space after any mistake.

Mr. Vincent's letter went on: "I would have preferred a younger bride, but I decided to marry the old window **[sic]** anyway."

If *sic* can be placed outside of the quotation itself, it appears between parentheses, not brackets.

Molly's paper was entitled "Understanding *King Leer*" **(sic).**

➤ **Tailor your language so that direct quotations fit into the grammar of your sentences.** You may have to tinker with the introduction to the quotation or modify the quotation by careful selection, an ellipsis, or a bracketed addition.

{**Awkward**} The chemical capsaicin that makes chili hot: "it is so hot it is used to make antidog and antimugger sprays" (Bork 184).

{**Revised**} Capsaicin, the chemical that makes chili hot, is so strong "it is used to make antidog and antimugger sprays" (Bork 184).

{**Awkward**} Computers have not succeeded as translators of languages because, says Douglas Hofstadter, "nor is the difficulty caused by a lack of knowledge of idiomatic phrases. The fact is that translation involves having a mental model of the world being discussed, and manipulating symbols in the model."

{**Revised**} "A lack of knowledge of idiomatic phrases" is not the reason computers have failed as translators of languages. "The fact is," says Douglas Hofstadter, "that translation involves having a mental model of the world being discussed, and manipulating symbols in the model" (603).

➤ **Place prose quotations shorter than four typed lines (MLA) or forty words (APA) between quotation marks.**

In *On Liberty* (1859), John Stuart Mill declares that "If all mankind minus one were of one opinion, mankind would be no more justified in silencing that one person than he, if he had the power, would be justified in silencing mankind."

38 D
Quotes

▶ **Indent any prose quotations longer than four typed lines (MLA) or forty words (APA).** MLA form recommends an indention of ten spaces; APA form requires five spaces. Quotation marks are not used around the indented material. If the quotation extends beyond a single paragraph, the first lines of subsequent paragraphs are indented an additional three typed spaces (MLA) or five spaces (APA). In typed papers, the indented material—like the rest of the essay—is double-spaced.

You may indent passages of fewer than four lines when you want them to have special emphasis. But don't do this with every short quotation or your paper will look choppy.

▶ **Indent more than three lines of poetry (MLA).** Up to three lines of poetry may be handled just like a prose passage, with slashes marking the separate lines. Quotation marks are used.

> As death approaches, Cleopatra grows in grandeur and dignity:
>
> "Husband, I come! / Now to that name my courage prove my title! / I
>
> am fire and air" (V.ii.287–89).

More than three lines of poetry are indented ten spaces and quotation marks are not used. (If the lines of poetry are unusually long, you may indent fewer than ten spaces.) Double space the indented passage. Be sure to copy the poetry accurately, right down to the punctuation.

> Among the most famous lines in English literature are those that
>
> open William Blake's "The Tyger":
>
> > Tyger tyger, burning bright,
> >
> > In the forests of the night;
> >
> > What immortal hand or eye,
> >
> > Could frame thy fearful symmetry?

When possible, you should attempt to duplicate any special typographical arrangement in the original text.

> George Herbert's poem "Easter Wings" (1633), among the most
>
> famous of the seventeenth century's "shaped poems," acknowledges
>
> the weakness of human nature.
>
> > My tender age in sorrow did begin
> >
> > And still with sickness and shame
> >
> > Thou did so punish sin,
> >
> > That I became
> >
> > Most thin.

▶ **Refer to events in works of fiction, poems, plays, movies and television shows in the present tense.** When discussing passages from novels, scenes from a movie, or events in a poem, think about the actions as performances that occur over and over again.

> In his last speech, Othello **orders** those around him to "Speak of me as I am. Nothing extenuate, / Nor set down aught in malice" (V.ii.338–39). Then he **stabs** himself, and **dies, falling** on the bed of the innocent wife he has murdered only moments before: "I kissed thee ere I killed thee. No way but this, / Killing myself, to die upon a kiss" (354–55).

38 E COMBINING INFORMATION FROM SOURCES

Troubleshooting

Don't rely on a single source for any large portion of your essay. Among the least successful research papers—explanatory or exploratory—are those that simply lump the opinions of five or six authors together like a five-course meal, one author per paragraph. For a successful essay, you have to do more than report the gist of several books and articles. You have to consider how the sources work in relationship to each other. Do they agree? Disagree? Offer different points of view? Support each other? Suggest new issues?

To use your sources effectively . . .

➤ **Draw the major ideas in your paper from several sources.** Your job as a writer is to create the relationship between the authors you have read and to add your own ideas. Odds are good that the sources you have selected for your research paper have never been examined in exactly the fashion you have read them. Your perspective on the subject can be unique, but only if you take the time to think seriously about your materials, your topic, your readers, and yourself.

38 E

Sources

> The following paragraph, for example, from James Balarbar's research paper draws upon five different writers. But the paragraph doesn't seem like a patchwork because all the different sources are marshalled to prove one clear point— that the sales bank concept used for marketing cars was a disaster. Each source simply provides evidence that enables James to draw his conclusions at the end of the paragraph.

> As an indirect result of the sales bank, between September 1966 and July 1978, Chrysler made "2447 recalls involving 71 million cars, some of which were recalled several times" **(Yates 236).** The company at one time was widely respected for the dependability of its cars and for engineering innovations such as the high compression engine, the alternator **(McDowell, "Behind Chrysler" I 12),** automatic transmission, power brakes, and power steering **(Vitullo-Martin 23).** However, the corporate reputation

was tarnished after the introduction, in 1975, of the Plymouth Volaré and Dodge Aspen, which both earned the Center for Auto Safety's "Lemon of the Year" citation in 1977 **(Sobel 253–54).** According to **Iacocca,** the Volaré and Aspen were introduced while they "were still in the development phase" and "should have been delayed a full six months" before they were released to the marketplace **(160).** Engines stalled, brakes failed, hoods flew open at "high speeds," and fenders rusted because of improper galvanization **(Sobel 254).** Chrysler lost $200 million "and much of its good will" because of the costly recalls the Volaré and Aspen required. <u>These recalls and losses, however, could have been prevented had the company concentrated more on quality rather than quantity as prescribed by the sales bank practices. Hence, even Lynn Townsend's objective of smooth-running plants was defeated.</u>

After learning from his sources, James took command of them, extracting the material he needed to support his ideas. The result is a paper that belongs primarily to him—even though it is based on information borrowed from sources. He is the one who chose to write on the sales bank problem; he is the one who, in a sense, gathered together Lee Iacocca, Brock Yates, Robert Sobel, and others to discuss that management technique for his readers.

You should strive for the same creative collaboration in writing your research paper. Don't allow a few sources to dictate the contents, point of view, and organization of your essay.

38 F

Draft

38 F WRITING A FIRST DRAFT

Troubleshooting

All the preparatory work that goes into a research paper can make writing the first draft a bit intimidating. You've got so much capital invested that you are suddenly afraid to take a risk. Yet all that work makes sense only when you begin writing.

To assure a successful paper . . .

➤ **Write a first draft early.** Think of the first draft as the testing ground for your thesis. Many months before new automobiles are introduced to the public, hand-built prototypes are run thousands of miles on test tracks that simulate road conditions. In a similar way, your draft tests your thesis under difficult situations: will it stand up to demands for facts, evidence, proof? Will it sustain itself against possible counterarguments? Will it be interesting and surprising enough to keep readers on the road?

You really won't know until you try your ideas out. So get them down on paper early—perhaps even before you have completed all your research. Remember that you don't have to write any essay—especially a long one—straight through from beginning to end. While doing your research, write any portion of the essay that seems "ready." But as your research draws to a preliminary conclusion, commit yourself to composing a full draft. Plan on finishing this draft about halfway through the time allotted for the essay. If, for example, you have a month for the paper, resolve to have a draft in hand in two weeks.

Why so early? Because you'll want time to fill in gaps and solidify your positions. You may have to return to the library to read more and gather additional facts. You may need to revise your stance entirely or restructure your essay. You will also want to polish your style. Early versions can afford to be ragged and cluttered; a final draft cannot.

Remember, too, that the final stages of producing a research paper may involve steps not required in other essays: doing an outline, managing documentation, preparing a *Works Cited* page, and so on. So get the prototype—your first draft—on the test track as early as possible.

38 G   REVISING AND EDITING A RESEARCH PAPER

Before turning in your final draft . . .

➤ **Get feedback from readers.** You've encountered this advice before in this handbook, but it bears repeating. Because of the length and complexity of most research papers, you'll benefit from the perspective offered by friendly but critical readers—classmates, writing lab personnel, instructors, friends. They'll read the paper without the background information and sense of context you have gained in research. Trust them to tell you where more information is needed—and where you've given too much. Ask them about focus, clarity, and style.

38 G

Rev/Edit

Here's a checklist for reviewing a classmate's paper.

Comments on a Research Paper Draft

Name _____ Date _____

➤ **Focus and development**
_____ Narrow your topic. The paper is
        ____ too general
        ____ too ambitious
        ____ too dull.
_____ Revise your thesis sentence. Your thesis needs
        ____ more substance
        ____ a clearer commitment.
_____ Revise your thesis statement so that it forecasts your intended development.
_____ Reconsider your major points. Your treatment seems too basic.
_____ Develop your points more comprehensively. Your treatment seems thin.
_____ Do more reading.

➤ **Structure**

_____ Reorganize. Your organization is
   _____ too simple
   _____ too complicated
   _____ confusing.
_____ Introduce your topic more effectively.
_____ Write a more effective conclusion.
_____ Organize your paragraphs more carefully. Use topic sentences to make a point. Then support that point with explanations, examples, or illustrations.
_____ Develop your paragraphs more fully; provide more illustrations and examples.
_____ You need better connections between paragraphs. Consider some transitional words or phrases.

➤ **Sources**

_____ Find better sources. Your sources are
   _____ dated
   _____ unconvincing
   _____ inappropriate.
_____ You need _____ more _____ fewer direct quotations.
_____ Introduce your quotations with a phrase identifying the author or source.
_____ You rely too heavily on just a few books or articles. Build ¶s from several different sources.
_____ You may be following the language of your sources too closely. Watch out for plagiarism.

➤ **Style and Mechanics**

_____ Work on your sentences.
   _____ They need more vigor: add action and people.
   _____ They are wordy.
   _____ They need better structures. Consider combining some of your shorter sentences.
   _____ They are tangled or confused. Simplify your sentences by focusing on clear subjects and strong action verbs.
_____ Note problems with
   _____ spelling
   _____ word choice
   _____ level of vocabulary
_____ Other mechanical problems: _____

_____ .

_____ Problems with the form of your parenthetical notes.
_____ Problem with the form of your _Works Cited/References_ page.

➤ **Summary**

_____ Your draft needs a _lot_ of work.
_____ Your draft is ok; needs _some_ work.
_____ Your draft is good; needs work.

38 G

Rev/Edit

➤ **Test your conclusions against your introduction and make any needed modifications.** Sometimes the end of your essay will not agree with your opening. What's happened is that your original idea has matured and developed: you've learned something.

Yet a surprising number of writers don't bother to readjust their opening paragraphs to reflect their new conclusions. They aren't necessarily lazy; they just may not realize how far they have traveled since they wrote that introduction hours or, more likely, days earlier. When you've completed a draft, put it aside for a day or two and then reread the entire piece. Does it all hang together? If not, revise.

➤ **Test your organization.** Organizing a long paper is rarely an easy job, so don't be surprised if readers or colleagues offer some suggestions for improving the structure of your draft. You can anticipate their objections by reading your own essay critically. One approach, while fairly mechanical, works well for many writers.

—**Underline the topic idea or thesis in your draft.** It should be clearly stated somewhere in the first few paragraphs.

—**Underline just the first sentence in each subsequent paragraph.** If the first sentence is unusually short or the second is directly related to the first, underline the first two sentences.

—**Read the underlined sentences straight through** the paper as if they formed an essay in themselves, always asking yourself how each sentence advances or develops the main point or thesis statement. If the sentences—read together—sound reasonably coherent, the chances are good that the paper is effectively organized.

➤ **If the sentences taken together don't make clear sense:**

—**Examine those paragraphs that open with sentences not convincingly related to the topic idea.** If the ideas really are not clearly related, cut the whole paragraph. If the ideas *are* related, consider how to revise the paragraph to highlight that relationship. Often, a new lead sentence for the paragraph will solve the problem.

—**Give more attention to transitions** (see Chapter 15). What words, phrases, or sentences might help readers find their way through your ideas? Is the piece long enough to require headings? Can you use parallel expressions or even sequences (first, second, third) to make the relationships between the separate sections clearer?

Don't be reluctant about making large-scale revisions in organization. Even if you end up discarding or substantially rearranging most of what you have written, the effort won't have been wasted if the result is a clearer, more convincing piece of research.

➤ **Edit the body of your research essay carefully.** Below is a list of some of the problems you might look for in editing your draft.

38 G

Rev/Edit

Editing Guide: the Research Paper

_____ Check spelling. Look for transposed letters, slips of the pen, illegible words, and omitted endings, especially *-ed* and *-s.* See Chapter 50.

_____ Check possessive forms. Don't forget the apostrophe (') before or after the *-s:* boy*'s,* boys*'.* Don't confuse *its* (possessive form) with *it's* (contraction for *it is*). See pp. 402–403.

_____ Check capitalization. See pp. 502–508.

_____ Check punctuation. Eliminate comma splices and fused sentences. See pp. 421–426.

_____ Check to see that titles of books, plays, and other long or major works are underlined: The Hunt for Red October. See pp. 492–494.

_____ Check to see that titles of articles, songs, and short poems are set between quotation marks: "Straight from the Heart." See p. 492.

_____ Check for words or phrases that have been omitted from your text or words that have been inadvertently repeated.

_____ Check for errors that crop up habitually in your papers. See p. 65.

38 H CHECKING THE FORM OF A RESEARCH PAPER

Terms you need to know

ABSTRACT. A prose summary of an article or paper, usually no more than a hundred words.

FRONT MATTER. Any material that precedes the body of an essay: dedication, table of contents, foreword, preface, acknowledgments, introduction, abstract, and so on. These features are usually optional in undergraduate essays.

38 H

Form

Troubleshooting

You can recognize a research paper almost as much by appearance as by what it says. Because these essays represent a first level of serious academic and professional research, most teachers expect research papers to have features not found in ordinary essays and to look more formal. These requirements vary from discipline to discipline and from teacher to teacher. Some instructors are flexible about their standards, provided that your handling of textual matters (margins, headings, documentation) is reasonably consistent throughout your essay. Other instructors allow little deviation from prescribed standards. To play it safe, be consistent and careful when writing a research paper.

Many writers, however, worry too much about format requirements, forgetting that the most important feature of a research paper is its content—what it has to offer. A beautiful text is worthless if it presents no new ideas. Yet neither is it good strategy to do fine research and then make it look incompetent—the format requirements of a research paper are relatively easy to manage.

To be sure your research paper looks right . . .

▶ **Type your paper.** If you type only one paper during a term, this should be it. If you aren't a good typist, you may want to take this essay to a typing service. A research paper shouldn't look like an amateur effort, full of strike-overs, white-outs, and wandering margins. Also, be sure the keys in your typewriter are clean and the ribbon has some ink in it. Don't experiment with colors. Use good quality paper, type only on one side, and double-space the body of your essay and the notes. Avoid onionskin paper—the kind that is so thin it's almost transparent.

If you write your research paper by hand, try to approximate a typed text: neat margins, clean surface, legible sentences. Use dark ink (blue or black), double-space (unless your instructor says otherwise), and write on only one side of the paper. Try to put a reasonable number of words on a page. Some students who sprawl their words fit no more than three or four sentences on a sheet. Such handwriting is difficult to read and looks juvenile.

If you use a word-processor, be sure your printer produces acceptable copy. If necessary, change the ribbon. Some computers can vary type fonts and produce boldface and italics. Keep the fonts simple and use boldface strategically to highlight important headings. Never type an entire paper in boldface. In bibliographies and notes, you may use italics for titles you would have underlined on a typewriter. Buy good quality computer paper, and be sure to separate the pages and pull off the tractor tabs before handing in an essay. (For more detailed advice about writing with a computer, see Chapter 51.)

► **Be consistent.** Whatever scheme or format you decide upon for your research essay, stick with it throughout the paper. Keep your margins even, all around the page: a one-inch margin works well, top, bottom, left, and right. Don't change typewriters or paper. Don't vary the way you handle titles or headings.

Locate page numbers in the same place throughout an essay (usually in the upper right-hand corner, one inch from the right margin, half an inch from the top of the page). In a paper that uses MLA documentation form, include your last name and first initial before the page number (beginning with page two)—just in case the body of your paper gets separated from its title page.

J. Balarbar   2

38 H

Form

```
Corporation's near-bankruptcy in 1979-80 was a concept

called "the sales bank" which exemplified the lack of
```

In an APA paper, place a shortened version of the title above the paper number on every page of the text, including the title page.

Chrysler's Sales

2

```
Corporation's near-bankruptcy in 1979-80 was a concept

called "the sales bank" which exemplified the lack of
```

► **Include all the parts your assignment requires.** Before you turn a paper in, reread the assignment sheet to review your instructor's requirements for the essay. In some cases, the assignment will require you to follow a documentation scheme or style sheet different from the MLA or APA forms described in this text. Be sure to do so.

Check to see what leeway (if any) you have in handling title pages or other features. The sample research essays on pp. 608–623 and pp. 636–647 present models in MLA and APA style.

➤ **Assemble the parts of your essay in the proper order.** Your paper may not have all the parts listed below, but here is the order of a typical undergraduate essay.

• **Title page** (optional in MLA; required in APA)

• **Outline** (optional; begins on its own page; requires separate title page)

• **Abstract** (optional, but common in APA; usually on its own page)

• **Body of the essay** (Arabic pagination begins with body of the essay in MLA; in APA, Arabic pagination begins with title page)

• **Content or bibliographic notes**

• **Works Cited/References** (begins on its own page separate from the body of the essay or any content or bibliographic notes)

For a more complex paper such as a Master's thesis or a dissertation, follow the order recommended either by an instructor or a volume such as *The MLA Style Manual* or *Publication Manual of the American Psychological Association.*

➤ **Follow the rules for documentation right down to the punctuation and spacing.** Accurate documentation is part of professional research. Instructors and editors notice even minor variances in documentation form. Perhaps the two most common errors in handling the MLA format, for example, are forgetting to put a period at the end of entries in the "Works Cited" list and placing a comma where none is needed in parenthetical documentation.

{**Wrong**} Clancy, Tom. *The Hunt for Red October.* Annapolis: Naval Insti-
          tute, 1984

{**Right**} Clancy, Tom. *The Hunt for Red October.* Annapolis: Naval Insti-
          tute, 1984.

{**Wrong**} (Clancy, 368–369)

{**Right**} (Clancy 368–369)

You will survive both errors, but they are easy to avoid. For full coverage of MLA and APA documentation, refer to the next two chapters.

➤ **Check special research paper requirements.** Follow this roster of questions.

Research Paper Requirements

_____ Name, date, course on first or title page?

_____ Title centered? Only major words capitalized? (Your title should *not* be underlined.)

_____ Did you number the pages? Are they in the right order?

_____ Have you used quotation marks and parentheses correctly and *in pairs?* The closing quotation mark and parenthesis are often forgotten.

_____ Have you placed quotation marks (" ") around all direct quotations shorter than four lines?

____ Have you indented all direct quotations over four lines long or forty words? (Remember that indented quotations are not placed between quotation marks.)

____ Did you introduce all direct quotations with some identification of their author, source, or significance?

____ Did you use the correct form for parenthetical notes?

____ Did you include a list of *Works Cited* or a *Reference* list? Is your list of *Works Cited* alphabetically arranged? Did you indent the entries correctly?

▶ **Bind your paper sensibly.** Be proud of your research paper, but don't treat it like a Gutenberg Bible. Bind it together modestly with a paper clip. Nothing more elaborate is needed—unless your teacher also asks you to hand in all the drafts, bibliography cards, note cards, photocopies, and other materials used in preparing the essay. If so, place the essay and related materials in a sturdy envelope.

Check with your instructor before stapling a research paper; some teachers like to read essays with the outline or *Works Cited* list placed alongside the body of the paper so that they can keep track of your organization and references. If you staple the essay, they can't do this as easily.

Don't even consider handing in an essay that is not clipped together.

▶ **Examine a sample research paper.** It may help you to check your paper against the sample essays provided in Chapters 39 or 40. The papers demonstrate many of the features discussed in this section.

Research Paper Checklist	**Calendar**
Find a topic	
____ Size up the assignment.	
____ Explore several potential topic areas.	
____ Do exploratory reading in the topic areas.	
____ Choose a preliminary topic and thesis.	By ____
Look for information	
____ Check the card catalog.	
____ Locate suitable bibliographies.	
____ Check indexes and data bases.	
____ Check other sources (experts, interviews).	
____ Prepare a working bibliography.	By ____
Write a draft	
____ Formulate a clear thesis or assertion.	
____ Organize the information.	
____ Write a first draft.	By ____
Revise	
____ Review the original assignment.	
____ Get feedback on the first draft and revise.	
____ Review documentation.	
____ Review format requirements.	
____ Edit for mechanical problems.	
____ Turn in final version.	By ____

38 H

Form

39 Writing an MLA Paper

A Using MLA documentation
B MLA form directory
C Sample MLA paper

39 A USING MLA DOCUMENTATION

Troubleshooting

In most college English and humanities courses, you will be expected to follow the conventions of documentation and format recommended by the Modern Language Association (MLA). The basic procedures for MLA documentation are spelled out in the following section. If you encounter documentation problems not discussed below or go on to do advanced work in a discipline that follows MLA guidelines, you may want to refer to the *MLA Handbook for Writers of Research Papers* or *The MLA Style Manual,* both edited by Walter S. Achtert and Joseph Gibaldi. These books are available in most college libraries and bookstores.

For common sources (books, magazines, articles by single authors), systems of documentation are almost always more difficult to explain than to use. Once you get the hang of MLA style, you'll find it easy and efficient. But it is important to follow the rules carefully. Seemingly small matters, such as spacing and punctuation, *do* count when you are preparing notes and bibliographies. And be prepared to consult this handbook when you encounter an unfamiliar source: a computer program, a film, a government document, an interview.

The best advice for efficient documentation is this: know the basic procedure and verify the details. The basic procedure is summarized in the following overview; the details are explained throughout the rest of this section.

MLA Overview: Follow these two basic steps:

➤ **Step 1: Insert an in-text note to identify the source of each passage or idea you must document.**

> While Beethoven enjoyed prosperity and success through 1815, his
> deafness continued to grow until he became "morose, irascible, and
> morbidly suspicious even toward his friends" **(Grout 540).**

➤ **Step 2: On a separate page at the end of the paper, list every source cited in a parenthetical note. This alphabetical list of sources is labeled** *Works Cited.*

Works Cited

Grout, Donald Jay. A History of Western Music. 3rd. ed. New York:

  Norton, 1980.

To use MLA documentation . . .

➤ **Step 1: Insert an in-text note to identify the source of each passage or idea you must document.** The basic form of the MLA note consists of the author's last name and a page number between parentheses. A single typed space separates name and page number(s). The number is *not* preceded by *p.* or *pp.,* or a comma.

(Grout 540)

(Iacocca 254–55)

The note is located right after a passage requiring documentation, typically at the end of a sentence and within the final punctuation mark. However with a quotation long enough (four typed lines or more) to require indention (ten spaces), the parenthetical note falls outside the final punctuation mark. Compare the following examples.

{Indented quotation (note placed outside final punctuation)}

> Problems in the Chrysler factories grew steadily worse:
>
> > Sometimes the quality deteriorated to such an extent that the
> >
> > [assembly] lines were stopped. One engineer (now retired)
> >
> > made some spot checks. He discovered a Plymouth sitting at a
> >
> > Detroit railhead with no engine mountings, the engine just
> >
> > resting on the frame. **(Moritz and Seaman 92)**

{Short quotation (note placed inside final punctuation)}   While Beethoven en-

  joyed prosperity and success through 1815, his deafness continued

  to grow until he became "morose, irascible, and morbidly suspicious

  even toward his friends" **(Grout 540).**

You can shorten a note by naming the author of the source in the body of the essay; then the note consists only of a page number. This is a common and readable form, one you should use regularly.

> **Grout, a musicologist,** explains that while Beethoven enjoyed
>
> prosperity and success through 1815, his deafness continued to
>
> grow until he became "morose, irascible, and morbidly suspicious
>
> even toward his friends" **(540).**

39 A

MLA

> **TIP: Make all parenthetical notes as inconspicuous and brief as possible. Don't make notes so intrusive that a paper becomes hard to read.**

The MLA directory on pages 588–606 lists the correct forms for many kinds of parenthetical notes and for their corresponding *Works Cited* entries.

➤ **Special Circumstances:**

• When two or more sources are cited within a single sentence, the parenthetical notes appear conveniently after the statements they support.

> While the ecology of the aquifer might be hardier than originally suspected **(Porter 42–48)**, there is no reason to believe that "the best interests of all the people of the county" **(Dixon 62)** would be served by the creation of a mall and shopping district in a vicinity described as "one of the last outposts of undisturbed nature in the state" **(Martinez 28).**

• When you introduce quoted or borrowed material with the author's name, you don't have to repeat the name in the parenthetical note.

> While Councilwoman **Porter** argues that the ecology of the aquifer might be hardier than originally suspected **(42–48)**, there is no reason to build a mall and shopping district in a vicinity described by naturalist **Joe Martinez** as "one of the last outposts of undisturbed nature in the state" **(28).**

39 A

MLA

Similarly, you don't have to repeat an author's name in subsequent references to the same source if no other sources are mentioned between these references. Page numbers are sufficient until another citation intervenes.

> . . . the creation of a mall and shopping district in a vicinity described by naturalist **Joe Martinez** as "one of the last outposts of undisturbed nature in the state" **(28).** The aquifer area provides a unique environment for several valuable species of birds and plant life **(31).** The birds, especially the endangered vireo, require breeding areas free from the encroaching signs of development: roads, lights, and human presence **(Harrison and Cafiero 189).** The plant life is similarly susceptible to soil erosion that has followed land development in other areas of the county **(Martinez 41).**

• When a work has more than one author, you can either put the names of all the authors in the note or just the name of the first author followed by the expression ***et al.*** (Latin abbreviation for *and others*). The form you use should match your entry on the *Works Cited* page.

Note with all authors named: (Brooks and Heilman 24)

Works Cited

Brooks, Cleanth, and R. J. Heilman, eds. Understanding Drama:

Twelve Plays. New York: Holt, 1945.

Note with *et al.*:   (Eastman et al. xxi–xxii)

Works Cited

Eastman, Arthur M., et al., eds. The Norton Reader. 5th ed. New York:

Norton, 1980.

• When more than one work by an author is cited in a paper, a parenthetical note that gave only the author's last name could refer, reasonably, to more than one book or article on the *Works Cited* page by that author. To avoid such confusion, place a comma after the author's name and add the title of the work being cited, followed by the page number. You may use a very shortened version of the title.

Possible parenthetical notes (for author listed below with more than one work cited in a paper):

(Altick, Shows 345)

(Altick, Victorian People 190–202)

(Altick, Victorian Studies 59)

Works Cited

Altick, Richard D. The Art of Literary Research. New York: Norton,

1963.

—. The Shows of London. Cambridge: Belknap-Harvard, 1978.

—. Victorian People and Ideas. New York: Norton, 1973.

—. Victorian Studies in Scarlet. New York: Norton, 1977.

Of course, if in introducing a quotation you name the author, you do not repeat the name in the parenthetical note.

Richard Altick reports that a record of the trial of Victorian

murderer William Corder bound in his own skin is on exhibit at

Moyse's Hall Museum in England, making Corder "one of the select

39 A

MLA

company of murderers who are hanged, drawn, and quartoed"

(Victorian Studies 64n).

> [The *n* following the page number indicates that the quotation is found in a footnote on page 64.]

• When you want to refer to an entire work, not just to certain pages, omit page references from the parenthetical note. Let's say that you use the following article in preparing a paper on *Hamlet*.

Works Cited

Wentersdorf, Karl P. "Hamlet's Encounter with the Pirates." Shake-

speare Quarterly 34 (1983): 434–40.

To cite the complete essay in your paper (not any particular pages), give only the author's name in parentheses.

> Entire articles have been written about Hamlet's encounter with the
>
> pirates in Act IV (Wentersdorf).

• When you need to document a work without an author—an article in a magazine, for example, or a newspaper story—simply list the title, shortened if necessary, and the page number.

> ("Aid to Education" 11)
>
> ("Subtle Art" 62)

39 A

MLA

Works Cited

"Aid to Education and Health Cut by \$38-Million." The Chronicle of

Higher Education. 18 Dec. 1985: 11.

"The Subtle Art of Stubble." Newsweek. 9 Dec. 1985: 62.

• When you want to cite more than a single work in a note, separate the citations with a semicolon.

> (Polukord 13–16; Ryan and Weber 126)

But if a parenthetical citation contains so many sources that it interrupts the smooth reading of a sentence, a **bibliographical note** (see p. 561) may be a reasonable alternative. In a bibliographical note, you may list as many sources as you need and comment on them.

> [3]On this matter see Polukord 13–16; Granchi and Guillen 126;
>
> Valusek and Syrek 188–94; and Shortell 23–64. Holding the opposite
>
> view are Lyon 120–55 and Greely 148–201. Elton is widely regarded
>
> as unreliable.

➤ **Step 2: On a separate page at the end of the paper, list every source cited in a parenthetical note. This alphabetical list of sources is labeled *Works Cited.*** The *Works Cited* page follows the body of the essay itself (and a footnote page—when there is one). Be sure to double-space all entries. The first line of each entry touches the lefthand margin and subsequent lines are indented five spaces. The format for a *Works Cited* page is explained on p. 623.

Entries on the *Works Cited* page are listed alphabetically, by last names of authors. If a work has no given author, it is listed by title and alphabetized by the first word, excluding *a, an,* and *the.* When an author has more than one work on the list, those works are listed alphabetically under the author's name.

Works published since 1900 include a publisher's name. Publisher's names should be shortened whenever possible. Drop words such as *Company, Inc., LTD, Bro., Books,* and so on. Abbreviate *University* to *U* and *University Press* to *UP.* When possible, shorten a publisher's name to one word. Here are some suggested abbreviations.

Barnes and Noble Books	Barnes
Doubleday and Co., Inc.	Doubleday
Harvard University Press	Harvard UP
D. C. Heath and Co.	Heath
Rand McNally and Co.	Rand
Scott, Foresman and Co.	Scott
University of Chicago Press	U of Chicago P

A typical MLA *Works Cited* entry for a book includes this basic information:

- Name of author(s), last name first, followed by a period and two spaces.

Altick, Richard D.

- Title of work, underlined, followed by a period and two spaces.

Victorian Studies in Scarlet.

- Place of publication, followed by a colon.

New York:

- Publisher, followed by a comma.

Norton,

- Date of publication, followed by a period.

1977.

Altick, Richard D. Victorian Studies in Scarlet. New York: Norton,
    1977.

A typical MLA *Works Cited* entry for an article in a scholarly journal (where the pagination is continuous throughout a year) includes the following basic information:

39 A

MLA

- Name of author(s), last name first, followed by a period and two spaces.

Robinson, Jay L.

- Title of work, followed by a period and between quotations. Leave two spaces after the closing quotation mark.

"Literacy in the Department of English."

- Name of the periodical, underlined.

College English

- Volume number, followed by the date in parentheses, and a colon.

47 (1985):

- For the date, you usually need to give only the year; however, if necessary to avoid confusion, you may add the season or month of the issue.

33 (Fall 1984): *or* 27 (May 1962):

- Page or location, followed by a period. Page numbers should be inclusive, from the first page of the article to the last, including notes and bibliography.

482–98.

Robinson, Jay L. "Literacy in the Department of English." College English 47 (1985): 482–98.

39 A

MLA

A typical MLA *Works Cited* entry for an article in a popular magazine or news-paper includes the following basic information.

- Name of author(s), last name first, followed by a period and two spaces.

Hoberman, Barry.

- Title of work, followed by a period and between quotations. Leave two spaces after the closing quotation mark.

"Translating the Bible."

- Name of the periodical, underlined.

The Atlantic

- Date of publication, followed by a colon. Abbreviate all months except May, June, and July.

Feb. 1985:

- Page or location, followed by a period. Pages should be inclusive.

43–58.

Hoberman, Barry. "Translating the Bible." The Atlantic Feb. 1985:

43–58.

There are so many variations to these general entries, however, that you will want to check the MLA form directory on the following pages for the correct format of any unusual entry.

39 A

MLA

39 B MLA Form Directory

Below, you will find the MLA *Works Cited* and parenthetical note forms for more than sixty kinds of sources. Simply find the type of work you need to cite in either the Format Index or Alphabetical Index and then locate that work by number in the list that follows.

MLA Format Index

➤ **Books/Dissertations:**

1. Book, one author
2. Book, two or three authors
3. Book, four or more authors
4. Book, revised by a second author
5. Book, edited—focus on the editor
6. Book, edited—focus on the editor, more than one editor
7. Book, edited—focus on the original author
8. Book, authored by a group
9. Book, no author
10. Book, focus on a foreword, introduction, preface, or afterword
11. Work, multi-volume
12. Book, translation—focus on the original author
13. Book, translation—focus on the translator
14. Book, in a foreign language
15. Book, republished
16. Book, part of a series
17. Book, a collection or anthology
18. A work within a collection or anthology
19. Book, chapter within
20. Book, published before 1900
21. Book, issued by a division of a publisher—a special imprint
22. Book, title includes the title of another work normally between quotation marks
23. Book, title includes the title of another work normally underlined
24. Dissertation—published
25. Dissertation—unpublished
26. Proceedings of a conference or meeting

➤ **Articles and Magazine Pieces**

27. Article in a journal paginated by the year or volume, not issue by issue
28. Article in a journal or magazine paginated issue by issue
29. Article in a weekly or biweekly magazine
30. Article in a monthly magazine—author named
31. Article in a monthly magazine—author not named
32. Article reprinted in a collection citing original place of publication

➤ **Newspapers**

33. Article in a newspaper—author named
34. Article in a newspaper—author not named
35. Editorial in a newspaper
36. Letter to the editor
37. Cartoon

➤ **Reference Works/Computers**

38. Encyclopedia, entry in a familiar
39. Reference work
40. Bulletin or pamphlet
41. Government document
42. Map
43. Computer software
44. Computer disk
45. Data base or information service, data from
46. Microfilm or microfiche

➤ **Miscellaneous entries**

MLA Alphabetical Index

39 B

MLA

39 B

MLA

1. Book, One Author—MLA

Works Cited

Magnuson, James. Ghost Dancing. New York: Doubleday, 1989.

Parenthetical note: (Magnuson 26)

2. Book, Two or Three Authors or Editors—MLA

Works Cited

Cassata, Mary, and Thomas Skill. Life on Daytime Television: Tuning in American Social Drama. Norwood, NJ: Ablex, 1983.

Notice that only the name of the first author—Cassata, Mary—is reversed for purposes of alphabetization. Names of additional authors and editors follow their normal order—Thomas Skill.

Parenthetical note: (Cassata and Skill 76–77)

3. Book, Four or More Authors or Editors—MLA

Works Cited

Abrams, M. H., et al., eds. The Norton Anthology of English Litera-

ture. 3rd ed. 2 vols. New York: Norton, 1974.

Although it is a Latin abbreviation, *et al.* is neither italicized nor underlined. Commas are needed around *et al.* only when it is followed by a
specification such as *eds.* (editors) or *trans.* (translators).

Parenthetical note: (Abrams et al. 1: 9)

This is a work in two volumes, so the note must specify which volume is
being cited. The volume number (1) occurs after *et al.* and is followed by a
colon and a page number.

4. Book Revised by a Second Author—MLA

Works Cited

Guerber, Hélène Adeline. The Myths of Greece and Rome. Ed. Dorothy

Margaret Stuart. 3rd ed. London: Harrap, 1965.

Parenthetical note: (Guerber 20)

5. Book, Edited—focus on the editor—MLA

Works Cited

Noyes, George R., ed. The Poetical Works of John Dryden. By John

Dryden. Boston: Houghton, 1950.

Parenthetical note: (Noyes v–vi)

6. Book, Edited—focus on the editor, more than one editor—MLA

Works Cited

Detweiler, Robert, John N. Sutherland, and Michael S. Werthman, eds.

Environmental Decay in its Historical Context. Glenview:

Scott, 1973.

Parenthetical note: (Detweiler et al. 3)

7. Book, Edited—focus on the original author—MLA

Works Cited

Dryden, John. Of Dramatic Poesy and Other Critical Essays. Ed.

George Watson. 2 vols. Everyman's Library 568–69. London:

Dent, 1962.

39 B

MLA

Everyman's Library is a series name. If a book is part of a series, the series name appears, as above, just before the publishing information and followed by the series number and a period. Series are not underlined.

Parenthetical note: (Dryden 1: 92)

Notice that the citation includes a volume number (1), followed by a colon and then the page number (92).

8. Book Written by a Group—MLA [The author may be a committee, commission, board, publisher, and so on.]

Works Cited

Reader's Digest. Fix-It-Yourself Manual. Pleasantville, NY: Reader's

Digest, 1977.

Parenthetical note: (Reader's Digest 54–55)

The note may be clearer if you name the group author or work in the sentence itself and place the relevant page numbers in parentheses: The Reader's Digest *Fix-It-Yourself Manual* lists the basic tools you need for furniture repair (54–55).

9. Book with No Author—MLA

Works Cited

Illustrated Atlas of the World. Chicago: Rand, 1985.

Parenthetical note: (Illustrated Atlas 88–89)

Be sure that a shortened title begins with the same word by which the full title is alphabetized in *Works Cited.* In this case, if the title had been shortened to *Atlas,* a reader would waste time searching for the citation under the A's in *Works Cited.*

39 B

MLA

10. Book, Focus on a Foreword, Introduction, Preface, Afterword—MLA

Works Cited

Tanner, Tony. Introduction. Mansfield Park. By Jane Austin. Har-

mondsworth: Penguin, 1966. 7–36.

Parenthetical note: (Tanner 9–10)

11. Work of More Than One Volume—MLA

Works Cited

Barker, Nancy Nichols. The French Legation in Texas. Vol. 1. Austin:

Texas State Historical Association, 1971. 2 vols.

Parenthetical note: (Barker 17–18)

Notice that it is not necessary to give a volume number here since the item in the *Works Cited* list specifies Volume 1. If both volumes were used in the paper, then individual citations *would* include the volume number: (Barker 1: 17–18); (Barker 2: 369).

12. Book, Translation—focus on the original author—MLA

Works Cited

Küng, Hans. The Council, Reform and Reunion. Trans. Cecily Has-

tings. New York: Sheed, 1962.

Parenthetical note: (Küng 46–49)

13. Book, Translation—focus on the translator—MLA

Works Cited

Hastings, Cecily, trans. The Council, Reform and Reunion. By Hans

Küng. New York: Sheed, 1962.

Parenthetical note: (Hastings 15)

14. Book in a Foreign Language—MLA

Works Cited

Bablet, Denis, and Jean Jacquot. Les Voies de la création théâtrale.

Paris: Editions du Centre National de la Recherche Scienti-

fique, 1977.

Copy the title of the foreign work exactly as it appears on the title page, paying special attention both to accent marks and capitalization, which may differ from English conventions.

Parenthetical note: (Bablet and Jacquot 59)

15. Book, Republished—MLA

Works Cited

Herbert, Frank. Dune. 1965. New York: Berkeley, 1977.

The date of the original publication follows the title. Then cite the edition you are using, giving full publication information.

Parenthetical note: (Herbert 146)

16. Book, Part of a Series—MLA

Works Cited

Kirk, Grayson, and Nils H. Wessell, eds. The Soviet Threat: Myths and

Realities. Proceedings of the Academy of Political Science 33.

New York: Academy of Political Science, 1978.

39 B

MLA

Proceedings of the Academy of Political Science is a series name. See 7.

Parenthetical note: (Kirk and Wessell 62)

17. Book, a Collection or Anthology—MLA

Works Cited

DeBell, Garrett, ed. The Environmental Handbook. New York: Ballantine, 1970.

Parenthetical note: (DeBell xiv–xv)

The small Roman numerals indicate that the quoted material appears in
the foreword of the volume.

18. Work within a Collection or Anthology—MLA

Works Cited

Erlich, Paul. "Too Many People." The Environmental Handbook.
Ed. Garrett DeBell. New York: Ballantine, 1970. 219–32.

Notice that page numbers are provided for the article ("Too Many People")
within the collection. Compare with 17.

Parenthetical note: (Erlich 219)

19. Chapter within a Book—MLA

Works Cited

Clark, Kenneth. "Heroic Materialism." Civilisation. New York:
Harper, 1969: 321–47.

Parenthetical note: (Clark 321)

20. Book Published Before 1900—MLA

Works Cited

Bowdler, Thomas, ed. The Family Shakespeare. 10 vols. London,
1818.

The publisher's name is usually omitted in citations to works published
prior to 1900.

Parenthetical note: (Bowdler 2: 47)

21. Book Issued by a Division of a Publisher—a special imprint—MLA

Works Cited

Fulbright, J. William. The Arrogance of Power. New York: Vintage-
Random, 1966.

The special imprint, Vintage in this case, is attached to the publisher's name by a hyphen.

Parenthetical note: (Fulbright 50)

22. Book Whose Title Includes the Title of Another Work Normally Between Quotation Marks—MLA

Works Cited

Crossley-Holland, Kevin, and Bruce Mitchell, eds. "The Battle of Maldon" and Other Old English Poems. London: Macmillan, 1965.

Parenthetical note: (Crossley-Holland and Mitchell 29)

23. Book Whose Title Includes the Title of Another Work Normally Underlined— MLA

Works Cited

Levin, Harry. The Question of Hamlet. London: Oxford UP, 1959.

Hamlet, the title of a play, would ordinarily be underlined if it stood alone. But as a part of a title, it is not underscored. If you use a computer capable of setting italics, the title would look like this: *The Question of* Hamlet.

Parenthetical note: (Levin 10)

24. Dissertation—published (including publication by UMI)—MLA

Works Cited

Rifkin, Myra Lee. Burial, Funeral and Mourning Customs in England, 1558–1662. Diss. Bryn Mawr, 1977. Ann Arbor: UMI, 1977. DDJ78–01385.

Many dissertations are made available through University Microfilms International (UMI). If the dissertation you are citing is published by UMI, be sure to provide the order number, the last item in the example above.

Parenthetical note: (Rifkin 234)

25. Dissertation—unpublished—MLA

Works Cited

Altman, Jack, Jr. "The Politics of Health Planning and Regulation." Diss. Massachusetts Institute of Technology, 1983.

Titles of unpublished dissertations appear between quotation marks. The abbreviation *diss.* indicates that the source is a dissertation, in this case, one written at the Massachusetts Institute of Technology.

Parenthetical note: (Altman 150)

39 B

MLA

26. Proceedings of a Conference or Meeting—MLA

Works Cited

Hairston, Maxine, and Cynthia L. Selfe. Selected Papers from the
1981 Texas Writing Research Conference. 24–25 Mar. 1981.
Austin: Dept. of English, U. of Texas, 1981.

Parenthetical note: (Hairston and Selfe iii–iv)

27. Article in a Scholarly or Professional Journal Paginated by the Year or Volume, Not Issue by Issue—MLA

Works Cited

Wentersdorf, Karl P. "Hamlet's Encounter with the Pirates." Shakespeare Quarterly 34 (1983): 434–40.

The citation for a scholarly journal paginated issue by issue differs in only one respect: a period and an issue number follow the volume number. For example, if the journal above were paginated issue by issue and the cited article were on pages 70–79 in the third issue of the 1983 volume, the citation would end: 34.3 (1983): 70–79.

Parenthetical note: (Wentersdorf 434)

28. Article in a Popular Magazine Paginated Issue by Issue—MLA

Works Cited

Lemonick, Michael D. "Jupiter's Second Ring." Science Digest Dec.
1985: 13.

The *Works Cited* entry lists a single page number (13) because the article is only one page long.

Parenthetical note: (Lemonick 13)

29. Article in a Weekly or Biweekly Magazine—MLA

Works Cited

Lindberg, Tod. "The World According to Moyers." National Review 10
Mar. 1989: 22–25.

Parenthetical note: (Lindberg 23)

30. Article in a Monthly Magazine—author named—MLA

Works Cited

Graham, Don. "When Myths Collide." Texas Monthly Jan. 1986: 42+.

39 B

MLA

The plus sign following the page number (42 +) indicates that the article continues beyond p. 42, but not necessarily on consecutive pages. The plus sign may also appear in citations of newspaper articles, which similarly carry across several pages.

Parenthetical note: (Graham 98)

31. Article in a Monthly Magazine—author not named—MLA

Works Cited

"Engineered Plants Resist Herbicide." High Technology Jan. 1986: 9.

The *Works Cited* entry lists a single page number (9) because the article is only a page long.

Parenthetical note: ("Engineered Plants" 9)

32. Article Reprinted in a Collection—MLA

Works Cited

Hartman, Geoffrey. "Milton's Counterplot." ELH 25 (1958): 1–12.

    Rpt. in Milton: A Collection of Critical Essays. Ed. Louis L.

    Martz. Twentieth Century Views. Englewood Cliffs, NJ: Spec-

    trum-Prentice, 1966: 100–08.

Notice that the book in which the article is reprinted is part of a series: Twentieth Century Views. The name of the series is not underlined. The book does not have a series number (compare to 7).

Parenthetical note: (Hartman 101)

33. Article in a Newspaper—author named—MLA

Works Cited

Branson, Louise. "Soviet TV Changing." The Dallas Morning News

    13 Jan. 1986, A1 + .

How you designate a page number for a newspaper is complicated. If the paper is divided into sections and the page numbers themselves include the section markers (A4, B12, C2), then the page numbers are handled as in the entry above. If, as in the Sunday *New York Times,* the paper is divided into numbered sections, but those sections are not a part of the actual page number, then a form like the following is used: sec. 3: 7 + . If the paper is numbered consistently from first to last page, just the page number is given. A plus sign following the page number (7 +) indicates that the article continues beyond the designated page, but not necessarily on consecutive pages.

Parenthetical note: (Branson 4)

39 B

MLA

34. Article in a Newspaper—author not named—MLA

Works Cited

"Nervous Robber Accidently Shoots Himself in the Mouth." Houston
Chronicle 15 Jan. 1986, state final ed., sec. 1: 17.

Parenthetical note: ("Nervous Robber" 17)

35. Editorial in a Newspaper—MLA

Works Cited

"How to Honor Dr. King—and When." Editorial. New York Times
15 Jan. 1986, nat. ed., sec. A: 23.

Parenthetical note: ("How to Honor" 23)

36. Letter to the Editor—MLA

Works Cited

Cantu, Tony. Letter. San Antonio Light 14 Jan. 1986, southwest ed.,
sec. C: 4.

Parenthetical note: (Cantu 4)

37. Cartoon—MLA

Works Cited

Mathis, Miles. "Squib." Cartoon. Daily Texan 15 Jan. 1986: 19.

Parenthetical note: (Mathis 19)

It might be better to describe the cartoon in the text of your essay, rather
than in a parenthetical note: "In 'Squib' by Miles Mathis. . . ."

38. Reference Work or Encyclopedia (Familiar)—MLA

Works Cited

Benedict, Roger William. "Northwest Passage." Encyclopaedia Britannica: Macropaedia. 1974 ed.

With familiar reference works, especially those revised regularly, you
need only identify the edition you are using by its date. You may omit the
names of editors and most publishing information. The authors of entries
in the Britannica and other reference works are sometimes identified by
initials. To find the full names of authors, you will need to check an index
or, in the case of Britannica, the *Guide to the Britannica* included with
the set. (Note carefully the spelling of *Encyclopaedia Britannica.*)

39 B

MLA

Parenthetical note: (Benedict)

No page number is given in the parenthetical note when a work is arranged alphabetically.

39. Reference Work (less familiar, see 38 for comparison)—MLA

Works Cited

Kovesi, Julius. "Hungarian Philosophy." The Encyclopedia of Philosophy. Ed. Paul Edwards. 8 vols. New York: Macmillan, 1967.

Notice that, with less familiar reference tools, a full entry is required, including the name of editors and publishing information.

Parenthetical note: (Kovesi)

40. Bulletin or Pamphlet—MLA

Works Cited

Finding Film Reviews. UGL Study Guide. Austin: The General Libraries, 1984.

Treat pamphlets as if they were books: underline titles and provide publishing information.

Parenthetical note: (Finding Film 4)

41. Government Document—MLA

Works Cited

United States. Cong. Joint Committee on Printing. 1985–86 Official Congressional Directory. 99th Cong.,1st sess. Washington: GPO, 1985.

Give the name of the government (national, state, local) and agency issuing the report; title of the document; publishing information. If it is a congressional document other than the *Congressional Record* (as in the case above), identify the Congress and, when important, the session (99th Cong., 1st sess.) after the title of the document. For the *Congressional Record,* give only the date and page number: *Cong. Rec.* 8 Feb. 1974: 3942–43.

Parenthetical note: (United States. Cong. Joint Committee on Printing 182–84).

Because the parenthetical note would be so long, identify the work in the body of a sentence and place only the relevant page numbers between parentheses: These facts are based on information gathered from the *1985–86 Official Congressional Directory* (182–84).

39 B

MLA

42. Map—MLA

Works Cited

<u>Cosmopolitan World on Mercator's Projection.</u> Map. New York: Rand.

Provide a year of publication if listed on the map.

Parenthetical note: Refer to the map directly in the body of your essay, not in a parenthetical note:

"Rand McNally's <u>Cosmopolitan World</u> map warns of the distortion in a Mercator projection. . . ."

43. Computer Software—MLA

Works Cited

<u>PageMaker.</u> Computer software. Aldus Corporation, 1985. Macintosh, 512K, disk.

If the author of the software is known, his or her name precedes the name of the product. If the software has a volume number, it follows the name of the software:

Microsoft Word. Vers. 3.0.

After the name of the manufacturer and the date, you may specify the computer(s) the software is written for, the amount of memory it requires, and the form of the software.

Parenthetical note: (PageMaker)

Name the software in the body of your essay, rather than in a note:

"Software, such as Aldus' *PageMaker.* . . ."

44. Computer Disk—MLA

Works Cited

"Enrollment and Placement—Math 302" Disk 47. Austin: The University of Texas Department of Mathematics, 1985.

An actual file name might be given from the document directory.

Parenthetical note: Name the source of the information in the body of your essay rather than in a parenthetical note.

45. Information Service or Data Base—MLA

Works Cited

Croll, Valerie J., and Kathleen S. Shank. <u>Teacher Training Resources: Preparing Teachers for Mainstreaming. A Selected Bibliography.</u> Charleston, IL: Eastern Illinois U, 1983. ERIC ED 232 971.

ERIC is the name of the information service; the numbers following identify the particular article in case readers wish to order it.

Parenthetical note: (Croll and Shank 10–15)

46. Microfilm or Microfiche—MLA

Works Cited

"How Long Will the Chemise Last?" <u>Consumer Reports</u>. Aug. 1958:

> 434–37.

Material seen on microfilm or microfiche is listed exactly as if it were seen
in the original hard-copy publication. You need not mention that you used
microfilm or microfiche unless the source you are using was originally
printed on microfilm or microfiche.

Parenthetical note: ("How Long?" 434)

47. Biblical Citation—MLA

Works Cited

The Jerusalem Bible. Ed. Alexander Jones. Garden City: Doubleday,

> 1966.

MLA style states that the titles of sacred works are not underlined, including all versions of the Bible.

Parenthetical note: (John 18:37–38)

Your parenthetical note does not have to indicate the edition you are
using.

48. Videotape—MLA

Works Cited

<u>Othello</u>. Videocassette. By William Shakespeare. Dir. Jonathan

> Miller. With Anthony Hopkins and Penelope Wilton. BBC Tele-
>
> vision, 1981.

The amount and order of information you give in this entry will vary,
depending upon what you intend to emphasize. If your focus is on the
author, the entry could begin:

Shakespeare, William. *Othello*. . . .

If your paper focuses on the director of the production, your entry would
begin this way:

Miller, Jonathan, dir. *Othello*. . . .

You could also give more (or less) information about the producer, designer, performers, and so on.

Parenthetical note: (Othello)

49. Movie—MLA

Works Cited

<u>Tender Mercies</u>. Dir. Bruce Beresford. With Robert Duvall and Tess

Harper. EMI Films, 1983.

The amount and order of information you give will vary, depending upon what you want to emphasize. If your focus is on the screenwriter, for example, the entry would begin:

Foote, Horton, screenwriter. <u>Tender Mercies</u>. Dir. Bruce Beresford. . . .

You could also give more (or less) information about the producer, designer, performers, and so on.

Parenthetical note: (<u>Tender Mercies</u>)

50. Television Program—MLA

Works Cited

"Mood Music." Prod. Peter Schindler. Dir. Matthew Diamond. With

Jamie Lee Curtis and Richard Lewis. <u>Anything But Love</u>.

KVUE, Austin. ABC. 25 Oct. 1989.

Note that the name of an episode appears between quotation marks; the name of the program is underlined. Information about narrator, producer, and director follows the episode name, but precedes the name of the program. If no episode name is given, the production information follows the program name.

Parenthetical note: ("Mood Music")

51. Radio Program—MLA

Works Cited

<u>Death Valley Days</u>. Created by Ruth Cornwall Woodman. NBC Radio.

WNBC, New York. 30 Sept. 1930.

Parenthetical note: (<u>Death Valley Days</u>)

Naming the program in the essay itself will usually be preferable to a parenthetical reference.

39 B

MLA

52. Interview, Personal—MLA

Works Cited

Michener, James. Personal interview. 4 Oct. 1984.

Parenthetical note: Refer to the interview in the body of your essay rather than in a parenthetical note: "In an interview, James Michener explained. . . ." If the person you are interviewing is not widely known, explain his or her credentials in your essay.

53. Musical Composition—MLA

Works Cited

Joplin, Scott. "The Strenuous Life, A Ragtime Two Step." St. Louis:

John Stark & Son Sheet Music Publishers, 1902.

If you don't have a score or sheet music to refer to, provide a simpler entry:

Porter, Cole. "Too Darn Hot." 1949.

Parenthetical note: (Joplin)

Naming the musical work in the essay itself will usually be preferable to a parenthetical reference.

54. Recording—MLA

Works Cited

Pavarotti, Luciano. Pavarotti's Greatest Hits. London PAV 2003, 1980.

Notice that the "publishing" information for a recording includes the record label and recording number: London PAV 2003.

39 B

MLA

Parenthetical note: (Pavarotti)

Naming the recording in the essay itself will usually be preferable to a parenthetical reference.

55. Speech—no printed text—MLA

Works Cited

Reagan, Ronald. "The Geneva Summit Meeting: A Measure of Prog-

ress." U.S. Congress. Washington, D.C., 21 Nov. 1985.

Parenthetical note: If you do not have a copy of a speech, refer to it by name or speaker in your essay itself and avoid the need for a parenthetical note:

"When President Reagan delivered his Geneva Summit address to

Congress. . . ."

56. Speech—printed text—MLA

Works Cited

Reagan, Ronald. "The Geneva Summit Meeting: A Measure of Progress." U.S. Congress. Washington, D.C., 21 Nov. 1985. Rpt. Vital
Speeches of the Day. 15 Dec. 1985: 130–32.

Parenthetical note: (Reagan 131)

57. Lecture—MLA

Works Cited

Emig, Janet. "Literacy and Freedom." Opening General Sess. CCCC
Annual Meeting. San Francisco, 18 Mar. 1982.

Parenthetical note: (Emig)

58. Letter—published—MLA

Works Cited

Eliot, George. "To Thomas Clifford Allbutt." 1 Nov. 1873. in Selections
from George Eliot's Letters. Ed. Gordon S. Haight. New Haven:
Yale UP, 1985: 427.

Parenthetical note: (Eliot 427)

59. Letter—unpublished—MLA

Works Cited

Newton, Albert. Letter to Agnes Weinstein. 23 May 1917. Albert Newton Papers. Woodhill Library, Cleveland.

Parenthetical note: (Newton)

It would be better to refer to the letter in the body of the essay:

"In a letter to Agnes Weinstein, dated 23 May 1917, Albert Newton
blames. . . ."

60. Artwork—MLA

Works Cited

Fuseli, Henry. Ariel. The Folger Shakespeare Library, Washington,
D.C.

Parenthetical note: (Fuseli)

It would be better to refer to the painting in the body of your essay rather than in a note:

"Fuseli's Ariel depicts. . . ."

61. Book Review—titled—MLA

Works Cited

Keen, Maurice. "The Knight of Knights." Rev. of William Marshall:
   The Flower of Chivalry, by Georges Durby. The New York Review of Books 16 Jan. 1986: 39–40.

Parenthetical note: (Keen 39)

62. Book review—untitled—MLA

Works Cited

Baym, Nina. Rev. of Uncle Tom's Cabin and American Culture, by
   Thomas F. Gossett. The Journal of American History 72
   (1985): 691–92.

Parenthetical note: (Baym 691–92)

A Table of Abbreviations

The following abbreviations are often used in notes or on a *Works Cited* page. Limit these abbreviations to such uses; spell the terms out fully whenever they occur in the body of your paper—except in parenthetical notes or explanations. Don't use abbreviations you think might confuse your readers.

assn.	association
bibliog.	bibliography
biog.	biography
©	copyright (usually followed by a date)
c.	"about" (usually followed by a date)
ch.	chapter
col.	column
coll.	college
Cong.	Congress
DAB	*Dictionary of American Biography*
dir.	director, directed by
diss.	dissertation
div.	division
DNB	*Dictionary of National Biography*
ed(s).	editor(s)
e.g.	for example
et al.	and others
etc.	and so forth
ex.	example

fig.	figure
fwd.	foreword
govt.	government
GPO	Government Printing Office
i.e.	that is
jour.	journal
l., ll.	line, lines
mag.	magazine
misc.	miscellaneous
mo., mos.	month, months
ms., mss.	manuscript, manuscripts
nar.	narrator, narrated by
n.d.	no date
ns	new series
obs.	obsolete
OED	*Oxford English Dictionary*
orig.	original
p., pp.	page, pages
Ph.D.	Doctor of Philosophy
pl.	plural
pref.	preface
proc.	proceedings
PS	postscript
pseud.	pseudonym
pub.	publisher, published by
publ.	publisher, published by
rev.	review, reviewed by
rpt.	reprint, reprinted by
ser.	series
sess.	session
sic	thus
sing.	singular
soc.	society
supp.	supplement
trans.	translator, translated by
U	University
UP	University Press
var.	variant
vol., vols.	volume, volumes
yr., yrs.	year, years

39 B

MLA

39 C   A SAMPLE MLA PAPER

This final version of an essay by James Balarbar has been reworked slightly to enhance its usefulness as a model; most of these modifications occur in quotations and notes. As a result of these additions, some transitions have been changed and James' original paragraphing is altered in one place. Phrases have been tightened, mechanical errors edited, paragraphs numbered. Yet the bulk of the essay remains just as James Balarbar wrote it in his freshman year.

James' paper, though written for a college class in rhetoric and composition, straddles the disciplines, using the research methods taught in an *English* course to present a *historical* account of a *business* problem. Such movement between disciplines is common in college writing, but also—increasingly so—in the professional fields themselves.

Accompanying the sample research paper is a series of checksheets to help you set up a research paper correctly. When your research paper meets the specifications described on the checksheets, the essay should be in proper form.

▶ **If your instructor asks for a separate title page, follow the form on the following page.** MLA style does not require such a separate cover sheet; many instructors, however, will expect one. If your instructor does *not* want a separate title page, turn to page 614.

✓ Arrange and center the title of your paper, your name, the course title (and section number if required), your instructor's name, and the date of submission.

✓ Use the correct form for your title. Capitalize the first word and the last word. Capitalize all other words in the title *except* articles (*a, an, the*), and prepositions and conjunctions under five letters—unless they are the first or last words.

{**Right**}   Chrysler's Sales Bank

Do not underline a title, capitalize every letter in it, place it between quotation marks, or terminate it with a period:

{**Wrong**}   Chrysler's Sales Bank

{**Wrong**}   CHRYSLER'S SALES BANK

{**Wrong**}   "Chrysler's Sales Bank"

{**Wrong**}   Chrysler's Sales Bank.

Titles may, however, include words or phrases that appear between quotation marks or are underlined. They may also end with question marks:

{**Right**}   Marriage in Shakespeare's As You Like It

{**Right**}   Dylan's "Like a Rolling Stone" Reconsidered

{**Right**}   Who Really Wrote Hamlet?

✓ Identify your instructor by an appropriate title. When uncertain about academic rank, use Mr. or Ms.

Dr. Lynda Boose   Professor Rodi   Ms. Nancy Peterson

39 C

MLA

Chrysler's Sales Bank

by

James Balarbar

English 306

Prof. John Ruszkiewicz

10 November 1985

➤ **If your instructor requires an outline,** place it immediately after the title page. Whether you use a sentence or phrase outline, be sure to observe correct form. (If your instructor does not require such an outline, go to p. 612.)

✓ Begin the outline with the thesis statement of the paper.

✓ Double-space the entire outline and align headings and subheadings carefully. Both sentence and phrase outlines should be double-spaced and consistently aligned, following this pattern:

I. -

   A. - - - - - - - - - - - - - - - - - -

   B. - - - - - - - - - - - - - - - - - -

      1. - - - - - - - - - - - - - - - -

      2. - - - - - - - - - - - - - - - -

      3. - - - - - - - - - - - - - - - -

         a. - - - - - - - - - - - - - -

         b. - - - - - - - - - - - - - -

   C. - - - - - - - - - - - - - - - - - -

II. -

39 C

MLA

Outline

Thesis: A major cause of the Chrysler Corporation's near-bankruptcy in 1979-80 was a concept called "the sales bank," which exemplified the lack of coordination between the company's management, manufacturing, and sales divisions.

I. Introduction
   A. Chrysler's poor management
   B. The sales bank
II. Definition and purpose of Chrysler's sales bank concept
III. Problems with sales bank
   A. No input from dealers or consumers in deciding what kinds of cars to manufacture
   B. High costs for storing and maintaining inventories of unsold cars
   C. Poor quality of cars built under quota pressures
IV. Consequences of sales bank
   A. Loss of the goodwill of consumers
   B. Loss of leverage over dealers
   C. Loss of control over accounting procedures
V. Conclusions
   A. Drain on Chrysler's finances
   B. Erosion of consumer confidence in Chrysler as auto manufacturer

An outline preceding a short paper will probably not need to go beyond the second or third level. If a line runs beyond the right margin, it carries over to the left and picks up at a point directly below where it started (see line **B.** above). No number or letter at any level of a formal outline stands alone. If you have a point **A.,** there must be a point **B.;** a point **1.** requires a corresponding point **2.**

✓ Do not number an outline that runs only a single page. One that requires more pages is numbered—along with all other items in the front matter—in small Roman numerals (i, ii, iii, iv). However, the first page is still unnumbered.

39 C

MLA

Chrysler's Sales Bank

¶1   The old Chrysler Corporation was an excellent example of how not to run a business. Its management was shortsighted and disorganized; its method of conducting business, completely unorthodox. In fact, according to Lee Iacocca, chairman of the reformed company,

> . . . Chrysler didn't really function like a company at all. Chrysler in 1978 was like Italy in the 1860's--the company consisted of little duchies, each one run by a prima donna. It was a bunch of mini-empires, with nobody giving a damn about what anyone else was doing. (152)[1]

¶2   However, if a business is to prosper, it must have a central authority, "coordination and a unity of purpose" (Albers 206). Unfortunately, the company lacked this focused collaboration and was almost financially destroyed. A major cause of the Chrysler Corporation's near-bankruptcy in 1979-80 was a concept called "the sales bank," which exemplified the lack of coordination between the company's management, manufacturing, and sales divisions.

¶3   Before Lee Iacocca arrived at the company, the sales bank was Chrysler's method of manufacturing and selling automobiles. The idea of a sales bank was conceived by Lynn Townsend, chairman of the corporation from 1960 to 1975, described as a good manager, "a long ball hitter who occasionally struck out" (McDowell, "Reassessing Townsend" 7). By this method, the management would set a quota on the number of cars to be built. Manufacturing produced the cars at regular rates, filled its production quota, and stored the cars on huge lots--sales bank lots. Marketing of these cars was left to the sales division. The sales bank method was supposed "to compensate for the disadvantages of [Chrysler's] relatively small size," "to keep plants running smoothly," and "to keep pressure on the salesmen and dealers" (Moritz and Seaman 87).

➤ **First page of the text of an essay with a separate title page (MLA).** If your paper has a separate title page, the first page of the body of your paper will look like the facing page. Be sure to check all the items in the list.

✓ Repeat the title of your paper, exactly as it appears on the title page, on the first page of the body of the paper about two inches from the top of the sheet.

✓ Center the title and capitalize it properly.

✓ Begin the body of the essay two lines (a double space) below the title.

✓ Double-space the entire body of the essay, including all quotations.

✓ Use one-inch margins at the sides and bottom of this page; use one-inch margins all around (including at the top) on all subsequent pages.

✓ Indent the first lines of paragraphs five spaces.

✓ Indent long quotations (more than four typed lines) ten spaces.

✓ Number this first page in the upper right-hand corner, one half inch from the top, one inch from the right margin. Include your name.

39 C

MLA

James Balarbar

Prof. Ruszkiewicz

English 306

10 November 1985

Chrysler's Sales Bank

¶1   The old Chrysler Corporation was an excellent example of how not to run a business. Its management was shortsighted and disorganized; its method of conducting business, completely unorthodox. In fact, according to Lee Iacocca, chairman of the reformed company,

> . . . Chrysler didn't really function like a company at all. Chrysler in 1978 was like Italy in the 1860's--the company consisted of little duchies, each one run by a prima donna. It was a bunch of mini-empires, with nobody giving a damn about what anyone else was doing. (152)[1]

¶2   However, if a business is to prosper, it must have a central authority, "coordination and a unity of purpose" (Albers 206). Unfortunately, the company lacked this focused collaboration and was almost financially destroyed. A major cause of the Chrysler Corporation's near-bankruptcy in 1979-80 was a concept called "the sales bank," which exemplified the lack of coordination between the company's management, manufacturing, and sales division.

¶3   Before Lee Iacocca arrived at the company, the sales bank was Chrysler's method of manufacturing and selling automobiles. The idea of a sales bank was conceived by Lynn Townsend, chairman of the corporation from 1960 to 1975, described as a good manager, "a long ball hitter who occasionally struck out" (McDowell, "Reassessing Townsend" 7). By this method, the management would set a quota on the number of cars to be built. Manufacturing produced the cars at regular rates, filled its production quota, and stored the cars on huge lots--sales bank lots. Marketing of these cars was left to the sales division. The sales bank method was supposed "to compensate for the disadvantages of [Chrysler's] relatively small size," "to keep plants running smoothly," and "to keep pressure on the salesmen and dealers" (Moritz and Seaman 87).

➤ **If your instructor does not require a separate title page (MLA),** the first page of your paper should look like the facing page.

✓ Place your name, instructor's name, course title, and the date in the upper left-hand corner, beginning one inch from the top of the paper. The items are double-spaced.

✓ Identify your instructor by an appropriate title. When uncertain about academic rank, use Mr. or Ms.

Dr. James Duban	Professor Farmer
Mr. Richard Sha	Dr. Charlton Ryan

✓ Center the title a double-space under the date. Use the correct form for the title. (See p. 607 for the complete guidelines.)

✓ Begin the body of the essay two lines (a double space) below the title. Double-space the entire body of the essay, including quotations.

✓ Use one-inch margins at the sides and the bottom of this page.

✓ Number this first page in the upper right-hand corner, one-half inch from the top, one inch from the right margin.

39 C

MLA

¶4   However, the sales bank strategy backfired--disastrously. To begin with, the management almost never consulted the sales division or dealers before deciding what kinds of cars to produce. Manufacturing, which was geared primarily toward filling the inventory quotas, haphazardly added options to each car. Consequently many of the cars were not equipped the way buyers wanted them to be and proved difficult to sell. At the close of 1979, the sales bank routine had piled 80,000 cars into Chrysler's central inventory and 355,000 automobiles sat in dealer showrooms (Vitullo-Martin 22). Those 80,000 cars in inventory alone were worth $700 million. Moreover, the cost of storing the vehicles in the inventory lots was a staggering $2 million per week (22). The money covered rising interest rates on the storage lot rentals and regular maintenance and repairs on the stored cars, such as "recharging batteries, pumping and changing tires, [and] replacing broken windshields" (Moritz and Seaman 93). These were all expenses Chrysler didn't need, especially in times of economic slowdown (Reginald 15).

¶5   Unfortunately, the storage costs were not the only drain on Chrysler's resources. Because the manufacturing division was pressed for time in filling its quotas, it built poor-quality automobiles. In Going for Broke, Moritz and Seaman explain how bad the production situation could get:

> Sometimes the quality deteriorated to such an extent that the [assembly] lines were stopped. One engineer (now retired) made some spot checks. He discovered a Plymouth sitting at a Detroit railhead with no engine mountings, the engine just resting on the frame. (92)

¶6   As an indirect result of the sales bank, between September 1966 and July 1978, Chrysler made "2447 recalls involving 71 million cars, some of which were recalled several times" (Yates 236). The company at one time was widely respected for the dependability of its cars and for engineering innovations such as the high compression engine, the alternator (McDowell, "Behind Chrysler's Decline" 12), automatic transmission, power brakes, and power steering (Vitullo-Martin 23). However, the corporate reputation was tarnished after the

39 C

MLA

➤ **Body of the essay.** The body of an MLA research paper continues uninterrupted until the separate *Notes* page (if any) and the *Works Cited* page. Be sure to type or handwrite the essay on good quality paper.

✓ Use margins of at least one inch all around. Try to keep the right-hand margin reasonably straight. But avoid hyphenating words whenever possible. If you must divide longer words, be sure to break them at syllable divisions (see the discussion of hyphens in Section 34B).

✓ Place page numbers in the upper right-hand corner, one inch from the right edge of the page and half an inch from the top. Type your first initial and last name before each page number.

✓ Indent the first line of paragraphs five spaces.

✓ Indent long quotations ten spaces.

39 C

MLA

introduction, in 1975, of the Plymouth Volaré and Dodge Aspen, which both
earned the Center for Auto Safety's "Lemon of the Year" citation in 1977 (Sobel
253-54). According to Iacocca, the Volaré and Aspen were introduced while they
"were still in the development phase" and "should have been delayed a full six
months" before they were released to the marketplace (160). Engines stalled,
brakes failed, hoods flew open at "high speeds," and fenders rusted because of
improper galvanization (Sobel 254). Chrysler lost $200 million and much of its
good will with the public because of the costly recalls the Volaré and Aspen required. These recalls and losses, however, could have been prevented had the company concentrated more on quality rather than quantity as prescribed by the
sales bank practices. Hence, even Lynn Townsend's objective of smooth-running
plants was defeated.

¶7   Not only did Chrysler lose good will; it lost respect as an automobile sup-
plier as well. As Iacocca explains it, dealers learned to take advantage of the
company. Since the manufacturer immediately sold its cars to the wholesalers
who stored them on the inventory lots, the retailers bargained directly with the
wholesalers. Because the sales bank foolishly focused on quantity and kept putting cars into the inventories, monthly "fire sales" were needed to make room for
the new incoming units. The dealers soon learned that the wholesalers became
desperate to move the older cars. So the retail marketers capitalized on that
panic by waiting until the last week of each month to barter for less than the
regular "wholesale price" (Iacocca 163). The sales bank system, in effect, removed from sales personnel and dealers the pressure it was designed to create.
The retailers were in control. The company lost more money.

¶8   When the sales bank inventory became too large and the sales division
could not unload all of the cars to the dealers, the company covered up its losses
on quarterly sales reports with stealthy accounting tricks. The manufacturing
division concealed its losses by recording its profits immediately after passing
the inventory to the sales division even though the cars had not actually been

sold to customers (Moritz and Seaman 91). Furthermore, the corporation shuffled the excess inventory between its major divisions, such as the Chrysler Leasing Company, so that the corporation could show sales to balance its sales reports. One leasing official conceded that "We were robbing Peter to pay Paul" (93). Ronald Horwitz, a business professor at the University of Michigan, observed at the time that this type of action makes the company "look better on the profit-and-loss statements but . . . does great harm over the long haul" (McDowell, "Behind Chrysler's Decline" 12).

¶9   The old Chrysler did eventually have to pay Peter. The management was only fooling itself with its cover-ups and inefficient sales bank practices. Although the sales bank was designed to improve Chrysler, it actually drained the corporation of both its financial resources and its credibility. The unusual business procedure had put the company under the "millstone effect" (Skinner 533-34). According to this business theory, the old corporation failed to "recognize the relationship between manufacturing decisions and corporate strategy [so it became] saddled with seriously noncompetitive production systems which [were] expensive and time-consuming to change" (533-34). The sales bank's inability to pressure retail dealers, the production of poorly-built vehicles, and the chaotic shuffling of inventories were all results of Chrysler's "noncompetitive production systems." The bottom line is that the sales bank and other management mistakes eventually cost the old Chrysler Corporation $3.3 billion (Nicholson and Jones 64). It took Lee Iacocca and a new team of managers more than five grueling years to reform the company, deliver it from red ink, and restore the good will of its customers.[2] But that's another story.

39 C

MLA

Notes

[1]Lee Iacocca joined Chrysler in November 1978 after Henry Ford II removed him from the Presidency of the Ford Motor Company. See Iacocca 120-53; Moritz and Seaman 196-97.

[2]According to Stuart Reginald, within his first year as President of Chrysler, Iacocca had abolished the sales bank: "Come hell or high water, we are never going to do it again!" (15).

▶ **The Notes page (MLA).** If a paper includes any content or bibliography notes (see p. 561), they appear on a separate page entitled *Notes* immediately after the body of the essay.

✓ Center the title *Notes* at the top of the page.

✓ List all the notes in the order they occur in the paper.

✓ The number of the note is raised slightly above the regular line. If typing, turn the carriage a half line. On a computer, select "superscript" in the character menu. Skip a space after the number.

✓ Be sure to number the notes page in the upper right-hand corner.

39 C

MLA

Works Cited

Albers, Henry H. Principles of Management. 3rd ed. New York: Wiley, 1969.

Iacocca, Lee. Iacocca: An Autobiography. New York: Bantam, 1984.

McDowell, Edwin. "Behind Chrysler's Long Decline: Its Management and Competi-
    tion." New York Times 17 Aug. 1979, A1+.

---. "Reassessing Lynn Townsend." New York Times 12 Aug. 1979, sec. 3: 7.

Moritz, Michael, and Barrett Seaman. Going for Broke: Lee Iacocca's Battle to Save
    Chrysler. Garden City, New York: Anchor-Doubleday, 1984.

Nicholson, Tom, and James C. Jones. "Iacocca's Little Miracle." Newsweek 3 Aug.
    1981: 64-65.

Reginald, Stuart. "On the Firing Line at Chrysler." New York Times 16 Sept. 1979,
    C7+.

Skinner, Wickman. "Manufacturing Link in Corporate Strategy." Harvard Busi-
    ness Review on Management. New York: Harper, 1975.

Sobel, Robert. Car Wars. New York: Dutton, 1984.

Vitullo-Martin, Julia. "Chrysler in Chaos: Is the Chrysler Company Beyond Re-
    pair?" Saturday Review 19 Jan. 1980: 22-25.

Yates, Brock W. The Decline and Fall of the American Automobile Industry. New
    York: Empire, 1983.

39 C

MLA

➤ **The Works Cited page (MLA).** The *Works Cited* list contains full bibliographical information on all the books, articles, and other resources used in composing the paper. For more information about the purpose and form of this list, see pp. 588–606.

✓ Center the title "Works Cited" at the top of the page.

✓ Include in the "Works Cited" list all the sources actually mentioned in the paper. Do not include materials you examined but did not cite in the body of the paper itself.

✓ Arrange the items in the "Works Cited" list alphabetically by the last name of the author. If no author is given for a work, list it according to its title, excluding articles (*the, a, an*).

✓ Be sure the first line of each entry touches the left-hand margin. Subsequent lines are indented five spaces.

✓ Double-space the entire list. Do not quadruple-space between entries unless that is the form your teacher prefers.

✓ Punctuate items in the list carefully. Don't forget the period at the end of each entry.

✓ Follow this form if you have two or more entries by the same author:

Altick, Richard D. The Shows of London. Cambridge: Belknap-

Harvard, 1978.

---. Victorian Studies in Scarlet. New York: Norton, 1977.

39 C

MLA

40 Writing an APA Paper

A APA documentation

B APA form directory

C Sample APA paper

40 A USING APA DOCUMENTATION

Troubleshooting

In many college courses (anthropology, astronomy, business, education, home economics, linguistics, political science, psychology, and sociology), you may be expected to follow the conventions of documentation recommended by the American Psychological Association (APA). A full explanation of APA procedures is provided by the *Publication Manual of the American Psychological Association,* 3rd edition (1983) available in most college libraries and bookstores. The basic procedures for APA documentation are summarized in the remainder of this section.

APA Overview: Follow these two basic steps.

➤ **Step 1: Insert an in-text note to identify the sources of each passage or idea you must document.**

> While Beethoven enjoyed prosperity and success through 1815,
>
> his deafness continued to grow until he became "morose, irascible,
>
> and morbidly suspicious even toward his friends" **(Grout, 1980,**
>
> **p. 540).**

➤ **Step 2: On a separate page at the end of the paper, list every source cited in a parenthetical note. This alphabetical list of sources is labeled** *References.*

References

Grout, D. J. (1980). A history of western music. 3rd. ed. New York:

Norton.

To use APA documentation . . .

➤ **Step 1: Insert an in-text note to identify the source of each passage or idea you must document.** The basic form of the APA parenthetical note consists of the author's last name and a date. A comma follows the author's name.

> (Grout, 1980)

A page number may be given for indirect citations and *must* be given for direct quotations. A comma follows the date if page numbers are given. Page numbers are preceded by **p.** or **pp.**

> (Grout, 1980, p. 540)
>
> (Iacocca, 1984, pp. 254–55)

The note is ordinarily located conveniently after a passage requiring documentation, often at the end of a sentence.

> While Beethoven enjoyed prosperity and success through 1815, his deafness continued to grow until he became "morose, irascible, and morbidly suspicious even toward his friends" **(Grout, 1980, p. 540).**

More typical of APA documentation is the note that cites the work of a researcher rather than a specific passage. In such cases, the researcher is ordinarily named and the year of his or her publication follows in parentheses.

> According to **Grunman (1984),** children fed a diet free of the chemical additive had fewer behavioral problems than those who ingested it regularly.

The documentation may also be distributed throughout the passage.

> **Grout (1980)** observes that while Beethoven enjoyed prosperity and success through 1815, his deafness continued to grow until he became "morose, irascible, and morbidly suspicious even toward his friends" **(p. 540).**

When a single source provides a series of references, the name of the author is not repeated until other sources interrupt the series. After the first reference, page numbers are sufficient until another citation intervenes.

> . . . The council vetoed the zoning approval of a mall and shopping district intended for an area described by **Martinez (1982)** as one

40 A

APA

of the last outposts of undisturbed nature in the state. The aquifer
area provides a "unique environment for several endangered species
of birds and plant life" **(p. 31).** The birds, especially the endangered
vireo, require breeding areas free from the encroaching signs of
development: roads, lights, and human presence **(Harrison &
Cafiero, 1979).** The plant life is similarly susceptible to soil
erosion that has followed land development in other areas of the
county **(Martinez, 1982).**

As with MLA notes, APA parenthetical notes should be as brief and incon-
spicuous as possible. The exact forms for many kinds of parenthetical notes
(books, articles, movies, collections, and so on) and their accompanying *References* entries are provided in the **APA form directory** on pp. 629–635.

Special Circumstances:

▶ **When two or more sources are used in a single sentence,** the notes are inserted
as needed conveniently after the statements they support.

While Porter **(1981)** suggests that the ecology of the aquifer might
be hardier than originally suspected "Given the size of the drainage
area and the nature of the subsurface rock **(p. 62),** there is no
reason to believe that the best interests of the county would be
served by the creation of a mall and shopping district in a vicinity
described as "one of the last outposts of undisturbed nature in the
state" **(Martinez, 1982, p. 28).**

40 A
APA

Notice that a parenthetical note is placed outside of quotation marks but before a
period ending a sentence.

• When a work has two authors, both names are given in all references.

(Harrison & Cafiero, 1979)

Notice that an ampersand **(&)** is used between the authors' names rather than
the *and* used in MLA.

• When a work has three or more authors, all of them are named in the first
parenthetical note.

(Harrison, Cafiero, & Dixon, 1979).

All subsequent notes then use **et al.** (Latin abbreviation for *and others*).

(Harrison et al., 1979)

• When more than one work written by an author in a single year is cited in a paper, assign a small letter after the date to distinguish between the author's works from the same year.

> (Harrison, 1981a)
>
> (Harrison, 1981b)

> The charge is raised by Harrison (1981**a**), quickly answered by Anderson (1981), and then raised again by Harrison (1981**b**).

• When you must document a work without an author, list the title, shortened if necessary, and the date. For a direct quotation, provide a page number.

> ("Aid to education," 1985)
>
> ("Subtle art," 1985, p. 62)

References

Aid to education and health cut by $38-million. (1985, December

18). The Chronicle of Higher Education, p. 11.

The subtle art of stubble. (1985, December 9). Newsweek, p. 62.

▶ **Step 2: On a separate page at the end of the paper, list every source cited in a parenthetical note. This alphabetical list of sources is labeled *References*.** The *References* page appears after and separate from the body of the essay itself and a footnote page—when there is one. The format for a *References* page is given on p. 646. Be sure to double space all entries in your list. The first line of each entry touches the left-hand margin and subsequent lines are indented three spaces.

Entries on the *References* page are listed alphabetically, by the last names of authors. If a work has more than one author, all authors are listed in the entry. An ampersand **(&)** is used where MLA documentation uses *and*.

> Clark, M., & Stadtman, N.

40 A

APA

If a work has no given author, it is listed by title and alphabetized by the first word in the title, excluding *a, an,* and *the*. Several works by the same author are listed alphabetically under that author's name.

A typical APA References entry for a book includes the following basic information.

• Name of author(s), last name first, followed by a period. Initials are substituted for first names unless two authors mentioned in the paper have identical last names and first initials.

> Peterson, R. T.

• Date in parentheses, followed by a period.

> (1963).

- Title of work, underlined, followed by a period. Only the first word and proper nouns are capitalized.

    <u>A field guide to the birds of Texas.</u>

- Place of publication, followed by a colon.

    Boston:

- Publisher, followed by a period.

    Norton.

    Peterson, R. T. (1963). <u>A field guide to the birds of Texas.</u> Boston:

    Norton.

A typical APA References entry for an article in a scholarly journal (where the pagination is continuous through a year) includes the following basic information.

- Name of author(s), last name first, followed by a period. Initials are substituted for first names unless two authors mentioned in the paper have identical last names and first initials.

    O'Meara, J. T.

- Date in parentheses, followed by a period.

    (1989).

40 A

APA

- Title of the article, followed by a period. Only the first word and proper nouns are capitalized. The title does not appear between quotation marks.

    Anthropology as empirical science.

- Name of the periodical, underlined, followed by a comma. All major words are capitalized.

    <u>American Anthropologist,</u>

- Volume number, underlined, followed by a comma, page numbers, and a period.

    <u>91,</u> 354–69.

    O'Meara, J. T. (1989). Anthropology as empirical science. <u>American</u>

    <u>Anthropologist, 91,</u> 354–69.

A typical APA *References* entry for an article in a popular magazine or newspaper includes the following basic information.

- Name of author(s), last name first, followed by a period. Initials are substituted for first names unless two authors mentioned in the paper have identical last names and first initials.

> Cole, D.

- Date in parentheses, followed by a period and two spaces. Give the year first, followed by the month (do not abbreviate it), followed by the day, if necessary.

> (1989, June).

- Title of work, followed by a period. Only the first word and proper nouns are capitalized. The title does not appear between quotation marks.

> The entrepreneurial self.

- Name of the periodical, underlined, followed by a comma. All major words are capitalized.

> Psychology Today,

- Page or location indicated by the abbreviation *p.* or *pp.,* followed by a period.

> pp. 60–63.

> Cole, D. (1989, June). The entrepreneurial self. Psychology Today,
>
> pp. 60–63.

There are so many variations to these generic entries, however, that you will probably want to check the *Publication Manual of the American Psychological Association* (1983) when you do a major APA-style paper.

40 B

APA

40 B APA FORM DIRECTORY

Below, you will find the APA *References* page and parenthetical note forms for a variety of sources. Simply find the type of work you need to cite in either the Format Index or the Alphabetical Index and then locate that work by number in the list that follows the indexes. The numbers for the entries below pick up where the *MLA Form Directory* entries leave off. Numbers 1–62 are MLA forms (see pages 588–606.)

APA Format Index

63. Book, one author
64. Book, two authors
65. Book, three or more authors
66. Book, revised
67. Book, edited
68. Book with no author

69. Book, a collection or anthology
70. Work within a collection or anthology
71. Chapter within a book
72. Article in a journal paginated by the year or volume, not issue by issue
73. Article in a journal or magazine paginated issue by issue
74. Article in a weekly or biweekly magazine
75. Article in a monthly magazine, author named
76. Article in a monthly magazine, no author named
77. Newspaper article, author named
78. Newspaper article, no author named
79. Computer software
80. Movie/videotape/audiotape
81. Review of a book

APA Alphabetical Index

40 B

APA

63. Book, One Author—APA

References

Pearson, G. (1949). Emotional disorders of children. Annapolis, MD: Naval Institute Press.

Parenthetical notes:

Pearson (1949) found . . .

(Pearson, 1949)

(Pearson, 1949, p. 49)

64. Book, Two Authors—APA

References

Lasswell, H. D., & Kaplan, A. (1950). Power and society: A framework for political inquiry. New York: Yale University Press.

Parenthetical notes:

Lasswell and Kaplan (1949) found . . .

(Lasswell & Kaplan, 1949)

(Lasswell & Kaplan, 1949, pp. 210–213)

65. Book, Three Authors or More—APA

References

Rosenberg, B., Gerver, I., & Howton, F. W. (1971). Mass society in crisis: Social problems and social pathology (2nd ed.). New York: Macmillan.

Parenthetical notes:

First note. Rosenberg, Gerver, and Howton (1971) found . . .

Subsequent notes. Rosenberg et al. (1971) found . . .

First note. (Rosenberg, Gerver, & Howton, 1971)

Subsequent notes. (Rosenberg et al., 1971)

66. Book, Revised—APA

40 B

APA

References

Edelmann, A. T. (1969). Latin American government and politics (rev. ed.). Homewood, IL: Dorsey.

Parenthetical notes:

Edelmann (1969) found . . .

(Edelmann, 1969)

(Edelmann, 1969, p. 62)

67. Book, Edited—APA

References

Journet, D., & Kling, J. (Eds.). (1984). Readings for technical writers. Glenview, IL: Scott, Foresman.

Parenthetical notes:

Journet and Kling (1984) observe . . .

(Journet & Kling, 1984)

68. Book with No Author—APA

References

Illustrated atlas of the world. (1985). Chicago: Rand, McNally.

Parenthetical notes:

in Illustrated Atlas (1985) . . .

(Illustrated Atlas, 1985, pp. 88–89)

69. Book, a Collection or Anthology—APA

References

Feinstein. C. H. (Ed.) (1967). Socialism, capitalism, and economic growth. Cambridge: Cambridge University Press.

Parenthetical notes:

Feinstein (1967) found . . .

(Feinstein, 1967)

70. Work within a Collection or Anthology—APA

References

Patel, S. (1967). World economy in transition (1850–2060). In C. H. Feinstein (Ed.), Socialism, capitalism, and economic growth (pp. 255–270). Cambridge: Cambridge University Press.

40 B

APA

Parenthetical notes:

Patel (1967) found . . .

(Patel, 1967)

71. Chapter within a Book—APA

References

Clark, K. (1969). Heroic materialism. In Civilisation (pp. 321–47). New York: Harper.

Parenthetical notes:

Clark (1969) observes . . .

(Clark, 1969)

72. Article in a Journal Paginated by the Year or Volume, Not Issue by Issue—APA

References

Kroll, B. (1984). Audience adaption in children's persuasive letters. Written Communication, 1, 407–27.

Parenthetical notes:

Kroll (1984) observes ...

(Kroll, 1984, p. 409)

73. Article in a Journal or Magazine Paginated Issue by Issue—APA

References

Lemonick, M. D. (1985, December), Jupiter's second ring. Science Digest, p. 13.

Parenthetical notes:

Lemonick (1985) notes ...

(Lemonick, 1985)

74. An Article in a Weekly or Biweekly Magazine—APA

References

Day, K. (1989, March 20). When hell sleazes over. The New Republic, pp. 26–30.

Parenthetical notes:

Day (1985) notes ...

(Day, 1985)

(Day, 1985, p. 27)

40 B

APA

75. Article in a Monthly Magazine, Author Named—APA

References

White, C. P. (1986, January). Freshwater turtles—designed for survival. National Geographic, pp. 40–59.

Parenthetical notes:

White (1986) observes ...

(White, 1986)

76. Article in a Monthly Magazine, No Author Named—APA

References

Engineered plants resist herbicide. (1986, January). <u>High Technol-</u>
<u>ogy,</u> p. 9.

Parenthetical notes:

in the article "Engineered plants" (1986) . . .

("Engineered plants," 1986)

Notice that quotation marks surround the shortened title of the article cited in the body of the paper but not in the references list.

77. Newspaper Article, Author Named—APA

References

Pine, A. (1989, July 15). Bush promises to help Mexico reduce its
debt. <u>The Austin American-Statesman,</u> pp. 1, 12.

When an article appears across several discontinuous pages, they are listed as in the entry above.

Parenthetical notes:

Pine (1989) reports . . .

(Pine, 1986, p. 12)

78. Newspaper Article, No Author Named—APA

References

S&L bailout panel mired in bickering. (1989, July 14). <u>The Austin</u>
<u>American-Statesman,</u> p. G1.

Parenthetical notes:

in the article "S&L bailout" (1989) . . .

("S&L bailout," 1989)

79. Computer Software—APA

References

Crawford, C. (1985). <u>Balance of power</u> [Computer program]. North-
brook, IL: Mindscape, SFN.

Parenthetical notes:

Crawford (1985) includes . . .

(Crawford, 1985)

80. Movie/Videotape/Audiotape—APA

References

Zeffirelli, F. (Director). (1968). <u>Romeo and Juliet</u> [Videotape].

   Hollywood, CA: Paramount Home Video.

This is the basic form for films, audiotapes, slides, charts, and other non-print sources. The specific type of media is described between brackets, as shown above for a videocassette.

Parenthetical notes:

Zeffirelli (1968) features . . .

(Zeffirelli, 1968)

81. Book Review—APA

References

Farquhar, J. (1987). [Review of <u>Medical power and social knowl-</u>

   <u>edge</u>]. <u>American Journal of Psychology, 94,</u> 256.

Notice that brackets surround the description of the article, which in this case has no title. If the review had a title, that title would precede the description—which would still be included in the entry.

Parenthetical notes:

Farquhar (1987) observes . . .

(Farquhar, 1987)

40 C

APA

40 C SAMPLE APA PAPER

This final version of an essay by Lori S. McWilliams has been revised to enhance its usefulness as a model. As a result of these changes, some material has been dropped and a few paragraphs reshaped. The language has been sharpened and mechanical errors edited. Yet the bulk of the essay remains just as Lori McWilliams wrote it in her freshman year.

Acupuncture: Energy or Nerves?

Lori S. McWilliams

The University of Texas at Austin

40 C

APA

▶ **The title page for a paper (APA).** APA style requires a separate title page; use the facing page as a model and review the following checklist.

Arrange and center the title of your paper, your name, and your school.

Use the correct form for the title, capitalizing all important words and all words of four letters or more. Articles, conjunctions, and prepositions are not capitalized unless they are four letters or more. Do not underline the title or use all capitals.

Number the cover sheet and all subsequent pages in the upper right-hand corner. Place a short title for the paper a double-space above the page number as shown; the short title consists of the first two or three words of the title.

40 C

APA

Abstract

Western science has long had doubts about acupuncture, an oriental technique for relieving pain. But both eastern and western traditions offer useful perspectives on how acupuncture works. According to Chinese tradition, acupuncture operates by directing the flow of energy through the body, which flows along channels called meridians. Western scientists think that acupuncture works either by interrupting pain messages conveyed by the nervous system or by stimulating the production of natural pain-killing substances in the body called endorphins. These explanations are not necessarily incompatible with the explanations of Chinese tradition.

40 C

APA

➤ **An abstract (APA).** Abstracts are common in papers using APA style. For information on preparing an abstract, see Chapter 43. (If your instructor does not require an abstract, go to p. 641.)

✓ Place the abstract on a separate page, after the cover sheet.

✓ Center the word *Abstract* at the top of the page.

✓ Include the short title of the essay and the page number (2) in the upper right-hand corner.

✓ Double-space the abstract.

✓ Do not indent the first line of the abstract. Type it in block form.

40 C

APA

Acupuncture: Energy or Nerves?

Pain plagues many people. A person who experiences chronic pain experiences an invasive problem: the pain becomes part of every aspect of life. All too often, a victim tries to find relief through over-the-counter or prescription drugs. But the pain persists. Western science has continually manipulated chemistry to produce analgesics; science has also tried to relieve pain through surgery. Despite advances in treatment, Holzman (1986) notes that "there is still no satisfactory set of treatments to consistently and permanently alleviate all sources of pain" (p. 2). One technique that is effective in up to 65% of all cases of chronic pain is the ancient Chinese technique of acupuncture (Langone, 1984). Physicians and scientists in the United States, however, have long been suspicious of acupuncture, in part because of doubts about how it works. Eastern practitioners believe acupuncture relieves pain by adjusting the innate energy within the body; western scientists believe that acupuncture must work through the nervous system. In fact, both of these views--eastern and western--can contribute to an understanding of how acupuncture works.

40 C

APA

According to Langone, the process of acupuncture involves "the insertion of hair-thin needles, singly or in combination, into the strategic points on the body to ease pain and treat a myriad of ailments" (p. 70). Needles used for insertion vary in length, anywhere from ½ an inch to 3 inches. In the past, acupuncture needles have been made of gold, silver, copper, brass, bone, flint, and stone (Duke, 1972). Rose-Neil (1979) notes that the earliest acupuncture needles were made of stone and called "stone piercers" or "stone borers" (p. 56). The material used for the needles today is 26-32 gauge stainless steel.

Acupuncture needles are inserted into the body at approximately 360 different locations from head to toe. Since the points or acupoints to be needled depend upon a patient's ailment, an acupuncturist must assess a patient's condition and needs. After a diagnosis, the acupuncturist inserts the needles and manipulates them either by manual or electrical rotation. As the points are stimulated, pain relief follows.

➤ **The body of the paper (APA).** The body of the APA paper runs uninterrupted until the separate *References* page. Be sure to type or handwrite the essay on good-quality paper. The first page of an APA paper will look like the facing page.

✓ Repeat the title of your paper, exactly as it appears on the title page, on the first page of the research essay itself.

✓ Be sure the title is centered and properly capitalized.

✓ Begin the body of the essay two lines (a double-space) below the title.

✓ Double-space the body of the essay.

✓ Use 1-½-inch margins at the sides, top, and bottom of this and all subsequent pages.

✓ Indent the first lines of paragraphs five spaces.

✓ Indent long quotations (more than forty words) five spaces. In student papers, APA permits long quotations to be single-spaced.

✓ Include the short title of the essay and the page number (3) in the upper right-hand corner. Number all subsequent pages the same way.

✓ Do not hyphenate words at the right-hand margin.

40 C

APA

In China, time and tradition have proven the effectiveness of acupuncture. Chang (1976) traces the origins of acupuncture back 6000 years, but Langone (1984) believes that the Chinese have been using acupuncture medically for only about 2000 years. Rose-Neil (1979) gives this account of acupuncture's development in China:

> It was noted that soldiers wounded by arrows sometimes recovered from illnesses which had afflicted them for many years. The idea evolved that, by penetrating the skin at certain points, diseases were, apparently, cured. It was observed that the size of the wound did not matter, but only its location and depth. The Chinese began to copy the effects of the arrow, puncturing the skin with needles (p. 56).

Though the East believes in acupuncture, western doctors tended to dismiss acupuncture as almost whimsical. McGarey (1974) attributes this attitude to a western focus on the process of disease rather than on the body itself. Not until Richard Nixon's historic trip to China in 1970, however, did the West take a serious interest in the mechanisms of acupuncture. It was obvious that acupuncture worked, but the two cultures did not agree on how.

40 C

APA

To the Chinese, health is maintained by the flow of energy in the body. Chang (1976) cites this passage from the *Nei Ching*, an ancient collection of writings on acupuncture:

> The root of the way of life, of birth and change is Qi (energy); the myriad things of heaven and earth all obey this law. Thus Qi in the periphery envelopes heaven and earth, Qi in the interior activates them. The source wherefrom the sun, moon, and stars derive their light, the thunder, rain, wind, and cloud their being, the four seasons and the myriad things their birth, growth, gathering and storing: all this is brought about by Qi. Man's possession of life is completely dependent upon this Qi (p. 17).

As the passage suggests, the energy flowing within a body governs its existence. Stiefvater (1971) observes that "the Chinese viewed man as being ruled by the 'two great forces' which govern also our earth and our heaven" (p. 14). The two forces are the Yin and the Yang. Since Yin and Yang compose the energy that governs man and woman, when Yin and Yang are in balance, health results. If the equilibrium created by the forces is disturbed, the result is discomfort or disease.

To maintain health, the energy must be transported through the body by means of lines called meridians that conduct energy. Twelve acupuncture meridians exist in the body. Six of the meridians represent the six bowels: the gall bladder, the small and large intestines, the stomach, the bladder, and the triple heater. Kruger (1974) explains that the triple heater is an "imaginary organ . . . that controls [the flow of energy] Ch'i" (p. 46). Five other meridians represent the five major organs--the lungs, the heart, the spleen-pancreas (together forming one meridian), liver, and kidneys. The remaining meridian represents the pericardium. These meridians join the 360 acupuncture points, each corresponding to its organ. Thus, needling a specific point will affect a corresponding organ.

Meridians must constantly conduct energy throughout the body. Each meridian has a point of entry and a point of exit. The energy enters the meridian, flows through its entire length, then exits. Upon exit, the energy promptly enters another meridian and repeats its course (Chang, 1976). If the continuous flow is disrupted, pain and disease will occur. Since the body expends energy coping with the pain of an ailment, acupuncture intervenes by restoring energy so that the body may heal.

Western scientists, dismissing this concept of energy, prefer to explain acupuncture by reference to the nervous system. One early explanation--called the gate theory--suggested that pain is controlled by gates located in the brain and the spinal cord. Needles stimulating the body produce large impulses that flood the gates, thus preventing them from transmitting additional impulses and blocking pain. This theory was gradually refined. Benson (1979) suggests, for

40 C

APA

example, that acupuncture relieves pain by "either altering the capacity of the
nerves which carry impulses . . . or by changing the programming of the central
nervous system itself" (p. 128). Stimulating a nerve close to an acupoint inhibits
pain impulses to the brain. As Frank Warren puts it, "It's as if a fat man and a
thin man want to go through a doorway, and the fat man blocks the way" (Kruger,
1974, p. 66).

More recently, western scientists have proposed that the pain relief
achieved by acupuncture may be caused by endorphins. Endorphins are
naturally occurring, pain-killing substances produced by the body. Endorphins
kill pain as effectively as morphine; hence the name, endorphin, which
means "the morphine within" (Olshan, 1980, p. 6). Bruce Pomeranz of the
University of Toronto has conducted experiments based on endorphins and their
relationship to acupuncture. Using anesthetized animals, Pomerantz "located
cells that fire rapidly [within the brain] when the animal's toe was pricked with
a pin. Acupuncture slowed down those cells' firing, and within about 90 minutes
after acupuncture they recovered their normal response to pain" ("Neural,"
p. 234). Pomeranz discovered that acupuncture no longer worked when the
pituitary glands of his experimental animals were removed. This suggested that
the pituitary, not the brain, is the source of endorphins. Further studies on
animals and humans have produced evidence that some of the main acupuncture
points are near nerves. Tests also verified that the amount of endorphins in the
cerebro-spinal fluid and the blood increased after an acupuncture treatment
(Langone, 1984). Thus needling the skin stimulates nerve endings and releases
endorphins. Once within the blood, the endorphins bind with receptors in the
brain to block the transmission of pain signals. Interestingly, the Chinese have
long known that the closer an acupuncture point was to a nerve, the greater the
pain relief achieved by acupuncture (Chan, 1976).

The East believes that acupuncture relieves pain and sickness by restoring
an energy balance in the body. The West attributes its effects to the normal

workings of the nervous system. But both explanations have merit. In trying to understand the folk medicine of the East, western scientists have finally come to understand a pain-suppression mechanism not previously understood. Langone (1984) quotes a New York doctor who now asserts that "for pain, [acupuncture] is probably the safest treatment, with the fewest side effects and the greatest benefit. It should be the first line of defense, not the last" (p. 72).

40 C

APA

References

Benson, H. (1979). The mind / body effect. New York: Simon.

Chan, P. (1973). Wonders of Chinese acupuncture. Alhambra, CA: Borden.

Chang, S. T. (1976). The complete book of acupuncture. Millbrae, CA: Celestial
    Arts.

Duke, M. (1972). Acupuncture. New York: Jove.

Holzman, A. D. (1986). Pain management: A handbook of psychological treatment
    approaches. New York: Pergamon.

Kruger, H. (1974). Other healers, other cures: A guide to alternative medicine.
    Indianapolis: Bobbs-Merrill.

Langone, J. (1984, August). Acupuncture: A new respect for an ancient remedy.
    Discover, pp. 70-73.

McGarey, W. A. (1974). Acupuncture and body energies. Phoenix: Gabriel Press.

A neural mechanism for acupuncture. (1976, November 20). Science News, p. 234.

Olshan, N. H. (1980). Power over your pain without drugs. New York: Rawson,
    Wade.

Rose-Neil, S. (1979). Acupuncture. In Ann Hill (Ed.), A visual encyclopedia of
    unconventional medicine (pp. 64-65). New York: Crown.

Stiefvater, E. H. W. (1971). What is acupuncture? How does it work? Bradford:
    Health Science Press.

40 C

APA

➤ **The References page (APA).** Sources contributing directly to the paper are listed alphabetically on a separate sheet immediately after the body of the essay. For more information about the purpose and form of this list, see pages 629–635.

✓ Center the title *References* at the top of the page.

✓ All sources mentioned in the text of the paper must appear in the *References* list; similarly, every source listed in the *References* list must be mentioned in the paper.

✓ Arrange the items in the *References* list alphabetically by the last name of the author. Give initials only for first names. If no author is given for a work, list and alphabetize it by title.

✓ The first line of each entry is flush with the left-hand margin. Subsequent lines are indented three spaces.

✓ The list is ordinarily double-spaced. In student papers, APA style does permit single-spacing of individual entries; double-spacing is preserved between the single-spaced items.

✓ Punctuate items in the list carefully. Do not forget the period at the end of each entry.

✓ In the *References* list, capitalize only the first word and any proper names in the title of a book or article. Within a title, capitalize the first word after a colon.

✓ If you have two or more entries by the same author, list them by year of publication, from earliest to latest. If an author publishes two works in the same year, list them alphabetically by title.

40 C

APA

SPECIAL ASSIGNMENTS

This section provides basic advice about a variety of writing projects common in school and the professional world.

Chapter 41 briefly introduces the literary analysis—an assignment more manageable than most students realize. Chapter 42 outlines some practical strategies for writing effective essay examinations. Chapter 43 describes the abstract—a feature that introduces professional papers in many fields. Chapter 44 explains how to write a position paper, in which you are invited to register a frank opinion or reaction to something you have read or considered.

Both in school and in the professional world, you'll need to know how to write a business letter (Chapter 45), a memo (Chapter 46), and a résumé—with accompanying job application letter (Chapter 47). Finally, in Chapter 48, you'll find tips for delivering a successful oral report.

PART 6

41 Writing a Literary Analysis

Troubleshooting

Writing a literary analysis is a common assignment in most English courses, even in composition classes. But requirements and approaches vary from teacher to teacher and course to course. Clearly, instructors think about literature in different ways, depending upon their background, training, inclinations, and familiarity with literary theory. How you write about works of literature may depend as much upon how you are taught as what you are taught. Critical approaches to literature today can range from close readings of individual texts to wide-ranging confrontations with issues of politics and culture.

What then is the point of a literary analysis? It can be to heighten your appreciation for works of literature, to demonstrate your ability to support a thesis about a literary work, to give you skill at close reading and interpretation, to expand your appreciation for a particular culture, to explore what it means to read, to understand how readers respond to texts, or to heighten your sensitivity to other cultures, races, and peoples.

Obviously, in a few pages, we can't give you advice for dealing with all these possibilities. What we can do is give you a little practical advice for finding a subject and working with literary materials. Whatever your teachers' predilections, we hope that reading literature makes you wiser and gives you pleasure. Those two aims of literature have stood the test of time.

To write a successful literary analysis . . .

➤ **Begin by reading carefully.** The evidence you'll need to write a thoughtful, well-organized analysis may come from within the literary work itself and from outside readings and secondary sources. Your initial goal is to find a point worth making, an assertion you can prove with convincing evidence.

To find a point, you must obviously begin by reading the work (or works) carefully and recording—at first—your general reactions or major questions. Don't interrupt your reading to take detailed notes yet. Instead, savor the literary experience.

Then think about what you have just read. What issues interest you immediately? What questions did the piece raise that you'd like to explore more? Examine your preliminary list of issues and questions. If you had been reading *Macbeth,* here are the kinds of jottings you might produce.

The problem of ambition in Shakespeare's *Macbeth*

The relationship between Lady Macbeth and her husband

41

Lit

How old are the Macbeths?

Is the story of the Macbeths true?

Why are some lines in this tragedy funny?

The nature of Shakespearean tragedy

To stimulate more questions, you may want to compare and contrast the work(s) you have read with other similar works.

What makes both *Macbeth* and *Romeo and Juliet* tragic plays?

Is Macbeth as ambitious as King Claudius in *Hamlet?*

Is Lady Macbeth a more influential character in *Macbeth* than Queen Gertrude is in *Hamlet?*

Does Macbeth resemble Darth Vader?

Why does Shakespeare use comedy in *Hamlet, Romeo and Juliet,* and *Macbeth?*

At this point, you might stimulate your thinking both by considering various ways of approaching a literary text (see next step) or by using one of the techniques described earlier in this handbook for finding and focusing ideas, particularly freewriting, brainstorming, and treeing (see Chapter 3).

➤ **Understand the various approaches you can take to a literary analysis.** A few basic types of literary analyses are outlined below. When you write a literary paper, you will ordinarily limit yourself to one or two of these types in making your point.

• **Close reading of a text.** When doing a "close reading," you carefully explain the meaning and possible interpretations of a literary passage, sometimes line by line. You look carefully at how the language of the work makes a reader experience or think about certain images. You might do a close reading of a short poem, a speech from a play, or a passage from a longer work.

• **Analysis of theme.** You may examine the ideas or messages a literary work conveys to readers. A literary work may explore any number of themes (some general ones might be *anger, jealousy, ambition, hypocrisy, greed*), but most poems, plays, and novels sound one or two consistent notes.

• **Analysis of plot or structure.** You may study the way a work of literature is put together and why a writer chooses a particular arrangement of ideas or plot elements to say what he or she wants. You may look for evidence of these patterns in works of literature from different cultures, seeking common structures and themes.

• **Analysis of character.** You may study the behavior of characters in a novel, poem, play, or short story to understand their motivations and the ways characters can relate to each other. Or you explore how a writer creates a character through description, action, reaction, and dialogue.

• **Analysis of setting.** You study a writer's creation of a setting to figure out how the environment of a literary work (where things happen in a

41

Lit

novel, short story, or play) affects what happens in the plot or to the characters. Settings can also be analyzed as the exterior representations of characters' inner being.

- **Archetypal criticism.** When generalized themes, plots, characters, and settings are seen to represent the characteristic myths of entire cultures—the quest, the sacrificial lamb, the descent into hell—they are called literary *archetypes.* You can explore literary texts to reveal the cultural patterns they embody and the archetypes they incorporate, modify, or even parody.

- **Analysis of literary type or genre.** You study a particular literary work by evaluating its form, as a tragedy, comic novel, sonnet, detective story, epic, and so on. You compare the work to other similar literary pieces, looking for similarities and differences and perhaps comparing the relative quality of the achievement.

- **Historical analysis.** You study a literary work as it reflects the society that produced it or as it was accepted or rejected by that society when it was published. Or you study the way historical information makes a literary work from an earlier time clearer to a reader today.

- **Cultural analysis.** You explore how a work of art embodies the culture that produced it, that is, what assumptions about the beliefs and values of a society can be traced in the literary work. Such analysis may reveal how certain groups gained or maintained power through the manipulation of literary myths or symbols. It may show how certain groups operated within supportive or repressive cultures—how, for example, blacks or women are represented in 19th-century American literature or the Irish in English novels.

- **Political analysis.** You may want to read literary works for what they reveal about the economic and political relationships between classes and groups of people. Some works of art represent the ideals of those in control while others may champion alternative arrangements of power.

- **Biographical study.** You study how a writer's life is expressed in or through a literary work. Obviously, such analyses may be related to cultural and political studies, but they may also focus on the individual psychology of a writer.

- **Study of the creative process.** You make a detailed study of how a work was composed. Such a paper might examine the sources, notes, influences, manuscripts, and revised texts of a literary work.

41

Lit

➤ **Consult secondary sources.** If reading the work itself hasn't stimulated enough questions about the literary work or if you now do have some issues you are eager to explore, consult secondary sources. There are many in the field of literary study.

To locate secondary sources on literary topics, begin with the following indexes and bibliographies available in a library reference room.

Essay and General Literature Index

MLA International Bibliography

New Cambridge Bibliography of English Literature

Here is a list of other useful reference works.

> **Reference Works for a Literary Analysis**

Beacham, Walton, ed. *Research Guide to Biography and Criticism.* Washington, DC: Research Publ., 1985.

Drabble, Margaret, ed. *The Oxford Companion to English Literature.* 5th ed. Oxford: Oxford UP, 1985.

Encyclopedia of World Literature in the Twentieth Century. New York: Ungar, 1981. 4 vols.

Evans, Gareth L. and Barbara. *The Shakespeare Companion.* New York: Scribner's, 1978.

Hart, James D., ed. *The Oxford Companion to American Literature.* 5th ed. New York: Oxford UP, 1983.

Harvey, Paul. *The Oxford Companion to Classical Literature.* Oxford: Clarendon, 1980.

Holman, C. Hugh. *A Handbook to Literature.* 4th ed. New York: Bobbs, 1980.

Magill, Frank Northen. *Magill's Bibliography of Literary Criticism.* Englewood Cliffs, NJ: Salem, 1979.

Mainero, Lina, ed. *American Women Writers: A Critical Reference Guide from Colonial Times to the Present.* New York: Ungar, 1979–82.

Modern British Literature. New York: Ungar, 1966. Supplement, 1976.

Patterson, Margaret C. *Literary Research Guide.* 2nd ed. New York: MLA, 1983.

Sampson, George. *The Concise Cambridge History of English Literature.* Cambridge: Cambridge UP, 1970.

> **Carefully develop a thesis about the literary work(s) you are studying.** You might begin with questions you are eager to explore in greater depth, a question generated perhaps by your reading of secondary sources or by your discussions with classmates or other readers.

41

Lit

Are some scenes missing from *Macbeth?*

What limits on the power of women in Elizabethan England might explain the behavior of Lady Macbeth?

Did the term *equivocation* have particular political significance to the original audience of *Macbeth?*

Did Shakespeare tailor *Macbeth* to please England's Scottish monarch, King James?

When you've put your question into words, test its energy. Is the answer to your inquiry so obvious that it isn't likely to interest or surprise anyone?

Is Shakespeare's *Macbeth* a great play?

If so, discard the issue. Try another. Look for a surprising, even startling, question whose answer you don't already know. Test your question on a friend or instructor.

Could Shakespeare's *Macbeth* actually be a comedy?

What role might the lower classes play in a dynastic struggle like that depicted in *Macbeth?*

Then turn your question into an assertion—your preliminary thesis statement.

Shakespeare's *Macbeth* is really a comedy.

The welfare of the lower classes seems to have been ignored in dynastic struggles like those depicted in *Macbeth*.

Is this an assertion you are interested in proving? Is it a statement other readers might challenge? If so, write it on a notecard and go on. If not, modify it or explore another issue.

➤ **Read the work(s) a second time with your thesis firmly in mind.** Read more slowly and analytically this time. Look for characters, incidents, descriptions, speeches, and dialogue that support or refute your thesis. Take careful notes. If you are using your own text, highlight significant passages in the work.

When you are done, evaluate the evidence you have gathered from a close reading of the piece. Modify your thesis to reflect what you have learned or discovered. In most cases, your thesis will be more specific and limited after you have gathered and assessed evidence.

The many unexpected comic moments in *Macbeth* emphasize how disordered the world becomes for murderers like the Thane of Cawdor and his wife.

If necessary, return to secondary sources or other literary works to supplement and extend your close reading. (For many kinds of analysis, much of your reading will be in secondary sources and journals of literary criticism.) Play with ideas, relationships, implications, and possibilities. Don't hesitate to question conventional views of a work or to bring your own cultural experiences to bear upon the act of reading and interpreting literature. Jot down random thoughts or freewrite.

If you use secondary sources, take careful notes. Be sure to prepare accurate bibliography cards for your *Works Cited* page. (See Section 37C for advice on note-taking.)

➤ **When you are ready to write a full draft, try out a few scratch outlines for the paper.** Choose the one you find most solid or most challenging.

41

Lit

Thesis: Comic moments in *Macbeth* emphasize how strange the world has become for the Macbeths.
  I. Comic moments after the murder of King Duncan
 II. Comedy at the feast for Banquo
III. Comedy in the sleepwalking scene
 IV. Conclusion

Now write the draft. Stay open to new ideas and refinements of your original thesis, but try not to wander off into a biography of the author or a discussion of the historical period unless such material relates directly to what you are trying to prove. If you do wander, consider whether the digression in your draft might be the topic you *really* want to write about.

➤ **Avoid the kind of paper that simply paraphrases the plot of a literary work or praises its author for a job well done.** Avoid extremely impressionistic judgments: "I feel that Hemingway must have been a good American. . . ." Don't expect to find a moral in every literary work either. And don't think a literary analysis requires you to search for "hidden meanings." Respond honestly to what you are reading—not the way you think your teacher expects you to. (To see how the paper on *Macbeth* sketched above might develop, see pp. 657–661.)

➤ **Follow the conventions of literary analysis.** A literary analysis may take many forms, but academic essays generally follow the conventions of the MLA research paper, including careful documentation. However, a few special conventions should be observed.

- Use the present tense to refer to events occurring in a literary work: Hester Prynne *wears* a scarlet letter; Hamlet *kills* Polonius. Think of a literary work as an ongoing performance.

- Identify passages of short poems by line numbers: ("Journey of the Magi," lines 21–31). Do not, however, use the abbreviations *l.* or *ll.* for *line* or *lines* because they are sometimes confused with Roman numerals; spell out *line* or *lines* completely.

- Provide act and scene divisions (and line numbers as necessary) for passages from plays. Act and scene numbers are now usually given in Arabic numbers, although Roman numbers are still common and acceptable: **Ham. 4.5.179–85** or **Ham. IV.v.179–86.** The titles of Shakespeare's works are commonly abbreviated in citations: *Mac.*. I.ii; *Oth.* 2.2. Check to see which form your teacher prefers.

- Make an effort to introduce all direct quotations. Do not insert a quotation from a literary work or a critic into your paper without identifying it in some way. And be sure quotations fit into the grammar of your sentences. Here are some examples.

  > **When an audience hears the king call his cowering servant a** "cream-fac'd loon," it begins to understand why Macbeth's men hate and distrust him.

  > **As we watch Lady Macbeth sleepwalking, we share the fears of the doctor who warns the gentlewoman:** "you have known what you should not" (V.i.46–47).

  > **Commenting on the play, Frank Kermode observes that** "*Macbeth* has extraordinary energy; it represents a fierce engagement between the mind and its guilt" (1311).

- Provide a date of publication in parentheses after your first mention of a literary work: Before publishing *Beloved* **(1987),** Toni Morrison had written. . . .

- Use technical terms accurately. Spell the names of characters correctly. Take special care with matters of grammar and convention.

Sample Literary Paper

Travis Beckwith III

Professor Sweno

English 321 Shakespeare

10 November 1990

The Comedy of Macbeth

Unlike Greek or French tragedians, Shakespeare seems more than willing to add
a lively comic scene to even his most serious plays. Everyone instantly recognizes the humor of the gravedigger in *Hamlet,* the fool in *King Lear,* the porter
in *Macbeth.* Yet *Macbeth* (1606?) also contains moments that seem funny, but
perhaps shouldn't be--so audiences aren't sure whether to laugh. Bolder actors
might be tempted to play these troublesome lines comically, but do so at the risk
of offending critics who expect *Macbeth* to be serious. In my view, Shakespeare
creates these uneasy comic situations in *Macbeth* deliberately to emphasize the
absurdity of the world created by the Macbeths after they decide to murder
King Duncan.

The first few such comic lines come early in the play and could pass
unnoticed if actors play them with straight faces. Yet it is hard not to smile when
Lady Macbeth boldly claims victory after drugging the grooms who guard Duncan's bedchamber, discovering that "That which hath made them drunk hath
made me bold" (*Mac.* II.ii.1). Then, just the way a slightly drunk person would,
she goes on to apologize gruesomely for not killing Duncan herself, almost surprised by her reluctance to murder: "Had he [King Duncan] not resembled / My
father as he slept, I had done't" (12-13).

Macbeth has the next comic line, this one his reaction to Lennox's description of the horrible storm that blows while Macbeth is murdering Duncan.
Deadpans Macbeth: " 'Twas a rough night" (II.iii.61). The audience laughs sympa-
thetically, knowing much better than Lennox how rough it has been for the new
Thane of Cawdor. Then, when a horrified Macduff discovers that Duncan has been

murdered, Lady Macbeth screams: "Woe, alas! / What, in our house?" (II.iii.87-88).
Any audience that hears those lines wants to laugh at Lady Macbeth's self-centeredness. Even Banquo notices her inappropriate concern for her household's
reputation when he replies: "Too cruel any where" (88). The remainder of the
scene has a comic edge to it, as Duncan's sleepy sons rouse themselves to learn
that their father has been assassinated: "O, by whom?" (100). Then Macbeth almost gives away the whole plot by trying to explain why he killed the grooms, the
only possible witnesses to the murder. Lady Macbeth understands the problem, so
she faints to draw attention away from her babbling husband. The entire ghastly
episode teeters on the brink of explosive laughter.

  For several scenes afterward, though, the action turns serious enough to
make an audience almost forget the moments of comedy in the play, as Macbeth
consolidates his power and hires men to kill his friend Banquo. But then, at the
feast visited by Banquo's ghost (III.iv), the comedy revives as a desperate Lady
Macbeth tries to convince the assembled thanes that her husband's odd behavior
when seeing Banquo is not unusual: "my lord is often thus, / And hath been from
his youth" (52-53), little comfort for men now serving a king who talks to chairs.
Lady Macbeth admits as much when she criticizes her husband: "Why do you
make such faces? When all's done, / You look but on a stool" (66-67). Macbeth's
major complaint is that the murdered Banquo isn't playing fair. Macbeth longs
for the good old days:

>   . . . the time has been,
>
> That when the brains were out, the man would die,
>
> And there an end; but now they rise again
>
> With twenty mortal murthers on their crowns,
>
> And push us from our stools. (77-81)

  If Macbeth sounds absurd in these passages, Lady Macbeth suffers the
same fate in her famous sleepwalking scene (V.i), most of which is pathetic and
serious. But in recalling the sight of murdered Duncan, whose blood she earlier

41

Lit

smeared on the grooms, she speaks one comic line: "Yet who would have thought the old man to have had so much blood in him?" (39-40). "Old man" seems to mean about the same thing here as "old geezer." The remark suggests that all the blood on Duncan surprises Lady Macbeth, in much the same way that the ghost of Banquo--also bloody--surprises Macbeth.

Is it possible to tie all these comic instances together? One last example hints at the connection. The line occurs very near the end of the play when Macbeth realizes exactly how the witches have lied to him (V.viii). Thinking he can't be killed by one born of woman, Macbeth fears no man during the battle with the rebels who have come to dethrone him. But then Macbeth's sworn enemy Macduff reveals that he was "untimely ripped" (14) from his mother's womb, making it possible for him to slay the tyrant. Macbeth curses the witches for deceiving his hopes, and then, like an angry little boy quitting a game and carrying his football home, he tells Macduff "I'll not fight with thee" (22). The remark sounds as absurd as all the others cited in this paper because Macbeth here feels the same emotions he and his wife have been experiencing at intervals throughout the play: surprise, outrage, and insult. Time and again, the Macbeths become comically absurd in the tragedy because they don't realize that their murderous actions have changed the world. After they seize the throne of Scotland, they expect everything to stay as it was before they killed Duncan, but they soon discover that the old game is being played according to rules they haven't learned yet. Repeatedly they must respond to situations they haven't anticipated:

> "Had he not resembled my father. . . ."
> " 'Twas a rough night" ʻ
> "What, in our house?"
> "Why do you make such faces . . .?"
> "Now they rise again . . . and push us. . . ."
> "Who would have thought . . .?"

41

Lit

Macbeth's comically pathetic "I'll not fight with thee" is a logical, but futile attempt to escape a game the Macbeths themselves have invented, one so horrible that, time and again, it frightens them out of their wits. Spectators feel the horror, but also detect the humor in the Macbeths' confusion. That's why audiences want to laugh, but usually don't.

T. Beckwith   5

Work Cited

The Riverside Shakespeare. Ed. G. Blakemore Evans. Boston: Houghton, 1974.

41
Lit

42 Writing an Essay Examination

Troubleshooting

Essay examinations are a special kind of writing assignment common in humanities courses, but also used in other classes as well. The point of taking an essay examination is to prove that you command the facts, vocabulary, and idiom of a subject area, to demonstrate that you can interpret and relate concepts, and to show that you can use information to support assertions and evaluate ideas. Not incidentally, you also want to pass the course.

A writer who hopes to do well on essay exams reads the questions carefully, provides clear, strategically organized answers, and furnishes evidence to prove any assertions made.

There are no established forms for essay exams. But because most such exams are both written and read under pressure, it makes sense to compose them in a way that makes writing efficient, reading easy, and a respectable grade likely.

To write a successful essay examination . . .

➤ **Plan ahead.** Read over the entire exam, estimate the time you can give to each question, make quick scratch outlines of your essays, work through them with an eye on the clock, and stick to your schedule. Answer every required question—even minimally if you have to. Instructors may give you a few points for a tentative answer, but no points at all for a blank space.

➤ **Read the questions carefully.** Answer the questions your instructor actually asked, not the ones you were hoping for. Underline key verbs that tell you what to do with the topic: **describe, analyze, classify, compare, contrast, discuss, evaluate.** Each of these words means something a little different. Underline other key terms—those that *identify* or *limit* the subject. If you don't understand a question, ask your instructor if a clarification is possible under the ground rules of the examination.

➤ **Use a commitment and response design (see Section 4C) to outline the essay in its first paragraph.** State your major point, repeating key words from the question and indicating what line of development you will follow. If appropriate, break the question down into parts you can discuss in separate paragraphs. If you don't complete an essay, the opening paragraph should make it possible for a reader to construct what your finished essay would have looked like—had you the time to write it.

➤ **Treat one major idea per paragraph.** State the main point of each paragraph in the first sentence—a topic sentence. Consider the possibility that an instructor may skim your essay and read only these topic sentences.

➤ **Provide specific supporting evidence for conclusions.** Because time is limited, choose your facts carefully. Look for evidence that will suggest you know more than you can write about in the time you have to complete the test. In particular, use terms, facts, and names you heard in lectures or came across in your reading—and be sure you know how to spell these terms.

➤ **Use transitions, numbers, and lists.** They help organize information and direct readers to important points: *first, second, third; consequently; as a result; by contrast;* and so on.

➤ **Don't pad your answers and don't wander from your subject.** Instructors will recognize a snow job.

➤ **Write clearly or print.** Illegible handwriting can drop a grade almost as fast as weak content. But don't hesitate to revise, cross-out, and rearrange the elements of your paper. Such changes show you are thinking. If necessary, use arrows or balloons to insert or relocate whole sentences or paragraphs, but be as neat as possible.

➤ **Allow time to edit and proofread your answer.** Instructors will appreciate the concern you show for correct spelling, punctuation, and grammar.

➤ **Sample Essay Exam Answer.** The following response to an essay question in a government course might be written in forty-five minutes to an hour. As a model, it is reproduced in a form and style more polished than might be possible given the time restriction. But the major features of the answer, explained in the comments, would be manageable within an hour-long class period.

> **Question: Explain** the system of **checks and balances** operating in the **federal** government.

The boldfaced key words in the question suggest that an effective answer will need to show what the checks and balances do. The question is specifically limited to the federal government only. Examples or illustrations from local or state government would be off the subject.

> To prevent any one group or individual from seizing control of the
>
> American federal government, the framers of the Constitution
>
> established a system of checks and balances that **imposed specific**
>
> **limitations** upon the **executive, legislative,** and **judicial**
>
> branches of government.

Again, key words in the reply are boldfaced. Immediately and briefly, the answer explains what the checks and balances *impose do: they specific limitations upon the . . . branches of government.* The three branches of government are named in order of their treatment in subsequent paragraphs, one paragraph per branch—executive, legislative, and judicial. This opening paragraph thus addresses the basic examination question and sketches out the organization for the remainder of the reply.

> **The executive branch of the federal government** is limited in its actions first by the authority of Congress, which controls the federal budget and passes laws and, secondly, by the actions of the courts. The President can veto laws passed by Congress, but the Congress can, by two-thirds majorities of both houses, override any veto. Similarly, while the President and executive branch control foreign policy and the military, treaties must be ratified by the Senate, the military budget is controlled by Congress, and only Congress can declare war. Domestic policies and federal appointments are administered by the executive branch, yet Presidential authority is again limited by Congressional review and budgetary power. In much the same way, actions of the executive branch fall under the scrutiny of the Federal Courts; the Supreme Court can declare presidential actions unconstitutional.

The answer first deals with the executive branch, explaining both its powers and its limitations—first those imposed by the Congress, and then those imposed by the judiciary. The writer shows command of the subject by referring to specific powers: foreign policy, treaties, federal appointments. But notice that particular historical examples aren't used. If this were a two-hour examination, such examples might be appropriate and workable. But they are probably too time-consuming to include here.

> **The legislative branch of the federal government** is limited by the authority of the President and the Federal Courts. The President can veto all acts of Congress; the Supreme Court can declare them unconstitutional. Moreover, the President can command the attention of the American people in ways simply not available to more than five hundred congressional representatives from different and antagonistic parties.

Just as the opening paragraph promises, this paragraph is about the checks on the legislative branch.

> **The judicial branch of the federal government**— particularly the Supreme Court—exercises enormous authority through the power of

judicial review of laws passed by the Congress and signed by the President. Theoretically, one vote on the Supreme Court (in a 5–4 split) could override the unanimous opinion of the Congress and the signature of the President. Yet members of the court are appointed by the executive branch and approved by the Senate. And ultimately, any act of the Supreme Court is subject to the power of the Congress, the President, and the people acting in concert to change the Constitution itself.

Here the answer explores checks on the judicial branch.

Thus, the American federal government is an elaborate system of checks and balances that has worked reasonably well for two hundred years to control the ambition of any one branch or person. Each of the branches has enjoyed periods of enhanced power and prestige, but none has been able to dominate or seize the government for any sustained period.

This effective conclusion suggests to a reader that the writer knows even more about checks and balances—and American history—than the essay contains.

43 Writing an Abstract

Troubleshooting

Most APA papers include an abstract, but abstracts are common across the disciplines—and for good reason. They save time by summarizing the contents of journal articles or other materials; after reading an abstract, a researcher can decide whether a piece needs to be read in its entirety. An abstract also can act as a sort of prologue or prose outline, helping readers follow the argument of a complicated essay by highlighting its premises, main ideas, and conclusions.

The qualities of a good abstract aren't difficult to enumerate. First, it outlines the major ideas in the abstracted material and provides a sense of how they are related. Second, it accurately represents the contents and organization of the abstracted piece. Third, it is written in a clear style that reflects the wording of the original piece. And last, it is concise, falling within any word-limit (100 words? 200 words?) imposed upon it.

To write an effective abstract . . .

▶ **Respect any requirements placed upon the abstract.** The correct form of an abstract is usually determined by where it will appear. A professional journal, for example, may have detailed requirements for abstracts, especially concerning length.

An abstract included in an undergraduate essay is typed on a separate page immediately before the body of the essay. The word *Abstract* appears as the title, centered on the page, a double-space before the body of the abstract. The abstract page is ordinarily numbered in APA form, unnumbered in MLA form. The abstract itself should be a single block paragraph (no indention), double-spaced, of approximately 75–150 words.

Abstracts separated from their original articles are often identified by the word *Abstract* followed by the title of the original piece (also see abstract 2 below).

Abstract: Characteristics of Rejection Letters

and Their Effects on Job Applicants

▶ **Construct the abstract systematically.** First, read through the article carefully, underlining or listing its main points and major supporting evidence. For a longer article, extract the gist of each section or cluster of related paragraphs, giving special attention to introductory and concluding paragraphs. Shape your abstract from the points you have underlined or the summaries you have made of each major part of the article, linking your points with helpful transitions. (Don't use direct quotations from the article in the abstract.) Finally, test the abstract against the article, evaluating how well it reflects what the original piece argues or presents.

In the abstract, try to follow the pattern of organization used in the original article. Don't try to rethink or restructure the piece, even if you discover a more economical way of arranging its argument or evidence. However, you need not summarize every topic discussed in an essay; you may, for example, explain how one type of analysis is applied to a variety of subjects rather than describe all the subjects individually (see abstract 2 below).

➤ **Be sure your abstract is easy to read.** Keep the piece short, but don't compress your style so much that the abstract reads like a telegram. Avoid sentence fragments and unnecessary abbreviations.

➤ **Sample Abstracts.**

1. **Abstract from an undergraduate research paper** (see pp. 608–623 for the complete paper):

Abstract

One major cause of Chrysler Corporation's near-bankruptcy in 1979–80 was a management concept called the sales bank. Originally intended to keep Chrysler's auto plants running smoothly by building autos according to quotas, the sales bank revealed a near-fatal lack of coordination between the corporation's management, manufacturing, and sales components. The quotas pressured the company into building low-quality vehicles consumers didn't want. The cars then had to be stored at great expense until sold at fire-sale prices to dealers profiting by Chrysler's overstock. For a while, Chrysler's losses were hidden by creative accounting methods, but the sales bank idea eventually cost Chrysler millions of dollars and the good will of many customers.

43

Abstract

2. **Abstract from a research journal:**

Abstract: Expanding Roles for

Summarized Information

At least seven types of summaries have emerged in common usage, especially during the past 250 years. They may be classified as either sequential summaries that retain the original order in which information was presented or synthesizing summaries that alter this sequence to achieve specific objectives. Each type of summary developed in response to challenges facing professions, government, business, and ordinary citizens—all of whom have sought to absorb increasing quantities of information being generated in a society that is becoming more complex. This taxonomy offers a definition and brief history for each of the seven techniques, describes the growth of corporations or other organizations that can be considered leading practitioners, and comments on the potential continuing role for each type of summary. The article also focuses on several contemporary issues that will affect future research, classroom writing instruction, and information management in modern computerized offices.

—Ratteray, O. M. (1985). Written Communication, 2, 457.

43

Abstract

44 Writing a Position Paper

Troubleshooting

In some courses, you may be asked to respond to particular readings, lectures, or issues by writing a position paper—a short (often only one-page) expression of your opinion on a topic. Obviously, such papers need to be thoughtful and coherent. But they should also be lively, inventive, and exploratory, particularly when they will be read aloud to stimulate classroom discussion, to sample a range of opinions, or to record "gut reactions" to readings. In these rhetorical situations, position papers may be only a degree or two more polished than freewriting assignments.

To write an effective and lively position paper . . .

➤ **Look for a problem to discuss.** Since position papers are so short, you want to get to the core of an issue quickly. But you can't ordinarily treat an entire book, article, issue, or problem in a page or two. Instead, open the paper in one of two ways: by focusing on some key point, or by exploring a small, but troublesome, issue that could have wider implications.

➤ **Trust your instincts.** If something in what you have read or heard disturbs you or seems, in academic jargon, "problematic," write about that. Allow your thoughts to percolate over the material, and then take some risks with your thinking. Identify the established position and wonder, "What if . . . ?"; consider the conventional wisdom and ask, "Why not . . . ?" In position papers, you can even afford to be argumentative—even combative—since such pieces are usually written to provoke discussion, not end it.

➤ **Keep the essay open-ended.** A position paper can defend a clear thesis, but it need not seem like a finished piece of work. Good position papers make a point at the same time that they invite speculation and hint at possible ties with other subjects, disciplines, and lines of inquiry. Depending upon the subject and course, position papers may even be leavened with wit, humor, and a degree of playfulness.

➤ **Be specific.** Even though they are tentative, position papers still need to argue from clear and convincing evidence. In fact, it's often helpful to build an argument from some concrete bit of evidence or text—a statement, a passage, a remark. The very brevity of a position paper should help you to select evidence carefully and strategically. If you have only a page to make a case, you can't rely on weak evidence.

➤ **Be brief; be neat.** Many instructors like to duplicate position papers for class discussion. That's why it's important to write clearly (or type), to be reasonably accurate about mechanics, and to adhere to any limitations on length.

Sample Position Paper

Dealing with Change in Eastern Europe

7/14/90

by Kathy Green

Kathy opens the position paper by describing the situation she intends to discuss.

It is easy to feel euphoric about recent nonviolent political revolutions in Eastern Europe that have reunited Germany and liberated Hungary, Czechoslovakia, and Poland from Marxist totalitarianism. Indeed, the spirit of western democracy seems to have spread clear across the continent like an irresistible tide, reaching the borders of Russia itself, heralding what everyone hopes will be an era of peace, freedom, and prosperity.

In the second paragraph, Kathy identifies what is bothering her, the "anomaly" in an otherwise hopeful political situation. Notice the transitional sentence that opens the paragraph.

Still one thing worries me and keeps my enthusiasm in check: the potential for conflict between states and ethnic groups that were at each other's throats long before Marxism split Europe conveniently between East and West. Although the tension between NATO and Warsaw Pact adversaries was often high between 1945 and 1989, the fearsome prospect of all-out nuclear war kept ethnic and national rivalries from escalating into wider conflicts. Animosities within the alliances, especially in Eastern Europe, always seemed petty when played out against the greater East-West conflict. Moreover, the Soviet and American superpowers often enforced a kind of discipline, the Soviets even invading their East German, Hungarian, and Czechoslovak "allies" to maintain the integrity of the Warsaw Pact.

The third paragraph now expands upon the single issue Kathy has identified. Here, she moves from the abstract to the concrete, from talking about general tensions to worrying about Russia, Poland, and Yugoslavia. She reminds readers that conflicts in small countries have led to more general European conflagrations.

> With the various peoples of Europe now freer to act on their own,
> one wonders whether even the growing influence of the European
> Community can temper Balkan rivalries, stifle anti-Semitism,
> constrain German ambition, or enable the Poles to feel secure
> within their borders. Will renewed conflicts between Serbs and
> Croats tear Yugoslavia apart? Will a democratic Russia necessarily
> be a less aggressive state? Or will new tangled alliances of the kind
> that drew Europe into two world wars develop again, pitting
> members of political groups, national groups, and even religious
> sects against each other—fostering frictions of the sort we've
> already seen lead to violence in Yugoslavia and several Russian
> republics?

Now Kathy gets more argumentative, risking statements that may provoke arguments. She's painting in broad strokes, but the picture is vivid and thought-provoking.

> Some day soon we may be forced to consider whether the old bipolar
> arrangement of Europe—East versus West; capitalist versus
> communist; democrat versus totalitarian—wasn't an inherently
> more stable and peaceable structure than what we face in the post-
> Cold War era. Each of the newly democratic states will be developing
> political systems and parties. There's nothing to guarantee that
> such developments will occur smoothly or within the bounds of
> moderation. Extremist or ethnic parties, propelled by old rivalries
> or hatreds, may reemerge with goals that are incompatible with
> current international political arrangements or borders. Lacking a
> long democratic tradition, such radical groups may find it difficult
> to operate within the democratic frameworks of their new
> governments. What happens if they win power? Will a continent
> that managed to survive the danger of total nuclear war for four
> decades experience the return of the local, conventional war?

44

Pos Paper

The conclusion is more hopeful than the paragraph that precedes it. Notice that the conclusion does not summarize what Kathy has written, but draws out the implications of her thinking.

Of course, such fears are, at present, based on little more than speculation. Europe and the world are not today what they were in 1914 or 1939. The prospects for prosperity are greater, trade between nations is freer, travel is more routine, communication is instantaneous. The continent—which has to a large extent surrendered its cultural dominance—has learned some brutal lessons not only from two world wars, but from forty years of sustained superpower rivalry. Perhaps, then, we should all breathe easy and enjoy a well-earned period of international good will. But I think all nations involved in the old Cold War now need to consider building new diplomatic and cultural relationships that will ensure stability, defuse old hatreds, and guarantee the security of all racial, ethnic, and religious groups. We shouldn't take peace for granted.

45 Writing a Business Letter

Troubleshooting

Any time you write to or for a business, institution, or office, you are expected to follow the conventions of the business letter. These conventions may seem arbitrary at first, but they provide information necessary to make a communication clear, significant, recordable, and (if necessary) continuing: institutional names and addresses; dates; titles; issues, questions, and problems; signature(s); routing information; and so on. Don't regard business letter *form* as a mere *form*ality. Remember that letters must both communicate accurate information *and* furnish a record of a business transaction. Both jobs are important.

To write a successful business letter . . .

➤ **Understand the function of all eight major components of a business letter.**

1. **Heading.** It includes the address of the person sending the letter followed by the date.

> Clear Lake Clarion
> 102 Rebhorn Hall
> Ruralia, IL 61803
> May 31, 1987

2. **Inside address.** It is the name and address of the person or institution to whom the letter is written. When you don't know exactly to whom you are writing, you can address the letter to an office or a position: Office of Admissions; Director of Personnel; Manager.

> Dr. Tiffany Shade, President
> Clear Lake College
> Mammoth Hall 201
> Ruralia, IL 61802

3. **Salutation.** In business letters, the conventional greeting is followed by a colon, not a comma. The most common titles are abbreviated (Mr., Mrs., Ms., Dr.), but others are spelled out in full (Senator, President, Professor, Reverend).

> Dear President Shade: Dear Mr. Kuanahura:
> Dear Sister Constance: Dear Mrs. Bellona:
> Dear Professor Upton: Dear Ms. Lim:

Use a title when you don't have a particular person's name to address.

> Dear Director of Personnel:
>
> Dear Admissions Officer:
>
> Dear Sir or Madam:

When you need to make a general announcement, you may use the formal greeting.

> To Whom This May Concern:

However, this impersonal greeting seems to be losing favor.

4. Body. Here is where the message of the letter is conveyed, arranged to highlight key ideas or facts. Keep paragraphs short and "chunk" the material so that you present one major idea per paragraph.

5. Closing. Like the greeting, the closing is a conventional expression. A variety of closings are available, some formal, others less so.

More formal	Respectfully yours,
	Yours very truly,
	Yours truly,
	Sincerely yours,
	Sincerely,
	Yours sincerely,
	Best regards,
Less formal	Best,

Notice that only the first word in the closing is capitalized and that the phrase is followed by a comma.

6. Signature. The letter is signed in ink just beneath the closing. Because some signatures are hard to read, the writer's name is typed below the signature. A title or position is often included.

> Yours truly,
>
> *Connie Lim*
>
> Connie Lim
> Editor, *Clear Lake Clarion*

7. Notations. Beneath the signature but nearer the left margin, it is common to include a pair of initials, the first identifying the person who dictated the letter, the second the secretary who typed it. The letter may also indicate whether any other materials are enclosed and to whom copies of the original have been sent.

> CL/dw
> Enclosures: 2
> cc: Avery Sweno
>   Doris Upton
>   Diana Bellona

8. Envelope. The envelope includes the inside address found on the letter plus the writer's return address in block form.

```
Connie Lim
Clear Lake Clarion
102 Rebhorn Hall
Ruralia, IL 61803




                        Dr. Tiffany Shade, President
                        Clear Lake College
                        Mammoth Hall 101
                        Ruralia, IL 61802
```

➤ **Give your letter a consistent form and appearance.** Later in this section you will find models of the three most common formats for business letters.

- the **block form,** in which all the components of the letter are aligned flush left and paragraphs are not indented (letter 1);

- the **modified block form,** in which the heading, closing, and signature are aligned at approximately the midpoint of the page, and the inside address and body paragraphs remain flush left; body paragraphs are not indented (letter 2);

- the **indented form,** in which the heading, closing, and signature are aligned at approximately the midpoint of the page, and the inside address and body paragraphs remain flush left; body paragraphs are, however, indented (letters 3 and 4).

Business letters should always be typed on standard 8-½ X 11 inch paper of good quality. If you are writing for a firm or institution, use its printed letterhead.

Use wide margins (one inch or more) all around the letter to form a kind of frame. A business letter should never look crowded. If necessary, break up long paragraphs into more readable chunks.

➤ **Choose an appropriate tone—usually formal, but cordial.** Business letters vary as much as people and institutions do. Some letters are extremely formal, conveying information of legal significance between writers who represent the opinions of their companies, institutions, even governments. Other letters may be almost as casual as personal notes—though they still arrive in business form.

You may find it easier to decide on a tone if you put yourself in the reader's position for a moment. Ask yourself how you might feel or react if you received the letter you are sending.

If you were writing a job application letter, for example, (see p. 689 for a model), you would want to assure the prospective employer that you are qualified for the position and eager to have it. But how do you show that? By taking time to find out what you can about your prospective employers and demonstrating that your strengths fill their needs. You wouldn't write the same job application letter to General Motors that you would to Joe's Auto Supply because the needs and scale of the two operations would be vastly different.

45

Letter

Similarly, when writing a letter of complaint, you need to consider the point of view of the person likely to read your letter. Even if you are outraged and upset, what will you accomplish by venting your anger on that employee? You are more likely to get what you want by recognizing that your reader is—in most cases—being paid to resolve complaints like yours. A calm but firm explanation of your problem will work better than an insulting diatribe.

Remember, too, that your letter might be read by several people or become part of a permanent record. Keep these other possible readers in mind as you decide on the tone of your communication. And, again, provide enough background information so that your letter would make sense if examined several weeks, months, or years in the future.

➤ **Be sure the reader understands why you are writing.** Anticipate the *who, what, where, when,* and *why* questions your readers might have when they pick up your letter. Give all the necessary information as briefly as possible: name names; supply dates; explain circumstances. Don't make a reader plow through paragraphs of narrative before they get to the point.

{**Not**}

Dear Ms. Flowers:

The accident occurred last week when my cat knocked over a soft drink into the keyboard of my computer, causing a short circuit, which then ignited some papers on my desk, leading to a fire that destroyed my computer, hard disk, and printer. Fortunately, I was able to put out the fire before it spread beyond the desk. But the computer and related equipment are, I am afraid, a total loss.

My roommate called the local fire department, who provided a full report on the incident (enclosed), but by the time they arrived, there really wasn't anything for them to do.

Fortunately, I carry full apartment owner's insurance with a separate rider covering my computer. Consequently, I am asking you to explain to me how to make a claim under that policy to replace my damaged computer, printer, and other properties destroyed in the fire on September 15. . . .

{**But**}

45

Letter

Dear Ms. Flowers:

On September 15, my computer, printer, hard disk, and other related equipment were destroyed by a small fire in my office. This equipment is covered by a special rider to the apartment owner's insurance policy I carry with your company: Policy No. 342-56-88709-3.

Please tell me how to make a claim against that policy.

The fire occurred as a result of an accidental short circuit caused when my cat knocked a soda onto the computer keyboard. I am enclosing a copy of the fire department's report on the incident which provides full details. . . .

➤ **Tell readers what you want from them.** Don't leave them guessing.

Please tell me how to make a claim against my insurance policy.

Could you send me information explaining New Zealand's current immigration policies?

WRITING A BUSINESS LETTER **677**

Could you send me information explaining New Zealand's current immigration policies?

If you do not make payment by the end of this month, we will be forced to take legal action to recover the property we sold to you.

➤ **Make the letter easy to read.** Present information in chunks. Use lists if you need them.

I have enclosed the information you have requested.
—a copy of my birth certificate
—copies of my medical and dental records
—my high school and college transcripts
—letters of recommendation from two previous employers

➤ **Keep the style natural, personal, and positive.** Avoid canned expressions such as:

pursuant to
at your earliest convenience
the aforementioned document
as per your letter of
enclosed please find

Be polite. Many business letters end with a pleasantry that affirms the good will or good intentions of both parties.

I am confident we can resolve this problem promptly.

I look forward to seeing you in Chicago next month.

With your help, the project is sure to stay on track.

Let me know if I can be of any further assistance.

Sample Business Letters

Letters 1–4 are part of a sequence relating to a problem caused by a review of the production of *Macbeth* described in the exercises in Chapters 23–24. As you read, notice that each letter is written with more than one reader in mind; check the notations to learn who receives copies.

45

Letter

You might also notice the degree of formality in these letters. They are written by people who know each other well enough to sit down and talk their problems out. Once the issue is put in writing, however, the stakes are raised and these communications become more serious matters. Observe how carefully letter 3 is phrased. President Shade attempts to resolve the dispute firmly and judicially. She balances praise and blame between both parties, but also takes firm action. Letter 4 implies a personal conversation to follow, so it is far less detailed.

Business letters you write may not be as complicated as those presented here. But every business letter—even a simple request—entails acting strategically and with consideration for the reader.

1 Full Block Form (with letterhead)

Clear Lake Clarion	**What you needed to know yesterday—today!**
102 Rebhorn Hall	Ruralia, IL 61803

23 April 1990

Dr. Tiffany Shade, President
Clear Lake College
Mammoth Hall 101
Ruralia, IL 61802

Dear President Shade:

I request that you promptly review recent actions by Professors Bellona
and Sweno restricting freedom of the press on this campus.

As you may know, several days ago Brian McVicker, a reporter from the
Clear Lake Clarion, reviewed the current English and Drama departments' production of the annual Shakespeare play. McVicker's review of
the dress rehearsal of Macbeth sharply criticized the acting, directing,
and staging of Professors Bellona and Sweno's production. A copy of the
review is enclosed.

Because of McVicker's unfavorable review of Macbeth, renamed Macbeth:
The Musical, Professor Bellona has established a policy banning Clarion
reporters from all future drama department dress rehearsals. She has
also warned students in the drama department not to talk with reporters
and denied backstage permissions freely granted to Clarion reporters in
the past.

Professor Sweno has taken similar action in the English department,
even warning Brian McVicker, an English major, that his work in an
English course might be subject to an evaluation as tough as that he gave
to Macbeth.

I am asking you to investigate these attempts by Professors Bellona and
Sweno to limit freedom of expression at Clear Lake College. I hope specifi-
cally that you will rescind the gag orders imposed by the Drama and
English departments on the Clear Lake Clarion.

Respectfully yours,

Connie Lim

Connie Lim
Editor, Clear Lake Clarion

Enclosure
cc. Avery Sweno
    Diana Bellona
    Brian McVicker
    Central Illinois ACLU

45

Letter

2 Modified Block Form

1425 Laudanum Dr.
Ruralia, IL 61802
April 25, 1990

Dr. Tiffany Shade, President
Clear Lake College
Mammoth Hall 101
Ruralia, IL 61802

Dear President Shade:

I have just read--with mounting outrage--the letter Connie Lim, editor of the Clear Lake Clarion, sent you on April 23, demanding that you rescind the guidelines Professor Bellona and I have promulgated to define the relationships our departments and faculty will have with the local press.

I strongly urge you to deny the petition and to consider taking further action against the Clarion for its unprofessional attacks upon my reputation. To permit the editor of the Clarion to dictate how the departments and faculties under our authority will behave toward reporters would set a dangerous precedent for this college.

The production of Macbeth supervised by me and directed by Professor Bellona may have had flaws. But we felt compelled to take risks this year to be sure that the annual Spring Shakespeare Festival--which I initiated and developed into a major campus event--continues to attract a large audience.

I would point out that Brian McVicker's review of Macbeth strayed well beyond the margins of good taste and criticism. May I remind you that he described Professor Bellona's choreography of the banquet at Macbeth's castle as "ten sweaty gymnasts tripping over a volleyball net"? And, for agreeing to play the title role, I have been branded as "the biggest ham since Hormel."

While I will admit that the Clarion's review has not hurt attendance at the festival production, the students and townspeople jamming our auditorium are attending for all the wrong reasons. I deeply resent the cheers that news of my character's death raises from this mob.

I hope you will act with your characteristic speed and determination to show Ms. Lim and Mr. McVicker the difference between anarchy of the press and reasonable supervision exercised by those who know better.

Yours truly,

Avery Sweno
Professor of English
Chair, Department of
English

c. Diana Bellona

45

Letter

3 Indented Form (with letterhead)

Clear Lake College   *Give the People Light . . .*

Office of the President
Mammoth Hall 101

April 27, 1990

Avery Sweno
Chair, Department of English
Clear Lake College
12 Praline Hall
Ruralia, IL 61802

Dear Avery:

    Like you, I was startled by the unusual sharpness of Brian McVicker's review of your and Professor Bellona's production of Macbeth: The Musical. I regret the personal tone he takes in the piece, but let us attribute that to his youth and a subject ripe for shaking.

    It pains me to be this blunt, but the Macbeth I watched last week was quite the worst play I have ever seen. McVicker's review, in most respects, accurately describes a troubled and unintentionally humorous production. Let us just say that your decision to transform Macbeth into a musical-tragedy was not a wise one.

    Yet even if the play had been entirely successful and the Clarion's review were as irresponsible a piece of journalism as your letter (25 April) suggests it is, I would feel obligated to rescind the restrictions you and Professor Bellona have imposed upon the college paper. I understand your personal feelings in this matter and applaud your professional regard for good order within your department. But the authority of a chair--even of a university president--must always take second place to the principles of free speech and a free press.

    Consequently, I am directing you and Professor Bellona to give reporters from the Clear Lake Clarion full access to your departments. I am confident that neither you nor Professor Bellona will take action of any kind against Ms. Lim and Mr. McVicker. I will, however, talk to both students and urge greater sensitivity in reviewing nonprofessional theatrical productions in the future.

    Should you have any questions about my actions, please do not hesitate to discuss them with me.

                  Sincerely,

                  Tiffany Shade

                  Tiffany Shade
                  President, Clear Lake College

45

Letter

TS/cr
c. Diana Bellona

4 Indented Form (with letterhead)

Clear Lake College _____   *Give the People Light . . .*

Office of the President
Mammoth Hall 101

                                        April 29, 1989

Connie Lim, Editor
Clear Lake Clarion
Clear Lake College
102 Rebhorn Hall
Ruralia, IL 61803

Dear Ms. Lim:

   Responding to your letter of 25 April, I have reviewed the restrictions placed on Clarion reporters as a result of Brian McVicker's recently
published review of Macbeth: The Musical. I am directing Professors
Bellona and Sweno to rescind those limitations immediately. Clarion reporters are to have the same access to the Drama and English departments they have always enjoyed.

   I would, however, like to discuss this entire issue with you and
Brian McVicker some time soon. Please call my secretary to arrange a
time when the three of us can talk this week.

   I appreciate your action and your concern for the Clarion.

                                        Sincerely yours,

                                        Tiffany Shade
                                        Tiffany Shade
                                        President, Clear Lake College

45

Letter

46 Writing a Memo

Troubleshooting

While in school, you may never have to write a memo—unless you become the officer of a club or student organization. But on the job, memos are the lifeblood of institutions, whether the messages circulate in paper form or on the computer screen as "electronic mail."

Memos serve many obvious, even mundane, purposes: they carry information, report recommendations, establish or affirm policies, and provide a record of an institution's activities. But they also can serve as a conduit for ideas, attitudes, and emotions. A good memo carries with it some of the spirit of an institution's "culture." It says "this is how we talk to one another" and such talk can be direct, clear, and efficient or cold, indirect, and clogged with jargon.

To write an effective memo . . .

➤ **Be sure the heading contains the correct routing information.** A memo really has two basic parts: a heading and a body. The heading explains whom the memo is from, to whom it is directed, what its subject is, and on what date it was sent.

> To:
> From:
> Subject:
> Date:

Other information may be included.

➤ **State your purpose clearly in the body of the memo—right in its first paragraph.** Don't think that the subject line of the heading of the memo guarantees that readers will know what a memo is about. Headings are designed (in part) to make filing the memo easier; many readers ignore headings and plunge right into the body of a memo itself. If you don't state your purpose in the first paragraph of a memo, you may confuse readers.

So it makes sense to open a memo with an action-oriented statement—one that makes a recommendation, states a policy, or summarizes the results of an investigation, report, or analysis. This opening statement may then be followed by more information that explains or justifies the action. The longer a memo, the more important it is that its opening paragraph explain the purpose of the communication and the actions expected. When drafting the memo, consider the possibility that a reader might examine only its opening paragraph and scan the remainder.

Sample Memo

SPARTAN Sporting Goods, Inc.   Interoffice Memo
Chicago, Illinois

To: Barry Meyer, Mgr.
From: H. Ross Pinkerton
Subject: Christmas sales at SPARTAN Sporting Goods stores
Date: Dec. 10, 1991

SPARTAN Sporting Goods has set three priorities for the 1991 holiday sales period:

1. Successful introduction of SPARTAN nutrition supplements.
2. Successful introduction of SPARTAN sporting clothes for men and women.
3. A 30 percent increase in sales of upscale exercise machines, including exercise cycles, self-contained gyms, abdominal machines, and slant boards.

The first two items reflect SPARTAN's intention to develop a full line of its own low-priced athletic/health products as an alternative to higher-cost national brands currently offered in our stores. Sales literature and suggestions for displays will follow.

The third item reflects a need to correct an overstock in what has proven to be the relatively low-volume home gym equipment area. Because of the overstock, we can offer you substantial discounts (see attached wholesale list) on home gym devices, which you may pass on to your customers.

Healthy sales during this important season!

HRP/dw
Enclosure: 1
cc: B. Twombly
    J. Velz
    K. Frost

46

Memo

➤ **Arrange the memo to highlight key information.** The body of the memo can be arranged like an outline, with major points flush with the left margin and supporting evidence indented neatly below, as in the Sample Memo. Use headings in longer memos to minimize the time readers spend searching for information.

A memo should never look crowded. Information should be "chunked" and surrounded by plenty of white space. Whenever possible, arrange information into readable lists. Items in a list should be parallel.

➤ **Remember that a memo may be filed as a record** of some report or transaction within a company. A memo needs to be clear enough to make sense a year or a decade after it was written.

➤ **Provide other information as necessary.** A memo ordinarily contains notations (in the lower left) explaining

- who typed the memo,
- whether it is accompanied by other documents (enclosures),
- who will receive copies; copies are indicated by the abbreviation *c.* (singular) or *cc.* (plural).

47 Writing A Résumé

Troubleshooting

Imagine for a moment that you are the personnel officer of a large firm thumbing through a stack of job applications. At this stage, the only impression you have of the people under consideration is what you gather from their résumés and accompanying job application letters. These pieces of paper will determine which candidates are examined more seriously—perhaps interviewed—and which are dropped from consideration. With so formidable a pile of applications, you are just looking for reasons to eliminate candidates. Under these circumstances, how would *you* react to a résumé that lacked basic information, was poorly arranged, or was full of spelling errors? Obviously, résumés and job letters need to be thoughtfully written, handsomely packaged, and proofread maniacally.

A résumé is a brief (usually one-page) outline of your academic and employment history, listing achievements, skills, and available references. It should give a prospective employer a sense of who you are, what you have done, and what you might be qualified to do. In preparing a résumé, you want to present an honest outline of your academic and employment record, yet one that enhances your chances of getting a job interview.

The job application letter that accompanies a résumé explains exactly how your expertise and experience make you the logical candidate for a particular job. In it, you subtly sell yourself, conveying to the employer a sense of your fitness for a job.

To write an effective résumé . . .

➤ **Include all the basic items.** A standard résumé includes:

- Your **name, current address, and phone number.** You may also want to list a second, more permanent, address if your current residence (an apartment or dormitory) might change during the period of your job application.

- *Relevant* **personal data.** Limit personal information only to what is essential for a particular job. Employers are, in fact, limited in what they can require employees to reveal about age, marital status, and so on. Don't include a photograph with your résumé.

- **Educational background.** In most cases, include the dates and institutions of your college and university degree(s) and other post-high-school training. List this information either in reverse chronological order (most recent experiences first) or in order of relevance to the job you are seeking. Information about elementary and secondary school education should not be mentioned unless directly related to the prospective job. You may need to name your academic major or areas of concentration, language skills, and significant academic honors, especially competitive scholarships, grants, and fellowships. A résumé you prepare immediately after graduation might list significant positions held while in college: on committees, in programs, and in clubs and social organizations.

• **Work experience.** List your employment record in reverse chronological order (most recent position first) or in an order relevant to the job you are seeking, most important first. Be sure to state the position(s) you have held, the names of your employers, and the dates of employment. As far as possible, make sure that all recent years are accounted for; don't leave gaps in your employment history that a prospective employer might worry about. Your job record should give an employer a sense of your experience, qualifications, and reliability.

• **Recommendations, credentials, or employment services.** Let a prospective employer know whom he or she may contact to get more information about you. You don't actually have to list the names of references on the résumé. A line at the bottom of the page to this effect will suffice: *References available upon request.* Be sure you can, indeed, supply these references. Discuss the matter with potential references *before* you cite them as such.

▶ **Tailor the résumé to the specific job or employer.** Since a résumé should be short, your criterion for including an item is its relevance to the position you are seeking. Depending upon the job description, you might, for example, add or delete lines about club memberships, college committee work, church or community service, references to high-school honors and achievement, and so on. In some circumstances, you may want to identify your career intentions (junior accountant; medical examiner; dental hygienist); in other cases, such a line might limit your potential.

For practical reasons, however, a résumé is often generic: you need one sheet suitable for many occasions. But tailoring the résumé is shrewd when you can manage it, particularly if you store your statement in a computer file and can add or delete items as needed. When you cannot, use the job application letter to fill in the details that your résumé cannot cover.

▶ **Pay attention to organization.** Most résumés resemble an outline, but there is actually no standard form. So use common sense. When you need to show a steady record of employment and achievement, arrange the items on your résumé chronologically; when you want to highlight accomplishments suited to a particular job, arrange items by importance.

In either case, locate the items on your résumé so that major points stand out. Use headings to highlight major divisions and always allow for margins and white space. Don't crowd a résumé, but do try to fit everything onto a single page. A longer résumé is acceptable only if you have a lengthy employment history and significant experiences to chronicle. Here's a workable order for the items on a résumé.

47

Résumé

1. Personal information
2. Educational background
3. Job experience
4. References

Once you have significant job experience, you may want that information to precede the section on education.

A handsomely typed résumé reproduced on high-quality white paper is all an employer expects. You need not have your résumé professionally printed—though such services are widely available and relatively inexpensive.

➤ **Proofread your finished résumé and job application letter several times; then get someone else to review them.** Errors on these documents make you look careless and irresponsible and can cost you a job interview.

➤ **Never send your résumé without a job application letter.** A résumé should always be accompanied by a typed cover letter explaining your interest in a position, your specific qualifications for the job, your willingness to meet for an interview, and so on. Like the résumé itself, the job application letter should ordinarily not exceed one page.

➤ **Use a job application letter to draw attention to the best reasons an employer should consider you for a job or interview.** The letter can be more specific about these major points than the résumé; don't merely repeat information already on the résumé. Mention your notable strengths in the job application letter and make it sound tailored for the occasion—which it should be.

47

Résumé

Sample Résumé

Sean M. O'Brian
2853 Sophia Ave.
Ruralia, IL 61802
(217) 123-4567

OBJECTIVE   Beginning position as cinematographer, film editor, script writer

EDUCATION   Seminar Participant: The American Cinema
American Film Institute, Los Angeles, CA
June–July, 1989. Worked with Francis Ford Coppola and
Sydney Pollack. Won "Outstanding Film Student" citation.

B.A. in Radio, Television, Film, 1990
Clear Lake College, Ruralia, IL
Senior Thesis: "The Art of Paddy Chayefsky"
Courses in Film Production, Script Writing,
History of the Film I, II, & III, Editing

President: Clear Lake College Film Club, 1988–89
Founded college film journal: "Frame & Shoot," 1988
Coordinated Central Illinois Film Fest, 1989

Manager: Clear Lake Photography Lab, 1988–90
Managed campus photo lab. Held informal classes on photography, lab work. Maintained and repaired cameras and equipment.

AWARDS   Best Student Film: "Treed" 35 mm. 13 min.
Central Illinois Film Festival (1988)

Best Animated Film "Bayou By You" 16 mm. 7 min.
Midwestern Film Conference (1990)

EXPERIENCE   1989–1990. Production Assistant
University Films, Inc., Ruralia, IL 61803
Gained experience with casting, script writing and revision, crew management, film stocks, development, editing.

Summer, 1987. Intern, KYUU-TV, Cleveland, OH
Worked as editor, guest coordinator, newswriter.
Summer, 1986. Gofer, Heliotrope Studios
Los Angeles

References available upon request.

47

Résumé

Sample Job Application Letter

2853 Sophia Avenue
Ruralia, IL 61802
May 23, 1990

Ms. Carina Obregon
Director of Personnel
Lamontier Films and Documentaries
5400 E. 133 St.
Garfield Heights, OH 44125

Dear Ms. Obregon:

I would like to be considered for the assistant production supervisor position advertised by Lamontier Films in the current issue of <u>Film Monthly</u>.

As my résumé demonstrates, I have a recent degree in cinema and wide-ranging practical knowledge of film production. My experience includes work with major movie companies and directors in California; I have also been active in movie productions, companies, and clubs in the Illinois area.

At KYUU-TV in Cleveland, I worked on several projects that involved technicians from Lamontier who helped us develop films about local area businesses and institutions, including a feature on the Western Reserve Historical Museum. Such experiences have made me particularly eager to be involved with the kind of film production Lamontier specializes in-- locally supported, community-oriented documentaries.

Having worked part-time with a small local film company, I believe I have the skills required of an assistant production supervisor--especially the ability to manage on-the-spot assignments. I have handled more than a few crises in the field, from revising a shooting script to accommodate the sudden laryngitis of an actor to repairing a jammed film transport on a camera forty feet off the ground. I have also managed more routine tasks.

Since I expect to be in Cleveland early in June, an opportunity for an interview then would be ideal. But I can be available at any time convenient to Lamontier Films.

I look forward very much to talking with you.

Sincerely,

Sean M. O'Brian

Sean M. O'Brian

47

Résumé

Encl.

48 Preparing an Oral Report

Troubleshooting

Instructors often require oral reports in their courses as a way of preparing students for a responsibility common to many professions—delivering a presentation, lecture, discussion, or talk. People often feel uneasy when speaking before a group, but public speaking is a valuable skill that can be mastered with practice—particularly in the friendly environment a classroom provides. There, the audience is usually forgiving and already well-disposed toward what colleagues have to say. A class is also a fine place to develop group presentations, which put less pressure on the individual speaker.

Good speaking requires many of the same qualities evident in good writing—coherent organization, a highly developed sense of audience, well-expressed transitions, and memorable illustrations. But if you have ever been to a conference where lecturers have read perfectly competent papers word-by-word to an audience, you know (from the audience's coughs and snores) that there's more to public speaking than just *reading* a well-crafted text. So much more, in fact, that all we can offer you here are a few tips. But we think you'll find them helpful.

To present an effective oral report . . .

➤ **Speak on a subject you want to learn more about;** chances are your classmates will want to discover more about it, too. Or talk on a subject about which you already know enough to feel like an expert. Look particularly for topics that provide illuminating perspectives on important general concepts or that make connections between an academic subject and realistic applications. In a biology class, a report might explain one link between evolutionary theory and Darwin's adventures on *The Beagle*. In a class on marketing, you might present facts about one famous (or infamous) political ad campaign from the 1980s. In a sociology course, you might explore the impact of a local plant closing on a surrounding neighborhood or a particular family.

➤ **Adapt your subject to your audience.** In school presentations, your audience will not be some imaginary group, but the instructor and classmates right in front of you—smiling, frowning, coughing, agreeing, or disagreeing. Adapting your subject to this audience is crucial to getting the response you want.

How do you make this match? Fortunately, you usually know your instructor and classmates fairly well—you know their interests, expectations for style (formal or informal), tolerance for humor, and attention span. If you are speaking about a course topic, you don't have to cover the basics, unless your report introduces new and difficult concepts.

➤ **Don't lull your listeners to sleep with a monotonous tone or rhythm.** Modulate the tone and intensity of your voice. Raise and lower it to underscore key points. Use pauses to mark punctuation and shifts in topic. Worry less about overdoing it than droning like a fan through an entire presentation.

➤ **Don't speak too swiftly or garble your words.** These are among the most common problems of inexperienced speakers. They may start out fine, but begin speaking faster and faster (and softer and softer) until they become almost unintelligible. An oral report is not a race to the finish line.

If you have too much material to cover in the allotted time, it is better to edit your material silently than to rush through it or to extend your presentation into another speaker's time.

➤ **Don't stare relentlessly at your paper on the podium** or hold your text up in front of you, blocking the audience's view. Make frequent eye contact with your audience. Keep your eyes moving and don't be afraid to look at individuals directly for a second or two. Give the impression that you are as interested in them as in your material. To make eye contact effectively, you'll need to practice your presentation so you can pull your eyes away from your notes comfortably and without stumbling.

➤ **Use *nonverbal* means to get points across,** including tone of voice, gestures, head movements, body movements, and shifts of position. Don't freeze up before an audience. If you stand stiffly, you'll give the impression that you aren't interested in the topic.

Use bodily movements deliberately. A shrug, nod, casual turn, sweep of the arm, even a scratch of the head can all be used to reinforce a point. If appropriate, move away from the podium and change position during the speech a few times. Compel your listeners to refocus their attention. But don't move incessantly and don't pace. Shifts of position should seem purposeful.

➤ **Prepare props and visual materials.** Charts, models, overhead projections, slides, and blackboards can all be important tools in an oral report. If visual elements are handsomely constructed and sensibly integrated into the presentation, they'll leave a favorable impression. A chart can summarize the main points you have made; a graph can turn dull statistics into a powerful image; slides can enliven the places or people you are discussing. Don't, however, let visual media dominate your report.

Before your presentation, check that all the equipment works and that you know how to operate it. Locate the electrical sockets, and focus the slide and overhead projectors. If you are showing a videotape, keep the TV off until you are ready to use it; don't compete with a glowing screen. For the same reason, turn off an overhead projector as soon as you are done with it. Plan a version of the report that takes into account the possibility of equipment failure. But do consider using visuals. They have impact and show that you've made an effort to please your listeners.

➤ **Dress up.** Students are ordinarily so casual about their classroom appearance that wearing more formal clothing on the day of a report can make a surprising difference. Try it.

TOOLS FOR WRITERS

As a writer, you are rarely on your own. Instructors, editors, friends, and colleagues are often eager to help you refine a rough draft into a polished essay.

This section of the handbook is similarly intended to make writing a little easier and surer for you. It provides a guide to the one essential book for every writer—the dictionary; there's a full chapter of advice about spelling, too. A more recent tool for writers is the computer; if you don't yet know what it's like to write with one, an introduction to word processing awaits. You'll also find a full glossary of usage and grammatical terms.

PART 7

49 References for Writers

A Choosing a dictionary
B Using a dictionary
C Developing a strong vocabulary
D Special-purpose dictionaries
E A writer's bookshelf

Terms you need to know

UNABRIDGED DICTIONARY. A dictionary that attempts to survey the English language comprehensively, providing spellings and meanings for all its standard vocabulary items. At any given time, however, many technical, regional, slang, colloquial, and newly invented words are absent from even the most authoritative volumes.

ABRIDGED DICTIONARY. A dictionary based on items selected from a more complete dictionary. Many desk or collegiate dictionaries are abridgments of larger dictionaries. For example, *The Random House College Dictionary* is a condensed version of the more comprehensive *Random House Dictionary of the English Language.*

ETYMOLOGY. The history of a word—its origins, developments, and changes in meaning.

IDIOM. Any expression in a language that does not seem to make literal sense. Idioms often mean more than the sum of their parts.

The aircraft **bit the big one** over Montana.

Let's **get cracking.** We're late.

49 A CHOOSING A GOOD DICTIONARY

49 A

Dict

Troubleshooting

Everyone needs at least one dictionary. But which of the many available volumes is right for you? Does the authority and comprehensiveness of an unabridged dictionary justify its bulk and expense? Does the portability of a pocket dictionary compensate for its limited lexicon and bare-bones definitions? Is size the only important difference between dictionaries? If not, what should you look for in making a selection?

For academic work, you should . . .

➤ **Own a desk-sized college dictionary.** So-called desk or collegiate dictionaries are an almost ideal compromise between large, unabridged dictionaries and paperback pocket dictionaries. They usually contain between 140,000 and 200,000 entries—enough for most writing jobs. Reasonably priced and usually hardbound, they offer many helpful features, from brief histories of the English language to style manuals, lists of foreign terms, and addresses of two- and four-year colleges.

Some dictionaries list meanings historically; that is, the first definition given for a word is its earliest known meaning. Subsequent definitions reflect changes in meaning the word may have undergone over the centuries. A historically-based dictionary provides a perspective on current language by showing how definitions grow and change. But you have to be careful. The first meanings listed for an item in a historically-organized entry may be archaic or rare—not the way the term is used today.

For that reason, other dictionaries arrange their definitions in order of use, from the most common meaning of a term to the least familiar. In such a dictionary, you lose some of the chronological feel gained from a historical arrangement, but you are less likely to use a word in a sense inappropriate or unfamiliar to modern readers.

Dictionaries also differ in their willingness to give you advice about how words ought to be used. A few tend to be *prescriptive,* offering ample guidance. Most dictionaries, however, comment on usage sparingly, preferring to be *descriptive.* They explain how words *are* used, not how they *should* be used.

The most popular desk dictionaries vary in their emphases and features. But any one of them will serve you well. Here are just a few:

• *The American Heritage Dictionary of the English Language*

  —Approximately 200,000 entries

  —Meanings listed in order of use, most common first

  —Usage notes based on the opinions of a panel of writers, scholars, editors, columnists, and so on

  —Lists the addresses of American and Canadian colleges and universities

  —Ample front matter: history of the language, dialects, computers

  —Numerous illustrations in ample margins

• *The Random House College Dictionary*

  —Based on the unabridged *Random House Dictionary of the English Language*

  —Approximately 170,000 entries

  —Meanings listed in order of use: most common part of speech first and most often encountered meaning

  —Good coverage of scientific, biographical, and geographic items

  —Includes essays on the history of the language, pronunciation, and dialect

49 A

Dict

—End matter includes directory of colleges and universities, list of names, style manual

—Some illustrations

- *Webster's Ninth New Collegiate Dictionary*

    —Based on the unabridged *Webster's Third New International Dictionary*

    —Approximately 160,000 entries

    —Meanings listed historically, with items dated

    —Biographical, geographic, and foreign terms listed separately at the back of the book

    —Lists the addresses of American and Canadian colleges and universities

    —Includes a list of abbreviations and a handbook of style

    —Some illustrations

- *Webster's New World Dictionary of the American Language*

    —Meanings listed "in semantic order from the etymology to the most recent sense"

    —Includes an essay on "Language and the Dictionary"

    —Provides guides to usage

    —Ample coverage of Americanisms

    —Geographical and foreign terms included in main listing

    —Lists American and Canadian colleges and universities

    —Provides sections on punctuation, manuscript form, and weights and measures

- *Webster's II New Riverside University Dictionary*

    —Definitions arranged by "central meaning clusters"

    —Emphasizes American regional terms indicated by boldface daggers

    —Definitions illustrated by quotations from American authors

    —Provides occasional "word histories"

    —Separate listings of abbreviations, biographical terms, geographic terms, and foreign words

    —Lightly illustrated

49 A

Dict

- *The Concise Oxford Dictionary of Current English*

    —Based on *The Oxford English Dictionary* and its supplements

    —Meanings listed according to "frequency and convenience"

    —Appendices on weights and measures, the Greek and Russian alphabets, and monetary units

> The name "Webster" is virtually synonymous with dictionaries in the United States. Noah Webster (1758–1843), an influential scholar, author, and language authority, wrote grammars and spellers that served as basic textbooks for Americans throughout the nineteenth century. His most important work was *The American Dictionary of the English Language* (1828). Revised and enlarged many times, Webster's *Dictionary* became a recognized standard. The Webster name has since entered the public domain—which means it cannot be copyrighted. Hence many works today bear Webster's name even though they may have no connection to him or his famous *Dictionary*.

➤ **Consult an unabridged dictionary when necessary.** On some occasions you may need more information about a word than your desk dictionary provides. Or the word you are looking for may be a form too rare, obscure, or old to appear in a dictionary designed for daily work. Then you need to consult one of the large **unabridged** dictionaries—works that attempt to record standard English vocabulary items as fully as practicable. If you have the wherewithal to own one of these imposing collections—some are single books, others are multi-volume sets—you'll enjoy easy access to the wealth of information they contain. Most people, however, examine such books in the reference rooms of their libraries. Here are three you should know.

• *The Oxford English Dictionary, Second Edition*

    —Over 500,000 items: 20 volumes and 22,000 pages

    —Perhaps the greatest dictionary in any language

    —Definitions listed historically, with quotations (about 2.4 million of them) providing the earliest recorded use of a word and its subsequent appearances through the centuries

    —Entries treated exhaustively: often more useful to scholars than to writers

    —The second edition of the OED, which appeared in 1989, is available in book and machine-readable (that is, computerized) form; it combines all entries from the original OED and its four supplements as well as five thousand new words.

49 A

Dict

• *Webster's Third New International Dictionary of English*

    —Approximately 450,000 items in one volume

    —Best-known American dictionary

    —Illustrated

    —Definitions listed historically and amply illustrated through quotations

    —Regarded as complete and authoritative

—Descriptive rather than prescriptive; caused great controversy when first published in 1961 because it printed nonstandard and controversial usages without commentary

- *The Random House Dictionary of the English Language*

    —Approximately 260,000 items in one volume

    —Includes many idioms, synonym and antonym lists

    —Usage labels steer middle course between fully prescriptive and fully descriptive

    —Full-color atlas of the world; gazetteer

    —French/Spanish/Italian/German-English dictionaries

What about pocket dictionaries?

Though no substitute for desk-size dictionaries, pocket dictionaries (and thesauruses) are certainly convenient. You can rely on them for correct spellings and basic meanings. But they do contain many fewer entries, shorter definitions, and sketchier etymologies than college dictionaries. See Section 49D.

EXERCISE 49.1

A checklist of dictionary features follows. How many of the features does the dictionary you usually use have? Is it time to consider upgrading?

✓ Does the volume have at least 100,000 words in its lexicon?
✓ Are the definitions full and clear?
✓ Are definitions arranged in an order suited to your purposes (frequency of use; historically; functionally)?
✓ Does an entry indicate a word's origin (etymology) and roots?
✓ Does an entry provide other useful information (capitalization, division, variations in spelling, synonyms, antonyms, and homonyms)?
✓ Is the pronunciation guide helpful and available in large enough type?
✓ Are helpful stylistic labels provided *(archaic, slang, chiefly British)*?
✓ Does the dictionary give you advice about usage?
✓ Does the dictionary provide examples of the word in use, especially for difficult items of usage *(affect/effect; allusion/illusion)*?
✓ Does the dictionary provide other useful information—the names of important persons, places, things, countries, cities?
✓ Are the introductions and appendixes useful? What do they cover?
✓ Are pages well laid out and readable? Does it offer helpful drawings, maps, charts, tables, and illustrations? Is this a dictionary you might enjoy using?
✓ Is the book well-bound? Will it lay open flat on a desk? Will it survive several semesters in a backpack?

49 A

Dict

49 B USING A DICTIONARY

Term you need to know

FRONT MATTER. Material that precedes the main body of a work. In a dictionary, the front matter may include a guide to the dictionary, a pronunciation key, a history of English, and various essays on language topics.

Troubleshooting

Dictionaries are as dependable as gravity. Once you know alphabetical order, you can usually navigate one with few problems. But a great many writers, put off by all the signs and symbols that seem to clutter entries, ask no more of a dictionary than that it furnish accurate spellings and clear meanings. In fact, a dictionary can tell you a great deal more, if you know how to interpret the information it presents.

To use a dictionary well . . .

➤ **Consult the front matter.** Every dictionary includes a kind of owner's manual, usually a thorough explanation of how to use the information contained in its thousands of entries. You may not want to read all this material every time you consult a new dictionary, but remember that this guide is available whenever you face an unfamiliar word, symbol, or feature.

Don't underestimate the number of features a dictionary entry can contain. The guide to *The American Heritage Dictionary* (Second College Edition), for example, lists all these headings (boldfaced items are discussed in the section that follows):

Guide Words	Illustrative Examples
The Entry Word	Variants
Superscript Numbers	Phrasal Verbs
Syllabication	Modifiers
Pronunciation	Idioms
Sound-Spelling Correspondences	**Etymologies**
Part-of-Speech Labels	Undefined Forms
Inflected Forms	**Usage Notes**
Labels *(Nonstandard, Slang)*	**Synonyms**
Cross-References	Biographical Entries
Order of Definitions	Geographical Entries
Sense-Division	Abbreviations
Explanatory Notes in Entries	

Each of these headings represents some feature you may encounter when you look up a word.

➤ **Know how to use key features in a dictionary: spelling, syllabication, pronunciation, part-of-speech, usage labels, definitions, etymologies, usage notes, synonyms, and antonyms.**

● **Spelling and Syllabication.** Obviously, the alphabetical listing of words in a dictionary is a guide to accurate spelling. The main entry, printed in boldface type, will be separated into syllables to indicate where to divide the word at the end of a line. Spellings will also be given for various forms of the entry: verb endings, unusual or potentially troublesome plurals, suffixes.

> **com•press**   **-pressed, -press•ing, -press•es**
> **mouse**   pl. **mice**
> **lush**   **-er, -est**
> **trav•el**   **-eled, el•ing, els** or **-elled, el•ling, els**

Many words have alternative spellings. In most cases, choose the first spelling listed, which is usually the more common.

> **mov•a•ble** also **move•a•ble**
>
> **me•di•e•val** also **me•di•ae•val**

Avoid archaic and British spellings unless you have a special reason to use them.

> **col•or** also Brit. **col•our**
>
> **lic•o•rice** also Brit. **li•quo•rice**

● **Pronunciation.** Hearing a word is the best way of learning to pronounce it correctly. However, dictionaries will help you figure out the sound of an entry if you are patient enough to interpret the pronunciation key usually printed at the top or bottom of every page. The front matter will explain how the pronunciation key in any given dictionary works, but most follow the same basic principles.

Each major entry in a dictionary is followed by a pronunciation, which often looks like an odd spelling of the word decorated with accent marks, strange vowels, and unusual markings: ü, ø, é, û. Every consonant and vowel sound in the pronunciation is keyed to familiar words in the pronunciation guide that also use those sounds.

For example, let's say you aren't sure how to say the word *harlequin.* Checking the American Heritage Dictionary again, you find this pronunciation listed:

> **(här′li-kwin, -kin)**

It tells you several things even before you check the pronunciation key. The word is accented on its first syllable **(här′),** the two unaccented syllables **(li-kwin)**— joined by a hyphen—are pronounced together, and there are two possible pronunciations, **här′li-kwin** and **här′li-kin.**

In *harlequin,* the consonants *h, r, l,* and *n* all have their most familiar sounds. But were you unsure of any of them, a check of the pronunciation key at the bottom of the page shows that they have these values:

> h   **h**at
> r   **r**oar
> l   **l**id
> n   **n**o, sudde**n**

In the pronunciation, the *qu* in *harlequin* is written as *kw* and pronounced exactly as you would expect.

49 B

Dict

k **kick**
w **with**

The key also gives approximate pronunciations for each of the vowels, often the most troublesome part of the sound in a given word. Because vowels often have different sounds, the marks over them indicate important distinctions. Again, each vowel sound in the pronunciation is explained by a familiar key word.

ä father
i pit

Notice especially that the *e* in *harlequin* appears as an *i* in the pronunciation.

Put all the sounds together, pay attention to the accent marks and syllable groupings, and you have a reasonably accurate rendering of an unfamiliar word. Sound difficult? Only because the pronunciation key is one feature of a dictionary easier to use than to explain.

Remember that pronunciations vary from region to region. Ohioans fill their crankcases with *oy-al* while Texans pump *awl.* Dictionaries strive to provide "standard" pronunciations, but standard doesn't necessarily mean *the only correct* pronunciation.

• **Part-of-Speech.** The meaning or pronunciation of a word may change according to the role it plays in a sentence. *Brave,* for example, can be a noun, verb, and adjective.

{As a noun}   Kyle once dreamed of wearing the uniform of an Atlanta **Brave.**

{As a verb}   Instead, he **braved** the difficulties of electrical engineering and chemistry.

{As an adjective}   It takes a **brave** student to pursue a double major.

Dictionaries, of course, must account for all these meanings in an entry. Or separate entries may be provided for words with the same spelling but different pronunciations and meanings. Consider, for example, the uses of the word *deserts* in the following sentences.

{Noun}   The **deserts** were hot and barren, yet full of life.

{Noun}   Martin received his just **deserts** for deceiving Alicia.

{Verb}   If Kyle **deserts** the team, he'll lose some friends.

Most dictionaries provide particularly useful information about verbs, indicating whether they are *transitive* or *intransitive* and furnishing the *principal parts* of irregular verbs.

49 B

Dict

• **Labels.** The labels used to describe words vary from dictionary to dictionary.

It is common, for example, to find **field** labels that identify words (or definitions) with special significance in specific disciplines. A word like *floppy* has a general meaning that describes the condition of rabbits' ears. But one definition of the term might be accompanied by a field label: *Computer Sci.* Then *floppy* refers to a magnetic disk that stores computer information.

Other labels describe the status of particular words in the language. The *American Heritage Dictionary,* for example, uses these labels: *nonstandard, informal, slang, vulgar, obscene, offensive, obsolete, archaic, regional,* and *chiefly British.* Each label is carefully defined in the front matter. Since people don't agree on how far a dictionary should go in saying what words are acceptable or offensive, such labels can be controversial. Yet they can also prevent blunders and embarrassing usages.

Be sure to check how any dictionary you use defines and applies its labels.

• **Order of Definitions.** Check the front matter of a dictionary to determine how it arranges the definitions of an entry when more than one meaning is possible. Some dictionaries list the most common meaning first. Others arrange their entries historically; that is, the first meaning records how the word was used when it initially appeared in the language. Subsequent meanings then show how the term changes in meaning over the years. Still other dictionaries arrange their definitions according to different principles—such as "meaning clusters."

Knowing how the definitions are arranged is important in understanding the meaning of a term. The *Oxford English Dictionary,* for example, lists "Strong, powerful, mighty" as its first definition for *crafty*—not a sense we use today, but the first meaning the term had in English. If you didn't know that the *Oxford* arranged its entries historically, you might be misled in this case by what seems like a peculiar definition.

• **Etymologies.** Most dictionaries make an effort to trace the origins of words, explaining what languages they, or their roots, come from. Etymologies may not be supplied for compounds *(homework, bloodshot)*, words derived from other words *(escapee)*, words derived from geographical names *(New Yorker)*, and so on. You can usually trace these etymologies by going back to the more basic words *(home, work, blood, shot, escape, New York)*.

Etymologies in desk dictionaries have to be brief, so they rely on various abbreviations and symbols. Some etymologies are easy to interpret, like the following explanation of *kumquat:*

[Cantonese *kumquat,* golden orange]

Others can seem quite complicated, especially when a word is derived from several earlier forms or several languages. This is how the *American Heritage Dictionary* traces the history of *rummage.*

[Obs. *rummage,* act of packing cargo <OFr. *arrumage<arumer,* to stow: *a-,* to (<Lat. *ad-*) + *run,* ship's hold, of Germanic orig.]

For help in interpreting such etymologies, check the guide to etymologies usually located in the front matter of a dictionary. It will explain the meaning of the symbols (<, :, +) and the abbreviations (OFr., Lat.).

• **Usage Notes.** Many dictionaries now offer advice about how the more troublesome words and expressions in a language ought to be used. The advice usually follows the main body of an entry. For example, *American Heritage* provides this comment on the word *critique.*

49 B

Dict

Usage: *Critique* is widely used as a verb, but is still regarded by many as pretentious jargon. The use of phrases like *give a critique* or *offer a critique* will forestall objections.

• **Synonyms.** Most writers search for synonyms in a thesaurus, but in a pinch a dictionary may help. Some desk dictionaries now list synonyms for many important words, and a few even attempt to explain the differences between synonyms—a useful feature.

EXERCISE 49.2

Browse through your dictionary to find examples of the following.

1. A word with a variant spelling.
2. A word that includes a usage note (if your dictionary provides such notations).
3. A word pronounced with a regional slant in your area. Compare your regional pronunciation with the dictionary's version.
4. Several words that can be used as more than one part of speech. Look especially for nouns that can also be used as verbs.
5. A word with a field label. You may want to begin with a technical term you sometimes use *(chip, touchdown)*. Check to see whether your dictionary gives it a field label.
6. A word that might be considered slang, vulgar, offensive, archaic, or informal. See how your dictionary treats the entry.
7. A word with a simple etymology.
8. A word with a complicated etymology.
9. A word you aren't sure how to pronounce. Use the pronunciation key to figure it out; then test your version on someone familiar with the word.
10. A word for which synonyms are offered (if your dictionary offers synonyms).

EXERCISE 49.3

Pick a full page of your dictionary at random. Read it completely and write a short summary of what you have learned about the words on that page or about your dictionary. What is the most interesting word on that page? Which has the most impressive etymology? The most complicated definition? The most meanings? The oddest or most difficult pronunciation? Do any words on the page require labels or remarks about usage? Are illustrations on the page (if any) useful?

---

49 C   DEVELOPING A STRONG VOCABULARY

Terms you need to know

49 C

LEXICON. A dictionary; or a list of words used in a particular discipline—a political *lexicon,* the *lexicon* of physics.

Etym   **NEOLOGISM.** A newly created word.

PREFIX. A cluster of letters attached to the beginning of a word or root. The addition of a prefix usually alters or expands the meaning of the expression to which it is attached. Consider the following examples.

re + gain

de + mystify

proto + type

SUFFIX. A cluster of letters attached to the end of a word or root. The addition of a suffix usually alters or expands the meaning of the expression to which it is attached or defines its function.

gain + **fully**

mystifi + **cation**

typ + **ical**

Troubleshooting

Dictionaries remind us how vast the resources of English are. While it is impossible to count the exact number of words available to the speaker and writer of English, the Oxford English Dictionary defines more than a half-million terms. And that number does not include many slang items, special terms, items of jargon, local expressions, neologisms, and creative variations on English vocabulary that we encounter almost every day.

Given this great wealth, it makes sense for writers to exploit the resources of English. Yet many writers fear that using "big" words or an impressive vocabulary interferes with clarity; they recall the George Orwell dictum drilled into them by teachers from high school through college: "Never use a big word where a small one will do." If words are used to confuse readers or conceal meaning, then Orwell would be right. But perhaps the rule needs a corollary: "Never use a big word just to use a big word."

After all, the whole point of a rich vocabulary is to furnish writers with precise instruments for description and analysis. Is it better to write "a ditch or gully formed by an intermittent flow of water" than to use *arroyo,* a word English offers (thanks to Spanish)? Do *evil* and *diabolical* mean precisely the same thing? Is it jargon to use technical terms like *dyslexia* or *philately* when a writer can safely assume that most readers understand them? The answer to all these questions is *no.* Big words aren't necessarily worse—or better—than small ones. They are simply *options.* But if writers know only the most basic items of English vocabulary (in 1930, Charles Kay Ogden suggested a version of English with only 850 words), then precision and choice suffer. After all, you can't choose to use a word you don't know.

A strong vocabulary enhances your ability both to read and to write, so it makes sense to develop word skills. In addition, words are fun, and English offers more such pleasures than just about any other language on Earth. But who's counting?

To develop a strong vocabulary . . .

➤ **Learn a little about the history of English.** Good writers obviously need adequate vocabularies to express themselves powerfully, memorably, and accurately. But since the earliest times, writers have argued about how inclusive English should be and how freely it should borrow from other languages.

When the Angles, Saxons, and Jutes began their invasion of the island of Britain in A.D. 449, they brought with them a Germanic tongue. This language, which we know as Old English (A.D. 450–1150), expanded its comparatively limited vocabulary—one as yet unenriched by significant Latin and French addi-

49 C

Etym

tions—by means of prefixes, suffixes, and ingenious compounds. The Anglo-Saxons drank, for example, at an *ealohus (ale + house);* fought on a *waelfeld (slaughter + field);* and followed a *leod-fruma (people + leader)*. This way of building a lexicon gave the Anglo-Saxons a language subtle enough to produce some of the finest European poetry of the period, including masterpieces like *Beowulf* and "The Wanderer."

By the Middle English period (1150–1450), English shows extensive borrowing from many languages, including **Celtic** (the language of the natives of Britain), **Latin** (following the Christian conversion of the Anglo-Saxons, begun in 597), **Scandinavian** (as the result of Viking invasions, 787–850, and subsequent Danish settlement in Britain), and **French** (as a result of the Norman conquest of England in 1066). Indeed, for a significant portion of the Middle Ages in England, French was the prestige tongue, the dominant language of Britain's upper classes and court. But by the thirteenth century, English was in ascendancy, spreading through the aristocracy once again, so that in the fourteenth century, it was spoken by all Britons, used by all classes, and established as the official language of the law courts (1362). But the French influence proved to be deep and long-lasting, contributing to English many terms that now seem completely native: *servant, messenger, statute, oppress, tax, nobility, accuse, perjury, adultery, defense, garment, button, appetite, mansion,* and so on.

In the Early Modern period (1450–1700), the vocabulary of English grew even more rapidly, with the dialect of London becoming the national standard, at least in writing. At the same time that it was beginning to displace Latin as the language of scholarship, English was also absorbing many Latin words—as well as terms of Greek, Italian, and Spanish origin. Indeed, the infusion of foreign terms into English was extensive enough to lead a writer like Thomas Wilson in his *Arte of Rhetorique* (1553) to condemn "strange ynkehorne termes."

During the last century of this period, the English language followed explorers and colonists into the New World, where what would someday become American (and Canadian) English came into contact with Native Americans, Africans, and Spaniards and acquired terms like *bayou, petunia, moccasin, toboggan, tobacco, banana, gumbo, okra, mesa, lariat,* and *rodeo*.

In the Modern Period (1700 to present), English rose to the stature of a world language, chiefly because of the political, military, and economic dominance first of Great Britain and then of the United States, but also as the result of the willingness of English speakers to absorb and use "foreign" terms. In the eighteenth century, Samuel Johnson hoped that his dictionary (1755) might "fix the English language" and make it more orderly; grammarians at about the same time labored to describe its operations and to establish a standard of correctness. But neither Johnson nor the grammarians could have anticipated the impact English would eventually have on the world. In the newly independent United States (1776), the American language became a patriotic expression. The language spread with pioneers and settlers across the entire North American continent, gained its own dictionary, and acquired distinct regional pronunciations and even some uniquely American spellings.

49 C

Etym

American	***British***
color	colour
wagon	waggon

ax	axe
tire	tyre
center	centre
plow	plough

Today, an estimated 700 million to one billion people can speak or read English with varying degrees of fluency. More important than sheer numbers, the language is employed on all continents and dominates the realms of diplomacy, science, and communications (especially the storage and transmission of information). English has official or semiofficial status in countries ranging from the United States, Canada, Australia, New Zealand, Ireland, and Great Britain to India, the Philippines, Nigeria, Jamaica, South Africa, Sri Lanka, and Kenya. In one way or another, all these lands and peoples now contribute to the lexicon of English, a language that once belonged only to obscure Germanic tribes settling an isolated corner of Europe.

Landmark Dates in the History of the English Language

700	Approximate date of earliest written records of Old English.
750?	Composition of the Old English epic *Beowulf.*
1066	Norman invasion and beginning of a strong French influence on the English language.
1086	Compilation of William I's *Domesday Book.*
1400	Death of Geoffrey Chaucer, greatest writer of Middle English.
1476	Introduction of the printing press to England by William Caxton.
1499	First dictionary printed in England, a Latin-English work.
1607	Settlement of Jamestown, first English colony in North America.
1611	Publication of the King James Bible.
1623	Publication of the First Folio of Shakespeare's plays.
1755	Publication of Samuel Johnson's two-volume *A Dictionary of the English Language.*
1781	Coinage of the term "Americanism" by John Witherspoon, President of Princeton University.
1794	Publication of Lindley Murray's influential *English Grammar:* "Two negatives, in English, destroy one another."
1828	Publication of Noah Webster's *An American Dictionary of the English Language.*
1884–1928	Publication of *The Oxford English Dictionary.*

49 C

Etym

Landmark Dates in the History of the English Language

1939 Beginning of the *Linguistic Atlas of the United States and Canada,* an attempt to record and study the regional speech of English speakers in North America.

1961 Publication of the controversial *Webster's Third New International Dictionary of the English Language,* which avoided prescriptive judgments.

1989 The second edition of *The Oxford English Dictionary.*

EXERCISE 49.4

Use a dictionary to determine from what language groups the following words entered English—Arabic, Bantu, Italian, French, German, Hebrew, Italian, Latin, Russian, Sanskrit, Slavic, Scandinavian. (You may want to do only one column.)

1. bomb	11. sable	21. banjo
2. face	12. ozone	22. salmon
3. Gulag	13. jukebox	23. zero
4. helicopter	14. volcano	24. parka
5. cherub	15. waltz	25. sugar
6. mesa	16. nickel	26. episode
7. radius	17. sapphire	27. chassis
8. plaza	18. pantomime	28. corral
9. ghetto	19. candy	29. robot
10. yam	20. mammoth	30. pagoda

EXERCISE 49.5

Provide an American alternative for the following British words. If necessary, consult a dictionary to establish the differences.

1. bonnet	6. dustman
2. windscreen	7. underdone
3. motorway	8. nappy
4. petrol	9. kip
5. lorry	10. lift

49 C

Etym

➤ **Read carefully.** You can pick up a surprising number of vocabulary items just by paying closer attention to what you read—pausing to notice words you don't fully comprehend. Such careful study will be rewarded most often with material filled with new information—like textbooks, scholarly articles, or informative pieces. But even a popular magazine or newspaper will contain words you probably haven't encountered before—the name of a geographic area, a verb describing a scientific procedure, an adjective describing a sports car.

You can discover the meaning of the term by checking a dictionary, atlas, or encyclopedia. But the context in which the word appears also provides a sense of meaning and proper use.

> What began as a nimble sports car developed over its production life into a **porcine** luxury coupe.

Even lacking a precise understanding of *porcine,* you'd probably guess that the word implies the opposite of *nimble.* And you'd be right.

While reading, you might not want to pause over every unknown or imprecisely understood word (we often read well enough even when a few terms are only vaguely understood), but you might circle unfamiliar items and come back to learn them later.

When you pick up a new word and learn its meaning, begin looking for it elsewhere. You'll be amazed how often the previously unrecognized word pops up in your reading and conversation. Of course it has always been there; you just tuned it out, the way you ignore an unfamiliar face in a crowd. Once you are confident that you know what a word means—both denotatively and connotatively—begin working it into your writing and conversation.

EXERCISE 49.6

Try to construct the meaning of the boldfaced terms from context only. Check a dictionary or encyclopedia to determine whether your constructed definition is accurate.

1. Supporting prison reform proved an **egregious** error, one the political party would regret for decades.
2. Kent's foot doctor indicated that his shoes were wearing oddly because of improper **pronation.**
3. The book was so full of praise and kind words about its subject that the newspaper's **acerbic** reviewer suggested it was nearer to **hagiography** than biography.
4. A splendid view opened to the group of tourists as they rounded the corner of the chateaux and approached a **ha-ha** that separated the formal gardens from a broad and pleasant field.
5. The character walks with **Kafkaesque** gloom through a surreal and unpredictable city we barely recognize as Boston.

> **Pay attention to the meaning of roots.** You can often construct the meaning of an unfamiliar term if a portion of the word is familiar—particularly its core or root. In an earlier example, if you recognized that *porcine* shares the same root as *pork,* you probably sensed that *porcine* means "resembling a pig or swine"; both words are derived from the Latin word for pig, *porcus.*

49 C

Etym

Because so many English words are derived from Latin, Greek, and French roots, learning any one root often opens up an entire family of words. For example, the Latin word *finis*—meaning "limit, conclusion, end"—is the root of all the following English terms, which form a word family.

affinity	finalist
confine	finality
confinement	finance
define	financier
definition	finesse
definitive	finicky
final	finish
finale	finite
indefinite	infinitive
infinite	refine
infinitesimal	unrefined

Clearly, knowing the meaning of basic roots (as well as some basic prefixes and suffixes—see below) is a quick way of expanding the range of one's vocabulary. Here is a list of a few important Latin and Greek roots.

Root (Latin)	Meaning	English terms
qus	equal	equality, equitable
amare	love	amorous
annus	year	biannual
aud	hear	auditorium
bene	good	benefit
cap	head	decapitate, capital
dic	speak, say	diction, dictate
disc	dish	dish, disk
duc	lead	induct, ductwork
expend	spend	expenditure
fac	do, make	factory, manufacturer
fix	fasten	transfix, fixate
judicium	judgment	judicial, injudicious
loqui	speak	elocution, eloquent
luc	light	lucid, translucence
man	hand	manipulate
med	middle	medium, intermediate
mit	send	transmission, remit
omni	all	omnidirectional
port	carry	portage, import
quar	question	inquisition, query
rog	ask	interrogatory
scrib	write	inscribe, description
secur	safe	security, insecure
sent	feel	sense, sentimental
spec	look, look at	inspect, spectrograph
spir	breathe	inspiration, expire
tend	stretch	tendon, extend
ter	earth	terrestrial, territory
torn	turn	return
verb	word	verbal, verbose

Root (Greek)	Meaning	English terms
aster	star	asteroid, astronomy
bio	life	biosphere

chrono	time	chronology, synchronic
geo	land, earth	geographical
graph	write	biography
kyrios	lord	church
logos	word, speech	monologue, dialogue
meter	measure	kilometer
pathos	feeling, suffering	empathetic, sympathy
photo	light	photograph
phys	nature	physical
psych	soul	psychiatry
pyr	fire	pyromaniac
tele	distant	telescope
thermo	heat	thermometer
xeros	dry	xerophyte

➤ **Pay attention to prefixes and suffixes.** Root words are transformed in their meaning by the addition of prefixes and suffixes. Prefixes appear before a root or word; suffixes show up afterward. Prefixes tend to change the meaning of a term, specifying such things as time (*pre-*; *post-*), negation (*un-*; *non-*; *ir-*), or number (*bi-*; *tri-*; *sesqui-*). Suffixes similarly affect the meaning of a word, but may also indicate its grammatical function, showing whether it is a noun (*-ness, -er, -ment,* among others), adjective (*-ive, -ish, -less,* among many others), or adverb (usually *-ly*). Suffixes that expressly change or indicate the grammatical function of a word are called **inflectional.** Such inflectional suffixes include verb endings, the *s* at the end of a plural word, and the comparative (*-er*) and superlative (*-est*) endings.

Knowing the meaning of a given prefix or suffix may help you decipher an unfamiliar term. Here's a partial list of prefixes and suffixes useful to recognize.

Prefix	*Meaning*	*Example*
a-	without	**a**symmetrical, **a**moral
ante-	before	**ante**chamber
anti-	against	**anti**aircraft
bi-	two	**bi**cameral
centi-	hundred	**centi**pede
circum-	around	**circum**ference
counter-	opposite	**counter**act, **counter**feit
dec-	ten	**dec**ade, **dec**asyllabic
dis-	do the opposite	**dis**enfranchise
ex-	out, out of, formerly	**ex**claim, **ex**tirpate **ex**-president
fore-	before	**fore**see
hemi-	half	**hemi**spherical
hyper-	above, beyond	**hyper**active
hypo-	below, beneath	**hypo**dermic
in-	not	**in**hospitable
inter-	together, between	**inter**coastal
intra-	within, inside	**intra**mural
kilo	thousand	**kilo**meter
mal-	bad, unpleasant	**mal**odorous, **mal**content
milli-	thousand, thousandth	**milli**second

49 C

Etym

Prefix	Meaning	Example
mini-	small	**mini**skirt
mis-	incorrectly, badly	**mis**manage
non-	not	**non**repeating
oct-	eight	**oct**agon
per-	through, very	**per**petual
peri-	surrounding	**peri**cardium
post-	after	**post**war
pre-	before	**pre**menstrual
pro-	before, for, in favor of	**pro**tuberance **pro**-capitalist
re-	do again, behind, back	**re**write **re**fract
retro	back	**retro**rocket
semi-	half	**semi**circle
super-	above, beyond	**super**sonic
trans-	across	**trans**national
tri-	three	**tri**color, **tri**motor
uni-	one	**uni**corn

Suffix	Meaning	Example
-ful	full of, having	use**ful**, plenti**ful**
-hood	in the condition of	brother**hood**, state**hood**
-ish	like, the state of	boy**ish**, squeam**ish**
-ist	one who does	tour**ist**, chem**ist**
-ize	to do, to make	legal**ize**, catego**rize**
-less	without, free of	hap**less**, law**less**
-ous	full of, state of	nox**ious**, beaut**eous**
-ology	study of	ge**ology**, ast**rology**

Of course, just combining roots with prefixes and suffixes will not tell you precisely what a word means. But often, these elements, aided by the context of your reading, will enable you to infer the meaning of words you have never before encountered. When you have the time, check their meaning in a dictionary and get a feel for their proper use.

EXERCISE 49.7

49 C

Etym

Companies often coin names for new products by using Greek and Latin roots, prefixes, and suffixes. The combinations produce new, but familiar expressions that suggest something about the products to which they are attached. Discuss the meanings of the following brand and product names and the connotations that attach to the product as a result. If necessary, use a dictionary.

1. Quattro (an all-wheel drive automobile)
2. Lucite (paint)
3. Dictaphone (an office device)
4. Magnavox (a brand of TV, radio, stereo)

5. Xerox (a photocopier)
6. Nautica (a clothing line)
7. Technics (a brand of audio equipment)
8. Infiniti (a brand of luxury car)
9. Geo (a line of economy cars)
10. Thermos (a container)

EXERCISE 49.8

1. The Latin words for the members of a family have shaped a number of English words: *pater* (father), *mater* (mother), *frater* (brother), *soror* (sister). List as many as you can without checking a dictionary.
2. Check a dictionary for the derivation of *kaleidoscope.*
3. Use the lists of roots, prefixes, and suffixes in this section to come up with at least five existing words. For example *psych + ology = psychology.*
4. Using the same lists as in the previous exercise, coin at least five new words. (You may use other endings as well.) Then define your neologisms and use them in sentences. For example, *super + aster + ic = superastric,* which means "above and beyond the stars": Joe's grand slam in the ninth inning was *superastric*!

▶ **Master words in key academic subjects, especially in your major.** You show your command of any field by how well you use its language. Observe professionals in any field talking or writing to each other and you'll encounter many specialized terms and expressions. Their language may be filled with very technical terms or with efficient abbreviations and acronyms. Just walking into a service station these days can be an education.

> "Sorry ma'am, but your *fuel injectors* may be clogged and you'll need to replace the *oxygen sensor* this time if you don't want to invalidate your *emissions control system* warranty. There's also a glitch in your *ABS* system computer, but we'll *scope* it and replace the faulty *module* if necessary."

Whatever your major may be, it will have a vocabulary all its own, one that you will acquire gradually over the years. To hasten that process, try to understand completely any words that keep appearing in the headings of your textbooks, in articles you read, or in the lectures of your instructors. Don't be ashamed to ask for a definition of a term that really puzzles you. Sometimes you may understand the denotation of a word well enough, without being sure about its connotations. In such cases, watch where and how the term is used and question your teachers about its proper use. Don't use it yourself in a paper or examination until you are confident you can handle it.

49 C

Etym

EXERCISE 49.9

1. If you have a major, make a list of key terms that you think might puzzle people outside your field. Then briefly try to define these words.

2. If you have not yet declared a major, make a list of puzzling terms you have encountered in various subjects. Define these terms to the best of your ability. In a group of fellow classmates, compare the puzzling terms and see whether members can help improve the less successful definitions.

> **If you enjoy reading about language, two valuable books are Albert C. Baugh and Thomas Cable's *A History of the English Language* (1978) and David Crystal's *The Cambridge Encyclopedia of Language* (1987).**

49 D SPECIAL-PURPOSE DICTIONARIES

Every field and interest is served by dictionaries. Your library reference room contains dictionaries of art, history, philosophy, physics, social science, photography, film, television, music, sports, opera, theater, ballet, and so on. Rest assured that for any serious subject you can name, someone has compiled an alphabetical collection of significant terms.

Regular English dictionaries cover general aspects of language—spelling, pronunciation, word meaning; other dictionaries deal with specialized interests. The reference room of a large library will house row after row of such special-purpose volumes. Such books can solve special needs you have while writing or reading.

What do you do, for example, when you read or hear an unfamiliar bit of slang, but can't find the expression in a desk dictionary or even in an unabridged volume? For such an item, consult a dictionary of slang such as:

A Dictionary of Slang and Unconventional English (Eric Partridge)

Mainstream dictionaries do list many slang and colloquial expressions, but they don't pretend to cover all the less formal terms English has acquired over the centuries. Go to Partridge for terms like *beer-slinger, flipside, give the heat, mosey, pintle-de-pantedly, put the bite on, ratbaggery, undress a sheep,* or *wharf-rat.*

Partridge's huge dictionary contains unconventional items from both past and present. If you are more interested in current idioms, you'll find a number of dictionaries catering to the subject, including:

Oxford Dictionary of Current Idiomatic Usage. 2 Vols. (A. P. Cowie)

and Stuart B. Flexner *Dictionary of American Slang* (Harold Wentworth)

Dictionaries of idioms explain these expressions from a language that means something more than the sum of its parts. Such a dictionary is handy for phrases such as *bite the dust, easy money, full of oneself, a long shot, a slip of the tongue, weak at the knees, stink to high heaven, tee up,* or *waltz off with.* Dictionaries of idioms are not only useful; they can be fun.

If you meet an abbreviation or acronym you don't recognize—perhaps the name of a new government agency or a corporate conglomerate recently merged—where do you go? To a specialized dictionary of abbreviations. One compilation of these terms, updated regularly, is:

Acronyms, Initialisms & Abbreviations Dictionary. 10th Ed. 1986–87, 3 Vols. (Julie E. Towell and Helen E. Sheppard, eds.)

The work covers abbreviations from many fields and areas: aerospace, associations, electronics, labor, government, military, religion, sports, and so on.

Perhaps the problem is understanding a proper noun—the name of an unknown person, place, or thing. Ordinary dictionaries make an effort here, sometimes providing separate geographic and biographical listings. But for the more obscure allusion, literary character, place, or person, check a specialized dictionary of proper nouns such as:

Webster's Dictionary of Proper Names (Geoffrey Payton)

Here you'll find listed terms as varied as *Angkor Wat, Birnam Wood, Bushido, Dear Abby, Krazy Kat, Mickey Finn, Politburo, Reynard the Fox, Sardi's,* and *Zond.*

Perhaps your problem is less exotic: you need help with your spelling. Your best friend might be a word list, a handy, pocket-sized dictionary without the definitions, pronunciations, etymologies, and other side dishes that fatten collegiate dictionaries. What word lists provide are words, word divisions, and occasional warnings about homonyms. Or you might consider one of these volumes:

The Word Book. (Kaethe Ellis)

20,000 Words (Louis A. Leslie)

If you are a *really* bad speller—so bad that you have trouble locating correct spellings in a dictionary—you might need something like *Webster's New World Misspeller's Dictionary.* In this tiny book, which lists 15,000 common errors, misspellings are used to locate correct spellings. Looking up the incorrect *laggon,* for example, provides the correct *lagoon; auxilary* gives *auxiliary;* either *medecine* or *medisine* gives *medicine.* Of course, the book cannot anticipate every misspelling, but it may get you out of a jam.

Regular dictionaries try to answer basic questions of usage, but more advice is available in a dictionary of usage, such as:

Current American Usage (Margaret M. Bryant)

A Dictionary of Contemporary American Usage (Bergen Evans and Cornelia Evans)

Modern American Usage: A Guide (Wilson Follett)

A Dictionary of Modern English Usage (Henry W. Fowler)

Harper Dictionary of Contemporary Usage (William and Mary Morris)

49 D

Resource

These volumes and others like them establish their authority on matters of usage and convention in a variety of ways. Fowler's book, for example, relies to a great extent on the authority and good sense of its original author; its orientation is

British. The *Harper Dictionary*, on the other hand, refers disputed questions of convention to the authority of a usage panel of 165 writers, editors, and speakers. Should *author* be used as a verb (as in "Richard Nixon *authored* the chapter")? The panel votes no. Is *parenting* a useful new word? The panel thinks not. Can *hopefully* be used in the sense of *we hope*? No, not in writing.

An interest in the origins of words and regional expressions can be satisfied by many dictionaries, among them:

> *The Oxford Dictionary of English Etymology* (C. T. Onions)
>
> *Dictionary of American Regional English* (Frederic G. Cassidy)
>
> *Dictionary of Word and Phrase Origins* (William and Mary Morris)

Even poets in search of a rhyme need not feel neglected in the reference room. There's a dictionary just for him or her:

> *The Penguin Rhyming Dictionary* (Rosalind Fergusson)

Arranged somewhat like a thesaurus, this computer-compiled volume includes entries for words that have at least one rhyme. Individual words are listed in an index at the back of the volume, keyed to groupings of words with rhyming endings.

49 E   A WRITER'S BOOKSHELF

Troubleshooting

What books should a writer keep within easy reach on a desktop? Any "essential" collection will vary according to professional needs and interests. A business major might want to own a reference book like Clark and Gottfried's *University Dictionary of Business and Finance*. For the typical English major, the micro-printed edition of the *Oxford English Dictionary* anchors any serious scholarly collection. A sports nut might regard Brander's *Dictionary of Sporting Terms* as required reading.

But professional concerns aside, we would like to suggest a core collection for all writers—a personal library of essential reference tools. We think such a desktop collection should include the following volumes.

> ➤ **A dictionary.**

A dictionary is the first and most important item in your collection. Many fine college dictionaries are available. If you can afford an unabridged dictionary (and have the space), consider purchasing one. But for desk use, the dictionaries discussed in Section 49A are more convenient.

> ➤ **A thesaurus.**

A thesaurus is a collection of synonyms—a book designed to help you discover a word better than one you have in mind or simply an alternative to avoid using one word too often.

The first English thesaurus was published by Peter Mark Roget in 1852. In the first part of his book, Roget grouped words by meaning according to a complex arrangement of categories: *Abstract Relations, Space, Matter, Intellect, Volition, Affections.* Within this scheme, words of similar meaning (and also of opposite meaning) were clustered together. To locate a particular word and its synonyms in the first part of the book, you started by consulting the alphabetical index in the back of the volume.

Roget's arrangement has been retained in some contemporary thesauruses, including:

Roget's International Thesaurus, 3rd ed.

The St. Martin's Roget's Thesaurus of English Words and Phrases

The traditional structure has the disadvantage of requiring two steps to find a synonym. In addition, the words listed in the thesaurus are often far from exact synonyms. More than one writer has chosen unwisely from the full slate of related words and synonyms traditional thesauruses offer. Yet the variety of words grouped in meaningful clusters is the strength of these reference books. Many experienced writers find that Roget's groupings stimulate their ideas and consequently they prefer his arrangement to the alternative.

That alternative to Roget's design is a thesaurus arranged alphabetically. Such a book is as convenient to use as a dictionary: to find a synonym for a word, you check a single alphabetical list. Two alphabetically-arranged thesauruses are:

Roget's II The New Thesaurus

Webster's Collegiate Thesaurus

In most cases, you will find fewer but more precise suggestions for synonyms in these works and much more guidance about meaning. *Roget's II* defines words briefly and uses the words in context, lessening the likelihood of choosing an inappropriate synonym. *Webster's* also uses synonyms in context and warns against terms that might be misconstrued. An alphabetical thesaurus is probably the best choice for most writers—at least initially. Eventually, you may want to graduate to Roget's more challenging design.

➤ **A handbook of writing, grammar, and usage.**
You need a handbook to give you advice and guidance about writing and usage. Consult a handbook when you have questions about composition, punctuation, grammar, usage, format, and documentation. Since you are reading this, you know what a general handbook looks like. But at some point you might want to purchase a manual specifically for your field: technical writing, business writing, scientific writing, and so on.

➤ **A one-volume encyclopedia.**
A multivolume encyclopedia is a superb reference tool, but too large for a desktop and usually very expensive. Consider, instead, a single-volume work, such as:

49 E

Ref

The Random House Encyclopedia

The New Columbia Encyclopedia

These handy tools supply you with information about thousands of subjects, from historical personalities to philosophical and scientific concepts. Keeping an encyclopedia within reach can save you dozens of trips to a library.

➤ An almanac.

An almanac provides facts and figures on thousands of subjects. And because paperback almanacs are relatively inexpensive, you can usually afford to buy a new one every few years to keep your information up to date. So when you need to know the population of Lagos, Nigeria, or who won the World Series in 1952, or the per-capita income of farmers in Wisconsin last year, you know where to turn. Most almanacs include information about topics as varied as elections, current events, astronomy, aviation, business, disasters, geography, awards (Nobel, Pulitzer, Oscar, Emmy, Grammy), nutrition, science, and weights and measures. They provide statistics on countries and states, and often include maps. Two familiar almanacs, updated annually, are:

> *The World Almanac and Book of Facts*
>
> *Information Please Almanac*

➤ An atlas.

When you write about a place, you should know where it is. A good atlas puts the political and geographical world at your fingertips with its full collection of maps. Atlases vary greatly in their focus and coverage. In addition to providing maps, they may also include detailed information about astronomy, geology, history, geography, ecology, and environments. Some atlases worth considering are:

> *The Prentice-Hall New World Atlas*
>
> *Rand McNally Illustrated Atlas of the World*
>
> *Rand McNally Cosmopolitan World Atlas*
>
> *The Times Atlas of World History*

➤ A dictionary of quotations.

The most famous advocate for dictionaries of quotations was Winston Churchill who wrote:

> It is a good thing for an uneducated man to read books of quotations. Bartlett's *Familiar Quotations* is an admirable work, and I studied it intently. The quotations when engraved upon the memory give you good thoughts. They also make you anxious to read the authors and look for more.

Even if such collections don't inspire "good thoughts," you will still find dictionaries of quotations handy for discovering what others have said about a subject or locating impressive support for ideas. Such dictionaries are indexed in various ways—usually by some combination of author, date, and subject. As Churchill suggests, *Bartlett's Familiar Quotations* is the best-known work in this field, but many useful books are available.

49 E

Ref

➤ A Bible.

No book is as well known or is quoted as often in the Western world as the Bible. Whether a believer or not, a writer should consider including a Bible among his or her reference works. Because of its literary power, the King James Version of 1611, along with its subsequent revisions, is still the edition of choice for writers of English.

➤ **A volume of Shakespeare.**
Among speakers of English, only the Bible is better known or quoted more often
than the works of Shakespeare. No matter what your discipline or profession, an
edition of Shakespeare can become a well-thumbed and cherished reference tool.
There are numerous reliable editions available, among them:

> *The Complete Works of Shakespeare.* (Scott, Foresman)
>
> *The Riverside Shakespeare.* (Houghton Mifflin)
>
> *The Complete Signet Classic Shakespeare.* (Harcourt Brace Jovanovich)

49 E

Ref

50 Spelling

Term you need to know

HOMONYMS. Words that have different meanings, but are pronounced alike: *altar/alter; to/too/two; hear/here.*

Troubleshooting

The first problem with spelling English right is that English is hard to spell. A second difficulty is that misspellings upset people far more than you might expect. You will pay a penalty for every significant error. Many readers will take you, your facts, and your ideas—whatever their merit—less seriously if your spelling is just slightly askew. If your spelling is atrocious, expect serious trouble.

But be clear on this point: good writing and reliable spelling are not the same thing. Many people incorrectly assume that accurate spelling automatically translates into good writing. In fact, the relationship is not that simple. You may be a perfectly sound writer, but a poor speller—or vice versa.

Fortunately, adults typically misspell only about 1 percent of the words they write, so the problem should be manageable. What's more, unlike many other issues of language, spelling is—for the most part—a matter of right or wrong. Words are either spelled correctly or they aren't. With the help of a dictionary and the techniques suggested below, you should be able to fix spelling errors more reliably than difficulties with organization, development, sentence structure, or style.

To be sure your spelling is right . . .

➤ **When in doubt, look it up.** Look up words in the dictionary even when you are only mildly suspicious of a misspelling; this will take less time than you imagine. To keep from interrupting the flow of writing, postpone trips to the dictionary until you have completed a section or need a break. But don't forget to do the checking. While composing, circle questionable spellings and then return to them.

If you are an especially poor speller, you'll need to verify the correctness even of some words that look right. If they are of a type you often misspell—words that end in *-ible,* for example, or technical terms—go for the security that extra checking gives.

Keep a dictionary close by while you write. A convenient alternative for frequent misspellers might be a word list, which is simply a dictionary stripped of just about everything but its words, accent marks, and syllable divisions. You can locate words much more quickly using this book, which fits in spaces too small for a dictionary. But don't toss out the dictionary. You'll need it for information other than spellings.

If you can't locate a word you are seeking in a dictionary or word list, don't assume Webster forgot it. Here are some strategies when searching a dictionary for a word you don't know how to spell.

• Look around in the neighborhood. In a dictionary or word list, you can quickly scan several columns near where you expected to find a word. It may turn up.

• Consider alternatives to the way you think a word is spelled. In English an *f* sound can be spelled *ph,* a *c* sound like an *s,* a *u* like a *y,* and on and on. Make a list of possible spellings and then check them out.

> fagocite?
> faygosight?
> faigocyght?
> phaygocite?
>
> ↓
>
> *phagocyte*

• Consider alternatives to the vowel sound after an initial consonant. You are pages away if you expect to find *tyranny* spelled *tiranny.*

• If you know what the word means, look up one of its synonyms in a thesaurus. Chances are the word you are seeking will be listed under the entry. For example, if you can't figure out how to spell *eulogy* (uelegy? yewlegie? huelogy?), but know it suggests a *tribute* or *sermon,* examine those entries in your thesaurus—where you will find *eulogy.* This method is too time-consuming to use regularly, but it can help.

• For proper nouns or adjectives you can't locate or technical terms, consider the telephone book. You may not be able to locate *Szechuan* in a dictionary, so look under restaurants (Chinese) in the yellow pages.

• Consult textbook indexes. These may list technical terms and proper names you need for a particular course and paper.

• Ask someone. But be sure to use a dictionary to verify any spelling offered to you.

EXERCISE 50.1

50

Sp

Below, three spellings are given for each word. Using memory alone, underline the spelling you think is correct. Then check the dictionary. Compute the percentage you guessed right. Can you afford to rely on memory alone for spelling?

1. parrallel   parallel   paralell
2. accommodate   acommodate   accomodate

3.	unecessary	unnecessary	unneccesary
4.	drunkeness	drunkness	drunkenness
5.	miniature	minature	minaiture
6.	exstacy	ecstacy	ecstasy
7.	rememberance	remembrance	remembrence
8.	rhythm	rythmn	rhythmn
9.	governement	governmant	government
10.	silouette	silhouete	silhouette
11.	exxagerate	exaggerate	exagerate
12.	ommission	ommision	omission
13.	lieutenant	leiutenant	leuitenant
14.	ocurrence	occurence	occurrence
15.	camoflage	camouflage	camoflaige
16.	guarentee	gaurantee	guarantee
17.	questionnaire	questionaire	questionnare
18.	miscellaneous	miscelaneous	miscelanious
19.	pshychology	pyschology	psychology
20.	resterant	restaurant	restuarant

Percent right: No. right x 5 = _____ %

➤ **Proofread carefully to eliminate obvious errors.** There's no easy way around the need to proofread carefully all your academic and professional writing. This means seeing a text you've worked on for days as clearly as the reader coming to it for the first time.

To proofread, you have to turn off the automatic pilot in your reading, focus on words and syllables, and locate potential trouble spots. These are special operations, separate from other kinds of revising.

—Read a paper with a pencil in hand, touching each word as you read.

—Read a paper aloud, slowly.

—Read an article backwards to isolate individual words.

Use any combination of these methods to spot the reversed letters, the omitted endings, the accidentally doubled vowels that may appear in something you have written.

Trouble spots to look for include contractions and possessives. Apostrophes can be murder. Many writers forget the apostrophes in the contractions *won't,* *don't,* and *can't.* Always check *it's* / *its.*

When you have found an error, check the next few words very carefully. Finding a mistake sometimes makes a writer think that another error in the immediate vicinity is unlikely. But there's no reason to make that assumption. Don't let locating one error blind you to a second coming up right behind.

50

Sp

EXERCISE 50.2

Edit Brian McVicker's review of *Gone with the Wind.* Circle misspelled words and mark them with the appropriate proofreading mark {**sp**} in the margin. One misspelling has been marked for you. Since you are editing the piece, you aren't responsible for providing the correct spellings.

1. *Gone with the Wind* has it's flaws, but it is a better film than most serious critics will admit. ⟨Sp⟩
2. Its faults are admittedly signficant.
3. Audiences today cannot approve of its glorificaton of a slave-holding Southern aristocrasy or its prejudice and demeaning portraits of African Americans.
4. The acting in *Gone with the Wind* is often overdone, at times verging on the histerical, as when Scarlett O'Hara swears by the clay of Tara never to be hungary again.
5. Clark Gable, as the dashing Rhett Butler, is admittedly just playing hisself, the charming, charismatic Clark Gable of Hollywood legend.
6. And the characters of Melanie and Ashley are to sacharine to stomach.
7. Yet, despite these and other problems, *Gone with the Wind* has remained popular with audiences around the world for more than fifty years, excepting only a sour cadre of film critics.
8. What the untrained and supposedly unsophisticated popular audiences understand that suttle critics dont is that *Gone with the Wind* is not a history lesson, but a romance full of larger-than-life heroes and heriones.
9. Ordinary viewers are enthralled by an epick tail about the destruction of a world purer and simpler than there own—where grand politcal forces and the power of passionate love collide.
10. And that is precisely the point: *Gone with the Wind* is an excercise of the imagination, an adult version of the dreams of childhood, where great men and women find themselfs locked in elemental struggles of love and war.

➤ **Read more to eliminate errors that result from mispronunciation or mishearing.** No one spells English right just because he or she pronounces it correctly or consistently. The regional differences in pronunciation that make English lively and interesting also make pronunciation an unreliable guide to spelling. Even if we all spoke the same way, the language itself refuses to be consistent. Just consider what English does with these words spelled roughly the same: en*ough*, c*ough*, thr*ough*, th*ough*. So you shouldn't feel surprised when the English you spell looks different from the English you speak.

Ghoti = fish?

According to George Bernard Shaw, English spelling is irregular enough to justify this odd version of the word *fish.* **Shaw assembles** *ghoti* **from the sounds and spellings of common English words:**

f = cou<u>gh</u>
i = w<u>o</u>men
sh = na<u>ti</u>on

50

Sp

The difficulties of English pronunciation, however, don't free you from the responsibility to spell English right. If you consistently drop syllables, add syllables, or leave off endings, you need to know it. Study corrected copies of your papers and try to classify your typical mistakes. Then, when proofreading, shift into an editing mode whenever you run up against a word you are likely to misspell. That's easier said than done.

Let's say that, like many writers, you tend to drop the -*d* or -*ed* after verbs or verbals or to use *of* instead of *have* as a helping verb.

{**Original**}   Sister Anne thought the sermon sounded confuse. She was convince she could of described the Promise Land better herself.

{**Revised**}   Sister Anne thought the sermon sounded confuse**d.** She was convince**d** she could **have** described the Promise**d** Land better herself.

Your job is to uncover such patterns in your misspellings.

Other errors may be harder to categorize and eliminate. You may not recognize that some of your errors come from mispronunciation.

Wrong	*Right*
suprise	su**r**prise
knowlege	knowle**d**ge
perscription	p**r**escription
hankerchief	han**d**kerchief
temperture	tempe**ra**ture
privlege	privi**l**ege
surppress	sup**p**ress

Occasionally, you may mishear entire phrases, such as writers who complain about a *doggy-dog* world (instead of *dog-eat-dog*) or describe people who are mere *ponds of faith* (instead of *pawns of fate*). Errors of this kind can't be eliminated magically or even with the aid of a spelling checker. You have to rely on trial and error—or as one writer preferred it, trial *in* error.

In fact, the only reliable way to eliminate pronunciation errors is to read a lot. Spelling relies on visual memory, and reading reinforces your familiarity with spelling patterns. You are less likely to misspell a word you have seen often.

EXERCISE 50.3

Build up a personal spelling list of words you tend to misspell for reasons of pronunciation. Use the list as an editing tool whenever you write a paper.

➤ **Be alert for words that sound or look alike.** Words similar in appearance often differ widely in meaning. Unfortunately, no simple tricks prevent the misspelling (or misuse) of such terms. The best you can do is gradually accumulate a personal list of troublemakers. When you write *principal,* be sure that you don't mean *principle;* when *affect* seems right, be sure you don't need *effect.* A dictionary or glossary of usage are your best tools for figuring out these troublesome sets. Here is a sampling of the many problem clusters.

Homonyms

all ready   already
   [set to go]   [by now]

50

Sp

altar
[table]

alter
[change]

bare
[empty, clear]

bear
[carry]

board
[group/plank/climb on]

bored
[uninterested]

brake
[stop]

break
[fracture]

buy
[purchase]

by
[near]

canvas
[fabric]

canvass
[examine]

capital
[seat of gov't, city]

capitol
[gov't building]

cite
[point out]

sight
[see]

site
[location]

coarse
[rough]

course
[class]

complement
[make complete]

compliment
[praise]

council
[group]

counsel
[advice/lawyer]

desert
[abandon/arid locale]

dessert
[treat]

die
[cease living]

dye
[change color]

fare
[cost]

fair
[just]

forth
[forward]

fourth
[next after third]

gorilla
[large ape]

guerilla
[soldier]

hear
[perceive sound]

here
[this place]

holy
[sacred]

wholly
[entirely]

holey
[full of holes]

its
[possessive form]

it's
[contraction for *it is*]

lead
[to direct/metal]

led
[past of *to lead*]

lessen
[decrease]

lesson
[instruction]

meat
[flesh]

meet
[encounter]

passed
[go by/meet standards]

past
[what has occurred]

patience
[tolerance]

patients
[people under medical care]

peace
[harmony]

piece
[part or portion]

50

Sp

Homonyms

plain
   [simple/level ground]
plane
   [aircraft/flat surface/tool]
principal
   [head of school/
   most important]
principle
   [standard/moral
   guide]
rain
   [precipitation]
reign
   [rule]
rein
   [pull in]
right
   [correct]
rite
   [ritual]
write
   [compose]
road
   [highway]
rode
   [past tense of *to ride*]
stationary
   [not moving]
stationery
   [writing material]
straight
   [not curved]
strait
   [body of water]
their
   [possessive]
there
   [in that place]
they're
   [they are]
threw
   [past tense of *to throw*]
through
   [across]
throne
   [royal seat]
thrown
   [past part. of *to throw*]
weak
   [not strong]
week
   [seven days]
wear
   [to *have on*]
where
   [place]
weather
   [climate]
whether
   [if/choice]
which
   [one of several]
witch
   [a magical person]
whose
   [possessive]
who's
   [contraction for *who is*]
your
   [possessive]
you're
   [contraction for *you are*]

Troublesome Pairs

accept [allow]   except [not including]
access [entry to]   excess [too much]
adverse [difficult]   averse [opposed to]
advice [n.—counsel]   advise [v.—give counsel]
affect [to influence]   effect [consequence]
allude [to refer to]   elude [to escape]
allusion [a reference]   illusion [a false impression]
are [form of *to be*]   our [possessive]
breath [n.—an inhalation]   breathe [v.—to inhale]
conscience [moral guide]   conscious [aware of]
device [a thingamajig]   devise [to fashion]
elicit [to evoke]   illicit [illegal]
eminent [famous]   imminent [about to occur]
faith [belief/confidence]   fate [doom]
loose [not fastened]   lose [to misplace]

moral [virtuous]	morale [spirit, feeling]
personal [private]	personnel [work force]
quiet [not noisy]	quite [very]
than [compared with]	then [at that time]
through [across]	thorough [complete, entire]
wear [to have on]	were [past of *to be*]

EXERCISE 50.4

Use the list above and a dictionary to choose the correct word in the sentences below.

1. Because three years had **(passed/past)** since the company paid dividends to **(its/it's)** investors, stockholders began to lose **(patients/patience)** with the management team.
2. The **(plain/plane)** truth was that the **(Board/Bored)** of Directors was **(averse/adverse)** to heeding the **(advice/advise)** of its lawyers.
3. As a result, the **(moral/morale)** of corporate **(personal/personnel)** declined.
4. Good employees began to **(dessert/desert)** what they saw as a sinking ship, taking **(there/their)** skills and talents to companies **(whose/who's)** management could make better use of them.
5. Yet no one was sure **(whether/weather)** the corporation's decline was an **(allusion/illusion)** or a fact.

EXERCISE 50.5

Select five pairs of homonyms or troublesome words from the lists immediately above (or other comparable pairs). Then write sentences in which both words in the pair are used correctly in a single sentence. For example:

> The air conditioner was **quite quiet.**

➤ **Check even familiar words whenever you suspect that some part might be wrong.** It may seem tedious to consult a dictionary or word list every time you are unsure about an ending, a vowel sound, or a doubled consonant, but until you know how to spell a word, safe is better than sorry. Some of the most familiar words and expressions are notorious spelling demons.

a lot	independent	receive
all right	misspell	roommate
athlete	necessary	separate
believe	neighbor	their
business	occasion	truly
environment	occurred	until
government	professor	villain

50

Sp

➤ **Identify trouble spots.** Be extra careful at those points where English spelling is most apt to go wrong. Review the following list to identify your trouble spots.

- Words that contain *ei* or *ie: receive, perceive, foreign.*
- Words with silent letters: *pneumonia, debt, answer.*
- Words that end in

    -able or *-ible: laughable, visible.*

    -ance or *-ence: guidance, obedience.*

    -ant or *-ent: attendant, different.*

    -cede, -ceed, or *sede: precede, proceed, supersede.*

- Words with double consonants: *occurrence, embarrass, exaggerate, accumulate, accommodate, recommend.*
- Homonyms: *right, write, rite.*
- Contractions: *who's, it's, you're, don't, won't, can't.*
- Possessive forms: *Jones's, Boz's.* (Section 25B.)
- Irregular plurals: *geese, media, spaghetti.* (Section 25A.)
- Hyphenated words: *much-loved, mothers-in-law.* See Section 34B.

➤ **Apply spelling rules—if helpful.** Spelling rules for English tend to be complicated, hard to remember, and unreliable. Because of all the exceptions to such guidelines, you are usually better off relying on a dictionary. Still, you may want to review the basic spelling rules listed below.

1. *I* comes before *e* except after *c*—except when *ei* has a long *A* sound.

bel**ie**ve	repr**ie**ve	p**ie**ce
rec**ei**ve	perc**ei**ve	conc**ei**ve
eight	w**ei**gh	sl**ei**gh

Significant exceptions weaken this guideline.

counterf**ei**t	**ei**ther	s**ei**ze
w**ei**rd	for**ei**gn	

2. When adding on to a word that ends with *e,* keep the final *e* if the addition begins with a consonant.

rid**e**	ride**r**
absolut**e**	absolute**ly**
retir**e**	retire**ment**

Drop the *e* if the addition begins with a vowel.

rid**e**	rid**ing**
advis**e**	advis**able**
tribut**e**	tribut**ary**

There are significant exceptions to these guidelines, among them:

tru**e**	tru**ly** (instead of *truely*)
argu**e**	argu**ment** (instead of *arguement*)
judg**e**	judg**ment** (*judgement* is a British spelling)
dy**e**	dye**ing** (instead of *dying*)
cano**e**	canoe**ing** (instead of *canoing*)
sing**e**	singe**ing** (instead of *singing*)

3. When adding a suffix beginning with a vowel or *y* to a word ending with a consonant, double the consonant if the word has only one syllable and the final consonant is single and preceded by a single vowel. This rule makes clearer sense when seen in operation, but it also demonstrates how complicated spelling rules can be.

drop	dro**pp**ing
flip	fli**pp**ed
star	sta**rr**y

Also, you double the consonant when the word has more than one syllable, if the last syllable is accented, and the final consonant is single and preceded by a single vowel.

reset'	rese**tt**ing
uncap'	unca**pp**ed
omit'	omi**tt**ed

In most other situations, a final consonant is not doubled.

lea**n**	leaning
offe**r**	offering
desi**gn**	designer
combat	combatant

In some cases, either the single or double consonant may be acceptable. American English, however, usually prefers the single consonant.

travel	traveled	trave**ll**ed
imperil	imperiled	imperi**ll**ed
kidnap	kidnaping	kidna**pp**ing

4. When adding to a word that ends in a *y* preceded by a consonant, change the *y* to *i*—except when the addition begins with an *i*.

cit**y**	cities	
happ**y**	happiness	
marr**y**	married	marrying

Retain the *y* when the *y* is preceded by a vowel.

vall**ey**	valleys
env**oy**	envoys
st**ay**	staying

5. When faced with a decision between *-able* and *-ible* at the end of the word, it may help you to recall that *-able* tends to attach itself to words that could stand alone without it.

comfort**able**	laugh**able**	advis**able**
admir**able**	unread**able**	desir**able**

In contrast, many of the words that take *-ible* would be incomplete without the ending.

hor**rible**	ter**rible**	respons**ible**
eli**gible**	le**gible**	incred**ible**

As always, there are exceptions.

improb**able**   perfect**ible**   forc**ible**

6. When faced with a decision between *-cede, -ceed,* and *-sede,* remember that *-cede* is by far the most common ending. Only three words end with *-ceed.*

pro**ceed**   suc**ceed**   ex**ceed**

Only one word ends with *-sede.*

super**sede**

All others end with *-cede.*

con**cede**   pre**cede**   se**cede**
inter**cede**   re**cede**   ac**cede**

7. Form plurals and possessives with care. See Chapter 25.

▶ **Use a spelling checker.** Spelling checkers help if you are writing on a word processor and have access to such a program. Because these programs compare your writing to the words stored in their internal dictionaries, they will question every word you produce that they don't recognize. All typos and errors in a paper will be found—as long as they don't form legitimate words on their own.

A spelling checker, for example, will let you know you forget an *m* in *imminent,* but it probably will be silent if you mistakenly use *eminent* instead—unless it has a homonym feature that flags potential problems. Some do.

If you use a word not on your spelling checker's dictionary, the word will be highlighted even if it is spelled right. In most cases, you will have the option of adding that new word to your program's dictionary.

Spelling checkers will catch many errors quickly and accurately. But even after a spelling checker has read through a draft, you still need to proofread it on your own to detect the kinds of errors computers can't read. A typical spelling checker, for example, would find no mistakes in the following sentence:

Their our to many excuses for the prejudice attitudes we sea every wear in the whirled around us.

▶ **Check all difficult words.** Don't avoid using words that are difficult to spell. But be honest enough to admit that you might need a dictionary to spell words like *entrepreneur, espresso, quiescent, laryngitis, fluorescent, fuchsia,* or *zucchini.*

Make a list of troublesome words you use frequently. Then memorize them, using whatever devices help you to visualize the words and get them down accurately on paper. For example, it may help to recall that *espresso* has a pair of *es's* (*espresso*), or that there is *a rat* in sep*ar*ate. Or simply dividing a word into more spellable units may work: *zuc-chini; entre-pre-neur; fluor-e-scent.*

If you write with a word processor, you might use the search-and-change function to locate and correct words you typically misspell. For example, if *thier* is one of your most common misspellings, direct the computer to replace all occurrences of *thier* with *their*. If your personal spelling list is short, you can quickly check a whole document this way.

➤ **Get to know the technical terms in a field. Don't guess on proper nouns.** Every discipline or profession has a technical vocabulary you need to master to write successfully in that area. The same is true of proper names in any kind of writing. Imagine the impression made by someone who composes a serious paper on Banquo, a character from Shakespeare's *Macbeth,* but spells the name Bango throughout.

When it comes to unfamiliar words, technical terms, or proper names, use whatever resources prove necessary to get the spelling right—regular dictionaries, dictionaries of technical terms, dictionaries of biography, newspapers, almanacs, indexes, reference librarians.

This advice applies especially to foreign terms and names.

EXERCISE 50.6

Make a short list of technical terms, proper nouns, or names of importance either in your major or some personal area of expertise. Which of the words give you a spelling challenge? Do you avoid using them because of their difficult spelling?

◆ **FINE TUNING** ◆

1. Not all words in English have a single correct spelling. Dictionaries will sometimes present you with variant spellings. In most cases, you should avoid variants labeled *chiefly British (e.g. colour, judgement, theatre), archaic,* or *obsolete* unless you have a special reason for using them. You would use British spellings, for example, in quoting a London newspaper or a speech by the British Prime Minister.
2. Avoid spellings made fashionable by advertising or the popular media: *nite, lite, thru, shur.*

EXERCISE 50.7

Read the following student paper. Then circle and correct any spelling errors you find in it. If you use a computer, underline those errors that a spelling checker probably would not be able to catch.

1. As I was flipping thru a magzine, my attention focused on a handsome sailer with muscular arms, a dark tan, and baby blew eyes.
2. Only after starring at the gorgeus guy for several seconds did I noticed that he was their on the page to sell a famous soft drink.
3. No doubt, like thousands of other female readers, Id been seduced by a cute smile just long enough to notice a product name.

50

Sp

4. In another ad, the first thing I notice is an attractive, dark-skinned girl on the beach in a white bikini, a bottle of suntan lotion tucked into her bikini bottoms.
5. In the background are six males, all holding surfboardes and smiling at the gorgious girl—who has a glow of a dark tan and oil on her body.
6. Men will notice the girl in the bikini and women will long for her taning secret—and the six handsome surfers.
7. Our consummers helpless in these situations? I almost think so.
8. After all, who doesnt want to look at an attractive man or woman—and imagine themselfes in the picture?
9. The problem comes if we allow such advertisements to enfluence important purchases or decisions.
10. Then we realy become victims of the clever, seductive technigues of Madison Avenue.

51 Writing with a Computer

A What word processing does

B Writing with a word processor

C Planning and organizing on a computer

D Drafting on a computer

E Revising on a computer

Terms you need to know

HARDWARE. The equipment that makes up a computer: keyboard, monitor, central processing unit, storage devices (disk drives, hard drives, CD-ROMs), printer.

SOFTWARE. The electronic directions or programs that run the hardware. The software determines whether the hardware will process words, crunch numbers, organize files, play games, and so on.

WORD PROCESSING. Writing on a computer with a software program specifically designed to produce documents. Word processing programs vary greatly in their features.

CURSOR. A line that blinks on a computer screen at the point where you are working on your text. You move the cursor to the place in your document where you want to add or delete words or perform some other operation. Cursors can be moved either by keyboard commands or with the aid of a pointing device called a *mouse*.

MEMORY. The capacity of a computer to process and store information. The speed and power of a computer is, in part, determined by the size of its memory.

51 A   WHAT WORD PROCESSING DOES

Troubleshooting

Almost everyone has heard of word processing by now, but many writers still hesitate to entrust their work to electronic devices. Some believe that pounding keys on a manual typewriter or dragging a pen across a legal pad gives more texture to their sentences and ideas. But writers who use word processors suspect that such physical drudgery produces nothing but calluses.

If you have little experience with computers or word processors, you may find the information in this section helpful. Eventually you will have to investigate individual systems or products on your own to discover exactly what they offer. Not all computers or programs have all the features described below. Nor are all the capacities of word processors covered in these few pages.

Understand, though, that computers are nothing to fear. The days when computer users had to be part engineer, part programmer, part fanatic are long gone. You need to know no more about the innards of a computer to process words than you need to understand the mechanics of an automatic transmission to shift gears. It *is* important, however, to understand just what writing with a computer will and will not do for you.

A word processor may help you . . .

➤ **To revise quickly and easily.** Most people find that writing on a computer takes the busywork out of revising and editing a text. Because a paper you are developing exists on the equivalent of a TV screen, you can make all the changes you want without manually erasing, recopying, or rearranging any of the document. The computer handles the alterations for you.

When you cut a portion of a paper, the deleted material disappears while the rest of the text rearranges itself to fill in the gap. You can also add anything you want any place in a paper. Left out a word? Just move the cursor to the spot where the word ought to be and begin typing. Need to move an entire paragraph? Mark it, then move it wherever you choose. Misspell a word? Change it before anyone notices.

When you have made all the necessary revisions, you can then print out a draft, turning the screen image into *hard copy,* that is, a printed version of the paper. If reviewing the hard copy suggests more changes, you can go back to your computer, revise the document again, and print out still another version. Since you don't have to retype an entire paper every time you make significant alterations, revisions aren't nearly as burdensome as they were formerly.

Moreover, since to the computer your document is just a series of electronic signals stored magnetically, you can make copies of your documents quickly and easily, saving various versions of a paper on your disks as records, or sending the document via disk or *modem* (an electronic telephone hookup) to anyone who has a compatible computer system.

➤ **To work with several documents or programs at the same time.** Many software programs make it possible for you to have several documents on the screen at the same time. This would enable you, for example, to compare several versions of the same paper, or to move words from one paper to another.

Depending upon the kind of computer you have, you may even be able to copy material from different kinds of programs into your word-processing document: a chart from a graphics program, columns of data from a spreadsheet, a design from a drawing program.

➤ **To share your work with others.** Computers in different locations can be connected through phone lines via devices called modems. Computers in the same location can be *networked* by cables and software that allow writers at different terminals to "talk" to each other.

A computer thus enables writers to respond almost immediately to texts, information, and commentary from across the room or across the country. When all the computers in a classroom are "networked," it's even possible to hold electronic conversations on any topic—a social issue, an essay, a poem. As each party to the conversation types in comments, the remarks become visible on every participant's monitor, thus provoking immediate reaction and debate. Not only do such conversations encourage people who are ordinarily silent in discussions to express their ideas, but the computer stores all the comments. At the end of the session, a complete transcript of the "class discussion" can be printed and shared.

▶ **To arrange and rearrange the format of a paper.** Because a word processor allows you to manipulate such things as margins, tabs, and spacing easily, you can print out a paper using any format you like: wide margins, narrow margins, single-spaced, double-spaced, centered, right margin justified, single-column, double-column, and so on. You can produce multiple versions of any paper, one perhaps double-spaced to hand in, another single-spaced for your own records.

The computer also takes care of moving you automatically from line to line as you type. You don't have to return a carriage or watch your spacing as you near the left margin; a feature called *word wrap* takes care of that, automatically fitting as many words as possible onto a line, and then dropping down to the next while you just keep on typing.

Computers enable you to place page numbers and running heads wherever they are required—top, bottom, centered, left-hand corner of a sheet—and they keep track of page numbering. If you add or cut pages as you revise, the paper repaginates itself automatically. No more fumbling with pages 8a and 8b.

▶ **To arrange and rearrange the appearance of a paper.** Most computers allow you to underline or print words in **boldface**. Some programs also allow a writer to vary both type style and size. Others, with even more flexibility, produce italics, small caps, outlines, and border boxes.

▶ **To check features of a paper.** Most word processors can search for a given word or phrase in a paper. This search feature helps a writer to locate and replace misspelled words or lame expressions used too often (*to be* verbs; *there is; it was*). Or the search can be used to save time. In place of a lengthy expression that will appear frequently in an essay (Mikhail Gorbachëv, for example), you can type in a short code—*mg*. Then, when you are nearly done, you simply instruct the computer to replace all occurrences of *mg* with the full name, Mikhail Gorbachëv.

Most word processors now are compatible with spelling checkers and thesauruses. Spelling checkers help a writer catch spelling and typographical errors (see p. 730 for more details); electronic thesauruses suggest synonyms for words selected in a paper. Some spelling checkers and thesauruses are built right into word-processing programs. Others operate separately.

Programs are also available to check selected stylistic features in a paper. Most style programs will calculate the number of words a passage contains, the average length of its sentences, and its readability level. Others will flag clichés and suggest alternatives; some highlight *to be* and other weak verbs to encourage writers to make livelier choices. Or the programs will draw attention to words repeated in close proximity. Style checkers vary enormously in their power and features; they can't make anyone a better writer automatically, but they can provide feedback on aspects of prose worth watching.

51 A

Word Pr

Other programs widely available to writers with access to personal computers make outlining, note-taking, and indexing easier. Again, such programs differ in power and features.

➤ **To print professional-looking texts.** The quality of the hard copy you produce with your computer depends, naturally, on the printer to which it is connected. Early dot matrix printers earned word processors a bad reputation, producing pages just barely more readable than cash register tapes. Most dot matrix machines today do much better, producing copy as good as an average typewriter can manage—and without erasures and white-outs.

A range of middle-level printers can produce texts of near letter quality—that is, their printing is as good as that of a top-of-the-line electric typewriter. These printers use several different output technologies, including daisy wheels and ink jets.

Computers can also be connected to laser printers that produce texts and graphics that look professionally printed. A whole industry called desktop publishing has evolved from the combination of computers, laser printers, and graphics software. In fact, the personal computer has become the driving force behind many small print shop operations that produce brochures, newsletters, books, slides, indeed almost any kind of printed material—some of it even in color. Anyone with adequate computer skills now has the ability to reach a wider audience than ever before.

Most writers, however, find the relatively inexpensive dot matrix printers adequate for typical academic jobs. When a particular assignment (a senior thesis, an annual report, a dissertation) merits special attention, you can usually arrange to print it at a typing service that rents access to letter-quality or laser machines. Writing on a word processor thus offers a variety of printing options even for the writer on a limited budget.

But a word processor probably will not . . .

➤ **Save you time.** You might get an argument here, but many users of word processors will admit that the machines don't always speed up composing. Instead, writing on a word processor encourages more tinkering with a text and, consequently, more revision. What a writer gains in not having to recopy a paper every time a change is made can be lost in the tendency to make more frequent changes and more serious revisions. So, on balance, you aren't likely to save much time by producing a paper on a word processor.

Don't forget, too, that it takes time to learn how to use a word processor. Some word-processing programs are devilishly complex, though many have become more user-friendly in recent years. Even simple-to-use software involves a writer in numerous computer routines that devour minutes eagerly: booting the machine, initializing disks, saving copy, backing up disks, transferring files, naming documents, formatting paragraphs, positioning running heads, repaginating, and so on. It all adds up.

➤ **Improve the quality of your writing dramatically.** Computers do make writing less frustrating. They keep track of items (like pagination, spacing, paragraph formats) that writers would just as soon ignore; they help out with outlining,

51 A

Word Pr

invention, spelling, and vocabulary; they make revision swift and entertaining; they churn out handsome copy with ease and speed.

But word processors don't perform miracles. The old rule holds: garbage in, garbage out. You still have to furnish the ideas to build a paper. You have to find the statistics that support an assertion or the illustrations that clinch an argument. You have to arrange sentences that suit both your ideas and your audience. The machine won't do the thinking.

▶ **Find and eliminate your errors.** Computers can help you locate typographical and spelling errors in a paper and suggest alternative vocabulary items. Some programs point out weaknesses in your style and potential grammar difficulties. But computers are a long way from being able to address all the complex issues even a "simple" paper raises. Don't think that a computer can take charge of the writing you do. It can't.

EXERCISE 51.1

1. In a small group, discuss what you believe might be the advantages and disadvantages of a class discussion held entirely between students seated in front of networked computers. Would you be more or less likely to participate in such a discussion? Why? Would such conversations be more intense than an ordinary discussion? More random?
2. If you have never written on a computer, list those questions and reservations you have about composing on a machine; if you have worked with computers, list what you regard as their strengths and weaknesses. Discuss the items on your list with several colleagues.
3. If you could ask a computer to perform any one task (short of actually writing papers for you), what would it be? In class, assemble a wish list and discuss how likely it is that computers one day will be able to do all that you have requested.
4. Have you seen laser-printed materials in class, on the job, or in other situations? What impression has the print quality of such materials made on you?
5. Have you ever lost material you have written on a computer either through a power failure, a glitch, or some other problem? In class, trade such stories. Who or what was responsible for your loss?

51 B   WRITING WITH A WORD PROCESSOR

51 B

Terms you need to know

Word Pr

DOCUMENT/FILE. A paper, article, or text prepared on a computer and stored on a disk. Documents are identified by their file names.

DISK. A plastic, record-like device used to compile and store information. Disks are inserted into a disk drive either to load a program into the computer or to record newly created files. (Some computers have sealed *hard disks* that store significantly more information than portable 3-½" or 5-¼" disks.)

SAVE. An important command that tells the computer to make a permanent copy of a document. Until you *save* a document, the file (or any change made in it since the last *save*) exists only in the computer's memory and can be wiped out if the computer is turned off or power is interrupted. *Save* is one of the first commands a beginner at word-processing needs to learn.

Troubleshooting

Some writers grow frustrated with a computer because they expect too much of the device. But it's just a machine that does exactly what you tell it—at times with maddening literalness. Some of your frustration and difficulties can be removed by following simple procedures.

To use a word processor effectively . . .

➤ **Learn to use your computer and software correctly.** You can waste a lot of time—and miss important features in your software—if you hunt and peck your way through it. Learn as much as you can about the operating system that manages the way information is handled by your computer. (For some computers, that system is known as MS-DOS, OS/2, or CP/M; on others, you learn to manipulate a desktop to open, close, name, and store files.) Think of the operating system as the lobby of your computer, a place for signing in and learning where everything in the building is located. Or think of it—as one system does—as a desktop, with all your software and files spread out, waiting to be opened.

When you are sufficiently familiar with a computer's operating system, learn the basics of any particular piece of software you are using. Word processors can be quite complicated, but it is usually not necessary to master each feature: in academic writing, for example, you may never need to use *print merge* or *index*. But keep the software manual handy to deal with complications.

➤ **Follow lab procedures carefully.** Many students meet word processors for the first time in writing labs. These labs use many different kinds of machines and accommodate a great many writers, so they must insist upon careful routines to protect their hardware, software, and the files of their patrons. Respect these rules and tolerate occasional problems and bottlenecks.

➤ **Initialize disks correctly.** Initializing a disk makes it available to receive information and gives it a name your computer will recognize. The procedure for initializing a new disk depends upon the machine and software you are using; in some cases, you may have to initialize the disk before entering a word-processing program. In most cases, initializing is a simple procedure that you need to do only once.

It is possible to erase and reinitialize a disk, but doing so eliminates whatever information was stored there. Be careful not to erase a disk that contains files and programs you need.

➤ **Use the correct start-up procedure.** Most computer systems are easy to boot up, but you do need to know the proper procedure. Consult a computer manual

51 B

Word Pr

or follow lab instructions. These instructions will explain whether to insert a program and document disks before or after turning on the power. If you have two disk drives, you'll need to know which drive takes the system disk and which the program disk. If your computer is running off a hard drive, the start-up will again be somewhat different and the word processing software programs will probably already be on the hard disk. (You'll still need a program disk for backup copies of any new files you create.)

When you start up a machine correctly, you can then ask for (or you'll be presented with) a directory of available files. Select the existing files you wish to work on or create a new text file by opening the word-processing program itself.

▶ **Learn to create a file.** This procedure will vary depending upon computer and software program. Creating a text file simply means to establish the electronic version of a paper; you do that, typically, by naming the file. The text file has to have a name so that the computer operating system can identify it on a disk and display it on the screen when you request it. On some systems, you can't type a word until you have named the file. Others will open an unnamed file for you, but you won't be able to save any information until you've named the document.

Give your file a name that is easy to remember and that conveys some sense of what the text contains. A cryptic title that seemed clever the day you created it may draw a blank three months later when you are searching your directory for a particular piece of information. Some computers limit the length of a filename to just a few letters, so you may have to be inventive with your abbreviations. But even with computers that allow longer names, you're better off choosing short, clear, and sensible designations.

▶ **Learn how to format your text.** It is important to learn how to manipulate all the major format features of a word-processing program, especially margins and spacing. If you have never used a word processor before, you may be confused by all the options available. But take them one at a time and don't be intimidated. It is typically possible to place page numbers exactly where you need them, to include running heads, to justify text, to center titles, to vary spacing (double, single), to place tabs (regular or decimal), and so on. Some computers allow you to vary the characters on the screen and to underline, italicize, or boldface words. If your computer has this capacity, you may have to resist the temptation to mix fonts and sizes. The appearance of a paper shouldn't attract more attention than its contents. On the other hand, having the ability to produce boldface headings or different type sizes gives you additional control over your contents. You can use bold headings, for example, to signal important sections or select a font or size likely to be pleasing to a given set of readers.

Be sure to determine how closely what you see on the screen matches what you will get on the printed page. With some computers, the match will be nearly exact; with others, you'll have to guess at what your printed text will eventually look like.

51 B

Word Pr

▶ **Remember to save the text you are working on at regular intervals,** about every fifteen minutes or any time you leave the keyboard. It is difficult to overemphasize this advice, but once you've lost a file to a power blip or surge, you'll never ignore it again. A momentary electrical interruption can erase hours of work.

If your computer is slow to save a document, use the interval for a stretch. You'll feel better and your document will be safely recorded on a disk. In fact, it's good advice to take regular breaks when working at the computer. Staring at a monitor is more fatiguing than you might realize. Be sure the screen is at a level comfortable for your eyes and that the keyboard is conveniently located. If you feel cramped or uncomfortable, your writing may show it.

➤ **Learn how to print your text.** Printing is easy, but be certain you know what you are doing. The printer must be on and capable of receiving information from your machine. (If you are part of a network, you'll be given careful instructions to follow.) Be sure the printer has paper.

You'll usually have several print options from which to choose, including speed and quality. A printer in *draft* mode, for example, does its job very quickly, supplying a text adequate for editing though not for final submission. (Many writers prefer to edit from hard copy than to look for errors on screen.)

When you need to prepare the final copy of a paper, you can select a slower printing mode—which usually produces cleaner, clearer type. Use a fresh ribbon in the printer and paper of adequate quality.

> **TIP: If you are using pin-fed paper pulled into a printer by tractor tabs, remove these tabs and *separate the pages* before submitting the essay to an instructor.**

➤ **Use the correct shutdown procedure.** Shutting a word processor down properly is as important as starting it up correctly. You usually begin a shutdown by saving a document. When the text has been saved, you then exit the word-processing program—returning you to the operating system, which may have its own exit procedure. Skipping any step can lead to lost information or prevent a computer from doing its own in-house record keeping. Most machines, for example, will automatically record information about a file: its size, time of creation, date of latest modification. Switching the machine off at the wrong moment disrupts this careful management.

➤ **Treat your disks with care.** If you brush them against a magnetic field (in your printer, a telephone receiver, a stereo speaker) or expose them to undue heat (direct sunlight, radiator) or moisture (shower, spilled coffee), you may scramble the information on the disk. Good-bye, term paper.

51 B

Word Pr

➤ **Always make backup copies of important software and documents,** both on disk and in hard copy. A single electronic copy of a paper or program is vulnerable to many accidents and system errors. Better safe than sorry, especially when copies are so easy to make. If you are working with a computer with a hard disk, it is still necessary to make disk copies of important files in case the hard disk ever crashes.

➤ **Respect software copyrights.** Producing good software takes enormous time and knowledge. Respect the rights of software authors by resisting the temptation to copy software you haven't purchased or are not authorized to own.

EXERCISE 51.2

1. In class, list the names of different software programs that members of the class know how to operate. Then categorize these software items according to their general functions (word processing; file program; spreadsheet; game; and so on). For the benefit of classmates not familiar with computers, explain what each category of software does.
2. Have you ever been tempted to copy a software program that you should have purchased? Discuss the issue of software copyright and the rights of software programmers.
3. Computers should make it easier to format a paper properly—that is, to make sure page numbers are in the right place, margins are even, and page breaks sensible. But have you ever had problems transferring what you see on the screen to what you get on the page? Compare your experiences with those of your colleagues.
4. Have you ever lost a file because you misnamed it? How might you prevent such errors? Do you have any suggestions for naming files?

51 C PLANNING AND ORGANIZING ON A COMPUTER

Terms you need to know

INVENTION. That part of the writing process during which a writer searches for ways of developing a subject or an argument. Some common invention techniques include brainstorming, freewriting, and outlining. (See Chapter 3.)

INVENTION PROGRAM. Any software program designed to help a writer find or develop a topic. Some encourage writers to list details about subjects; others ask systematic questions intended to draw out key issues and arguments.

OUTLINER/IDEA PROCESSOR. Software programs designed to help a writer develop and organize a topic. Typically, the program produces outlines that can be expanded, contracted, or rearranged until a satisfactory design for the paper is found.

Troubleshooting

Computers can't think for themselves, but they can stimulate your thinking, especially early in the writing process when ideas about topics may be hazy and untested. Computers can also help you detect relationships between ideas. The speed and ease of word processing encourages a writer to take risks at precisely the time when a little daring is needed—at the beginning.

51 C

Plan

To develop and organize a topic using a computer . . .

➤ **Try freewriting.** A computer makes freewriting especially easy, even for the less-than-skilled typist. If you already have a topic, begin the freewriting by placing that topic idea at the top of the page, boldfacing or underlining it for emphasis. If you are freewriting to find a topic, just start typing words onto the screen. Hammer away nonstop at the keyboard for a predetermined length of time. (If your computer has an alarm, set it to go off in five, ten, or fifteen minutes.) Don't worry about misspellings, missed letters, or faulty grammar. The freewriting is between you and the computer.

Some people find that they freewrite with less inhibition if they turn down the screen brightness until the text becomes invisible. (Brightness is usually controlled by a rotary switch on the monitor.) Darkening the on-screen text makes it impossible to scan words already written, so there's less of an inclination to pause in the freewriting or to be controlled by ideas already stated. Turning up the brightness at the end of the time limit may reveal surprising ideas, interesting themes, or significant repetitions. Underline such discoveries.

A second round of freewriting can be used to examine a topic idea even more closely. In your first freewriting exercise, look for a sentence, phrase, or cluster of words that seems to be the focal point, key idea, or "center" of the piece. It may be one of the striking phrases you have underlined or simply the concept that interests you most. Mark that passage, copy it, and then move the selection to the bottom of the screen or (if your computer has the capability) to a new file entirely. In either case, the focal point of the first exercise can now serve as the opening line of a second freewriting stint. Type away on this idea just as you did earlier—but perhaps for a shorter period of time. Repeat the process a third time if necessary to refine an idea.

➤ **Use an invention program.** Many writing labs are equipped with fairly sophisticated invention programs that walk you through a topic by asking numerous questions about a subject, recording your replies, and then presenting them to you as stimuli for composing. These programs may be open-ended or tailored to support a specific kind of writing: narrative, descriptive, or persuasive. Depending upon the program, you may be asked to list a series of events, to supply adjectives and adverbs describing a person, place or thing, or to find arguments in support of an idea. When you exit an invention program, it's often with a printout full of good ideas for a paper, usually arranged in some logical order. If you have access to invention software, give it a try.

➤ **Make an invention program.** If commercial invention software isn't available, make your own. A helpful prompt can be no more complicated than the list of journalist's questions discussed in Section 3C.

Who?	What?	Where?
When?	How?	Why?

To use them as an invention program, simply create a file named *Journ?* (or something similar) containing just these questions. Then, whenever you are writing an informative paper (the kind most appropriately controlled by these questions), copy the contents of this brief file into the document at its beginning. If you have a split-screen feature, keep the questions visible at the top of the monitor while you compose on the remainder of the screen. The journalist's questions will remind you to supply all the needed facts.

A slightly different list of questions may help you keep ideas on track.

What is my purpose in writing?
For whom am I writing this?

What is my key point or assertion?
What is my evidence?

Again, you can create a simple file to store these questions and then transfer them into whatever document you are creating.

Perhaps a list of familiar patterns of organization may give you directions for exploring and arranging a subject. The simple list of modes may be an invention prompt.

Description	Narration	Process
Cause/effect	Division	Classification
Comparison	Contrast	Definition
Evaluation	Illustration	Evidence

Each mode then might be expanded into its basic structure and inserted at the beginning of an essay to suggest the paper's general direction.

Process
    Introduction
        Step One
        Step Two
        Step Three
    Conclusion.

Obviously, the best such custom programs will be those that suit the type of writing you typically do.

➤ **Try brainstorming and listing.** If you have access to an outlining program (see immediately below), making a list may seem like a crude device for invention and organization. But it works just fine for many writers.

Write the topic or topic area for the exercise at the top of the blank screen; underline it for emphasis. Then quickly list any items related to it, from profound to profane. Set the ideas down just as they come to you, without regard for order or arrangement. (You may want to work with a team to speed the process along, assigning one person to the keyboard.) Brainstorm the whole topic or just some key item within it—a person's physical characteristics; the features of a landscape.

When you've completed your list, use the editing features of your word processor to group related ideas, to arrange clusters of ideas, to delete irrelevant notions, and to add new ideas. By a careful manipulation of tabs, you might even begin constructing a crude outline for your paper.

➤ **Use an outlining program.** Some outliners are stand-alone items while others are fully integrated with word-processing programs.

51 C

Plan

What makes outlining on a computer preferable to doing the job on paper is the ease with which an on-screen outline can be expanded, contracted, rearranged, and otherwise altered. Rather than constraining like a rigid skeleton, a computer outline encourages a writer to be flexible because there's no drudgery involved in experimenting. Adding new ideas is as easy as moving the cursor and typing; moving an idea from heading to subheading involves no more than marking a line and hitting a few keys. Whole categories within the outline structure can be lifted, renumbered, or rearranged.

When the ideas are sufficiently rich and a satisfactory design is found to house them all, the outline can then usually be fleshed out in a word-processing mode. Some programs allow a writer to switch back and forth to assess how a document is shaping up. Changes made in the outlining mode then are reflected in the paper itself.

➤ **Highlight your thesis.** For many people, the most difficult aspect of academic writing may be the need to develop a point. If you have this problem and need help keeping a paper on track, the computer can help.

When you know that a paper needs a clear thesis statement (see Section 11A), underline, boldface, or italicize that sentence on the screen as soon as you have written it. Just knowing that you have to highlight *some* sentence will prompt you to think about a thesis. If you finally can't find a sentence to highlight, you probably have an organizational problem. If the sentence you highlight isn't really what all the subsequent paragraphs are about, you need either to modify the thesis or to revise the paper substantially.

➤ **Test your structure.** When writing a paper that requires a traditional structure or tight organization (a research report, for example), you may want to test both its structure and transitions. A way to do that is to copy the thesis statement, and the first and last sentence from each subsequent paragraph into a separate file and then to assemble them into a short essay. This cut-and-paste job is relatively easy to do with a computer.

If the thesis and other sentences do, in fact, form a reasonably coherent unit, you've probably got an essay that reads smoothly and develops a clear point. If not, you may need to revise your organization and transitions. The method isn't infallible, but it's worth a try.

EXERCISE 51.3

1. Try brainstorming on any subject with the computer monitor darkened. Were you able to write well that way? Why or why not?
2. If you were to compose an invention program of your own, what questions would it include? Specify the kind of writing your questions might work with best.
3. Many writers claim to dislike outlining. If you are one of them, try to explain why. Would computerized outlining resolve some of the difficulties you have had with handwritten versions?

51 D

Draft

51 D DRAFTING ON A COMPUTER

Terms you need to know

DRAFT. Any relatively complete version of a paper leading up to a final, carefully edited document. The initial version of a paper is the *first draft;* a quick, tentative, trial version may be termed a *rough draft.*

WINDOW. On a computer screen, a box of adjustable size that contains a text or graphic. Some computers can display a number of windows on the screen at the same time, each with its own text. Multiple windows, which can be layered on the screen and can be opened and closed independently, enable a writer to work with several documents simultaneously.

Troubleshooting

A computer can seem almost magical to a writer working with one for the first time. All the drudgery of composition seems to drop away, as words and sentences appear and disappear with simple keystrokes. But a computer can do more than just reduce frustrations; as this section suggests, it enhances a writer's ability to deal with ideas, encourages risk-taking, and shows how one text can grow from another.

To write on a computer effectively . . .

➤ **Take advantage of the freedom of a computer text.** There is no one correct way to produce a paper. Some writers prefer to produce multiple drafts, each more refined than the first; others work steadily, line by line, making sure each sentence is satisfactory before moving on to the next. A writer's habits, however, probably have been acquired from experiences working with pen and paper or perhaps a typewriter. A computer changes the ground rules so much that even an experienced writer may want to trade in old habits that constrain revision and risk-taking.

Consider the fact that a computer text is no more than a display of light on a screen; altering that display requires just the stroke of a key. Consequently, you can afford to explore new ways of assembling papers, perhaps writing quick, deliberately incomplete rough drafts—part scratch outline, part full sentences, part rambling phrases—leaving gaps where you'll need examples, statistics, or just more material, and inserting notes to yourself about decisions yet to be made. You can go over and over such drafts, gradually expanding them and refining their separate parts until they evolve into the papers you want. A fully polished sentence or paragraph can be entered at any point while surrounding material remains rough. There's no need to begin at the beginning, to end at the end, or to worry about initial clutter, a preliminary absence of transitions, or any fine points of grammar. Remember that a reader will see only the final products.

This great flexibility should encourage you to start on a paper early, especially when a deadline remains days or weeks away. Think of a paper not as a distant responsibility, but as a continuing process. Record your initial impressions on a topic in a file the day the assignment is made and then, in the same file, gradually accumulate observations from your reading, illustrations and quotations from sources, shrewd or helpful remarks from discussions, and any tentative conclusions. Whole sentences or paragraphs might be entered at the moment you feel compelled to write them. Over time, you'll gradually assemble materials for the entire paper and will find—already keyboarded—a surprising amount of the prose you'll need to shape into the final text. If you are comfortable composing this way, you'll be surprised by how intriguing the process of assembling an essay can become. And you'll be taking full advantage of the freedom your word processor offers.

51 D

Draft

▶ **Work through separate drafts.** Occasionally, you may be satisfied with the progress you've made on a paper, but also feel tempted to experiment with a new strategy—perhaps deleting a huge chunk of the body of the paper, adding some dialogue, or rearranging several complicated paragraphs. With a computer, it's easy to take such risks. Just duplicate your existing file and give it a new version number. For example, if the first draft of a paper on hypochondria is named *Hypo,* the second experimental version could be *Hypo2,* the third *Hypo3,* and so on. So long as you have disk space, you can create new versions while preserving all the work you've already done—should you prefer to go back to an earlier version. (After all, revising a text does not automatically improve it.)

You probably should also create a new file version of a document whenever you respond to a review of your work—by your instructor, fellow students, or colleagues. Keep a copy of the original text and begin any revisions in a new file.

▶ **Use split screen and multiple windows.** If your computer can split the screen of a file you are working in, type any commitment you've made to readers at the top of the screen while responding to it in the bottom section. For example, if the first paragraph of a paper contains a very specific thesis statement announcing the four or five major points to be developed, keep that thesis visible on screen as you work through each point in the order promised. Or, when working on the conclusion of the paper, display the introductory paragraph on screen to remind yourself where the paper began and what commitments were made there.

If your computer can display multiple windows, open all files related to the paper you're developing—that is, all preliminary versions, any files that contain notes, any related papers you have written. Then you can move between versions as necessary, borrowing lines you liked from earlier drafts, transferring statistics you've gathered in note files, and so on. You can even compare versions of a paper by sizing the separate files so that you can view two at the same time. Don't forget occasionally to save the latest version of your paper. You can't afford to lose it.

▶ **When appropriate, use graphics.** Many computers now make it easy to create boxes, line drawings, charts, and illustrations and to import them into a written text. If your computer has this capacity, take advantage of it. Don't clutter a paper with graphics for their own sake, but do use charts, diagrams, or other illustrations when your material warrants them.

Have you written any papers recently in which you would have found it helpful to incorporate illustrations, tables, or other graphics? What makes using graphics difficult? What advantages might there be to employing illustrations?

51 E REVISING ON A COMPUTER

Terms you need to know

HARD COPY. A printed version of any material produced on a computer.

SEARCH/FIND. A command that enables a computer to look for a designated word or phrase in a document. *Search* usually is paired with a *change* command that allows the writer to substitute one word or phrase for another.

Troubleshooting

The ease of revising a paper composed on a word processor is perhaps the computer's greatest attraction for a writer. But there are more advantages to revising with a computer than just the ability to add, delete, and rearrange material at will. Some suggestions for revising are presented below.

To revise on a word processor . . .

➤ **Begin with hard copy.** Whether making large-scale changes in theme, strategy, and organization; small-scale revisions in sentence style or paragraph sense; or editing fine points of grammar, you'll probably work more efficiently from a hard-copy version of your paper than from the text on the screen. The printed version provides a surer feel for the size and shape of a paper and a better sense of paragraph divisions and the flow of your style. Just as important, errors that seem all but invisible on the screen (repeated words, dropped endings, transposed or deleted letters) show up more easily on a printed page.

Most printers have draft modes to produce quick hard-copy texts suitable for revision. So don't avoid hard-copy revision just because it may take a little more time. Be sure that you accurately transfer any corrections made on the printed version to the computer file. But don't accidentally introduce new errors.

➤ **Use a spelling checker.** Running a paper through a spelling check is a logical editing step. Spelling checkers are either separate programs designed to spot misspellings in any text produced with a computer or programs incorporated directly into particular word processors. Few programs are more helpful to a writer, but spelling checkers do have significant limitations. For a detailed discussion of spelling checkers, see page 730 in Chapter 50, Spelling.

➤ **Use a style checker.** You may have access to programs described as style checkers. Such programs can have a variety of functions: determining the readability level and average length of sentences in a paper; finding weak verbs; highlighting racist and sexist terms; highlighting clichés; spotting repetition; and so on. The diversity of such programs is so great that no detailed discussion of them is possible here, but be aware that most can only describe writing problems in limited ways. Readability levels and average sentence length, for example, are purely mechanical computations insensitive to content, purpose, and style. Not every use of a *to be* verb is inappropriate. Not every repetition is incorrect. Still, if you have access to such a program, give it a try, especially if you have a problem with precisely the features a given program examines.

➤ **Create your own style checker.** You can use the *search/change* function in your word-processing program selectively to look for specific weaknesses or flaws in your writing. If you are prone to use *to be* verbs too frequently, direct the computer to find all uses of *be, is, are, was,* and *were* and replace them, when possible, with more action-oriented expressions. If expletive expressions such as *there is,*

51 E

Rev

there were, and *it was* are your weakness, ask the computer to locate these constructions in your paper. If punctuation around the word *however* baffles you, double-check each occurrence of the word. Do you usually misuse semicolons? Order the computer to find each one, and then be sure you can explain its function well enough to justify its use in the paper. Obviously, the longer the paper, the more helpful the *search/change* command can be.

If your computer lacks a spelling checker, you can even use the *search/change* command to search out words you routinely misspell and to correct all occurrences of words you might have misspelled more than once (*their/there; too/to; who's/whose*).

▶ **Clean up your text.** A last step important to anyone writing on a computer is to be sure the final text looks good. Be sure you've instructed the computer to paginate the paper in the right spot, and, when required, add a running head (often a last name).

Set the margins correctly and review the page breaks. You don't want the computer to leave a heading at the bottom of a page or to separate an illustration from its caption. You can usually edit the appearance of a paper best either from hard copy or from a "page preview" feature in your word-processing program.

51 E

Rev

Glossary

Within a single alphabetical list, this glossary defines grammatical terms, discusses fallacies of argument, and treats questions of usage. Many words defined in the first five parts of *The Scott, Foresman Handbook for Writers* appear again in this glossary, usually illustrated with different examples. Key terms of grammar and mechanics have been marked by the symbol §.

A, AN. Indefinite articles. *A* and *an* are **indefinite articles** because they indicate something generally (*a* book, *a* church) while the **definite article** *the* points to a specific thing (*the* book, *the* church). *A* is used when the word following it begins with a consonant sound: *a* house, *a* year, *a* boat, *a* unique experience. *An* is used when the word following it begins with a vowel sound: *an* hour, *an* interest, *an* annoyance, *an* illusory image.

Notice that you choose the article by the *sound* of the word following it. Not all words that begin with vowels actually begin with vowel sounds, and not all words that begin with consonants have initial consonant sounds.

§ **ABSOLUTE.** A phrase that stands alone as a sentence modifier. Absolutes are often infinitive or participial phrases. Unlike other modifying phrases, absolutes do not necessarily modify a word or phrase standing near them.

To put it politely, Connie is irritating.

She will publish the entire story, **space permitting.**

Scripts discarded, props disassembled, costumes locked away in trunks, the annual Shakespeare festival concluded.

(See *misplaced modifiers* and *dangling modifiers.*)

§ **ABSOLUTE ADJECTIVE.** A word such as *unique, dead,* or *equal* that ought not to be qualified to suggest some degree. One cannot be 'more unique,' 'less equal,' or 'more dead.'

§ **ABSTRACT NOUN.** A noun that names ideas, concepts, and qualities without physical properties: *softness, Mother Nature, democracy, humanism.* Abstract nouns exist in the mind as ideas. They are defined in contrast to **concrete nouns.**

ACCEPT/EXCEPT. Very commonly confused. *Accept* means to take, receive, or approve of something. *Except* means 'to exclude,' or 'not including.'

I **accepted** all the apologies **except** George's.

ACCIDENTLY/ACCIDENTALLY. *Accidently* is a misspelling. The correct spelling is *accidentally.*

§ **ACTIVE VERB/VOICE.** See **VOICE.**

ACRONYM. A single term created by joining the first letters in the words that make up the full name or description. Acronyms are pronounced as single words and are ordinarily capitalized:

NATO—North Atlantic Treaty Organization

NASA—National Aeronautics and Space Administration.

Some common acronyms are written as ordinary words without capitalization: **laser, radar.** See **INITIALISMS**, also 36C.

AD/ADVERTISEMENT. In academic and formal writing, you should use the full word: *advertisement.*

AD HOMINEM ARGUMENT. A logical fallacy. The Latin term means "to the man." An *ad hominem* argument is an attack on the character of an individual rather than on what he or she stands for. In politics, *ad hominem* arguments are often vicious.

The senator is a wealthy man; how can he be concerned about the homeless?

She probably supports gun control only because she lives in a safe neighborhood.

Such an argument is often an attempt to divert attention from an issue. For example, a candidate for the U.S. Senate who is regarded as weak on defense issues might defend himself with an *ad hominem* attack on his opponent, pointing out that she has never served in the armed forces. The accusation may be true, but it would not necessarily affect the positions or records the two candidates have on defense matters.

§ **ADJECTIVAL.** A word, phrase, or clause that modifies a noun or pronoun.

noun   adjectival
the engagement **of Ike and Bernice**

adjectival   noun   adjectival
the **never-ending** battle **between the sexes**

noun   adjectival
the ceremony **they would have preferred**

§ **ADJECTIVE.** A word that modifies a noun or pronoun. Some adjectives describe the words they modify:

an **unsuccessful** coach   a **green** motel
the **lucky** one   a **sacred** icon

Such adjectives frequently have comparative and superlative forms:

the **blacker** cat   the **happiest** people
the **direst** prophecy

Other adjectives limit or specify the words they modify:

this adventure   **every** penny
neither video   **each** participant

Proper nouns can also serve as adjectives.

Italian marble   **African** sculpture
Cantonese cuisine

See also **demonstrative adjective** and **predicate adjective.**

§ **ADJECTIVE CLAUSE.** A subordinate (or dependent) clause that functions as an adjective, modifying a noun or pronoun.

Margery Hutton, the woman **who writes mystery stories,** lives in the mansion **that Dr. Horace Elcott built.**

Her gardens were tended by Elmer Smith, **who learned to garden from his father.**

§ **ADVERB.** A word that modifies a verb, adjective, or another adverb.

adverb   verb
Bud **immediately** *suspected* foul play at the Hutton mansion.

adverb   adjective
It seemed **extremely** *odd* to him that Mrs. Hutton should load a large burlap sack into the trunk of her Mercedes.

adverb   adverb
Mrs. Hutton replied **rather** *evasively* when Bud questioned her about what she was up to.

Some adverbs modify complete sentences.

adverb
Obviously, Mr. Hutton had been murdered!

§ **ADVERB CLAUSE.** A subordinate clause that functions as an adverb.

After Mrs Hutton left, Bud slipped into the Hutton mansion.

Bud was startled **when Mr. Hutton greeted him in the living room.**

§ **ADVERBIAL.** A word or phrase that functions like an adverb but is not actually an adverb. Adverbials can be nouns, clauses, and phrases.

{**Noun as adverbial**}   They are going *home.*   [explains *where*]

{**Clause as adverbial**}   They go jogging *whenever they can.*   [explains *when*]

{**Phrase as adverbial**}   They go jogging *in the morning.*   [explains *when*]

ADVERSE/AVERSE. Often confused. *Adverse* describes something hostile, unfavorable, or difficult. *Averse* indicates the opposition someone has to something; it is ordinarily followed by *to.*

Travis was **averse to** playing soccer under **adverse** field conditions.

ADVICE/ADVISE. These words aren't interchangeable. *Advice* is a noun meaning an opinion or counsel. *Advise* is a verb meaning to give counsel or advice.

I'd **advise** you not to give Maggie **advice** about running her business.

AFFECT/EFFECT. A troublesome pair! Both words can be either nouns or verbs, although *affect* is ordinarily a verb and *effect* a noun. In its usual sense, *affect* is a verb meaning 'to influence' or 'to give the appearance of.'

How will the storm weather **affect** the plans for the outdoor concert?

The meteorologist **affected** ignorance when we asked her for a forecast.

Affect is only rarely a noun—a term in psychology meaning 'feeling' or 'emotion.' On the other hand, *effect* is usually a noun, meaning 'consequence' or 'result.'

The **effect** of the weather may be serious.

Effect may, however, also be a verb, meaning 'to cause' or 'to bring about.'

The funnel cloud **effected** a change in our plans.

[Compare with: The funnel cloud *affected* our plans.]

AGGRAVATE/IRRITATE. Most people use both of these verbs to mean 'to annoy' or 'to make angry.' But formal English preserves a fine—and useful—distinction between them. *Irritate* means 'to annoy' while *aggravate* means 'to make something worse.'

It **irritated** Greta when her husband **aggravated** his allergies by smoking.

§ **AGREEMENT, PRONOUN AND ANTECEDENT.** A grammatical principle which requires that singular pronouns stand in for singular nouns (*his* surfboard = *Richard's* surfboard) and plural pronouns stand in for plural nouns (*their* surfboard = *George and Martha's* surfboard). When they do, the pronoun and its antecedent agree in **number;** when they don't, you have an agreement problem. See Chapter 27.

Pronouns and their antecedents also must agree in **gender.** That is, a masculine pronoun (*he, him, his*) must refer to a masculine antecedent, and a feminine pronoun (*she, her, hers*) must refer to a feminine antecedent.

Finally, pronouns and antecedents must agree in **case,** whether objective, subjective, or possessive. For example, an antecedent in the possessive case (*Lawrence's* gym) can be replaced only by a pronoun also in the possessive case (*his* gym). See Chapter 28.

§ **AGREEMENT, SUBJECT AND VERB.** Verbs and nouns are said to agree in number. This means that with a singular subject in the third person (for example, *he, she, it*), a verb in the present tense ordinarily adds an *—s* to its base form. With subjects not in the third person singular, the base form of the verb is used.

Third person, singular, present tense:	Barney sit**s.**
	He sit**s.**
	She sit**s.**

First person, singular, present tense:	I sit.
Second person, singular, present tense:	You sit.
First person, plural, present tense:	We sit.
Second person, plural, present tense:	You all sit.
Third person, plural, present tense:	They sit.

Most verbs—with the notable exception of *to be*—change their form to show agreement only in third person singular forms (*he, she, it*). See Chapter 22.

AIN'T. It may be in the dictionary, but *ain't* isn't acceptable in academic or professional writing. Avoid it.

ALL READY/ALREADY. Tricky, but not difficult. *All ready,* an adjective phrase, means 'prepared and set to go.'

Rita signalled that the camera was **all ready** for shooting.

Already, an adverb, means 'before' or 'previously.'

Rita had *already* loaded the film.

ALL RIGHT. *All right* is the only acceptable spelling. *Alright* is a misspelling.

ALLUDE/ELUDE. Commonly confused. *Allude* means to refer to. *Elude* means to escape.

Kyle's joke **alluded** to the fact that it was easy to **elude** the portly security guard.

ALLUDE/REFER. The difference between these words is significant. *To allude* is to mention something indirectly; *to refer* is to mention something directly.

The freshmen were not sure to what Kyle was **alluding.**

Kyle did, however, **refer** to ancient undergraduate traditions and the honor of the college.

ALLUSION/ILLUSION. These terms are often misused. An *allusion* is an indirect reference to something. An *illusion* is a false impression or a misleading appearance.

The entire class missed Professor Sweno's **allusion** to the ghost in *Hamlet.*

Professor Sweno entertained the **illusion** that everyone read Shakespeare as often as he did.

A LOT. Often misspelled as one word. It is two. Many readers consider *a lot* inappropriate in academic writing, preferring *many, much,* or some comparable expression.

ALREADY. See **ALL READY.**

ALRIGHT. See **ALL RIGHT.**

AMONG/BETWEEN. Use *between* with two objects, *among* with three or more.

Francie had to choose **between** Richard and Kyle.

Francie had to choose from **among** a dozen actors.

AMOUNT/NUMBER. Use *amount* for quantities that can be measured, but not counted. Use *number* for things that can be counted, not measured: the *amount* of water in the ocean; the *number* of fish in the sea. The distinction between these words is being lost, but it is worth preserving. Remember that *amount of* is followed by a singular noun while *number of* is followed by plural nouns.

amount of money	number of dimes
amount of paint	number of colors
amount of support	number of voters

AN. See **A/AN.**

ANALOGY. An extended comparison between something familiar and something less well known. The analogy helps a reader visualize what might be difficult to understand.

A transitional word in a paper serves **as a road sign, giving readers directions to the next major idea.**

See also *false analogy.*

AND ETC. A redundant expression. Use *etc.* alone or *and so on.* See *etc.*

AND/OR. A useful form in some situations, especially in business and technical writing, but some readers regard it as clumsy. Work around it if you can, especially in academic writing. *And/or* is usually typed with no space before and after the slash.

ANGRY/MAD. The distinction between these words is rarely observed. But some people use *angry* to describe irritation, *mad* to describe insanity.

§ **ANTECEDENT.** The person, place, or thing a pronoun stands in for or refers to: *she = Marisa; it = the radio; they = the joggers in Central Park.* The antecedent is the word you would have to repeat in your sentence if you couldn't use a pronoun. See Section 17A.

ANTONYMS. Words with directly opposite meanings: *bright/dull; apex/nadir; concave/convex.*

ANYONE/ANY ONE. These expressions mean different things. Notice the difference highlighted in these sentences:

Any one of those problems could develop into a crisis.

I doubt that **anyone** will be able to find a solution to **any one** of the equations.

ANYWAYS. A nonstandard form. Use *anyway.*

{**Wrong**}   It didn't matter **anyways.**

{**Right**}   It didn't matter **anyway.**

§ **APPOSITIVE.** A word or phrase that stands next to a noun and modifies it by restating or expanding its meaning. Note that appositives ordinarily are surrounded by commas.

Fred the Fearless Aviator, **owner of a legendary Z-car,** sometimes mistook highway on-ramps for runways—and had the speeding tickets to prove it.

Connie Lim, **editor of the paper and an arch-liberal,** was furious when President Bush decided to give his only campus interview to Richard Wesley, **chair of the Young Republicans.**

§ **ARTICLES.** The words *the, a,* and *an* used before a noun. *The* is called a **definite article** because it points to something specific: *the* book, *the* church, *the* criminal. *A* and *An* are *indefinite articles* because they point more generally: *a* book, *a* church, *a* criminal. (See Section 25D and *a/an.*)

AS BEING. A wordy expression. You can usually cut *being.*

In most cases, telephone solicitors are regarded **as (being)** nuisances.

§ **AUXILIARY VERBS.** Verbs, usually some form of *be, do,* or *have,* that combine with other verbs to show various relationships of tense, voice, mood, and so on. All the words in boldface are auxiliary verbs: **has** *seen;* **will be** *talking;* **would have been** *going;* **are** *investigating;* **did** *mention;* **should** *prefer.* See Chapter 22.

AWFUL. In most academic writing, *awful* is inappropriate as an adverb.

> {**Inappropriate**}   The findings of the two research teams were **awful** close.

> {**Better**}   The findings of the two research teams were **quite** close.

AWHILE/A WHILE. The expressions are not interchangeable. *Awhile* is an adverb; *a while* is a noun phrase. After prepositions, always use *a while.*

> Bud stood **awhile** looking at the grass.

> Bud decided that the lawn would not have to be cut for **a while.**

BAD/BADLY. These words are troublesome. Remember that *bad* is an adjective describing what something is like; *badly* is an adverb explaining how something is done.

> Stanley's taste in music wasn't **bad.**

> Unfortunately, he treated his musicians **badly.**

Problems usually crop up with verbs that explain how something feels, tastes, smells, or looks. In such cases, use *bad.*

> The physicists felt **bad** about the disappearance of their satellite.

> The situation looked **bad.**

BEGGING THE QUESTION. The logical fallacy of assuming that something is a fact when it is precisely the issue in question. A lawyer begs the question, for example, when he defends an embezzler by insisting that the accused is an honest person: he wants a jury to accept as a fact what is very much in doubt. Sometimes it is difficult to spot this fallacy because assertions can be phrased to hide plausible but unproven assumptions. If you argued, for example, that the lives saved by the fifty-five mile-per-hour speed limit made it a good traffic law, you are assuming that the law had, indeed, saved lives. That's possible, but hardly proven.

BEING AS/BEING THAT. Both of these expressions are wordy when used in place of *because* or *since.* Use *because* and *since* in formal and academic writing.

> {**Inappropriate**}   **Being that** her major was astronomy, Jenny was looking forward to the eclipse.

> {**Better**}   **Since** her major was astronomy, Jenny was looking forward to the eclipse.

BESIDE/BESIDES. *Beside* is a preposition meaning 'next to' or 'along side of'; *besides* is a preposition meaning 'in addition to' or 'other than.'

> **Besides** a sworn confession, the detectives also had the suspect's fingerprints on a gun found **beside** the body.

Besides can also be an adverb meaning 'in addition' or 'moreover.'

> Professor Bellona didn't mind assisting the athletic department, and, **besides,** she actually liked coaching volleyball.

BETWEEN. See **AMONG.**

BUNCH. The expression is too casual for academic writing.

> {**Too casual**}   President Shade reported that the college faced a **bunch** of problems.

> {**Better**}   President Shade reported that the college faced **many** problems.

BUT WHAT. In most writing, *that* alone is preferable to the colloquial *but that* or *but what.*

{**Colloquial**}   There was little doubt **but what** he'd learned a few things.

{**Revised**}   There was little doubt **that** he'd learned a few things.

CAN/MAY. Understand the difference between the auxiliary verbs *can* and *may.* (See also *modal auxiliaries.*) Use *can* to express an ability to do something:

Charnelle **can** work differential equations.

According to the Handbook of College Policies, Dean Rack **can** lift the suspension.

Use *may* to express either permission or possibility:

You **may** compare my solution to Charnelle's.

Dean Rack **may** lift the suspension, but I wouldn't count on his doing it.

CANNOT. *Cannot* is ordinarily written as one word, not two.

CAN'T. Writers sometimes forget the apostrophe in this contraction and others like it: *don't, won't.*

CAN'T HARDLY. A common expression in speech that is, technically, a double negative. Use *can hardly* instead when you write.

{**Double negative**}   I **can't hardly** see the road.

{**Revised**}   I **can hardly** see the road.

CARDINAL NUMBERS. Numbers that express a count: *one, two, three.* In contrast, **ordinal numbers** show a sequence: *first, second, third.* See 36D.

§ **CASE.** The form a noun or pronoun takes to indicate its function in a sentence. Nouns have only two cases: the **possessive** form to show ownership (*girl's; Greta's; swimmers'*) and the **common** form to serve all other uses (*girl; Greta; swimmers*). See Chapter 25.

Pronouns have three forms: **subjective, objective,** and **possessive.** (See Chapter 28.) The subjective (or *nominative*) case is the form a pronoun takes when it is the subject of a sentence or a clause. Pronouns in this case are the doers of actions: *I, you, she, he, it, we, they, who.*

A pronoun is in the *objective case* when something is done to it. This is also the form a pronoun has after a preposition: [to] *me, her, him, us, them, whom.* For the pronouns *you* and *it,* the subjective and objective forms are identical.

A pronoun is in the *possessive case,* when it shows ownership: *my, mine, your, yours, her, his, its, our, ours, their, theirs, whose.*

CENSOR/CENSURE. These words have different meanings. As verbs, *censor* means 'to cut, to repress,' or 'to remove'; *censure* means 'to disapprove' and 'to condemn.'

The student editorial board voted to **censor** the four-letter words from Connie Lim's editorial and to **censure** her for attempting to publish the controversial piece.

§ **CLAUSE.** A group of related words that has a subject and verb. Clauses can be independent or dependent.

dependent clause   independent clause

Whenever it could, **the Astronomy Club scheduled meetings at an isolated hilltop observatory.**

An independent clause can stand alone as a complete sentence:

The Astronomy Club scheduled meetings at an isolated hilltop observatory.

A dependent (or subordinate) clause is a group of words which cannot stand alone as a sentence, but which contains a subject and verb.

Whenever it could, the Astronomy Club scheduled meetings at an isolated hilltop observatory.

CLICHÉ. A tired expression or conventional way of expressing something: *guilty as sin, hungry enough to eat a horse, sleep like a log, dumb as a rock.*

§ **COLLECTIVE NOUN.** A noun that names a group: *team, orchestra, jury, committee.* Collective nouns can be either singular or plural, depending upon how they are used in a sentence.

§ **COMMA SPLICE.** The mistaken use of a comma to join two groups of words, each of which could be a sentence by itself. Also called a "comma fault." See Sections 24B and 30B.

{**Comma splice**}   David liked Corvettes, they were fast cars.

{**Corrected**}   David liked Corvettes because they were fast cars.

§ **COMMON NOUN.** A noun that names some general object, not a specific person, place, or thing: *singer, continent, car.* Common nouns are not capitalized.

§ **COMPARATIVE AND SUPERLATIVE.** Adjectives and adverbs can express three different levels or degrees of intensity—the **positive,** the **comparative,** and the **superlative.** The positive level describes a single object; the comparative compares two objects, the superlative ranks three or more.

Positive	*Comparative*	*Superlative*
cold	colder	coldest
angry	more angry	most angry
angrily	more angrily	most angrily

§ **COMPLEMENT.** A word or phrase that completes the meaning of a verb, a subject, or an object. A **verb complement** is a direct or indirect object. A **subject complement** is a noun, pronoun, or adjective (or a comparable phrase) that follows a linking verb (a verb such as *to be, to seem, to appear, to feel,* and *to become*) and modifies or explains the subject.

Eleanor is Bruce's **cat.**

Eleanor is grossly **overweight.**

Eleanor is the **one** on the sagging couch.

Object complements are nouns or adjectives (or comparable phrases) that follow direct objects and modify them.

A pet food company named Eleanor **"Fat Cat of the Year."**

Mackerel makes Eleanor **happy.**

COMPLEMENT, COMPLEMENTARY/COMPLIMENT, COMPLIMENTARY. The words are not synonyms. *Complement* and *complementary* describe things completed or compatible. *Compliment* and *complimentary* refer to things praised or given away free.

Travis' sweater **complemented** his green eyes.

The two parts of Greta's essay were **complementary,** examining the same subject from differing perspectives.

Travis **complimented** Greta on her successful paper.

Greta found his **compliment** sincere.

She rewarded him with a **complimentary** sack of rice cakes from her health food store.

§ **COMPLEX SENTENCE.** A sentence that combines an independent clause and one or more dependent (subordinate) clauses.

dependent clause +
When Rita Ruiz first saw the announcements for the carnival,
independent clause
she began to get nervous.

§ **COMPOUND SENTENCE.** A sentence that combines two or more independent clauses, usually joined by a coordinating conjunction *(and, or, for, but, yet, so)* or a semicolon.

independent clause +
Recruiters from industry have set up booths on campus, and
independent clause
several corporations are sending recruiters to interview students.

§ **COMPOUND-COMPLEX SENTENCE.** A sentence that combines two or more independent clauses and at least one dependent (subordinate) clause.

dependent clause +
Although business is slow,
independent clause +
recruiters from industry have set up booths on campus, and
independent clause
several corporations are sending recruiters to interview students.

§ **CONCRETE NOUNS.** Nouns that name objects or events with physical properties or existences: *butter; trees; asteroid; people.* Concrete nouns are defined in contrast to **abstract nouns.**

§ **CONJUGATION.** The forms of a given verb as it appears in all numbers, tenses, voices, and moods. See Anatomy of a Verb, p. 356.

§ **CONJUNCTIONS, COORDINATING.** The words *and, or, nor, for, but, yet,* and *so* used to link words, phrases, and clauses that serve equivalent functions in a sentence. That is to say, a coordinating conjunction is used to join two independent clauses or two dependent clauses; it would not link a subordinate clause to an independent clause. See also **CONJUNCTIONS, SUBORDINATING.**

Oscar **and** Marie directed the play.

Oscar liked the story, **but** Marie did not.

§ **CONJUNCTIONS, SUBORDINATING.** Words or expressions such as *although, because, if, since, before, after, if, when, even though, in order that,* and *while* that relate dependent (that is, subordinate) clauses to independent ones. Subordinating conjunctions introduce subordinate clauses:

dependent clause

Although *Oscar and Marie both directed parts of the show,* Marie got most of the blame for its failure.

dependent clause

Oscar liked the story **even though** *no one else did.*

dependent clause

When *the show opened,* audiences stayed away.

§ **CONJUNCTIVE ADVERBS.** Words such as *however, therefore, nevertheless, moreover,* and so on, used to link one independent clause to another. Conjunctive adverbs are weaker links than **coordinating conjunctions** (such as *and, but, or, yet*) and must be preceded by a semicolon when used to join independent clauses:

Darwin apologized; **nevertheless,** Rita considered suing him.

CONNOTATION. *Connotation* is what a word suggests beyond its basic dictionary meaning— that is the word with all its particular emotional, political, or ethical associations. While any number of words may describe a street, for example, and so share the same **denotation** (dictionary meaning), such words as *avenue, alley, boulevard, alley, lane, court,* and *highway* differ significantly in what they imply—in their connotations. When using a list or collection of synonyms, such as you would find in a thesaurus, be sure you understand the connotation of any words you decide to use. See Section 16B.

CONSCIENCE/CONSCIOUS. Don't confuse these words. *Conscience* is a noun referring to an inner ethical sense; *conscious* is an adjective describing a state of awareness or wakefulness.

The linebacker felt a twinge of **conscience** after knocking the quarterback **unconscious.**

CONSENSUS OF OPINION. This expression is redundant; *consensus* by itself implies an opinion. Use *consensus* alone.

{**Redundant**}   The student senate reached a **consensus of opinion** on the issue of censorship.

{**Revised**}   The student senate reached a **consensus** on the issue of censorship.

CONTACT. Some people object to using *contact* as a verb meaning 'to get in touch with' or 'to call.' The usage is common, but you might want to avoid it in formal or academic writing.

§ **CONTRACTION.** A word shortened by the omission of a letter or letters. In most cases, an apostrophe is used to indicate the deleted letters or sounds: it is = *it's;* you are = *you're;* who is = *who's.* See 36A.

§ **COORDINATING CONJUNCTION.** See *conjunction, coordinating.*

Darwin apologized, **so** Rita forgave him.

Either Kelly **and** Maggie **or** Sue Ellen **and** Travis will be paired in the experiment, **but** I'd be surprised if they cooperated.

§ **CORRELATIVES**. Words that work together as conjunctions: *either . . . or; neither . . . nor; whether . . . or; both . . . and; not only . . . but.*

> **Whether** Darwin **or** Travis plays makes little difference.

> Brian attributed the failure of the play **not only** to a bad script **but** also to incompetent direction.

COULD OF/WOULD OF. Nonstandard forms when used instead of *could have* or *would have.*

> {**Wrong**}   Coach Rhoades imagined that his team **could of** been a contender.

> {**Right**}   Coach Rhoades imagined that his team **could have** been a contender.

§**COUNT NOUN**. A noun that names any object that exists as an individual item: *car; child; rose; cat.* Compare with *mass noun.*

COUPLE OF. Too casual an expression for formal or academic writing.

> {**Informal**}   The article accused the admissions office of a **couple of** major blunders.

> {**Revised**}   The article accused the admissions office of **several** major blunders.

CREDIBLE/CREDULOUS. *Credible* means 'believable'; *credulous* means 'willing to believe on slim evidence.' (See also **INCREDIBLE/INCREDULOUS**.)

> Klinkhamer found Mr. Hutton's excuse for his speeding **credible.** However, Klinkhamer was known to be a **credulous** police officer, capable of accepting almost any story.

CRITERIA/CRITERION. *Criteria,* the plural form, is more familiar, but the word does have a singular form—*criterion.*

> John Maynard, age sixty-four, complained that he was often judged according to a single **criterion,** age.

> Other **criteria** ought to matter in hiring.

CURRICULUM/CURRICULA. *Curriculum* is the singular form; *curricula* is the plural.

> President Shade believed that the **curriculum** in history had to be strengthened; in fact, the **curricula** in all the liberal arts departments needed rethinking.

§ **DANGLING MODIFIER**. A modifying phrase that doesn't seem connected to any word or phrase in a sentence. Dangling modifiers are usually corrected by rewriting a sentence to provide a better link between the modifier and what it modifies. See Section 18B.

> {**Dangling**}   **After finding the courage to ask Richard out,** the evening was a disaster.

> {**Improved**}   After finding the courage to ask Richard out, Francie had a disastrous evening.

DATA/DATUM. *Data* has a singular form—*datum*. In speech and informal writing, *data* is commonly treated as both singular and plural. In academic writing, use *datum* where the singular is needed. If *datum* seems awkward, try to rewrite the sentence to avoid the singular.

> {**Singular**}   The most intriguing **datum** in the study was the percentage of population decline.

> {**Plural**}   In all the **data,** no figure was more intriguing than the percentage of population decline.

§ **DEMONSTRATIVE ADJECTIVE.** An adjective that points to a specific object: *this* house, not *that* one; *those* rowdies who disrupted *these* proceedings last month.

§ **DEMONSTRATIVE PRONOUN.** A pronoun that points something out: *this; that; these; those.*

DENOTATION. A relatively neutral or objective meaning for a term. Sometimes called the "dictionary meaning," the denotation of a word attempts to explain what the word is or does stripped of particular emotional, political, or cultural associations. See *connotation.*

§ **DEPENDENT CLAUSE.** See **CLAUSE**.

§ **DETERMINER.** A word which indicates that a noun must follow. Determiners in English include articles (*a, an, the*) and certain possessive pronouns (*my, your*).

DIFFERENT FROM/DIFFERENT THAN. In formal writing, *different from* is usually preferred to *different than.*

> {**Formal**}   Ike's account of his marriage proposal was **different from** Bernice's.

> {**Informal**}   Ike's account of his marriage proposal was **different than** Bernice's.

DIRECT DISCOURSE. The actual words of a speaker or writer. Direct discourse is enclosed within quotation marks. [See *indirect discourse.*]

> {**Direct**}   As she approached the altar, Bernice yelled, "I won't marry you!"

> {**Indirect**}   As she approached the altar, Bernice declared that she would not marry Ike.

DISCREET/DISCRETE. *Discreet* means 'tactful' or 'sensitive to appearances' (discreet behavior); *discrete* means 'individual' or 'separate' (discrete objects).

> Joel was **discreet** about the money spent on his project. He had several **discrete** accounts at his disposal.

DISINTERESTED/UNINTERESTED. These words don't mean the same thing. *Disinterested* means 'neutral' or 'uninvolved'; *uninterested* means 'not interested' or 'bored.'

> Kyle and Richard sought a **disinterested** party to arbitrate their dispute.

> Stanley was **uninterested** in the club's management.

DON'T. Writers sometimes forget the apostrophe in this contraction and others like it: *can't, won't.*

§ **DOUBLE NEGATIVE.** Two negatives in a sentence that emphasize a negative idea. Such expressions are not standard English.

{Wrong} **Don't never** use a double negative.

{Wrong} Ike **won't** say **nothing** about his wedding plans.

To correct a double negative, eliminate one of the negatives in the sentence.

{Right} **Never** use a double negative.

{Right} **Don't** use a double negative.

{Right}-Ike will say **nothing** about his wedding plans.

{Right} Ike **won't** say anything about his wedding plans.

DUE TO. Some writers prefer *because of* to *due to* in many situations.

{**Considered awkward**} The investigation into Bud's disappearance stalled **due to** Officer Klinkhamer's sudden concern for correct procedure.

{**Revised**} The investigation into Bud's disappearance stalled **because of** Officer Klinkhamer's sudden concern for correct procedure.

However, *due to* is often the better choice when it serves as a subject complement after a linking verb. The examples illustrate the point.

> subj.   lk. vb   subj. compl
> Klinkhamer's discretion seemed ***due to cowardice.***

> subj.   lk. vb   subj. compl
> His discretion was ***due to the political prominence
> of the Huttons.***

DUE TO THE FACT THAT. Wordy. Replace it with *because* whenever you can.

{**Wordy**} Coach Meyer was fired **due to the fact that** he won no games.

{**Revised**} Coach Meyer was fired **because** he won no games.

EFFECT/AFFECT. See **AFFECT/EFFECT.**

EITHER/OR. The logical fallacy of reducing a complicated problem to simplistic alternatives. This is a favorite ploy of politicians trying to tar the opposition.

Either you are a socialist or you aren't.

Anyone who favors nuclear weapons **is either a criminal or an idiot.**

Such politicians suggest that an issue comes down to two choices, only one of which is really acceptable: war or peace; poverty or prosperity; repression or freedom; death or life. They, of course, side with the favorable alternative while their opponent offers war, poverty, repression, and death. The easiest way of breaking down an ''either/or'' situation is to show that other alternatives are possible.

ELICIT/ILLICIT. These words have vastly different meanings. *Elicit* means 'to draw out' or 'bring forth'; *illicit* describes something illegal or prohibited.

The detective tried to **elicit** an admission of **illicit** behavior from Bud.

§ **ELLIPTICAL CONSTRUCTION.** A phrase or sentence from which words have been deleted without obscuring the meaning. Elliptical constructions are common.

When [she is] asked about Rodney, Sue Ellen groans.

She likes reading books better than [she likes] writing them.

Kyle is a tough guy at heart, but [he is] a softie on the surface.

EMINENT/IMMINENT. These words are sometimes confused. *Eminent* means 'distinguished' and 'prominent'; *imminent* describes something about to happen.

The arrival of the **eminent** scholar is **imminent.**

ENTHUSED. A colloquial expression that should not appear in your writing. Use *enthusiastic* instead.

{**Unloved**}   Francie was **enthused** about Bruce's latest album.

{**Better**}   Francie was **enthusiastic** about Bruce's latest album.

EQUALLY AS. The expression is redundant. Use either *equally* or *as* to express a comparison—whichever works in a particular sentence.

{**Redundant**}   Sue Ellen is **equally as** concerned as Hector about bilingual education.

{**Revised**}   Sue Ellen is **as** concerned as Hector about bilingual education.

{**Revised**}   Sue Ellen and Hector are **equally** concerned about bilingual education.

ETC. This common abbreviation for *et cetera* should be avoided in most formal writing. Instead, use *and so on* or *and so forth.*

EVEN THOUGH. *Even though* is two words, not one.

EVERYONE/EVERY ONE. These expressions mean different things. Notice the differences highlighted in these sentences:

Every one of those problems could develop into a crisis **everyone** would regret.

I doubt that **everyone** will be able to attend **every one** of the sessions.

EXCEPT/ACCEPT. See **ACCEPT/EXCEPT.**

§ **EXPLETIVE.** An obscene word or exclamation. The phrase *expletive deleted* gained national currency during the Watergate Hearings when it was used to indicate where vulgar expressions had been cut from transcripts of the Watergate tapes. More generally, an expletive is any word that serves only as filler in a sentence.

§ **EXPLETIVE CONSTRUCTION.** The words *there* and *it* used as sentence lead-ins. In an expletive construction, there is no intended antecedent for the pronoun.

It is going to be a day to remember.

There were hundreds of spectators watching the demonstrators.

Expletive constructions can contribute to wordiness. Cut them whenever appropriate.

{**Revised**}   Hundreds of spectators were watching the demonstrators.

FACT THAT, THE. Wordy. You can often replace the entire expression with *that.*

{**Wordy**}   Bud was aware of **the fact that** he was in a strange room.

{**Revised**}   Bud was aware **that** he was in a strange room.

FAITH/FATE. A surprising number of writers confuse these words and their variations: *faithful, fateful, faithless.*

Faith is confidence, trust, or a religious belief; *fate* means destiny or outcome.

FALLACIES OF ARGUMENT. Forms of argumentation generally considered to be illogical, inappropriate, or indefensible. Recognizing these fallacies will make you a shrewder analyst of persuasive writing. Avoiding these errors in logic will make your own writing more mature and compelling.

For particular fallacies, see *ad hominem argument; begging the question; either/ or; false analogy; hasty generalization; non sequitur; post hoc, ergo propter hoc;* and *red herring.*

FALSE ANALOGY. A logical fallacy. A false analogy is a comparison that does not hold true or proves misleading. Analogies ordinarily help make ideas clearer to a reader; they work by comparing what is unfamiliar to something better known and understood. A writer, for example, might explain how the turbocharger in an automobile works by comparing it to a windmill, waterwheel, or compressor.

A false analogy trades on the assumption that readers can be persuaded to accept a comparison that is only partially true. Because one part of an analogy works, readers tend to buy the entire comparison, even when it misrepresents or simplifies the truth. Thus, comparing a touchdown drive in a football game to a military operation might reveal interesting tactical similarities, but the analogy would become false if casualties on the playing field were considered justified because casualties occur in battle as well.

FARTHER/FURTHER. The distinction between these words is not always observed, but it is useful. Use *farther* to refer to distances that can be measured.

It is **farther** from El Paso to Houston than from New York to Detroit.

Use *further,* meaning *'more'* or *'additional,'* when physical distance or separation is not involved.

The detective decided that the crime warranted **further** investigation.

§ **FAULTY PREDICATION.** A term used to describe verbs that don't fit their subjects. In many cases of faulty predication, a subject could not logically perform the action specified by the verb. See Section 19D.

{**Possible problem**} The purpose of radar detectors **is banned** in a few states. [What is forbidden—radar detectors or their purpose?]

{**Possible revision**} Radar detectors **are banned** in a few states.

At other times a linking verb is used incorrectly to connect nouns that aren't really equivalent.

{**Problem**} A common problem with some exotic cars **is** *when* you have them serviced.

[A *problem* cannot be *when.*]

{**Revised**} A common problem with an exotic car **is** getting it serviced.

FEWER THAN/LESS THAN. Use *fewer than* with things you can count; use *less than* with quantities that must be measured or can be considered as a whole.

The express lane was reserved for customers buying **fewer than** ten items.

Matthew had **less than** half a gallon of gasoline.

She also had **less than** ten dollars.

FINALIZE. Some readers object to this word, regarding it less appropriate than its synonyms: *conclude, close, bring to an end.*

§ **FINITE VERB.** A verb that changes form to indicate person, number, and tense. (See Section 24B.) A complete sentence requires a finite verb. Finite verbs stand in contrast to *non-finite* verb forms such as infinitives, participles, and gerunds which do not change form and which cannot stand as the only verb in a sentence. Compare the following finite and non-finite forms.

{**Non-finite verbs**}

To assure freshness, Jean-Pierre buys eggs from local farms.

The baker **kneading** the dough sneezed.

{**Finite verbs**}

He **assures** freshness.

The baker **kneads** the dough.

FLAUNT/FLOUT. These words are confused surprisingly often. *Flaunt* means 'to show off'; *flout* means 'to disregard' or 'to show contempt for.'

Mr. Butcher **flaunted** his muscles at every opportunity.

Flouting a gag order, the newspaper published its exposé of corruption in the city council.

FUN/FUNNER/FUNNEST. Used as an adjective, *fun* is not appropriate in academic writing; replace it with a more formal expression:

{**Informal**}   Skiing is a very **fun** sport.

{**More formal**}   Skiing is a very **enjoyable** sport.

The comparative and superlative forms, *funner* and *funnest,* while increasingly common in spoken English, are also inappropriate in writing. In writing, use *more fun* or *most fun:*

{**Spoken**}   Albert found tennis **funner** than squash.

{**Written**}   Albert found tennis **more fun** than squash.

{**Spoken**}   He thought racquetball the **funnest** of the three sports.

{**Written**}   He thought racquetball the **most fun** of the three sports.

§ **FUNCTION WORD.** A word in a sentence that helps to explain the relationship between other words in a sentence. The common function words include articles (*the, a, an*), conjunctions (*but, yet, either . . . or*), and prepositions (*on, between, over*).

§ **FRAGMENT.** A group of words that does not fully express an idea even though it is punctuated as a sentence. May also be called a 'broken sentence.' See Chapter 30.

{**Fragment**}   Despite the fact that Professor Chase had an impressive portfolio of investments.

{**Complete sentence**}   Despite the fact that Professor Chase had an impressive portfolio of investments, she was careful with her money.

{**Fragment**}   A safe investment most of the time.

{**Complete sentence**}   Bonds are a safe investment most of the time.

FUSED SENTENCE. See *run-on*.

§ **GENDER.** A classification of nouns and pronouns as masculine (actor, muscleman, he), feminine (actress, midwife, she), or neuter (tree, it).

§ **GERUND.** A verb form used as a noun: *smiling, biking, walking.* (See Section 24A.) Most gerunds end in —*ing* and, consequently, look identical to the present participle:

{**Gerund**}   **Smiling** is good for the health.

{**Participle**}   A **smiling** critic is dangerous.

The difference is that gerunds function as nouns while participles act as modifiers. Gerunds usually appear in the present tense, but they can take other forms:

Having been criticized made Brian angry.
>   [Gerund in past tense, passive voice, acting as subject of the sentence]

Being asked to play an encore was a compliment Otto enjoyed.
>   [Gerund in present tense, passive voice, acting as subject of sentence]

Gerunds have many functions:

{**Gerund as subject**}   *Being* solvent posed a problem for the Ericsons.

{**Gerund as object**}   They enjoyed *spending* money.

{**Gerund as complement**}   Spending was *enjoying* life.

{**Gerund as appositive**}   Mrs. Ericson rarely resisted her weakness, *buying* **expensive cars.**

GET. The principal parts of this verb are:

Present	*Past*	*Past Participle*
get	got	got, gotten

Gotten usually sounds more polished than *got* as the past participle, but both forms are acceptable:

Rita has **gotten** an *A* average in microbiology.

Rita has **got** an *A* average in microbiology.

Many expressions, formal and informal, rely on *get.* Avoid these less formal ones:

get it together

get straight

get real

GOOD AND. An informal expression. Avoid it in academic writing.

{**Informal**}   The lake was **good and** cold when the sailors threw Sean in.

{**Better**}   The lake was **icy** cold when the sailors threw Sean in.

GOOD/WELL. These words cause many problems. As a modifier, *good* is an adjective only; *well* can be either an adjective or an adverb. Consider the difference between these sentences where each word functions as an adjective:

Katy is **good.** (adj.)

Katy is **well.** (adj.)

Good is often mistakenly used as an adverb.

{**Wrong**}   Katy conducts the orchestra **good.**

{**Right**}   Katy conducts the orchestra **well.**

{**Wrong**}   The bureaucracy at NASA runs **good.**

{**Right**}   The bureaucracy at NASA runs **well.**

Complications occur when writers and speakers—eager to avoid using *good* incorrectly—substitute *well* as an *adjective* where *good* used as an *adjective* may actually be more accurate.

{**Wrong**}   After a shower, Coach Rhodes smells **well.**

{**Right**}   After a shower, Coach Rhodes smells **good.**

{**Ok**}   I feel **good.**

{**Also ok**}   I feel **well.**

GREAT. Don't use this vague word to describe every appealing object and circumstance.

The band did a **great** update of "Positively 4th Street." Lee was especially **great** on the lead guitar.

HANG UP. A slang term when used to mean 'problem.' Avoid it in academic writing.

{**Slang**}   Kyle has a **hang up** about learning French.

{**Revised**}   Kyle has a **problem** about learning French.

HANGED/HUNG. *Hanged* is the past participle conventionally reserved for executions; *hung* is used on other occasions. The distinction is a nice one, probably worth observing.

Connie was miffed when her disgruntled editorial staff decided she should be **hanged** in effigy.

Portraits of the faculty were **hung** in the student union.

HASSLE. Used either as a noun or verb to mean 'trouble,' *hassle* is not appropriate in academic writing.

HASTY GENERALIZATION. A logical fallacy in which a conclusion is based on too little evidence. While a single experience may suffice to teach that fires burn and cats scratch, most assertions require much fuller demonstration. You usually cannot construct a broad generalization from just a few examples, incidents, or illustrations: *Flying can't be safe: two jets crashed last month.* Nor should you try to reduce a complicated issue to a single statement: *Everyone knows most politicians are on the take.* Most generalizations need the precision of qualifying words and phrases: *some; many; a few; in many cases; in some situations; almost.*

§ **HELPING VERB.** Another name for *auxiliary verb.*

HE/SHE. Using *he/she* (or *his/her* or *s/he*) is one way of avoiding a sexist pronoun reference. However, many readers find expressions with slashes clumsy and prefer *he or she* and *his or her* or some alternative construction.

HISSELF. A nonstandard form. Don't use it.

HOMONYMS. Words of different meanings pronounced alike: *straight/strait; peace/piece; their/there.*

HOPEFULLY. As a sentence modifier, *hopefully* has been attacked about as fiercely as the beaches of Normandy. Unless you want to get caught in the crossfire, avoid using *hopefully* when you mean 'I hope' or 'it is hoped.'

{**Not**}   Hopefully, the weather will improve.

{**But**}   I hope the weather will improve.

Use *hopefully* only when you mean 'with hope.'

Geraldo watched **hopefully** as the safe was pried open.

IDIOM. A widely accepted expression that does not seem to make literal sense. Idioms often mean more than the sum of their parts:

The aircraft **bit the big one** over Montana.

Let's **get cracking.** We're late.

Kyle hoped that Richard would **cough up** the money for the fine.

'Idiom' can also describe a vocabulary and language style shared within certain groups or professions: the *idiom* of medical personnel, the *idiom* of computer specialists, the *idiom* of literary critics.

ILLICIT/ELICIT. See **ELICIT/ILLICIT.**

ILLUSION/ALLUSION. See **ALLUSION/ILLUSION.**

IMMINENT/EMINENT. See **EMINENT/IMMINENT.**

§ **IMPERATIVE MOOD.** The form of a verb which expresses a command (see *mood*):

Go! Find that missing cannister of film. **Bring** it back to the lab.

IMPLY/INFER. Think of these words as opposite sides of the same coin. *Imply* means 'to suggest' or 'to convey an idea without stating it.' *Infer* is what you might do to figure out what someone else has implied: you examine evidence and draw conclusions from it.

By joking calmly, the pilot sought to **imply** that the aircraft was out of danger. But from the hole that had opened in the wing, the passengers **inferred** that the landing would be exciting.

INCREDIBLE/INCREDULOUS. *Incredible* means 'unbelievable'; *incredulous* means 'unwilling to believe' and 'doubting.' (See also **CREDIBLE/CREDULOUS.**)

The press found the governor's explanation for his wealth **incredible.** You could hardly blame them for being **incredulous** when he attributed his vast holdings to coupon savings.

§ **INDEFINITE PRONOUN.** A pronoun that does not refer to a particular person, thing, or group: *all, any, each, everybody, everyone, one, none, somebody, someone,* and so on. See Section 27D.

§ **INDEPENDENT CLAUSE.** See *clause.*

§ **INDICATIVE MOOD.** The form of a verb which states facts or asks questions (see *mood*):

Did he **find** the cannister of film? It **was** in the lab yesterday.

INDIRECT DISCOURSE. The substance of what a speaker or writer has said, but not the exact words. Indirect discourse is not surrounded by quotation marks. [See *direct discourse.*]

{**Direct**}   At the altar Ike told Bernice, "If you don't marry me, I'll sue."

{**Indirect**}   At the altar Ike told Bernice that he would sue her if she didn't marry him.

§ **INFINITIVE.** A verbal that can be identified by the word *to* preceding the base form of a verb: *to strive; to seek; to find; to endure.* Infinitives also take other forms to show various tenses and voices: *to be seeking; to have found; to have been found.* Infinitives can act as nouns, adjectives, and adverbs (see 24A):

{**Infinitive as noun**}   **To capture** a market is not easy.
  [subject of the sentence]

{**Infinitive as adjective**}   Greta had many posters **to redesign.**
  [modifies the noun *posters*]

{**Infinitive as adverb**}   Mr. Stavros laughed **to forget** his troubles.
  [modifies the verb *laughed*]

An infinitive can also serve as an *absolute,* that is, a phrase, standing alone, that modifies an entire sentence.

***To be* blunt,** the paper is plagiarized.

The sign of the infinitive—*to*—is deleted in some sentence constructions.

The cast of the Broadway show chewed antacid tablets to help them **[to] deal** with horrible reviews.

INFLECTION. A change a word undergoes to specify its meaning or to reflect a relationship to other words or phrases in a sentence. For instance, verbs change to reflect shifts in tense, person, and number (*walk, walks, walked*). Nouns change to indicate number and possession (*antenna, antennae; Pearl, Pearl's*). Adverbs and adjectives change to show degrees of comparison (*cold, colder, coldest; happily, more happily, most happily*).

INITIALISM. A single term created by joining the first letters in the words that make up the full name or description. Unlike acronyms, however, initialisms are pronounced letter by letter:

IRS—**I**nternal **R**evenue **S**ervice

CIA—**C**entral **I**ntelligence **A**gency

HBO—**H**ome **B**ox **O**ffice.

See *acronyms* and Section 36C.

§ **INTENSIFIER.** A modifier that adds emphasis: *so, very, extremely, intensely, really, certainly.*

so cold   **very** bold   **extremely** complex

§ **INTENSIVE PRONOUN.** A pronoun form, created when *-self* or *-selves* is added to personal pronouns (*myself, yourself, herself, himself, itself, oneself, ourselves, yourselves, themselves*), that modifies a noun to add emphasis. (See Section 29A.)

Otto **himself** admitted he was the winner.

The managers did all the printing **themselves.**

§ **INTERJECTION.** A word that expresses emotion or feeling but that is not grammatically a part of a sentence. Interjections can be punctuated as exclamations (!) or attached to a sentence with a comma. Common interjections include *oh, hey, wow, ouch, well.* Avoid opening sentences with *well.*

§ **INTERROGATIVE PRONOUN.** A pronoun used to pose a question: *who, which, what, whose.*

INTO. Avoid this word in its faddish sense of being 'interested in' or 'involved with.'

{**Informal**}   The college was finally **into** computers.

{**More formal**}   The college was finally **involved with** computers.

§ **INTRANSITIVE VERB.** A verb that does not take a direct object. This means that the action of an intransitive verb does not pass on to someone or something; the sentence is complete without an object:

{**Intransitive**}
I **slept** well.   [You cannot **sleep** *something.*]

Lawrence **sat** down.

Compare intransitive verbs to transitive ones that require an object to complete the action of a sentence:

{**Transitive**}
Travis accidentally **slugged** *Kyle.*   [You can **slug** *someone.*]

Sister Anne **bit** her *lip.*

Linking verbs are intransitive:

{**Intransitive**}
I **am** happy.

You **have been** absent.

§ **INVERSION.** A reversal in the normal subject/verb/object order of a sentence:

Off came the wheel.

Our lives we hold less dear than our honor.

IRREGARDLESS. A nonstandard form. Use *regardless* instead.

§ **IRREGULAR VERBS.** A verb that does not form its past and past participle forms by adding *-d* or *-ed* to the infinitive (see *principal parts of a verb* and Section 23D). Irregular verbs are both numerous and important. They change their forms in various ways; a few even use the same form for all three principal parts.

Infinitive	*Past*	*Past Participle*
burst	burst	burst
drink	drank	drunk
arise	arose	arisen
lose	lost	lost

IRRITATE/AGGRAVATE. See **AGGRAVATE/IRRITATE.**

ITS/IT'S. Don't confuse these terms. *It's* is a contraction for *it is*. *Its* is a possessive pronoun meaning 'belonging to it.' See Section 28G for a discussion of this problem.

JUDGMENT/JUDGEMENT. The British spell this word with two *e*'s. Americans spell it with just one: *judgment*.

KIND OF. This expression is colloquial when used to mean 'rather.'

> {**Colloquial**}   The college trustees were **kind of** upset by the bad publicity.

> {**More formal**}   The college trustees were **rather** upset by the bad publicity.

LESS THAN. See FEWER THAN/LESS THAN.

LIE/LAY. These two verbs cause much confusion. Here are their parts:

Present	*Past*	*Present Participle*	*Past Participle*
lie (to recline)	lay	lying	lain
lay (to place)	laid	laying	laid

Notice that the past tense of *lie* is the same as the present tense of *lay*. It may help you to remember that *to lie* (meaning to recline) is *intransitive*—that is, it doesn't take an object. You can't lie *something*.

Travis **lies** under the cottonwood tree.

He **lay** there all afternoon.

He was **lying** in the hammock yesterday.

He had **lain** there for weeks.

To lay (meaning to place or to put) is *transitive*—it takes an object.

Jenny **lay** a *book* on Travis' bed.

Yesterday, she **laid** a *memo* on his desk.

Jenny was **laying** the *memo* on Travis' desk when he returned.

Travis had **laid** almost three *yards* of concrete that afternoon.

LIKE/AS. Many readers object to using the preposition *like* to introduce clauses of comparison. *As, as if,* or *as though* are preferred in situations where a comparison involves a subject and verb:

> {**Not**}   Mr. Butcher is self-disciplined, **like** you would expect a champion weightlifter might be.

> {**But**}   Mr. Butcher is self-disciplined, **as** you would expect a champion weightlifter might be.

> {**Not**}   It looks **like** he will win the local competition again this year.

> {**But**}   It looks **as if** he will win the local competition again this year.

Like is acceptable when it introduces a prepositional phrase, not a clause.

Francie looks **like** her mother.

The sculpture on the mall looks **like** a rusted Edsel.

§ **LINKING VERB.** A verb, often a form of *to be,* that connects a subject to a word or phrase that extends or completes its meaning. Common linking verbs are *to seem, to appear, to feel,* and *to become.*

> Wolfgang Rack **is** Dean of Humanities.

> *She* **seems** *tired.*

LITERALLY. When you write that something is *literally* true, you mean that it is exactly as you have stated. If you write, for example,

> Bernice **literally** steamed when Ike ordered her to marry him.

you are asserting that Bernice emitted heated water vapor, an unlikely event no matter how angry she was. If you want to keep the image (*steamed*), omit *literally:*

> Bernice **steamed** when Ike ordered her to marry him.

LOGICAL FALLACIES. See *fallacies of argument.*

LOSE/LOOSE. Be careful not to confuse these words. *Lose* is a verb, meaning 'to misplace,' 'be deprived of,' or 'be defeated.' *Loose* can be either an adjective or verb. As an adjective, *loose* means 'not tight'; as a verb, *loose* means 'to let go' or 'to untighten.'

> Without Kyle as quarterback, the team might **lose** its first game of the season.

> The strap on Kyle's helmet had worked **loose.**

> It **loosened** so much that Kyle lost his helmet.

MAD/ANGRY. See **ANGRY/MAD.**

MAJORITY/PLURALITY. There is a useful difference in meaning between these two words. A *majority* is more than half of a group; a *plurality* is the largest part of a group when there is *less than a majority.* In an election, for example, a candidate who wins 50.1 percent of the vote can claim a *majority.* One who wins a race with 40 percent of the electorate may claim a *plurality,* but not a majority.

MAN/MANKIND. These terms are considered sexist by many readers since they implicitly exclude women from the human family:

> **Man** has begun to conquer space.

> **Mankind's** greatest invention may be language.

Look for alternatives, such as *humanity, men and women, the human race,* or *humankind.*

> **Humankind** has begun to conquer space.

> **Humanity's** greatest invention may be language.

MANY TIMES. Wordy. Use *often* instead.

§ **MASS NOUN.** A noun that names something that does not exist as a separable or individual unit: *blood; money; work; time.* Compare with *count noun.*

MAY/CAN. See **CAN/MAY.**

MEDIA/MEDIUM. *Medium* is the singular of *media.*

> Connie believed that the press could be as powerful a **medium** as television.

The visual **media** are discussed in the textbook.

Media is commonly used now to refer in particular to the electronic press:

President Shade declined to speak to the **media** about the fiscal problems facing the college.

METAPHOR. A comparison that does not use the words *like* or *as:*

All the world's a stage.

I'm a little teacup, short and stout.

See *mixed metaphor.*

MIDST/MIST. Some people write *mist* when they mean *midst,* but the words mean different things. *Midst* means 'between' or 'in the middle of.' A *mist* is a mass of fine particles suspended in the air.

MIGHT OF. A nonstandard form. Use *might have* instead.

{**Not**}   Ms. Rajala **might of** never admitted the truth.

{**But**}   Ms. Rajala **might have** never admitted the truth.

§ **MINOR SENTENCE.** A group of words that does not have all the usual parts of a sentence but can act as a sentence because it expresses an idea completely.

{**Minor sentences**}   So what? Big deal!

§ **MISPLACED MODIFIER.** A modifying word or phrase that is ambiguous because it could modify more than one thing. See Section 31F.

{**Misplaced modifier**}   Some of the actors won roles *without talent.*

{**Improved**}   Some of the actors *without talent* won roles.

MIXED METAPHOR. An metaphor in which the terms of the comparison are inconsistent, incongruent, or unintentionally comic.

Unless we tighten our belts, we'll sink like a stone.

The fullback was a bulldozer, running up and down the field on winged feet.

§ **MODAL AUXILIARY.** An auxiliary verb that indicates possibility, necessity, permission, desire, capability, and so on. These modal auxiliaries include *can, could, may, might, will, shall, should, ought,* and *must.*

Hector **can** write.

Hector **might** write.

Hector **must** write.

§ **MODIFIER.** A word, phrase, or clause that gives information about another word, phrase, or clause. Writers use modifiers, mainly adjectives, adverbs, and modifying phrases, to make important qualifications in their writing, to make it more accurate, and sometimes to give it color and depth. See Chapter 31.

§ **MOOD.** A term used to describe how a writer regards a statement: either as a fact (the *indicative* mood), as a command (the *imperative* mood), or as a wish, desire, supposition, or improbability (the *subjunctive* mood). Verbs change their form to show mood. See Section 23F.

Indicative: The engineer **was** careful.

Imperative: **Be** careful!

Subjunctive: If the engineer **were** careful . . .

MORAL/MORALE. Don't confuse these words. As a noun, *moral* is a lesson. *Morale* is a state of mind.

The **moral** of the fable was to avoid temptation.

The **morale** of the team was destroyed by the opponents' touchdown.

MUST OF. Nonstandard. Use *must have* instead.

{**Not**} Someone **must of** read the book.

{**But**} Someone **must have** read the book.

NICE. This adjective has little impact when used to mean 'pleasant': *It was a nice day; Sally is a nice person.* In many cases, **nice** is damning with faint praise. Find a more specific word or expression. *Nice* can be used effectively to mean precise or fine:

There was a **nice** distinction between the two positions.

§ **NOMINAL.** A word, phrase, or entire clause that acts like a noun in a sentence. *Pronouns* and *gerunds* often function as nominals.

The wild applause only encouraged **them.**   [pronoun *them* acts as an object]

Keeping a straight face wasn't easy.   [gerund phrase acts as a subject]

§ **NOMINALIZATIONS.** Nouns coined by adding endings to verbs and adjectives: *acceptability, demystification, prioritization,* and so on. Clumsy, polysyllabic nominalizations can usually be replaced by simpler words. See Section 17D.

§ **NONFINITE VERB.** See *finite verb* and *verbal.*

§ **NONRESTRICTIVE ELEMENTS.** A modifier, often a phrase, not essential to the meaning of a sentence. If the nonrestrictive element is removed, the basic meaning of the sentence is not altered:

The senator, *who often voted with the other party,* had few loyal friends and a small constituency.

The agent, *a tall fellow from the FBI,* looked a bit self-conscious when he introduced himself.

Nonrestrictive phrases are ordinarily set off by commas. (See *restrictive elements.*)

NON SEQUITUR. A logical fallacy. A non sequitur is a conclusion that does not follow logically from previous statements or evidence. A non sequitur can sometimes slip through in an argument because it often has a degree of plausibility, but the assertion falls apart under more careful scrutiny:

He's from Massachusetts—a liberal, no doubt.

I'm sure Marisa voted for Bush; she makes $150,000 per year.

It does not follow that a person from Massachusetts is a liberal, or that someone with a six-figure income is automatically a Republican.

Here is a more complex example. If a writer claimed that the national economy must be healthy because inflation is under control, the assertion might sound reasonable. But it does not follow necessarily that an economy with low inflation must be thriving. Low inflation might be the result of slow growth, recession, or other conditions. So other factors would have to be considered and the relationship between the economy and inflation drawn more precisely to avoid a charge of non sequitur.

§ **NOUN.** A word that names a person, place, thing, idea, or quality. In sentences, nouns can serve as subjects, objects, complements, appositives, and even modifiers. There are many classes of nouns: *common, proper, concrete, abstract, collective, mass,* and *count.* See individual entries for details of each type.

NOWHERES. Nonstandard version of *nowhere* or *anywhere.*

{**Colloquial**}   The chemist couldn't locate the test tube **nowheres.** It was **nowheres** to be found.

{**Revised**}   The chemist couldn't locate the test tube **anywhere.** It was **nowhere** to be found.

NUMBER. The form a word takes to indicate whether it is singular or plural. See Section 25A.

{**Singular**}	boy	his	this
{**Plural**}	boys	their	these

NUMBER/AMOUNT. See **AMOUNT/NUMBER.**

§ **OBJECT, DIRECT/INDIRECT.** A word or phrase that receives the action of a verb. An object is direct when it states to whom or to what an action was done.

direct object
Kyle gave us *the signal.*

An object is indirect when it explains for whom or for what an action is done or directed. It precedes the direct object.

indirect object
Kyle gave *us* the signal.

§ **OBJECTIVE CASE.** The form a noun or pronoun takes when it serves as a direct or indirect object in a sentence or as the object of a preposition. See *case.*

OFF OF. A redundant expression. *Off* alone is enough.

Travis drove his Jeep **off** the road.

O.K./OK/OKAY. Not the best choice for formal writing. But give the expression respect. It's an internationally recognized nod of approval. OK?

ON ACCOUNT OF. Can seem wordy. Replace it with *because of* whenever appropriate.

{**Wordy**}   Dukakis lost **on account of** poor strategy.

{**Better**}   Dukakis lost **because of** poor strategy.

ORDINAL NUMBERS. Numbers that express a sequence: *first, second, third.* In contrast, *cardinal numbers* express a number, or count: *one, two, three.*

PARAGRAPH. A cluster of sentences working together for some purpose: to develop a single idea, to show relationships between separate ideas, to move readers from one point to another, to introduce a subject, to conclude a discussion, and so on. Paragraphs are marked by separations (indentions or open spaces). Paragraphs vary greatly in length but may be as short as a single sentence. See Chapters 13–14.

The symbol ¶ meaning *paragraph* is sometimes inserted by editors and instructors where a new paragraph is needed in a paper. *No* ¶ indicates that an existing paragraph should be combined with another.

§ **PARALLEL STRUCTURE.** A sentence pattern in which related words, clauses, or phrases follow similar patterns. The shared pattern reinforces the notion that these ideas are related or equivalent.

The band had difficulty *marching in step, maintaining straight rows,* and *preserving straight faces.*

§ **PARALLELISM.** Ideas or items expressed in matching grammatical forms or structural patterns. Words, phrases, sentences, and even whole paragraphs can demonstrate parallelism:

{**Parallel verbs**}   The child was *waving, smiling, jumping,* and *laughing—* all at the same time.

{**Parallel phrases**}   *On the sea, in the air, on the ground,* the forces of the Axis powers were steadily driven back.

{**Parallel clauses**}   He was the best of clowns; he was the worst of clowns.

{**Parallel sentences**}   The child was waving, smiling, jumping, and laughing—all at the same time. Her mother was yelling, screaming, berating, and threatening—all to no avail.

§ **PARENTHETICAL ELEMENT.** A word or phrase that contributes to a sentence but is not an essential part of it. Parenthetical items are usually separated from sentences by commas, dashes, or parentheses. When the element occurs in the middle of a sentence, it is surrounded by punctuation.

Kyle, **a wiry fellow who could pass for a gymnast,** climbed the sycamore tree easily.

Francie decided to climb an elm and—**still clutching her purse and camera**—soon waved from its topmost branches.

All the while, Richard **(the most vocal advocate of tree-climbing)** remained on *terra firma.*

§ **PARTICIPLE.** A verb form used as a modifier (see Section 24A). The present participle ends with —*ing.* For regular verbs, the past participle ends with —*ed;* for irregular verbs, the form of the past participle will vary. Participles have these forms:

To perform (a regular verb)

Present, active:	performing
Present, passive:	being performed
Past, active:	performed
Past, passive:	having been performed

Participles can serve as simple modifiers:

Smiling, Officer Klinkhamer wrote the traffic ticket.   [modifies 'Officer Klinkhamer']

But they often take objects, complements, and modifiers of their own to form verbal phrases that play an important role in shaping sentences:

Writing **the ticket for speeding,** Klinkhamer laughed at his own cleverness in catching Travis.

Having been ridiculed **often in the past by Travis,** Klinkhamer now had his chance for revenge.

Travis, *knowing* **what his friends were doing to Officer Klinkhamer's car,** smiled as he took the ticket.

Like an infinitive, a participle can also serve as an *absolute,* that is, a phrase, standing alone, that modifies an entire sentence.

All things *considered,* the prank was worth the cost of the ticket.

§ **PARTS OF SPEECH.** The eight common categories by which words in a sentence are categorized according to what they do, how they are formed, where they are placed, and what they mean. Those basic categories are **nouns, pronouns, adjectives, verbs, adverbs, prepositions, conjunctions** and **interjections.** See Part IV: Minigrammar.

PASSED/PAST. Be careful not to confuse these words. *Passed* is a verb form; *past* can function as a noun, adjective, adverb, or preposition. The words are not interchangeable. Study the differences in the sentences below:

{**Passed as verb, past tense**}   Tina **passed** her economics examination.

{**Passed as verb, past participle**}   Earlier in the day, she had **passed** an English quiz.

{**Past as noun**}   In the **past,** she had done well.

{**Past as adjective**}   In the **past** semester, she got straight A's.

{**Past as adverb**}   Tina smiled at the teacher as she walked **past.**

{**Past as preposition**}   **Past** midnight, Tina was still celebrating.

§ **PASSIVE VERBS/VOICE.** See *voice.*

PERSECUTE/PROSECUTE. *Persecute* means 'to oppress' or 'to torment'; *prosecute* is a legal term, meaning 'to bring charges or legal proceedings' against someone or something.

Connie Lim felt **persecuted** by criticisms of her political activism.

She threatened to **prosecute** anyone who interfered with her First Amendment rights.

§ **PERSON.** A way of classifying personal pronouns in sentences:

1st Person: the speaker—*I, we.*

2nd Person: spoken to—*you.*

3rd Person: spoken about—*he, she, it, they* + all nouns.

Verbs also change to indicate a shift in person.

1st Person: I **see.**

3rd Person: She **see***s*.

§ **PERSONAL PRONOUN.** A pronoun that refers to particular individuals, things, or groups: *I, you, he, she, it, we, you, they.*

PERSONAL/PERSONNEL. Notice the difference between these words. *Personal* refers to what is private, belonging to an individual. *Personnel* are the people staffing an office or institution.

> Drug testing all airline **personnel** would infringe upon **personal** freedom.

PHENOMENA/PHENOMENON. You can win friends and influence people by spelling these words correctly and using *phenomenon* as the singular form.

> The astral **phenomenon** of meteor showers is common in August.

> Many other astral **phenomena** are linked to particular seasons.

§ **PHRASE.** A group of related words that does not include both a subject and a finite verb. Among the types of phrases are *noun phrases, verb phrases, verbal phrases* (infinitive, gerund, and participial), *absolute phrases,* and *prepositional phrases.*

> {**Noun phrase**}   *The members of the Astronomy Club* will be going to the observatory in a van.

> {**Verb phrase**}   The members of the Astronomy Club *will be going* to the observatory in a van.

> {**Verbal phrase—infinitive**}   Their intention is *to observe the planet Mars.*

> {**Verbal phrase—gerund**}   *Driving to the observatory* will be half the fun.

> {**Verbal phrase—participial**}   The instructor *sponsoring the trip* will drive the van.

> {**Absolute phrase**}   *All things considered,* the trip was time well spent.

> {**Prepositional phrase**}   Whenever it could, the Astronomy Club scheduled its meetings *at the hilltop observatory.*

PLUS. Don't use *plus* as a conjunction or conjunctive adverb meaning 'and,' 'moreover,' 'besides,' or 'in addition to.'

> {**Not**}   Mr. Burton admitted to cheating on his income taxes this year. **Plus** he acknowledged that he had filed false returns for the last three years.

> {**But**}   Mr. Burton admitted to cheating on his income taxes this year. **Moreover,** he acknowledged that he had filed false returns for the last three years.

§ **POSSESSIVE CASE.** The form a noun or pronoun takes to show ownership: *Barney's; Jean-Pierre's; mine; yours; hers; theirs.* See Sections 25B and 28F.

§ **POSSESSIVE PRONOUN.** The form a pronoun takes when it shows ownership: *my, mine, your, yours, her, his, its, our, ours, their, whose, anyone's, somebody's.* See Section 28F.

POST HOC, ERGO PROPTER HOC. A logical fallacy also known simply as *post hoc.* The Latin expression means *after this, therefore because of this.* It describes the faulty assumption that anything that happens after some phenomenon is caused by it. In its most extreme form, this fallacy produces superstitions: breaking a mirror causes seven years' bad luck; finding a penny brings good fortune. More subtly, *post hoc, ergo propter hoc* reasoning can induce belief in plausible, but unproven, causal relationships. For example, when traffic deaths fell the year after the imposition of a national 55 mph speed limit, safety crusaders immediately credited the slower highway speeds with saving lives. Yet subsequent studies showed that the dip in highway fatalities was more accurately related to Americans driving significantly fewer miles because of high gas prices and an economic recession.

Post hoc, ergo propter hoc is among the most common, tempting, and persuasive fallacies because the facile solutions it finds for serious problems are often more appealing than more realistic answers. Thus, it might be easier to blame rock and roll for rising teen pregnancies than to try to understand complex social and economic relationships; it is easier to blame foreigners for domestic factory closings than to examine labor and management relationships, productivity, and quality control.

PRECEDE/PROCEED. Spelling, not meaning, is the problem with these terms. Though their second syllables sound alike, they are not spelled the same. Check these puzzlers in the dictionary when you are stumped.

§ **PREDICATE.** A verb and all its auxiliaries, modifiers, and complements.

The pregnant cat, enormous and fierce, **kittened in the back seat of Officer Klinkhamer's car, where Travis and friends had deposited her.**

§ **PREDICATE ADJECTIVE.** An adjective that follows a linking verb and describes the subject.

Coach Rhodes is **inept.**

It was **cold.**

§ **PREDICATE NOMINATIVE.** A noun or pronoun that follows a linking verb and says what the subject is.

Rhodes is the **coach.**

It was **she.**

PREJUDICE/PREJUDICED. Many writers and speakers use *prejudice* where they need *prejudiced. Prejudice* is a noun; *prejudiced* is a verb form.

{**Wrong**} Joe Kamakura is **prejudice** against Liberals.

{**Right**} Joe Kamakura is **prejudice*d*** against Liberals.

{**Wrong**} **Prejudice** people are found in every walk of life.

{**Right**} **Prejudice*d*** people are found in every walk of life.

{**Compare**} **Prejudice** is found in every walk of life.

§ **PREPOSITION.** A word that links a noun or pronoun to the rest of a sentence. Prepositions point out many kinds of basic relationships: *on, above, to, for, in, out, through, by.*

§ **PREPOSITIONAL PHRASE.** The combination of a preposition and a noun or pronoun. The following are prepositional phrases: *on our house, above it, to him, in love, through them, by the garden gate.*

§ **PRINCIPAL PARTS OF A VERB.** The three basic forms of a verb from which all tenses are built. See 23A, 23D.

> **infinitive (present).** This is the base-form of a verb, the shape it takes when preceded by *to: to* **walk;** *to* **go; to choose.**

> **past.** This is the simplest form the verb takes to show action that has already occurred: **walked; went; chose.**

> **past participle.** This is the form a verb takes when it is accompanied by an **auxiliary verb** to show a more complicated past tense: *had* **walked;** *might have* **gone;** *would have been* **chosen.**

PRINCIPAL/PRINCIPLE. Two terms commonly confused because of their multiple meanings. *Principal* means 'chief' or 'most important.' It also names the top gun in elementary and secondary school. (Remember, the *principal* is your "pal"?). Finally, it can be a sum of money lent or borrowed.

> Ike intended to be the **principal** breadwinner of the household.

> Bernice accused Ike of acting like a power-mad high school **principal.**

> She argued that they would need two incomes just to meet their mortgage payments—both interest and **principal.**

A *principle,* on the other hand, is a guiding rule or fundamental truth.

> Ike declared it was against his **principles** to have his wife work.

> Bernice said he would just have to be a little less **principled** on that issue.

PRIORITIZE. Some readers object to this word, regarding it less appropriate than its equivalents: *rank* or *list in order of priority.*

§ **PROGRESSIVE VERB.** A verb form that shows continuing action. Progressive tenses are formed by the auxiliary verb *to be* + the present participle.

> (to be) + (present participle)
> Katy **is conducting** her string orchestra.

> (to be) + (present participle)
> Katy **had been conducting** the orchestra for many years.

> (to be) + (present participle)
> Katy **will be conducting** the orchestra for many years to come.

§ **PRONOUN.** A word that acts like a noun, but doesn't name a specific person, place, or thing—*I, you, he, she, it, they, whom, who, what, myself, oneself, this, these, that, all, both, anybody,* and so on. There are many varieties of pronouns: **personal, relative, interrogative, intensive, reflexive, demonstrative, indefinite,** and **reciprocal.** See Chapters 26–29 and individual entries for details about each type.

§ **PROPER ADJECTIVE.** An adjective based on the name of a person, place, or thing treated as a proper noun. Proper adjectives are capitalized.

> **British** cuisine

> **Machiavellian** politics

> **Cubist** art

§ **PROPER NOUN.** A noun that names some particular person, place, or thing; *Bryan Adams, Australia, Ford.* The first letter in proper nouns is capitalized.

§ **QUALIFIER.** A modifier. Sometimes the word refers to particular classes of modifiers: **intensifiers** (*so, too, surely, certainly*), **restrictive expressions** (*many, most, both, some, almost*), or **conjunctive adverbs** (*however, nevertheless*).

QUOTE. Some people do not accept *quote* used as a noun—that is, as a shortened form of *quotation.* To be safe, use *quotation* in formal writing.

REAL. Often used as a colloquial version of *very: I was real scared.* This usage is inappropriate in academic writing.

REALLY. An adverb too vague to make much of an impression in many sentences: *It was really hot; I am really sorry.* Replace *really* with a more precise expression or delete it.

REASON IS . . . BECAUSE. The expression is redundant. Use one half of the expression or the other—not both:

{**Redundant**}   The **reason** the cat is ferocious is **because** she is protecting her kittens.

{**Revised**}   The **reason** the cat is ferocious is **that** she is protecting her kittens.

{**Revised**}   The cat is ferocious **because** she is protecting her kittens.

§ **RECIPROCAL PRONOUN.** A compound pronoun that shows a mutual action: *one another; each other.*

The members of the jury whispered to **one another.**

RED HERRING. Red herrings are distractions in an argument—facts, statements, accusations that have no bearing on the main point. They serve to throw an opponent off balance or readers off course. An accused car thief uses a red herring when he blames his crime on the owner having left her keys in the vehicle. Politicians may be employing a red herring when they attempt to blame a political problem on the press or other media: terrorism occurs because of news coverage; drugs are rampant because movies popularize them.

REDUNDANCY. A word or expression that is repetitious or unnecessary: *final* end; *ultimate* conclusion; *initial* start.

§ **REFERENCE.** The connection between a pronoun and the noun it stands in for (antecedent). This connection should be clear and unambiguous. When a reader can't figure out who *he* is in a sentence you have written, or what exactly *this* or *it* may mean, you have a problem with unclear reference:

{**Unclear references**}   The sun broke through the mists as Jim and Jack, fully recovered from their accident, arrived with news about the award and the ceremony. **This** pleased us because **he** hadn't mentioned anything about **it.**

{**References clarified**}   The sun broke through the mists as Jim and Jack, fully recovered from their accident, arrived with news about the award and the ceremony. **The news** pleased us because **Jim** hadn't mentioned anything about **a ceremony.**

See Chapter 26.

§ **REFLEXIVE PRONOUN.** A pronoun form created when *-self* or *-selves* is added to personal pronouns (*myself, yourself, herself, himself, itself, oneself, ourselves, yourselves, themselves*). These words are *reflexive* when both the subject and object of an action are the same person or thing (see Section 29A).

subject   object
Corey had only *himself* to rely on.

subject object
They took *themselves* too seriously.

§ **REGULAR VERB.** A verb that forms its past and past participle forms (see *principal parts of a verb*) simply by adding *-d* or *-ed* to the infinitive.

Infinitive	*Past*	*Past Participle*
talk	talk**ed**	talk**ed**
coincide	coincid**ed**	coincid**ed**
advertise	advertis**ed**	advertis**ed**

RELATE TO. A colloquial expression used vaguely and too often to mean 'identify with' or 'appreciate'.

{**Vague**} Bud could **relate to** being a campus football hero.

{**Better**} Bud liked being a campus football hero.

§ **RELATIVE CLAUSE.** See *relative pronoun.*

§ **RELATIVE PRONOUN.** A pronoun such as *that, which, whichever, who, whoever, whom, whomever, whose* and *of which* that introduces subordinate clauses.

subordinate clause
Whichever **car you choose to buy** will cost a small fortune.
   [*Whichever* introduces a noun clause that forms the subject of the complete sentence.]

        subordinate clause
Stanley sold the club *which* **he had owned for twenty years.**
   [*Which* introduces an adjective clause modifying *club*.]

A clause introduced by a relative pronoun is called a **relative clause.**

§ **RESTRICTIVE ELEMENTS.** A modifier, usually a phrase, essential to the meaning of a sentence. If the restrictive element is removed, the sentence no longer makes sense:

Only the senator *who voted "nay"* remained in the chamber.

The agent *from the CIA* was the one who called.

Restrictive phrases are *not* set off by commas. (See *nonrestrictive elements.*)

§ **RUN-ON SENTENCE.** A sentence in which two independent clauses (groups of words which could stand alone as sentences) are joined without appropriate punctuation marks or conjunctions. May also be called a "fused sentence." See Section 30D.

{**Run on**} Reading *Ulysses* is one thing understanding it is another.

{**Corrected**} Reading *Ulysses* is one thing; understanding it is another.

SENTENCE. A group of words that expresses an idea and is punctuated as an independent unit.

Whenever it could, the Astronomy Club scheduled meetings in an isolated hilltop observatory.

Is that true?

Explain the situation to me.

§ **SENTENCE FRAGMENT.** See *fragment.*

§ **SENTENCE STRUCTURE.** The way a sentence is put together—its shape or arrangement of phrases and clauses. Sentences can be described in many ways, for example, as *simple, complex, compound,* or *compound-complex; periodic* or *cumulative;* or *direct, complicated, tangled,* and so on. See Chapters 17–20.

§ **SEQUENCE OF TENSES.** The way the tense of one verb in a sentence limits or determines the tense of other verbs.

SET/SIT. See **SIT/SET.**

SEXIST LANGUAGE. Language that reflects prejudiced attitudes and stereotypical thinking about the sex roles and traits of both sexes, but most frequently about women. See Chapter 16.

S/HE. Many readers object to this construction which, like *he/she* and *she/he,* is an alternative to the nonsexist, but clumsy *he or she.* Avoid *s/he* if possible.

SHOULD OF. Mistaken form of *should have.* Also incorrect are *could of* and *would of.*

SIMILE. An explicit comparison between two things. Similes include a word, such as *like* or *as,* that underscores the comparison:

Driving a Mercedes 560 SEC is *like* meeting the Pope.

Kelly is *as* flaky *as* Wheaties.

SIMPLE SENTENCE. A sentence that has only one clause.

Mardi Gras is celebrated on the Tuesday before Ash Wednesday.

SIT/SET. These two verbs can cause problems. Here are their parts:

Present	*Past*	*Present Participle*	*Past Participle*
sit (take a seat)	sat	sitting	sat
set (put down)	set	setting	set

It may help you to remember that *to sit* (meaning 'to take a seat') is *intransitive*—that is, it doesn't take an object. You can't sit *something.*

Travis **sits** under the cottonwood tree.

He **sat** there all afternoon.

He was **sitting** in the hammock yesterday.

He had **sat** there for several weeks.

To set (meaning 'to place' or 'to put') is *transitive*—it takes an object.

Jenny **set** a *plate* on the table.

At Christmas, we **set** a *star* atop the tree.

Alex was **setting** the *music* on the stand when it collapsed.

Connie discovered that Travis **had set** a *subpoena* on her desk.

SLANG. Casual, aggressively informal language.

The punk wanted to bum a cigarette off of us, but we told him to get lost.

Slang expressions are out of place in academic and business writing. See Section 16A.

SO. Vague when used as an intensifier, especially when no explanation follows *so: Sue Ellen was so sad. So* used this way can sound trite (How sad is *so* sad?) or juvenile: *Professor Sweno's play was* so *bad.* If you use *so,* complete your statement:

Sue Ellen was **so** sad she cried for an hour.

Professor Sweno's play was **so** bad that the audience cheered the scenery.

§ **SPLIT INFINITIVE.** An infinitive interrupted by an adverb; *to boldly go; to really try.* Split infinitives offend some readers, and should be avoided in formal writing, except when the revised version is more awkward than the split infinitive. To revise a split infinitive, simply place the adverb somewhere else in your sentence: *to go boldly.* See Section 24C.

STATIONARY/STATIONERY. *Stationary,* an adjective, means 'immovable, fixed in place.' *Stationery,* a noun, means 'writing material.' The words are not interchangeable.

§ **SUBJECT.** A word or phrase that names what a sentence is about. The **simple subject** of a sentence is a single word; the complete subject is the simple subject and all its modifiers:

               subject   verb

{**Simple Subj.**} The **captain** of the volleyball team *quit*.

               subject   verb

{**Complete Subj.**} **The captain of the volleyball team** *quit*.

§ **SUBJECT COMPLEMENT.** A word or phrase that follows a linking verb, completing its meaning. Subject complements can be nouns, pronouns, or adjectives. See *predicate adjective* and *predicate nominative.*

    subj.   l.v.   subj. comp.

David Barrett is **student representative.**

      subj.   l.v.   subj. comp.

The director is **she.**

     subj.   l.v.   subj. comp.

Kelly McKay seems **mysterious.**

§ **SUBJUNCTIVE MOOD.** The form of a verb which expresses a wish, desire, supposition, or improbability (see *mood* and Section 23F).

If he **were to find** the cannister of film, we would be delighted. It is necessary that the film **be** locked in the vault overnight.

SUBORDINATING CONJUNCTION. See *conjunction, subordinating.*

§ **SUPERLATIVE.** The highest degree in a comparison of at least three things:

The *worst* play in thirty-seven years . . .

The *most vicious* of three published reviews . . .

SUPPOSED TO. Many writers forget the *d* at the end of *suppose* when the word is used with auxiliary verbs:

{**Incorrect**}   Maggie was **suppose** to check her inventory.

{**Correct**}   Maggie was **supposed** to check her inventory.

SYNONYMS. Words of approximately the same meaning: *street/road; angry/mad; home/ domicile.* While synonyms may share their **denotation** or basic meaning, they often differ in **connotation,** that is, what the words imply. Both *skinny* and *svelte,* for example, denote thinness, but the terms differ significantly in how they would be used. In most situations, *skinny* sounds disparaging while *svelte* is a positive, even glamorous description.

§ **SYNTAX.** The arrangement and relationship of clauses, phrases, and words in a sentence.

§ **TENSE.** That quality of a verb that expresses time and existence. Tense is expressed through changes in verb forms and endings (*see, seeing, saw; work, worked*) and the use of auxiliaries (*had seen, will have seen; had worked, had been working*). Tense enables verbs to state complicated relationships between time and action—or relatively simple ones. See Sections 23A–D.

THAN/THEN. These words are occasionally confused. *Than* is a conjunction expressing difference or comparison, *then* an adverb expressing time.

If the film is playing tomorrow, Shannon would rather go *then than* today.

THEIRSELVES. A nonstandard form. Use *themselves* instead.

{**Incorrect**}   All the strikers placed **theirselves** in jeopardy.

{**Correct**}   All the strikers placed **themselves** in jeopardy.

THIS. As a pronoun, *this* is sometimes vague and in need of clarification (see Section 26C).

{**Vague**}   We could fix the car if you had more time or I owned the proper tools. Of course, **this** is always a problem.

{**Clearer**}   We could fix the car if you had more time or we owned the proper tools. Of course, **my lack of proper tools** is always a problem.

This (and *these*) may be inappropriate when used informally as demonstrative adjectives that refer to objects not previously mentioned:

{**Inappropriate *this***}   Jim owns **this** huge Harley motorcycle.

{**Inappropriate *these***}   After she moved out, we found **these** really huge roaches in her apartment.

Such forms are common in speech, but should not appear in writing:

{**Better**}   Jim owns **a** huge Harley motorcycle.

{**Better**}   After she moved out, we found huge roaches in her apartment.

THRONE/THROWN. A surprising number of writers use *thrown* when they mean *throne*.

Charles I was **thrown** from his **throne** by an angry army of Puritans.

THUSLY. A fussy, nonstandard form. Don't use it. *Thus* is stuffy enough without the *-ly.*

TILL/UNTIL. *Until* is used more often than *till* in school and business writing, though the words are usually interchangeable. No apostrophe is used with *till*. You may occasionally see the poetic form *'til,* but don't use it in academic or business writing.

TO/TOO. Most people know the difference between these words. But a writer in a hurry can easily put down the preposition *to* when the adverb *too* is intended. If you make this error often, check for it when you edit.

{**Incorrect**}   Coach Rhodes was **to** surprised to speak after his team won its first game in four years.

{**Revised**}   Coach Rhodes was **too** surprised to speak after his team won its first game in four years.

TOWARD/TOWARDS. *Toward* is preferred, though either form is fine.

TRANSITIONS. Connecting words, phrases, and other devices (repetitions, headings) that help readers move from one unit to the next in your writing. Transitions help to hold a piece of writing together, bridging gaps and linking sentences and paragraphs. *Transitional words* are individual terms used to link ideas: *therefore, moreover, nevertheless, nonetheless, consequently,* and so on. See Chapter 15.

§ **TRANSITIVE VERB.** A verb that takes an object. The action of a transitive verb passes on to someone or something; the sentence would be incomplete without an object.

{**Transitive**}
Travis accidentally **slugged** *Kyle.*   [You can **slug** *someone.*]

Sister Anne **wrecked** the *van*.

Transitive verbs (unlike intransitives) can usually be changed from the active to passive voice:

{**Active**}   Travis accidentally **slugged** *Kyle.*

{**Passive**}   Kyle **was** accidentally **slugged** by Travis.

Compare transitive verbs to intransitive ones that do not require an object to complete the action of a sentence:

{**Intransitive**}
I **slept** well.   [You cannot **sleep** *something.*]

Lawrence **sat** down.

TRY AND. An informal expression. In writing, use *try to* instead.

{**Incorrect**}   After its defeat, the soccer team decided to **try and** drown its sorrows.

{**Revised**}   After the victory, the soccer team decided to **try to** drown its sorrows.

TV. This abbreviation for 'television' is common, but in most writing it is still preferable to write out the entire word. The abbreviation is usually capitalized. You may, of course, abbreviate the names of television networks and services: *CBS, ABC, NBC, CNN, MTV, HBO.*

TYPE. You can usually cut this word.

> {**Wordy**}   Hector was a polite **type** of guy.

> {**Revised**}   Hector was polite.

UNINTERESTED/DISINTERESTED. See **DISINTERESTED/UNINTERESTED.**

UNIQUE. Something *unique* is one of a kind. It can't be compared with anything else, so expressions such as *most* unique, *more* unique, or *very* unique don't make sense. The word *unique*, when used properly, can stand alone.

> {**Incorrect**}   Joe Rhodes' coaching methods were **very unique.**

> {**Revised**}   Joe Rhodes' coaching methods were **unique.**

Quite often *unique* appears where another, more specific, adjective is appropriate.

> {**Incorrect**}   The **most unique** merchant on the block was Tong-chai.

> {**Improved**}   The **most inventive** merchant on the block was Tong-chai.

USED TO. Many writers forget the *d* at the end of *use:*

> {**Incorrect**}   Leroy was **use to** studying after soccer practice.

> {**Correct**}   Leroy was **used to** studying after soccer practice.

UTILIZE. Many readers prefer the simpler term *use.*

> {**Inflated**}   Mr. Ringling **utilized** his gavel to regain the crowd's attention.

> {**Better**}   Mr. Ringling **used** his gavel to regain the crowd's attention.

§ **VERB.** The word or phrase that establishes the action of a sentence or expresses a state of being (see Chapters 22–23).

verb

The music **played** on.

verb

Turning the volume down **proved** to be difficult.

A verb and all its auxiliaries, modifiers, and complements is called the **predicate** of a sentence.

complete subject   predicate

David's band **would have played throughout the night.**

complete subject   predicate

Turning the volume down on the band **proved to be much more difficult than the neighbors had anticipated it might be.**

§ **VERBALS.** Verb forms that act like nouns, adjectives, or adverbs (see Chapter 24). The three kinds of verbals are *infinitives, participles,* and *gerunds.* Like verbs, verbals can take objects to form phrases. But verbals are described as *non-finite* (that is, "unfinished") verbs because they cannot make complete sentences alone. A complete sentence requires a *finite* verb, that is a verb that changes form to indicate person, number, and tense.

> {**Non-finite verb—infinitive**}   **To have found** security . . .

> {**Finite verb**}   I **have found** security.

{**Non-finite verb—participle**}   The actor **performing** the scene . . .

{**Finite verb**}   The actor **performs** the scene.

VERY. Many teachers and editors will cut *very* almost every time it appears. Overuse has deadened the impact of the word. Whenever possible, use a more specific term or expression.

{**Weak**}   I was **very angry.**

{**Stronger**}   I was **furious.**

§ **VOICE.** Transitive verbs can be in either the *active voice* or the *passive voice*. They are in the active voice when the subject in the sentence actually performs the action described by the verb.

      subject   action

Professor Chase **donated** the video camera.

They are in the passive voice when the action described by the verb is done *to* the subject.

      subject   action

The video camera **was donated** by Professor Chase.

WELL/GOOD. See **GOOD/WELL**.

WHO/WHOM. Use *who* when the pronoun is a subject; use *whom* when it is an object.

Who wrote the ticket?

To whom was the ticket given?

See Section 28E.

-WISE. Don't add *-wise* to the end of a word to mean 'with respect to' or 'as far as the _____ is concerned.' Many people object to word coinages such as *weatherwise, sportswise,* and *healthwise*. However, a number of common and acceptable English expressions do end in *-wise: clockwise, lengthwise, streetwise, otherwise*. When in doubt about the appropriateness of an expression, check the dictionary.

WITH REGARDS TO. Drop the *s* in regards. The correct expression is *with regard to*.

WON'T. Writers often forget the apostrophe in this contraction and others like it: *can't, don't.*

WOULD OF. Mistaken form of *would have*. Also incorrect are *could of* and *should of.*

Y'ALL. Southern expression for *you,* singular or plural. Not used in academic writing.

YOUR/YOU'RE. Homonyms that often get switched. *You're* is the contraction for *you are; your* is a possessive form.

You're certain Maxine has been to Paris?

Your certainty on this matter may be important.

Credits

American Heritage Dictionary—From *The American Heritage Dictionary, Second College Edition*. Copyright © 1985 by Houghton Mifflin Company. Reprinted by permission.

Balarbar—"Chrysler's Sales Bank" by James B. Balarbar. Copyright © 1985 by James B. Balarbar. Reprinted by permission of the author.

Barnett—Lincoln Barnett, *The Universe and Dr. Einstein*. William Morrow, 1968, p. 84.

Bedard—From "Showdown" by Patrick Bedard, *Car and Driver,* December 1989, p. 56. Copyright © 1989 *Car and Driver*. Reprinted by permission.

Bennett—Hal Zina Bennett, *The Doctor Within*. Clarkson Potter, 1981, p. 184.

Blumenthal—"We're Taking a Trip—All of Us?" by Ruth Blumenthal. Copyright © 1988 by Ruth Blumenthal. Reprinted by permission of the author.

Bork—Robert H. Bork, "Give Me a Bowl of Texas," in *Forbes,* September 1985, p. 184.

Brody—Jane Brody, *Jane Brody's Nutrition Book*. W. W. Norton & Co., 1981, p. 7.

Bronowski—J. Bronowski, *The Ascent of Man*. Little, Brown and Company, 1973, p. 83.

Burke—James Burke, *Connections*. Little, Brown and Company, 1978, p. 45.

Callahan—From "Advertising the Army" by Tom Callahan. *American Way,* November 26, 1985, Vol. 18, No. 24. Reprinted by permission of the author.

Cheers—From "Cheers." Copyright © 1986 Paramount Pictures Corporation. All rights reserved. Reprinted by permission.

Colligan—From "The Light Stuff" by Douglas Colligan, *Technology Illustrated,* February/March 1982. Copyright © 1982 by Douglas Colligan. Reprinted by permission of the author.

Contreras—"Beware of the Dark Side" and "Grackles?" by Michael Contreras. Copyright © 1989 by Michael Contreras. Reprinted by permission of the author.

Cousins—Norman Cousins, *The Healing Heart*. W. W. Norton & Company, 1983, p. 137.

Darman—Richard Darman, quoted in *The New York Times,* January 25, 1990, p. 10.

Davies—From "A Few Kind Words for Superstition" by Robertson Davies, *Newsweek,* November 20, 1978. Copyright © 1978 by Robertson Davies. Reprinted by permission of the author.

Dyson—Freeman J. Dyson, *Infinite in All Directions*. Harper & Row, Publishers, Inc., 1988, pp. 100, 216.

Ellis—Bret Easton Ellis, *Less Than Zero*. Simon and Schuster, 1985, p. 47.

Epstein—Daniel Mark Epstein, "The Case of Harry Houdini," in *Star of Wonder*. Overlook Press, 1986, p. 42.

Fallows—James Fallows, "Containing Japan." *The Atlantic Monthly,* May 1989, p. 41.

Garcia—"No Competition," "The Crimes of the Rising Sun" and "The Right to Burn" by Luis F. Garcia III. Copyright © 1989 by Luis F. Garcia III. Reprinted by permission of the author.

Gilligan—Carol Gilligan, *In a Different Voice*. Harvard University Press, 1982, p. 17.

Goodman—"The Chem 20 Factor," from *Close to Home*, by Ellen Goodman. Copyright © 1979 by The Boston Globe Newspaper Company/Washington Post Writers Group. Reprinted by permission of Simon & Schuster, Inc. and The Washington Post Company.

The Graying of Silicon Valley—"The Graying of Silicon Valley." *U. S. News & World Report*, Oct. 2, 1989, p. 44.

Grout—Donald Jay Grout, *A History of Western Music*. W. W. Norton, 1980, p. 540.

Hoberman—From "Translating the Bible" by Barry Hoberman as originally published in the February 1985 issue of *The Atlantic Monthly*, Vol. 255, No. 2. Copyright © 1985 Barry Hoberman. Reprinted by permission of the author.

Hofstadter—Douglas Hofstadter, *Gödel, Escher, Bach: An Eternal Golden Braid*. Vintage Books/Random House, 1979, p. 603.

Jack—Dana Jack and Rand Jack, "Women Lawyers: Archetype and Alternatives," from *Mapping the Moral Domain*. Ed. Carol Gilligan et al. Harvard University Press (Cambridge), 1988. 264–65.

Jeffreys—William J. Jeffreys and Robert Robbins, *Discovering Astronomy*. John Wiley and Sons, 1981, p. 14.

Johnson—Paul Johnson, *Intellectuals*. Harper & Row, Publishers, Inc., 1988, p. 73.

Karnow—Stanley Karnow, *Vietnam: A History*. Penguin Books, 1984, p. 135.

Kiesler—Sara Kiesler, Lee Spoull, and Jacquelynne S. Eccles, "Second Class Citizens?" *Psychology Today*, March 1983, p. 47.

King—Excerpted from *I Have a Dream* by Martin Luther King, Jr. Copyright © 1963 by Martin Luther King, Jr. Reprinted by permission of Joan Davies.

King—From "The Novelist Sounds Off," *Time*, October 6, 1986. Copyright © 1986 by Time, Inc. All Rights Reserved. Reprinted by permission of Time, Inc. and Stephen King.

McMurtry—Larry McMurtry, *Lonesome Dove*. Simon and Schuster, 1985, pp. 386–87.

McWilliams—"Acupuncture: Energy or Nerves?" by Lori S. McWilliams. Copyright © 1989 by Lori S. McWilliams. Reprinted by permission of the author.

Minor—"The Voices" by Michael Jarrett Minor. Copyright © 1989 by Michael Jarrett Minor. Reprinted by permission of the author.

Morrison—Toni Morrison, *The Bluest Eye*. Simon and Schuster, 1970, p. 97.

Mowat—Farley Mowat, *Never Cry Wolf*. Little, Brown and Company, 1963, p. 80.

Oxford English Dictionary—"Crafty" from *The Compact Edition of the Oxford English Dictionary*, Vol. I, A–O, 1971, p. 1129. Copyright © 1979 by Oxford University Press. Reprinted by permission.

Ratteray—From "Expanding Roles for Summarized Information" by Oswald M. T. Ratteray. *Written Communication*, Vol. 2, No. 4, October 1985, p. 457. Reprinted by permission.

Readers' Guide—"Venus" (surface): From *Readers' Guide to Periodical Literature*. Copyright © 1983–1984 by The H. W. Wilson Company. Reprinted by permission of the publisher.

Rodriguez—Richard Rodriguez, *Hunger of Memory*. David R. Godine, Publisher, Inc., 1982, p. 184.

Rose—Mike Rose, *Lives on the Boundary*. The Free Press, 1989, p. 8.

Ruszkiewicz—From "Using the Library For Research—Avoiding Plagiarism" by John Ruszkiewicz. Copyright © 1985 by The General Libraries, The University of Texas at Austin. Reprinted by permission.

Sagan—Carl Sagan, *The Dragons of Eden*. Random House, Inc., 1977, p. 21.

Shaw—Jane S. Shaw & Richard L. Stroup, "Getting Warmer?" *National Review*, July 14, 1989, p. 26.

Stanlis—Peter J. Stanlis, Editor, *Edmund Burke: Selected Writings and Speeches*. Regnery-Gateway, 1963, p. 491.

Starr—From "The Case For Nuclear Energy" by Roger Starr, *The New York Times,* November 8, 1981. Copyright © 1981 by The New York Times Company. Reprinted by permission.

Stern—Barbara Lang Stern, "Tears Can Be Crucial to Your Physical and Emotional Health," in *Vogue,* June 1979. Conde Nast Publications.

Stone—Robert Stone, "A Higher Horror of the Whiteness: Cocaine's Coloring of the American Psyche," *Harper's,* December 1986, p. 49. Reprinted by permission of Candida Donaldo & Associates.

Strehlo—Kevin Strehlo, "Talk to the Animals," in *Popular Computing,* June 1982.

Thomas—From "The Health-Care System" from *The Medusa and the Snail* by Lewis Thomas. Copyright © 1975 by Lewis Thomas. Originally published in *The New England Journal of Medicine.* Reprinted by permission of Viking Penguin Inc.

Thomas—Lewis Thomas, "Humanities and Science," in *Late Night Thoughts on Listening to Mahler's Ninth Symphony.* Viking Press, 1983, p. 154.

Walker—Alice Walker, "The Black Writer and the Southern Experience," *In Search of Our Mothers' Gardens.* Harcourt Brace Jovanovich, Publishers, 1983, p. 21.

Weinberg—Steven Weinberg, *The First Three Minutes.* Basic Books, Inc., Publishers, 1977, p. 9.

Weiner—Jonathan Weiner, "Glacier Bubbles Are Telling Us What Was in the Ice Age Air," *Smithsonian,* May 1989, p. 78.

What's Behind the Rankings—"What's Behind the Rankings." *U. S. News & World Report,* Oct. 16, 1989, p. 58.

Wheeler—John Wheeler, "Black Holes and New Physics," *Discovery.* The University of Texas at Austin, Winter 1982, p. 5.

When the Earth Rumbles—"When the Earth Rumbles." *U. S. News & World Report,* Oct. 30, 1989, p. 38.

Wolfe—Tom Wolfe, *The Right Stuff.* Farrar, Straus, & Giroux, 1979, p. 27.

Yankelovitch—Daniel Yankelovitch, "The Work Ethic is Underemployed," in *Psychology Today,* May 1982. Ziff-Davis Publishing Co.

Zinsser—William Zinsser, *Willie and Dwike: An American Profile.* Harper & Row, Publishers, Inc., 1984, pp. 3–4.

Index